Marvin A. Sweeney, Ph.D.,
is professor of Hebrew Bible at the Schoo
of Theology at Claremont and professor
of religion at the Claremont Graduate
School. He has served as the Dorot
Research Professor at the W. F. Albright
Institute and as Yad Hanadiv/Barecha
Foundation Fellow at the Hebrew
University of Jerusalem. He is the author
of *Isaiah 1–39*, with an *Introduction to
Prophetic Literature* (FOTL 16; Grand
Rapids: William Eerdmans, 1995); *Isaiah
1–4 and the Post-Exilic Understanding of
the Isaianic Tradition* (BZAW 171; Berlin
and New York: Walter de Gruyter, 1988),
and other studies on biblical literature.

THE TWELVE PROPHETS

BERIT OLAM
Studies in Hebrew Narrative & Poetry

The Twelve Prophets

VOLUME ONE

Hosea
Joel
Amos
Obadiah
Jonah

Marvin A. Sweeney

David W. Cotter, O.S.B.
Editor

Jerome T. Walsh
Chris Franke
Associate Editors

A Michael Glazier Book
THE LITURGICAL PRESS
Collegeville, Minnesota

A Michael Glazier Book published by The Liturgical Press.

Cover design by Ann Blattner.

Unless otherwise indicated, the translations of Scripture that appear in this volume are the author's own. Others are taken from the New Revised Standard Version Bible, Catholic edition, © 1989 by the Division of Christian Education of the National Council of Churches of Christ in the U.S.A. Used by permission. All rights reserved.

1   2   3   4   5   6   7   8   9

Library of Congress Cataloging-in-Publication Data

Sweeney, Marvin A. (Marvin Alan), 1953–
    The twelve prophets / Marvin A. Sweeney ; David W. Cotter, editor ;
Jerome T. Walsh, Chris Franke, associate editors.
        p.   cm. — (Berit olam)
    Includes bibliographical references and index.
    ISBN 0-8146-5095-3 (alk. paper)
    1. Bible.   O.T.   Minor Prophets—Commentaries.   I. Cotter, David W.
II. Walsh, Jerome T., 1942–   III. Frank, Chris.   IV. Title.   V. Series.

BS1560 .S94   2000
224'.907—dc21   00-035651

For
Terry and Candy

Georgia, Walter Issac, Jake, Lakie,
and Mary

CONTENTS

ACKNOWLEDGMENTS

It is a great pleasure to acknowledge the various forms of support, advice, and encouragement that have enabled me to complete this commentary. I would like to thank the editors of the Berit Olam series, David Cotter, OSB, Chris Franke, and Jerome Walsh, for their invitation to contribute this volume to such an interesting and exciting new series. I am particularly grateful for their interest in including a group of scholars who represent such methodological and religious diversity. I would also like to thank the Lilly Theological Endowment for its award of a Lilly Theological Research Grant, which enabled me to take a full year research leave in 1997–1998, and the Claremont School of Theology, which granted a sabbatical in the Fall 1997 semester and a leave of absence in the Spring 1998 semester so that I might pursue this project. I am indebted to Lori Anne Ferrell, David L. Petersen, Rolf Rendtorff, Odil Hannes Steck, and Marjorie Suchocki for their efforts to make my leave possible. My student assistants, Seungil Whang, Geri Newberge and Jami Flatt, provided invaluable assistance. The Institute for Antiquity and Christianity of the Claremont Graduate University provided research support funds that allowed me to test some ideas before colleagues at various conferences. My colleagues in Hebrew Bible, Tammi Schneider and Kristin De Troyer, and my students at the Claremont School of Theology and the Claremont Graduate University have proved to be constant sources of insight. None of this would have been possible without the love and support of my wife, Muna, and my daughter, Leah.

Finally, I would like to dedicate this work to my brother Terry and his family, who constantly remind me of the joys of life in the world.

San Dimas, California   August 1999

ABBREVIATIONS

AASOR	*Annual of the American Schools of Oriental Research*
ABD	*The Anchor Bible Dictionary*, ed. D. N. Freedman et al. 6 volumes. New York: Doubleday, 1992.
ABS	*Archeology and Biblical Studies*
AnBib	*Analecta Biblica*
ANEP	*The Ancient Near East in Pictures Relating to the Old Testament*, ed. J. Pritchard. Princeton: Princeton University Press, 1969.
ANET	*Ancient Near Eastern Texts Relating to the Old Testament*, ed. J. Pritchard. Princeton: Princeton University Press, 1969.
AOAT	Alter Orient und Altes Testament
ARAB	*Ancient Records of Assyria and Babylonia*, ed. D. D. Luckenbill. London: Histories and Mysteries of Man, 1989.
AT	Altes Testament
ATSAT	*Arbeiten zu Text und Spruche im Alten Testament*
BA	*Biblical Archaeologist*
BASOR	*Bulletin of the American Schools of Oriental Research*
BBET	*Beiträge zur biblischen Exegese und Theologie*
B.C.E.	Before Common Era
BDB	Brown, Driver, Briggs: *Hebrew and English Lexicon of the Old Testament*, ed. F. Brown, S. R. Driver, and C. A. Briggs. Oxford: Clarendon, 1972.
BEATAJ	*Beiträge zur Erforschung des Alten Testaments und des Antike Judentums*
BibSem	*Biblical Seminar*
BJS	Brown Judaic Studies
BLS	Bible and Literature Series
BN	*Biblische Notizen*
BO	*Biblica et Orientalia*
BTS	*Biblisch-Theologische Studien*
BZAW	Beihefte zur Zeitschrift für die Alttestamentliche Wissenschaft
CAH	*The Cambridge Ancient History*. Cambridge: Cambridge University Press.

CBQ	*The Catholic Biblical Quarterly*
C.E.	Common Era
ConBibOT	*Coniectanea Biblica, Old Testament Series*
CR:BS	*Currents in Research: Biblical Studies*
CRINT	Compendia Rerum Iudaicarum ad Novum Testamentum
DDD²	*Dictionary of Deities and Demons in the Bible,* ed. K. van der Toorn, B. Becking, and P. van der Horst. 2nd edition; Leiden: E. J. Brill; Grand Rapids, MI: Eerdmans, 1999.
DJD	*Discoveries in the Judaean Desert*
EB	*Études bibliques*
EvT	*Evangelisches Theologie*
Fest.	Festschrift
FOTL	Forms of the Old Testament Literature Commentary Series
FRLANT	Forschungen zur Religion des Alten und Neuen Testaments
GCT	Gender, Culture, and Theory Monograph Series
HBD	*HarperCollins Bible Dictionary,* ed. P. Achtemeier et al. 2nd edition; San Francisco: HarperSanFrancisco, 1996.
HKAT	Handkommentar zum Alten Testament
HSM	Harvard Semitic Monographs
HUCA	*Hebrew Union College Annual*
ICC	*International Critical Commentary*
IDB	*Interpreter's Dictionary of the Bible,* ed. G. Buttrick. 4 volumes. Nashville: Abingdon, 1962.
IDB[S]	*Interpreter's Dictionary of the Bible. Supplementary Volume,* ed. K. Crim. Nashville: Abingdon, 1976.
IEJ	*Israel Exploration Journal*
JAOS	*Journal of the American Oriental Society*
JBL	*Journal of Biblical Literature*
JCS	*Journal of Cuneiform Studies*
JNES	*Journal of Near Eastern Studies*
JR	*Journal of Religion*
JSOT	*Journal for the Study of the Old Testament*
JSOTSup	Journal for the Study of the Old Testament, Supplement Series
JSS	*Journal of Semitic Studies*
JTS	*Journal of Theological Studies*
KAT	Kommentar zum Alten Testament
KHAT	Kurzer Hand-Commentar zum Alten Testament
LXX	Septuagint
MT	Masoretic Text
NEAEHL	*New Encyclopedia of Archaeological Excavations in the Holy Land,* ed. E. Stern et al. 4 volumes. Jerusalem: Carta and the Israel Exploration Society.
NICOT	New International Commentary on the Old Testament
NRSV	New Revised Standard Version
OBO	Orbis biblicus et orientalis
OT Guides	Old Testament Guides
OTL	Old Testament Library Commentary Series

OTS	*Oudtestamentische Studiën*
RB	*Revue biblique*
RBL	*Review of Biblical Literature*
SBLDS	Society of Biblical Literature Dissertation Series
SBLMS	Society of Biblical Literature Monograph Series
SBLResBS	Society of Biblical Literature Resources for Biblical Study Monograph Series
SBS	Stuttgarter Bibelstudien
SBT	Studies in Biblical Theology
SJOT	*Scandinavian Journal of the Old Testament*
TA	*Tel Aviv*
TB	Theologische Bücherei
TDOT	*Theological Dictionary of the Old Testament*, ed. H. Ringgren et al. Grand Rapids: Eerdmans, 1977ff.
VT	*Vetus Testamentum*
VTSup	Vetus Testamentum Supplements
WMANT	Wissenschaftliche Monographien zum Alten und Neuen Testaments
ZAW	*Zeitschrift für die Alttestamentliche Wissenschaft*
ZDPV	*Zeitschrift des deutschen Palästina Vereins*

INTRODUCTION

The Book of the Twelve Prophets is a multifaceted literary composition that functions simultaneously in all Jewish and Christian versions of the Bible as a single prophetic book and as a collection of twelve individual prophetic books. Each of the twelve individual books—Hosea; Joel; Amos; Obadiah; Jonah; Micah; Nahum; Habakkuk; Zephaniah; Haggai; Zechariah; and Malachi according to the Masoretic version of the Twelve—begins with its own superscription or narrative introduction that identifies the prophet and usually provides some details concerning the historical setting, literary characteristics, or overall concerns and circumstances of the book. In this manner, each book is clearly distinguished from the others within the overall framework of the Twelve. There is generally no introduction or other common material that binds together the works of the individual prophets that comprise the Twelve, but they almost invariably stand together as a clearly defined book with the other prophetic books of the Bible, i.e., Isaiah; Jeremiah; Ezekiel; and, in Christian Bibles, Daniel.

Although manuscripts and printed editions of the various versions of the Bible frequently lack a comprehensive title for the Book of the Twelve, it is generally identified in Jewish tradition as *tĕrê ʾăśār*, Aramaic for "the Twelve," and in Christian tradition as *ʿoi dōdeka prophētai* or *ton dōdekaprophēton*, Greek for "the Twelve Prophets." The apocryphal Wisdom of Jesus son of Sirach (a.k.a. Ecclesiasticus), dated to the second century B.C.E., refers in Sir 49:10 to "the bones of the twelve prophets," which suggests that ben Sirach knew the Twelve as a single book. The first century C.E. Jewish historian Flavius Josephus apparently considers the Book of the Twelve as one of the twenty-two books of the Bible (*Against Apion* I.8). Likewise, 4 Ezra 14:41 considers the Twelve to be one of the twenty-four holy books transcribed by Ezra. The Twelve are apparently omitted by accident from the canon list of the second–third century Church Father Origen, who counts twenty-two Jewish books for the Old Testament but names only twenty-one (Eusebius, *Ecclesiastical History* vi 25). Most see this as evidence that he considered the Twelve to constitute a single book.[1]

The dual character of the book is evident in Talmudic tradition, which considers the Twelve as a single prophetic book that follows Isaiah; Jeremiah; and Ezekiel (or alternatively, Jeremiah; Ezekiel; and Isaiah) in the "Latter Prophets" (see *bBaba Batra* 14b) and counts them as one book among the twenty-four of the Bible.[2] But the Talmud also stipulates that whereas the books of the Bible are to be separated in manuscripts by four blank lines, the individual books of the Twelve Prophets are to be separated from each other by three blank lines (*bBaba Batra* 13b) which indicates their dual status as separate books that nevertheless comprise a single book. Likewise, the Masorah of the Twelve Prophets tallies the number of verses at the end of each individual prophetic book, but it also provides a count of verses for the Book of the Twelve as a whole. Similar considerations appear in Christian tradition, which nearly consistently groups the Twelve Prophets together, but counts them as twelve individual books among the thirty-nine books of the Old Testament.[3] The first century C.E. Bishop Melito of Sardis refers to the Twelve as *tōn dōdeka ʿen monobibiōi*, "the twelve in one book" (Eusebius, *Ecclesiastical History* iv 26). The term "Minor Prophets," *Prophetae minores* in Latin, first appears in Latin Christian Patristic sources, such as the work of Augustine (*City of G–d* 18:29), and refers only to the relative length of the individual works of the twelve prophets when compared to the larger books of Isaiah, Jeremiah, Ezekiel, and Daniel. Apparently, the term refers to the Twelve both as a collection and as individual works.

The various versions of the Book of the Twelve show a great deal of fluidity in their overall arrangements of the books. The Jewish version

[1] See Henry Barclay Swete, *An Introduction to the Old Testament in Greek* (1902; New York: KTAV, 1968) 203.

[2] For a general discussion of the canon in Jewish tradition, see Sid Leiman, *The Canonization of Hebrew Scripture: The Talmudic and Midrashic Evidence* (Hamden, CT: Connecticut Academy of Arts and Sciences/Archon, 1976); Roger T. Beckwith, "Formation of the Hebrew Bible," *Mikra: Text, Translation, Reading, and Interpretation of the Hebrew Bible in Ancient Judaism and Early Christianity*. CRINT, ed. M. J. Mulder, 2/1 (Assen: Van Gorcum; Philadelphia: Fortress, 1988) 39–86; Christian D. Ginsburg, *Introduction to the Massoretico-Critical Edition of the Hebrew Bible* (New York: KTAV, 1966).

[3] For an overview of the form of the Bible in the Septuagint and Patristic literature, see Swete, *Introduction*, 197–230; cf. Roger Beckwith, *The Old Testament Canon of the New Testament Church* (Grand Rapids, MI: Eerdmans, 1986).

of the Book of the Twelve is based upon the Masoretic Text (MT), a standardized Hebrew consonantal text that is supplied with vowel pointing, accents, and notations that are intended to preserve and transmit accurately the text and the means to read it properly. The earliest manuscript of the entire Masoretic version of the Bible is the so-called St. Petersburg or Leningrad codex (B 19A) which dates to 1009 C.E., although an earlier Masoretic manuscript dated to 916 C.E., also located in St. Petersburg, presents only the Prophets.[4] As noted above, Jewish Bibles from the Talmudic period to the present place the Twelve Prophets as the fourth book of the "Latter Prophets." Although the order of the first three prophetic books could vary considerably prior to the introduction of printed editions of the Rabbinic Bible in the late-fifteenth and early-sixteenth centuries, the order of the Twelve Prophets remained constant as Hosea; Joel; Amos; Obadiah; Jonah; Micah; Nahum; Habakkuk; Zephaniah; Haggai; Zechariah; and Malachi. *Targum Jonathan*, an authoritative Aramaic version of the Prophets ascribed to a pupil of Rabbi Hillel (fl. 30 B.C.E.–10 C.E.) named Jonathan ben Uzziel (*bMegillah* 3a), likewise presents the Twelve Prophets according to the order of the MT.[5]

The Greek Septuagint (LXX) constitutes the basis for the Old Testament canon from the time of the early Church, although the version is believed to have originated in the Alexandrian Jewish community.[6] The name Septuagint recalls the famous tradition related in the *Letter of Aristeas* that the seventy or seventy-two Rabbis engaged by Ptolemy II of Egypt (3rd century B.C.E.) to produce a Greek translation of the Torah or Pentateuch produced a Greek text in seventy-two days. Later Church Fathers embellished the legend by claiming that the Rabbis each worked separately, but produced identical translations. The earliest manuscripts of the LXX, *Codex Vaticanus* and *Codex Sinaiticus*, date to the fourth century C.E.[7] *Vaticanus* presents the order of the Twelve as Hosea;

---

[4] For discussion of the Masoretic manuscripts, see Ginsburg, *Introduction* 207–37, 475–6; David Noel Freedman, ed., *The Leningrad Codex: The Facsimile Edition* (Grand Rapids, MI: Eerdmans, 1998).

[5] For discussion of the Targum, see Philip S. Alexander, "Jewish Aramaic Translations of the Hebrew Scriptures," *Mikra*, 217–54. An English translation of the Targum to the Twelve Prophets with commentary appears in Kevin J. Cathcart and Robert P. Gordon, *The Targum of the Minor Prophets, Translated with a Critical Introduction, Apparatus, and Notes*, Aramaic Bible, no. 14 (Wilmington, DE: Michael Glazier, 1989).

[6] For discussion of the Septuagint, see Swete, *Introduction*; Emanuel Tov, "The Septuagint," *Mikra*, 161–88.

[7] See Swete, *Introduction*, 126–8, 129–31.

Amos; Micah; Joel; Obadiah; Jonah; Nahum; Habakkuk; Zephaniah; Haggai; Zechariah; and Malachi. Although the leaves that contained Hosea; Amos; and Micah are missing from *Sinaiticus*, the remaining nine books appear in the same order as *Vaticanus*. Most later LXX manuscripts present the same order, but there are a few variations. The LXX order of the Twelve appears also in 4 Ezra 1:39-40 (2 Esdras 1:39-40), a Jewish apocalyptic work written in the aftermath of the destruction of the Second Temple in 70 C.E. that appears now in the Apocryphal or Deutero-canonical books.

Later Christian versions of the Bible present the Twelve Prophets in the same order as the MT. The Latin Vulgate, prepared by Jerome in the land of Israel in 390–405 C.E., is a self-conscious attempt to render the Hebrew of the Old Testament into Latin as faithfully as possible.[8] Jerome's work was controversial, because he ultimately rejected the LXX as inspired scripture for the Church. Since the Council of Trent in 1546, however, the Vulgate has been established as the authoritative text of the Roman Catholic Church. The Syriac Peshitta constitutes the version of the Bible employed by Syrian Christians as early as the fourth or fifth century C.E.[9] Syriac is an Aramaic dialect, and there is a great deal of speculation that the Peshitta may well have originated in part as a Jewish Targum of the first century C.E. or at least among Jewish communities in Syria who were converted to Christianity.

Some nine manuscripts of the Book of the Twelve appear among the scrolls of the Judean wilderness. Chief among them is the Wadi Muraba'at scroll (MurXII), a deteriorated second century B.C.E. Hebrew manuscript, that presents a "proto-Masoretic" text nearly identical with that of the MT.[10] The beginning and end of the manuscript are lost so that the text begins with Joel 2:20 and ends with Zechariah 1:4, but it presents partial texts of the remaining books of the Twelve in the same order as the MT (Joel; Amos; Obadiah; Jonah; Micah; Nahum; Habakkuk; Zephaniah; Haggai; Zechariah). A first century B.C.E. Greek version of the Twelve from Nahal Hever (8HevXIIgr) presents a somewhat wooden Greek translation of the proto-Masoretic text that differs significantly from the old Greek of the LXX.[11] It, too, is fragmentary, but it presents portions of the books of Jonah; Micah; Nahum; Habakkuk; Zephaniah; and Zechariah in the same order as the MT. Fragments of

---

[8] See Benjamin Kedar, "The Latin Translations," *Mikra*, 299–338, esp. 313–34.

[9] See Peter Dirksen, "The Old Testament Peshitta," *Mikra*, 255–97.

[10] See P. Benoit, ed., *Les grottes de Muraba'at, DJD*, vol. 2 (Oxford: Clarendon, 1961).

[11] Emmanuel Tov, ed., *The Greek Minor Prophets Scroll from Nahal Hever (8Hev XIIgr)*, DJD, vol. 8 (Oxford: Clarendon, 1990).

seven Hebrew scrolls of the Twelve, which correspond largely to the MT, were found in Qumran cave 4.[12] Noteworthy among them is 4QXII[a], dated to the mid-second century B.C.E., which presents portions of Zechariah; Malachi; and Jonah. Although only a few heavily deteriorated fragments of the scroll survive, it is quite clear that Jonah follows Malachi in the sequence of the Twelve. Unfortunately, the order of the other nine books cannot be known, but this manuscript suggests the possibility that a third major version of the Twelve existed in antiquity. The remains of the other manuscripts of the Twelve from Qumran cave 4 indicate a sequence like that of the MT.

Several variations in the order of the Twelve appear in the pseudepigraphical literature of the period following the destruction of the Second Temple. The *Martyrdom and Ascension of Isaiah* 4:22, a Jewish work of the first century C.E. that was later expanded by Christian circles in the late-first or early-second century, presents the order Amos; Hosea; Micah; Joel; Nahum; Jonah; Obadiah; Habakkuk; Zephaniah; Haggai; Zechariah; and Malachi. The presentation of the prophets in the *Lives of the Prophets,* also a first century C.E. Jewish composition that was later reworked in Christian circles, presents the order Hosea; Micah; Amos; Joel; Obadiah; Jonah; Nahum; Habakkuk; Zephaniah; Haggai; Zechariah; and Malachi. There is no evidence, however, that either of these orders represents an authoritative sequence of the Twelve from antiquity.

Current Research on the Book of the Twelve

For the most part, modern biblical scholarship has treated the Book of the Twelve as twelve distinct prophetic compositions that have relatively little to do with each other apart from having been placed in the same collection. This applies even to a number of commentaries written during the past century by single authors who paid only perfunctory attention to the overall form of the Book of the Twelve.[13] Such treatment reflects the general interests of much modern historical-critical scholarship that, during the latter part of the nineteenth century and most of

---

[12] Russell Fuller, "The Form and Formation of the Book of the Twelve: The Evidence from the Judean Desert," *Forming Prophetic Literature: Essays on Isaiah and the Twelve in Honor of J.D.W. Watts,* ed. J. W. Watts and P. R. House, JSOTSup 235 (Sheffield: Sheffield Academic Press, 1996) 86–101; E. Ulrich, ed., Qumran Cave 4, X: *The Prophets, DJD,* vol. 15 (Oxford: Clarendon, 1997).

[13] Examples of major commentaries on the Twelve Prophets written by one author include, Karl Marti, *Das Dodekapropheton,* KHAT, vol. XIII (Tübingen: J.C.B.

the twentieth century, was primarily concerned with the study of biblical literature in relation to its original or earliest historical contexts.[14] The later editing and interpretation of biblical literature was generally considered irrelevant and even counterproductive to the task of recovering the supposed original meaning of the biblical text. Indeed, such an approach was largely concerned with identifying and stripping away the work of later editors and interpreters so that the original or earliest form of the biblical text could be reconstructed. Insofar as the final form of biblical books, whether it was the final form of an individual book such as Hosea or Zechariah or even the final form of the entire Book of the Twelve, was considered to be the work of such later editors, tradents, and interpreters, scholars generally treated it as an obstacle to interpretation.

Nevertheless, the twentieth century has seen a growing preoccupation with the final form of biblical books, especially under the influence of developing models of redaction-critical, canon- and canonical-critical, and newer literary-critical models of exegesis. Redaction-critical work has been instrumental throughout the twentieth century as it is concerned with reconstructing the compositional and editorial process by which earlier texts are taken up to be reread, reinterpreted, edited, and rewritten in relation to the concerns of later times. Whereas early redaction-critical work viewed redactors largely as mechanical tradents who frequently misunderstood the significance of the texts with which they worked, more recent redaction-critical models have stressed the role of redactors as creative thinkers, historians, theologians, etc., who play a major role in shaping the historiographical and theological perspectives of the books that now form the Bible. Canon- and canonical-

---

Mohr [Paul Siebeck], 1904); A. Van Hoonacker, *Les douze petits prophètes, EB* (Paris: J. Gabalda, 1908); W. Nowack, *Die kleinen Propheten,* HKAT, vol. III/4, 3rd ed. (Göttingen: Vandenhoeck & Ruprecht, 1922); Ernst Sellin, *Das Zwölfprophetenbuch,* KAT, vol. XII, 2nd–3rd ed. (Leipzig: A. Deichert, 1929–1930). The more recent KAT series by Wilhelm Rudolph treats the books separately without even a general introduction to the Book of the Twelve, and is cited in the commentary in relation to each of the twelve prophetic books.

[14] For overviews of biblical interpretation, see John Barton, *Reading the Old Testament: Method in Biblical Study* (Louisville: Westminster John Knox, 1996); Robert Morgan with John Barton, *Biblical Interpretation* (Oxford: Oxford University Press, 1988). See also, Rolf Knierim, "Criticism of Literary Features, Form, Tradition, and Redaction," *The Hebrew Bible and Its Modern Interpreters,* ed. D. A. Knight and G. M. Tucker (Chico: Scholars Press, 1985) 123–65; Marvin A. Sweeney, "Formation and Form in Prophetic Literature," *Old Testament Interpretation: Past, Present, and Future,* ed. J. L. Mays, D. L. Petersen, and K. H. Richards (Nashville: Abingdon, 1995) 113–26.

criticism grew out of redaction-criticism and theological interpretation
to raise questions concerning the meaning of biblical books both in relation to their formative contexts as they were undergoing the process
of composition into their present forms and in relation to the communities that read them once they were completed and found their places
within the various forms of the Bible in both Judaism and Christianity.
Newer forms of literary criticism have raised questions concerning the
ability of scholars to reconstruct the process of composition and redaction, and have consequently stressed the synchronic analysis of biblical
writings. In all three cases, interpretation of the final form of the biblical text has become paramount and, in the present case, demands consideration of the present form of the Book of the Twelve.

Two early attempts by Ewald and Steuernagel employ the superscriptions of the twelve prophets as a basis for explaining the order in
which each of the books was introduced into the collection as a whole.[15]
Ewald argues that the Book of the Twelve was formed in a three-stage
process that began in the seventh century with Joel, Amos, Hosea, Micah,
Nahum, and Zephaniah. The second stage in the post-exilic period saw
the addition of Obadiah, Jonah, Habakkuk, Haggai, and Zechariah 1–8,
and the third stage in Nehemiah's later years saw the addition of
Zechariah 9–14 and Malachi. Steuernagel argues for seven stages that
began during the seventh century reign of Josiah and extended through
the third century. The stages include: 1) Hosea, Micah, Zephaniah; 2)
Amos; 3) Haggai and Zechariah 1–8; 4) Nahum 2–3; 5) Habakkuk and
Nahum 1; 6) Zechariah 9–14; and 7) Joel, Obadiah, and Jonah.

The earliest major attempt by a modern critical scholar to treat the
issue in relation to the redaction-critical study of the individual books
of the Twelve appears in Karl Budde's 1922 study of the Book of the
Twelve.[16] Budde notes the dual nature of the Book of the Twelve as a
collection of individual prophetic works and attempts to explain how
such a collection was brought together. Noting the relative lack of narrative material in the Twelve when compared to the larger prophetic
books of Isaiah; Jeremiah; and Ezekiel, Budde argues that the Twelve

---

[15] H. Ewald, *Die Propheten des alten Bundes,* vol. 1 (Göttingen: Vandenhoeck &
Ruprecht, 1867) 73–81; C. Steuernagel, *Lehrbuch der Einleitung das Alte Testament*
(Tübingen: J.C.B. Mohr, 1912) 669–72. For full discussions of the history of research
on the Book of the Twelve, see Barry Alan Jones, *The Formation of the Book of the
Twelve: A Study in Text and Canon,* SBLDS, vol. 149 (Atlanta: Scholars Press, 1995)
13–42; James D. Nogalski, *Literary Precursors to the Book of the Twelve,* BZAW, vol. 117
(Berlin and New York: Walter de Gruyter, 1993) 3–12.

[16] Karl Budde, "Eine folgenschwere Redaction des Zwölfprophetenbuchs," *ZAW*
39 (1922) 218–29.

Prophets were brought together to provide authoritative prophetic scripture in the fourth-third centuries B.C.E. The absence of narrative material represented a self-conscious redactional attempt to eliminate the so-called "human" material, much like the Priestly redaction of the Pentateuch was believed to have done, so that the divine word of the prophets could be presented as scripture together with the Torah.

Although Budde's work was largely dismissed, it prompted a 1935 article by R. E. Wolfe, who likewise attempts to reconstruct the redactional process by which the Book of the Twelve was formed.[17] Wolfe applies a source-critical analysis to the individual prophetic books in order to determine what was "authentic" to the prophet and what was "unauthentic." The result is the reconstruction of a redactional process that extended from the seventh through the third centuries B.C.E. in which the earliest prophetic writings of the Twelve from the eighth century were expanded and reworked into the present form of the Twelve. Unfortunately, he relies on his own subjective feelings and appreciation for what must have been the original words of the prophets, and his work is easily dismissed.

The issue received little further attention until the 1979 dissertation by Dale Schneider which emphasizes a combination of canon-critical and redaction-critical considerations.[18] He argues that the present form of the Twelve is the result of a four-stage process in which various collections within the Twelve were formed and added. The first is the eighth century collection of Hosea, Amos, and Micah, which is reflected in the order of the LXX. The second is the seventh century collection of Nahum, Habakkuk, and Zephaniah added during the Exile by a Josianic reform party. The third is the late Exilic collection of Joel, Obadiah, and Jonah. The fourth stage is the fifth century collection of Haggai, Zechariah (both 1–8 and 9–14), and the later book of Malachi.

A renewed interest in the redaction-critical study of the individual books of the Twelve in relation to the whole appears among a circle of scholars based in the redaction-critical and traditio-historical methodological approach of Odil Hannes Steck, who stresses the need to assess the entire history of composition from the earliest layers to the final glosses.[19] Peter Weimer's 1985 redaction-critical study of Obadiah, for

---

[17] Ronald E. Wolfe, "The Editing of the Book of the Twelve," *ZAW* 53 (1935) 90–129.

[18] Dale A. Schneider, "The Unity of the Book of the Twelve" (Ph.D. diss., Yale University, 1979).

[19] Odil Hannes Steck, *Old Testament Exegesis: A Guide to the Methodology*, SBLResBS, vol. 39 (Atlanta: Scholars, 1998). By the same author, *Der Abschluss der Prophetie im Alten Testament. Ein Versuch zur Frage der Vorgeschichte des Kanons*, BTS, vol. 17 (Neukirchen-Vluyn: Neukirchener, 1991).

example, identifies six layers of redaction in Obadiah.[20] Through the use of lexical similarities, he associates these layers with passages from other books of the Twelve Prophets that are also considered to be the products of later redaction. The result is a model by which the individual books of the Twelve are taken up and redacted as part of the Book of the Twelve as a whole. A 1987 study by Erich Bosshard points to lexical similarities and thematic parallels between the Book of the Twelve and the Book of Isaiah.[21] He argues that both are the products of the same redactional circles that emphasized the roles of the "Day of YHWH" tradition and Edom as a symbol of the nations as part of their overall portrayals of YHWH's purposes in bringing punishment upon Israel/ Judah and the nations prior to a restoration in Jerusalem. In the case of the Twelve, Joel 2:1-11; Obadiah 5–6, 15–21; and Zeph 2:13-15; 3:14-18 were added to establish the parallels with Isaiah. A later 1990 study by Bosshard together with Reinhold Gregor Kratz argues for a three stage process by which Malachi was added as part of the final redaction of the Book of the Twelve and indeed the Prophets as a whole.[22] Bosshard-Nepustil's massive 1997 monograph attempts to explain the redactional interrelationship between Isaiah 1–39 and the Book of the Twelve in detail by defining two major redactional layers common to both books.[23] An "Assyrian-Babylonian layer" appears in texts from Joel, Habakkuk, and Zephaniah. It begins in the eighth century and ultimately reflects upon the fall of Jerusalem in 587. A "Babylonian layer" appears in texts from Joel, Micah, Nahum, Habakkuk, Zephaniah, and Zechariah from the late-sixth century and reflects upon the significance of Cyrus.

A substantial two-volume 1993 study by Steck's student James Nogalski employs a combination of catchword associations, thematic associations, and redaction-critical arguments to posit a five-stage redaction for the Book of the Twelve.[24] The initial layer appears in a collection of Hosea, Amos, Micah, and Zephaniah that was edited by Deuteronomistic circles in the sixth century. A second collection appears in

---

[20] Peter Weimer, "Obadja: Eine redaktionskritische Analyse," *BN* 27 (1985) 35–99.

[21] Erich Bosshard, "Beobachtungen zum Zwölfprophetenbuch," *BN* 40 (1987) 30–62.

[22] Erich Bosshard and Reinhold Gregor Kratz, "Maleachi im Zwölfprophetenbuch," *BN* 52 (1990) 27–46.

[23] Erich Bosshard-Nepustil, *Rezeptionen von Jesaja 1–39 im Zwölfprophetenbuch*, OBO, vol. 144 (Freiburg: Universitätsverlag; Göttingen: Vandenhoeck & Ruprecht, 1997).

[24] James D. Nogalski, *Precursors*. By the same author, *Redactional Processes in the Book of the Twelve*, BZAW, vol. 218 (Berlin and New York: Walter de Gruyter, 1993).

Haggai and Zechariah 1–8. Both of these collections were united and systematically edited in redactional stages that added Joel, Obadiah, Nahum, Habakkuk, and Malachi in the late-fourth century. Successive additions of Zechariah 9–14 and later Jonah completed the Book of the Twelve in the early third century B.C.E. following the time of Alexander. A 1997 study by Burkard Zapff attempts to relate the redactional formation of Micah to the overall models posited by Steck, Bosshard-Nepustil, and Nogalski.[25] Aaron Schart's 1998 monograph likewise builds upon and slightly modifies the work of these scholars by pointing to a six-stage process that sees the expansion of an initial layer in Hosea, Amos, Micah, and Zephaniah by layers in Nahum-Habakkuk; Haggai-Zechariah; Joel-Obadiah; and Jonah and Malachi.[26]

In addition to the redaction-critical models, a number of synchronic studies have recently appeared. Paul House's 1988 monograph attempts to argue that the Book of the Twelve represents a prophetic drama that highlights the themes of sin (Hosea-Micah), punishment (Nahum-Zephaniah), and restoration (Haggai-Malachi).[27] Herbert Marks' brief 1987 literary commentary on the Twelve emphasizes the text and the various voices that appear within the various prophets that make up the whole.[28] Terence Collins' 1993 treatment of the Twelve attempts to demonstrate the roles that the themes of covenant-election, fidelity and infidelity, fertility and infertility, turn and returning, the justice and mercy of G–d, the kingship of G–d, the place of G–d's dwelling (Mt. Zion/Temple), and the nations as enemies and allies play in uniting the Book of the Twelve as a coherent literary work.[29] John Barton's 1996 study argues for a canonical interpretation of the Twelve.[30] He emphasizes a deliberate attempt in the Twelve to challenge the message of judgment by Amos, Hosea, etc., with calls for the preservation of Israel by keeping YHWH's Torah faithfully in anticipation of the last days.

---

[25] Burkard M. Zapff, *Redaktionsgeschichtliche Studien zum Michabuch im Kontext des Dodekapropheton*, BZAW, vol. 256 (Berlin and New York: Walter de Gruyter, 1997).

[26] Aaron Schart, *Die Entstehung des Zwölfprophetenbuch*, BZAW, vol. 260 (Berlin and New York: Walter de Gruyter, 1998).

[27] Paul House, *The Unity of the Twelve*, JSOTSup, vol. 97; BLS, vol. 27 (Sheffield: Almond, 1990).

[28] Herbert Marks, "The Twelve Prophets," *The Literary Guide to the Bible*, ed. R. Alter and F. Kermode (Cambridge: Belknap, 1987) 207–32.

[29] Terrence Collins, *The Mantle of Elijah: The Redaction Criticism of the Prophetical Books*, BibSem, vol. 20 (Sheffield: JSOT Press, 1993) 59–87.

[30] John Barton, "The Canonical Meaning of the Book of the Twelve," *After the Exile: Essays in Honor of Rex Mason*, ed. J. Barton and D. J. Reimer (Macon, GA: Mercer University, 1996) 59–73.

The studies cited above point to a growing interest in the question of the form and formation of the Book of the Twelve as a whole, but they also reveal two very serious problems that have been brought to light in more recent study.

First, these studies are based upon the presumption that the Masoretic Text constitutes the authoritative basis for evaluating the final form of the Book of the Twelve and for reconstructing its compositional or redactional history.[31] Nevertheless, there are at least two authoritative forms of the Book of the Twelve as represented by the Masoretic Text (Hosea; Joel; Amos; Obadiah; Jonah; Micah; Nahum; Habakkuk; Zephaniah; Haggai; Zechariah; Malachi) and the Septuagint (Hosea; Amos; Micah; Joel; Obadiah; Jonah; Nahum; Habakkuk; Zephaniah; Haggai; Zechariah; Malachi) and perhaps even three if one considers the evidence of 4QXII[a] (Zechariah; Malachi; Jonah). This is a particularly significant issue for Nogalski's study because his argument depends upon a close analysis of the catchwords that he claims links the books of the Twelve into their present sequence—according to the MT.

Analyses of Nogalski's work by Ehud Ben Zvi and Barry Jones both point to the rather mechanical or arbitrary fashion in which Nogalski employs the catchwords identified in his studies to establish the sequence of the books within the Twelve and the basis for a redaction-critical reconstruction.[32] One might observe, for example, that the catchwords in Nahum 1 and Micah 7 are crucial for establishing the sequence between these two books in the MT (and indeed, in arguing that Micah 7 is the result of later redaction), but the extensive citation of Obadiah in Joel does not entail that these two books must stand together in the sequence of the Twelve.

Jones in particular calls for consideration of the different sequences of books among the different versions of the Twelve.[33] He observes that Jonah holds a very unstable position within the sequence of the Twelve as indicated by its placement after Malachi in 4QXII[a]. Likewise, a comparison of MT and LXX shows that, like Jonah, the respective placements of Joel and Obadiah are also unstable. He notes the relatively stable arrangements of the eighth century prophets, Hosea, Amos, Micah; the seventh century prophets, Nahum, Habakkuk, Zephaniah; and the sixth century prophets, Haggai, Zechariah, Malachi, and posits that there must have been a Book of the Nine that grew successively through

---

[31] See esp. Jones, *The Formation*; Marvin A. Sweeney, "Three Recent European Studies of the Composition of the Book of the Twelve," *RBL* 1 (1999) 22–37.

[32] Ehud Ben Zvi, "Twelve Prophetic Books or 'The Twelve': A Few Preliminary Considerations," *Forming*, 125–56, esp. 139–42; Jones, *Formation*, 32–40.

[33] Barry Jones, *Formation*.

the centuries as each collection was added. The final form of the book was produced when first Joel and Obadiah and later Jonah were added to produce books of eleven and twelve prophets respectively. The differences between 4QXII[a], LXX, and MT reflect the different forms of the Twelve during the course of their evolution. Nevertheless, it is striking that although Jones is concerned with the final sequence of the Twelve, he never offers a full synchronic interpretation of the sequence in any of the versions. Instead, he primarily addresses the implications of the respective sequences for reconstructing the redactional formation of the Twelve. This is particularly problematic because recent advances in redaction criticism call unequivocally for a full synchronic analysis of the final form of the text prior to engaging in the diachronic enterprise of reconstructing the compositional and redactional history of a text.[34]

The second major issue is the extent to which many of these studies argue for the redactional formation of the Book of the Twelve as a whole. The arguments for this position are based upon the identification of secondary elements in the constituent prophetic books and their correlation in a larger redactional scheme to form collections that transcend the boundaries of the individual books. But Ben Zvi in particular points to the role that the titles, superscriptions, and introductions for each of the constituent books of the Twelve play in establishing their identities as separate composition or literary units within the larger framework of the Twelve, i.e., the *books* of the Twelve are meant to be read as twelve distinct books that are brought together in one collection.[35] Although previous research points to some broad thematic interrelationships among the Twelve, such as the "Day of YHWH," images of natural fertility or the lack thereof, and general concerns with judgment and restoration, the relatively mechanical association of catchwords in these passages does not establish their character as redactional additions that are *intentionally* designed to unite the various constituent books. The many cases of intertextual citation among the Twelve, however, such as Joel's citation of Obadiah and other books or Zechariah's citation of Micah, do point to interrelationships that must be evaluated.

On this basis, Ben Zvi calls for a reception-centered approach that emphasizes the role of the reader rather than a production-centered approach that emphasizes the role of the author.[36] Was the Book of the Twelve read as a whole? Or was it read as twelve individual prophetic books? Again, the question of synchronic analysis that requires analysis of the whole comes to the forefront. The individual titles and introduc-

---

[34] Knierim, "Criticism"; Sweeney, "Formation and Form."

[35] Ben Zvi, "Twelve Prophetic Books."

[36] Ibid., 149–54.

tions to the constituent books of the Twelve indicate that each book is presented as a coherent and self-contained unit that requires evaluation on its own terms. Furthermore, the individual books are arranged in sequence—and that sequence differs between the three versions of the Twelve identified above. In order properly to understand the Book of the Twelve, each version of the Twelve must first be analyzed synchronically—both according to its final form and the forms of its constituent units—before any attempt can be made to establish its interpretation or to reconstruct its redactional history.

The Masoretic and Septuagint Versions of the Book of the Twelve

A full sequence of books for the Book of the Twelve appears only in the Septuagint and Masoretic versions of the book. Although 4QXII[a] may well represent a third version of the Twelve, the manuscript is fragmentary and preserves portions of only three books. It is impossible to know whether or not all twelve of the books of the Twelve Prophets were originally present in this manuscript. Furthermore even if all twelve books were present, it is impossible to know in what sequence they appeared. It is well known that the Qumran scribes frequently rearranged and rewrote biblical texts to suit their own purposes.[37] Consequently, 4QXII[a] cannot be considered as definitive evidence for a third major version of the Book of the Twelve.

Most attempts to explain the sequence of both the LXX and MT versions of the Book of the Twelve have focused on chronological factors, although the relative size of the books and thematic concerns are sometimes considered.[38] The reason for such a contention is that the books representing prophets from the eighth century (Hosea; Amos; Micah) appear generally at the beginning of the sequences, those representing

[37] See, for example, the Psalms Scroll (11QPss), which rearranges Psalms according to its own purposes; the Habakkuk Pesher (1QpHab), which eliminates Habakkuk 3 and interprets Habakkuk 1–2 in relation to the early history of the Qumran sect; the Temple Scroll (11QTem), which rewrites the Book of Deuteronomy in relation to other halakhic texts in the Torah, and the Great Isaiah Scroll (1QIsa[a]), which frequently rewrites the text of Isaiah in relation to the ideology of the Qumran sect.

[38] For a full discussion of the problem of the sequence of books in the various versions of the Book of the Twelve, see Marvin A. Sweeney, "Sequence and Interpretation in the Book of the Twelve" (paper presented at the Society of Biblical Literature International Meeting, Lausanne, Switzerland, July 1997), which will appear in a volume of essays to be edited by James D. Nogalski and the author.

prophets from the seventh century (Nahum; Habakkuk; Zephaniah) appear in the middle of the sequences, and those representing prophets from the sixth century (Haggai; Zechariah) appear at the end. The books of Joel; Obadiah; and Malachi are problematic, however, because they do not provide clear evidence of the historical setting in which their respective prophets are to be placed. Indeed, each is associated somehow with figures from the ninth century, i.e., the reference to the Valley of Jehoshaphat in Joel 4:12 (NRSV: 3:12) recalls the Judean King Jehoshaphat's (r. 873–849 B.C.E.) defeat of Ammon, Moab, and the men of Seir (Edom) in the Valley of Berachah near Teqoa as related in 2 Chronicles 20; Obadiah is the name of Elijah's associate who announced the presence of the prophet to the Israelite King Ahab (r. 869–850 B.C.E.) and hid the prophets of YHWH (1 Kings 18); and Malachi is likewise associated with Elijah in Mal 3:1, 23-24 (NRSV: Mal 3:1; 4:5-6). None of these associations can be taken as evidence for the actual historical settings of these prophets, but they do provide the only evidence for establishing the representation of setting in each.

Ironically, the ninth century settings presupposed in these books would require them to begin the sequence of the Twelve if indeed the book was arranged according to chronological principles, but of course they do not. Even the supposed chronological arrangement of the other prophets is questionable. Among the eighth century prophets, Jonah and Amos would have to come first as they are set in the reigns of Jeroboam ben Joash of Israel (786–746 B.C.E.) and Uzziah of Judah (783–742 B.C.E.), whereas Hosea is placed from the reign of Jeroboam ben Joash through the reign of Hezekiah of Judah (715–687/6 B.C.E.) and Micah is placed in the reigns of the Judean kings Jotham (742–735 B.C.E.), Ahaz (735–715 B.C.E.), and Hezekiah. Of the seventh century prophets, Habakkuk would have to be last as the reference to the rise of the Neo-Babylonians and the threat they posed to Judah presupposes the period after the time of Josiah when both Zephaniah and Nahum are set. Although chronological factors may have played some role, perhaps at an earlier stage in the formation of the Twelve, clearly the present form of neither the LXX nor the MT version of the Book of the Twelve is arranged in a chronological sequence.

At the same time, both the LXX and the MT appear to presuppose a progression from concerns with the judgment or punishment of Israel and Judah in the monarchic period to the restoration of Jerusalem and the Temple in the post-exilic period. In this regard, it is noteworthy that both versions begin with Hosea, which metaphorically employs the figures of Hosea and Gomer to represent the divorce or disruption of the relationship between YHWH and Israel, and conclude with Malachi, in which YHWH expresses opposition to divorce and calls upon the

people to hold firm to the covenant as YHWH's messenger approaches.
Furthermore, the theme of the Day of YHWH as a day of punishment of
both Israel and the nations as well as the manifestation of YHWH's
sovereignty in Zion likewise permeates the books that comprise the
Twelve. Nevertheless, this progression from judgment to restoration is
configured differently in each version of the Twelve.

The LXX version of the Twelve appears to present an initial concern
with the punishment and restoration of the northern kingdom of Israel,
which then provides a model for understanding the experience of Jeru-
salem/Judah and the nations. The initial concern with the northern
kingdom of Israel appears in Hosea; Amos; and Micah, which constitute the first three books of the LXX sequence. As noted above, Hosea is
fundamentally concerned with the relationship between YHWH and
Israel, and employs the metaphor of Hosea's marriage to Gomer to
portray the potential dissolution of that relationship as well as the potential for its restoration or continuation. Although the book is concerned primarily with the northern kingdom of Israel, it points to
concern with Judah as well, and ultimately calls upon Israel to return to
YHWH at the end of the book. In this respect, it is ideally suited to begin
the sequence of the Twelve as this model of disruption and the anticipation of the restoration underlies the sequence of the entire book. The
second book in the LXX sequence of the Twelve, Amos, focuses especially on the prophet's condemnation of the northern kingdom of Israel
for corruption, including both its king, Jeroboam ben Joash, and its
sanctuary at Beth El, prior to calling for the restoration of Davidic rule
over the north, which entails the reunification of Israel and Judah as in
the days of David and Solomon, as an expression of the will of YHWH.
Micah, the third book in the LXX sequence of the Twelve, likewise begins with a focus on the punishment of northern Israel and Samaria,
but explicitly compares the north with Judah and Jerusalem. In this
scenario, the experience of Israel becomes the paradigm for that of
Jerusalem and Judah. But Micah also looks to restoration, and the
Babylonian Exile becomes the catalyst by which Israel and Judah return to YHWH at Zion, the nations recognize YHWH's sovereignty, and a
new Davidic monarch rises to exercise just rule on YHWH's behalf over
all. Although only Amos explicitly mentions the "Day of YHWH" (Amos
5:18-20), all three books explicitly anticipate the "day" when this process will be realized.

The fourth book in the LXX sequence of the Twelve, Joel, marks the
transition to a new concern with Jerusalem and the nations. Joel portrays the threat posed to YHWH's land by the nations metaphorically
represented as a locust plague that threatens creation. It envisions
YHWH's response to that threat on the Day of YHWH in which YHWH will

bring the heavenly hosts to defeat the threatening nations and restore the fertility of the land. The anonymity of the book and its many inter-textual references to other books within the Twelve enable Joel to as-sume a programmatic role within the sequence of the Twelve as it presents a typological scenario of threat to Jerusalem, punishment of the offending nations, and restoration that expresses the basic themes of the Book of the Twelve as a whole.[39]

The next three books in the LXX sequence of the Twelve, Obadiah; Jonah; and Nahum, then focus on the nations. Obadiah specifically identifies Edom as the object of a diatribe that accuses the nation of standing by, gloating, and assisting as foreigners ravage Jerusalem. It employs the motif of the "Day of YHWH," which enables Edom to stand as a symbol of the nations at large. This is especially important within the Twelve since Edom appears once again in Malachi as the object of YHWH's wrath. The book of Jonah likewise addresses the issue of the nations, but it points to the possibility of YHWH's mercy should the na-tions repent. Within the LXX sequence of the Twelve, Hosea and Micah have already pointed to the possibility of repentance for Israel, and Jonah holds out the same possibility for the Assyrian capital of Nineveh. The issue is especially poignant because Jonah ben Amittai, a prophet from the time of Jeroboam ben Joash (2 Kgs 14:25), presumably knows that Assyria will one day destroy his native northern Israel. Certainly, the reader of the Twelve knows that this is the case. The book of Nahum then makes it very clear that in the absence of repentance, Nineveh will suffer YHWH's judgment for its abusive actions and arrogance in de-stroying Israel and defying YHWH. Nahum also looks forward to the restoration of Israel and therefore points to the balance of the Book of the Twelve.

The next four books in the LXX sequence of the Book of the Twelve then turn to a concern with Jerusalem. Habakkuk begins this portion of the sequence by directing attention to the emergence of the Chaldeans or the Neo-Babylonian empire as a threat to Judah (Hab 1:6; cf. 1:2-4). Through the course of a report of a dialogue between the prophet and YHWH, it becomes clear that YHWH is responsible for bringing the Baby-lonians, but the book seemingly resolves the issue by pointing to the ultimate downfall of the oppressor as a result of its excessive greed. Nevertheless, it also raises the issue of theodicy in that it is never clear that Judah deserves punishment. The book of Zephaniah then follows

---

[39] For a full discussion of Joel's place and function within the LXX and Masoretic versions of the Book of the Twelve, see Marvin A. Sweeney, "The Place and Func-tion of Joel in the Book of the Twelve," *Society of Biblical Literature 1999 Seminar Papers* (Atlanta: Scholars, 1999) 570–95.

with its call for a purge of all that is evil from Jerusalem and Judah. Chronologically speaking, Zephaniah should precede Habakkuk as it is set during the reign of Josiah prior to the emergence of Babylon as a threat to Judah, but its placement in the present position enables Zephaniah to function as justification for the destruction of Jerusalem at the hands of the Babylonians. Again, the Day of YHWH is prominently featured as the day when YHWH will bring the punishment—and the subsequent restoration—about. The destruction of Jerusalem and the Temple is never explicitly portrayed in the Book of the Twelve, but the scenario of Temple reconstruction and the restoration of the exiles by the nations portrayed in Haggai clearly presupposes the events of 587–6 B.C.E. The book is set in the second year of the Persian king Darius (520 B.C.E.), and exhorts the people to support the process of Temple reconstruction. The ultimate goal of the process is the recognition of YHWH by the nations as sovereign. YHWH's overthrow of the throne of the kingdoms and the establishment of Zerubbabel as YHWH's signet, a clear call for the restoration of the Davidic dynasty in Jerusalem. The book of Zechariah is set in the same general period of the second through fourth years of Darius, and points to the eschatological combat that will take place successively against Judah, Israel, and the nations as YHWH's sovereignty is once again established and recognized at Zion. Zechariah's references to Micah's scenario in which Israel and the nations are purged prior to the establishment of world peace at Zion (Zechariah 8; 14; Micah 4–5) play a major role in binding the Book of the Twelve together. Of course, such a portrayal constitutes the ultimate outcome of the Day of YHWH when read in the context of the Book of the Twelve.

Finally, the Book of Malachi sums up the major concerns outlined throughout the Book of the Twelve, i.e., the potential divorce or disruption of the covenant between Israel and YHWH; the polluted state of the Temple, priesthood, and land; the Day of YHWH; and the called for renewed adherence to the covenant. It points to the time when YHWH's messenger will come to announce YHWH's appearance, and it calls for renewed observance of YHWH's Torah in keeping with the scenario laid out in Micah 4–5. The concluding references to Elijah point to the references in Joel and Obadiah to the ninth century when Jehoshaphat ruled in Jerusalem and Edom broke away from Israelite rule. Overall, the portrayal of YHWH's judgment against Edom in Malachi is designed to provide a threat that will motivate the descendants of Jacob to maintain their relationship with YHWH.

The Masoretic version of the Twelve employs a very different principle of organization than that of the LXX in which the initial books concerned with the northern kingdom of Israel are interspersed with those concerned with Jerusalem and the nations. The result is a sequence that emphasizes the role of Jerusalem and its relationship to both Israel and the nations throughout the Masoretic form of the Book of the Twelve. Such a concern is evident in the placement of the two major programmatic books of the Twelve, Hosea and Joel, at the beginning of the sequence. Like the LXX sequence of the Twelve, the Masoretic sequence begins with Hosea and ends with Malachi so that the metaphorical portrayal of YHWH's relationship with Israel as a marriage that potentially results in divorce appears at the outset of the sequence. Once again, the question of the relationship or covenant between YHWH and Israel is addressed at the beginning by portraying the potential dissolution of the marriage between Hosea and Gomer. Likewise, the book of Malachi points to the potential resolution of the issue at the end of the Twelve by stating that YHWH hates divorce and calling upon the readers of the book to observe YHWH's expectations as defined by the Torah. Although Hosea clearly focuses on the northern kingdom of Israel and calls upon Israel to return to YHWH, the book has implications for Jerusalem and Judah as well in that it also envisions Judah's punishment for transgressing YHWH's commandments (Hos 12:3 [NRSV: 12:2]; 1:7; 5:5, 10, 14; 6:4, 11; 8:14; 10:11) and looks forward to the restoration of Davidic rule over Israel (Hos 3:1-5). Although Jerusalem is not explicitly mentioned, the restoration of Israel to Davidic rule would entail the reestablishment of Jerusalem as the political and religious center of all Israel.

Such a contention is particularly important when read in relation to the following book of Joel. As noted above, Joel takes up the threat posed to Jerusalem by the nations and YHWH's response to that threat on the Day of YHWH. Hosea had already made it clear that Israel would be punished at the hands of the nations, but it did not envision a threat against Jerusalem. Joel postulates just such a threat and portrays it in historically open terms so that the book cannot be tied to any specific historical situation; rather, it functions as a typological portrayal of the threat posed to Jerusalem—and indeed, the natural order of creation—that can apply to any historical setting in which a threat is posed to Jerusalem. In this manner, Joel defines the Leitmotif of the Masoretic form of the Book of the Twelve,[40] i.e., Jerusalem will be threatened by the nations and the natural order will be threatened by the forces of chaos, but YHWH will step in to deliver Jerusalem and creation from that threat on the Day of YHWH when the forces of the nations and chaos are defeated and subsumed to YHWH's sovereignty at Zion. This

---

[40] Sweeney, "The Place and Function of Joel."

motif builds upon the presentation of Hosea, particularly its portrayal of the threat posed by Israel's actions to the natural world of creation and YHWH's efforts to restore Israel and the natural world. More importantly, it appears to function as the major concern throughout the rest of the Masoretic form of the Book of the Twelve.

This is evident in the third book of the MT sequence, Amos, which takes up the issue of YHWH's judgment of the northern kingdom of Israel and the nations, and points to the restoration of Israel to Davidic rule. The book highlights Judean concerns from the outset by portraying YHWH's roaring from Zion (Amos 1:2) as an introduction to the oracles against the nations that culminate in the judgment of Judah and northern Israel (Amos 1–2). The prime target of Amos' oracles appears to be the northern dynasty and the royal altar at Beth El, both of which are to be destroyed according to Amos, so that ultimately, the fallen booth of David will be restored together with the natural fecundity of the land (Amos 7–9). Again, the restoration of the Davidic house points to the importance of Jerusalem. Statements concerning Israel's possession of Edom appear in the concluding portion of the Masoretic form of the book, which facilitates the transition to Obadiah, the fourth book of the sequence. Insofar as Obadiah takes up the condemnation of Edom and its submission to Israel at Zion on the Day of YHWH, it constitutes a projected fulfillment of the scenarios laid out in both Joel and Amos. Many note that Edom fills a typological role as a symbol of the nations, but it should be noted that Edom was an early vassal of the Davidic house that broke free during the eighth century B.C.E. Its submission to Israel at Zion entails an element in the restoration of the Davidic house and the role of Jerusalem as holy center of Israel and the world in the Masoretic form of the Book of the Twelve.

The book of Jonah then follows as the fifth in the Masoretic sequence of the Twelve. As noted above, it raises the question of YHWH's mercy to the nations, here represented by Nineveh, and this tempers Obadiah's portrayal of judgment against Edom as it does in the LXX sequence. But Jonah's placement prior to Micah in the Masoretic sequence of the Twelve is also noteworthy insofar as Micah takes up the issue of the punishment (and restoration) of Israel and Jerusalem, and Nineveh, the capital of the Assyrian empire, is the major figure in the realization of that scenario. Readers of Jonah and the Twelve are aware of Nineveh's role in bringing about the destruction of northern Israel and threatening Jerusalem. The recognition that even Nineveh might repent and receive YHWH's mercy is cause for reflection, especially since Nineveh's repentance in Jonah enables the city to survive and ultimately to destroy Jonah's homeland. Jonah thereby points to YHWH's ultimate plans as articulated in the Masoretic Book of the

Twelve to punish Israel and the nations as part of the process by which both will recognize YHWH's sovereignty at Zion. Micah, the sixth book in the Masoretic sequence, likewise serves this role by pointing to Jerusalem's destruction as an analogy to that of Samaria. But Micah also outlines the process by which a new and righteous Davidic monarch will rise to defeat the nations that punished Israel and Jerusalem, resulting ultimately in a universal peace as both the nations and Israel submit to YHWH's rule at Zion. Such a scenario points ultimately to the portrayal of the nations and Israel at Zion in Zechariah 14.

The balance of the Masoretic sequence of the Twelve then follows the same order as the LXX sequence. Nahum celebrates Nineveh's downfall as an expression of YHWH's power and justice in the world. Although many criticize it as vindictive, it announces Nineveh's downfall as punishment for its abusive treatment of those placed under its authority. Nahum therefore points to YHWH's justice as a basic principle of creation and as the foundation for Judah's (and Jerusalem's) ultimate restoration. Habakkuk then follows with its assertions that YHWH is responsible for bringing the Neo-Babylonian empire to threaten Judah, and thereby reaffirms Nahum's portrayal of Israel's or Judah's judgment as a part of YHWH's plans from the outset. It also looks forward to YHWH's punishment of the Neo-Babylonians who, like Nineveh, also overstep their bounds. Whereas Habakkuk does not make it clear that Judah has committed any wrongdoing that justifies punishment at the hands of the Babylonians, Zephaniah calls upon the nation of Judah to purge itself from the influence of foreign gods. Zephaniah's portrayal of Judah's purification on the Day of YHWH clearly represents the destruction of Jerusalem by the Babylonians, although the book appears to have been written early in Josiah's reign prior to the time when Babylon posed a threat to Judah.

The book of Haggai, the tenth book in the Masoretic sequence, then takes up the issue of the restoration of the Temple in Jerusalem as the holy center of Israel and the nations. Essentially, it views the rebuilding of the Temple as a symbol of YHWH's world-wide sovereignty that will see the nations streaming to Jerusalem to bring gifts to YHWH at the Temple. As noted earlier, the rebuilding of the Temple also signals YHWH's intentions to overthrow the throne of the kingdoms and to restore Zerubbabel—and thus the house of David—to the role of YHWH's regent in Jerusalem. Zechariah, once again, portrays the significance of the building of the Jerusalem Temple in a series of visions in which the rebuilding of the Temple is represented as an event of world-wide significance. That significance is portrayed in the second half of the book which depicts Zion as the scene of combat in which the old shepherds or rulers are removed and both Israel and the nations ultimately submit to YHWH at Zion in the midst of cosmic upheaval that concludes with the celebration of Sukkoth.

Finally, Malachi once again concludes the sequence by pointing to the time when YHWH's messenger will ultimately return as the basis for an appeal to observe YHWH's Torah. The readers of the book are presented with a choice, to suffer like Esau or to return like Jacob and ultimately reap the benefits of living under YHWH's rule. The coming day of YHWH's return in Malachi of course provides the capstone for the repeated articulation of the coming Day of YHWH that appears throughout the Book of the Twelve. The concluding references to Moses and Elijah likewise aid in linking the Book of the Twelve to the Pentateuch and the Former Prophets.

Implications for the Setting and Compositional History of the Book of the Twelve

Clearly, the LXX and Masoretic forms of the Book of the Twelve point to two very different organizational principles and underlying conceptualizations by which the sequence of prophets in the Twelve is presented and read. Both are ultimately concerned with questions concerning the relationship or covenant between YHWH and Israel, including both an understanding of the punishment or suffering that Israel and Judah underwent in the Assyrian (eighth-seventh centuries B.C.E.) and Babylonian (seventh-sixth centuries B.C.E.) periods as well as the implications of the restoration of Jerusalem and the Temple in the early Persian period (sixth-fifth centuries B.C.E.). Nevertheless they differ in that the LXX sequence indicates an interest in portraying the experience of the northern kingdom of Israel as a model for understanding that of Jerusalem and Judah whereas the Masoretic sequence focuses on Jerusalem throughout. This suggests that the two forms of the Book of the Twelve were composed or arranged to meet different needs or to address different concerns in the period following the restoration of Jerusalem and the Temple.

The LXX form of the Book of the Twelve, with its interest in comparing the experience of the northern kingdom of Israel with that of Judah and Jerusalem, appears to reflect concerns within Judah during the late-monarchic, exilic, and early post-exilic periods when Judean thinkers were attempting to come to terms with the Assyrian destruction of the northern kingdom of Israel and the threat to Jerusalem and Judah posed and later realized by the Babylonian empire. Indeed, such concerns appear in a number of other biblical works. Many argue for a Josianic

or late-monarchic edition of the Deuteronomistic History in Joshua-
Kings that identifies the worship of foreign gods as the reason for the
collapse of northern Israel and thereby encourages Judah to adhere to
YHWH's commands.[41] The LXX version of the book of Jeremiah, believed
by many scholars to be an earlier form of the book, likewise points in
chapters 2–6 to the punishment of northern Israel as a model for what
might happen to Judah if it does not adhere to YHWH's expectations.[42]
LXX Jeremiah also resembles LXX Twelve by placing materials concerning the nations in the middle of the book—the oracles concerning the
nations appear in LXX Jeremiah 25–32 rather than in Jeremiah 46–51 as
they do in the MT. The portrayal of Jerusalem's fall and potential for
restoration then follows in LXX Jeremiah 33–52. The proposed Josianic
edition of Isaiah in chapters 5–32; 36–37 points to the destruction of
northern Israel as an act of YHWH from which Judah must learn in order
to avoid a similar fate.[43] Following the analogy between Israel and
Judah in Isaiah 5–12, the oracles concerning the nations appear in
Isaiah 13–23 and material concerning Jerusalem and Judah follow in
Isaiah 28–32; 36–37. Likewise, the sixth century edition of Isaiah,[44]
which contains the writings of Second Isaiah, also employs the model
of Jacob's or Israel's Exile in Isaiah 40–48 prior to turning to the issue of
the restoration of Jerusalem in Isaiah 49–55. Whereas Judean thinkers
in the late-monarchic period saw the destruction of northern Israel as a
sign of YHWH's intentions to reunite the north and south under Davidic
rule, later Judean thinkers during the Exile and the early years of the
restoration would have seen northern Israel's experience of punishment and projected restoration as a model for interpreting the experience of Jerusalem and Judah. The LXX form of the Book of the Twelve
reflects such an outlook, and may indeed represent an early form of the
Book of the Twelve that began to take shape in the late-monarchic pe-

---

[41] For example, Frank M. Cross, Jr., "The Themes of the Book of Kings," *Canaanite
Myth and Hebrew Epic* (Cambridge: Harvard, 1973) 274–89. For full discussion of
scholarship on the Deuteronomistic History, see Steven L. McKenzie, "The Deuteronomistic History," *ABD* II:160–68, and Thomas Römer and Albert de Pury,
"L'historiographie deutéronomiste (HD). Histoire de la recherche et enjeux du
débat," *Israël construit son histoire. L'histriographie deutéronomiste à la lumière des
recherches récentes*, ed. A. de Pury and J.-D. Macchi (Geneva: Labor et Fides, 1996)
9–120. See also Marvin A. Sweeney, *King Josiah of Judah: The Lost Messiah of Israel* (Oxford and New York: Oxford University Press, 2000).

[42] Jack Lundbom, "Jeremiah, Book of," *ABD* III:706–21.

[43] See Marvin A. Sweeney, *Isaiah 1–39, with an Introduction to Prophetic Literature*,
FOTL, vol. 16 (Grand Rapids, MI: Eerdmans, 1996), for discussion.

[44] Sweeney, *Isaiah*.

riod. The full form of the book would range from the restoration of the Temple through the time of Ezra and Nehemiah in the fifth century B.C.E. and perhaps beyond. Unfortunately, such a proposal must remain hypothetical as the earliest manuscripts that reflect this sequence are Greek Christian manuscripts, such as *Codex Vaticanus* or *Codex Sinaiticus,* that date to the fourth century C.E.

The Masoretic version of the Book of the Twelve, which focuses especially on the role of Jerusalem at the center of creation and the nations, appears to reflect the concerns of the later Persian period, particularly in the time of Ezra and Nehemiah, when concern shifted away from the north to focus almost entirely on Jerusalem as the holy center of Persian-period Yehud. The appointment of Nehemiah and later Ezra by the Persians apparently signaled an attempt to establish a new administrative center in Jerusalem that would have been taken from territory formerly under the control of figures based in Samaria or Damascus, and prompted the conflicts between such administrative figures from the north and the community based in Jerusalem as portrayed in the books of Ezra and Nehemiah. Such concern with Jerusalem appears throughout the books of Ezra–Nehemiah and 1–2 Chronicles, which were apparently composed separately from the late-fifth through the fourth centuries B.C.E.[45] The shift from concern with the north to concern with Jerusalem is especially evident in Chronicles, which reworks Samuel–Kings by eliminating most material pertaining to northern Israel in order to present a history that focuses on Judah, Jerusalem, and the Temple. A similar shift may be observed in the Masoretic form of Jeremiah, which many take to be a later edition that expands the LXX form of the book.[46] MT Jeremiah focuses on Jerusalem from the outset, as indicated by Jeremiah 2:2, which adds the statement that Jeremiah's oracles are addressed to the people of Jerusalem. Likewise, the oracles concerning the nations are placed at the end of the book in chapters 46–51 so that Jeremiah 1–45 focuses entirely on Jerusalem and Judah. This shift is also evident in the final form of the book of Isaiah, which may derived from the fifth century B.C.E., which frames the entire book by focusing on Jerusalem at the beginning (Isaiah 1; 2–4) and the end (Isaiah 56–66; cf. Isaiah 49–54).[47] A similar concern with Jerusalem permeates the book of Ezekiel, dated to exilic or early-post-exilic times,[48] which begins by portraying YHWH's departure from the city and ends

---

[45] Ralph Klein, "Ezra-Nehemiah, Books of," *ABD* II:731–42. By the same author, "Chronicles, Books of 1–2," *ABD* I:992–1002.

[46] Lundbom, "Jeremiah, Book of."

[47] Sweeney, *Isaiah.*

[48] Lawrence Boadt, "Ezekiel, Book of," *ABD* II:711–22.

with a portrayal of the projected Temple in Jerusalem. The earliest manuscripts that reflect the sequence of the Masoretic version of the Twelve, MurXII and 8HevXIIgr, date to the Hasmonean period in the second-first centuries B.C.E., a period in which the role and sanctity of Jerusalem were of paramount concern. Such considerations suggest that the Masoretic version of the Twelve derives from later periods and concerns than those of the LXX version of the Book, ranging from the period of Ezra–Nehemiah through the early Hasmonean period.

This relative dating of the LXX and Masoretic forms of the Book of the Twelve may also contribute to discussion of its diachronic formation. As noted above, the LXX form of the book begins with the grouping Hosea; Amos; and Micah. Schart, Nogalski, and others have noted that these books all derive from eighth century prophets and that their respective superscriptions are somewhat consistent in form in that they all employ similar phraseology to identify the words of their respective prophets and the reigns of the Israelite and Judean kings in which they prophesied.[49] The same observations may be made for the superscription of Zephaniah, but no other books among the Twelve share this form. It therefore seems likely that an early grouping of Hosea; Amos; Micah; and Zephaniah may have been extant in the reign of Josiah in order to support his efforts to restore Davidic rule over all Israel with Jerusalem as the religious center. Other books, perhaps in groups, would have entered the sequence over time as the collection developed in relation to reflection on later historical events. Nahum and Habakkuk would reflect the post-Josian period when Babylon replaced Assyria as Judah's primary enemy. Haggai and Zechariah would reflect the early Persian period when the Temple was reconstructed. Joel, Obadiah, and Jonah would reflect the fifth century when the question of Judah's continuing relationship with Persia, the ruler of the nations at the time, would have been raised. Malachi likewise reflects fifth century concerns with adherence to YHWH's covenant in the aftermath of the Temple's reconstruction. Of course, no full manuscript evidence exists to confirm this hypothetical reconstruction of the formation of the Book of the Twelve. However, 4QXII[a], which places Jonah after Malachi, may well indicate that Jonah was a relatively late entry among the Twelve Prophets.

In any event, the various forms of the Book of the Twelve and the potential they have for reconstructing the compositional history of the book point to the important role that the Twelve Prophets play in addressing the concerns and defining the theological/ideological views

---

[49] Nogalski, *Precursors*. By the same author, *Processes*; Schart, *Entstehung*.

of Jewish thinkers from the late-monarchic period and beyond. Although the concerns of the *Berit Olam* commentary series do not include a full redaction-critical analysis and reconstruction of the compositional history of the Book of the Twelve, it is clear there is great potential for future research in this area.

The Commentary

This commentary focuses on a synchronic literary analysis of the Book of the Twelve Prophets. Insofar as the above discussion points to the Book of the Twelve as a collection of twelve individual prophetic books that were placed together to form at least two major versions of the Twelve, it treats the individual books as discrete units within the Twelve and considers their interrelationships within the sequences of both the Masoretic and Septuagint forms of the book. The commentary necessarily includes diachronic considerations in order for the synchronic analysis to make sense. Such diachronic considerations include the historical settings of the prophets included among the Twelve, the historical, cultural, and linguistic contexts and circumstances in which the prophets and other authors of the twelve prophetic books spoke or wrote, and some indication of redaction-critical problems where necessary. Nevertheless, the commentary does not engage in a full redaction-critical analysis of the Book of the Twelve or of its component books. Instead, it focuses on the formal literary structure of the present text of each of the twelve prophetic books that comprise the Book of the Twelve, the various genres of oral and written expression that appear within, the rhetorical characteristics and conventions that play roles in shaping the text, philological and linguistic analysis of the Hebrew words, syntax, and forms of expression that comprise the text, and the historical, social, religious, and cultural settings in which the texts were formed and read. The analysis is based upon the Hebrew Masoretic text of the Twelve, because the MT constitutes the most commonly accepted scriptural base for the Twelve in both Judaism and Christianity. Nevertheless, the Greek Septuagint and the other versions are considered at times to clarify text-critical issues or to illustrate the differences between the various forms of the Book of the Twelve.

In keeping with some forms of traditional Jewish practice, this commentary does not spell the Name of G–d. Rather, names applied to G–d are rendered as Yhwh, jhwh, G–d, L–rd, etc. It also does not apply the masculine pronoun to G–d, except where required by the citation of Bible translations.

FOR FURTHER READING

COMMENTARIES

Marti, Karl. *Das Dodekapropheton*. Kurzer Hand-Commentar zum Alten Testament, XIII. Tübingen: J.C.B. Mohr (Paul Siebeck), 1904.

Nowack, Wilhelm. *Die kleinen Propheten*. Handkommentar zum Alten Testament, III/4. Göttingen: Vandenhoeck & Ruprecht, 3rd edition, 1922.

Robinson, Theodore H. and Friedrich Horst. *Die zwölf kleinen Propheten*. Handbuch zum Alten Testament, 14. Tübingen: J.C.B. Mohr (Paul Siebeck), 3rd edition, 1964.

Sellin, Ernst. *Das Zwölfprophetenbuch*. Kommentar zum Alten Testament, XII. Leipzig: A. Deichert, 2nd–3rd edition, 1929–1930.

Van Hoonacker, A. *Les douze petits prophètes*. Études bibliques. Paris: J. Gabalda, 1908.

Weiser, Arthur and Karl Elliger. *Das Buch der zwölf kleinen Propheten*. Das Alte Testament Deutsch, 24–25. Göttingen: Vandenhoeck & Ruprecht, 1956.

Wellhausen, Julius. *Die Kleinen Propheten*. Berlin: Walter de Gruyter, 1963 (1898).

STUDIES

Barton, John. "The Canonical Meaning of the Book of the Twelve." *After the Exile: Essays in Honour of Rex Mason*. Ed. J. Barton and D. J. Reimer, 59–73. Macon, GA: Mercer University, 1996.

Ben Zvi, Ehud. "Twelve Prophetic Books or 'The Twelve': A Few Preliminary Considerations." *Forming Prophetic Literature: Essays on Isaiah and the Twelve in Honor of J.D.W. Watts*. Ed J. W. Watts and P. R. House, 125–56. JSOTSup Series, 235. Sheffield: Sheffield Academic Press, 1996.

Bosshard, Erich. "Beobachtungen zum zwölfprophetenbuch." *Biblische Notizen* 40 (1987) 30–62.

Bosshard-Nepustil, Erich. *Rezeptionen von Jesaja 1–39 im Zwölfprophetenbuch.* Orbis Biblicus et Orientalis, 144. Freiburg: Universitätsverlag; Göttingen: Vandenhoeck & Ruprecht, 1997.

Bosshard, Erich and Reinhold Gregor Kratz. "Maleachi im Zwölfprophetenbuch." *Biblische Notizen* 52 (1990) 27–46.

Budde, Karl. "Eine folgenschwere Redaction des Zwölfprophetenbuchs." *Zeitschrift für die alttestamentliche Wissenschaft* 39 (1922) 218–29.

Collins, Terrence. *The Mantle of Elijah: The Redaction Criticism of the Prophetical Book.* Biblical Seminar, 20, 59–87. Sheffield: JSOT Press, 1993.

Fuller, Russell. "The Form and Formation of the Book of the Twelve: The Evidence from the Judean Desert." *Forming Prophetic Literature: Essays on Isaiah and the Twelve in Honor of J.D.W. Watts.* Ed. J. W. Watts and P. R. House. JSOTSup Series, 235, 86–101. Sheffield: Sheffield Academic Press, 1996.

House, Paul. *The Unity of the Twelve.* JSOTSup Series, 97. Bible and Literature Series, 27. Sheffield: Almond, 1990.

Jones, Barry Alan. *The Formation of the Book of the Twelve: A Study in Text and Canon.* SBLDS, 149. Atlanta: Scholars Press, 1995.

Marks, Herbert. "The Twelve Prophets." *The Literary Guide to the Bible.* Ed. R. Alter and F. Kermode, 207–32. Cambridge: Belknap, 1987.

Nogalski, James D. "Intertextuality and the Twelve." *Forming Prophetic Literature: Essays on Isaiah and the Twelve in Honor of J.D.W. Watts.* Ed. J. W. Watts and P. R. House. JSOTSup Series, 235, 102–24. Sheffield: Sheffield Academic Press, 1996.

_____. *Literary Precursors to the Book of the Twelve.* Beiheft zur Zeitschrift für die alttestamentliche Wissenschaft, 117. Berlin and New York: Walter de Gruyter, 1993.

_____. *Redactional Processes in the Book of the Twelve.* Beiheft zur Zeitschrift für die alttestamentliche Wissenschaft, 118. Berlin and New York: Walter de Gruyter, 1993.

Schart, Aaron. *Die Entstehung des Zwölfprophetenbuch.* Beiheft zur Zeitschrift für die alttestamentliche Wissenschaft, 260. Berlin and New York: Walter de Gruyter, 1998.

Schneider, Dale A. "The Unity of the Book of the Twelve." Ph.D. diss., Yale University, 1979.

Steck, Odil Hannes. *Der Abschluss der Prophetie im Alten Testament. Ein Versuch zur Frage der Vorgeschichte des Kanons.* Biblisch-theologische Studien, 17. Neukirchen-Vluyn: Neukirchener, 1991.

Sweeney, Marvin A. "The Place and Function of Joel in the Book of the Twelve." *Society of Biblical Literature 1999 Seminar Papers,* 570–95. Atlanta: Scholars, 1999.

_____. "Three Recent European Studies of the Composition of the Book of the Twelve." *Review of Biblical Literature* 1 (1999) 22–37.

Van Leeuwen, Raymond C. "Scribal Wisdom and Theodicy in the Book of the Twelve." *In Search of Wisdom: Essays in Memory of John G. Gammie.* Ed. L. G. Perdue, B. B. Scott and W. J. Wiseman, 31–49. Louisville: Westminster John Knox, 1993.

Weimer, Peter. "Obadja: Eine redaktionskritische Analyse." *Biblische Notizen* 27 (1985) 35–99.

Wolfe, Ronald E. "The Editing of the Book of the Twelve." *Zeitschrift für die alttestamentliche Wissenschaft* 53 (1935) 90–129.

Zapff, Burkard M. *Redaktionsgeschichtliche Studien zum Michabuch im Kontext des Dodekapropheton.* Beiheft zur Zeitschrift für die alttestamentliche Wissenschaft, 256. Berlin and New York: Walter de Gruyter, 1997.

HOSEA

HOSEA

Overview

Hosea is the first book in both the Masoretic and Septuagint versions of the Book of the Twelve. Rabbinic tradition considers Hosea to be the earliest of the Twelve (*bBaba Batra* 14b; *bPesahim* 87a; *bSota* 48b), which would suggest the reason for its placement in this position. Amos and Micah are considered to follow chronologically, however, which suggests that the Septuagint employed a chronological principle in its arrangement of the Twelve. Nevertheless, the references to Jotham, Ahaz, and Hezekiah in Hos 1:1 suggest that Hosea should be placed chronologically later than Amos which mentions only Jeroboam ben Joash and Uzziah (Amos 1:1). Hosea seems to be particularly well suited for its position at the head of the Twelve on thematic grounds. It employs the metaphor of Hosea's marriage to Gomer and the birth of their children as a metaphor for YHWH's relationship with Israel. As Hosea accuses Gomer of harlotry and names their children symbolically to represent the divorce of his wife, so YHWH condemns the "wife" Israel for pursuing other lovers and thereby abandoning its covenant with G–d. Likewise, just as Hosea takes back his wife, so YHWH calls upon Israel to return. The book therefore stands as a programmatic statement of one of the primary issues addressed throughout the Book of the Twelve, the condemnation of Israel/Judah and the restoration of the relationship with YHWH following punishment at the hands of various foreign nations. The statements in Malachi concerning YHWH's disdain for divorce are particularly important when read in relation to Hosea because they point to the resolution of the disrupted relationship between YHWH and Israel/Judah at the end of the Book of the Twelve.

The book is clearly intended to be read against the background of the rise of the Assyrian empire in the mid-eighth century B.C.E. and the

3

threat it posed to the northern kingdom of Israel. Although Rabbinic tradition considers Hosea to be the earliest of the Twelve Prophets, most modern scholars place Hosea after the time of Amos.[1] Whereas Amos speaks in the mid-eighth century at a time when Assyria is just beginning to pose a threat, Hosea's references to the corruption and demise of Israel's kings (Hos 7:7; 13:10-11), battle in the land of Israel (Hos 5:8–6:6), the breaking of the calf of Samaria (Hos 8:6), the demise of Israel (Hos 8:8), and the explicit reference to Shalmaneser's (generally identified as Shalmaneser V, the Assyrian monarch who invaded Israel in 724–722 B.C.E.) sack of Beth Arbel (Hos 10:14), point to a time when Israel actually suffered invasion by the Assyrian army. From the death of the Israelite king Jeroboam II in 746 B.C.E., six kings sat on the Israelite throne (Zechariah, Shallum, Menahem, Pekahiah, Pekah, Hoshea) and only two of them were not assassinated by their successors (Menahem and Hoshea). The Assyrian army invaded Israel during the course of the Syro-Ephraimitic War in 735–732 B.C.E., when Tiglath Pileser III stripped Israel of its outlying territories in the trans-Jordan, Galilee, and the coastal plain, and again in 724–722 B.C.E. when Shalmaneser V and Sargon II destroyed the kingdom and exiled much of its population (cf. 2 Kings 17).

There are problems with this view. Although many commentators see Hosea as opposed to kingship in general,[2] his criticism of the monarchy focuses especially on the dynasty of King Jehu (842–815), insofar as his son Jezreel is named for the site at which Jehu killed the Omride King Jehoram and his mother Jezebel in order to portray YHWH's disrupted relationship with Israel. This reference to the house of Jehu makes little sense if Hosea is placed in a much later period when the Assyrians actually attacked, as the Jehu monarchs were long gone. Instead, the following commentary attempts to demonstrate that the book of Hosea does not portray the actual Assyrian invasions of Israel. Rather, it was written largely in the period following the death of Jeroboam and prior to the Assyrian assault in 735–732 in an effort to convince Israel to abandon its alliance with Assyria, concluded initially by

---

[1] For a summary of discussion concerning historical issues in the interpretation of Hosea, see G. I. Davies, *Hosea*, OT Guides (Sheffield: Sheffield Academic Press, 1993) 13–20. See also the treatments of Israelite history during the eighth century B.C.E. in John H. Hayes and J. Maxwell Miller, eds., *Israelite and Judaean History*, OTL (Philadelphia: Westminster, 1977) 381–434 and A. K. Grayson in the *Cambridge Ancient History*, vol. 3, part 1. *The History of the Balkans: The Middle East and the Aegean World, Tenth to Eighth Centuries B.C.*, ed. J. Boardman et al. (Cambridge: Cambridge University Press, 1982).

[2] A. Gelston, "Kingship in the Book of Hosea," *OTS* 19 (1974) 71–85.

King Jehu and maintained by his successors, Jehoahaz (815–801), Jehoash (801–786), Jeroboam II (786–746), and Zechariah (746), throughout the rule of the Jehu dynasty. Hosea lived at a time when the future
of Israel's foreign alliances was the subject of intense debate, and it appears that Zechariah was assassinated by Shallum in order to force a
change in Israel's relations from alliance with Assyria to alliance with
Aram. Menahem apparently killed Shallum in order to return to a policy
of alliance with Assyria, which he and his son Pekahiah maintained
throughout their reigns. Pekahiah was assassinated by Pekah, who
formed the anti-Assyrian Syro-Ephraimitic alliance with Rezin of
Damascus, and ultimately led Israel into a confrontation with the Assyrians. Pekah was assassinated during the course of the Assyrian invasion of Israel by Hoshea, who promptly surrendered. When Hoshea
was unable to stop a revolt in 724 B.C.E., he was imprisoned and deported by Shalmaneser V.

Hosea apparently was heavily involved in the debate over Israel's
future from the end of the Jehu dynasty until the emergence of Pekah.
His position is markedly anti-Assyrian as he portrays Israel's relationship with Assyria as a rejection of YHWH (cf. Hos 8:9; 10:6; 11:5, 11; 12:2
[NRSV: 11:12]; 14:4 [NRSV: 14:3]). He draws heavily on Israel's traditional
history from the time of the patriarch Jacob through the Exodus, wilderness wandering, and conquest of the land of Israel, to portray Israel's
constant rejection of YHWH.[3] It is noteworthy that he sees Jacob as a
positive role model, however, in order to point to his roots in Aram and
his conclusion of a treaty with Laban, as a means to argue for Israel to
establish relations with Aram in his own day (see Hosea 12). Indeed
Hosea's message may well have formed part of the background against
which Shallum assassinated Zechariah or Pekah assassinated Pekahiah.
Hosea's message appears to send a strong signal of support to those
who opposed alliance with Assyria and who sought to return the nation
to its YHWHistic roots by allying with Aram, the early home of Abraham, Sarah, and Rebekah, and the place where Jacob found his brides
Leah and Rachel at the home of their father (and his mother's brother)
Laban. Insofar as the book of Hosea presupposes a Judean setting (cf.
Hos 1:1, which identifies the kings of Judah from Uzziah to Hezekiah
but mentions only Jeroboam ben Joash for the Israelite kings) and includes many statements concerning Judah that are considered redactional,[4] it would appear that Hosea had to leave northern Israel at some

[3] See esp. Heinz-Dieter Neef, *Die Heilstraditionen Israels in der Verkündigung des
Propheten Hosea*, BZAW, vol. 169 (Berlin and New York: Walter de Gruyter, 1987).

[4] See G. I. Emmerson, *Hosea: An Israelite Prophet in Judean Perspective*, JSOTSup,
vol. 28 (Sheffield: JSOT Press, 1984); Gale A. Yee, *Composition and Tradition in the Book*

point and that he settled in Judah. Support for Shallum or Pekah would certainly motivate him to leave the country once Menahem or Hoshea eliminated these figures. Indeed, the book of Hosea appears to have been completed in Judah, and points to the restoration of Judean Davidic rule over the northern kingdom of Israel (Hos 3:1-5)!

Hosea's relationship with Gomer has been the subject of a great deal of speculation.[5] She is called "a woman of harlotry" (Hos 1:2) and portrayed as an unfaithful wife in the early chapters of the book. Many have tried to identify her as a cult prostitute and devotee of Baalistic worship, and others have commented extensively on her marital infidelity. Although this presentation of Gomer forms an important component of the book and stands at the basis of Hosea's conception of Israel's relationship with YHWH, feminist scholars have correctly noted that Gomer is first and foremost a woman and that she never speaks in the book.[6] We do not know if she was indeed a cultic prostitute or if she ever betrayed her husband; we only know that Hosea accuses her of such actions in the book. Interpreters rarely question Hosea on this point, but scholars are increasingly willing to consider that Hosea's portrayal of Gomer does not tell the full story. Indeed, Landy speculates on what it must have been like for Gomer to see this angry man continually brooding and accusing her of base infidelity.[7] Such questions must be posed, particularly as YHWH accuses Israel of infidelity throughout the book, and yet it is YHWH who will bring the Assyrians to punish Israel. Israel was destroyed by the Assyrians, and the book of Hosea explains this reality theologically by arguing that Israel sinned against YHWH. Hosea raises a question of theodicy to the modern reader in a personally pointed way, viz., did Israel sin by failing to be true to YHWH, or did YHWH sin by failing to be true to Israel? In the case of the latter, YHWH would not be the first husband who failed his wife and tried to cover his actions by accusing her of adultery. The question is as relevant to the contemporary world as it was in the past. In the face of the modern experience of the Shoah (Holocaust), one may ask why G–d allowed such evil to take place.

_____

of Hosea: A Redaction Critical Investigation, SBLDS, vol. 102 (Atlanta: Scholars Press, 1987).

[5] See Davies, *Hosea*, 79–93.

[6] See esp. Yvonne Sherwood, *The Prostitute and the Prophet: Hosea's Marriage in Literary-Theological Perspective*, JSOTSup, vol. 212; GCT 2 (Sheffield: Sheffield Academic Press, 1996); Marie-Theres Wacker, *Figurationen des Weiblichen im Hosea-Buch*, HBS, vol. 8 (Freibourg: Herder, 1996); and the essays on Hosea and Gomer in *A Feminist Companion to the Latter Prophets*, ed. A. Brenner (Sheffield: Sheffield Academic Press, 1995).

[7] Landy, *Hosea*, 23–4.

Despite the implications of responsibility for evil, whether by YHWH or by Israel, the book of Hosea is formulated to call for Israel's return and the restoration of its relationship with YHWH. This point is frequently lost in early redaction-critical study of the book as scholars frequently assign passages concerned with the hope for restoration to the post-exilic period, and argue that Hosea's message was one of stern judgment against a recalcitrant people.[8] In light of modern advances in the field of redaction criticism and the emergence of the acceptance in Christian circles of the theological legitimacy of post-biblical Judaism, scholars are increasingly coming to the conclusion that the message of hope and restoration for Israel derives from the prophet himself. Indeed, such advances lead also to a reconceptualization of the structure of the book of Hosea as diachronic readings of the prophet's oracles no longer govern views of its synchronic literary structure. Past scholarship views the book as forming two parts, Hosea 1–3 and 4–14,[9] based upon the generic character of the largely narrative material in chapters 1–3 and the poetic character of chapters 4–14 as well as the view that later messages of hope have been appended to oracle collections concerned with judgment. But full consideration of the generic character of Hosea as a rhetorical work in which several voices speak points to a different understanding.[10] The book contains three basic components: the superscription in Hos 1:1, which identifies the work of Hosea; the body of the work in Hos 1:2–14:9 [NRSV: 14:8], in which the book presents the message of Hosea; and the concluding exhortation to the reader in Hos 14:10 [NRSV: 14:9], in which the reader is encouraged to find YHWH's wisdom in the book. The message of Hosea in Hos 1:2–14:9 [NRSV: 14:8] breaks down further into two components: the report of YHWH's speaking to Hosea concerning his marriage to Gomer and the birth of his children in Hos 1:2–2:3 [NRSV: 1:9] and the presentation of Hosea's oracles, in which the prophet frequently presents YHWH's speech, in Hos 2:4–14:9 [NRSV: 1:10–14:8]. Altogether, the book is intended to persuade its audience to adopt a specific course of action insofar as it presents Hosea as a prophet who called upon Israel to return to YHWH and thereby to prevent the punishment announced in the book.

[8] See esp. Yee, *Composition*, 1–50, for a history of research and critical reevaluation.

[9] Or alternatively three parts: Hosea 1–3; 4–11; 12–14, each of which concludes with a redactional message of hope (Wolff, *Hosea*, xxix–xxxii; Yee, *Composition*, 51–2).

[10] For a full discussion of the synchronic structure and generic character of the book of Hosea as well as their implications for redaction-critical analysis of the book, see the relevant sections of my forthcoming study, *King Josiah of Judah: The Lost Messiah of Israel* (Oxford and New York: Oxford University Press, 2000).

The Superscription: 1:1

The superscription for the entire book of Hosea appears in Hos 1:1. Superscriptions stand as generically and structurally distinct entities within their larger literary contexts in that they are designed to introduce and to identify the material that follows.[11] They are formulated in a third person titular style and generally do not constitute full sentences. This is in contrast to the material that they introduce which is formulated either in prose or poetry as syntactically complete statements. When placed before prophetic material, they generally identify the genre of literature, the identity of the prophet to whom it is attributed, and the time period in which it was purportedly first communicated. In the present case, Hos 1:1 identifies the following material in Hos 1:2–14:10 [NRSV: 14:9] as "the word of YHWH that was unto Hosea ben Be'eri," and places it chronologically "in the days of Uzziah, Jotham, Ahaz, Hezekiah, kings of Judah, and in the days of Jeroboam ben Joash, king of Israel." Hosea 1:1 thereby stands as the first major structural component of the book of Hosea.

The overall form of the superscription in Hos 1:1 is similar to those found in Joel 1:1; Mic 1:1; Zeph 1:1; and LXX Jer 1:1, and variant forms that appear in Jer 1:2; Ezek 1:3; Jonah 1:1; Zech 1:1; Hag 1:1; and Mal 1:1. It appears to be a variation of the typical formula employed in prophetic literature, "and the word of YHWH was unto X" (see Jer 1:4, 11, 13; Ezek 3:16; 6:1; Jonah 3:1; Zech 4:8; 6:9, etc.) that introduces oracular speech by YHWH to a prophet. By identifying the book generically as "the word of YHWH," Hos 1:1 attributes divine authority to the statements by the prophet and the narratives about him. Apart from the contents of the book of Hosea, nothing is known of Hosea or of his father Be'eri. The name Hosea *(hôšēʿa)* means "YHWH saves." In Hebrew, it is identical to the name of Hoshea ben Elah, the last king of the northern kingdom of Israel (2 Kgs 17:1) and the alternative name of Joshua ben Nun, i.e., Hoshea ben Nun (Num 13:8; Deut 32:44). The name Be'eri *(bǝʾērî)* is identical to the Hittite father of Esau's wife Judith (Gen 26:34).

The identities of the kings of Judah and Israel listed in the superscriptions present somewhat of a problem. Although the language and contents of the book demonstrate clearly that Hosea is a prophet from the northern kingdom of Israel, the Judean kings are listed first. Furthermore, the dates of their reigns (Uzziah, 783–742 B.C.E.; Jotham,

---

[11] See Gene M. Tucker, "Prophetic Superscriptions and the Growth of the Canon," *Canon and Authority: Essays in Old Testament Religion and Theology,* ed. G. W. Coats and B. O. Long (Philadelphia: Fortress, 1977) 56–70.

742–735 B.C.E.; Ahaz, 735–715 B.C.E.; Hezekiah 715–687/6 B.C.E.) extend well beyond the dates of the one northern king, Jeroboam ben Joash (reigned 786–746 B.C.E.). The last six kings of northern Israel (Zechariah, 746 B.C.E.; Shallum, 745 B.C.E.; Menahem 745–738 B.C.E.; Pekahiah, 738–737 B.C.E.; Pekah, 737–732 B.C.E.; and Hoshea 732–722/1 B.C.E.) are not mentioned even though they are contemporaries of the Judean kings. Because Hosea consistently criticizes the northern monarchy, particularly for allying with the Assyrians (Hos 5:13; 7:11; 8:9; 9:6; 12:1 [NRSV: 11:12]; 14:3), many scholars argue that Hosea's message must be placed in the period following the reign of Jeroboam ben Joash when northern Israel struggled with the question of whether to submit to or ally with Assyria as Menahem, Pekahiah, and Hoshea (initially) did (2 Kgs 15:17-26; 15:30-31; 17:1-6) or to oppose Assyria militarily as Pekah did (2 Kgs 15:25-31). Some argue that Hosea viewed these kings as illegitimate, and therefore they are not acknowledged in the superscription.

Such a view overlooks two important considerations. First, the present form of the book of Hosea addresses both the northern kingdom of Israel and the southern kingdom of Judah from a relatively pro-Judean perspective. Whereas Israel and Judah are frequently condemned, Israel or Ephraim receives the brunt of the criticism while Judah is singled out as the recipient of YHWH's mercy (see Hos 1:7) and is still associated with G–d (see Hos 12:1 [NRSV: 11:12]). Judah thereby provides the means by which Israel will be restored insofar as Israel will return to YHWH and to David their king (Hos 3:4-5); i.e., when Israel returns to YHWH in Jerusalem and to Davidic/Judean rule, Israel will be restored. Second, Israel's policy of alliance with or submission to Assyria did not begin with Menahem, but with the kings of the dynasty of Jehu. According to Assyrian records, both Jehu (842–815 B.C.E.) and his grandson Jehoash (801–786 B.C.E.) submitted to Assyrian power, which comes as no surprise since Israel needed Assyrian support to fend off incursions by Aram/Syria (see 2 Kgs 10:32–36; 13:1-25). It seems likely that Jeroboam ben Joash, the fourth ruler of the house of Jehu, was able to establish hegemony over Aram/Syria as far north as Lebo-Hamath (2 Kgs 14:23-29) with the aid of Assyria. Assyrian records are relatively scarce for this period, but they indicate that the Assyrian monarch Assur Nirari V was able to assert control in northern Syria over Mati'ilu of Arpad in 751 B.C.E., although Mati'ilu quickly broke free of Assyrian hegemony to conclude a new treaty with Bargayah of KTK.[12] It appears

---

[12] For the treaty between Assur Nirari V and Mati'ilu of Arpad, see Luckenbill, *ARAB*, vol. I:749–60. For Mati'ilu's treaty with Bar Gayah of KTK, see Pritchard, *ANET*, 651–59. See also, W. W. Hallo and W. K. Simpson, *The Ancient Near East: A History* (New York: Harcourt, Brace, Jovanovich, 1971) 131–2.

that Israel's resurgence under Jeroboam ben Joash was due in part to an alliance with Assyria in which Israel and Assyria divided Aram/Syria. Insofar as Hosea initially condemns the house of Jehu (Hos 1:2–2:2 [NRSV: 1:9]), it would appear that Hosea argues that the policy of accommodation to Assyria began with the Jehu dynasty.

These considerations could well explain the enumeration of the kings of Israel and Judah in Hosea 1:1. Shallum's assassination of Zechariah in 745 B.C.E. may have been motivated by an interest in breaking the alliance with Assyria in order to join with Aram/Syria in a renewed effort to oppose the Assyrian resurgence under Tiglath Pileser III (745–727 B.C.E.). Certainly, Menahem's assassination of Shallum and his submission to Assyria would subdue parties interested in such an effort. But Pekah's assassination of Menahem's son Pekahiah and his alliance with Rezin of Aram/Syria constitutes the revival of the anti-Assyrian party in Israel, insofar as the Syro-Ephraimitic alliance was designed to oppose Tiglath-Pileser III. The book of Hosea indicates that the prophet consistently opposed plans to ally with Assyria, and argued that the Assyrian alliance was the ultimate cause for Assyria's interest in subduing Israel. It seems likely then that Hosea, as an opponent of Jeroboam's, Zechariah's, Menahem's, and Pekahiah's policy of alliance with Assyria, would have left Israel to settle in Judah, perhaps as early as the reign of Zechariah when forces opposed to such a policy began to assert themselves. The pro-Judean sentiments expressed in the book of Hosea seem to support such a scenario, and a location in Judah would provide Hosea with a secure base from which to criticize the northern monarchy without fear of retribution.

Parenetic Appeal for Israel's Return:
1:2–14:9 [NRSV: 14:8]

Interpreters generally argue that the structure of the book of Hosea comprises three basic elements: 1) the largely narrative material concerning Hosea's marriage and the birth of his children in Hosea 1–3; 2) the collection of oracular material in Hosea 4–11 in which the prophet announces his message of judgment against Israel for abandoning YHWH; and 3) the oracular material in Hosea 12–14 which employs past tradition to rehearse the history of Israel's relationship with YHWH in order to lead up to a concluding appeal for Israel's return. This understanding of Hosea's structure is based largely on the view that Hosea 1–3 must be a distinct unit because of its primarily prose literary form and because of its thematic focus on Hosea's marriage to Gomer. It is also based on the thematic distinction between judgment against Israel and salvation for Israel, in that each section of the three sections takes up the theme of judgment, but ends with material that looks forward to the restoration of Israel (e.g., Hos 3:1-5; 11:1-11; 14:2-9 [NRSV: 14:1-8]). Scholars tend to explain this arrangement as the product of the later redaction of the book of Hosea, in that they view Hosea as a prophet who announced a message only of judgment against Israel whereas later writers or redactors attempted to soften the blow by adding material that calls for Israel's restoration as well.

Nevertheless, this view is problematic for several reasons. First, interpreters are increasingly abandoning the view that prophetic messages of hope for Israel must be assigned only to the post-exilic period as they recognize that prophecy is a much more complex phenomenon than previously believed. Essentially, prophets represented a variety of viewpoints in ancient Israelite and Judean society, and they were heavily involved in the public political and religious debates of their day. Prophecy did not represent one consistent theological position, but many, as prophets and others debated concerning the proper understanding of YHWH's actions in the world and the policies that the kings and people of Israel and Judah should follow. As part of public discussion, prophets announced either judgment or salvation, depending on how they viewed YHWH's intentions and the choices for action that people might take. In attempting to convince the people of Israel to adhere to YHWH's will, Hosea announced judgment against Israel if the kingdom continued its policy of alliance with Assyria and salvation for Israel if it abandoned Assyria and thereby returned to YHWH.

Second, the common view of the structure of Hosea does not take full account of the literary features of the book, particularly the narrative voice of the book that identifies the speakers and addressees in any given text. Although both Hosea 1 and 3 are generally grouped together because they are prose and concerned with Hosea's marriage(s), they present very different narrative voices that must be accounted for in any assessment of the literary form and perspective of the book. Hosea 1:2–2:2 [NRSV: 1:2–1:11] is basically a third person narrative in which an unidentified narrator reports YHWH's initial instructions to the prophet to marry the harlot Gomer, to have children by her, and to give the children symbolic names that embody YHWH's and the prophet's message to the nation of Israel. Although Hos 2:3 [NRSV. 2:1] is frequently included with 1:2–2:2 [NRSV: 1:2–1:11] because of its reference to Hosea's children, the command, "say to your brother . . ." indicates that the verse is formulated as an address to Jezreel rather than as an instruction by YHWH to Hosea as reported in Hos 1:2–2:2 [NRSV: 1:1-11]. It therefore must be grouped together with Hos 2:4ff. [NRSV: 2:1ff.], which is an address by the prophet to Jezreel that culminates in the reversal of the symbolic names given to Lo Ruhamah and Lo Ammi. In contrast to Hos 1:2–2:2 [NRSV: 1:2–1:11], Hos 3:1-5 is an autobiographical narrative in which the prophet describes YHWH's instructions to marry an adulterous woman who will then symbolize YHWH's decision to take back the people of Israel and restore them to Davidic rule. The autobiographical character of Hos 3:1-5 is particularly important in that it represents the same narrative voice of the poetic material in Hos 2:3-25 [NRSV: 2:1-23], which presents the prophet as the speaker who addresses the people of Israel in order to explain the significance of his marriage, i.e., just as Hosea's wife rejected him to pursue other lovers, so Israel had rejected YHWH. Insofar as both Hos 2:3-25 [NRSV: 2:1-23] and 3:1-5 represent the same narrative perspective in which the prophet speaks in order to establish his marriage as a paradigm for YHWH's relationship with Israel, Hos 2:3–3:5 [NRSV: 2:1–3:5] must be considered together as a distinct literary unit which employs Hosea's marriage as a means to announce both the punishment of Israel and eventual restoration to YHWH.

This assessment of Hos 2:3–3:5 [NRSV: 2:1–3:5] has implications for both the preceding and following material. Although Hos 1:2–2:2 [NRSV: 1:2–1:11] takes up the issue of Hosea's marriage to Gomer and the birth of their children, the objective narrative form of this text indicates that Hosea is not the speaker. Hosea 1:2–3:5 thereby constitutes a distinctive textual unit that establishes Hosea's marriage as a symbolic act and thereby provides the means by which the prophet's own statement may be interpreted. Hosea 1:2–2:2 [NRSV: 1:2–1:11] is the narrator's report of YHWH's instructions to Hosea to marry Gomer and to name their children, but Hos 2:3–3:5 [NRSV: 2:1–3:5] is a presentation of Hosea's own words concerning these matters. Furthermore, the book presents Hosea as the speaker throughout Hos 4:1–14:9 [NRSV: 14:8] in a series of oracles that explore the various dimensions of the relationship between YHWH and Israel in Hosea's time as well as the implications for the future. Overall, the prophet condemns Israel for its actions but calls upon the nation to return to YHWH throughout this section. There is no evidence of an objective narrator other than the prophet until Hos 14:10 [NRSV: 14:9], a wisdom saying that calls upon the reader of the book to be wise in discerning the ways of YHWH. Insofar as Hos 14:10 [NRSV: 14:9] addresses the reader of the book and calls upon him/her to evaluate its message, Hos 14:10 [NRSV: 14:9] stands as an afterward or conclusion to the book analogous to the superscription in Hos 1:1. The narrative perspective of the book therefore indicates a very different structure for the book of Hosea. Following the superscription in Hos 1:1, the body of the book in Hos 1:2–14:9 [NRSV: 14:10] breaks down into two primary sections: 1) the anonymous narrator's report of YHWH's initial instructions to Hosea to marry the harlot Gomer to assign symbolic names to their children (Hos 1:2–2:2) [NRSV: 1:2–1:11] and 2) the presentation of Hosea's speeches to Israel that outline judgment against Israel for abandoning YHWH and call for Israel's return to YHWH (Hos 2:3–14:9) [NRSV: 2:1–14:8]. When read as a whole, Hosea 1:2–14:9 [NRSV: 14:8] constitutes a report or presentation of Hosea's parenetic appeal to Israel to return to YHWH. The anonymous narrator's instruction to the reader to be wise in reading the book and in discerning the ways of YHWH constitutes the third major component of Hosea.

The Report of YHWH's Initial Instruction to Hosea to Marry the Harlot Gomer: 1:2–2:2 [NRSV: 1:11]

As noted above, Hos 1:2–2:2 [NRSV: 1:11] clearly constitutes a report of YHWH's initial instructions to Hosea by the anonymous narrator of the book. Specifically, the section relates YHWH's instructions to Hosea that he should marry a woman described as a harlot and have "children of harlotry" by her. In addition, the section relates Hosea's compliance with these instructions together with YHWH's instructions to give the children symbolic names as they are born. By this means, the marriage and the birth and naming of the children becomes a symbolic act by the prophet that portrays YHWH's relationship with Israel. Symbolic actions by a prophet in the ancient world represent a form of drama in which the prophet, through his or her own actions, symbolically represents the actions or intentions of YHWH in the world.[13] The symbolic naming of children, such as Isaiah's sons Shear Jashub, "a remnant shall return" (Isa 7:3-9; 10:20-23); Immanuel, "G–d is with us" (Isa 7:10-17; 8:5-10); and Maher-shalal-hash-baz, "the spoil speeds the prey hastens" (Isa 8:1-4) or the grandson of the high priest Eli at Shiloh, Ichabod, "no glory" (1 Sam 4:19-22) frequently constitute such symbolic acts. Some other symbolic actions include Isaiah's walking about Jerusalem naked to symbolize the captivity and humiliation of the city (Isaiah 20); Jeremiah's walking about Jerusalem with a yoke on his back to symbolize the need to submit to Babylon (Jeremiah 27–28); and Ezekiel's various actions, such as employing a brick to represent the siege of Jerusalem, lying on his sides for three hundred ninety and forty days to represent the captivity of Israel and Judah respectively,

---

[13] See W. D. Stacey, *Prophetic Drama in the Old Testament* (London: Epworth, 1990).

preparing a meal with dung, and cutting and dividing his hair to represent the fate of the people of Jerusalem (Ezek 4:1–5:7). As conceived in antiquity, such symbolic dramas not only represent or express the Deity's actions, they play a role in bringing them about as well so that symbolic actions serve as a means to motivate YHWH or to appeal to YHWH for action.

The section begins in verse 2a with a brief statement that functions somewhat as a superscription for the entire episode, "the beginning of YHWH's speaking to Hosea." This statement is frequently considered as a temporal introduction to verse 2b, "when YHWH began to speak to Hosea, YHWH said to Hosea," based upon the analogy to Gen 1:1, "when G–d began to create the heavens and the earth . . ."[14] Unlike Gen 1:1 (*bĕrēʾšît bārāʾ ʾĕlōqîm*, "when G–d began to create"), however, the phrase in Hos 1:2a lacks a temporal particle, such as *bĕ-, kĕ-, ʾăšer*, or the like, which would enable it to serve as temporal relative clause. Furthermore, if verse 2a is intended to introduce only verse 2b, it would be unnecessary to repeat both YHWH's and Hosea's names in the speech report formula. It therefore does not introduce only the first report of YHWH's speech to Hosea in 1:2b; instead, it introduces the entire sequence of YHWH's speeches to Hosea and Hosea's compliance with YHWH's instructions in Hos 1:2b–2:2.

The report of YHWH's initial instruction to Hosea appears in Hos 1:2b. It begins with a speech formula which identifies YHWH as the speaker and Hosea as the person to whom YHWH's speech is directed. The quotation of YHWH's speech to the prophet follows in which YHWH commands Hosea to "take a woman of harlotry and children of harlotry." Furthermore, YHWH's statement makes it very clear that this action is meant to symbolize YHWH's relationship with the land or nation of Israel, insofar as verse 2bβ states that the motivation for this action is "because the land indeed commits harlotry from after YHWH."

The imperative verb, "take," is generally understood as a command to "marry," based upon analogies in Gen 4:19 in which Lamech "takes" Ada and Zillah as "wives" and Gen 34:16 in which the sons of Jacob proposed to "take" the daughters of the city of Shechem as wives. The reference to "a woman of harlotry and children of harlotry" has caused considerable comment. In keeping with the overall context of marriage, many translators render "woman" as "wife" in that Hebrew does not have a special word for "wife" other than "woman." Although many presume that in an ancient context, a "woman" would necessarily be a "wife," such an understanding seems to read a modern presupposition into the translation. The Hebrew word *ʾiššâ*, "woman," can be employed

---

[14] See the comments by Rashi on Gen 1:1.

to express "wife," but it may also be applied to women who lack husbands, such as a widow (2 Sam 14:5; 1 Kgs 11:26), or to express other roles that have little or nothing to do with marriage, such as "wet-nurse" (Exod 2:7); "prophetess" (Judg 4:4); "harlot" (Josh 2:1); "foreign women" (1 Kgs 11:1); or "wise woman" (2 Sam 14:2).

The reference to "harlotry" has been interpreted from various angles. Some consider Gomer to be a Canaanite "cultic prostitute" who would sell herself as part of the fertility rites to worship Baal, Ashtoreth, and other agricultural deities, although no Canaanite texts testify to such forms of worship. A variant of this interpretation holds that Canaanite women would engage in ritual sexual intercourse immediately prior to marriage as a way to insure fertility, although this model is based upon relatively late portrayals of Babylonian or Phoenician practice.[15] Others argue that Gomer is labeled a harlot because she betrays Hosea after marriage to sleep with other men. In this scenario the reference to "children of harlotry" would suggest that Hosea does not know if he is in fact the father of his own children. Nevertheless, the book of Hosea provides no indication that this is the case. Much of the discussion of Gomer's harlotry is based on the view that prostitution constitutes a moral crime that women choose to engage in for lack of moral character, but when considered in relation to its ancient context, it seems to constitute a matter of economic necessity. In order to understand the references to "woman of harlotry" and "children of harlotry," it seems best to recognize that in an ancient, agriculturally-based economy with a patriarchal social structure such as that of ancient Israel, women would typically be dependent upon male relatives, such as a father, husband, sons, or brother, for support insofar as men would have the rights to land and its produce. If a woman could not depend upon such support, she would have to support herself in a manner that forced her to stand outside the "normal" social structure. If she lacked access to land, this would mean that she would support herself through whatever means were available, such as begging or taking whatever assistance was available to people who lacked means of support, agricultural labor or other industries such as weaving, wetnursing, innkeeping, prostitution, or any combination of these activities. Gomer may well have been a woman who lacked her own means of support, and turned to prostitution to support herself. This does not require that the children born to her after she married Hosea were not necessarily Hosea's; the term "children of harlotry" may only signify the status of their mother.

---

[15] See H. W. Wolff, *Hosea,* trans. G. Stansell, Hermeneia (Philadelphia: Fortress, 1974) 14.

In turning to this explanation, however, an important point must be kept in mind. Gomer does not label herself as a harlot—indeed, she does not even speak in the entire book. Rather, the book of Hosea labels her as such. This means that the prophet or other writers of the book decide that she is to be considered a harlot, which indeed serves the theological agenda of the book of Hosea to portray Israel as turning from YHWH. It would be very interesting to learn Gomer's perspective on this issue, particularly since she would find herself in a marriage in which her husband publicly calls her a harlot and names their children with names that reflect his estimation of her. The book does not provide the reader with information concerning the quality of the marriage between Hosea and Gomer, but it does not appear to have been a happy one. Insofar as Gomer represents Israel in Hosea's symbolic action, this has some rather important implications for Israel's view of YHWH. What incentive does Israel/Gomer have not to pursue other lovers? Having failed to control Gomer/Israel by providing "gifts," will Hosea/YHWH beat her into submission by bringing the Assyrians? Clearly, the relationship between Gomer and Hosea is in deep trouble, whether it is because Gomer is indeed a harlot or because Hosea calls her one. In this regard, the portrayal of Hosea's marriage to Gomer reflects a great deal of frustration for both Hosea and Gomer, and indeed for YHWH and Israel at a time when the relationship is about to collapse because of the impending onslaught of the Assyrian empire. As a husband in the ancient world, Hosea/YHWH is expected to "protect" Gomer/Israel, but instead charges her with harlotry so that he is released from his marital obligation. One might ask from Gomer's perspective, does he lack the power or the will to fulfill his role? Indeed, the text does not ask this question. It is written by an Israelite or Israelites who choose not to question the character of G–d, but choose instead to take responsibility for their own fate by portraying Israel/themselves as a harlotrous wife.

Hosea 1:3–2:2 [NRSV: 1:11] then reports Hosea's fulfillment of YHWH's initial instruction by relating the births of three successive children together with YHWH's instructions concerning the naming of each child. The first stage appears in Hos 1:3-5, which portrays Hosea's "taking" Gomer bat Diblaim, the birth of her son, and YHWH's instructions to name the boy Jezreel. The name Gomer bat (daughter of) Diblaim is somewhat unusual. The name Gomer is generally applied to a male (Gen 10:2, 3; 1 Chr 1:5, 6; Ezek 38:6). The root on which it is based means "to complete, accomplish" and it is employed as a slang reference to sexual activity in modern Hebrew. The name Diblaim is hardly a suitable name for a father in that it is a dual form of *dĕbēlâ* which means "a pair of fig cakes." Some have taken this as a reference to the price of Gomer's prostitution. Others see it as a corrupted reference to a place name from which she comes (cf. Diblataim in Jer 48:22; Num 33:46, 47) or perhaps to a Canaanite name such as Debal-Yam, but neither name is attested securely elsewhere. It should be noted, however, that the male name Ephraim is likewise formulated as a dual noun based on a root that means "agility" or "enclose."

The report of YHWH's command to name the baby boy Jezreel is particularly significant in that it alludes to the coup d'etat that brought the dynasty of Jehu, the ancestor of Jeroboam ben Joash (see Hos 1:1), to power. According to 2 Kings 9–10, Jehu ben Jehoshaphat was a military commander serving against the Arameans in Ramoth-Gilead under King Joram ben Ahab of Israel. Joram had been wounded in battle against the Arameans, and returned to Jezreel to recover from his injuries. The prophet Elisha sent a young man to anoint Jehu as king and to prompt him to undertake a coup d'etat against Joram. Upon receiving the support of the other military commanders in Ramoth Gilead, Jehu drove his chariot to Jezreel, and there assassinated King Joram of Israel, Joram's cousin King Ahaziah ben Jehoshaphat of Judah, and Joram's mother Jezebel. Following these assassinations, the seventy sons of Ahab were killed in Jezreel by the "great men of the city" of Jezreel who apparently supported Jehu. Jehu saw to the destruction of Joram's other supporters, including the priests and prophets of Baal, and thereby secured his throne by wiping out the Omride dynasty and all of its supporters. Jehu is presented in 2 Kgs 10:28-31 as a monarch who wiped out Baal from Israel although he is criticized for failing to observe YHWH's commandments. Insofar as Jehu's coup was initiated and supported by the prophets Elijah and Elisha (see also 1 Kings 19 for Elijah's role), it is presented in very positive terms in the Deuteronomistic History.

It is therefore somewhat surprising to see that YHWH instructs Hosea to name his son Jezreel in Hos 1:4 in order to symbolize the punishment of the house of Jehu for the blood of Jezreel. The narratives concerning the reigns of the Omride kings and Jehu's coup certainly portray the Omrides as idolaters who richly deserved the punishment brought against them by Elijah, Elisha, and Jehu. Why then should an Israelite prophet such as Hosea condemn the house of Jehu for eliminating a clearly syncretistic dynasty from Israel? Many interpreters assume that the prophets of ancient Israel represented a relatively consistent theological and political viewpoint as they spoke on behalf of YHWH. Obviously, there is only one G–d, YHWH, and the prophets who speak on YHWH's behalf must therefore represent the will of the one true G–d. Unfortunately, such a view does not take full account of the individual perspectives that prophets might bring to bear in their understandings

and portrayals of YHWH. Prophets frequently disagreed with one another in ancient Israel and Judah as indicated by Jeremiah 27–28 which
portrays the conflict between the prophet Hananiah, whose message of
YHWH's deliverance for Jerusalem from Babylon represents the theological stance of Isaiah more than a century earlier, and Jeremiah, whose
message of submission to Babylon was based in a very different understanding of YHWH from that of the Isaiah tradition. Prophets in ancient
Israel and Judah all claimed to represent the will of YHWH, but they frequently had different understandings of what exactly constituted that
will, whether they were contemporaries or removed in time by a century or more.

Insofar as Hosea is instructed to condemn the house of Jehu for the
blood of Jezreel, it appears that he holds a very different view than that
presented for the prophets Elijah and Elisha in 1–2 Kings. Several factors
must be considered. First, although the destruction of the Omride dynasty in Israel removed the influence of Phoenician Baal worship from
the nation, 2 Kgs 10:28-31 indicates that Jehu did not eliminate religious
apostasy entirely in that Jehu continued the worship of the golden
calves at Dan and Beth-El. Politically speaking, the coup ended the alliance between Omride Israel and the Phoenicians, but Israel was unable
to sustain itself in complete independence in the aftermath of Jehu's
coup. As noted above, Israel was subject to repeated attacks by the
Arameans during the reigns of Jehu, Jehoahaz, and Joash, and it was
only under the rule of Joash and Jeroboam that Israel was finally able to
defeat the Arameans and to restore Israelite control over Aram (2 Kgs
13:14-25; 14:23-29). As Assyrian records indicate, Israel did not accomplish this reversal on its own, but apparently relied on alliances with
Assyria to divide and conquer Aram. This represents quite a reversal
from the policy of the Omride King Ahab, who together with Aram
fought the Assyrians under Shalmaneser III in 853 B.C.E. According to
the so-called "Black Obelisk" of Shalmaneser III, Jehu paid tribute to
Assyria making him an Assyrian ally.[16] A fragment from Shalmaneser
III's annals at Calah indicates that Jehu submitted to Assyria in the
aftermath of Shalmaneser's defeat of Hazael of Aram in his eighteenth
year.[17] Likewise, Adad Nirari III (810–783) lists Israel (lit., "the land of
Omri") as one of his tributaries,[18] presumably during the reign of Jehoahaz, and later he specifically names Joash the Samaritan as a tributary.[19]

[16] See Luckenbill, *ARAB*, vol. I: 590; Pritchard, *ANET*, 281.

[17] Luckenbill, *ARAB*, vol. I: 672.

[18] Pritchard, *ANET*, 281.

[19] S. Page, "A Stela of Adad Nirari III and Nergal-ereš from Tell al Rimlah," *Iraq*
30 (1968) 139–53.

While Jeroboam ben Joash extended his rule to Lebo-Hamath (2 Kgs 14:23-29), Assur Nirari V concluded treaties to control the northern part of Aram in Arpad, although Arpad subsequently broke away.[20]

Although the house of Jehu removed Israel from the Phoenician orbit, it initiated the alliances with Assyria that Hosea so severely criticizes throughout the book. This seems to provide the basis for Hosea's charges that Israel has abandoned YHWH, and committed harlotry in doing so. For this reason, YHWH's instruction to Hosea indicates the intent to "bring the kingdom of the house of Israel to an end" and to "break the bow of Israel in the Jezreel valley." This latter reference to the Jezreel valley is significant as well. It not only calls to mind the previously mentioned reference to Jehu's coup against the Omride house, but it points to the significance of this region in Hosea's time as well. The Jezreel valley is a broad plain that lies to the south of the Galilee and to the north of the hill country of Ephraim or Samaria. It extends from the mountain passes at Megiddo in the west to Beth Shean and the Jordan river in the east. In antiquity, it was one of the "bread baskets" of ancient Israel in that it was a very fertile agricultural area that produced vast quantities of grain and other crops. Insofar as it cut through the hilly regions of Galilee and Samaria, it constituted a major trading route in that it provided access to the coastal plains of the Mediterranean in the west and the highway to Damascus in the east.

Indeed, the highway that ran through the Jezreel valley gave the region its strategic significance. Israel was able to establish itself as an independent state in the tenth century because it was able to wrest control of the Jezreel valley and the coastal plain from the Philistines, which enabled Solomon and later kings to dominate the trade between Egypt to the south and both Asia Minor and Mesopotamia to the north. It was the strategic significance of the Jezreel valley and the access it provided to the coastal plain and to Egypt that attracted the attention of the Assyrian empire in the late eighth century B.C.E. Control of the Jezreel and the coastal plain would enable Assyria to realize its interests in establishing and controlling a trade route to Egypt that would allow them to dominate commerce in the eastern Mediterranean and eventually to conquer Egypt.[21] When the Assyrian king Tiglath Pileser III attacked Kings Rezin of Aram and Pekah of Israel in 735–732 B.C.E., the Jezreel valley, the coastal plain, and the King's Highway in Trans-Jordan were his primary targets. In the aftermath of the Assyrian invasion, the Trans-Jordan, the Galilee, and the Phoenician coast by Dor

---

[20] See note 2 above.

[21] See M. Elat, "The Economic Relations of the Neo-Assyrian Empire with Egypt," *JAOS* 98 (1978) 20–34.

were stripped from Israel and turned into Assyrian provinces.[22] Not only did control of these regions allow him to dismember the kingdom of Israel and reduce it to a weakened rump state under the rule of King Hoshea, it also gave him control of the trade routes that were the key to economic and military power in the ancient Near East.

Hosea 1:6-7 reports the birth of Hosea's daughter and Yʜᴡʜ's instructions concerning the naming of the girl. The narrative statements in verse 6aα laconically report Gomer's second pregnancy and the birth of a daughter prior to the speech formula that introduces Yʜᴡʜ's instructions to the prophet. Yʜᴡʜ's instructions to name the girl Lo Ruhama constitutes a symbolic action in that the name means "no mercy." As noted in the explanation of this name in verse 7bα, it signifies Yʜᴡʜ's intention to show no mercy to Israel. This statement is relatively clear in and of itself, but it also must be considered in relation to Israelite tradition which maintains that one of Yʜᴡʜ's qualities is to show mercy to Israel. Thus, the formulaic statement in Exod 34:6 of Yʜᴡʜ's attributes spoken in Yʜᴡʜ's self-revelation to Moses states, "Yʜᴡʜ, Yʜᴡʜ, G–d of mercy (ʾēl raḥûm) and favor, patient and loyal and true, keeping loyalty for thousands, forgiving iniquity and rebellion and sin, and not pardoning the guilty, visiting the iniquity of the fathers upon the sons and the sons of the sons upon three and four generations" (for variations of this formula, see also Deut 4:31; Pss 78:38; 86:15; 103:8; 111:4; 145:8; 2 Chr 30:9; Neh 9:17, 31; Joel 2:13; Jonah 4:2). Likewise, in an *idem per idem* rhetorical statement to Moses in Exod 33:19 reminiscent of the initial revelation of the Divine Name in Exod 3:14, Yʜᴡʜ states, "I will cause my goodness to pass before you, and I shall call the name of Yʜᴡʜ before you, and I will show favor to whom I shall show favor, and I will show mercy (wĕriḥamtî) to whom I will show mercy (ʾăraḥēm)." Thus, the name Lo Ruhamah clearly signifies the reversal of the relationship between Yʜᴡʜ and Israel as it is portrayed in the Mosaic tradition, the foundational tradition of Israel's existence and sense of identity.

The following explanatory statement, "but I shall surely forgive them," is somewhat enigmatic when considered in relation to the name Lo Ruhamah and its explanation in that it seems to negate Yʜᴡʜ's intention no longer to show mercy to Israel. There have been various attempts to emend the ᴍᴛ statement, *kî nāśōʾ ʾeśśāʾ lāhem*, to variations such as *kî nāśōʾ ʾeššāʾ lāhem*, "for I will surely oppress them," a change that only requires the movement of a single dot to change the Hebrew letter *śin* to *šin*; *kî nāśōh ʾessâ lāhem*, "for I will surely test them," which requires a change from *śin* to *samekh* and other minor alterations; or *kî*

[22] Pritchard, *ANET*, 283–4.

śānōʾ ʾaśnāʾ lāhem, "for I surely hate them," which involves a transposition of letters. When read in relation to the formulaic statement of Exod 34:6, however, such emendations are unnecessary as the formula states that YHWH will "forgive iniquity and rebellion and sin" without declaring the guilty to be innocent. The statement thereby holds out some hope that although Israel will suffer punishment, it will eventually be forgiven so that it might restore its relationship with YHWH. In this case, the initial *kî* does not function as a causative particle ("for"), but as an asseverative particle ("but") that expresses an exception to the preceding statement that YHWH will no longer show mercy to Israel, "but I will surely forgive them."

Verse 7 offers a rather interesting qualification to YHWH's statement of forgiveness in that it specifies that YHWH "will show mercy to the house of Judah," and "deliver them by YHWH their G–d" and not by military means such as the "bow, sword, war, horses, and cavalry." Many interpreters consider this to be a redactional expansion by a Judean redactor to a text originally directed to northern Israel that is designed to reformulate the statement so that it looks forward to a Judean restoration. This may well be the case, but in the present form of the book, it prepares the reader for later statements, such as those in Hos 3:1-5, that call upon Israel to return to YHWH and the Davidic king, i.e., when Israel returns to Judah, the forgiveness and restoration will take place. Although such notions are frequently considered to be the products of post-exilic messianism, pre-exilic Judean kings, such as Hosea's eighth century contemporary Hezekiah (2 Chronicles 30) and the seventh century Josiah (2 Kings 22–23) are reported to have attempted to extend their influence over the territory of the former northern kingdom of Israel.

Finally, Hos 1:8–2:2 [NRSV: 1:8–1:11] reports the birth of Hosea's and Gomer's third child, a son who is to be named Lo Ammi. Verse 8 contains the narrative report of Gomer's weaning Lo Ruhamah, her third pregnancy, and the birth of the son. Following the initial speech formula at the beginning of verse 9, Hos 1:9–2:2 [NRSV: 1:9-11] contains YHWH's instructions to Hosea concerning the naming of the boy. Verse 9 presents the basic instruction to name the boy Lo Ammi, which means "not my people" in Hebrew, followed by the explanation, "because you are not my people, and I am Lo Ehyeh to you." Again, the statement "not my people" functions as a somewhat self explanatory statement much like Lo Ruhamah. But like Lo Ruhamah, Lo Ammi also takes up Israel's foundational traditions from the Mosaic literature. For example, in YHWH's self revelation in Exod 6:2-9 to Moses as the Deity who appeared to Abraham, Isaac, and Jacob, and who made a covenant with them, YHWH states the intention to relieve Israel from its suffering under Egyptian bondage and to remember the covenant. YHWH instructs Moses in verses 6–7,

> say therefore to the people Israel, 'I am YHWH, and I will bring you out
> from under the burdens of the Egyptians and I will deliver you from
> their slavery and I will redeem you with an outstretched arm and with
> great judgments, and I will take you to myself for a people and I shall be
> to you G–d . . .'

Variations of this last statement appear elsewhere as well in the foundational traditions of the nation Israel and in later prophetic literature that takes up this theme, viz., in Lev 26:12, "and I shall be G–d to you, and you shall be to me for a people," and elsewhere (Deut 26:17-19; 27:9; 28:9; 29:12; 2 Sam 7:24; Jer 7:23; 11:4; 24:7; 30:22; 31:1, 33; 32:38; Ezek 11:20; 14:11; 36:28; 37:23, 27; Zech 8:8). In all cases, this statement and its variants functions as the basic expression of the relationship between YHWH and the people Israel. As in the case of Lo Ruhamah, YHWH's explanation for the name, "for you are not my people," signals the disruption of the relationship between YHWH and Israel. The point is reinforced by the following statement, "and I am Lo Ehyeh to you." The Hebrew term Lo Ehyeh means "I am not." When the phrase is translated literally, "and I am not I am to you," it is somewhat awkward, but this misses the point. In the narrative concerning the burning bush in Exodus 3, Moses asks YHWH to reveal the divine name. YHWH does not respond with "YHWH," but with the *idem per idem* statement *ʾehyeh ʾăšer ʾehyeh*, "I am who I am," in Exod 3:14, and follows up with the statement, "Thus you shall say to the people of Israel, 'ʾEhyeh has sent me to you.'" In this case, the term Ehyeh functions as the name of G–d, or at least in place of G–d's name, and signifies the initial statement of YHWH's identity at the beginning of the relationship between YHWH and Israel at the time of Moses. When employed in Hos 1:9 in the statement, "and I am Lo/not Ehyeh to you," it again signifies the disruption of the relationship between YHWH and Israel.

YHWH's explanation of the name Lo Ammi continues in Hos 2:1-2 [NRSV: 1:10-11]. Many consider it to be a separate unit from Hos 1:2-9 because it appears in poetic rather than in prose form and because it refers objectively to YHWH as "the living G–d" (verse 1) when YHWH is the speaker in Hos 1:9. Nevertheless, the text does not indicate that anyone other than YHWH is speaking, and the introductory conjunction *wĕhāyâ*, "and it shall be," ties Hos 2:1-2 [NRSV: 1:10-11] syntactically to YHWH's speech in Hos 1:9. The objective reference to "the living G–d" appears in the context of a statement that will be made by others about the people of Israel. It follows immediately upon a reference to the people as "not my people," which indicates that YHWH is still the speaker in this text.

YHWH's instructions to Hosea again draw upon past tradition to draw out the significance of the marriage to Gomer and the naming of the children, but whereas YHWH's previous statements focused on the disruption of the relationship between YHWH and Israel, they now address the restoration of that relationship once punishment is complete. In stating that "the number of the people of Israel shall be like the sand of the sea which cannot be measured nor counted," Hos 2:1 [NRSV: 1:10] draws upon the traditions of YHWH's promises to the ancestors of Israel. Upon returning to the land of Israel to face Esau in Gen 32:13, Jacob reminds YHWH of the promise, "and you said, 'I shall do good with you, and I shall make your seed like the sand of the sea which is too numerous to be counted.'" When Abraham is prepared to sacrifice Isaac at Moriah in Gen 22:17, YHWH reiterates the promise, "for I will surely bless you and I will surely multiply your seed like the stars of the heavens and like the sand upon the shore of the sea, and your seed shall possess the gate of its enemies."[23] Although there are other versions of the promises to the ancestors, these texts are particularly important in relation to the present context because they both relate specifically to the foundational traditions of the northern kingdom of Israel. Jacob is the eponymous ancestor of the northern kingdom of Israel, and the narrative in Gen 32:1-13 relates Jacob's return to the land of Israel. The narrative concerning Abraham's binding of Isaac in Genesis 22 is generally recognized as the product of the Elohistic stratum of the Pentateuch which derives from the northern kingdom of Israel. Insofar as it expresses YHWH's promise to Abraham and Isaac, it recognizes that they are the ancestors of Jacob. Not only do both traditions express the foundational promise to the ancestors of Israel, they recount the ancestors' overcoming of calamity, Jacob's return from exile in Aram and reconciliation with Esau, the brother who sought to kill him, and Isaac's deliverance from death. Just as the ancestors of Israel escaped disaster based upon YHWH's promise that their descendants would be as numerous as the sand of the sea, so Israel would escape the upcoming disaster because YHWH's promise still holds true. Insofar as these promises are directed to the "seed" (*zeraʿ*) of the ancestors, the use of this tradition in Hos 2:1 [NRSV: 1:10] plays upon the name Jezreel (*yizrĕʿeʾl*), which means "G–d sows."

---

[23] The metaphorical comparison to the stars of the heavens also appears in YHWH's promise to Abram in Gen 15:5 and in Moses's attempt to dissuade YHWH from destroying Israel in Exod 32:13.

Hoses 2:1a [NRSV: 1:10a] reiterates the theme of Israel's restoration by noting the reversal of the symbolic name given to Hosea's son. No longer would the people of Israel be known as "Lo Ammi/Not my people," but they would be called, "sons of the living G–d." The term "sons of the living G–d" reflects terminology that appears in the psalms of the sons of Korah, believed by some to represent a priestly line that may once have had ties to the northern kingdom (Pss 42:3 [NRSV: 42:2]; 84:3), and in the traditions concerning Joshua, the Ephraimite or northern Israelite hero who led the conquest of the land of Israel (Josh 3:10). Verse 2 [NRSV: 1:11] then specifies the nature of the restoration of Israel's fortunes by stating that both the people of Judah and the people of Israel would be gathered together, appoint for themselves one head, and go up from the land. Many interpreters understand this as a reference to return from exile, and therefore place the passage in the post-exilic period. No exile is mentioned here, however, as the verse merely speaks to the reunification of the people. The statement is highly charged politically in that it looks to the reunification of Israel and Judah as a time when they will appoint one head. This apparently is a reference to a leader or king, and recalls the rule of the house of David over both Israel and Judah in the days of both David and Solomon. Although this sentiment is not made explicit in the present context, the references to restored Davidic rule in Hos 3:1-5 make it clear that this is the ultimate goal of the present statement. Likewise, the enigmatic reference to the reunited people who "will go up from the land" reiterates the common terminology for traveling to Jerusalem, the site of YHWH's Temple, to which one always "goes up." Again, Hos 3:1-5 makes it clear that the people return not only to the house of David, but to YHWH as well. The passage concludes with the explanatory statement, "for great is the day of Jezreel." Just as Jezreel signifies the bloodshed that will be visited upon the dynasty of Jehu, so the metaphor of sowing seeds conveys the imagery of restoration and regrowth. Once Israel and the Jehu dynasty suffers punishment, it will be restored—to YHWH, the house of David, and to Judah.

Presentation of Hosea's Speeches Concerning Appeal for Israel's Return: 2:3–14:9 [NRSV: 2:1–14:8]

Following the report of YHWH's instructions to Hosea in Hos 1:2–2:2 [NRSV: 1:2-11], the book of Hosea turns to a presentation of Hosea's prophetic speeches in Hos 2:3–14:9 [NRSV: 2:1–14:8]. This section lacks the narrative form of Hos 1:2–2:2 [NRSV: 1:1-11] that identified the speaker and the addressee, but various other features of these chapters make it clear that Hosea is the speaker throughout. Introductory statements, such as those in Hos 4:1; 5:1; 6:1; 9:1; and 14:2 [NRSV: 14:1], explicitly identify Israel as the addressee and refer to YHWH in third person form. At times these statements introduce words by YHWH, but the references to Israel and YHWH demonstrate that the prophet is the speaker and that he conveys or quotes statements attributed to YHWH within the framework of his own statements. The situation is somewhat ambiguous in Hos 2:3–3:5 [NRSV: 2:1–3:5] in that Hosea appears to be the speaker at the beginning of the passage who addresses his children and his wife in keeping with the themes of a wife and children of harlotry in Hos 1:2–2:2 [NRSV: 1:1-11]. But as the passage progresses, it becomes increasingly evident that the speaker is YHWH who addresses Israel rather than Hosea who addresses Gomer. This ambiguity is part of the rhetorical strategy of the passage, which establishes Hosea's marriage to Gomer as the paradigm for YHWH's relationship with Israel and draws the reader into the paradigm gradually. It thereby appeals to the audience's empathy with Hosea's human predicament as a means to establish support for YHWH's position and the resulting condemnation of Israel. Nevertheless, the oracular formulas beginning in Hos 2:15 [NRSV: 2:13], the explicit references to the relationship between YHWH and Israel in Hos 2:16-25 [NRSV: 2:14-23], and the autobiographical form of Hos 3:1-5 make it very clear that Hosea is the speaker throughout Hos 2:3–3:5 [NRSV: 2:1–3:5] as well as in Hos 4:1–14:9 [NRSV: 4:1–14:8]. Consequently, all of Hos 2:3–14:9 [NRSV: 2:1–14:8] is presented as speech by Hosea.

The overall character of Hosea's speech as an appeal for Israel to return to YHWH is evident from both the beginning and the concluding sections of Hos 2:3–14:9 [NRSV: 2:1–14:8]. Hosea 2:3–3:5 [NRSV: 2:1–3:5], the first major segment of Hosea's speeches, introduces the theme of Israel's return to YHWH at the outset with a command addressed to the son Jezreel, "Say to your brother, 'Ammi (my people),' and to your sister, 'Ruhama (mercy),'" thereby reversing the themes of their rejection that were inherent in their names. The following material in Hos 2:4-25 [NRSV: 2:2-23] then addresses the return of the straying wife to her husband, Hosea/YHWH, and the acknowledgment of the children. The autobiographical material in Hos 3:1-5 employs the analogy between Hosea's experience with his wife and YHWH's experience with Israel to call upon Israel to return to YHWH and to the House of David. Likewise, the concluding segment of Hosea's speeches in Hos 14:2-9 [NRSV: 14:1-8] is formulated as an appeal for Israel to return to YHWH and to abandon its alliance with Assyria. Whereas the intervening material takes up the various accusations against Israel, the appeals for Israel's return to Y<small>HWH</small> at both the beginning and the conclusion provide contextualization and set the rhetorical agenda of Hos 2:3–14:9 [N<small>RSV</small>: 2:1–14:8] as a whole so that the accusations against Israel are subsumed into the overall strategy to call for Israel's return to Y<small>HWH</small>.

The overarching structure of Hos 2:3–14:9 [N<small>RSV</small>: 2:1–14:8] likewise serves the rhetorical goal to appeal for Israel's return. The structure of this text is defined by the appearance of a series of imperative statements directed to Israel in Hos 2:3, 4 [N<small>RSV</small>: 2:1, 2]; 4:1; 5:1; and 14:2 [N<small>RSV</small>: 14:1] that introduce each key segment of the text. The commands to Jezreel/Israel to rename the siblings and to plead or contend with the mother in Hos 2:3, 4 [N<small>RSV</small>: 2:1, 2] introduce the segment in Hos 2:3–3:5 [N<small>RSV</small>: 2:1–3:5] that states the initial appeal for Israel's return to Y<small>HWH</small> and thereby sets the theme of the entire section devoted to the presentation of Hosea's speeches. The command to hear the word of Y<small>HWH</small> addressed to the people of Israel in Hos 4:1 introduces a section in Hos 4:1-19 that reports Y<small>HWH</small>'s contentions against Israel and thereby sets the terms of the disagreement between Y<small>HWH</small> and Israel that requires resolution. The command to hear the legal case in Hos 5:1, directed to the priests, the people of Israel, and the house of the king, introduces a lengthy segment in Hos 5:1–14:1 [N<small>RSV</small>: 13:16] that specifies the issues between Y<small>HWH</small> and Israel in great detail and that establishes Y<small>HWH</small>'s willingness to reconcile if possible. Finally, the imperative appeal for Israel to return to Y<small>HWH</small> in Hos 14:2 [N<small>RSV</small>: 14:1] introduces the segment in Hos 14:2-9 [N<small>RSV</small>: 14:1-8] that calls for Israel's return to Y<small>HWH</small> and rejection of Assyria. Overall, Hos 2:3–14:9 [N<small>RSV</small>: 2:1–14:8] is designed to convince its audience that in spite of the accusations made against Israel throughout this text, a reconciliation between Israel and Y<small>HWH</small> is possible.

Hosea's Appeal to Jezreel for Mother's Return: Restoration of a United Israel under Y<small>HWH</small> and Davidic Monarch: 2:3–3:5 [N<small>RSV</small>: 2:1–3:5]

Hosea 2:3–3:5 [N<small>RSV</small>: 2:1–3:5] sets the theme and overall rhetorical goal of the speeches by Hosea to call for the return of Israel to Y<small>HWH</small>. The passage builds upon the themes established in Hos 1:2–2:2 [N<small>RSV</small>: 1:1-11] of Hosea's marriage to a woman of harlotry and the birth of their children, and employs two major textual sub-units to achieve its aim. Hos 2:3-25 [N<small>RSV</small>: 2:1-23] is formulated as a prophetic speech in which the husband, first presumed to be Hosea but later identified as Y<small>HWH</small>, calls upon the children to appeal to their mother so that the marriage, and indeed the entire family, might be restored. The autobiographical material in Hos 3:1-5, which is joined syntactically to Hos 2:3-25 [NRSV: 2:1-23] by its *waw-consecutive* narrative formulation, outlines the prophet's marriage to an adulterous woman in order to call for Israel's return to YHWH. Although the prophet's speech in Hos 2:3-25 [NRSV: 2:1-23] makes the intention of the passage clear enough, Hos 3:1-5 makes the agenda explicit in that it equates Hosea's marriage to the adulterous woman with Israel's return to YHWH following a period of separation. By the end of the passage, it is clear that Israel's return to YHWH entails its return to Davidic rule as well, indicating that the agenda is simultaneously religious and political, viz., the restoration of the Solomonic ideal of a united Israel based upon the worship of YHWH and Davidic rule in Jerusalem.

The presentation of Hosea's speech in Hos 2:3-25 [NRSV: 2:1-23] employs the theme of the prophet's marriage to Gomer in order to convey its appeal for Israel's restoration to YHWH. It is deliberately ambiguous in that it does not initially identify the speaker(s) in the text. Based upon the preceding narrative material concerning Hosea's marriage to Gomer and the birth of their children, it would seem initially that the passage conveys Hosea's appeals to his children to assist in calling for the mother's return from her other lovers. But as the passage progresses, it becomes clear from the oracular formula in Hos 2:15 [NRSV: 2:13] and the contents of Hos 2:16-25 [NRSV: 2:14-23] that the prophet conveys YHWH's words addressed to Israel. These words portray Israel's abandonment of YHWH for other lovers as well as Israel's anticipated return to YHWH and the restoration of the entire family relationship. The text thereby appeals to its audience by portraying YHWH in human terms that virtually anyone could understand from personal experience, viz., the pain and frustration of a lost love and the desperation that fuels an attempt to restore the relationship to its original state. In this manner, the passage is designed to arouse sympathy for YHWH on the part of the audience and thereby to convince the audience to accept the proposal that they have done wrong and that they must rectify the situation by returning to YHWH. At this point, the passage operates on a very personal level to express its metaphors of abandonment and return in relatively general terms; the specific referents of these metaphors, viz., the rejection of alliance with Assyria and the return to Davidic rule, will be spelled out later.

The prophet's speech begins in Hos 2:3 [NRSV: 2:1] with the imperative instruction, "say to your brothers, 'Ammi (my people),' and to your sisters, 'Ruhama (mercy).'" The statement of these names obviously reverses the significance of the names originally applied to the children, i.e., Lo Ammi, "not my people," and Lo Ruhama, "no mercy,"

in order to signal the anticipated reversal of the relationship between
YHWH and Israel. Interpreters frequently view this verse as the concluding statement of Hos 2:1-2, [NRSV: 1:10-11] but several features
demonstrate that it begins a new unit. Hos 2:1-2 [NRSV: 1:10-11] is part
of the instruction by YHWH to Hosea reported in Hos 1:9–2:2, [NRSV: 1:9-
11] but Hos 2:3 [NRSV: 2:1] is clearly not addressed to Hosea. The masculine plural imperative verb *ʾimĕrû*, "say," cannot be addressed to the
prophet as that would require a singular formulation. Some have presupposed that the plural imperative must be read in relation to the
plural references to the people of Israel in Hos 2:1-2 [NRSV: 1:10-11], but
these verses speak *about* the people of Israel; they are not addressed *to*
them as is the case in Hos 2:3 [NRSV: 2:1]. Furthermore, Hos 2:3 [NRSV:
2:1] takes up both Hosea's son Lo Ammi and his daughter Lo Ruhama,
but Hos 2:1-2 [NRSV: 1:10-11] only deals with Lo Ammi in keeping with
its role as part of YHWH's instruction concerning the naming of Lo
Ammi beginning in Hos 1:9. Hosea 2:3 [NRSV: 2:1] builds upon the themes,
language, and imagery of Hos 1:2–2:2 [NRSV: 1:2-11], but it is generically
different in that it is neither a report of action in Hos 1:2–2:2 [NRSV: 1:2-
11], nor a part of YHWH's reported instructions to Hosea in Hos 1:9–2:2
[NRSV: 1:9-11], nor even a part of a general announcement of Israel's
restoration in Hos 2:1-2 [NRSV: 1:10-11]. Instead, it is a plural address to
Israel, here portrayed as Hosea's son Jezreel, instructing Israel/Jezreel
to announce the restoration of Lo Ammi and Lo Ruhama, and thereby
to announce the restoration of Israel. The significance of the plural address form continues in the use of the plurals, "your brothers" and
"your sisters," to indicate that the passage takes up the restoration of
the people of Israel. By employing the metaphor of the children to announce the restoration of Israel, Hos 2:3 [NRSV: 2:1] signals a motif to
which this passage will return in Hos 2:23-25 [NRSV: 2:21-23], viz., the
restoration of Israel portrayed as Jezreel, Lo Ruhama, and Lo Ammi.

The speech then turns in Hos 2:4-7 [NRSV: 2:2-5] to Hosea's/YHWH's
initial appeal to the children to intercede with their mother in order to
restore the marriage relationship. The basic appeal appears in Hos 2:4
[NRSV: 2:2] to "plead" with their mother. The appeal to "plead" employs
a masculine plural imperative verb *rîbû*, which generally means, "contend, strive, quarrel." It can be employed in reference to a physical
struggle between two individuals (see the legal case concerning bodily
injury in the event of an altercation in Exod 21:18) or a verbal quarrel or
dispute (see Jacob's protests against Laban for pursuing him without
justification in Gen 31:36). It is also employed as a technical term that
signifies legal complaint or lawsuit (see YHWH's stance to judge peoples
in Isa 3:13-15; cf. Job 10:2; Isa 27:8; Jer 50:34; Mic 7:9; Prov 25:8). The
legal connotations of the term apply here as it is employed in the con-

text of a divorce proceeding, as indicated by the statement, "for she is not my wife and I am not her husband." Although there is no clear evidence that the expression is employed as part of a divorce procedure in the Bible, many interpreters understand this as a formal statement of divorce (see Deut 24:1-4 which specifies a written document of divorce but does not state its contents). The desired result of the appeal by the children, and perhaps the grounds for the divorce, is specified in verse 4b [NRSV: 2b] which opines that perhaps the mother will remove "her harlotries *(zĕnûnêhā)* from her face and her adulteries *(naʾăpûpêhā)* from between her breasts." There has been a great deal of speculation that the terms, "her harlotries *(zĕnûnêhā)*" and "her adulteries *(naʾăpûpêhā)*," refer to some sort of jewelry or ornamentation that signifies the status of a harlot. Perhaps the terms allude to the nose ring and necklace mentioned in Hos 2:15 [NRSV: 2:13] which seem to function as ornaments or jewelry worn by a bride. In this respect it is noteworthy that when Abraham's servant identifies Rebekah as the potential bride for Isaac in Genesis 24, he places a ring in her nose and bracelets on her arms to signify her betrothed status (verses 22, 30, 47). If this is the case, then the terms are employed sarcastically here to signify both the wife's married state and the adultery with which the husband charges her. Despite the sarcasm, the husband's statements in verse 4 [NRSV: 2] indicate that he wishes for his wife to return to him.

As indicated by the introductory particle *pen,* "unless," Hos 2:5-6 [NRSV: 2:3-4] outlines potential consequences for the wife should she fail to return to the husband. The threat to strip the wife naked conveys several dimensions of the marriage relationship in ancient Israel. According to Exod 21:10-11, a husband is obligated to provide a wife with food, clothing, and conjugal relations. All of these obligations are designed to support the wife, including the conjugal relations as the birth of sons to the wife will ensure the security of her marriage to the husband and her support in the event of the husband's death.[24] In the present case, the charge of adultery against the wife of course negates the obligation of conjugal relations and becomes the basis for denying both food and clothing. Not only does the husband threaten the removal of clothing, but water as well (n.b., the topic of food for the wife will appear below beginning in verse 7 [NRSV: 5]), which enables her to

---

[24] For full discussion of this law, see Shalom Paul, *Studies in the Book of the Covenant in the Light of Biblical and Cuneiform Law,* VTSup, vol. 18 (Leiden: E. J. Brill, 1970) 52–61. Based upon parallels with Mesopotamian texts, Paul concludes that the law refers not to conjugal rights but to a supply of oil. The Hebrew term employed in this law, *ʿōnātāh,* never refers to oil, but is based upon the root *ʿnh,* which means "to respond" or "to be occupied," and apparently serves as a euphemism for conjugal rights.

live. The reference to water is particularly important here in that Hosea
or the husband will later charge the wife with pursuing other lovers or
husbands, and in doing so will refer specifically to Baal (see verses 10,
18 [NRSV: 8, 16]). Baal is the Canaanite god of rain who brings water to
the earth and thereby insures fertility and the growth of new crops.
Based upon the Bible's various references to the sexual activities of the
Canaanites and the many nude female goddess figurines found
throughout ancient Israel, Judah, and Canaan,[25] many argue that sacred
prostitution is a part of Baal worship, but evidence from Canaanite
texts is lacking.[26] Indeed, such practice may be Israelite as well. An interesting portrayal of Israelite sexual activity in relation to agricultural
procedures, such as the harvest of the vineyards, appears in Judg 21:16-
23 in which the men of Benjamin "take" their wives from the maidens
who dance in the vineyards around the sanctuary at Shiloh, perhaps in
conjunction with an Israelite observance of the festival of Sukkoth.
Sukkoth, coincidentally, marks the beginning of the rainy season in
Israel. In any case, the emphasis on the withholding of water and the
references to a dry wilderness and death by thirst signal a concern with
cultic apostasy within the text in that it will charge that the bride Israel
has rejected YHWH to pursue the Canaanite fertility/rain god Baal.

Verse 6 [NRSV: 4] relates the husband's rejection of the wife's children; because he charges that they are "sons/children of harlotry" and
therefore not his own, he is not obligated to support them either. Some
commentators charge that the children have incurred the guilt of their
mother.[27] They are not guilty of anything; they are simply not his. Likewise, commentators note that the children are no longer directly addressed as at the beginning of verse 4 [NRSV: 2]. Again, verses 5-6 [NRSV:
3–4] (cf. verse 7 [NRSV: 5]) simply describe the consequences for the
mother (and her children) if she does not return to the husband.

Hoses 2:7 [NRSV: 2:5] presents the basis for the husband's threats; he
charges that the wife has committed adultery. Some note that Deut
22:22 conflicts with the present passage in that it requires that a man
and a woman who willfully engage in adultery are to be put to death.
Likewise, Deut 22:23-24 applies the same standard to a woman who is
betrothed (contra Deut 22:25-27 which excuses a betrothed woman

---

[25] For discussion of the goddess figurines, see William Dever, "The Silence of the
Text: An Archaeological Commentary on 2 Kings 23," *Scripture and Other Artifacts:
Essays on the Bible and Archaeology in Honor of Philip J. King*, ed. M. D. Coogan, J. C.
Exum, L. E. Stager (Louisville: Westminster John Knox, 1994) 143–68 and the litera-
ture cited there.

[26] See the discussion in Wolff, *Hosea*, 14.

[27] E.g., Wolff, *Hosea*, 34.

who could not call for help). But both of these cases apply only in instances in which the adultery is observed. Deuteronomy 24:1-4 indicates that a man may divorce his wife if he finds some impropriety in her, presumably sexual, but it does not indicate that this impropriety needs to be witnessed or even proven. In any case, it is not clear to what extent these laws represent actual legal practice, or merely state legal principle. According to 2 Samuel 12, neither David nor Bath Sheba suffered legal penalty for their adultery, although the text makes it very clear that such actions were theoretically subject to penalty. After stating that the wife has committed harlotry, the husband goes on to "quote" the wife who "states," "I will go after my lovers, who give my bread and my water, my wool and my flax, my oil and my drink." Again, the basic means of support to be provided by a husband are listed here. At the same time, the text portrays the husband as the one who speaks for the wife. In fact, she does not speak for herself. In speaking for her, the husband is establishing the grounds on which he claims the right to divorce.

Hosea 2:8-10, 11-15 and 16-25 [NRSV: 2:6-8, 9-11, 14-23], each of which is introduced by the particle *lākēn*, "therefore," relate the consequences or results of the situation described in verses 4-7 [NRSV: 2-5]. The first segment in Hos 2:8-10 [NRSV: 6-8] presents the husband's statements addressed to the wife that he will block her way so that she will not be able to return to her lovers. The images of ancient Israelite agricultural life predominate in this portrayal in that the husband states that he will block the wife's path with thorns and build a fence so that she can not find her paths. The vineyard song in Isa 5:1-7 offers an interesting parallel in that it describes the singer's, i.e., YHWH's, efforts to care for the vineyard by clearing it, hoeing it, building a wine vat, etc. When the singer's efforts fail in Isa 5:5-6, he states that he will break down its fence so that it will be trampled and refuse to hoe it so that it will be overgrown with briers and thorns. The husband states in Hos 2:9 [NRSV: 2:7] that the purpose of his actions is to prevent the wife from finding her lovers. He then places words in her mouth once again to justify her actions, claiming that she states, "I will go and I will return to my first husband, because it was better for me then than now." This is quite an ironic statement since the goal of the husband's actions and statements has been the return of the wife throughout. It is doubly ironic in that Deuteronomic law in Deut 24:1-4 forbids the return of a wife to her first husband after she has married another man, but this situation is presented as a case of adultery, not marriage and remarriage. In any case, the ironic intent of the passage continues to be served in verse 10 [NRSV: 8] which states that the wife did not know that the husband was the one who provided "the grain, the wine, and the oil" as well as the "silver" and "gold made for Baal" all along. At this point, the text presents the first clue that YHWH in fact is the husband. The terms "grain, wine, and oil *(haddāgān wĕhattîrôš wĕhayyishār)*" are formulaic terms for the agricultural produce of the land that YHWH provides the people and that they are obligated to present as offerings in Deuteronomy (see Deut 14:23; 18:4). Likewise, the reference to "gold made for Baal" signals that YHWH is the husband and that cultic apostasy is the issue. Although YHWH is not yet explicitly identified as the husband, the alert reader will recognize the significance of these references.

Hosea 2:11-15 [NRSV: 2:9-13] presents the second set of consequences that proceed from those outlined in verses 8-10 [NRSV: 6-8], i.e., the husband announces that he will take back the gifts which he has given to the wife in order to punish her. The textual clues that YHWH is the husband continue to mount. The husband states that he will return to take "my grain in its time *(bĕ⁽ittô)* and my wine in its season *(bĕmô⁽ădô)*," employing technical terms for the time when these crops are to be harvested and thus when they are to be presented for sacrifice at a Temple festival (see Ps 1:3; 2 Chr 30:22; cf. Deut 31:10; Hos 9:5; 12:10 [NRSV: 12:9]; Lam 2:7, 22). The husband's statement that he will recover the wool and the flax "to cover her nakedness" not only defines the function of these commodities as clothing, but recalls the sexual nature of the issue in that the term "nakedness *(⁽erwâ)*" is employed to describe some breach of modesty as the grounds for divorce in Deut 24:1. Likewise, when the husband states that he will "uncover her lewdness *(nablūtāh)* to the eyes of her lovers," he employs the term *nablût*, "lewdness, immodesty," which conveys sexual impropriety.

The husband continues by stating that he will bring to an end "all her mirth, her festival *(ḥaggāh)*, her new moon *(ḥādĕšāh)*, and her Sabbath *(wĕšabbattāh)*, and all her appointed feast *(wĕkōl mô⁽ădāh)*," employing the technical terms for the times of Temple observances and sacrifices. The statement that the wife's vine and fig tree shall be made into a forest reverses a common formula for peace and prosperity in the Bible, "but every man shall sit under his vine and under his fig tree, and none shall make them afraid" (Mic 4:4; cf. Zech 3:10; Isa 36:16=2 Kgs 18:31). The term normally translated as "forest" *(ya⁽ar)* more properly describes thick, wild growth that may include trees or thickets. It signifies the return of cultivated, well maintained agricultural land to wild growth and abandonment, as signified by the references to the wild animals who will eat the wife's vine and fig tree. Again, the husband places words in the mouth of the wife to describe the vine and fig tree, "They are my hire/gift which my lovers gave to me." Once more, the statements placed into the mouth of the wife are designed to establish her guilt and thereby to justify the husband's divorce action. The term for "hire" or "gift" (*ʾetnâ*) is frequently emended to *ʾetnan*, "the hire of a harlot" (see Deut 23:19 [NRSV: 23:18]; Ezek 16:34, 41; Hos 9:1), although the term is derived either from the root *tnh* which means simply "to hire" or perhaps from *ntn* which means "to give." In verse 15 [NRSV: 13], the identity of the husband as YHWH becomes explicit. He states that he will punish the wife for "the days of the Baalim when you burned incense to them," thereby identifying the wife's "harlotry" as the cultic offense of serving other gods. As noted above, the adornment of the wife with ring and necklace to pursue her "lovers" employs the imagery of wedding adornment (see Genesis 24) and thereby incorporates the motif of sexual infidelity once again. When the oracular formula, "utterance of YHWH," appears at the end of the verse, the identity of the husband as YHWH is secure.

Hosea 2:16-25 [NRSV: 2:14-23] presents the third section that outlines the consequences or results of the husband's, i.e., YHWH's appeal for intercession with the wife. This section is climactic, not only because it is the final segment in a sequence of three section, but because it outlines the future restoration of the marriage relationship and the restoration of the children as well. In this respect, he returns to the themes of both Hos 2:3 [NRSV: 2:1], which call for the restoration of the daughter Lo Ruhama and the son Lo Ammi and of Hos 2:4-7 [NRSV: 2:2-5] which calls upon the children to plead with their mother to return. The passage begins with the husband's/YHWH's statements that he is wooing the wife and bringing her back to the wilderness in order to renew the marriage. The initial statement, "behold, I am alluring her (*mĕpattêhā*)," employs the verb commonly used to express seduction, enticement, and even deceit. Thus, it appears in Exod 22:15 to describe the case of a man who seduces a virgin, and thereby is obligated to marry her. It also appears in Judg 14:15; 16:5 to describe Samson's seduction by his Philistine wives who were intent on discovering the secrets of his strength. It likewise appears in Jeremiah's laments (Jer 20:7, 10), where it expresses YHWH's enticement and deceit of the prophet, who was compelled by G–d to embark upon a path that he did not want. The husband's/YHWH's statement that he will guide the wife back into the wilderness functions on several levels. It invokes the imagery of seduction once again as a man leads a woman away from others in order to seduce her. Indeed it may also have a cultic context insofar as it also expresses the marriage practices of the tribe of Benjamin at the sanctuary at Shiloh as described in Judg 21:16-25 [NRSV: 21:15-24] in which the men lie in wait for maidens who dance in the vineyards at harvest time. It likewise plays upon the themes of the Exodus and YHWH's guidance of Israel through the wilderness into the promised land. Israelite tradition looks upon this period as the foundation of the nation in which the relationship between YHWH and Israel was firmly established (see Jer 2:2-3). The husband states that he "will speak upon her heart," an idiom that also refers to the language of lovers. It appears in Gen 34:3 to describe Shechem's attempt to woo Dinah; in Ruth 2:13 to describe Boaz's speech to Ruth; in Judg 19:3 to describe the Levite's attempt to win back his concubine; and in Isa 40:2 to describe YHWH's speech to Jerusalem, later identified as a bride and mother in Isaiah 54, indicating that her time of restoration is at hand (see also Gen 50:21; 2 Sam 19:8; 2 Chr 30:22). YHWH/the husband begins to list promises to the wife in verse 17 [NRSV: 15]. She will receive her vineyards from the wilderness, apparently a reference to land that the wife will receive as part of the marriage agreement. According to Judg 1:11-15, however, it is the father of the bride, Caleb, who presented land to his daughter Achsah when she married Othniel. Likewise according to 1 Kgs 9:16, Pharaoh conquered and presented the city of Gezer to Solomon when he married his daughter the Egyptian princess.

The presentation of the Valley of Achor as a "door of hope" is particularly interesting in this context in that it draws upon Israelite tradition to make a political statement concerning the future of Israel as well. The Valley of Achor is well known in biblical tradition as the site where Achan ben Carmi was executed in the time of Joshua for his theft of some of the booty from Jericho that had been devoted to YHWH. According to Joshua 7, Achan stole some of the booty devoted to YHWH prior to the Israelite assault against Ai, nearby to Beth-Aven and Beth-El. Thirty-six Israelites died in the initial attack on Ai because Joshua 7 claims that YHWH punished Israel for Achan's crime. After Joshua was informed by YHWH of the reason for the defeat, an investigation was undertaken and Achan was identified as the culprit. In order to remove the impurity of the crime from the people, Achan and his children and livestock were stoned, a heap of stones was erected as a monument, and the place was called the Valley/Plain of Achor (i.e., "trouble"). The Hebrew word ʿemeq is employed to describe the broad flat plain that defines the bottom of a valley floor. The exact location of the Valley of Achor is disputed, but it is identified in Josh 15:7 as defining the northern border of Judah with Benjamin. Most scholars follow Noth, who identifies the Valley/Plain of Achor with the modern El Buqeah, a small plain in the northern Judean wilderness between Hyrcania and Qumran, in the northwestern area of the Dead Sea.[28] It is bounded on the north by the Wadi Dabr system and on the south by the Wadi en-Nar or Kidron Valley. This latter reference is particularly significant for Hosea in that the Wadi Kidron extends all the way up to the city of

[28] See Carolyn Pressler, "Achor," *ABD* I:56.

Jerusalem and defines the eastern boundary of the City of David. In this regard, the identification of the Valley/Plain of Achor with *Petach Tiqvah*, "the door of Hope," employs the geographical features of the land to make the point that Israel's hope leads to Jerusalem. In this respect, the renaming of the Valley of Achor as *Petach Tiqvah* likewise involves a word play that signifies the reversal of the bride's or Israel's status from "Valley of Trouble *(Achor)*" to "Door of Hope *(Tiqvah)*."

Finally, the concluding statements of verse 17 [NRSV: 15] recap the themes of marriage in the wilderness and the Exodus/Wilderness tradition. The statement, "and she will answer there as in the days of her youth," recalls the tradition of a youthful Israel in the wilderness as the bride of YHWH that is cited in Jer 2:2-3. The statement, "and as the day of her going up from the land of Egypt," of course recalls the motif of the Exodus from Egypt and the journey through the wilderness to the promised land.

Hosea 2:18-25 [NRSV: 16-23] relates the anticipated restoration of the relationship between YHWH and Israel that YHWH attempts in verses 16-17 [NRSV: 14-15]. These results are outlined in two sub-units, each of which is introduced by the formula *wĕhāyâ bayyôm hahûʾ*, "and it shall come to pass in that day," in order to signify the restoration of the relationship in the future. The first appears in relation to the wife (verses 18-22) [NRSV: 16-20], and the second appears in relation to the children (verses 23-25) [NRSV: 21-23]. Hosea 2:18-22 [NRSV: 2:16-18] also employs the oracular formula *nĕʾūm YHWH*, "utterance of YHWH," to demonstrate that YHWH continues as the speaker. The presentation of YHWH's speech begins with a deliberate word play in a statement addressed to the wife, "you shall call me 'my husband/man,' and you shall not call me 'my Baal/husband.'" This statement encapsulates both the imagery of the marriage relationship and that of cultic apostasy. The term employed for "my husband/man," *ʾîšî*, conveys the common term for a "man," that can designate a "husband" as well. The term *baʿlî*, "my husband/Baal," employs a term that is frequently used to convey "lord," "husband," and the name of the Canaanite rain/fertility deity, Baal. YHWH continues with a statement indicating the intention to remove the names of the Baalim so that they are remembered no more, which of course plays upon the motifs of cultic apostasy and the marriage relationship once again.

YHWH then states in verses 19 20 [NRSV: 17-19] the intention to "make a covenant for them in that day," which is a formal statement of YHWH's intention to renew the relationship. The term to "cut a covenant" is commonly applied for the making of treaties between countries or their rulers (e.g., Joshua and the Gibeonites, Josh 9:6; Solomon of Israel and Hiram of Tyre, 1 Kgs 5:26 [NRSV: 5:12]), the relationship

between YHWH and Israel (e.g., Exod 19:5), or any relationship or agreement between human beings (e.g., Jacob and Laban, Gen 31:44), including the marriage relationship between man and woman (Prov 2:17; Mal
2:14). The statement indicates that the covenant will include the "animals of the field," the "birds of the heavens," and the "crawling things
of the ground," which relates all of the basic categories of living creatures mentioned as part of creation (see Genesis 1) with the exception
of fish and other sea creatures. The fish are obviously irrelevant since
Hosea is concerned with the land of Israel, but the presence of wildlife
in the relationship indicates that the covenant is conceived to embrace
all of the land of Israel, including both its human and animal inhabitants. YHWH states the intention to break "bow and sword and war"
from the land, indicating a cessation of war made by enemy nations, so
that the land might "lie down in security." This idyllic picture appears
elsewhere in biblical tradition as well. Leviticus 26:6 states as part of
the articulation of covenant blessings that YHWH "will give peace in the
land, and you shall lie down, and none shall make you afraid; and I
will remove evil beasts from the land, and the sword shall not go
through your land." Obviously, this statement is quite similar to that of
Hosea, and suggests that both are expressions of ancient Israelite con-
ceptions and formulations of covenant making between YHWH and Israel. Analogous expressions appear in Isa 11:6-9, which describes the
idyllic situation of the restoration of Davidic rule over Israel, Judah,
and the nations, and in Ezek 34:25-28, which portrays YHWH's "shepherding" of Israel in a time of peace.

Finally, YHWH states the intention "to betroth" the wife Israel in
verses 21-22 [NRSV: 19-20]. This clearly provides a sexual play of words
that builds upon the concluding statement of verse 21 [NRSV: 19], "and I
will cause you to lie down in security." The piel form of the verb *ʾrś* is
commonly employed to express an agreement of marriage between
man and woman (e.g., Deut 20:7; 28:30), including the payment of the
bride-price paid to the father by the prospective husband (2 Sam 3:14).
The qualities expressed for the relationship, "in righteousness *(běṣedeq)*
and in justice *(ûběmišpāṭ)* and in fidelity *(ûběḥesed)* and in mercy
(ûběraḥămîm)" and "in faithfulness *(beʾĕmûnâ)*" are qualities typically
ascribed to YHWH (e.g., Exod 34:6) or the ideal Davidic monarch (e.g.,
Isa 11:3-5). The concluding statement to the bride in this sequence,
"and you shall know YHWH," plays once again on the sexual innuendo
in that the verb *ydʿ*, "to know," conveys both acquaintance in a relationship and sexual union (e.g., Gen 4:1; 38:26).

Hosea 2:23-25 [NRSV: 2:21-23] relates the future restoration of the
relationship between YHWH and the children, who likewise represent
Israel. Again, the passage begins with the formula, "and it shall come to

pass on that day," and the oracular formula, "utterance of YHWH," to convey the future orientation of the passage and the identity of the speaker as YHWH. The first statement made by YHWH is a cryptic "I will answer (*ʾeʿĕneh*)," which conveys YHWH's assent to join in the relationship. Although the verb *ʿnh* commonly means "to answer," it frequently conveys a formal understanding of the action as an answer or testimony that might be given in a legal context (e.g., Exod 20:16; Deut 5:20; 31:21; 1 Sam 12:3; Isa 3:9; Mic 6:3; Job 9:14, 15; 15:6). In the present case, the legal ramifications of the verb convey YHWH's assent to the legal relationship of marriage or covenant with Israel, as the case may be, and the legal recognition of the children as YHWH's own. Likewise, YHWH's statement of intent to "answer" the heavens and the earth invokes common witnesses to legal covenant making in Israelite traditions (see Deut 32:1; Isa 1:2; cf. Mic 1:2; Jer 4:23). After invoking or "answering" heaven as a witness, heaven "answers" earth/the land, and earth/the land "answers the grain, the wine, and the oil," once again bringing in the formulaic reference from verses 10 [NRSV: 8] and 11 [NRSV: 9] that describes the produce of the land granted by YHWH that in turn is to be presented as an offering at the Temple (Deut 14:23; 18:4). The grain, wine, and oil, in turn "answer" Jezreel, and thereby seal the relationship with the first of the " sons" born to the marriage. At this point, the pronunciation and etymology of Jezreel become important. The term Jezreel, *yizreʿeʾl* in Hebrew, sounds like the term Israel (*yiśrāʾēl*) in Hebrew. It obviously signifies Israel, based upon its assonantal qualities and the symbolic significance of the name in the context of the marriage between Hosea/YHWH and Gomer/Israel. The term is derived from the verb *zrʿ*, "to plant, sow," and means "G–d plants/sows." It thereby conveys the imagery of planting, growth, and restoration that is so essential to the meaning of this passage, and it provides the basis for the following pun in verse 25 [NRSV: 23] that signals that new growth and restoration. At the beginning of verse 25 [NRSV: 23], YHWH states about Jezreel, "and I planted her (*ûzĕraʿtîhā*) for myself in the earth," employing the verb *zrʿ* as the basis for a pun on the name Jezreel. Many scholars emend the feminine singular suffix of the verb ("planted her") to a masculine singular suffix, insofar as Jezreel is described as a son of Hosea, but this is unnecessary as Jezreel is the name of a broad valley. Like all natural features of the land, it must be viewed grammatically as feminine. YHWH's statement then continues with two additional puns that convey restoration in relation to the other two children, "and I will show mercy (*wĕriḥamtî*) [to] Lo Ruhama, and I will say to Lo Ammi, 'you are Ammi/my people,' and he will say, 'My G–d.'" This last statement represents the formal response of the children/Israel accepting YHWH as G–d in the renewed marriage/covenant relationship.

Autobiographical Report of Hosea's Remarriage
to an Adulterous Woman: 3:1-5

Hosea 3:1-5 is an autobiographical report concerning the prophet's remarriage to an adulterous woman. It is linked syntactically by the initial *waw-consecutive* formulation to the prophet's speech in Hos 2:3-25 [NRSV: 2:1-23], which appeals for the return of his wife as a symbol for the return of Israel to YHWH. Hosea 3:1-5 presents YHWH's instructions to Hosea in verse 1 to marry an adulterous woman once again, followed by the report of the prophet's compliance in verses 2-5 which relate the significance of this action as a symbol for the return of Israel to YHWH and to the house of David. Because it follows upon the prophet's appeal in Hos 2:3-25 [NRSV: 2:1-23], it indicates that Hosea was successful in reestablishing his marriage thereby indicating that YHWH would be successful in reestablishing the relationship with Israel. It reinforces the message of Hos 2:3-25 [NRSV: 2:1-23] that YHWH's intention is to restore the nation Israel following a period of punishment and separation.

Hosea 3:1 is the first major section of this text. It reports YHWH's instructions to Hosea once again to love an adulterous woman. This statement has provoked a great deal of discussion among interpreters who raise questions as to whether or not this woman is Gomer or a different woman. The Hebrew word *'ôd*, "again," appears to relate to the report of YHWH's initial statement to Hosea, "and YHWH said to me again, 'go, love a woman . . .'" Insofar as YHWH's first instructions to Hosea are related in Hos 1:2–2:2 [NRSV: 1:2-11], the word "again" apparently refers to another speech by YHWH to Hosea, not necessarily to another marriage. The woman is never named, which raises the question as to whether or not Gomer is intended. Hosea is told to "love" a woman, and it is only clear later when he reports the amount of the bride price that this refers to a marriage. The woman is described as one "loved by a neighbor and an adulteress," but it is not clear that this necessarily refers to Gomer as there is no report that she ever abandoned Hosea in Hos 1:2–2:2 [NRSV: 1:2-11]. Gomer is described as "a woman of harlotry," but there is no indication that the harlotry took place after her marriage to Hosea. Many argue that the statements in Hos 2:7, 9, 15 [NRSV: 2:5, 7, 13], etc., demonstrate that Gomer was unfaithful to Hosea, but the nature of the oracle in Hos 2:3-25 [NRSV: 2:1-23] and the symbolic act of Hosea's marriage to Gomer make it unclear whether these statements refer to actual events in Hosea's personal experience. Certainly, public charges that she and her children were a "woman of harlotry" and "children of harlotry" and the symbolic naming of the children Jezreel, Lo Ruhama, and Lo Ammi could well lead to her departure from the marriage, whether by adultery or other means. Hosea does not seem to have been an easy man to live with, and the woman mentioned in Hos 3:1-5 might very well be someone different. In any case, the explanation of the significance of this action in Hos 3:3-5 does not require that this be a remarriage to the same woman. Furthermore, Deut 24:1-4 makes it clear that Israelite legal tradition forbade the remarriage of a man to his previous wife if she had been married to another man after the divorce. The reference to the marriage price in verse 2 suggests that this was indeed a marriage, and not a simple transaction with a prostitute (see the discussion of the price paid for the woman below). The text suggests that Hosea bought himself a prostitute for marriage in the aftermath of his failed marriage to Gomer. YHWH's instructions make it clear that Hosea's action is designed to serve as a paradigm for YHWH's relationship with Israel. Hosea's marriage is compared to YHWH's love for Israel, but Israel is said to have turned from YHWH to other gods and to love raisin cakes. Apparently raisin cakes were a common offering to deities, including YHWH (2 Sam 6:19; 1 Chr 16:3).

Hosea 3:2-5 reports Hosea's compliance with YHWH's instructions, and conveys the significance of his actions as a demonstration of YHWH's intention to restore Israel. Hosea reports in verse 2 that he "bought her for fifteen shekels of silver, a homer of barley (ca. eleven bushels), and a *lethech* of barley (half a homer)." The verb *krh*, "to buy," is unusual in the Hebrew Bible and generally signifies purchase by trade or bargaining (see Deut 2:6; Job 6:27; 40:30 [NRSV: 41:6]), which may suggest bargaining with a prostitute or bargaining for a marriage price. Wolff calculates the value of the *homer* and *lethech* of barley at fifteen shekels, and concludes that the total of thirty shekels worth of silver and barley is equivalent to the price demanded in the event that a (male) slave is gored according to Exod 21:32.[29] Likewise, Lev 27:4 indicates that the valuation of a woman for the Temple tax is thirty shekels. It is difficult to determine if these prices would have been in effect in Hosea's day, but the substantial amount of the transaction indicates that the purchase is for the purpose of marriage, not a simple transaction with a prostitute.

Hosea 3:3-5 then convey Hosea's statements to his wife and his explanation of the significance of his marriage. He tells her that "she shall remain many days" for him, that she shall not practice harlotry in order to be with another man and she shall not be with him either. As noted above, Exod 21:10-11 requires a husband to provide his wife with food, clothing, and sexual relations, and his failure to provide these three

[29] Wolff, *Hosea*, 61.

things is grounds for the wife to go free. Although Hosea seems to have transacted a real marriage, at least in financial terms, he seems to be setting himself up for another divorce! He then explains his actions by establishing once again the analogy between his marriage and YHWH's relationship to Israel, stating that "Israel will remain many days" without king, officer, sacrifice, Mazzebah (cultic pillar), Ephod, and Teraphim. This statement clearly indicates that Israel will lose its leaders, i.e., the king and the officers or government officials, and its cultic establishment, i.e., sacrifice, Mazzebah, Ephod, and Teraphim. The sacrifice is the common means of worship in Israelite Temples. The Mazzebah is a cultic pillar that symbolizes a sacred site (see Genesis 28 in which Jacob erects a Mazzebah at Beth-El, the site of the royal Temple of the northern kingdom of Israel) or other important place. The Ephod is the garment of priest which contains objects for the practice of divination or oracular inquiry of G–d (see Exod 28:5-15, 25-28 [NRSV: 28:6-14, 24-27]; Judg 8:27; 1 Sam 23:9-12; 30:7-9). Teraphim are apparently idols or statues of a deity (see Gen 31:19, 25-35; 35:1-4; Judg 17:5; 18:14-20). Finally, Hosea states in verse 5 that after the period of punishment or separation is over, Israel will "seek YHWH their G–d and David their king and they shall come in fear to YHWH and to his goodness in the latter days," indicating a return to YHWH and the rule of the house of David. Evidently, this points to the restoration of a united Israel under the rule of Davidic monarchy as it existed in the days of David and Solomon. The reference to "fear" is a common means in the Bible to indicate "respect." Many interpreters take the reference to "the latter days *(bĕ³aḥărît hayyāmîm)*" as a reference to the eschatological fulfillment of this statement, but the phrase *bĕ³aḥărît hayyāmîm*, "in the latter days," simply denotes the distant future (see Gen 49:1; Num 24:14; Deut 4:30; 31:29; Isa 2:2; Mic 4:1; Jer 23:20, etc.).[30]

Presentation of YHWH's Controversy against Israel:
Appeal to Reject Corrupted Priesthood and Cultic Places: 4:1-19

Hosea 4:1-19 has long been recognized as a key component of the book of Hosea. Its programmatic character in delineating YHWH's complaints against Israel and its position at the head of the prophetic oracles

---

[30] For discussion of the phrase *bĕ³aḥărît hayyāmîm*, see Simon J. De Vries, *Yesterday, Today, and Tomorrow* (Grand Rapids: Eerdmans, 1975) 50; Marvin A. Sweeney, *Isaiah 1–39, with an Introduction to Prophetic Literature*, FOTL, vol. 16 (Grand Rapids: Eerdmans, 1996) 99.

in Hosea 4–14, immediately following the narratives in Hosea 1–3 concerning the restoration of Hosea's relationship with his wife, have convinced many scholars that Hosea 4 functions as the introduction to an early collection of the prophet's oracles.[31] As noted above, there is little reason to accept the common conclusion among interpreters that Hosea 1–3 and 4–14 constitute the basic structural building blocks of the book of Hosea. Rather, Hos 1:2–2:3 [NRSV: 1:2-11] constitutes the report of YHWH's speaking to Hosea concerning his marriage to Gomer and the birth of their children, and Hos 2:4–14:19 [NRSV: 2:1–14:8] reports Hosea's speech concerning YHWH's appeal for Israel's return. In the context of this latter section, Hos 4:1-19 follows immediately upon the report of Hosea's appeal to his children for their mother's return. Based upon its formal literary features and contents, Hos 4:1-19 constitutes the prophet's report of YHWH's controversy against Israel and his appeal to abandon its corrupted cultic establishment. It points especially to the failure of the priesthood in its responsibility to educate the people concerning YHWH's expectations, and it therefore calls upon the people to abandon the cultic sites at Beth Aven (i.e., Beth El) and Gilgal. Hosea 4:1-19 thereby prepares the readers for the following segments in Hos 5:1–14:9 [NRSV: 5:1–14:8] that take up these issues in detail.

The literary structure of Hos 4:1-19 is notoriously difficult to assess due to the constant shifts in the pronouns that indicate the addressees of the text as well as various other textual difficulties. As a result, many interpreters have considered the chapter to be a collection of originally independent oracles that have been placed together into their present context by later redactors of the book.[32] A great deal of attention thereby is given to the interpretation of the individual elements of this text, particularly verses 1-3 and 4-10 that take up YHWH's condemnation of Israel and its priesthood. Verses 11-19 receive relatively less attention because of their textual difficulties, although scholars generally acknowledge that they continue the theme of the condemnation of the priesthood for its failure to educate the people properly in YHWH's expectations.

Because of the reference to YHWH's *rîb*, "controversy" or "lawsuit," in verse 1 and other examples of forensic language in these verses, such as the references to violations of the Ten Commandments in verse 2, interpreters tend to view Hosea 4 as an example of a covenant lawsuit in which YHWH places charges against Israel in a court of law for violating

---

[31] See Davies, *Hosea*, 35–6; Wolff, *Hosea*, 30; Gale A. Yee, *Composition*, 51–2.

[32] E.g., Davies, *Hosea*, 110–3; Wolff, *Hosea*, 65–6, 73–6; cf. Yee, *Composition*, 158–70.

the terms of the covenant that binds Yʜᴡʜ and Israel together.[33] Other examples of the form in prophetic literature include Isaiah 1; Jeremiah 2; Micah 6; and various texts from Deutero-Isaiah. The existence of a clearly defined covenant lawsuit speech is increasingly questioned by scholars, however, in that no standard literary structure or terminology is apparent throughout all of the various examples of the form that have been put forward, and there are great difficulties in portraying Yʜᴡʜ as both plaintiff and judge in a legal proceeding.[34] Nevertheless, the influence of forensic or trial language is evident throughout the text.

A particularly important and problematic issue in the assessment of the literary structure and genre of Hosea 4 appears in verse 15, "If you act as a harlot, O Israel, let not Judah incur guilt, and do not come to Gilgal, and do not go up to Beth Aven, and do not swear, 'By the life of Yʜᴡʜ!' This statement clearly addresses Israel and calls upon it to take action by abandoning the cultic sites—and their priests—that have played such a role in leading to the corruption of the people as articulated throughout Hosea 4. Because the verse takes up a concern for the welfare of Judah and because it considers the possibility that Israel might change its ways and avoid the punishment outlined throughout the chapter, many interpreters regard it as a later addition to the original text that was designed to consider the situation of Judah in later times and to qualify the harsh judgment called for throughout Hosea 4.[35] Even when it is not dismissed as a secondary accretion to the text, it is frequently overlooked in assessments of the literary structure and character of Hosea 4.

Nevertheless, Hos 4:15 must be recognized as the crucial element in Hosea 4 in that it defines the rhetorical goal of the chapter as a whole and points to the function of the forensic language within the larger literary context. Overall, Hosea 4 is designed to call upon its audience to take action; in this case, to recognize the failure of the priesthood to meet its responsibilities in educating the people of Israel and to reject the priesthood and its cultic sites as a means to begin the process of restoration to Yʜᴡʜ. The forensic language of the chapter builds the

---

[33] Davies, *Hosea*, 113; Stuart, *Hosea-Jonah*, 72–4. For discussion of the lawsuit form, see Claus Westermann, *Basic Forms of Prophetic Speech* (Cambridge: Lutterworth; Louisville: Westminster John Knox, 1991) 199–200; Kirsten Nielsen, Yʜᴡʜ *as Prosecutor and Judge: An Investigation of the Prophetic Lawsuit (Rîb-Pattern)*, JSOTSup, vol. 9 (Sheffield: JSOT Press, 1978); cf. Sweeney, *Isaiah 1–39*, 541–2.

[34] See Michael De Roche, "Yʜᴡʜ's *rîb* Against Israel: A Reassessment of the So-Called 'Prophetic Lawsuit' in the Preexilic Prophets," *JBL* 102 (1983) 563–74.

[35] Rudolph, *Hosea*, 112–4; Wolff, *Hosea*, 89–90; cf. Davies, *Hosea*, 128. For a full discussion, see Grace I. Emmerson, *Hosea: An Israelite Prophet in Judean Perspective*, JSOTSup, vol. 28 (Sheffield: JSOT, 1984) 77–83.

case for the failure of the priesthood and highlights the consequences: judgment against the people for their sins in failing to abide by Y<small>HWH</small>'s will and the deterioration of the created world because the people do not fulfill their proper role in maintaining the land and creation at large. The accusations and announcements of judgment directed against the Israelite priesthood and the people are not ends in and of themselves; they are designed to motivate the people to recognize the cause of their difficulties and to take action to correct the problems identified in the prophet's discourse. In this regard, the people are called upon to resume their responsibilities in relation to Y<small>HWH</small> and in relation to the created world in which Y<small>HWH</small> has placed them. This agenda appears in the three basic structural components of the chapter, each of which begins with direct address to the people or the priests: 1) Hos 4:1-3 constitutes the prophet's summons to the people of Israel to hear Y<small>HWH</small>'s *rîb* or "controversy"; 2) Hos 4:4-14 constitutes the prophet's presentation of Y<small>HWH</small>'s judgment speech against the priesthood for leading the people into sin; and 3) Hos 4:15-19 constitutes the prophet's appeal for Israel to abandon Gilgal and Beth El and thereby begin the attempt to restore the relationship with Y<small>HWH</small>.

HOSEA'S SUMMONS FOR ISRAEL TO HEAR YHWH'S RÎB OR "CONTROVERSY": 4:1-3

Hosea 4:1-3 introduces the entire sequence of the chapter by calling upon the people of Israel to hear Y<small>HWH</small>'s *rîb,* "controversy" or "lawsuit," against them for violating the terms of the covenant that defines the relationship between Y<small>HWH</small> and Israel. It begins with an example of the "Call to Attention" formula in verse 1a that appears throughout biblical literature as a common introduction to a public presentation or address.[36] Although it appears most frequently in prophetic literature (e.g., Isa 1:10; Ezek 6:3; Amos 3:1; Mic 6:1), it may also introduce hymnic compositions (Judg 5:3), wisdom discourses (Prov 7:24), or diplomatic messages from an official envoy (2 Kgs 18:28-29). Its basic function is to introduce and to call the audience's attention to the following presentation. It identifies both the audience, i.e., the people of Israel, and what the audience is to hear, i.e., the word of Y<small>HWH</small>.

Two explanatory clauses, each of which begins with the causative *kî,* "because, for," then follow the initial "call to attention" formula. The first appears in verse 1bα, "for Y<small>HWH</small> has a controversy *(rîb)* with the inhabitants of the land," which states the basic cause of the summons. The noun *rîb* is derived from the verb *ryb,* which commonly denotes a

---

[36] Wolff, *Hosea,* 66; cf. Sweeney, *Isaiah 1–39,* 544.

controversy or dispute between two parties, such as the dispute between the herdsmen of Gerar and those of Isaac concerning water
rights (Gen 26:20-22), the complaints of Israel against Moses for lack of
water in the wilderness (Exod 17:2), or Job's contentions against YHWH
(Job 9:3; 13:19; 23:6; 40:2). The noun frequently appears as a technical
term that designates a lawsuit or other formal legal dispute (e.g., Exod
23:2, 3, 6; Deut 21:5; 2 Sam 15:2, 4). In the present context, it denotes a
dispute between the two parties identified in verse 1bα, viz., YHWH and
the inhabitants of the land.

The second explanatory clause appears in verses 1bβ-3, which build
upon verse 1bα to explain the nature of the controversy between YHWH
and the inhabitants of the land. It first identifies the basic problem in
verse 1bβ as a lack of "truth" (*'emet*), "fidelity" (*ḥesed*), and "knowledge
(*daʿat*) of G–d in the land." Each of these terms identifies the abstract
qualities of the relationship between YHWH and Israel, particularly the
attitude of Israel toward YHWH, that are defined much more concretely
in verses 2-3. The term *'emet*, "truth," conveys the quality of trustworthiness in a relationship, as exemplified by those who are chosen to
serve as judges in Israel (Exod 18:21), or the trustworthiness of a report
(1 Kgs 10:6), witnesses in court (Prov 14:25), laws (Neh 9:13), or a teaching (Mal 2:6). The term *ḥesed* conveys fidelity in and to a relationship,
whether between human beings (e.g., Joseph and the chief butler, Gen
40:14; David and Saul, 1 Sam 20:15; Esther, Hegai and Ahashuerus,
Esth 2:9, 17), or between human beings and YHWH (by YHWH to Jacob,
Gen 32:11 [NRSV: 32:10]; by YHWH to David, Ps 89:1; by Israel the bride
to YHWH the groom, Jer 2:2).[37] Both terms frequently appear together to
express a secure and faithful relationship (e.g., Joseph and Jacob/Israel
in Gen 47:29; Joshua's spies and Rahab in Josh 2:14; YHWH and Israel in
Ps 85:11 [NRSV: 85:10]). The term "knowledge (*daʿat*) of G–d" is characteristically employed in Hosea to express the intimate relationship
between YHWH and Israel based upon the analogy of the marriage relationship and the cognitive knowledge of YHWH's laws and expectations. The verb *ydʿ*, "to know," from which *daʿat*, "knowledge," is
derived, frequently expresses intimate relations between husband and
wife (e.g., Gen 4:1; 24:16; 1 Sam 1:19) that embodies not only sexual
intercourse but a full interrelationship between the spouses in all aspects of life as well.

Specific indications of the disrupted state of the relationship between YHWH and Israel appear in verses 2-3, which elaborate upon the
current desolate state of the land. Verse 2 relates a series of problems

[37] See esp. Nelson Glueck, *Ḥesed in the Bible* (Cincinnati: Hebrew Union College,
1967).

that are drawn from the decalogue, including inappropriate swearing (*ʾālâ*) in which the name of YHWH would be invoked to curse another (Exod 20:7; Deut 5:11; see also the early form of the Decalogue in Lev 19:12; cf. Judg 17:2), lying (Exod 20:16; Deut 5:20; Lev 19:11), murder (Exod 20:13; Deut 5:15), stealing (Exod 20:15; Deut 5:19; Lev 19:11), and adultery (Exod 20:14; Deut 5:18). The problematic verb *pārāṣû*, "they have broken out," is generally understood as a reference to the outbreak of the crimes listed in verse 2a as the verb is frequently employed in reference to "breaking over limits" or "increasing" (e.g., Gen 30:30; Exod 1:12; Job 1:10). The statement "bloodshed follows (lit. touches) bloodshed" employs the noun *dāmîm*, literally "bloods" or "bloodshed," which conveys the outbreak of the most serious, violent, bloody crimes in the land. As indicated by the introductory *ʿal-kēn*, therefore, verse 3 then summarizes the situation outlined in verse 2 by stating that the land "mourns" *(teʾĕbal)* and all its inhabitants "wither" *(ʾumlal)*. The combination of the verbs *ʾbl*, "to mourn," and *ʾml*, "to languish, wither," employs the language of natural fertility in reference to the lack of rain that sustains life to convey the desolate state of the land (see Isa 24:4, 7; 33:9; Jer 14:2; Joel 1:10; Lam 2:8). In employing such language, Hosea draws upon the fertility imagery of the Canaanite Baal religion that looked to Baal to bring the rains necessary for life in the land. By employing such language, Hosea conveys the necessary interrelationship between human actions and the state of the natural world, i.e., the role of humans is to maintain the world of creation (cf. Gen 1:26).[38] If human beings fail to maintain the proper order of their lives, the entire world of creation suffers. In this case, Hosea's reference to the "gathering" of "the beasts of the field," "the birds of the heavens," and "the fish of the sea" employs the language of Gen 1:26 to express the consequences of the failure to live up to the human responsibility for their own actions and the welfare of the natural world. Similar sentiments and language appear in Zeph 1:2-3. Likewise, the covenant blessings and curses in Leviticus 26 and Deuteronomy 28–30 express the consequences of human moral failure in relation to the disruption of the natural world.

HOSEA'S PRESENTATION OF YHWH'S JUDGMENT SPEECH AGAINST THE PRIESTS: 4:4-14

Hosea 4:4-14 constitutes the prophet's presentation of YHWH's judgment speech against the priesthood for leading the people of Israel into

[38] Cf. M. DeRoche, "The Reversal of Creation in Hosea," *VT* 31 (1981) 400–9.

sin. Within the larger structure of Hosea 4 as a whole, this section presents the evidence for YHWH's "controversy" or "lawsuit" against the people of the land that is announced in Hos 4:1-3. Overall, it points to the responsibility of the priesthood to educate the people in YHWH's requirements, and it argues that the priests have failed to fulfill this responsibility. Hosea draws an analogy between the priesthood and the people in this passage; just as the priesthood is corrupted and acts as a harlot, so the people are corrupted and act as harlots because that is the example provided them. Although much of the passage is formulated as a first person speech by YHWH directed to the priests, the third person reference to YHWH in verse 10b indicates that Hosea conveys YHWH's words.

The literary structure of Hos 4:4-14 comprises two basic components in verses 4-5 and 6-14, each of which is built around a prophetic announcement of punishment. Hosea 4:4-5 lays out the issue in very general terms with a basic announcement of punishment that establishes the analogy between the people and the priesthood. It begins in verse 4 with a statement by YHWH directed to the priests that indicates their inability to challenge or argue against the following assertions. The reason for this is because the people are like those accused by or challenged by the priests, i.e., the people are likened to those judged by the priests to be somehow unsuitable or unclean.[39] Just as the people are unable to challenge such a contention by the priest, so the priests are unable to challenge the contention by YHWH. The terminology employed for this statement, "and your people are as those challenged of (the) priest *(kimĕrîbê kōhēn),*" is extremely problematic. The verb *mērîb* is a *hiphil* masculine plural construct participle from the root *ryb* which literally means "those who cause to contend." When prefixed with the preposition *kĕ,* "like," bound in construct to *kōhēn,* "priest," the expression translates literally, "like those causing contention of the priests." The only other example of a *hiphil* participle of *ryb* appears in 1 Sam 2:10 where it clearly designates those who contend against YHWH or act as adversaries to G–d. This indicates that the term refers to opponents or adversaries of the priests in Hos 4:4. A reference to the adversaries of the priests would not likely refer to some group which attempted to challenge the power of the priests or who attempted to depose them from their role in sacred practice, as any such challenge would have to come from another priestly line rendering the concept of adversaries of the *priests* meaningless. It seems likely that the "adversaries of the priests" would have to be those whose ritual purity had been chal-

---

[39] See the procedures for identifying leprosy and other impurities in Leviticus 13–15 and the question of sacrificial purity put before the priests in Hag 2:10-19.

lenged by the priests, i.e., those who were deemed unfit by the priests for cultic worship because some blemish or imperfection, such as leprosy, sexual intercourse, improper eating of meat or treatment of blood, robbery, murder, etc., had rendered them unfit to participate in Temple worship (cf. the purity laws of Leviticus; Ezekiel 18). Just as such persons were in no position to challenge the decisions of the priests, so the priests are in no position to challenge the decision of YHWH. According to verse 4b, YHWH considers the priests to be unfit for sacred service. As a result, the announcement of judgment in verse 5 states that they shall "stumble" or "fail," a common reference to punishment in the prophets (see Isa 3:8; 8:15; 31:3; Jer 50:30; cf. Hos 5:5; 14:2 [NRSV: 14:1]). The priests are condemned together with the prophets, who also frequently served as cultic functionaries in ancient Israelite and Judean Temples (cf. Isa 28:7; Jer 2:8; 4:9; 5:31; 6:13; 8:10; 14:18; 18:18; 23:11; Mic 3:11; note also that Moses, Samuel, Jeremiah, Ezekiel, and Zechariah are both prophets and priests). The concluding statement by YHWH, "and I will destroy your mother," is enigmatic and the cause of many suggestions to emend the text. It is very likely a reference to Israel portrayed as Gomer, the wife of Hosea in Hos 1:2-9, who bears him the children who symbolize Israel. Just as Hosea will punish his wife, the mother of his children, so YHWH will punish the "mother" of the priesthood.

Hosea 4:6-14 then provides a much more detailed portrayal of YHWH's announcement of judgment against Israel that points specifically to the actions of the priests as the cause of the punishment. Verse 6 begins this segment with a second person address by YHWH to the priests that notes the current compromised state of the people prior to announcing that YHWH will reject the priests and forget their sons because the priests have rejected "knowledge" and forgotten "the Torah of your G–d." Indeed, the parallel use of the verbs "reject" and "forget" indicates a principle of reciprocity in carrying out the punishment. The speech by YHWH then shifts to third person references to Israel and the priesthood as the Deity explains in verses 7-14 the background and causes of the preceding announcement of punishment. Verse 7 charges that the priests sinned even as they increased, perhaps in numbers, status, or power, which prompts YHWH to announce the intention to exchange their glory *(kĕbôdām)* for shame *(qālôn)*. The term "glory" *(kābôd)* frequently appears in reference to the Divine Presence at a cultic site such as the wilderness tabernacle (Exod 40:34-38) or the Jerusalem Temple (1 Kgs 8:10-12; Isa 4:2-6), and the verb root *kbd*, "to honor," can be applied to the status of the priesthood (see 1 Sam 2:30 which employs the verb roots *kbd* and *qll*, "to shame, despise," to describe the impending downfall of the Elide priesthood). Verse 8 offers an interesting play on words that takes up the roles of the priests in relation to the sacrifices of the people, "the sin (offering) of my people they eat, and they raise their throat to their guilt." Ancient Israelites and Judeans would present a "sin offering" (*ḥaṭṭaʾt;* see Leviticus 4–5, esp. 4:2-3 and 5:1) as part of the process for atoning for "sin" (*ḥaṭṭaʾt*) or "guilt" (*ʿāwōn*), and the "sin offering" would be eaten in part by the priests at the Temple as part of their income or due (Lev 6:24-30). Because the term for "sin offering" and "sin" is identical, verse 8 essentially portrays the sin and guilt of the priests by reference to their devouring the "sin offering" and "guilt" of the people. Likewise, the statement, "and they raise (*yiśʾû*) their throat to their guilt," employs the same verb that conveys the bearing of guilt as expressed for example in Lev 5:1, "he shall bear (*nāśāʾ*) his guilt" (see also Num 18:1). Again, the pun aids in portraying the guilt of priests who eat the sin offerings of the people even though they fail to instruct the people properly and thereby lead them into sin in the first place. The pun thereby suggests that they are eager to "bear their guilt."

Verses 9-14 then describe the consequences of the priests' actions. Verse 9a states the principle that the situation of the people applies also to the priests, i.e., as the people incur sin and guilt that must be punished, so the priests will be punished for their sin and guilt. YHWH states the intention to punish the priests for their deeds in verse 9b, and then lays out detailed consequences for the priests in verses 10-14. Verses 10-11 state the basic consequences, i.e., they will eat and not be satisfied, and they will "act as harlots," i.e., engage in sexual relations, but not "spread out" or "multiply." The reason is that they have abandoned YHWH to observe "harlotry and wine" and to be mindful of (literally, "take to heart") new wine. In this fashion, the passage portrays a people that is corrupted or compromised because they consult the priests. Verses 12-13a describe the actions of the people. Verse 12 states "my people consults his wood and his staff declares to him." Some understand "his wood" as a reference to the Canaanite fertility goddess Asherah who is frequently represented by a tree,[40] but it is more likely that the term "wood" is employed here as a reference to the Levitical rod or staff. The Levites and priests apparently carried a Levitical rod or staff that indicated their priestly status and perhaps played a role in the delivery of oracles from YHWH (see Aaron's rod in Num 17:16-28 [NRSV: 17:1-12], and Jeremiah's rod in Jer 1:11-12).[41] By referring to the Levitical rod as "wood," the passage perhaps raises doubts as to its efficacy (cf. Isa 44:9-20) and contributes to the imagery of an ineffective priesthood. Verse 12b continues this imagery by arguing that the

---

[40] E.g., Wolff, *Hosea,* 84.
[41] Note that Jeremiah is priest of the Elide line (Jer 1:1).

people are led astray by a spirit of harlotry so that they, too, engage in harlotry like the priests and thereby abandon their G–d. Verse 13a states that the people sacrifice and burn incense on the mountains and hills, which employs an image that frequently expresses apostasy from YHWH or pagan worship outside of YHWH's Temple (see Deut 12:2; 1 Kgs 14:23; Isa 65:7; Jer 2:20; Ezek 18:6, 11, 15). Verse 13b describes the consequence of this activity, "therefore, your daughters engage in harlotry and your brides commit adultery," i.e., the people have been led into harlotry by the actions of the priests. Finally, verse 14 concludes this segment with YHWH's stated intention not to punish the daughters and brides. The reason is quite simple; "they" (i.e., the men) have engaged or gone off with harlots and sacrificed with cultic prostitutes *(qĕdēšôt)*, and thereby led the women into harlotry and apostasy as well. The verse concludes with the statement, "and a people that does not understand will come to ruin." This statement brings the basic issue of the passage back to the forefront, i.e., the priests are responsible for the education of the people and their failure to meet this responsibility leads the people into apostasy (here expressed as harlotry and adultery) and punishment.

CONCLUDING EXHORTATION TO ISRAEL:
ABANDON GILGAL AND BETH EL: 4:15-19

Following the presentation of YHWH's judgment against the priests for failing to educate the people in the proper observance of YHWH, Hos 4:15-19 articulates the main purpose of this chapter, viz., an appeal to Israel to abandon the cultic sites at Beth El and Gilgal and thereby to begin to return to YHWH. As noted above, many interpreters argue that verse 15 is a secondary addition to the text by a late Judean writer. The reasons for this are the abrupt change in form in verse 15 from third person references to second person address, the concern for Judah's welfare in a context that otherwise treats only Israel, and the overall element of potential deliverance from punishment that such an appeal presupposes. And yet, Hos 4:15ff expresses very clearly the overall message of the book of Hosea as a whole. It appeals to Israel for a return to YHWH, which is completely in keeping with the similar appeals in Hos 2:3–3:5 [NRSV: 2:1–3:5] and 14:2-9 [NRSV: 14:1-8] that define the fundamental purpose of the book, and the expression of concern for Judah ties in well with the apparent Judean setting for the composition and message of the final form of the book. Although Hosea the prophet undoubtedly spoke to northern Israel, Hosea the book is addressed to Judah in the aftermath of the northern Israelite collapse.

The abrupt shift to second person address form marks verse 15 as the beginning of the unit, much as the second person address forms verses 1 and 4 mark the beginnings of the units in Hos 4:1-3 and 4:4-14. The reference to YHWH at the end of the verse suggests that Hosea is the speaker. He addresses Israel directly, and begins by stating that if Israel acts as a harlot, let not Judah become guilty. The verb *'šm*, "to become guilty," generally indicates cultic impurity or wrongdoing (see Lev 4:13, 22, 27, in which such guilt requires a "sin offering"). The expression of such a sentiment apparently recognizes the differences between Israel and Judah in the late-eighth century, i.e., they were two different countries that at times were allied and at other times opposed each other. Essentially the statement indicates that Judah is not included in the sins and punishment ascribed to Israel. For the Judean reader of the book, such a statement would help to explain why Israel was destroyed in the late-eighth century and why Judah was not. The prophet continues with the appeal not to go to Gilgal, not to go up to Beth Aven, and not to swear "by the life of YHWH." These statements call upon Israel to reject some of its fundamental cultic sites and practices. Gilgal is traditionally identified as the first sanctuary established in the land by Israel in the time of Joshua (Joshua 3–5; 10), and it is one of the sites where Saul was designated as Israel's first king (1 Sam 11:14-15). The exact site of ancient Gilgal is uncertain, but it appears to have been situated in the Jordan Valley, on the eastern border of Jericho (Josh 4:19), perhaps the later site of Hisham's Palace.[42] The reference to Beth El as Beth Aven, "house of falsehood," is clearly polemical as Beth El means "house of G–d" (see Genesis 28 in which Jacob names the site Beth El because of his vision of G–d). Beth El is situated in the south central hill country of northern Israel near the site of modern Beitin.[43] It served as the royal sanctuary of the northern kingdom of Israel (see 1 Kings 12–13; Amos 7:10-17), and together with Gilgal was also a primary target of Amos' polemics against the northern kingdom (see Amos 4:4; 5:5; cf. 9:1). Apparently both Hosea and Amos see Beth El and Gilgal as the primary cultic sites of northern Israel—perhaps Dan was too far north to be considered by prophets who are active in the central hill country of Israel. The final admonition to avoid swearing "by the life of YHWH" apparently takes up a northern cultic practice (see Amos 8:14; cf. Jer 4:2; 5:2 bearing in mind that Jeremiah is a northern priest and prophet from the Elide house), but it is well attested in the south as well (e.g., Jer

---

[42] Tamar Noy, "Gilgal," *NEAEHL* 2:517-8; Wade R. Kotter, "Gilgal," *ABD* II:1022-4; James Muilenberg, "The Site of Ancient Gilgal," *BASOR* 140 (1955) 11–27.

[43] James L. Kelso, "Bethel," *NEAEHL* 1:193-4; Harold Brodsky, "Bethel," *ABD* I:710-2.

44:26). Perhaps its appearance here indicates Hosea's desire to dissociate YHWH's name from Beth El and Gilgal. Altogether, Hosea's call for the rejection of central Israelite cultic installations and practices builds upon the earlier condemnation of the priesthood. According to Hosea, northern Israel's religious establishment is corrupt, and it will lead the people into disaster if they continue to support it.

The reasons for the prophet's appeal follow in verses 16-19, which are introduced by causative *kî*, "because." Verse 16a identifies a straying heifer that has turned aside (cf. Isa 1:2-3, 5). This simile is particularly apt in that it calls to mind the golden calf that is associated with the Beth El sanctuary (1 Kgs 12:28-33), and it employs feminine counterpart to the bull, a common Canaanite symbol of fertility. This statement is followed immediately in verse 16b by rhetorical question which employs the imagery of shepherding to assert that YHWH is not able to lead or guide Israel. Verses 17-19 then portray Israel's situation in relation to idols, drunkenness, and sexual relations. Verse 17 states that Ephraim (i.e., Israel) is joined to idols, and is to be left alone. The following imagery suggests that the reason for this instruction is that Ephraim is about to engage in intercourse. Verse 18 describes the scene: he turns to their (alcoholic) drink, he gives himself over to harlotry, they love, they give shame for her shields. This last statement is enigmatic, but it seems to convey the shamefulness of an illicit union. Finally, verse 19 completes the scene with the statement, "a wind binds her in her skirts, and they are shamed by their altars." Although many translate *biknāpêhā* as "her wings," the meaning "her skirts" is clear from the sexual imagery of the preceding verse (cf. Isa 8:8; Ezek 16:8; Ruth 3:9; cf. Deut 23:1 [NRSV: 22:30]; 27:20).[44] In essence, verses 17-19 portray Israel's apostasy in relation to sexual worship at the sacrificial altar, and thereby recap the imagery of the harlot Gomer that appears at the beginning of the book.

Report of Specific Grounds for YHWH's Controversy With Israel:
5:1–14:1

The basic core of Hosea's speeches concerning Israel appears in Hos 5:1–14:1, immediately following the report of Hosea's appeal to Jezreel for the mother's return in Hos 2:3–3:5 [NRSV: 2:1–3:5] and the presenta-

---

[44] Cf. Landy, *Hosea*, 65-6; Marvin A. Sweeney, "On *ûmᵉśôś* in Isaiah 8.6," *Among the Prophets: Language, Image and Structure in the Prophetic Writings*, ed. P. R. Davies and D.J.A. Clines, JSOTSup, vol. 144 (Sheffield: JSOT Press, 1993) 42–54.

tion of Yʜᴡʜ's controversy against Israel in Hos 4:1-19. This lengthy segment constitutes a detailed presentation of the specific grounds for Yʜᴡʜ's contentions against Israel that serve as the basis for the prophet's appeal to return to Yʜᴡʜ throughout the book. It thereby builds upon the generalized presentation of Yʜᴡʜ's complaints against Israel in Hosea 4. The unit comprises a series of addresses, each of which begins with an imperative or second person address form that calls the audience's attention to the material at hand. When read in sequence, the addresses take up the various aspects of the controversy between Yʜᴡʜ and Israel. The unit focuses not only on Israel in general, but specifically upon the monarchy and priesthood of Israel as the culpable parties. Each sub-unit of the whole addresses a specific aspect of the controversy. Thus, Hos 5:1-7 constitutes the initial statement of the issues addressed to the priests, the house of Israel, and the house of the king, viz., Israel's harlotry and the birth of "alien" children that point to Israel's "betrayal" of Yʜᴡʜ. It thereby builds upon the metaphor of Israel's "harlotry" previously presented in Hos 2:3–3:5 [ɴʀsᴠ: 2:1–3:5] and 4:1-19. Hosea 5:8–7:16 then focuses specifically on Israel's alliances with Assyria and Egypt, which the text presents as a transgression of the covenant with Yʜᴡʜ. Hosea 8:1-14 identifies the kings and the priests as the parties responsible for this violation of the covenant and continues to employ the imagery of harlotry and licentiousness as a metaphor for the transgression. Finally, Hos 9:1–14:1 [ɴʀsᴠ: 9:1–13:16] employs the metaphors of agricultural and animal fertility to characterize Israel's rejection of Yʜᴡʜ as cultic apostasy in which the prophet charges Israel with pagan or foreign cultic practice.

Tʜᴇ Iɴɪᴛɪᴀʟ Sᴛᴀᴛᴇᴍᴇɴᴛ ᴏғ ᴛʜᴇ Issᴜᴇs:
Isʀᴀᴇʟ's "Hᴀʀʟᴏᴛʀʏ" ᴀɴᴅ ᴛʜᴇ Bɪʀᴛʜ ᴏғ "Aʟɪᴇɴ" Cʜɪʟᴅʀᴇɴ: 5:1-7

Hosea 5:1-7 constitutes the initial statement of the issues in Yʜᴡʜ's controversy with Israel. It builds upon the imagery of Hosea's marriage to Gomer presented in Hos 1:2–2:2; 2:3–3:5 [ɴʀsᴠ: 1:2-11; 2:1–3:5]; and 4:1-19 by renewing the charges of "harlotry," and by emphasizing the motif of Israel's "betrayal" of Yʜᴡʜ and the birth of "alien" children. This unit constitutes a speech by the prophet that conveys, introduces, and elaborates upon Yʜᴡʜ's announcement of the intention to "chastise" Israel in verses 2b and 3. The text begins with an imperative formulation in verses 1-2 which marks the beginning of the unit. Overall, the speech by Yʜᴡʜ is based upon a judgment speech form in which Yʜᴡʜ first announces the chastisement of Israel in verse 2b and then provides the grounds for this action in verse 3. The passage employs the language and imagery of harlotry, divorce, and the birth of alien children throughout to convey YHWH's contentions against Israel. The imperative formulation in Hos 5:8 marks the beginning of the next textual block.

Hosea 5:1-7 contains two major sub-units which together present YHWH's announcement of Israel's chastisement. The first appears in Hos 5:1-2 which constitutes the prophet's own announcement of YHWH's statement of the intention to chastise Israel. The prophet speaks in verses 1-2a in order to introduce the statement by YHWH in verse 2b. The prophet's speech begins with a three-part imperative address, "Hear O priests, and pay attention O house of Israel, and give ear O house of the king." This is a modified version of the standard "call to attention" formula that is characteristically employed to introduce prophetic oracles, wisdom instruction, and other types of discourse.[45] It appears in three parts here in order to identify Israel in general and its leaders in particular, the priests and the monarch, as the parties responsible for the issues identified in YHWH's controversy with Israel. In identifying both the priests and the monarch, the text builds upon the identification of the priests as the culpable party in Hos 4:1-19 and points to the monarch as the primary human authority in the land. It thereby prepares the reader for the combination of the religious or cultic and the political/economic factors that will appear throughout the balance of Hos 5:1–14:1 [NRSV: 5:1–13:16]. Two explanatory clauses, each of which is introduced by the causative particle *kî*, "because," lay out the reasons why the parties addressed should give attention to the prophet's words. The statement, "because the judgment is for you," signals that the priests, Israel, and the monarch are the parties that are coming under judgment in the context of a legal proceeding brought against them by YHWH. The term *hammišpāṭ*, "the judgment," is characteristically employed in legal contexts to designate a sentence or a legal decision (see 1 Kgs 20:40; Deut 17:11; 19:6; 21:22; Jer 26:11, 16; Ezek 7:23) or the execution of a legal decision or judgment (see Jer 7:5; Ezekiel 18). It may also be employed to designate the decision of a judge in a legal case (Exod 21:31) or to laws in general (e.g., Exod 21:1; 24:3; Deut 4:1, 5; 7:12). In the present case, it apparently refers to the sentence or decision that is to be passed against the priests, Israel, and the monarch for the harlotry and betrayal of YHWH that occupies the concerns of the balance of the passage.

The second explanatory clause points to the causes of the judgment by arguing that Israel and its leaders have become some sort of trap, net, or pit in relation to three specific locations: Mizpah, Tabor, and

---

[45] See Wolff, *Hosea*, 66; Sweeney, *Isaiah 1–39* 544.

Shittim. It is not entirely clear how Israel serves as a "trap" or "snare" for itself unless the intention is to address the leaders who have "en-snared" the people. Some have therefore suggested that "house of Israel" in verse 1 must refer to the council of "seventy" elders that generally played a role in northern Israelite governance (see Exod 24:9-11; Judg 9:2; 1 Sam 8:4; 2 Sam 5:3; 2 Kgs 10:1), but this can only be speculative. Both "traps" and "nets" were employed to catch birds (for "trap" [*paḥ*], see Amos 3:5; Ps 124:7; Prov 7:23; for "net" [*rešet*], see Prov 1:17).[46] Certainly this imagery is applied to Israel or its leaders elsewhere in prophetic literature (e.g., for "trap" see Isa 24:17-18; for "net" see Ezek 12:13; 19:8; cf. Hab 1:14-17). Assyrian reliefs commonly portray the eighth century Assyrian monarchs hunting for lions with the aid of traps or nets to demonstrate their prowess and authority. The use of this motif in the present passage apparently constitutes an ironic reversal of a commonly understood image to convey Israel's ineptness in relation to YHWH. The statement, "and a pit (for) Shittim they have made deep" depends upon a textual emendation of the phrase *wĕšaḥăṭâ śēṭîm heᶜmîqû*, literally, "and slaughter of those who revolt has become deep," to *wĕšaḥaṭ haššiṭîm heᶜmîqû*.[47] The MT apparently has in mind the slaughter of the Israelites who engaged in sexual worship of the Moabite gods at Baal Peor in the wilderness wanderings (see Numbers 25), but the present context appears to call for the imagery of a pit at the site of Shittim. The issue may well involve a variant reading of the word "pit" (*šaḥat*) as *šaḥat*, which entails only the use of *taw* in place of *ṭet*, in the northern Israelite dialect.

Although most interpreters are puzzled over the selection of place names in this passage,[48] the choice of Mizpah, Tabor, and Shittim makes a great deal of sense in relation to the identification of the priests, the house of Israel, and the house of the king in the initial address of the passage. Mizpah is sometimes identified with the Trans-Jordanian site at which Jacob asserted that his wives and children were indeed his own, and set up a pillar to mark the boundary between his land (i.e., Israel's) and that of Laban (i.e., Aram), his father-in-law (Gen 31:36-43).[49] More appropriately, the Mizpah in Benjamin is the site where Israel se-

---

[46] See L. E. Toombs, "Traps and Snares," *IDB* IV:687-8; Göran Eidevall, *Grapes in the Desert: Metaphors, Models, and Themes in Hosea 4–11*, ConBibOT, vol. 43 (Stockholm: Almqvist & Wiksell, 1996) 96.

[47] See BHS note, Rudolph, *Hosea*, 116, and Wolff, *Hosea*, 94.

[48] E.g., Yee refers to "the random location of these places in Israel" ("Hosea," 244).

[49] See Davies, *Hosea*, 138–9; Heinz-Dieter Neef, *Die Heilstraditionen Israels in der Verkündigung des Propheten Hosea*, BZAW, vol. 169 (Berlin and New York: Walter de Gruyter, 1987) 216–20.

lected Saul by lot to serve as its first monarch. Tabor is the mountain at the northeastern edge of the Jezreel Valley that marked the boundary between the tribes of Issachar, Zebulun, and Naphtali (Josh 19:12, 22, 34). It is also identified in Judges 4 as the site where the tribes of Naphtali and Zebulun gathered under the leadership of Deborah to fight Jabin of Hazor and his general Sisera. Although the narrative in Judges 4 portrays this battle as a relatively localized action, the poetic account in Judges 5 indicates that the war presupposed the participation of all Israel as several tribes are cursed for failing to take part. This appears to be one of the oldest traditions in which all the tribes of Israel are to act together to repulse a common enemy, and it may indicate one of the earliest times at which the individual tribes united to form a single federation of Israel. As noted above, Shittim is the Trans-Jordanian site at which Israel stopped prior to its entry into the promised land, and engaged in sexual worship rites with the Moabites at Baal Peor (Numbers 25). Phineas ben Eleazar led the assault against the apostates and his line was established as priests over Israel as a result. The identification of Gibeah, later the capital of Saul (1 Sam 10:26; 11:4), as the home of Phineas (Josh 24:33) associates the line of Phineas with Saul's kingship and the origins of the Israelite monarchy. Each of these sites can be considered a snare or trap for Israel: Mizpah is the site of the selection of Israel's first king, which is portrayed as rebellion against YHWH in 1 Samuel 8–12; Tabor is the site of an early federation of the tribes of Israel in Judges 4–5 for which several of the tribes failed to show; and Shittim is the site of an early tradition of Israelite apostasy against YHWH in Numbers 25. All of these sites were important to the formation of the Israelite nation, including its monarchy, its identity as a united people, and its priesthood. Hosea roundly criticizes all three throughout the balance of his oracles.

Following the prophet's introduction in verses 1-2a, YHWH's statement of the intention to serve as a "chastiser" for Israel appears in Hos 5:2b. The shift in form, from second person address to Israel to a first person statement about Israel suggests that there is a literary history behind this text, but it also confirms the shift from the prophet to YHWH as speaker. The term for "chastise," *mûsār*, is a noun derived from the root *ysr*, which is commonly employed in the wisdom and legal literature as a term for the instruction, training, and discipline of sons and others who are to be instructed (see Prov 1:2, 7, 8; 4:1; 13:1; 19:18; 23:12, 23; cf. Lev 26:18; Deut 8:5; 21:18; 22:18).[50] The term is frequently

---

[50] For a full study of *mûsār* and its derivatives, see J. A. Sanders, "Suffering as Divine Discipline in the Old Testament and Post-Biblical Judaism," *Colgate Rochester Divinity School Bulletin* 28 (1955).

employed in prophetic texts as well to convey divine instruction or chastisement (Isa 26:16; 53:5; Jer 2:30; 5:3; 7:28; 17:23; 32:33; 35:13; Zeph 3:2, 7). It is joined to the prophet's introduction by the initial conjunctive *waw*. The statement functions as an announcement of punishment. The grounds for such action appear in the following verses.

The second major sub-unit of this passage appears in Hos 5:3-7, which constitutes the prophet's announcement of YHWH's statements concerning the basis for YHWH's punishment of Israel. The imagery, language, and procedures of divorce are evident throughout this section as Israel is charged with harlotry, betrayal, and the birth of alien children as the pretext for YHWH's "withdrawal" from the people. YHWH's statement in verse 3 constitutes the first major element of this section. The statement by YHWH is formulated as a first person speech direct address to Israel and Ephraim. The basic charge of harlotry is based upon the premise that YHWH has "known Ephraim," and that Israel "is not hid" from YHWH. As noted above, the verb *ydᶜ*, "to know," frequently conveys the intimate relationship between husband and wife (see Gen 4:1, etc.), and the statement that Israel is "not hid" from YHWH reinforces the intimacy of the relationship. YHWH charges that Ephraim has acted as a harlot, and states that Israel has become "defiled" (*niṭmāʾ*) as a result. The term "defiled" (*niṭmāʾ*) conveys uncleanness in relationship to cultic matters (Lev 15:31; Num 5:3), such as idolatry (Jer 2:7; Ezek 36:17, etc.), contact with dead bodies (Deut 21:23; Ezek 9:7), leprosy (Lev 13:3, etc.), unclean animals (Lev 11:44; 20:25), and sexual conduct (Lev 18:24; Gen 34:5, etc.; Ezek 18:6, etc.). The term is frequently employed in contexts that employ the image of sexual misconduct to express idolatry (Jer 2:23; Ezek 20:30, 31, etc.; 23:7, 13, etc.; cf. Hos 6:10). In the present case, such sexual misconduct construed as apostasy leaves the "wife" Israel defiled in relation to the "husband" YHWH (n.b., in Deut 24:1-4, sexual misconduct is presented as the primary grounds for divorce).

Hosea 5:4-7 provides the prophet's elaboration upon YHWH's statement in verse 3 as indicated by the third person references to "their G–d," "YHWH they do not know," etc., beginning in verse 4. In verses 4-5, the prophet states that the people are not able to return to "their G–d" because of their deeds, which he further specifies in relation to a "spirit of harlotry" which prompts the people not to "know" YHWH. This statement apparently presupposes the situation of a divorce in which the woman becomes the wife of another man. According to Deut 24:1-4, when the wife is divorced and becomes the wife of another man, she is no longer able to return to her first husband following a second divorce or the death of the second husband. According to Deut 24:4, she becomes "defiled" (*huṭṭammāʾâ*; a *hophal* formulation of the root for defilement *[ṭmʾ]* employed in Hos 5:3) in relation to her first husband. The prophet continues by stating that the "pride of Israel *(gĕʾôn yiśrāʾēl)* testifies *(wĕʿānâ)* in his presence," and charges that both Israel/Ephraim and Judah stumble in their iniquity. The term *gāʾôn,* "pride" or "majesty," apparently refers to Israel's honor or attitude, which must be diminished by the action of harlotry. The term is derived from the root *gʾh,* "to rise up," which in derivative forms sometimes refers to "haughtiness" or "arrogance" (e.g., *gaʾăwâ* in Ps 10:2; 31:19, 24 [NRSV: 31:18, 23]). Perhaps the connotation of arrogance is intended here to convey the attitude of adultery. The term "testify" *(ʿānâ bĕ)* basically means "to answer," and it is frequently employed to express legal testimony (e.g., Exod 20:16; Deut 5:20; Prov 25:18; Job 9:14, 15). In the present case, it indicates Israel's formal response to Yhwh's charges, and perhaps presupposes the setting of a legal divorce procedure. The reference to Israel's testimony to Yhwh's "face" or "presence" conveys the face-to-face confrontation of such a formal setting. The statement that Israel/Ephraim shall "stumble" employs the verb root *kšl,* which frequently refers to failure (see also Hos 4:5). Many consider the reference to Judah's "stumbling" together with Israel/Ephraim to be a later insertion into the text.[51] In the context of the final form of the book of Hosea, however, it indicates that the prophet's words are intended to have an impact in the southern kingdom of Judah as well as in the north.

The prophet's elaboration upon Yhwh's statement concerning the rejection or divorce of Israel continues in verses 6-7. The prophet portrays the people coming with their flocks and cattle "to seek Yhwh." The expression "to seek *(lĕbaqqēš)* Yhwh" indicates the intention to appear in Yhwh's presence at a Temple or other cultic site for worship, sacrifice, and petitioning for assistance (Exod 33:7; 2 Sam 12:16; Zeph 1:6; 2:3; Zech 8:21, 22; Ps 105:4). The presence of the flocks and herds clearly indicates an interest in worshiping Yhwh with sacrifices. The statement that the people will not find Yhwh and that Yhwh has "withdrawn" from them is particularly significant in relation to the imagery of divorce in this text. The verb *hlṣ,* "to draw off, withdraw," is not employed elsewhere in relation to divorce, but it is employed to describe the ceremony employed by a childless widow when her dead husband's brother refuses to fulfill his Levirate obligations to marry the widow and produce a child who will bear the dead man's name and inherit his property. Upon the refusal of the brother to meet this obligation, the widow shall "draw off" his shoe, spit in his face, and declare to the elders of the city that this is done to the man who refuses to meet his Levirate obligations. Apparently, the drawing off of the shoe symbolizes

---

[51] See Emmerson, *Hosea: An Israelite Prophet in Judean Perspective,* 65–8.

the withdrawal of the brother from his brother and his widow. In essence, it marks the end of the family relationship between the widow and the family into which she married, and it marks the end of the brother's line of descent and inheritance of family property. Likewise, it marks the end of the relationship between the "husband" YHWH and the "wife" Israel in the present context. The basic reasons are stated in verse 7. Israel has "betrayed" YHWH by producing "alien children." The verb "betray," *bgd*, is a general term for all types of treachery in relation to marriage, property, agreement, apostasy, and warfare. It is employed in Jer 3:20 to describe a "treacherous" wife who leaves her husband, again presenting a metaphor for Israel's relationship with YHWH. The birth of "alien children" is the proof of the contention of harlotry. The prophet presents a common charge employed by men who wish to divorce their wives on the grounds of adultery, i.e., the child is not mine; she has been with another. Again, the verse calls up the image of the birth of children to Gomer in Hos 1:2–2:2 [NRSV: 1:2-11]; because she is described as a harlot, the paternity of the children is implicitly in question. The concluding statement in verse 7b is difficult philologically, but it appears to mix the metaphors of a sacrificial meal and the inheritance of property in relation to the "alien children." The first part of the statement translates literally, "now, a new moon shall eat them," which some have rendered, "now he shall eat them at the new moon." Not only does the identification of "new moon" as the subject present difficulties, but the appearance of a second direct object for the verb, "their portions" (*ʾet-ḥelqêhem*), complicates the matter further.[52] It is possible that the term for "new moon," *ḥōdeš*, should be repointed to *ḥādāš*, "a new one," i.e., a new or another god shall eat them (their sacrifices).[53] The term *ḥādāš* appears in reference to new or other gods in Deut 32:17 and Judg 5:8. The rendition of "new moon" by the MT would eliminate a statement that "new gods" would eat the sacrifices of Israel. The direct object marker *ʾet* of the statement *ʾet-ḥelqêhem* is frequently read as the particle *ʾet*, "with," so that the phrase reads, "now (he) shall eat them at the new moon with their portions," which aids in mixing the metaphors of consumption of sacrifices and legal inheritance. The term *ḥeleq*, "portion," generally refers to a portion of land that is passed on as part of a property holding or inheritance. The term appears to be employed deliberately as a pun to suggest the consumption of a "portion" of a sacrifice that is consumed, as *ḥeleq* is sometimes used in reference to the portion of the sacrifices consumed by the priests at the altar

[52] For discussion, see BHS notes, Rudolph, *Hosea*, 117–8, Wolff, *Hosea*, 95.

[53] Cf. W. Kuhnigh, *Nordwestsemitische Studien zum Hoseabuch*, BO, vol. 27 (Rome: Pontifical Institute, 1974) 69–70.

(Lev 6:10 [NRSV: 6:17-18]; Deut 18:8; cf. Hab 1:16). By turning to other gods who will "eat" their "portions/sacrifices," Israel will lose the "portion/inheritance" of land on which it lives as alien nations or sons come to claim their share of the parents' inheritance (n.b., all children born to a father have a share of the father's inheritance in Deut 21:15-17).

PROPHET'S CONVEYANCE OF YHWH'S RELUCTANCE TO ANSWER ISRAEL AND JUDAH DUE TO BETRAYAL OF TRUST THROUGH FOREIGN ALLIANCES: 5:8–7:16

Hosea 5:8–7:16 constitutes the prophet's presentation of a lengthy speech by YHWH which articulates the Deity's reluctance to answer Israel and Judah in their time of distress. Many interpreters have questioned the literary integrity of this section because of its numerous and diverse literary forms,[54] but the text is held together by its consistent focus on Israel's alliances with foreign powers as the cause for its suffering or punishment by YHWH and by its characterization as a speech by YHWH that is transmitted by Hosea. Indeed, the first person perspective of the speaker appears throughout the unit beginning in Hos 5:9b and clearly identifies YHWH as the one who is speaking. The prophet's words appear in the introductory warning of impending disaster for Israel in Hos 5:8-9a and in the interpretative comment in Hos 7:10. Hosea 5:8–7:16 builds upon the general accusation of Israel's "harlotry" in Hos 5:1-7 in that it points specifically to Israel's and Judah's alliances with Assyria and Egypt (see Hos 5:13-14; 7:11-12) as the basis for the charge that they have "betrayed" YHWH (see Hos 5:7) by showing a lack of fidelity to YHWH (see Hos 6:4, 6), transgressing the covenant (see Hos 6:7), and refusing to turn to or seek YHWH (see Hos 7:10). Overall, YHWH claims to be the one who has brought punishment upon Israel and Judah for lack of fidelity in the first place (see Hos 5:9b-11), and raises questions as to why any response to the people's pleas for help is necessary when they do not acknowledge YHWH's power, involvement, and capacity to deliver (see Hos 6:4-6; 7:13-16).

The fundamental literary structure of this text is based upon the prophet's initial words in Hos 5:8-9a. This text includes a summons to alarm in verse 8 that calls upon various cities in the territory of Benjamin to sound an alarm against an impending threat. It also includes the identification of the cause for alarm in verse 9a which announces

---

[54] E.g., Rudolph, *Hosea*, 122–55; Mays, *Hosea*, 85–113; Andersen and Freedman, *Hosea*, 399–480; Jeremias, *Hosea*, 78–101; Davies, *Hosea*, 145; Landy, *Hosea*, 73–100. Wolff, *Hosea*, 108–12 considers Hos 5:8–7:16 to be a "kerygmatic unit," and Yee, "Hosea," 246, considers Hos 5:8–8:14 to be a composition composed of five oracular units.

that Ephraim is about to suffer destruction on a day of punishment. Hos 5:9a thereby states the basic premise for the entire unit, viz., that Ephraim is about to suffer punishment. Hosea's presentation of YHWH's speech then follows immediately in Hos 5:9b–7:16. It comprises three basic components, each of which begins with a syntactically independent first person statement by YHWH that sets the theme for the sub-unit. Hosea 5:9b–14 identifies YHWH as the cause and agent of Israel's punishment, and states that Israel's and Judah's alliances with Assyria are the cause of the punishment. Hosea 5:15–6:3 employs the simile of a lion returning to its lair to express YHWH's willingness to wait for Israel's and Judah's appeal for assistance in their distress. Finally, Hos 6:4–7:16 states in detail YHWH's reluctance to answer Israel's and Judah's pleas on account of their infidelity to YHWH, expressed once again in relation to their alliances with foreign powers and their unwillingness to turn to YHWH.

Most interpreters follow Alt's contention that the historical setting of this text, or at least of Hos 5:8–6:6, must be Judah's counterattack against Israel during the Syro-Ephraimitic War of 735–732 B.C.E.[55] The Syro-Ephraimitic War was prompted by an alliance between King Pekah of Israel and King Rezin of Damascus that was designed to resist Assyrian incursions into the Syro-Israelite region.[56] When King Jotham and later his son Ahaz refused to join this alliance, Israel and Aram attacked Judah in order to remove Ahaz from the throne, replace him with a more compliant ruler named Ben Tabeel (see Isa 7:6), and thereby present a united front against Assyria. Rather than succumb to this invasion, Ahaz appealed to Tiglath Pileser III of Assyria for assistance. In a series of campaigns, the Assyrians destroyed Damascus and killed Rezin, and stripped Israel of its territories in the Trans-Jordan, Galilee and the Jezreel Valley, and the coastal plain. Israel's resistance ceased when Pekah was assassinated by Hoshea ben Elah, who assumed the Israelite throne and promptly surrendered to the Assyrians. Alt argues that Judah attacked Israel in conjunction with the Assyrian invasions of the region, and that Hos 5:8 expresses the alarm felt in Benjamin as the Judean army moved northward.

There are several problems with this scenario, however, that raise questions as to whether this text should be understood in relation to the Syro-Ephraimitic War. First, there is no evidence that Judah ever at-

[55] Albrecht Alt, "Hosea 5,8-6,6. Ein Krieg und seine Folgen in prophetischer Beleuchtung," *Kleine Schriften* (München: C. H. Beck, 1964) II:163-87.

[56] For discussion of the Syro-Ephraimitic War, see the comments by H. Donner in *Israelite and Judean History,* ed. J. H. Hayes and J. M. Miller, OTL (Philadelphia: Westminster, 1977) 421–34.

tacked Israel during the war. Although such an attack might be possible or even expected, neither Assyrian nor biblical sources provide any evidence that Judah attacked the north. It took Tiglath-Pileser some two to three years to defeat Aram and Israel. Judah was much smaller than either Israel or Aram and although their forces might be preoccupied in the north with the Assyrians, Judah simply lacked the power to mount a full scale invasion of the north. Second, Hos 5:12-13 and 7:11-12 envision a situation in which both Israel and Judah turn to Assyria and Egypt for protection. This stands in conflict with the goals of the Syro-Ephraimitic alliance to oppose Assyria. Alt argues that these statements reflect the period following the Assyrian defeat of Aram and Israel in which Hoshea surrendered Israel to Assyria and thereby became an Assyrian vassal together with Judah. But it is not clear why Hosea would consider this to be the cause of Israel's punishment. The punishment had already begun during the reign of Pekah with the Assyrian assault against Israel; why should Hosea explain Israel's punishment in relation to an alliance that was not yet realized? Pekah's actions to oppose an Assyrian alliance would fit well with Hosea's objections to such a move and any postulated Judean attack would have preceded Hoshea's surrender. Furthermore, Hosea initially condemns the house of Jehu, which initiated a long period of Israel's alliance with Assyria, but he does not criticize Israel's alliance with Aram in any respect. He criticizes Israel's moves to ally with Egypt on various occasions (Hos 7:11-12; 12:1), but he does not mention Israel's alliance with Aram.

This calls for a somewhat different explanation for the setting of Hos 5:8–7:16 that would take Israel's alliances with Assyria and Egypt into account. It is important to note that the son of Jeroboam ben Joash, Zechariah, was assassinated in 746 B.C.E. only six months after assuming the throne. It may be assumed that Zechariah was willing to continue the policy of alliance with Assyria as his predecessors in the Jehu dynasty had done, particularly since the alliance kept Aram weak and enabled Israel to exercise power over a great deal of Aramean territory as far north as Lebo-Hamath. But the Assyrian empire was showing signs of becoming more aggressive during this period, and many in Israel would begin to question the wisdom of an alliance with Assyria, no doubt with a great deal of prompting from Aram which had the most to gain from opposing the Assyrians and much to lose by acquiescing to an Israelite-Assyrian alliance. It would seem that Shallum's assassination of Zechariah was motivated by an interest in breaking the alliance with Assyria in order to form a new anti-Assyrian alliance with Aram. Shallum was in turn assassinated after only one month on the throne by Menahem ben Gadi, who immediately submitted to Assyria and thereby restored Israel's alliance with Assyria, presumably on less favorable grounds as indicated by the tribute he paid when Pul (i.e., Tiglath-Pileser III) came against the land (2 Kgs 15:17-22). Menahem's own son Pekahiah was assassinated in 735, after only two years on the throne, by Pekah who immediately broke relations with Assyria, allied with Rezin of Damascus, and began to threaten Judah based upon the fear that Judah would ally with Assyria and thereby undermine the new Syro-Ephraimitic coalition. It would seem that the cycle of regicides that took place in Israel during the last years of the kingdom's existence were motivated in large measure by a conflict concerning Israel's foreign policy, particularly with regard to Assyria. The Jehu dynasty, including Jeroboam ben Joash and Zechariah ben Jeroboam, and the Menahem dynasty, including Menahem ben Gadi and Pekahiah ben Menahem, apparently supported alliance with Assyria. The challengers to these dynasties, Shallum and Pekah, were apparently opposed to alliance with Assyria and opted for alliance with Aram instead (at least in the case of Pekah).

Hosea's position seems to have a great deal in common with those of Shallum and Pekah, insofar as he too is opposed to alliance with Assyria and takes special pains to condemn the Jehu dynasty at the beginning of the book. Furthermore, it is well known that Assyrian interest in western Asia during this period was motivated by a desire to open trade relations with Egypt.[57] There is no indication that Hosea supported any policy of alliance with Aram; indeed, his hostility to foreign involvement in general would seem to place him in opposition to Pekah as well. Overall, Hosea's position is that Israel should turn to YHWH alone, and stay away from foreign involvement altogether. Hosea 5:8–7:16 expresses this hostility to foreign involvement, especially in relation to Assyria and Egypt. This would suggest that Hos 5:8–7:16 must be read in relation to the debate concerning Israel's future foreign relations that must have taken place in Israel late in the reign of Jeroboam and during the reign of Zechariah. Hosea opposed alliance with Assyria and with Egypt as a betrayal of the nation's relationship with YHWH. Shallum and later Pekah also opposed this alliance, and they were willing to assassinate the ruling monarch of Israel and remove the Davidic monarch of Judah in order to achieve their ends. Indeed, Hosea's alarms to Benjamin express the fear or threat of Judean attack, which apparently played a major role in prompting Israel and Aram to attack Judah at this time. Such actions could only have confirmed

---

[57] See especially Moshe Elat, "The Economic Relations of the Neo-Assyrian Empire with Egypt," *JAOS* 98 (1978) 20–34; Nadav Na'aman, "The Brook of Egypt and Assyrian Policy on the Border of Egypt," *Tel Aviv* 6 (1979) 68–90.

Hosea's opposition to foreign involvement, particularly with Assyria and Egypt, because it could only lead the nation to destruction.

Summons to Alarm directed to Benjamin: 5:8

The passage begins with an alarm directed to several important localities in the territory of Benjamin. The blowing of the Shofar, a horn made from the horn of a ram, frequently signals a summons to battle at a time when the people are threatened by outside enemies (see Num 10:9; Judg 3:27; 6:34; 1 Sam 13:3; Jer 4:5; Joel 2:1; Zeph 1:16). The Shofar was also employed in cultic contexts to signal a religious observance, such as Yom Kippur (the Day of Atonement; Lev 25:9), the new moon (Ps 81:4 [NRSV: 81:3]), or Shavuot (Pentecost; 2 Chr 15:4). The blowing of a metal horn frequently accompanied the blowing of a Shofar at times of war (Num 10:9) and cultic celebration (Ps 98:6; 1 Chr 15:28; 2 Chr 15:14). It is also employed to signal the movement of the camp during the period of wilderness wandering (Num 10:5, 6). The term "raise a shout" *(hārîᶜû)* typically appears in contexts of war (Judg 7:21; Joel 2:1) and cultic celebration (Ps 47:2 [NRSV: 47:1]; 95:1, 2; 98:6) as well.

The identity of the cities mentioned, Gibeah, Ramah, and Beth-Aven (=Beth El), is significant as well as they are the major sites along the route through the territory of Benjamin north from Jerusalem into the heart of the hill country of Ephraim. Gibeah, the capital of King Saul (1 Sam 10:26; 11:4) is identified with the present site of Tel el-Ful, about three miles north of Jerusalem.[58] Ramah, the site where the prophet Samuel anointed Saul as king (1 Sam 9:1–10:16) is identified with the present site of er-Ram, about five miles north of Jerusalem.[59] Beth-Aven, which means "house of iniquity," is frequently taken as a disparaging reference to Beth-El, "house of G–d," the site of the royal sanctuary of the northern kingdom of Israel (see Genesis 28; 1 Kings 12–13; cf. Hos 4:15; 10:5; LXX Hos 12:5; Amos 5:5).[60] The name is applied to Beth El elsewhere in biblical literature (see Josh 7:2; 18:12; 1 Sam 13:5; 14:23), although some claim that it refers to a site other than Beth El. It is unlikely that the term here refers to another site as Hosea also employs the name Aven for cultic high places (see Hos 10:8) and in reference to a city in Gilead (Hos 6:8; 12:12 [NRSV: 12:11]). The sequence of

---

[58] See Patrick M. Arnold, "Gibeah," *ABD* II:1007-9.

[59] See Patrick M. Arnold, "Ramah," *ABD* V:613-4.

[60] See Davies, *Hosea,* 153. On Beth-El, see Harold Brodsky, "Bethel (Place)," *ABD* I:710-2; William G. Dever, "Beitin, Tell," *ABD* I:651-52. On Beth Aven, see Patrick M. Arnold, "Beth Aven," *ABD* I:682.

cities suggests the route that an invader from Jerusalem would take in an assault against the northern kingdom (n.b. Baasha's fortification of Ramah was designed to protect Israel from a Judean invasion. See 1 Kgs 15:16-24). The phrase "behind you O Benjamin" (ʾaḥărêkā binyāmîn) is frequently emended to "tremble O Benjamin" (haḥărîdû binyāmîn) based upon the Greek, but this is unnecessary. The phrase also appears in Judg 5:14 as part of the Song of Deborah where it refers to those who followed the tribe of Benjamin into battle against Sisera. Because Benjamin appears to be part of the northern kingdom of Israel at this time, it likely refers here to a threat against Benjamin posed by Judah. In the context of Israel's shift from alliance with Assyria to an anti-Assyrian alliance with Aram in the days of Shallum or Pekah, a Judah still allied with Assyria would pose a clear threat to Israel in the event of war with the Assyrian empire.

REASON FOR THE ALARM:
THE DESTRUCTION OF ISRAEL AND JUDAH DUE TO THEIR ABANDONMENT
OF YHWH/ALLIANCE WITH ASSYRIA AND EGYPT: 5:9–7:16

The prophet introduces his presentation of YHWH's speech in Hos 5:9b–7:16 with his own announcement of Ephraim's impending destruction in Hos 5:9a. This announcement thereby provides the reason for his summons to alarm in verse 8, and it constitutes the premise for YHWH's speech which articulates the Deity's reluctance to come to Israel's aid. Hosea refers to the land as Ephraim, and thereby employs the name of the tribe that occupied the central hill country of Samaria and constituted the core of the northern kingdom of Israel around which the other tribes were arrayed. By using this name, the prophet emphasizes that the threat to Israel from Judah strikes at the very heart of the northern kingdom, and thereby impresses his audience with the severity of the danger. In the context of a shift in alliance from Assyria to Aram, the leaders of northern Israel feared an attack from Judah in the event that Judah did not also shift its alliance. Such concerns apparently were a major factor in prompting Israel to attack Judah during the Syro-Ephraimitic War in order to force Judah into the new anti-Assyrian coalition. Hosea describes Ephraim's destruction with the term šammâ, which means "desolation," and describes the threat in relation to a "day of chastisement" (yôm tôkēḥâ). The term tôkēḥâ, "chastisement," is relatively rare in the Hebrew Bible where it appears in contexts that refer to the assault of one nation upon another, such as Hezekiah's appeal to Isaiah during Sennacherib's siege of Jerusalem (2 Kgs 19:3/Isa 37:3) and YHWH's chastisement of the nations that threaten Jerusalem in

Ps 149:7. It is to be distinguished from the related *tôhahat*, "reproof," which refers to moral reproof, correction, or argument (Hab 2:1; Prov 1:23, 25; 3:11; 29:15; Ps 39:12 [NRSV: 39:11]; 73:14). The prophet apparently intends to portray the threat against Ephraim as retaliation from Judah.

Concerning YHWH's Role as the Cause of Israel's Punishment: 5:9b-14

YHWH's speech formally begins in Hos 5:9b as indicated by the first person speaker's perspective, viz., "I have made known," which clearly presupposes that YHWH is the speaker. YHWH begins in verses 9b-11 by establishing divine credibility for the discourse that is to follow. G–d points to the divine self as the source for true knowledge among the tribes of Israel, and thereby appeals to the past experience of the people of Israel as well as their sense of national identification with their own deity. By referring to the people as "the tribes of Israel," YHWH employs the designation for the united kingdoms of Israel and Judah, indicating that the concern is not only with the northern kingdom but with the south as well. The statement, "I have made known what is true," employs the term *ne'ĕmānâ*, "true, sure," which is based in the same root as the Hebrew word "Amen," and indicates what is certain, constant, and enduring (see Isa 7:9; Hab 2:4). YHWH then turns to Judah and Ephraim individually in order to take up the two major entities within the people of Israel at large and to address their respective situations. YHWH refers to the leaders of Judah in verse 10 as "those who remove a boundary." This expression appears in Deut 19:14 as part of a legal prohibition that forbids impinging on the borders or property of others, and thereby states a basic principle of a larger section in Deut 19:14–21:23 that is concerned with the maintenance of boundaries and rights among both nations and individuals. It also appears in Prov 22:28 as a prohibition that is part of a larger instruction from teacher to pupil in Prov 22:22-29 concerning the just treatment of others. In the present context, it portrays the leaders of Judah as those who would invade the territory of the northern kingdom and thereby violate the border between the two nations. As a punishment for such action, YHWH states the intention to pour out wrath against Judah like water, employing a metaphor that emphasizes the swiftness and thoroughness of divine chastisement.

YHWH turns to Ephraim in verse 11, describing it as "oppressed" and "crushed in justice." The term *ʿāšûq*, "oppressed," is derived from the root *ʿšq*, which is commonly employed in the Hebrew Bible to describe the victimization of the poor (Deut 24:14; Jer 7:6; Ezek 22:29; Amos 4:1; Zech 7:10; Prov 14:31; 22:16), extortion (Lev 5:23 [NRSV: 6:2];

Ezek 18:18; 22:29); and the oppression of nations (Deut 28:29; Ps 119:122; Isa 52:4). The term *rĕṣûṣ mišpāṭ*, "crushed in justice," likewise conveys the victimization of Ephraim by pointing to the illegal nature of Judah's border violation. YHWH presents the cause for Ephraim's victimization as its willingness to go after "what is right/worthless." The term *ṣāw* is frequently rendered as "worthless," but this is based on an emendation to *ṣāw'* in accordance with the LXX reading of the passage.[61] The meaning of *ṣāw* is uncertain, although the term also appears in Isa 28:10, 13, where many interpreters understand it as an expression for the gibberish spoken by the drunken leaders of Israel as they stumble about in their own vomit and filth. The term is sometimes understood in relation to the root *ṣwh*, "to command," or the noun *ṣîyûn*, "signpost, monument." This would suggest that it is intended here to refer Israel's attempt to abide by its agreements with Judah in that it could refer to the stipulated border between the two countries (n.b., in Isa 28:10, 13, *ṣāw* is parallel with *qāw*, "precept, measure," which supports those who maintain that the term refers to "line" in this passage). In any case, verse 11 continues to portray Ephraim as the victim of Judean aggression. It appears that YHWH, through Hosea, quotes a view circulating among the leadership and people of northern Israel that Judah constitutes a threat to the "righteous" Ephraim which only wishes to maintain its agreements. Such a charge reflects the deteriorating relations between the two nations as Israel abandoned its alliance with Assyria to ally with Aram, but Judah, once a vassal of Israel under the Jehu dynasty, refused to follow course. As noted above, this portrayal of Judah apparently played a major role in prompting Israel to attack Judah during the Syro-Ephraimitic War.

Whereas verses 9b-11 present Judah as the culprit and Ephraim as the victim, YHWH in Hos 5:12-14 claims responsibility for both Ephraim's and Judah's problems. The introductory conjunction, "and," in verse 12 therefore conveys the contrast between the scenario painted in verses 9b-11 and that of verses 12-14. Judah is no longer the cause of the problem; YHWH is. The Deity employs the metaphors of "moth" [NRSV: "maggot"] and "dry rot" to convey the divine role in undermining and punishing both countries. Many read "moth" (*ʿāš*) as "pus" based on a derivation of the term from the verb root *ʿšš*, which is rendered as "to putrefy" in LXX Ps 31:11,[62] but "moth" best conveys the image of slow deterioration as a moth eats away silently and thoroughly at a garment while the victim is unaware of the damage until it is entirely too late. The image is perfectly suited to be a parallel to "dry rot" (*rāqāb*), which

[61] See Wolff, *Hosea*, 104.
[62] Ibid.

conveys the same slow and unseen deterioration. YHWH employs the metaphor of "sickness" or "wound" to describe both Ephraim's and Judah's condition in verse 13aα, and again draws upon the metaphor of slow deterioration introduced in the preceding verse. The references to "moth" and "dry rot" may well support the image of a slowly worsening wound that festers and attracts gnats or small moths as it degenerates into gangrene or the like and slowly kills the victim.

YHWH identifies the true source of divine concern, viz., Ephraim's turn to Assyria and its king, in verse 13aβ-b. Although the reference to the Assyrian king currently reads *melek yārēb,* "a king who contends, a contentious king" in the Masoretic text, the expression is likely a misrendering or mispointing of the term *melek/malkî rāb,* "great king," which corresponds to the standard means by which the Assyrian kings referred to themselves in treaties and other inscriptions.[63] It is noteworthy that only Ephraim is identified as turning to Assyria in that it points to the northern alliance with Assyria under the Jehu dynasty as the fundamental cause of both Israel's and Judah's problems. In this respect, verse 13aβ-b identifies Ephraim and not Judah as the source of the problem. Judah turned to Assyria for assistance only after Israel and Aram invaded during the Syro-Ephraimitic War. As Israel had already abandoned its alliance with Assyria at this point, it is unlikely that this passage presupposes the events of the war itself, but the period leading up to the war. When Israel shifted its alliance from Assyria to Aram, it created the conditions that ultimately led to Assyrian invasion of the region. Many maintain that the passage refers to Israel's return to Assyria under Hoshea after the Assyrians invaded and Pekah was assassinated,[64] but such a view does not account for the failure to mention Judah's turn to Assyria as well. The intent of the passage is to shift the blame for calamity from Judah to northern Israel, and point to the long process by which such a change in alliance would hold consequences for both Israel and Judah. Like the damage done by a moth, dry rot, or a festering wound, the consequences of northern Israel's actions would slowly but certainly be realized. YHWH directly addresses the people with second masculine plural address forms in verse 13b stating that the Assyrian king is not able to heal the wounds of the people. By this means, YHWH highlights the divine role in this situation; only YHWH is able to bring about relief from the sickness/wounds.

Finally, YHWH employs the metaphor of a lion or young lion devouring its prey in verse 14 to convey the Deity's own role in the catastrophe

---

[63] See Davies, *Hosea,* 157.
[64] E.g., Wolff, *Hosea,* 110–2.

overtaking the two nations. The imagery is particularly pertinent in the present context as the Assyrian kings frequently portrayed themselves in palaces reliefs as hunters of lions, all the better to demonstrate their courage, prowess, and strength.[65] Instead, YHWH claims the role of lion which none can overcome. The three-fold use of the independent pronoun "I" and the three first person verbs especially highlight YHWH as the true cause for Israel's suffering. Like a lion/young lion, YHWH will tear the victim and toss it about as it eats, and no one will be able to save it. YHWH is the one to whom Israel and Judah must look as the cause for their punishment and for potential relief.

*Concerning Y*HWH's *Willingness to Wait for the People's Appeal: 5:15–6:3*

YHWH's speech shifts to a new concern in Hos 5:15–6:3 as the Deity states a willingness to withdraw and wait for the people's appeal for assistance rather than intervene to save them from a calamity that YHWH brings about as a punishment. This unit builds upon the preceding material in verses 9b-14 to portray YHWH as a lion who returns to its den in order to wait. Hosea 5:15 continues the first person statements by YHWH, who states the intention to return to "my place" (*mĕqômî*). The term "place" is ambiguous in English in that it can designate any "place" to which a lion might return, but in Hebrew the term *māqôm*, "place," frequently serves as a technical term to designate YHWH's Temple (e.g., Deut 12:5, 14; 14:23, 25; 1 Kgs 8:29, 30; Isa 18:7; Ezek 43:7). This prompts the following statements indicating that YHWH will wait "until they acknowledge their guilt and seek my face." The verb *ʾšm*, "to incur guilt," is a technical term employed within the context of the Temple cult to refer to the ritual and moral impurity or the profane state of a human being who appears before YHWH at the Temple in order to restore the state of ritual sanctity and moral propriety. Indeed, the offering that overcomes such "guilt" is called the *ʾāšām*, "guilt offering" (see Lev 5:6, 7, 15; 7:1-10) which must be presented at the Temple. Likewise, the verb *bqš*, "to seek," is frequently employed as a technical term to refer to the worship of YHWH or oracular inquiry of YHWH (see 2 Sam 21:1; Pss 24:6; 27:8; 105:4; 1 Chr 16:11; 2 Chr 7:14; cf. Deut 4:29; Zeph 1:6; 2:3; Hos 3:5; 5:6). The reference to the distress of the people indicates a situation of cultic lament in which the people beseech YHWH in the Temple (see Psalms 6; 7). The reference to the people's "searching" for YHWH employs the verb *šḥr*, which also appears in cultic contexts to express an appeal to G–d (Ps 78:34; cf. Isa 8:20; 47:11 where the

[65] See Pritchard, *ANEP* 184.

noun form *šaḥar* suggests oracular inquiry or divination). Although many English translations supply the word "saying" to introduce YHWH's quote of the people in Hos 6:1-3, the term does not appear in Hebrew.

Scholars have suggested a variety of interpretations for the song of the people quoted by YHWH in Hos 6:1-3. Most commonly, it is considered a penitential psalm that is designed to demonstrate or to express the people's repentance and attempt to return to YHWH in a time of crisis. Davies points to the exhortational character of the song as a summons to worship and repentance, and notes that a close parallel appears in Lam 3:40-41 which expresses the people's call for repentance in the aftermath of the fall of Jerusalem in 587 B.C.E.[66] Whether it is an actual song that was sung by the people or priests in the Beth El temple or a composition that is simply placed in the mouths of the people by the prophet/YHWH in the present text of Hosea is difficult to say. Its use of the verbs *ṭrp*, "to tear," and *rpʾ*, "to heal," certainly takes up terminology from the preceding statements that present YHWH as a lion "tearing" its prey (Hos 5:14) and the Assyrian monarch as unable to "heal" the people (Hos 5:13), but such correspondence might be the prophet's own creation or his attempts to employ language that actually appeared in the context of cultic lament or exhortation. Indeed, other major motifs of the song, such as the reference to smiting and binding, the focus on rain, the metaphorical portrayal of YHWH in relation to the sun, do not appear elsewhere in this context. This might suggest that the prophet is quoting a song that actually was sung in some northern Israelite context as he would have made use of these other motifs if he had in fact composed the song himself. Some have argued that the past tense references to YHWH's "tearing" and "smiting" the people and the future references to YHWH's "healing" and "binding" must presuppose some actual event that has already taken place, such as the Assyrian invasion of Israel during the Syro-Ephraimitic War, but such imagery is open to a wide range of interpretation and does not provide the means to assign it to a particular event.

The song comprises two basic proposals that are made by those who sing it. The first appears in verses 1-3aα[1], which calls upon the people to "return" to YHWH. The first part of the proposal is typically formulated as a summons to repentance or return that is very similar to the summons to worship that appears in Isa 2:3; Mic 4:2; Pss 95:1; 122:1; and 132:7.[67] It differs, however, in that it does not call upon the people to worship per se, but to "return" to YHWH and later to "know" YHWH,

[66] Davies, *Hosea*, 151.
[67] Ibid.

both of which are characteristic themes of Hosea. The verb *šûb*, "to return," is commonly employed to express the simple concept of return or the cultic concept of repentance when used in relation to a return to YHWH. An explanatory *kî*, "for, because," introduces the reasons for the people's return to YHWH, i.e., YHWH has "torn and will heal us" and YHWH "smites and will bind us." The combination of the perfect verb *ṭārāp*, "he has torn," and the imperfect verb *yak*, "he will smite," portrays both completed or past and incomplete or future action. Some have looked to the verbal forms to argue that the song refers to some actual event,[68] but Hebrew poetry commonly employs the combination of perfect and imperfect forms as a stylistic device that conveys parallel statements and continuous action. Christian exegesis in particular focuses on the statement "and he will make us live after two days, on the third day he will raise us up," as an expression of resurrection from death.[69] Certainly the surrounding pagan cultures portrayed the death and resurrection of their respective fertility gods, such as the Mesopotamian Tammuz, the Egyptian Osiris, and the Phoenician/Greek Adonis (=Baal) after periods of two to three days, but the period of time can vary. In the mythologies of these ancient cultures, the death and descent to the underworld of the fertility god marked the end of the rainy season and the beginning of the dry season when vegetation and crops would wither and die. The advent of the rainy season marked the return to life or resurrection of the god from the underworld. It is likely that such fertility concepts underlie the statement here, especially since the song refers to the coming of the rains in verse 3, but it does not express the physical resurrection of dead human beings. It simply stands as a poetic device that conveys the rejuvenation and rescue of the nation in a time of crisis. Whether by bringing rain or by delivering the people from enemies, YHWH gives life to the nation Israel so that the people "live before" YHWH.

The second proposal appears in Hos 6:3aα²-b, beginning with the statement, "Let us press on (literally, "pursue") to know YHWH . . ." It is deliberately designed to provide a parallel to the initial proposal to "return" to YHWH by adding the concept of "knowledge" of YHWH which is so foundational to Hosea's thought. As noted before, the verb *ydʿ*, "to know," conveys a sense of intimacy that oftentimes involves sexual relations. In this sense, the fertility background of the song is apparent, but the term is designed primarily to express the intimate and exclusive relationship between YHWH and the people of Israel. The metaphor of the sun and its rising appears in this proposal as well. The

[68] Ibid., 152.
[69] See Wolff, *Hosea*, 117–8.

statement, "like the dawn, sure is his (YHWH's) going forth," portrays the constant appearance of the sun at dawn as a sign of YHWH's constancy and fidelity. The use of the term *šaḥar*, "dawn," conveys YHWH's efficacy or power, as the root is also used to convey magical practice or divination (see Isa 8:20; 47:11) and the color black as a portrayal of beauty or the "dawn" of life and youth (see Cant 1:5; 5:11; Qoh 11:10). As noted in Hos 5:15, the root is also employed as a means to express "searching for" or "beseeching" YHWH, and thereby conveys a sense of efficacy as well, perhaps in relation to the dawn. The fertility elements of the song are made clear in the statements that YHWH's power to deliver the people will be expressed through the Deity's ability to come like "rain" *(gešem)* and to water the land like "spring rain" *(malqôš)*. The terms designate the rains that mark respectively the beginning and the end of the all-important rainy season in Israel. The term *yôreh*, "fall rain," is frequently read as *yarweh*, "it will soak/water," in accordance with the Peshitta and the Targum. Interestingly, the root of the term is also employed to express guidance, and appears as the root of the Hebrew terms Torah *(tôrâ)*, "guidance, instruction," and *môreh*, "teacher." This would suggest something of the means by which phenomena of the natural world were understood in relation to abstract notions of ethical and moral guidance in ancient Israel.

Concerning YHWH's Reluctance to Respond to Ephraim and Judah: 6:4–7:16

Hosea 6:4–7:16 relates the primary concern of Hos 5:8–7:16 as a whole, viz., YHWH's reluctance to answer Ephraim and Judah in their time of distress. This pericope comprises two major sub-units that are joined by a conjunctive *waw* in Hos 6:7. The first sub-unit, Hos 6:4-6, employs rhetorical questions to express YHWH's reluctance to respond, and the second sub-unit, Hos 6:7–7:16, provides a lengthy substantiation for YHWH's reluctance by charging Israel and Judah with transgression of their covenant with YHWH. With the exception of Hos 7:10, which employs third person references to YHWH and thereby demonstrates its character as a statement by the prophet, the pericope is presented as a speech by YHWH throughout.

Basic Premise: YHWH's Reluctance to Respond: 6:4-6

By stating YHWH's reluctance to answer Ephraim and Judah, Hos 6:4-6 presents a particularly challenging view of G–d that reverses the normal expectations of the relationship between a nation in the ancient world and its deities. Normally, an ancient nation would look to its deities for protection from outside enemies, but in the present instance Yhwh indicates a possible refusal to come to Ephraim's and Judah's aid. This clearly poses a question of theodicy, viz., why does Yhwh allow evil to take place? Alternatively, it questions divine power, viz., is Yhwh able to defend the people against enemies? In either case, the passage answers the question by placing the blame squarely on the people. Verse 4 employs a pair of rhetorical questions, "What shall I do for you, Ephraim? What shall I do for you, Judah?" in order to address the issue of Yhwh's protection of the people. By asking the question in this fashion, the answer is obvious. Yhwh will do nothing, and the reason for Yhwh's inaction follows immediately in a statement that employs the similes of morning mist and dew to describe the people's fidelity to Yhwh, "and your fidelity (*wĕḥasdĕkem*) is like morning mist/cloud and like dew that goes away early." The term *ḥesed*, "loyalty, love," is commonly employed in Hebrew to convey the loyalty or fidelity of parties to an agreement, particularly in relation to the covenant between Israel and Yhwh. The use of the similes of morning mist and dew continues the natural imagery of the dawn, the rain, and the spring rain that appears in verse 3, but it also provides a contrast by which to portray the people in relation to Yhwh. Whereas the dawn comes everyday and the rains come regularly at the beginning and end of the normal rainy season, the fidelity of the people to their relationship with Yhwh is presented as the fleeting morning mist and dew that appears briefly and then departs as soon as the morning heat makes its appearance. Clearly, the prophet sees in the natural world the paradigms for Yhwh's and Israel's interrelationship. In this regard, Hosea employs a typical wisdom perspective in which the natural world provides the models for the social world.

Verses 5-6 employ an introductory "therefore" (*ʿal-kēn*) to describe the consequences of the people's lack of fidelity to Yhwh. Yhwh claims to be the one who is responsible for sending the prophets to "hew" the people and to "slay" them with words of the mouth. The verb *ḥṣb*, "to hew," is normally employed to describe the hewing out of cisterns (Deut 6:11; 2 Chr 26:10; Neh 9:25), wine vats (Isa 5:2), tombs (Isa 22:16), stone (2 Kgs 12:13 [NRSV: 12:12]; 1 Chr 22:2), wood (Isa 10:15), and the like, but its use in parallel with the verb *hrg*, "to slay," indicates the "hewing" or killing of human beings. Again, this raises questions concerning Yhwh in that the Deity claims responsibility for killing people in Israel through the agency of the prophets, but such killing is justified by the charge that those who were slain were sentenced to death for their failure to abide by Yhwh's will. Earlier, Yhwh appeared as an abusive husband who charged the wife with adultery and thereby denied her support; now YHWH appears not as the protector of the people but as the one who brings about their death and defeat. Certainly the paradigm for such a conception appears in the presentation of prophets from earlier generations: the prophets Elijah and Elisha, for example, were principle supporters of Jehu's revolt against the house of Omri, which saw the massacre of the Omride family and its supporters (see 1 Kings 17–2 Kings 13). The statement, "and your judgments (*ûmišpāṭêkā*) go out like light," contributes to the assertion that the dead have been judged by YHWH. The term "judgment" (*mišpāṭ*), frequently denotes "justice" (e.g., Gen 18:25; Ps 106:3; Job 29:14) or a "judgment" in a legal case (e.g., Deut 19:6; 21:22; 1 Kgs 20:40). The use of the term here builds upon the preceding imagery of mist and dew by portraying rapid evaporation at the appearance of light, viz., the people "evaporate" in judgment as dew disappears in the morning sun.

Finally, the causative *kî*, "for," in verse 6 introduces YHWH's wishes for "fidelity" (*ḥesed*) rather than "sacrifice" (*zebaḥ*) and "knowledge of G–d" (*daʿat ʾĕlōqîm*) rather than "whole burnt offerings" (*ʿōlôt*). The "sacrifice of well-being/peace" (*zebaḥ šĕlomîm*) was normally presented in the Temple as a means to maintain the relationship between YHWH and the people (see Leviticus 3) that could be offered in thanks (see Lev 7:11-16) or as the fulfillment of a vow (see Lev 7:17-18). The "whole burnt offering" (*ʿōlâ*) was offered daily (see Leviticus 1) to honor YHWH continuously (see Lev 6:13 [NRSV: 6:20]). YHWH's statement indicates that sacrifices offered without the accompanying relationship of loyalty and intimacy with G–d are meaningless.

Substantiation: Concerning Israel's and Judah's Transgression of the Covenant with YHWH: 6:7–7:16

By charging that Israel and Judah have transgressed their covenant with YHWH, Hos 6:7–7:16 provides the explanation as to why YHWH will not protect the people in a time of crisis. Essentially, this provides the theological grounds by which Hosea explains the difficulties that are overtaking the country. Rather than charge YHWH with failing to abide by the divine obligations to the covenant or with incompetence, the prophet chooses to blame the people for their problems and to present YHWH as having little choice but to let the catastrophe take place. The passage comprises four basic sub-units, each of which constitutes a syntactically independent component of YHWH's speech with its own distinctive theme. Hosea 6:7-11a charges Israel with violation of its covenant with YHWH, and points specifically to the trans-Jordanian region, i.e., Gilead, in making this charge. Hosea 6:11b–7:2 charges Israel with impurity and performing evil deeds, even at a time when YHWH attempts to restore the captivity of the people and heal Israel. Hosea 7:3-7 employs the simile of a smoldering oven to portray a conspiracy that results in the assassination of the king and his officers. Hosea 7:8-12 points specifically to a treacherous and ill-advised alliance with a foreign power that saps the strength of the nation and leaves it vulnerable to its enemies. Finally, the concluding woe speech in Hos 7:13-16 reiterates the charges that the people have abandoned YHWH and consider their G–d to be evil even when YHWH attempts to strengthen them. Altogether, this concluding element of YHWH's speech conveys the Deity's (and the prophet's) deep frustration concerning Israel's foreign affairs.

Concerning Israel's Transgression of the Covenant: 6:7-11a

Hosea 6:7-11a charges Israel with violation of their covenant with YHWH, and it points specifically to the trans-Jordanian region and the traditional tribal center at Shechem in making this fundamental charge. The initial statement of this sub-unit, "and they, like Adam, transgressed the covenant; there they betrayed me," has prompted a great deal of discussion concerning the reference to "Adam." In the present form of the Masoretic text, the expression "like Adam" (*kĕʾādām*) appears to be a reference to Adam, the first human being created by YHWH in the first chapter of Genesis. Adam's betrayal of the covenant of course would have to be the decision to eat the fruit of the forbidden tree which prompted the subsequent expulsion from the Garden of Eden. Such an understanding of this reference is attractive, and Hosea frequently makes use of past tradition in his portrayal of Israel and its relationship with YHWH. But the statement, "there they betrayed me," suggests that Adam refers not to the first human being, but to a place instead. This requires the emendation of *kĕʾādām*, "like Adam," to *bĕʾādām*, "at Adam."[70] In this respect, interpreters have pointed to the city of Adam mentioned in Josh 3:16, where the people of Israel initially crossed the Jordan River into the promised land. According to Joshua 3, the waters of the Jordan River stood up and rose in a heap when the feet of the priests bearing the ark of the covenant stepped into the water, allowing the ark, the priests, and the people to cross into the promised land on dry ground. Of course this motif corresponds to the crossing of the Red Sea in the Exodus from Egypt, so that the two crossings provide a narrative framework for the beginning and the end of the period of wilderness wandering as the people depart from Egyptian bondage

[70] Ibid., 105.

and enter into the promised land.[71] This is particularly important in relation to the covenant, because Israel's crossing into and taking possession of the promised land constituted the fulfillment of YHWH's promises in the context of the covenant relationship with Israel. Once Israel took possession of the land, it was obligated to fulfill YHWH's expectations and thereby keep its own part of the covenant relationship.

Hosea's reference to Adam as the site of the transgression of the covenant therefore employs a motif from the conquest tradition to argue that Israel had transgressed the covenant from the very outset of its life in the land. In this manner, the prophet looks to the past in order to find paradigms that explain the problems of his present day. The next statement identifies the town of Gilead as "those who do evil" and as "tracked with blood." Gilead is not elsewhere in the Bible identified as a town or city; it is instead the name of the Trans-Jordanian region inhabited by the tribes of Gad, the half-tribe of Manasseh, and Reuben. Some have noted that the name may refer to the city of Ramoth Gilead, and Assyrian texts contain references to a town by the name of Gilead in this region.[72] The prophet clearly associates Gilead with the previous mention of the transgression of the covenant, and the references to Gilead's evil deeds that leave it tracked with blood certainly reinforces this image. Tradition associates the region with potential treachery. Joshua 22 contains a tradition concerning the building of an altar in the Trans-Jordanian region that the tribes west of the Jordan River took to be evidence that the Trans-Jordanian tribes intended to revolt from Israel. Potential war between the tribes was averted when the Trans-Jordanian tribes explained that the altar was not a symbol of revolt, but of loyalty, in that it was intended to serve YHWH and better to preserve the unity of the tribes of Israel despite the geographical division of the Jordan River. During the time of the prophets Elijah and Elisha, the region of Gilead served as the geographical base for Jehu's revolt against the Omride dynasty. It thereby played a role in bringing about Israel's alliance with Assyrian empire that Hosea so severely condemns throughout the book. In his own time, Gilead apparently provided the base for Pekah's overthrow of the pro-Assyrian Pekahiah ben Menahem, which plunged the country into the Syro-Ephraimitic War and resulted in Assyria's invasion and dismemberment of Israel. Clearly, Hosea considers Gilead to be a treacherous area that is heavily involved

[71] See Jan Wagenaar, "Crossing the Sea of Reeds (Exod 13–14) and the Jordan (Josh 3–4): A Priestly Framework for the Wilderness Wandering," *Studies in the Book of Exodus*, ed. M. Vervenne, BETL, vol. 126 (Leuven: Leuven University Press/Peeters, 1996) 461–70.

[72] Davies, *Hosea*, 173.

in instigating shifts in alliances throughout Israel's history that often led to disastrous consequences for the nation. As Hos 7:3-12 indicates, another such shift is taking place before his eyes, and he maintains that it will lead to Israel's downfall.

The language associated with Gilead in this verse also contributes to the portrayal of treachery and leads to the following statements concerning the murderous deeds of the priests. The designation of Gilead as "doers of evil" employs the Hebrew term *ʾāwen*, which the prophet elsewhere uses in references to Beth-El as Beth-Aven, "house of evil." Beth-El of course is the royal sanctuary of the northern kingdom of Israel. According to the conquest tradition in Joshua 7–8, when Israel attempted to conquer Ai, which is located near Beth-El, they were initially defeated due to Achan's theft of booty taken at Jericho. Even after Achan was identified and executed, Israel was only able to take Ai through a ruse. Likewise, Judg 1:22-26 associates the conquest of Luz/Beth El with similar deception. The use of *ʾāwen* here apparently calls to mind such traditions, and builds the prophet's case for Israel's infidelity to Yhwh. Likewise, the phrase "tracked with blood" (*ʿăqubâ middām*) employs the root *ʿqb*, which means "to follow at the heel" and "to act deceitfully." The root also forms the basis of the name Jacob, the eponymous ancestor of the northern kingdom. The association of this terminology with Beth El and Jacob or the northern kingdom provides a transition to the following statements concerning the priests who wait like bands of robbers and commit murder along the road to Shechem. Shechem is the old tribal center of the northern kingdom. According to Deuteronomy 27, the tribes swore loyalty to the covenant at Shechem in the time of Moses. According to Joshua 24, the tribes renewed their covenant with Yhwh at Shechem after completing the conquest of the land of Canaan. According to 1 Kings 12, the northern tribes gathered at Shechem to confirm Rehoboam's kingship, and formed the northern kingdom as an act of rebellion against the house of David when Rehoboam refused to meet their terms. Again, Hosea calls upon past tradition to depict the treachery of the kingdom of Israel and its major centers, the sanctuary at Beth El and the city of Shechem. He charges the priests with committing "villainy" (*zimmâ*), employing a term that is generally associated with plotting or secret scheming (Job 17:11; Isa 32:7; Prov 24:9) and adultery (Jer 13:27; Ezek 16:27; 22:9) or other sexual improprieties (Lev 18:17; 19:29; 20:14). Yhwh claims to have seen "a horrible thing" (*šaʿărurît, Qere*) in the house of Israel, employing a term that appears in various forms to refer to rotten figs (Jer 29:17), corruption among the prophets and priests (Jer 5:30; 23:14), and apostasy against Yhwh (Jer 18:13). The sexual connotations of the terms *zimmâ* and *šaʿărurît* lend themselves easily to Yhwh's charges concerning Ephraim's "harlotry" and Israel's "defilement." The "harvest" appointed for Judah likewise builds on the association of *šaʿărurît* with spoiled figs. Again, scholars have questioned whether this reference to Judah is original to the text,[73] but the present form of Hosea is addressed to Judah as well.

Concerning the Evil Deeds of Israel: 6:11b–7:2

YHWH's charges against Israel take on a somewhat new dimension in Hos 6:11b–7:2 when the Deity argues that Israel turns away from YHWH even when they are restored and healed. The reference to healing contrasts with Israel's attempt to seek healing from Assyria in Hos 5:13. One might expect a nation to question its gods in a time of trouble, but Hosea argues that Israel abandons YHWH even when things go well. The phrase "when I returned the captivity of my people" *(bĕšûbî šĕbût ʿammî)* employs a common expression for the restoration of Israel's exiles to their own land (cf. Jer 48:47; 49:6, 39; Zeph 3:20; Joel 3:1). Some argue that the term *šĕbût* is derived not from the root *šbh*, "to take captive," but from the root *šûb*, "to return," and render the expression "when I restored the fortunes of my people" or the like, but such an interpretation is not conclusive. Many consider the phrase to be eschatological, in that any reference to the return of exiles would have to presuppose the Babylonian exile and the return to the land in the post-exilic period, but such a perspective overlooks the many times throughout Israelite and Judean history when major territories and their populations were lost to Israel and Judah and later returned. One such instance would be the territory of Gilead, which was taken by Moab in the ninth century B.C.E. as indicated by the Moabite stone.[74] Insofar as the Israelite king Jeroboam ben Joash established an empire that extended from Lebo Hamath in the north to the Arabah in the south (2 Kgs 14:25), it seems reasonable to conclude that Jeroboam recovered this territory from Moab and thereby restored the captivity of Israel. Nevertheless, Hosea consistently portrays the Jehu dynasty as one that betrayed YHWH and led the country into apostasy on account of its alliance with the Assyrians, the very alliance that likely gave Jeroboam the power to extend his kingdom to such boundaries.

[73] See Grace Emmerson, *Hosea: An Israelite Prophet in Judean Perspective* (Sheffield: JSOT Press, 1984) 86–8.

[74] See Pritchard, *ANET* 320–1; see also J. A. Dearman, ed., *Studies in the Mesha Inscription and Moab*, ABS, vol. 2 (Atlanta: Scholars Press, 1989) for discussion of the stone.

Despite YHWH's attempts to heal or restore Israel, the Deity's speech continues with the charge that Ephraim's "guilt" *(ʿăwōn)* and Samaria's "evil deeds" *(rāʿôt)* are revealed, employing common terms for guilt and evil. Again, the prophet employs the metaphor of theft that appeared in conjunction with the priests in verse 9 above. Ephraim and Samaria are charged with committing "falsehood" *(šeqer)* like a thief who "enters" or bandits who raid "out" in the open. The speech portrays the lack of concern for YHWH in Ephraim and Samaria in that it charges the people with failure to acknowledge that YHWH remembers their evil deeds that are committed before the divine presence. This plays upon the motif of secrecy and conspiracy noted above in verses 7-10, in that YHWH (or Hosea) maintains that although the people think that they are acting in secret, their actions take place before YHWH. It is noteworthy that the text at this point is concerned only with Ephraim and Samaria; Judah does not appear. This may indicate something of the literary history of the passage in that Hosea 7 might well represent an older element of the text.

Concerning Conspiracy against the King: 7:3-7

Hosea 7:3-7 employs the metaphor of smoldering oven to portray the treachery of those whose hidden anger prompts them to assassinate the king and his officers after gaining his confidence through deception. It is not certain which particular assassination Hosea has in mind. The assassinations of Kings Zechariah (746 B.C.E.), Shallum (746 B.C.E.), Pekahiah (737 B.C.E.), and Pekah (732 B.C.E.) certainly indicates that there was no shortage of possibilities during his lifetime. Pekah's assassination of Pekahiah and his alliance with Aram is a common choice, but Hosea nowhere decries an alliance with the Arameans. Hosea's consistently anti-Assyrian perspective might indicate that Menahem's assassination of Shallum or Hoshea's assassination of Pekah are potential candidates. Menahem's killing of Shallum after one month on the throne hardly appears to be a secret conspiracy. Rather, it appears to be the work of an officer loyal to the murdered King Zechariah who strikes against his ruler's assassin and reinstates the policies of the dead king by submitting immediately to Assyria. Hoshea's assassination of Pekah is a possibility, particularly since 2 Kgs 15:30 states that Hoshea made a "conspiracy" against Pekah. The coup takes place at the time of Assyria's invasion of Israel, and this may explain the later reference to the sapping of Israel's strength through alliance with foreigners in verses 8-9. Nevertheless, these verses suggest a slow, unseen process that gradually weakens Israel, not the decisive blow of Hoshea who immediately submits to Assyria and thereby ends hostilities.

Given Hosea's criticism of the treachery of the house of Jehu in Hosea 1, it should be kept in mind that Jehu came to power as the result of a conspiracy against the house of Omri. Jehu was a military officer stationed at Ramot Gilead where King Ahab lost his life. He conspired against King Joram and killed him at Jezreel together with the Judean King Ahaziah while the former was recovering from his wounds. Joram's supporters were lured into the Temple of Baal at Samaria on the pretext of a cultic celebration, and they were killed by Jehu's soldiers when they were gathered inside the Temple and were unable to defend themselves. Interestingly, Jehu's coup against the house of Omri seems best to fit the circumstances described in Hos 7:3-7; it is possible that Hosea has this in mind when he condemns perhaps Menahem's killing of Shallum or Hoshea's killing of Pekah.

The passage begins in verse 3 with a reference to the "evil" of the conspirators in that they "gladden the king." The *piel* form of the verb *śmḥ* here lends itself well here to the description of a king and officers who are made drunk and then struck down. Likewise, the reference to their "deceptions" *(kaḥăšêhem)* that gladden the "officers" *(śārîm)* reinforces the imagery of a conspiracy, and lends itself to the simile of a deceptive and smoldering oven that characterizes the attitudes of the conspirators. The charge in verse 4 that they are "adulterers" *(mĕnā'ăpîm)* is sometimes challenged based on the claim that Hosea uses the term in reference to religious apostasy, but Hosea employs the metaphor for those who shift political alliances as well. In any case, adultery is an apt metaphor for the false loyalty of the conspirators who profess allegiance to the king while plotting his murder. Hosea then turns to the simile of the burning "oven" *(tannûr)*. The ancient Israelite oven is a conically shaped clay structure with openings at the top and bottom.[75] Flattened dough was slapped against the side of the oven from the top for baking, and coals were kept smoldering at the bottom to supply the necessary heat. When the coals were stirred they naturally flamed up, but continued to produce heat when they were left alone even when no flame was visible (a modern covered charcoal grill works on basically the same principle). Hosea describes a baker who ceases to stir the fire and "knead" *(lûš)* or prepare the dough for baking, and thereby builds the image of an oven that is left to smolder.

In verse 5, the prophet returns to the description of the king and the conspirators. The reference to the "day of our king" is somewhat enigmatic, but it seems to refer to some sort of a celebration on behalf of the king or in which the king is involved. In any case, it conveys an occasion of celebration and drunkenness when the officers of the king "are

---

[75] G. A. Barrois, "Oven," *IDB* III:612-3.

sick from the heat of wine," thereby building upon the image of the heated oven and providing the conditions in which the assassination is realized. The phrase, *māšak yādô ʾet lōṣĕṣîm*, "he stretched out his hand with mockers" should be translated literally, "his hand drew in the mockers," indicating the king's unwitting acceptance of those who intended to kill him. Verse 6 returns to the simile of the burning oven by stating "because they drew near like an oven, their hearts (burning) in their intrigue." The prophet describes the bakers as "sleeping all night," so that the oven lies untended all night while its coals smoulder. Although the fire appears to have died out, it flames up in the morning when the baker awakens and stirs the coals. Verse 7 then applies the simile to the conspirators when the prophet states that "all of them," i.e., the conspirators, "are hot like the oven." Just as one eats the bread that emerges from a smoldering oven, the conspirators "eat judges, and all their kings fall." The final statement of verse 7, that no one calls to YHWH, expresses the underlying premise of YHWH's speech, viz., that people are taking action with disastrous results because no one looks to YHWH for guidance.

Concerning Ephraim's Foreign Alliances: 7:8-12

Hosea 7:8-12 then shifts attention from the conspiracy and assassination of the king to Israel's alliances with foreign powers. It begins with the statement that "Ephraim has mixed himself with the peoples," employing a verb root that was also used to express the mixture of peoples and languages in the Tower of Babel story in Gen 11:1-9. Verse 8 is syntactically distinct from verse 7, which together with the shift in theme marks it as the beginning of a new sub-unit. At the same time, it builds upon the previous sub-unit by comparing Ephraim to unturned cake that burns when left too long on the side of the oven, and prepares for the image of a nation that is slowly being compromised by its entanglements with foreign powers. Verse 9 states the basic premise, "foreigners eat his strength, and he (Ephraim) does not know; indeed, grey (hair) is sprinkled in him, and he does not know." As a result of its alliances with foreigners, Israel is slowly but surely losing its strength and its independence.

The third person references to YHWH in verse 10 clearly mark it as a statement by the prophet that interrupts YHWH's speech. Indeed, the *waw-consecutive* verbal formation indicates that the verse is intended to elaborate upon or to explain the Deity's words. It does not mark the beginning of a new unit, as the first person references in verse 12 indicate that YHWH's speech resumes, probably in verse 11. Rather, it indicates that YHWH's speech is transmitted by the prophet; this is one of the few points where Hosea allows himself to speak. It is possible that the verse originated as a marginal comment, but in its present context it must be understood as a statement by the prophet. It draws out the obvious implications of the metaphorical speech in verses 8-9 and even in verses 3-7, viz., the people do not turn to YHWH (see especially verse 7bβ). It uses the legal term *ʿnh*, "to testify," to indicate the nature of the proof that is offered in the context of this passage. The claim is stated clearly in verse 10b, "and they do not return to YHWH their G–d, and they do not seek him (i.e., YHWH) in all this."

YHWH's discourse continues in verses 11-12, introduced by *wayĕhî*, which binds it syntactically to verse 10 and thus to verses 8-9 as well. YHWH employs the metaphor of the "dove" *(yônâ)* to describe Ephraim's actions with regard to its alliances with nations. The use of the dove is particularly apt in that the noun *yônâ* is a homonym in Hebrew for the participle form of the verb *yônâ*, which means "oppressing" or "maltreating" and thereby conveys the results of Ephraim's alliances. The "dove" is described as "fickle, silly" *(pôtâ)* and "without sense (literally, 'heart')." The verb *ptḥ*, "to be simple," is used to describe those who are easily deceived or seduced (Deut 11:16; Job 31:27), such as a woman who is seduced (Hos 2:16 [NRSV: 2:14]; Exod 22:15 [NRSV: 22:16]) or the prophet Jeremiah who charges G–d with deceiving him (Jer 20:7). The reason for such a portrayal is expressed in verse 11b, when Ephraim is described as calling to Egypt and going to Assyria. Again, the prophet condemns Israel's alliance with Egypt and Assyria because this leaves the country vulnerable to much stronger powers that are interested in enhancing their own trade connections and military power. In verse 12, YHWH continues the metaphor of the simple dove by stating the intention to cast a net over the dove and trap it, in order to bring it down from the heavens. The final statement in verse 11b reads literally, "I will chastise them as a rumor/report to their congregation" *(ʾayĕsirēm kĕšēmʿa lāʿdātām)*. It is frequently emended to "I will chastise them according to the report of their wickedness" *(ʾăyĕssĕrēm kĕšēmʿa lĕrāʿātām)* or the like.[76] It is possible that the reference to "the report of their congregation" should be understood as "according to the report of their testimony *(ʿēdûtâm)*" in which the word "testimony" *(ʿēdût)* refers to the terms of a treaty with a vassal, as indicated by the Akkadian cognate *adu*, "treaty." Such a rendering would indicate that the terms of a treaty with Assyria or Egypt could easily be turned against Israel, in this case, YHWH takes the role of the suzerain to chastise or punish the errant vassal.

---

[76] See Wolff, *Hosea*, 107–8.

Concluding Woe Speech Concerning Israel's Infidelity: 7:13-16

The concluding "woe" speech by YHWH builds upon the previous portrayal of Israel's fickleness in its foreign alliances by portraying a similar ambiguous attitude toward YHWH. The introductory "woe" (*ʾôy*) indicates a type of oracle or discourse that generally addresses a situation of punishment as a warning or condemnation that looks to future punishment or a lament that presupposes a situation of past or present punishment.[77] Such oracles typically begin with the particle *hôy*, "woe," which generally appears in the formal contexts of funeral laments, vocative appeals and addresses, warnings, and prophetic indictments (1 Kgs 13:30; Isa 5:8-24; 28-33; Amos 5:8-20; Nah 3:1; Hab 2:6-20). The particle *ʾôy* may simply be a dialectical variant, but it seems to appear in less formal exclamations (e.g., Isa 6:5; Jer 10:19; 15:10; Lam 5:16). The cause of YHWH's exclamation is Israel's "wandering" or "straying," which seems to build upon the prior imagery of the naive dove who simply flies away. The second part of the verse suggests that the "wandering" is deliberate in that it calls for punishment or desolation for the people because they have "rebelled" (*pāšĕʿû*) against YHWH, a term that conveys political rebellion against a nation (e.g., 1 Kgs 12:19; 2 Kgs 1:1; 3:5, 7) as well as religious apostasy (e.g., Isa 1:28; 46:8; Amos 4:4; Lam 3:42; cf. Hos 8:1; 14:10 [NRSV: 14:9]). YHWH follows up by pointing to the absurdity of the situation in verse 13b, viz., although YHWH "redeems" the people, they speak "lies" about their G–d. The verb *pdh*, "to redeem," is used to describe the ransoming of a family member from debt or slavery or the redemption of land from a creditor (see Exod 13:15; 34:20; Lev 27:27; Num 3:46; 18:15). It can also be applied figuratively to describe YHWH's deliverance of people in bondage to Egypt or other forms of trouble (see Deut 7:8; 13:6 [NRSV: 13:5]; Mic 6:4; Isa 35:10; 51:11; Jer 31:11; Zech 10:8). The Deity clearly indulges in some self-pity as the statements portray divine efforts on the part of the people that remain unrecognized or even scorned (cf. Isa 5:19; Zeph 1:12).

YHWH continues with a description of the actions of the people in verse 14 by stating that "they do not cry out to me in their heart," i.e., they continue to ignore YHWH. The description seems to shift to images of sexual fertility worship in that YHWH describes the people "wailing" on their beds. The verb *yêlîlû*, "they wail, howl," appears to serve as a parallel to "cry out," as it is typically employed in situations of lament or distress (e.g., Isa 14:31; Jer 47:2; 48:20; Mic 1:8). The association with "their beds," however, suggests that the cause of all the noise is some-

---

[77] See Sweeney, *Isaiah 1–39*, 543.

thing other than distress or an appeal to YHWH, particularly since Baal fertility worship involved cultic prostitution, drinking, and consequent hangovers (cf. Isa 28:7-8). The people are said to "gather themselves" *(yitgôrārû)* over grain and new wine. Grain and new wine describe the agricultural produce provided by Baal in Canaanite worship (and YHWH in Israelite worship). Many emend *yitgôrārû,* "they gather themselves," to *yitgôdādû,* "they gash themselves,"[78] in keeping with the practice of Baal priests to draw blood, probably to identify with the dead Baal in the underworld as they attempt to raise the deity from the dead in order to inaugurate the rainy season and thereby bring about the production of new crops (see 1 Kgs 18:28; Deut 14:1; Jer 41:5; cf. Jer 5:7 which describes such action at the house of a harlot). At the end of verse 14, the Deity sums up by stating, "they turn against me."

YHWH returns in verse 15 to a description of the Deity's own beneficent acts on behalf of the people, claiming to have "trained" *(ysr)* them and to have strengthened their arm, only to have the people "consider" or "reckon" *(hšb)* YHWH to be evil (see Nah 1:9, 11 for similar uses of *hšb* in relation to YHWH). Instead, they return to "Not High" *(lōʾ ʿāl),* a term that is frequently emended to *baʿal,* "Baal," the name of the Canaanite deity.[79] Some maintain, however, that *lōʾ ʿāl* is simply a derogatory means by which the prophet refers to Baal. YHWH likens the people to a "slack bow," indicating that the people lack the ability or the will to adhere to YHWH and therefore must be unreliable just as a bow is useless without a taught bowstring. YHWH concludes that the people "will fall by the sword of their masters because of the insolence of their tongue." This is a revealing comment because it seems to hark back to the charges of conspiracy in Hos 7:3-7, and suggests that such conspiracy was motivated by an outside power which will then turn against Israel. Again, there is no shortage of such scenarios in northern Israel. Jeroboam ben Nebat was sheltered from Solomon by Egypt, which then turned against Judah after Israel was divided (1 Kgs 11; 14:25-28). Hazael of Aram invaded Israel after Jehu's coup against Joram, which broke the Phoenician-Israelite alliance of the house of Omri and reduced Israel to a vassal of Aram for a while (2 Kgs 10:32-33). The Syro-Ephraimitic War was prompted by Aramean attempts to control both the thrones of Samaria and Jerusalem. The concluding reference to Egypt's mockery of Israel at the end of verse 16 suggests that the coup described by Hosea was instigated by Egypt, which of course is Assyria's partner in dividing western Asia in order to control trade. By allying with Egypt and Assyria, Israel placed itself into a trap.

[78] See Wolff, *Hosea,* 108.
[79] Ibid.; Davies, *Hosea,* 192.

PROPHET'S ANNOUNCEMENT OF YHWH'S CONDEMNATION OF ISRAEL
FOR VIOLATION OF COVENANT: 8:1-14

Hosea 8:1-14 turns to the heart of YHWH's controversy with Israel by conveying the charge that Israel has transgressed its covenant with YHWH. It builds upon the preceding section in which YHWH expresses reluctance to answer Israel because it has violated the covenant, but the charge is made explicit here. The passage points specifically to Israel's designation of kings as the core of the problem, but ties this concern together with charges of idolatry and illegitimate cultic activity on the one hand and charges that Israel has allied with foreign powers, i.e., Assyria, on the other hand as a result of its rejection of YHWH. These concerns are held together by the view that the kings were not authorized by YHWH in the first place, and that kings in the ancient world sponsor state sanctuaries or national forms of worship and enter into relations with other nations. Given the close associations between a nation and its god(s) in the ancient world, this means that Israel's relations with foreign nations entails relations with foreign gods as well.

Interpreters have offered a wide variety of proposals for the literary structure of this passage, based largely on a combination of thematic and formal features, but there is still no consensus.[80] The issue is complicated by difficulties in understanding the present form of the text and the many emendations that have been made as a result. It is further complicated by redaction-critical considerations as v. 14 and other segments of the passage are frequently judged to be later additions. A careful reading of the chapter, however, indicates that the prophet once again conveys the words of YHWH in that his words in vv. 1a, 5aα, and 13aα$^{3-5}$-b introduce YHWH's statements in vv. 1b-4, 5aβ-13aα$^{1-2}$, and 14. The result is a three-part structure for the chapter that appears to be based in a modified form of the basic prophetic judgment speech. Verses 1-4 constitute the prophet's presentation of YHWH's first statement in the chapter in which YHWH charges Israel with violation of the covenant. Verses 5-13aα$^{1-2}$ constitute the prophet's presentation of YHWH's second statement, in which YHWH makes specific accusations against Israel that support the more general charge. Verses 13aα$^{3-5}$-14 constitute the prophet's presentation of YHWH's final statement on the matter, in which YHWH announces punishment against Israel and Judah for its rejection of YHWH. Altogether, this chapter presents YHWH's basic charges against Israel in the book of Hosea.

[80] Examples include divisions such as verses 1-3, 4-14 (Wolff); 1-3, 4-10, 11-13, 14 (Davies), 1-3, 4-7, 8-10, 11-13, 14 (Rudolph); 1-3, 4-6, 7-8, 9-10, 11-13, 14 (Stuart); 1-2, 3-6, 7, 8-10, 11-14 (Yee); 1-8, 9-14 (Andersen and Freedman); 1-3, 4, 5-6, 7, 8-10, 11-13, 14 (Mays); 1-3, 4-6, 7-10, 11-13, 14 (Jeremias).

Hosea's announcement of YHWH's first speech in Hos 8:1-4 begins with the prophet's summons to alarm in v. 1a. The command, "set the trumpet to your lips," is reminiscent of the similar summons to Benjamin in Hos 5:8, but no specific audience is identified by the second masculine singular address form until YHWH's subsequent statement points to Israel as the addressee (v. 2). The sounding of the Shofar or "ram's horn" is a typical means to warn people of impending danger or to summon them to battle (Num 10:9; Judg 3:27; 6:34, etc.), but it is also employed to announce YHWH's presence (e.g., Exod 19:16) or to announce worship (Ps 98:6) and other cultic occasions, such as Rosh Ha-Shanah, i.e., the New Year (Num 29:1), or the Jubilee Year (Lev 25:9). The dual connotation of Shofar in this context signals both the danger to Israel and the concern with Israel's worship that appears later in the passage. Various features of the text present difficulties to interpreters, who have proposed numerous emendations for this verse.[81] The prophet's command lacks a verb so that it reads literally, "unto your lip, Shofar," but this may be explained by the prophet's attempt to convey the urgency of the situation with a cryptic cry of warning.[82] Likewise, *ḥikkĕkā* reads literally "your palate," but the term appears frequently as a poetic reference to the lips (Prov 5:3; 8:7; Cant 5:16; 7:10 [NRSV: 7:9]) or mouth (Job 20:13; 31:30; 33:2). The second part of the prophet's statement conveys the reason for the warning by portraying a "vulture" poised over "the house of YHWH." The use of the term "vulture" presents the image of a bird of prey that is about to devour Israel, and thereby prepares the reader for the statement that "Israel is swallowed" in v. 8. The Hebrew term *nešer* may also be translated as "eagle," which is a bird of prey. The imagery of the eagle frequently symbolizes the Assyrian kings or the god Assur, who is portrayed in a winged sun disk much like an eagle about to swoop down on prey. The phrase "the house of YHWH," sometimes understood as a reference to Israel in general,[83] must refer to a Temple of YHWH, especially since the balance of the passage is concerned with Israel's cultic worship. Because there is no known sanctuary in Samaria, many scholars assume that the passage refers to Beth-El or Dan.[84] The references to the "calf of Samaria" later in the passage (verses 5 and 6) suggest that a sanctuary did indeed exist in Samaria or that other sanctuaries are identified especially with the northern monarchy.

[81] See Andersen and Freedman, *Hosea*, 484–6.
[82] Cf. Davies, *Hosea*, 195.
[83] Wolff, *Hosea*, 137.
[84] Ibid., 139–41.

YHWH's statement in verses 1b-4 provides the basic reason for the prophet's warning, i.e., Israel has violated its covenant. Verse 1b contains the fundamental statement of this issue, "because they have violated my covenant and against my Torah (instruction) they have rebelled." The passage clearly builds upon the prophet's statement as YHWH in verse 1b identifies the speaker. The unspecified "they" is identified as Israel in verse 2. Some have followed Wellhausen in maintaining that verse 1b is a post-exilic addition to the text insofar as it equates YHWH's covenant with Torah understood as "law," but this is unwarranted.[85] The rendition of *tôrâ* as "law" is incorrect, and represents the Pauline and especially the later Protestant theological view that "law" or Mosaic covenant stands in opposition to "grace" or the revelation of Jesus. Wellhausen inappropriately read this theology back into the text of Hosea. The term actually means "instruction," and refers to various sorts of instruction, especially priestly instruction concerning cultic or worship matters (Hos 4:6; 8:12; Jer 2:8; 18:18; Ezek 7:26; Hag 2:11; Mal 2:6, 7, 8, 9). It cannot be equated here with the use of the term to refer to the full Mosaic Torah or Five Books of Moses that constituted the basis for Jewish thought and practice in the Second Temple period, although the equation of Torah and covenant in the present context would certainly support such an equation in later times. In the present context, it basically refers to YHWH's instructions concerning the observance of the covenant.

YHWH continues with a series of statements in verses 2, 3, 4a, and 4b that illustrate the initial statement that Israel has violated its covenant with YHWH. In verse 2, YHWH quotes the people who cry out, "My G–d, we Israel have known you." The quotation presents several problems beginning with the juxtaposition of the first common singular pronoun, "my G–d," with the first common plural pronoun, "we have known you," in the same statement. The issue is further complicated by the introduction of the name "Israel" together with "we," which may have originated as a marginal comment. Some emend the text with the versions in various ways, but no satisfactory solution has emerged as the ancient translators faced the same textual problems as those from modern times. Others maintain that Hosea or YHWH quotes formulaic language from Israelite worship, and simply combines two such statements in a single quotation, but the result remains awkward. The context of the passage indicates that the quote is meant to convey Israel's return to YHWH after consorting with other gods or nations. This is conveyed by verse 3, in which YHWH states that "Israel rejected what is good," but now "an enemy pursues him." The term "good"

[85] Davies, *Hosea*, 196–7.

seems clearly to refer to association with YHWH, and may denote adherence to YHWH's covenant and Torah (instruction) mentioned in verse 1. The reference to an enemy's pursuit of Israel indicates that Israel finds itself in trouble as a result of its relationships with other nations, and now returns to YHWH for help. Finally, YHWH points to the core issues of rejection of the covenant in verses 4a and 4b. The people appointed kings over themselves without YHWH's authorization, and they have used their silver and gold to make idols. Verse 4a reads literally, "they caused to rule *(himlîkû)* and not from me, they granted authority *(hēśîrû)* and I did not know." This statement is frequently read in relation to Israel's statement to Samuel in 1 Sam 8:5, "appoint over us a king like all the nations," which presents kingship as a foreign institution not wholly in keeping with YHWH's plans for Israel. Although the statement in verse 4a can be read in relation to the unauthorized appointment of Israelite kings, it also points to the realities of foreign alliances with major powers such as Assyria, in which the suzerain king in effect becomes king of the vassal or subject nation. From Hosea's perspective, Israelite kings entered into a relationship or covenant with the Assyrian kings and thereby betrayed its covenant with YHWH. This is especially clear from the use of the unusual term *hēśîrû*, "they granted authority." This is the only *hiphil* occurrence of this term in the Bible, and it may be that it is employed here to suggest the similar sounding term *hēsîrû*, "they removed, rejected," i.e., they abandoned or violated their covenant with YHWH. The reference to the silver and gold used to make idols refers not only to the materials used in such construction, but to the alliances with Assyria and Egypt which promote trade and bring wealth to Israel (cf. Hos 12:2 [NRSV: 12:1]). YHWH states instead that this wealth will result in Israel's being "cut off" from YHWH.

Hosea's announcement of YHWH's second speech in Hos 8:5-13aα[1-2] begins with the prophet's statement to Samaria in verse 1a that YHWH has rejected its calf. Many scholars attempt to emend the initial *zānaḥ*, "he has rejected," to *zānaḥtî*, "I have rejected," in an attempt to continue the speech by YHWH in verses 1b-4,[86] but this fails to recognize the prophet as the speaker, who introduces YHWH's speeches with his own words. Whereas YHWH speaks about Israel, the prophet addresses Israel/Samaria directly. Furthermore, Hosea links his statements into YHWH's words by repeating the verb *zānaḥ* from verse 3. He thereby re verses YHWH's statement that Israel rejects what is good, to a statement concerning YHWH's rejection of Israel's form of worship. The reference to the calf in Samaria presents problems as the Bible elsewhere relates

---

[86] See BHS, but cf. the comments by Wolff, *Hosea*, 132.

that such calves were erected by Jeroboam ben Nebat in the sanctuaries at Dan and Beth El (1 Kgs 12:26-33), but it says nothing about a calf or a sanctuary at Samaria. Samaria, however, was not established as northern Israel's capital until the reign of Omri (876–869 B.C.E.), about half a century after the time of Jeroboam (922–901 B.C.E.). The calf figure may well have served as a symbol of the northern Israelite kingdom,[87] and it would be somewhat unusual in the ancient world if the capital of the state did not have some kind of cultic installation, even if the primary royal temples were placed elsewhere. The calves at Dan and Beth El would certainly be associated with the northern Israelite monarchy (cf. Hos 10:5), and may have functioned in relation to a shrine at Samaria as well.

YHWH's speech in verses 5aβ-13aα[1-2] lays out specific reasons for YHWH's anger against the people of Israel in relation to its cultic practices and its relations with foreign nations. The passage begins with YHWH's first person statement concerning Israel, "My anger burns against them," which states the basic premise of the entire speech. The balance of the speech states the reasons for YHWH's anger in two sections, verses 5b-7 and 8-13aα[1-2], each of which begins with an initial assertion followed by a series of explanatory clauses introduced by *kî*, "because, for," that build upon and specify the initial assertion.[88]

The first section in verses 5b-7 raises questions about Israel's innocence or purity. It begins with the rhetorical question, "How long will they not be able to be innocent/pure?" or perhaps more idiomatically, "How long will they remain impure?" Essentially, the rhetorical question answers itself by the asking, and asserts that Israel will remain impure for an indefinite period. The term for purity, *niqqāyōn*, basically refers to cleanliness and is employed in situations of guilt and innocence. The initial words of verse 6, "because from Israel," are frequently grouped together with the rhetorical question in verse 5b to refer to innocence "in Israel" (see NRSV), but this is very awkward and overlooks the series of three statements introduced by *kî* in verses 6a, 6b, and 7 that explain the assertion of Israel's impurity. The first statement in verse 6a begins with astonishment by noting that such an occurrence takes place in Israel, i.e., that the calf or god that the people worship is made by an artisan and therefore cannot be G–d, "Because

---

[87] See the discussion in Helmut Utzschneider, *Hosea. Prophet vor dem Ende*, OBO, vol. 31 (Freiburg: Universitätsverlag; Göttingen: Vandenhoeck & Ruprecht, 1980) 88–110.

[88] Contra Wolff, *Hosea*, 135, who points to the deitic or emphatic function of *kî* in verse 7, but his position represents the difficulties that scholars have had in discerning the structure of this passage and relating its various components.

(it is) from Israel, and its maker is an artisan, and not G–d." The initial phrase *kî yiśrāʾēl*, "because/for from Israel," is an example of a verbless clause in which the subject, "and it," is defined in the subsequent phrase. The identification of the calf as the product of an artisan of course means that it cannot be considered as G–d in keeping with the commandment from the Decalogue, "You shall not make for yourself an image or any likeness, etc." (Exod 20:4-5; Deut 5:8-10). That such idolatry could take place in Israel is shocking to Yʜᴡʜ and to the prophet. The second statement in verse 6b builds upon the first by pointing to the fragile nature of the "calf of Samaria," i.e., it breaks into pieces. Some understand the term *šĕbābîm*, "pieces," to mean "flames" based upon the appearance of a similar term in Job 18:5 and cognate terms in Akkadian, Aramaic, Syriac, and Arabic.[89] The matter is uncertain as other cognates associate the term with hewing wood and splinters. In either case, the statement indicates that the calf may be destroyed. This of course demonstrates that it cannot be considered as G–d.

The third statement in verse 7 conveys the vacuous nature of the calf by associating it with wind and by indicating its inability to produce crops, both of which call to mind the natural elements that should be under the control of G–d. The verse contains three sub-statements. The first states that the people plant "wind" and harvest "whirlwind." This statement presupposes the interrelationship between divine power and natural produce, but indicates the empty nature of idol worship and the disastrous results of putting trust into something that lacks the power to provide crops. The second sub-statement builds upon the first by pointing to crop failure and the resulting lack of meal for food. The third sub-statement builds upon the previous two by pointing to the likelihood that aliens would devour or "swallow" any crop that was produced. This brings in the human dimension together with the natural in the conception of divine power, i.e., a deity that is unable to provide crops is also unable to protect the people from enemies. The statement thereby prepares the reader for the next section of Yʜᴡʜ's speech in verses 8-13aα[1-2], which take up the problem of Israel's relationships with foreign nations.

The reference to the aliens' "swallowing" Israel's crops leads into the statement that begins the next section of Yʜᴡʜ's speech in verses 8-13aα[1-2], "Israel is swallowed" (verse 8a). But as the subsequent statements indicate, the focus of Yʜᴡʜ's concerns have shifted from the vacuous nature of idol worship to Israel's alliances with foreign nations. Verses 8b-13aα[1-2] elaborate upon the initial statement that Israel is

[89] See Davies, *Hosea*, 203.

swallowed by employing a combination of metaphors pertaining to alien nations, sexual licentiousness, and sacrificial worship, all of which are bound together in Israel's images of foreign worship as cultic prostitution (cf. Numbers 25; Leviticus 18).

The elaboration begins with the blanket statement, "now they are among the nations like a useless vessel," which like the reference to wind in verse 7 conveys the vacuous nature of Israel's relationships with foreign nations. Two explanatory statements, each introduced by explanatory *kî*, "because," then relate verse 8b to Israel's "prostitution" with the foreign monarchs and officers (verses 9-10) and sinful sacrificial worship, presumably to foreign gods (verses 11-13aα$^{1-2}$). Verses 9-10 employ the image of a wild ass in heat and prostitution to describe Israel's relationship with Assyria. The reference to the ass wandering alone presents the imagery of an unbridled animal in pursuit of a mate (cf. Jer 2:23-25), and it metaphorically relates the image to Ephraim as the Hebrew term *pere³* constitutes a pun on the name Ephraim which employs the same Hebrew letters, i.e., *³eprayim*.[90] The use of the verb *hitnu*, "they hired (lovers)," likewise applies the metaphor of prostitution to Israel as the same root stands behind the noun *³etnâ*, "wages of harlot," in Hos 2:14 [NRSV: 2:12] (cf. *³etnan*, "wages of a harlot," in Hos 9:1; Deut 23:19 [NRSV: 23:18]; Ezek 16:34, 41; Mic 1:7; etc.). Many interpreters note the irony in Israel's hiring of lovers, in contrast to the normal practice of a prostitute, and indicate its willingness to pay foreign allies such as Assyria annual tribute for protection. The metaphor of prostitution continues with the statement, "indeed, they hire among the nations, now I will gather them." The initial *gam-kî*, "indeed," is unusual, but conveys emphasis together with causation. The reference to YHWH's "gathering" the people is sometimes understood as a later reference to YHWH's gathering the people from exile (Mic 2:12; Zeph 3:19, 20; Jer 31:10; Isa 54:7, etc.), but the verb can be applied to the gathering of lovers by YHWH to expose Jerusalem as a harlot as well (Ezek 16:37). Here it seems to be used to convey YHWH's gathering Israel for judgment (cf. Mic 4:12; Isa 66:18; Joel 4:2 [NRSV: 3:2]). The statement, "And while they shall cease for a little while from anointing king and princes," has caused considerable confusion as interpreters have presented a number of emendations to clarify this text.[91] Much of the confusion stems from the verb *wayyāḥēllû*, "and they began/ceased," and the assumption that the reference to the kings and officers indicates Israelite figures. Furthermore, interpreters have failed to recognize the sexual innuendo of this statement. As pointed, the verb *wayyāḥēllû* is

---

[90] Wolff, *Hosea*, 143.
[91] See MacIntosh, *Hosea*, 320–1; Wolff, *Hosea*, 133.

derived from the root *ḥll*, which means "to profane" or "to begin." When read in relation to the following *mĕ'āṭ*, "little," it is frequently taken as a reference to Israel's beginning to be diminished by the burden of bearing its kings and officers. But the term might best be understood in relation to the meaning "to profane" so that the statement indicates that "they are profaned a little from bearing king and officers." In this case, the reference to "bearing" *(maśśā')* would convey Israel's "sexual relations" with Assyria's king and officers, and thereby continue the metaphor of verses 9-10a.

The second explanatory statement in verses 11-13aα[1-2] focuses on Israel's illicit sacrificial worship, presumably to foreign gods. The reference to multiplying altars contradicts the command in Deuteronomy 12 that allows for only one altar, although some view this command as a Jerusalemite attempt to close down rival northern altars. Verse 11 makes it very clear that these altars are sinful, although it does not specify the nature of the sin. The previous references to Israel's sexual licentiousness with the Assyrians, however, suggests that the new multitude of altars are devoted to foreign gods. YHWH expresses frustration in verses 12-13aα[1-2], "I write for him (Israel) multitudes of my Torah/instruction; they consider my roasted sacrifices as foreign." Although the problematic "my roasted sacrifices" *(zibḥê habhābay)* is frequently read as the object of the verb "they sacrifice" in verse 13, "they sacrifice" already has an object, "flesh," in verse 13 and the first person possessive suffix "my" indicates that the term is part of YHWH's statement in verses 11-12. The meaning of the term is debated.[92] Some derive it from the root *yhb*, "to give" ("gift sacrifices") or *'hb*, "to love" ("love offerings"), but the Aramaic cognate *habhābā'*, "glow, heat," derived from the root *hbb*, "to be hot," suggests that the expression serves as a northern Israelite technical term for some sort of sacrifice that is roasted in fire. (Cf. the *'ōlâ*, "whole burnt offering," which is entirely consumed by fire on the altar in the Jerusalem Temple. Furthermore, the passages devoted to the sacrifices in Leviticus 1–7 are described as *tôrâ*, "instruction," in Leviticus 6–7.) The statement in verses 12-13aα[1-2] plays upon the previous reference to the multiplication of altars by reference to YHWH's many instructions and sacrifices. It likewise ironically plays upon the theme of foreigners by indicating that, as a result of its relations with foreigners, Israel now considers YHWH's instructions and sacrifices to be foreign.

The last major segment of the chapter is the prophet's presentation of YHWH's announcement of punishment against Israel in Hos 8:13aα[3-5]-14. The prophet's comments appear in verse 13aα[3-5]-b. He first describes

---

[92] MacIntosh, *Hosea,* 327–8.

the people's sacrificial activity, "they sacrifice flesh, and they eat," and then follows with a statement of Y<small>HWH</small>'s rejection of the sacrifices, "Y<small>HWH</small> does not desire them." The antecedent to them, "my roasted sacrifices," appears in Y<small>HWH</small>'s prior quote, which again points to the interdependence of Hosea's and Y<small>HWH</small>'s quotes in this passage (cf. the antecedent to "they" in verse 1b, which appears in the prophet's statement in verse 1a). The prophet continues with a statement that Y<small>HWH</small> will remember and punish the sins of the people in verse 13b. Some interpreters understand the phrase, "they shall return to Egypt," as a rhetorical inclusion with "for they have gone up to Assyria" (verse 9a) so that verses 9-13 form a single unit.[93] But this conclusion overlooks the differences in form between Y<small>HWH</small>'s speech in verses 8-13aα$^{1-2}$ and Hosea's speech in verse 13aα$^{3-5}$-b. The two phrases are interrelated, but the prophet's statement constitutes a play upon Y<small>HWH</small>'s, i.e., the people go up to Assyria, therefore they shall return to Egypt. Not only does this recognize the apparent relationship between Assyria and Egypt in Hosea's descriptions of Israel's covenant with foreign powers (Hos 12:2 [N<small>RSV</small>: 12:1]), it also calls to mind the tradition of Israel's slavery in Egypt prior to the Exodus. In this manner, Hosea draws upon the tradition to indicate that Israel's relations with Assyria will lead it back into Egyptian slavery and thereby reverse the exodus from Egypt which stands as Israel's formative experience as a nation.

Finally, Y<small>HWH</small>'s statement of judgment against Israel and Judah appears in verse 14. Many consider this verse to be redactional, particularly because it includes Judah and because it appears to draw upon the formulaic refrain of Amos' oracles against the nations (cf. Amos 1:4, 7, 10, 12, 14; 2:2, 5).[94] Although this conclusion is probably correct, the redactional character of verse 14 cannot justify treating it merely as a supplement. In the present context, Y<small>HWH</small>'s statement of judgment against Israel and Judah constitutes the climax of Hos 8:1-14. The inclusion of Judah not only points to a Judean reading audience for the present form of the book of Hosea, it acknowledges Judah's alliance with Israel throughout much of the eighth century prior to the Syro-Ephraimitic War. During the reigns of Jeroboam ben Joash and Uzziah (Azariah) ben Amaziah, Israel and Judah reached the peak of their combined power and would have fortified their cities (cf. 2 Kgs 14:23-27). The reference to Israel's building of "palaces" employs the same Hebrew term *(hêkālôt)* used for the main hall of the Solomonic Temple, and thereby relates to the issue of proper worship presented through-

---

[93] See Andersen and Freedman, *Hosea,* 502; J. R. Lundbom, "Poetic Structure and Prophetic Rhetoric in Hosea," *VT* 29 (1979) 300–8.

[94] Emmerson, *Hosea: An Israelite Prophet in Judean Perspective,* 74–7.

out the passage. Likewise, the reference to Judah's "multiplying" fortified cities employs the same verb as the statement concerning Ephraim's
multiplication of altars in verse 11. YHWH's charge that Israel has forgotten its maker again echoes themes that appear throughout Hosea 8.
The statement of punishment, "and I will send fire against his cities, it
shall consume his strongholds," speaks to the downfall of the Israelite-
Judean alliance.

The Prophet's Presentation of YHWH's Reasons for Condemnation of Israel: Historical Review Concerning Israel's Rejection of YHWH: 9:1–14:1 [NRSV: 9:1–13:16]

Hosea 9:1–14:1 [NRSV: 9:1–13:16] constitutes a lengthy discourse by
the prophet in which he presents YHWH's overview of the history of
G–d's relationship with Israel. Once again, the familiar pattern of
Hosea's style appears throughout this section in which the prophet first
speaks and provides the context by which the following words of
YHWH are to be understood. Overall, the passage presents the reasons
why YHWH chooses to bring punishment upon Israel. YHWH cites
episodes from throughout the history of the relationship to charge that
Israel has continually abandoned YHWH in order to pursue relationships with the Baals and other forms of idol worship. This provides
background for the current crisis in that Israel's turn to Assyria is entirely consistent with its history of turning away from YHWH to pursue
such idolatry. Just as Israel now turns to Assyria, YHWH announces the
intention to exile the people to Assyria and return them to Egypt,
thereby reversing the Exodus from Egypt which provided the foundation for Israel's national identity in relation to YHWH. Nevertheless, neither Hosea nor YHWH present this situation as a complete end. As the
passage progresses, both YHWH and the prophet express doubts about
the decision to destroy Israel and begin to call upon Israel to return to
YHWH. The passage thereby provides historical context or background
for the preceding condemnation of Israel in Hos 2:3–8:14 [NRSV: 2:1–
8:14] as well as for the following appeal for Israel's return to YHWH in
Hos 14:2-9 [NRSV: 14:1-8].

The entire passage is held together by a combination of two major
motifs that appear throughout. The first relates to the themes of fertility
and natural growth in the world. The prophet's words in particular are
filled with images of agricultural abundance, food, floral growth, and the
birth of children. All of these images speak to YHWH's role as the source
of fertility and life in the natural world, which presents an obvious

polemic against the Baals who are understood in pagan Canaanite religion to be the source of natural bounty. The second is YHWH's historical
experience with Israel at Baal Peor, Gilgal, Beth Aven (Beth El), Gibeah,
Egypt, and the wilderness, which appear especially in the words of
YHWH. These locations are the sites of major incidents in the history of
the relationship between YHWH and Israel, and they are presented in
order to highlight cases in which Israel turned from YHWH in some
manner or another.

The combination of natural or fertility imagery with historical experience is quite common in biblical tradition. It is particularly important
here in relation to the festival observance presupposed in Hos 9:1-9,
which many scholars have identified as Sukkoth, the festival of Tabernacles or Booths.[95] Sukkoth is observed from the fifteenth to the twenty-
second days of the seventh month (Tishri, September/October) in the
Jewish calendar (Lev 23:39-42). It marks the beginning of the rainy season
in Israel and thus the season for agricultural and natural growth. The
harvests of grapes and olives are gathered and the planting of grain begins so that it may be harvested in the spring between Pesah (Passover)
and Shavuot (Weeks or Pentecost). In historical terms, Sukkoth commemorates Israel's wandering in the wilderness and the entry into the
promised land (Lev 23:39-43). Temples and altars are dedicated at
Sukkoth (1 Kings 8, esp. verse 65; 2 Chronicles 6–7, esp. 7:8-10; Ezra 3:1-7;
cf. Numbers 7), and the priests are ordained for service in the Temple
(Exodus 29, esp. verses 30, 35-36; Leviticus 8, esp. verse 33-35; cf. Numbers 8). At the same time, Sukkoth is the occasion on which the Torah is
read publicly as a means to rehearse the history of Israel's relationship
with YHWH and to reinforce the observance of YHWH's expectations
(Deut 31:9-13; Nehemiah 8). One might also compare Psalms 78; 105;
106; 135; and 136, which likewise rehearse episodes from Israel's history or YHWH's acts on behalf of Israel. Apparently, these psalms were
composed for liturgical recitation at the three major festivals. With this
combination of natural and historical motifs, the prophet's concentra-
tion on the natural and historical images of Sukkoth constitutes his
own "reading of Torah" to the people, i.e., YHWH is about to bring punishment. Because Israel has abandoned YHWH by turning to Assyria,
the once fertile Israel will be overgrown with weeds and the people
will be exiled out of the land to Assyria. Unless Israel abandons its
relationship with Assyria and the Baals, Sukkoth will be a time of destruction, not a time of new growth and secure life in the land.

---

[95] For a general discussion of Sukkoth, see "Sukkot," *Encyclopaedia Judaica*
15:495-502.

HOSEA'S INITIAL WARNING TO THE PEOPLE:
SUKKOTH IS A DAY OF PUNISHMENT: 9:1-9

Hosea's initial speech calls upon the people not to rejoice at the festival of Sukkoth because it is to be a time of punishment rather than a time for feasting and celebration. The prophet makes his fundamental points with three direct second person addresses to the people in verses 1, 5, and 7b, each of which is followed by third person statements in verses 2-4, 6-7a, and 9 concerning the people and YHWH which elaborate upon the themes of the initial addresses.

The prophet's first address to the people in verse 1 begins with his commands that the people not celebrate to the point of "rejoicing like the peoples." This statement emphasizes the theme of Israel's pursuit of pagan gods at the outset, and it ties into the preceding theme of kingship in Israel (Hos 8:4-5, 10), which elsewhere is described as "like the nations" (1 Sam 8:5; cf. Deut 17:14). The prophet returns to his characteristic theme of harlotry in describing the reasons why Israel should not celebrate, viz., "because you have acted as a harlot against your G–d, etc." Hosea emphasizes the people's love for "a harlot's hire" (*'etnān)*, although the term may only designate wages in general,[96] the context gives it its specific meaning. The reference to "the threshing floors of grain" merely indicates the place where the people come to thresh and sell their grain, such as the one at the gate of Samaria (1 Kgs 22:10; 2 Chr 18:9). Threshing floors were convenient sites for Temples or cultic celebration as sacrifice included grain offerings (e.g., 2 Sam 6:6; 24:16, 18, 21, 24; cf. Num 15:20; 18:30; Deut 16:13). They provided a context in which prophets might speak (1 Kgs 22:10) or relationships between men and women might be established (Ruth 3:1-5).

The prophet elaborates upon this statement in verses 2-4, in which he states some of the basic theses of this passage and Hos 9:1–14:1 [NRSV: 9:1–13:16] as a whole. He begins by stating that neither "threshing floor" nor "wine vat" will feed the people, and that the "new wine" shall fail. Hosea thereby signals that this celebration is Sukkoth, which is especially known for the harvest of grapes and in which the produce of both "threshing floor" and "wine vat" are brought in for presentation at the Temple (Deut 16:13-15). Whereas Sukkoth also celebrates the wilderness wandering period and YHWH's bringing the people into the land of Israel, the prophet states that the people "will not dwell in the land of YHWH," but that they will return to Egypt and eat unclean food in Assyria. He thereby reverses the themes of the holiday by referring

---

[96] Davies, *Hosea*, 213–4 notes that the term in Ugaritic may refer only to "hire" without any relationship to prostitution.

both to tradition, i.e., return to Egypt, and to the contemporary situation, i.e., exile to Assyria. The latter reference raises a cultic issue as well in that food suitable for Israelite consumption would not be available in a foreign land that lacked sanctuaries for YHWH at which meat was properly slaughtered (cf. Deuteronomy 12). The cultic aspect continues with references to the inability of the people to present libations; as the beginning of the rainy season in Israel, Sukkoth is marked especially by libation offerings in the Temple (see Numbers 29 for an enumeration of sacrifices and libation offerings), especially in later Rabbinic tradition (*mSukkah* 4:9). The absence of suitable sacrifices would render food unclean, like that eaten by mourners (cf. Ezek 4:9-17; 24:17, 22). Contact or association with the dead in ancient Israel rendered one unfit for holy service (Num 19:11-22; cf. Lev 21:1-15). Likewise, food that was eaten during mourning or otherwise associated with rituals for the dead was considered unclean (Deut 26:14; cf. Num 19:15), and therefore unfit to enter the Temple of YHWH.

The prophet's second address to the people in verse 5 is a rhetorical question that asserts the inability of the people to observe the festival of Sukkoth. The terms "appointed time" and "day of the festival of YHWH," indicate holiday observance. "Appointed time" (*môʿēd*) is a general term for festival celebration (Lev 23:2) that can be applied to Passover (Lev 23:5); Sukkoth (Deut 31:10); Shabbat (Lam 2:6); etc. The term "festival" (*ḥag*), however, generally refers to the three pilgrimage festivals, Passover, Shavuot, and Sukkoth (e.g., Exod 23:15-16), but is most closely associated with Sukkoth (1 Kgs 8:2, 65; 12:32-33; Ezra 3:4; 6:22). By asking the people what they will do on this holiday, he rhetorically asserts that they can do nothing as destruction is coming. He elaborates upon this premise in the third person statements of verses 6-7a, which are tied syntactically to verse 5 by an explanatory *kî*, "because." The statement, "for behold, they have walked from destruction," is frequently emended to "for behold, they are going to Assyria."[97] This is not supported by any manuscript evidence, but represents a conjecture based upon the overall thrust of the passage. In its present form, the statement merely indicate that the people will go into exile from a ruined land. The references to Egypt's gathering them and Memphis' burying them simply indicates the fate of those who flee to a foreign land where they will eventually die (cf. Jer 43:8–44:30). Although the verb "to gather" (*qbṣ*) is frequently employed in reference to the gathering of exiles for return to the land of Israel (Mic 2:12; 4:6; Zeph 3:19, 20; Jer 31:10, etc.), it is employed here in reference to their exile from Israel. The statement, "Nettles shall possess their precious things of silver,"

[97] See NRSV; Wolff, *Hosea*, 150; MacIntosh, *Hosea*, 348–51.

has proved to be very difficult. "Precious things of silver" would hardly be left to be overgrown, and the Hebrew means literally, "precious for their silver." The term *maḥmad* refers generally to "precious things," but in Hos 9:16 it refers to "precious" children whom YHWH will slay. In the present context, the expression may refer to the ransoming of children as the people are taken captive or to their sale. The loss of children would certainly counteract the fertility associations of Sukkoth. Likewise, the references to overgrowth by nettles and thorns conveys the imagery of desolation and neglect in a conquered and abandoned land and thereby reverses the motif of fertile agricultural and floral growth. The prophet concludes this section with the bald statement that "the days of punishment have come, the days of recompense have come, Israel shall know." This presents his main contention, that Sukkoth this year will be a time of punishment rather than a time of celebration. Some argue that the phrase "Israel shall know" should be emended or that is has been displaced from another context. In its present position, it expresses a major motif of Hosea: Israel is to be punished because it does not "know" YHWH; when the punishment takes place, Israel will know.

The prophet's third address to the people appears in verse 7b. Although some interpreters imagine the prophet sparring verbally with hecklers at the festival, the statements that "the prophet is a fool" and "the man of the spirit is mad" constitute the antecedent to "concerning the multitude of your guilt and great enmity." Without the references to the foolish and mad prophets, this statement would be grammatically incomplete. Instead of verbal jabs thrown at Hosea by the crowd,[98] these statements represent Hosea's contention that the prophets of Israel are unable to cope with the disaster overtaking the people. This statement therefore corresponds to earlier charges by Hosea that the prophets and other leaders of the people are incompetent (cf. Hos 4:5-6).

This sentiment is continued in the prophet's explanatory statements in verses 8-9. He identifies the prophet as "the watchman of Ephraim with my G–d (is the prophet)." The statement is difficult and frequently emended to "The prophet is the watchman of Ephraim, the people of my G–d," but there is no textual basis for such a change.[99] The prophet Ezekiel likewise characterizes himself as "watchmen" of the people of Israel (Ezek 3:17; 33:7), and Jeremiah refers to prophets as "watchmen" (Jer 6:17). The irony of Hosea's statement becomes apparent when the "watchmen" are unable to protect the people from the snares that will trap them on all their paths, i.e., when the Assyrians come for conquest,

---

[98] So Wolff, *Hosea*, 156–7.
[99] MacIntosh, *Hosea*, 354–7.

and the resulting "hatred" that will appear in "the house of his G–d," i.e., in the temple of YHWH. This stands in striking contrast to the joy of the festival of Sukkoth. Hosea concludes this section with a reference to the people's deep corruption, much "like the days of Gibeah." Gibeah was the home of Saul (1 Sam 10:26), the first king of Israel, which aids the prophet in further expressing his dissatisfaction with northern Israelite kingship. Gibeah was also the site of the rape and murder of the Levite's concubine in Judges 19–21, which apparently stands in part as an anti-Saul polemic in the Deuteronomistic History. The tradition also relates the Benjaminite practice of seizing wives from the dancing maidens at Shiloh during the festival of Sukkoth (Judg 21:16-23). Such a practice in northern Israel might also contribute to the prophet's emphasis on the theme of harlotry. The prophet concludes with the ominous statements that YHWH will remember the guilt and sin of the people.

YHWH'S PRESENTATION OF ISRAEL'S ACTIONS AT BAAL PEOR: 9:10-13

YHWH's first statement focuses on the themes of natural and human fertility in relation to Israel's actions at Baal Peor (see Numbers 25), and thereby emphasizes the correlation between natural fecundity and historical events that is characteristic of the festival of Sukkoth. This passage draws upon the tradition of YHWH's marriage to Israel in the wilderness and Israel's subsequent rejection of YHWH the husband (see Hos 2:16-22 [NRSV: 2:14-20]; Jer 2:2-3; cf. Ezekiel 16) to present a scenario of lost fertility. YHWH compares Israel to the grapes of the wilderness and the first fruits of the fig harvest, but as a result of the apostasy at Baal Peor, YHWH maintains that Israel will lose its ability to bear children.

The passage begins in verse 10a with YHWH's first person statement concerning the finding of Israel in the wilderness and the comparison to grapes and figs. The correlation of nature and Israel is made explicit at the outset, "like grapes in the wilderness, I found Israel." Likewise, the statement, "like the first fruit *(bikkûrâ)* of the fig in its first growth *(rêšîtāh)*, I saw your fathers," employs the technical terminology for the first harvest of fruit in comparison to the ancestors of Israel (cf. Exod 23:19; 34:26; Deut 26:2, 10) so that Israel becomes in essence YHWH's "first fruits" (n.b., Jer 2:3 provides a similar analogy between the ancestors of Israel and the first fruits of the harvest). Many interpreters emend "your fathers" to "their fathers" in keeping with the LXX, but the LXX reading is an attempt to harmonize text.[100] Apparently, the MT read-

---

[100] Wolff, *Hosea*, 160.

ing indicates an attempt to address the audience directly, although the rest of the passage refers to Israel, both from the past and from the time of Hosea, in the third person. The correlation of Israel with grapes and the wilderness motif are particularly important elements in the observance of Sukkoth. This is the time that Israelites would go out into the fields from their cities and towns to bring in the fruit harvest. Rather than return to their homes at night, they would build temporary shelters or huts *(sukkôt)* so that they would sleep out in the fields until the work was completed. This movement to the "wilderness" for the harvest likewise symbolizes the wilderness period following the Exodus from Egypt, so that Sukkoth came to be associated with the traditions concerning Israel's dwelling in the wilderness and the incidents of rebellion against YHWH that are presented as part of that tradition (e.g., Exodus 16–17; 32–34; Numbers 11–25).

YHWH then turns to Israel's actions at Baal Peor, which constitute the culmination of the rebellion in the wilderness tradition. According to Numbers 25, Israelites accepted an invitation from the Moabites or Midianites to participate in the worship of Baal Peor at Shittim. When one of the Israelite men brought a Midianite woman into his tent during the course of the observance, Phineas ben Eleazar, the grandson of Aaron, took a spear and killed the two of them while they were together in the tent. For this, he was awarded a perpetual covenant of peace so that he and his descendants could serve as Israel's priests. Interestingly, the themes of harlotry, cultic prostitution, and wine are employed as part of an argument in which YHWH vows to forget the offspring of the priests in Hosea 4. YHWH's statement begins with a syntactically independent "they," and employs perfect and converted perfect verbs to convey an event that took place in the past. The statement, "and they consecrated themselves to Baal," should read literally, "and they consecrated themselves to shame." The verb "consecrate" *(nzr)* is commonly employed for religious vows, particularly for the Nazirite vow (Numbers 6) in which a man or woman devotes oneself for special service to YHWH (cf. Samson in Judges 13–16 and Samuel in 1 Samuel 1–3 who are both presented as Nazirites), and thereby forgoes contact with the dead, wine or grapes, and cutting of the hair. The term "shame" is frequently employed in place of the name "Baal" in Israelite names (2 Sam 2:8 employs Ish-bosheth, but 1 Chr 8:33; 9:39 refers to him as Esh-baal; cf. 2 Sam 11:21) and other statements (Jer 3:24; 11:13). The term "detestable" *(šiqqûṣîm)* is frequently applied to idols and idolatrous practice (Deut 29:16 [NRSV: 29:17]; 2 Kgs 23:13, 24; Isa 66:3; etc.). "Like the thing that they love" refers back to Baal.

YHWH then turns in verses 11-12 to the loss of fertility or children in Israel. This theme follows directly from the prior focus on sexual worship

at Baal Peor, i.e., as the sexual intercourse at Baal Peor is illicit, it will
not produce children for Israel. The reference to Ephraim's "glory" flying away apparently symbolizes the disruption of Israel's relationship
with YHWH, as "glory" frequently represents the presence of YHWH in
the Temple and world at large (Exod 33:18; 40:34, 35; 1 Kgs 8:11; Ezek
1:28, etc.). The metaphorical comparison to a bird flying away conveys
the image of divine departure by representing swift flight in the air (cf.
Isa 31:5; Ezek 3:12-15). The departure of (YHWH's) "glory" takes with it
the possibility of bearing children, which once again conveys the motif
of YHWH's marriage with Israel. Verse 12 elaborates upon this image
with two statements introduced by explanatory *kî's*. YHWH concedes in
the first that the people might still have children, but promises that the
children will have no offspring. The second statement, "for woe to
them when I contend/depart from them," employs a very unusual
form of the verb *śrh*, "to persevere, exert, contend" *(běśûrî)*, which is
pointed like the infinitive form of the root *swr*, "to depart, turn aside."
The association is probably meant to convey a pun, as *śrh* essentially
expresses the continued association of two parties, even if the relationship is contentious, whereas *swr* is frequently employed for apostasy.
The expression thereby presents YHWH's contentious departure from
Israel as a response to Israel's apostasy from YHWH.

YHWH concludes this speech in verse 13 with a statement that reiterates the basic themes of the passage, i.e., Ephraim/Israel is headed for
trouble and childlessness. The statement that Ephraim "is destined for a
prey" should read literally, "is spread out *(šětûlâ)* in the pasture for
trouble." The verb *štl* is commonly translated as "to transplant,"[101] but
its usage in relation to the spreading boughs and roots of a tree growing by the water (see Jer 17:8; Ezek 17:10, 23; 19:10) more properly conveys the imagery of roots that are spread out on the ground. In this
case, the statement presents a sexually-oriented image of Israel taking
lovers in the context of outdoor worship (cf. Numbers 25; Judg 21:16-
24). YHWH reiterates the results in verse 13b, i.e., Ephraim brings forth
children who will die.

HOSEA'S APPEAL FOR PUNISHMENT: 9:14

The prophet interjects with an appeal to YHWH to bring punishment
upon Israel. His first statement expresses this intention very generally,
"Give to them, O YHWH," and then follows up with a rhetorical question, "What shall you give?" in order to heighten the anticipation of his

---

[101] See BDB 1060.

audience. The answer follows immediately in terms that echo YHWH's previous statements concerning Israel's projected childlessness. The images of a miscarriage and dried up breasts contradict the normal expectations of fecundity in relation to Sukkoth and the sexual motifs of the marriage relationship between YHWH and Israel.

YHWH's CONDEMNATION OF ISRAEL IN RELATION TO GILGAL: 9:15-16

YHWH moves on to a condemnation of Israel's action in relation to Gilgal in Hos 9:15-16. No specific crime is identified, but commentators generally point to Gilgal as the location where Saul was made king over Israel following his deliverance of Jabesh Gilead from Nahash the Ammonite (1 Samuel 11, esp. verses 12-15). Gilgal is also the site at which Saul is rejected as king by the prophet Samuel and by YHWH. In the first case, he oversteps his royal authority by offering sacrifice to YHWH prior to a battle with the Philistines when Samuel failed to show up in time to fulfil his priestly functions (1 Sam 13:7-15). In the second case, Samuel announces YHWH's rejection of Saul as king at Gilgal when it becomes apparent that Saul has not observed YHWH's command to slay Agag the Amalekite together with all of his people and their livestock (1 Samuel 15). Certainly, Hosea emphasizes the role of the kings in his condemnation of Israel, and traces his condemnation of the kings all the way back to Saul. But it should also be noted that Gilgal is the site at which Israel first negotiated treaties with foreign people or nations, which is the fundamental reason why Hosea condemns Israel and its kings. At the time of Israel's initial entry into the land of Israel during the time of Joshua, the people encamp at Gilgal where they observe Passover for the first time (Josh 4:19–5:15). Joshua observes an agreement with Rahab, the Canaanite harlot who protected the Israelite spies in Jericho (Joshua 2), so that she and her family would be spared and would continue to live in Israel (Josh 6:22-25). Gilgal is also the location at which Joshua agrees to observe his covenant with the men of the Canaanite city of Gibeon, and as a result of Israel's victory of Gibeon's enemies, the people of Gibeon are allowed to live in Israel (Joshua 9–10). From Hosea's/YHWH's perspective, the roots of Israel's alliances with Assyria and Egypt may be found in its actions at Gilgal.

As a result, YHWH states, "for there, I hated them," and "I will drive them from my house." The reference to "my house" is generally taken to mean YHWH's Temple, but it should also be considered in relation to the language of divorce. Both of the verbs employed in YHWH's statement, śn', "to hate," and grš, "to drive out," are employed as technical language in relation to divorce. As part of the instruction in Deut 24:1-4 prohibiting the remarriage of man and a woman after the woman has been divorced and married to another man, verse 3 states, "and (if) the other man 'hates' her and writes for her a divorce document, etc." The root *grš* is employed to describe a divorced woman in Lev 21:7, 14; 22:13; Num 30:10 [NRSV: 30:9]; and Ezek 44:22 (cf. Gen 21:10 for the "expulsion" of Hagar by Abraham). The motif continues in verse 15b when YHWH vows never again to "love" them, which contrasts with Hos 9:10 which describes Baal as the object of Israel's "love."

YHWH returns to a fertility image in verse 16 to describe Ephraim's "smitten" state. The "root dries up" and the "flower does bloom," which once again speaks to the fertility themes of Sukkoth, the beginning of the rainy season in Israel, when the land blooms with new growth and blossoms. YHWH likewise turns to human fertility by vowing that the people will not give birth and promising to kill "the precious of their belly." The term *maḥămadê biṭnām*, "precious of their belly," recalls the enigmatic reference to the sale of the "precious" *(maḥmad)* in Hos 9:6.

HOSEA'S ALLEGORICAL STATEMENT OF YHWH'S INTENTION TO REJECT ISRAEL: 9:17–10:8

The prophet resumes his speech in Hos 9:17–10:8 with a presentation of YHWH's intentions to reject Israel for disobedience, which specifically targets Israel's king and cultic installations.

The passage begins with the prophet's statement of his basic premise in Hos 9:17, "My G–d will reject because they have not listened to him," followed by a statement of the results, "and they shall become wanderers among the nations." The imagery serves as a metaphor for exile, and corresponds to the portrayal of Cain, who is forced to wander in the land of Nod ("Wandering") desert as a result of the murder of his brother Abel (Gen 4:1-16). Many commentators point to this verse as a statement of the notion of the "wandering/eternal Jew," which plays such an important role in Christianity's understanding of the "eternal Jew."[102] The "eternal Jew" is a figure rejected by G–d and forced to wander among the nations for the rejection of Jesus as the Christ. Overall, this portrayal of the "eternal Jew" has been very influential in creating a climate of hostility against Jews, i.e., Jews lacked a homeland because they were sinful. It frequently led to restrictions on Jewish life, the establishment of ghettos, expulsion, pogroms against Jewish communities, and ultimately the Shoah or Holocaust in Europe.

---

[102] MacIntosh, *Hosea*, 381–2, provides a brief survey.

From Hosea's perspective, Israel has responsibilities to G–d, but the reader also has the responsibility not to put her/himself in the place of G–d in order to judge others.

The prophet follows with an allegorical announcement of YHWH's intentions to punish Israel in Hos 10:1-8. The prophet's announcement continues the emphasis on the interrelationship between natural elements and human events in Sukkoth by interweaving the presentation of Israel as a flourishing grapevine, its involvement in idolatry and treaties, and its ultimate submission to the Assyrian empire. In conjunction with the metaphorical portrayal of Israel, the language of the passage makes extensive use of double entendre to demonstrate the irony of Israel's actions and their results or consequences.

The allegorical portrayal is established in Hos 10:1, which presents Israel as "a luxuriant vine that yields its fruit." The vine, of course, presupposes the celebration of Sukkoth when the grape harvest is brought in. The use of the term *bôqēq*, "luxuriant," appears to convey the sense of fertility and abundance that one would expect from the festival, but the term more commonly means "to empty (a bottle)" or "to lay waste" (Isa 24:1; Nah 2:3 [NRSV: 2:2]). In the present context, the luxuriantly growing vine apparently indicates the overgrowth that will cover Israel's altars once the land submits to Assyria (see verse 8). A similar double entendre appears in the statement, "that yields its fruit," in that the verb *yĕšawweh*, "it shall yield, set, place," corresponds assonantally to *šāwʾ*, "emptiness, vanity" (e.g., Exod 20:7, "Do not take the name of YHWH in vain [*šāwʾ*]").[103] It thereby conveys the coming emptiness of the land. Israel "increases" *(hirbâ)* its altars according to the "multitude" or "increase" *(rōb)* of its fruits, and the "goodness" *(ṭôb)* in the land results in the "improvement" *(hêṭîbû* literally, "making good") of Masseboth or cultic pillars that are employed in both Israelite and pagan forms of worship (e.g., Gen 28:18-22; contra. Deut 12:3; 16:21-22).

Verses 2-5 then present YHWH's charges of idolatry and blasphemy against Israel while continuing to employ the metaphors of natural fertility. The statement in verse 2, "their heart is false," employs the verb *hlq*, which means both "to be smooth, deceptive," and "to divide." It thereby conveys a sense of duplicity and divided allegiance, and plays upon the description of Jacob, the eponymous ancestor of the northern kingdom as "smooth" and "duplicitous" (see e.g., Gen 27:11), and leads directly to the statement, "now they incur guilt." The verb *ʾšm*, "to incur guilt," a by-form of *šmm*, "to be desolate," generally describes cultic impurity or impropriety that must be remedied by sacrifice and other appropriate measures of repentance. Such a sacrifice appears

---

[103] Ibid., 389.

metaphorically in the statement, "He (YHWH) will break down their altars and destroy their pillars," in that the verb ʿrp, "to bring down," is generally used to describe the breaking of the neck of an animal that is dedicated to YHWH (e.g., Exod 13:13; 34:20; Deut 21:4, 6; cf. Isa 66:3).

The reason for YHWH's action appears in verse 3, introduced by causative kî which presents the statements of the people concerning their views of their king's and YHWH's ineffectiveness. The statement, "we have no king," is frequently taken as an indication that the passage refers to the aftermath of the Assyrian conquest of Israel in 722/1 B.C.E. when King Hoshea was removed and imprisoned (2 Kgs 17:4), but the following statements indicate that the people do not lack leadership; they simply do not respect the leadership that is in place. Their statement, "we do not fear YHWH," presupposes that nothing has happened, such as an Assyrian overthrow of the northern kingdom, that would strike fear into the people. Rather, it indicates that the people feel secure. Likewise, the rhetorical question, "and the king? What will he do for us?" indicates that the king is on the throne and considered ineffective or irrelevant. Insofar as the passage later refers to false covenants and submission to Assyria, these statements could well indicate lack of confidence in the dynasties of Jehu or Menahem, both of which concluded treaties with Assyria. Menahem in particular is known to have paid tribute to Assyria to secure his throne (2 Kgs 15:19-20). Verse 4a explicitly points to the hypocrisy of such treaties by referring to those who "speak words," and then qualify those words with "(with) false (šāwʾ) oaths they make covenants." Verse 4b follows with a simile that metaphorical portrayal portrays such dishonesty by comparing the "sprouting" of "justice" to the new growth of "poisonous weeds" or "poppies" in the furrows of the field. The Hebrew term rōʾš, translated here as "poisonous weeds," means both "head" and "venom" or "poppy." It thereby conveys the double entendre that the "heads" or leaders of Israel have attempted to deceive their own people (and perhaps themselves) by making a treaty with Assyria. The poisonous imagery of venom is clear enough (see Deut 32:33; Job 20:16). Likewise, poppies are known for both their rapid growth with the initial Sukkoth rains and their role in inducing drowsiness.[104]

Verse 5 concludes the metaphorical portrayal of Israel's apostasy with a portrayal of worship devoted to the calves of Beth El. The initial statement, "the inhabitants of Samaria tremble for the calf of Beth Aven," raises several problems. The literal statement, "inhabitant of Samaria," is frequently emended to the plural, but the use of the verb škn, "to settle, abide," commonly describes either the settling down of animals

---

[104] See "Flowers," *Encyclopaedia Judaica* 6:1364-8, esp. 1365.

(e.g., Deut 33:20; Ezek 17:23; Job 39:28) as well as the presence of G–d (Deut 12:11; 1 Kgs 8:12; Ps 78:60). The singular use might indicate a reference to the king. The verb "tremble" *(gûr)* also means "to sojourn" in reference to a resident alien, and may be intended to convey the transitory nature of the calf. The term "the calf of Beth Aven" in fact is plural, "calves." Some suggest a reference to the calf at Dan, but the imagery of the calf was probably pervasive in the northern kingdom. The reference to Beth Aven, "house of wickedness," is well known as a disparaging reference to Beth El in Hosea (4:15; 5:8). The portrayal of the people "mourning" simultaneously calls to mind the mourning worship of Canaanite and Babylonian religion which mourns the gods Baal or Tammuz while they are symbolically dead in the underworld and rise to life as the rains come to renew the natural world in the fall, i.e., at the time of Sukkoth. Likewise, the reference to the "idolatrous priests who exult over it" employs the term *kōmer,* perhaps an Assyrian loan word for "priest"[105] which always refers to idolatrous priests in the Bible (cf. 2 Kgs 23:5; Zeph 1:4). The term "exult" is frequently emended to "wail," but *yāgîlû,* "they exult," well conveys the dancing and exultation of Canaanite fertility worship (cf. 1 Kings 18), and relates assonantally to the following verb *gālâ,* "to go into exile," which describes the departure of the "glory" of the calves. The term "glory" also frequently describes the presence of YHWH (e.g., Exod 40:34).

Verses 6-8 then make the meaning of the allegory very explicit. Verse 6a describes the presentation of the calf to the king of Assyria. Apparently, it was a common practice for the gods of allied or subject nations to be presented to the Assyrian king, perhaps in relation to ceremonies that would establish or acknowledge the alliance and the payment of tribute. The reference to the Assyrian king as *melek yārēb,* "the king shall contend," is apparently an attempt to render the Akkadian term *šarru rabû,* "the great king" (cf. Hos 5:13).[106] The prophet clearly portrays this as a shameful moment for Israel. The statement, "he shall take the shame of Israel," likely refers to the appropriation of the Israelite calf by the Assyrian monarch.[107] The phrase, "and Israel shall be ashamed of his counsel *(mēʿăṣātô),*" is frequently emended to "and Israel shall be ashamed of his idol *(mēʿăṣabô).*"[108] There is no need for such emendation, however, as a textual basis is lacking and the Hebrew text probably refers to statements made by the Assyrian monarch

[105] See BDB 485.

[106] Davies, *Hosea,* 157.

[107] MacIntosh, *Hosea,* 403, cites the 10th–11th century Jewish commentator Ibn Janah, who understands "the shame of Israel" as a reference to the Israelite cult.

[108] See RSV and BHS notes. Cf. MacIntosh, *Hosea,* 403–4.

at the time that the tribute and gods of subject or allied nations is presented.

Verse 7a portrays the demise of the Israelite king with the term *nidmēh*, "is destroyed," which is frequently translated in the future tense, "the king of Samaria will be destroyed." The *niphal* participle form of the verb, however, does not predict the future destruction of the monarch; rather it presents his current situation and reflects the prophet's assessment of his efficacy in providing security for the land. The comparison of the king to "a chip on the face of the waters" likewise expresses his powerlessness to determine his own fate and that of his country. The term *qeṣep*, "chip," probably refers to a cut off branch from a tree or bush, and the image of the severed fragment floating helplessly on the water as it is carried off aptly conveys the prophet's views. In most of its occurrences, *qeṣep* means "wrath," and thereby provides another double entendre in reference to YHWH's wrath and the result for the king. Although many interpreters maintain that this passage refers to the destruction of Israelite kingship in 724–722/1 B.C.E., conquered kings were generally either killed or imprisoned. The portrayal of a humbled Jehu bowing before Shalmaneser III on the "Black Obelisk" apparently expresses the shameful experience of an Israelite king who submits to Assyria. Jehu after all was an ally of Assyria, not an opponent.[109] The prophet likewise portrays the destruction of the "altars of evil," perhaps a reference to the Temple at Beth El which is reinforced by the reference to them as "the sin of Israel" (cf. 2 Kgs 17:21-22). Many view the plural *bāmôt*, "altars," or more properly "high places," as a reference to the many worship sites that proliferated throughout Israel during the monarchic period. One might see another double entendre in the expression "sin of Israel" as the Hebrew term *ḥaṭṭāʾt* refers both to "sin" and "sin offering," so that the destruction of Israel's altars might be perceived as a sort of a sacrifice for sin. The prophet then returns to the imagery of natural growth and altars that appear at the beginning of the passage when he describes the thorns and nettles that will grow up over the ruined altars. In the final statement of this passage, the altars call upon the mountains and hills to collapse and bury them. The altars metaphorically appeal for their own suicide or burial as a further sign of their inefficacy and impurity. The dead represent extreme impurity in ancient Israelite thought, and a priest may not touch the dead or enter a cemetery (see Lev 21:10-12; cf. Num 11:19-22). The portrayal of the altars as dead and buried thereby expresses the end of their cultic use.

---

[109] James A. Pritchard, *The Ancient Near East: An Anthology of Texts and Pictures* (Princeton: Princeton University Press, 1958), figure 100A.

Yhwh's Chastisement of Israel for Sins from Gibeah: 10:9-11

Yhwh resumes speaking in Hos 10:9-11 with a speech that draws upon the prophet's preceding imagery of the calves at Beth Aven (Hos 10:5-8). Yhwh begins by promising chastisement of Israel for sins that began at Gibeah. Although some interpreters understand this statement as a reference to the origins of Israelite kingship under Saul, whose home and capital were located at Gibeah (1 Sam 10:26; 11:14), most consider it to be a reference to the rape of the Levite's concubine that took place at Gibeah (Judges 19–21). As a result of this outrage, war broke out between Benjamin, in which Gibeah is located, and the other Israelite tribes after the Benjaminites refused to turn over the guilty parties for judgment. The ensuing war resulted in the decimation of Benjamin until there were only six hundred men left who were able to fend off the Israelite attack at the Rock of Rimmon. As the tribes vowed never to marry their daughters to the men of Benjamin, wives were provided by sacking the city of Jabesh Gilead, which had not joined the war, so that the surviving virgins could be given to Benjamin. Only four hundred virgins survived the action, and the men of Benjamin were allowed to "capture" their wives from the maidens who danced in the vineyards at Shiloh during the festival of Sukkoth.

Yhwh's statement in verse 9 appears to refer to the battle. The Hebrew expression *šām ʿāmādû* is frequently translated, "there they have continued" (NRSV), in reference to the continuation of Israel's sin, so that the statement provides grounds for Yhwh's punishment of Israel. This is a forced translation, however, as the term actually means, "there they stood," apparently in reference to the six hundred men who survived and fought off the Israelite attack. The NRSV translation is based upon the view that this passage must be read in relation to the late-eighth century B.C.E. Assyrian invasions that led to the destruction of the northern kingdom of Israel, so that the "continuation" of Israel's sin provides justification for the attack as Yhwh's punishment. As noted above, Hosea's prophecies are better placed in an earlier period when the country was debating the wisdom of its alignment with Assyria. The reference to Israel's sin "from the days of Gibeah" then provides the basis for Yhwh's intentions to "chastise" or "correct" Israel, but not to destroy it. Indeed, the interpretation of Hosea's statements in relation to Assyrian assault also influences the NRSV translation of the following statement, "Shall not war overtake them in Gibeah?" Again, the introduction of the interrogative is a forced translation that is made in order to relate Yhwh's statements to an actual Assyrian invasion. Furthermore, the translation ignores the presence of the phrase, "against the sons of iniquity." Instead, the phrase should be read as a simple statement,

"the war against the sons of iniquity did not overtake them in Gibeah."
Several important conclusions concerning the meaning of this statement (and indeed the passage) then follow. First, "the war against the
sons of iniquity" not only accounts for the missing phrase, but it relates
it to the circumstances of the war against Benjamin; "sons of iniquity"
points to the causes of the war in the rape and murder of the Levite's
concubine in Gibeah and Benjamin's refusal to turn over the guilty parties. Second, "the war . . . did not overtake them in Gibeah," refers to
the ability of the six hundred men of Benjamin to fight off the Israelite
attack; they were never taken. Third, the verse as a whole refers to
YHWH's capacity to chastise wrongdoing and to prepare for the correction of those who have done wrong. Just as the men of Benjamin were
reintegrated back into Israelite life after the war, so YHWH prepares to
train Israel so that they might live after punishment is complete. This
view underlies YHWH's laments later in Hos 11:8, "How can I give you
up, O Ephraim, how can I hand you over, O Israel?"

YHWH's intention to chastise or correct Israel is already apparent in
verses 10-11 as well as in the following material spoken by the prophet.
Verse 10 is particularly problematic.[110] It reads literally, "In my desire
(*bĕʾawwātî*) I will chastise them, and nations shall be gathered against
them, when they are bound to their two iniquities." The Septuagint
reading of the first phrase presupposes *bāʾtî*, in place of *bĕʾawwātî*,
which requires that the letter *waw* be dropped and the consonants repointed, "I have come and I will chastise them." The Greek reading is
easier, but it appears to be an attempt to grapple with the difficulties of
the Hebrew text and to read YHWH's statement as an introduction to the
punishment of sin in verse 10b. The Hebrew term *ʾawwâ*, however, expresses both YHWH's desire to chastise or correct and YHWH's emotional
longing to do so, which builds upon the portrayal of the marriage relationship between Israel and YHWH elsewhere in the book and the later
portrayal of YHWH as parent in chapter 11. The expression, "and I will
chastise/correct them," is based upon the verb *ysr*, which generally
conveys discipline, instruction, and correction of human beings (Prov
9:7; Jer 31:18) or animals (Pss 6:2 [NRSV: 6:1]; 38:2 [NRSV: 38:1]). The notice that "nations shall be gathered against them" calls to mind the
image of the tribes of Israel gathered against Benjamin at Gibeah or
Rimmon, but the reference to the nations metaphorically transfers this
image to Hosea's contemporary situation in which he envisions a potential Assyrian attack. Like all empires, Assyria was well known for
incorporating foreign military units into its army so that an Assyrian

[110]For discussion of the problems in this verse, see especially MacIntosh, *Hosea*,
414–7.

campaign was literally an assault by the nations.[111] The final statement of verse 10, "when they are punished for their double iniquity" (NRSV), is a particularly problematic phrase which has greatly influenced the interpretation of the verse as a statement concerning YHWH's punishment of Israel for sin. The Hebrew reads literally, "when they are bound for their two iniquities" *(bĕʾāsrām lištê ʿōnōtām)*. The reference to "binding" is enigmatic, and is understood as a punishment for sin in the LXX, which reads the verb as *bĕhiwwārām*, "in their being chastised" (cf. NRSV). Likewise, the reference to "their two iniquities" is perplexing. Some have tried to relate this statement to the two calves at Dan and Beth El, but other passages in Hosea do not indicate that Hosea is concerned with the Dan calf. Other efforts to identify two sins for Israel are entirely speculative. Indeed, the ancient controversy over the meaning of this verse is indicated by the *Qere/Ketiv*[112] reading of "their iniquities," in which the Hebrew consonantal text presents the term *ʿênōtām*, "their rings," whereas the vowel pointing presupposes the word *ʿōnōtām*, "their iniquities." When read with the *Ketiv ʿênōtām*, "their rings," the phrase refers to the binding of draft animals into the two rings of a harness or yoke (i.e., "when they are bound to their two rings"), and provides an introduction to verse 11 which employs the image of a plowing ox for Israel.

At this point, YHWH's statement at the beginning of the verse, "in my desire, I will chastise them," becomes important once again in that the verb "chastise" is used for the training or guidance of animals as well as for human instruction. The passage points to YHWH's efforts to use punishment as a means to train Israel in proper conduct; it is not used as a means to announce Israel's final destruction. The portrayal of Israel as a trained ox set to the plow contributes to this agenda. A threshing ox is harnessed to a sledge or some other implement in order to trample grain and thereby separate grain from chaff. In this context YHWH's statement, "and I spared her fair neck" (NRSV), must be reconsidered. The verb *ʿābartî*, translated here as "I spared," means literally "I passed," and refers to the placement of such a harness on the neck of the draft animal. It is also supported by the Hebrew of the following statement, *ʾarkîb ʾeprayim*, "I mounted/harnessed Ephraim," which is

---

[111] See S. Dalley, "Foreign Chariotry and Cavalry in the Armies of Tiglath-Pileser III and Sargon II," *Iraq* 47 (1985) 31–48, who notes the presence of Samarian chariot units in the Assyrian army.

[112] The Masoretic scribes indicated variant readings by a *Qere/Ketiv* system, in which one reading is indicated by the Hebrew consonantal text whereas the other reading is indicated by the vowel pointing of the word. For discussion, see William S. Morrow, "Kethib and Qere," *ABD* IV:24-30.

improperly translated as "but I will make Ephraim break the ground" in NRSV. The following statements that both Judah and Jacob shall plow likewise contribute to the imagery of YHWH's efforts to "train" or "chastise" Israel in order to bring the people to a proper course.

HOSEA'S ANNOUNCEMENT THAT WAR WILL OVERTAKE BETH EL AND ISRAEL: 10:12-15

The prophet takes up YHWH's portrayal of Israel as an ox by calling upon the people to "plant righteousness," "harvest fidelity," "break up fallow ground," and otherwise "seek YHWH." Altogether, the prophet calls upon the people to change their ways before they suffer the consequences of destruction by an invading Assyrian army. The pastoral imagery of planting and harvesting of verses 12-13 well suits the prophet's purposes as he points to the agricultural season prior to the fall rains as a time for Israel to tend to the business of insuring its own future before the destructive deluge of rains makes planting and harvest impossible. Such a setting points once again to the festival of Sukkoth in which the final harvest is brought in prior to the beginning of the rainy season in Israel. Elements of double entendre permeate these verses. The "sowing" of "righteousness" and the "harvesting" of "fidelity" of course express the qualities expected of partners in a covenant or marriage relationship, and points to the fertility aspects of such a union. The statement, "break up your fallow land," employs the Hebrew term *nîr*, which means both "furrow" and "lamp, light," a term that is used to describe the future succession of the Davidic dynasty in 1 Kgs 11:36; 15:4; 2 Kgs 8:19/2 Chr 21:7 and prosperity or happiness in general in Prov 21:4; 2 Sam 21:17; Job 18:6, etc. The reference to "a time to seek YHWH," employs the term *ʿēt*, "time," which frequently refers to the "season" of rain (e.g., Deut 11:14; Jer 5:24). The statement, "until he comes and he rains righteousness for you," employs the verb *yōreh*, "he rains," which can also mean, "he teaches, guides" and underlies the noun form *tôrâ*, "Torah, instruction." Verse 13 uses the same metaphorical imagery to present the prophet's perception of Israel's state of being, i.e., they have "plowed wickedness," "harvested injustice," and "eaten the fruit of lies."

The prophet does not specify what such wickedness, injustice, etc., entails, but he points to Israel's reliance on its own "ways" and its own "warriors." As the following verses indicate, he has in mind the military implications of Israel's actions. He anticipates that Israel's actions raise the threat of military invasion by the Assyrians, and he clearly concludes that Israel will not be able to stand against an Assyrian assault. At this point, the preceding analogy between Hosea's eighth century Israel and the eleventh–tenth century stand made by Benjamin begins to break down in the prophet's presentation, i.e., Benjamin could stand against Israel (cf. verse 9), but Israel cannot stand against Assyria. The prophet attempts to demonstrate his case by citing Shalman's destruction of Beth-arbel in verse 14. Apparently, this would be an event that was well known to the prophet's audience, but unfortunately, it is not as well known to modern readers. Many interpreters assume that Shalman is to be identified with the Assyrian monarch Shalmaneser V, who ruled in 727–722 B.C.E. and invaded Israel in 724 B.C.E.[113] He is generally believed to have conquered Samaria, but he died around the time of Samaria's fall and his successor Sargon II claims credit for the conquest. Because of the brevity of his reign, there is very little information concerning his exploits other than a reference to his invasion of Israel. There is no record of his conquest of Beth-arbel. Consequently, many speculate that Beth-arbel is the same Galilean city mentioned in 1 Macc 9:2 and Josephus (*Antiquities of the Jews* 12.11.1 §421) where the Seleucid Syrian commander Bacchides defeated Judah the Maccabee in 161 B.C.E. Others identify the city with Arbela in the Trans-Jordan near Pella (modern Irbid, cf. Eusebius, *Onomast.* 14:18). As there is no evidence that Shalmaneser V ever attacked either site, some interpreters have suggested that Shalman is the Moabite king Salamanu who paid tribute to Tiglath-pileser III, but there is no evidence that he attacked Israel during this period. An alternative hypothesis, however, is that Shalman is Shalmaneser III (r. 858–824 B.C.E.) who campaigned against Aram and Israel on various occasions.[114] In 853, he was repulsed near Karkar on the Orontes River by a coalition that included chariotry and soldiers sent by King Ahab of Israel. Later in 841 B.C.E., he was able to subdue much of southern Aram and entered northern Israel where he erected a stele in the Carmel mountain range.[115] He is also the first Assyrian monarch to receive tribute from Israel as King Jehu (r. 842–815 B.C.E.) is portrayed on the "Black Obelisk" presenting tribute to Shalmaneser III.[116] Again, there is no mention of his assault against a Syrian or Israelite city called Beth-arbel, but his

[113] For a summary of interpretations, see Davies, *Hosea*, 248–9. See also Paul L. Redditt, "Arbela," *ABD* I:354.

[114] For an overview of Shalmaneser III's reign and campaigns, see A. K. Grayson's treatment in J. Boardman et al., eds. *Cambridge Ancient History. Second Edition. Volume III. Part I. The Prehistory of the Balkans: The Middle East and the Aegean World, Tenth to Eighth Centuries B.C.* (Cambridge: Cambridge University Press, 1982).

[115] Ibid., 263.

[116] See especially M. Elat, "The Campaigns of Shalmaneser III against Aram and Israel," *IEJ* 25 (1975) 25–35.

campaigns against the so-called "Damascus coalition," his incursions into northern Israel, and his submission of Jehu would be well-remembered in Israel. Hosea's argument against Assyria, after all, cites the beginning of Jehu's reign when he wiped out the Omride dynasty at Jezreel as the time when Israel's troubles began (Hos 1:4-5). Jehu was the first Israelite king to submit to or ally with Assyria, and his dynasty was well-known for its alliance with Assyria.[117]

The prophet concludes this section in verse 15 with references to the impending destruction of Beth El, the royal sanctuary of the northern kingdom of Israel. He likewise refers to the impending demise of the northern Israelite king. Although the LXX presents this scenario as a future event, the perfect and participial formation of the verbs suggest that it is a past event.[118] Many see this verse as a reference to Assyria's destruction of Beth El and the imprisonment and deportation of King Hoshea during the course of the campaign in 724–722/1 B.C.E. Others see it as the prophet's projection of Beth El and the king's fate. The reference to the king's demise "at dawn" suggests that the prophet anticipates this as a future event. Furthermore, Hosea does not name the king of Israel although he names Shalman, which is somewhat surprising if he refers to a past event.

YHWH'S PARENTAL CARE FOR ISRAEL
FOLLOWING THE EXODUS FROM EGYPT: 11:1-9

YHWH resumes speaking in Hos 11:1-11, but shifts to the metaphor of parent and child rather than husband and wife to describe the relationship with Israel. The passage clearly builds upon the motif of Israel's impending destruction from the previous pericope, and the introductory *kî* ties YHWH's speech syntactically to Hosea's words in Hos 10:12-15. Overall, it presents YHWH as an anguished parent who has raised a rebellious child from infancy only to see it rebel when it is able to make its own choices. In order to present this image, it draws upon two major traditions in biblical literature. The first is the motif of Israel's wandering in the wilderness following the Exodus from Egypt and the rebellions against YHWH that take place during this period in which the people complain that they should return to Egypt when faced with difficulties in the wilderness, worship other gods, and refuse to accept YHWH's promises of security and land (Exod 12:37-39; 14:10-14; 16:1-3;

---

[117] See S. Page, "A Stela of Adad Nirari III and Negal-ereš from Tell al Rimlah," *Iraq* 30 (1968) 139–53, which notes Joash's submission to Assyria.

[118] For discussion of the textual problems of this verse, see MacIntosh, *Hosea*, 431–5.

17:1-7; 32:1-35; Num 11:18-20; 14:1-25; 25:1-17). The second is the law pertaining to the rebellious son in Deut 21:18-21, which calls for the stoning of a son who refuses to accept the authority of his parents. In the end, YHWH is unable to consign the rebellious child to death. The passage includes two major sections: in verses 1-7 YHWH presents an overview of the parental relationship with the child Israel in which Israel rejects YHWH for other gods and thereby brings punishment upon itself, and in verses 8-9 YHWH exclaims the inability to give up the child Israel for punishment.

YHWH's description in verses 1-7 of the parental relationship with Israel points to Israel's rebellion in the wilderness period as the cause and analogy of its predicament in the late eighth century when Assyria poses a threat. The deity begins in verse 1 with a description of the divine overtures to Israel. YHWH describes Israel as a "child" (NRSV) although the Hebrew term *na'ar* more properly describes a "youth" or adolescent who is more prone to rebel against a parent. YHWH states, "I loved him, and I called him from Egypt for/as my son," and thereby sets the stages for the situation envisioned in the law concerning the rebellious son.

Verse 2 describes Israel's rejection of YHWH in order to worship the Baals and other idols, which calls to mind both the worship of the golden calf in the wilderness (Exodus 32) and the apostasy to Baal at Baal Peor (Numbers 25). The first half of the verse in enigmatic, "they called to them, and they went before them." Rabbinic tradition understands this statement as a reference to the prophets who called Israel and Israel's failure to heed them.[119] The LXX presents a somewhat different text, "as I called to them, they went from me," which underlies the NRSV translation. Basically, the LXX reworks the text, reading *qārĕʾû*, "they called," as *kĕqāĕʾrî*, "when I called," and *mippĕnêhem*, "from before them," as *mippĕnay*, "from before me," and *hem*, "they," which introduces the following verse. Many read this statement in relation to Hos 7:11, which states that Israel calls to Egypt and follows Assyria. Insofar as the passage later highlights the issue of the return to Egypt in verse 5, it seems likely that the passage refers to Israel's continuous expression of the desire to return to Egypt and its seeking of foreign gods while in the wilderness (Exod 14:10-14; 16:1-3; 17:1-7; 32:1-35; Num 11:18-20; 14:1-25) and the procession of Israelites before the "mixed multitude" which clearly includes Egyptians who perhaps are understood to play a role in stimulating Israel's wilderness apostasy (Exod 12:37-39). YHWH continues in verse 3 with a description of the parental role in which YHWH devotes time and effort to the child Israel, taking the offspring by the

---

[119] See MacIntosh, *Hosea*, 439–45 for treatment of verse 2.

arms in order to guide it and perhaps to teach it how to walk. Despite
YHWH's efforts, however, Israel does not "know" that YHWH is the one
who "sustained" them. Although the verb *rp⁾* commonly refers to healing, the parental image and the portrayal of YHWH as a mother who
feeds Israel suggests that it refers to sustenance in this context. The
NRSV rendering of verse 4a, "I led them with cords of humankindness
(ḥablê ⁾ādām), with bands of love," overlooks the significance of the expression *ḥablê ⁾ādām* in that *ḥebel,* "cord," should also be read as *ḥēbel,*
"labor pain" (cf. Hos 13:13), so that the passage should read, "with
human labor pains, I drew them out." The expression then creates a
word play with *ʿăbōtôt ⁾ahăbâ,* "bands of love," that expresses bonds of
love and childbirth that tie mother and child together. The imagery
continues in the balance of verse 4, although textual difficulties obscure
the portrayal. Verse 4aβ reads, "I was like those who raise the yoke *(ʿōl)*
on their jaws," which plays upon the image of Israel as a trained ox
who plows in Hos 10:9-11, 12-15. Various commentators have suggested that *ʿōl,* "yoke," should be read as *ʿûl,* "suckling infant," which
seems better to fit the imagery of the immediate context.[120] The statement would then read, "I was like those who raise a suckling infant
upon their cheeks" (cf. NRSV). It would also correspond well to the imagery of the following statement in verse 4b and the first word of verse
5, "and I bent down to him, I fed him." This reading takes *lō⁾,* "not," at
the beginning of verse 5 as *lô,* "to him," in keeping with the LXX. Verse 5
then expresses the irony of Israel's situation with a pun on the word
šûb, "to return, repent," "He (Israel) will return *(yāšûb)* to the land of
Egypt and Assyria will be his king, because they refused to return/
repent *(lāšûb).*" This reading presupposes the subjugation of Israel to
Assyria and Egypt mentioned elsewhere in the book (Hos 7:11; 12:2
[NRSV: 12:1]) due to their alliances with these countries. The reading of
the MT places *lō⁾,* "not," at the beginning of the verse, but expresses a
similar irony, "He (Israel) will not *(lō⁾)* return *(yāšûb)* to the land of
Egypt and Assyria will be his king, because they refused to return/re-
pent *(lāšûb).*" This reading builds upon the analogy of Israel's present
situation to that of the wilderness period, and asserts that Israel will
indeed not return to Egypt (a desire so commonly expressed in the
wilderness), because Assyria will be their new master in "slavery."
Both readings build upon the announcement of the demise of Israel's
king in Hos 10:15, and assert that Assyria will be Israel's new king as a
punishment or consequence of its failure to return/repent.

---

[120] For discussion of the metaphorical portrayal of YHWH in this verse and elsewhere in Hosea, see Birgitte Seifert, *Metaphorisches Reden von G–tt im Hoseabuch,*
FRLANT 166 (Göttingen: Vandenhoeck & Ruprecht, 1996) 183–216.

YHWH's speech then focuses on the theme of punishment in verses 6-7. YHWH describes the "twirling" sword that is set against Israel's cities to consume the "bars" *(bad)* that hold the city gates closed (cf. Job 17:16; Exod 25:13). The term *bad* is a very suggestive term as that it has several meanings that suggest the presence of a pun, e.g., "idle talker," "white linen" (the material used to make the garments of a priest, cf. Exod 28:42; 39:28) that connotes action against Israel's priests and/or counselors who engage in idle talk. The latter motif continues in the second part of the verse which states that the sword will consume their "counsels" or "resolutions." The statement recalls earlier criticism of both the priests and those who engage in diplomacy or plots that result in alliances with Assyria and Egypt (Hos 6:7–7:16). YHWH concludes this assessment of Israel with the statement in verse 7, "my people is inclined to apostasy." Verse 7b is problematic, reading, "and unto the 'high' *(ʿal)* they call, together he does not raise them."[121] Many interpreters argue that the Hebrew term *ʿal* is a deliberate alteration of the name of the pagan god "Baal" *(baʿal)* that was made to remove a religious offensive reference to Israel's worship of a forbidden deity. Others see it as a reference to YHWH who will not save the people, but this view is contradicted in the following verse. It most likely refers to the Assyrian king, referred to in verse 5 with the pronoun "he" (cf. "they will call him") who will not deliver the people in their time of distress (cf. Hos 5:13; 2:7 [NRSV: 2:5]). The statement, "together he will not raise them *(yĕrômēm)*," indicates a word play that recalls the image of mother YHWH raising the suckling *(mĕrîmê ʿûl)* Israel for feeding in verse 4. Most interpreters take "together" *(yaḥad)* as a reference to the entire nation. The Assyrian king will not do for the nation Israel what mother YHWH has done for Israel the child.

In verses 8-9, YHWH cries out concerning the inability to give up the rebellious child Israel for punishment as required by the law concerning a rebellious son in Deut 21:18-21. This statement builds upon the emotional bonds portrayed between YHWH and Israel, as YHWH is the mother, who give birth and feeds "with bonds of love" (verse 4). Many interpreters fail to consider that this was very likely a common reaction among parents affected by this law, and they would pursue such action only in the most extreme cases. YHWH employs a sequence of rhetorical questions to express the reluctance to give Israel up, "How can I give you up, O Ephraim? (How) can I hand you over, O Israel? How can I make you like Admah? (How) can I treat you like Zeboiim?" The references to Admah and Zeboiim of course refer to cities that were included in the destruction of Sodom and Gomorrah (cf. Deut 29:22 [NRSV: 29:22];

---

[121] For discussion, see MacIntosh, *Hosea*, 455–8.

Gen 14:2, 8; 19:24-28; 10:19; 13:10-12). The emphasis on YHWH's emotional bonds with Israel continues in verse 8b, which speak of the turning of YHWH's heart and the heated compassion within. In the end,
YHWH states the intention not to allow the divine wrath to decide the
destruction of Israel, "because I am G–d and not man." YHWH here
claims a capacity to forgive that is not attributed to human beings, but
as the analogy of YHWH and mother indicates, it is precisely such a
human relationship that underlies YHWH's compassion in the first
place. YHWH's final statement, "in your midst is the Holy One, and I
will not come against a city," refers to divine presence in Israel as symbolized by the Temple. YHWH gives in to the emotional bonds of mother
and child, and reverts to the traditional promise of protection for Israel
that the nation would presuppose in the first place.

HOSEA'S METAPHORICAL PORTRAYAL OF ISRAEL'S RETURN TO YHWH: 11:10-11

The absence of Israel as the explicit subject of verse 10 demonstrates
that Hos 11:10-11 is intended to follow upon Hos 11:1-9, but the third
person form of the verses indicates that Hosea is the speaker. The
prophet takes up the parental imagery of YHWH's reluctance to punish
Israel in Hos 11:1-9 by presenting a metaphorical image of Israel following YHWH much as lion cubs follow a roaring lion or birds return to
their nests. Hosea employs these images to project the potential return
of Israel to YHWH, and thereby presents the rhetorical goal of his oracles
as expressed at the end of the book in Hos 14:2-9 [NRSV: 14:1-8]. Both
images employ the motif of fear to explain the willingness of the respective animals to "return." This motif underlies much of Hosea's
message that Israel has much to fear if it does not return to YHWH.

The passage includes two basic components, each of which employs a distinctive animal image in a syntactically free standing statement. Verse 10 employs the image of a roaring lion and its cubs to
express the prophet's hope that Israel will "follow" YHWH. The prophet
states this premise at the outset, "after YHWH they will follow," and follows up with a simile that compares YHWH to a roaring lion. Although
such an image is well known from the natural world, it is politically
significant as well in that the lion is the symbol of the tribe of Judah and
its role as ruler of the other tribes (Gen 49:8-12; cf. Amos 1:2). It is possible that this statement reflects the prophet's location in Judah when
the final form of the book was produced or perhaps some Judean sym-
pathies on his part. The reaction of the cubs to the lion's roaring is also
important in that it employs the verb *ḥrd* to describe their fear and

trembling. Variations of the verb root are employed elsewhere as synonym for the piety of those who "tremble" before G–d (see Isa 66:2; Ezra 9:4; 10:3). The statement that they tremble "from the west" (literally, "from the sea") merely indicates that fear of the lion or YHWH extends to the farthest reaches of the land, i.e., all the way to the sea.

The prophet employs the images of a bird who "trembles from Egypt" or a dove who trembles "from Assyria" in verse 11. These images presuppose the natural migratory habits of birds who fly to more hospitable climates at times of inclement weather, such as the beginning of the rainy season that is marked in Israel by the festival Sukkoth. This imagery is particularly apt in that it is well known that the birds will return to the land once the rainy winter season concludes in the spring. The introduction of the motif of fear from Egypt and Assyria indicates the prophet's political intentions in that the birds have departed for fear of the two powers with which Israel is allied. Return is inevitable, however, and this motif is expressed in the prophet's quotation of an oracular statement by YHWH, "and I shall cause them to dwell in their homes." The NRSV follows the LXX in reading the verb *wĕhôšabtîm*, "and I will cause them to dwell," as *wahăšîbōtîm,* "and I shall cause them to return," which clarifies the function of the original Hebrew verb. The use of the term "homes" (literally, "houses") aids in conveying the metaphorical association between the birds and the people of Israel, i.e., like migrating birds who depart and return with the change of seasons, Israel will return to its home with YHWH after its fear of Assyria and Egypt has passed.

YHWH'S PREMISE:
ISRAEL IS NOT TO BE TRUSTED: 12:1A [NRSV: 11:12]

The first person style of Hos 12:1a [NRSV: 11:12] demonstrates that YHWH is the speaker, although this statement does not appear to be a part of the same statement quoted by the prophet in Hos 11:11b. The oracular formula of the preceding verse indicates that verse 11b is to be considered a part of the prophet's speech in Hos 11:10-11, and the contents of Hos 11:11b indicate that it is an entirely different statement from that in Hos 12:1a [NRSV: 11:12]. YHWH lays out the premise of the following sequence of passages, i.e., that Israel/Ephraim is not to be trusted. Although many interpreters look to the forensic language of verse 3 [NRSV: 2] to characterize this statement as a legal indictment that leads to judgment, the following material from YHWH and Hosea in Hos 12:1b-15 [NRSV: 11:12–12:14] presents a scenario in which Israel is offered the possibility to change its course of action. YHWH's accusation

that "Ephraim has surrounded me with a lie and the house of Israel
with deceit," indicates a sense of betrayal that must be read in relation
to Israel's decision to abandon its agreements with Aram (see Hos
12:12, 13-15 [NRSV: 12:11, 12-14]) in favor of treaties with Assyria and
Egypt (see Hos 12:2b [NRSV: 12:1b]). The term *kaḥaš,* "lie," denotes misrepresentation, particularly in cases where one party attempts to appear weak or thin, but is actually powerful (Deut 33:29; Josh 24:27; Jer
5:12; Isa 59:13; Job 8:18). The term *mirmâ,* "deceit," is frequently employed in relation to deceptive trading practices such as the use of false
balances (see Hos 12:8 [NRSV: 12:7] below; Amos 8:5; Prov 11:1; 20:23;
Mic 6:11).

HOSEA'S ASSERTION OF JUDAH'S FIDELITY: 12:1B [NRSV: 11:12B]

The third person form indicates that Hos 12:1b [NRSV: 11:12b] is
styled as a statement by the prophet that is linked to YHWH's statement
in verse 1a by the conjunction "and." Most scholars maintain that it is a
redactional addition to this text that was likely made when the final
form of the book was composed or edited in Judah.[122] The statement is
clearly favorable to Judah, but this stands in stunning contrast to verse
3 that announces YHWH's "lawsuit" against Judah. Furthermore, the
meaning of the verse is disputed in that the verb *rōd* is not well understood.[123] Most interpreters view it as a participle form of *rôd,* which
means "to wander, roam," and indicates that Judah still "roams" with
G–d, i.e., Judah remains constant with G–d as suggested by the second
part of the statement. Others argue that the verb derives from the root
rdh, "to rule," so that the statement would express Judah's preeminent
position following the collapse of northern Israel, but this would require the verb to have a final *hē* which is lacking in the text. Some take
qĕdôšîm, "holy ones," as a reference to idols that indicates Judah's apostasy, but this flies against the plain meaning of the text that presents
Judah as "constant, faithful" *(neʾĕmān)* with "the Holy One" in which
qĕdôšîm is a plural of majesty parallel with *ʾēl,* "G–d."

YHWH'S PREMISE:
ISRAEL HAS MADE TREATIES WITH ASSYRIA AND EGYPT: 12:2 [NRSV: 12:1]

Hosea 12:2 [NRSV: 12:1] lacks the first person form that would identify it conclusively as a speech by YHWH, and can be considered as a

---

[122] E.g., Emmerson, *Hosea,* 113–6.
[123] For a discussion of the term, see MacIntosh, *Hosea,* 473–4.

speech by the prophet that ties into verses 1b [NRSV: 11:12b] and 3-9 [NRSV: 2-8]. Nevertheless, it appears to have been composed as a speech by YHWH that continues YHWH's statement in verse 1a [NRSV: 11:12a] by specifying that Israel's "lie" or "deceit" is its conclusion of treaties with Assyria and Egypt. As noted above, verse 1b [NRSV: 11:12b] appears to be redactional, and the emphasis on YHWH's name in verse 3 [NRSV: 2] indicates that this verse was intended to mark the beginning of the prophet's speech. Once again, the statement in verse 2 [NRSV: 1] draws upon natural metaphors to express the futility of Israel's actions, "Ephraim shepherds wind and pursues the east wind all day." This provides an interesting contrast to the approach of the lion (YHWH) in Hos 11:10-11 as shepherds are supposed to protect their flocks from lions and other threats. The "east wind," known in modern times as the Hamsin (Arabic) or Sharav (Hebrew) is a dry desert wind like the Santa Ana winds of Southern California that periodically blows into Israel.[124] They are frequently powerful enough to cause a great deal of destruction, which is the premise for the following statement, "he multiplies lie(s) and destruction." The intent of the analogy is clear; Israel pursues what is destructive rather than what will benefit the nation. The specific meaning of these statements becomes clear in verse 2b [NRSV: 1b], i.e., Israel cuts a treaty with Assyria and presents oil to Egypt. It is well known that Assyria's goals in its westward expansion into Aram, Israel, and Philistia was to open trade relations with Egypt.[125] Indeed by the seventh century B.C.E. after Assyria had conquered the entire region, excavations at Tel Miqne (Philistine Eqron) demonstrate that Assyria turned Philistia into a major center for olive oil production that was able to supply the needs of the entire Assyrian empire.[126]

HOSEA'S USE OF THE JACOB TRADITION TO APPEAL FOR
ISRAEL'S RETURN TO YHWH: 12:3-9 [NRSV: 12:2-8]

Hosea 12:3-9 [NRSV: 12:2-8] is one of the most frequently debated passages in the book of Hosea because it employs elements from the Jacob tradition (cf. Genesis 25–35) to represent Israel's actions or character

---

[124] For discussion of the *hamsin* or *sharav,* see "Israel, Land of (Geographical Survey)," *Encylopaedia Judaica* 9:189-90.

[125] See especially M. Elat, "The Economic Relations of the Neo-Assyrian Empire with Egypt," *JAOS* 98 (1978) 20–34; N. Na'aman, "The Brook of Egypt and Assyrian Policy on the Border of Egypt," *TA* 6 (1979) 68–90.

[126] See S. Gitin, "Tel Miqne-Ekron: A Type Site for the Inner Coastal Plain in the Iron Age II Period," *Recent Excavations in Israel: Studies in Iron Age Archaeology,* ed. S. Gitin and W. G. Dever, AASOR, vol. 49 (Winona Lake: Eisenbrauns, 1989) 23–58.

in Hosea's own time.[127] Scholars are not entirely certain whether prophet draws upon the present form of Genesis 25–35, an earlier version of the tradition, or an alternative form, but it seems quite clear that some version of the tradition was extant in Israel during Hosea's lifetime. Indeed, Jacob is the eponymous ancestor of the northern kingdom of Israel, having been named Israel following his wrestling with the "man" at Jabbok (Gen 32:22-32), again at Beth El (Gen 35:1-15), and having founded the sanctuary at Beth El which served as the royal sanctuary of the northern kingdom (Gen 28:10-22; 35:1-15; cf. 1 Kgs 12:25–13:32). Interpreters generally view Jacob as a deceitful character as he was able to convince his brother Esau to trade his birthright for a bowl of lentil soup and to deceive his father Isaac into giving him Esau's blessing. This view of Jacob informs a great deal of the interpretation of Hosea 12 as many interpreters view Hosea's remarks as an accusation against Israel and an indication of Israel's immoral character. This is true to a certain extent, but it overlooks the prophet's clearly stated agenda of attempting to prompt Israel to return to YHWH (see verse 7 [NRSV: 6]). The Jacob tradition is very important to this strategy. Indeed, Jacob starts life as a deceitful figure, but his love for Rachel turns him into a righteous and faithful husband whom his father-in-law Laban is easily able to exploit. Interpreters frequently overlook this side of Jacob's character in the interpretation of Hosea 12 and the fact that Jacob ultimately does return to the land of Israel (and YHWH) at the end of the Jacob cycle. Even after Rachel dies, Jacob remains loyal to her and places her sons, Joseph and Benjamin, over those born to Leah, Bilhah, and Zilpah. It is Jacob's fidelity to Rachel and his return to Israel that prompts Hosea's use of the image to call for Israel's fidelity and return to YHWH. In the prophet's view, if Jacob could change, so can northern Israel.

The prophet begins in verses 3-6 [NRSV: 2-5] with a metaphorical description of YHWH's intentions to punish Israel for its deeds based upon the paradigm of the eponymous ancestor Jacob. This intention is stated explicitly in verse 3 [NRSV: 2], which presents Israel in its entirety, including both Judah and Jacob/Israel. The reference to Judah in verse 3a [NRSV: 2a] disturbs many commentators who view it is a later addition to the text analogous to that of Hos 12:1b [NRSV: 11:12b]. But this view overlooks the fact that Judah comprises a portion of the Israelite empire under the Jehu dynasty as Judah was allied as a vassal or partner with Israel during this period. Many interpreters note the presence of

---

[127] For recent discussion, see S. L. McKenzie, "The Jacob Tradition in Hosea xii 4–5," *VT* 36 (1986) 311–22; Utzschneider, *Hosea. Prophet vor dem Ende*, 186–230; Neef, *Die Heilstraditionen Israels in der Verkündigung des Propheten Hosea*, esp. 15–49.

the forensic term *rîb*, "lawsuit, case at law, indictment" (literally, "controversy"), and argue that the entire passage is presented as an indictment of Israel that leads to judgment. Although the actions specified in the following verses can certainly lead to judgment, and Israel's culpability is indicated in verse 15b [NRSV: 14b], the very clear address to Israel in verse 7 [NRSV: 6] calls upon the nation to return to YHWH and thereby demonstrates the rhetorical goal of the prophet's charges. Jacob or the northern kingdom of Israel is also included in verse 3b [NRSV: 2b], which states the principle that the people are subject to punishment for their actions.

The prophet then shifts to a presentation of the Jacob tradition in verses 4-6 [NRSV: 3-5] in order to establish the analogy between the eponymous ancestor Jacob and the nation of Israel from his own time. The cryptic style and poetic parallel structure of the rendition suggests that the prophet cites a liturgical form of the tradition; indeed, the refrain in verse 6 [NRSV: 5], "and YHWH, the G–d of Hosts, YHWH is his remembrance," indicates that the prophet draws upon a liturgical rendition of the tradition, perhaps one that was presented in the Beth El sanctuary founded by Jacob. The usual time for the dedication of an altar or the foundation of a sanctuary is Sukkoth, and Sukkoth would therefore be a suitable time for the recitation of the Jacob tradition at Beth El. Verse 4 [NRSV: 3] summarizes Jacob's conflicts with Esau and with G–d. It refers to the competition between Jacob and Esau even in the womb (Gen 25:19-26). The use of the verb *ʿāqab*, "he tried to supplant," derives from the Jacob tradition where the noun *ʿāqēb*, "heel," is used in Gen 25:26 to describe Jacob's seizing Esau by the heel at birth in an attempt to emerge as the first born (*ʿāqēb* means "heel," and the root *ʿqb* is the basis of the name Jacob [*yaʿāqōb*]). The verb also appears in Gen 27:36 where Esau uses it to describe Jacob's deceit in gaining Isaac's blessing. The reference to Jacob's struggle with G–d employs the verb *śārâ*, "he strove," also derives from the Jacob tradition concerning his wrestling with the "man" by Jabbok in which *śārâ* is employed to explain the meaning of Jacob's new name Israel (*yiśrāʾēl*), "because you have striven (*śārîtâ*) with G–d and with humans, and have prevailed" (Gen 32:29). Many note that the reference to Jacob's "manhood" (*ʾôn*) establishes a pun with the word *ʿāwōn*, "guilt," in verse 9 [NRSV: 8], and aids in building the image of Jacob as sinner.

The reference to Jacob's wrestling with the "angel," "he strove (*wāyāśar*) with the angel and he prevailed (*wayyukāl*)," draws upon the language of Gen 32:29, "because you have striven (*śārîtâ*) with G–d and with humans, and have prevailed (*watûkāl*)." The term "angel," however, does not appear in the Genesis version of the story. Many consider it to be a redactional addition to the text that is meant to specify an original reference to G–d *(ʾēl)* that could stand behind the present *ʾel,* "to," but this is speculative and creates even greater problems in that it would suggest that G–d is portrayed as the victor in Hos 12:5 [NRSV: 12:4], "and G–d struggled and prevailed." The statement, "he wept and sought his favor," is problematic in that Jacob neither weeps nor implores the "man" in Genesis 32. There is a great deal of weeping in the Jacob tradition in Gen 27:38; 29:11; 33:4; cf. Gen 35:8, but Hos 12:5 [NRSV: 12:4] probably refers to weeping by the "man/angel" with whom Jacob wrestled. The term, "he sought his favor," is indicative in that the "man" requests that Jacob release him in Gen 32:27, but Jacob refuses until he receives a blessing. It is the "angel" who seeks the favor of Jacob, not Jacob who seeks the favor of the "angel." The "man's" entreating of Jacob results in his new name, Israel. The verse continues with the statement, "at Beth El, he found him, and there he spoke with him," but it is not clear whether G–d found and spoke with Jacob at Beth El or whether Jacob found G–d and spoke with him. It is probably immaterial as the key point of Hos 12:5b [NRSV: 12:4b] is that G–d and Jacob met and spoke together at Beth El as indicated in both Genesis 28 and 35.

The prophet's recitation of the Jacob tradition concludes at this point with the liturgical refrain, "and YHWH, the G–d of Hosts, YHWH is his remembrance" (cf. Exod 15:3; Amos 4:13; 5:27). The term "his remembrance" *(zikrô)* is somewhat unusual, but it can function as a synonym for "his name" (Ps 135:13).

Hosea changes his literary style in verse 7 [NRSV: 6] to a second person direct address to Israel, "and you shall return to your G–d." Although the verb is formulated as a second person imperfect, "you shall return," the following imperatives in verse 7b [NRSV: 6b] indicate that this is not a prediction of the future, but a call by the prophet for a change of direction. The verb *šûb,* "to return," frequently conveys repentance, but the context indicates that the prophet calls not only for a return to YHWH, but a return to previous political commitments, such as Israel's treaty relationship with Aram, as well. The prophet's demand of Israel, "hold fast to love and justice" *(ḥesed ûmišpāṭ šĕmōr),* conveys both religious and political fidelity and righteousness. The expression is better translated, "observe fidelity and law." The term *ḥesed* frequently appears in contexts that suggest a sense of loyalty and constancy in a relationship between two parties, and *mišpāṭ* conveys fundamental righteousness, justice, and lawful action. The second phrase, "wait continually for your G–d," is somewhat misleading as it suggests that G–d will come to Israel. Rather, it expresses the prophet's view that Israel should place its hope or trust in G–d, "(place) hope unto your G–d." Obviously, the prophet does not identify such hope with an

Assyrian or Egyptian alliance, but subsequent verses make it clear that Israel's relationship with Aram constitutes adherence to Yhwh's expectation. Jacob's wife Rachel came from Aram (as did his mother Rebekah), which links the two countries together. Altogether, Hosea's appeal to Israel to return to Yhwh constitutes the fundamental goal of his discourse and his portrayal of Jacob/Israel.

Hosea then returns to third person objective language to characterize Israel as a deceiver. At this point, the language concerning the eponymous ancestor Jacob disappears as the prophet turns his attention to the nation Israel of his own day. He calls Israel, "Canaan" [NRSV: "trader"], which is frequently taken as a reference to Phoenician merchants (cf. Zeph 1:11; Ezek 16:29; 17:4) based upon the imagery of false scales and riches gained through trade in the balance of the verse. But the label also expresses Hosea's rhetorical goals by labeling Israel as the Canaanites who were displaced from the land at the conquest led by Joshua. Israelite tradition labels the Canaanites as those people who were removed from the land by Yhwh for immoral action, and Hosea employs this label as a means to make his point that Israel is now immoral and subject to a similar punishment if it does not change. The reference to "false balances" is particularly noteworthy in relation to the Jacob tradition in that the term *mirmâ,* "false," appears in Gen 27:35 to describe Jacob's deceit in convincing Isaac to give him Esau's blessing. The verb *ʿšq,* "to oppress," frequently refers to economic extortion (Amos 4:1; Deut 24:14; Jer 7:6; Ezek 22:29). The prophet places words in Ephraim's mouth in verse 9 [NRSV: 8] that draw upon the Jacob tradition in order to characterize Israel's wealth as a result of its trading relationship with Assyria and Egypt, "Indeed, I am rich, I have gained wealth for myself." The term "wealth" *(ʾôn)* also appears in verse 4 [NRSV: 3] to characterize Jacob's "adulthood" or "maturity." Here it contributes to a pun with *ʿāwôn,* "offense," that aids in presenting Jacob's wealth as ill-gotten gain. Overall, the statement draws upon the tradition concerning Jacob's confrontation with Laban after he departed for the land of Israel (Gen 31:22-42). After Laban searched Jacob's tents and did not find the teraphim or household gods that Rachel had stolen and hidden in her baggage, Jacob protests to Laban, "what is my offense *(pišʿî)*? How have I sinned *(ḥaṭṭāʾtî)* that you have hotly pursued me?" In Genesis, Jacob thought that he was innocent, and indeed, he had acted properly with Laban at every turn, whereas Laban tried repeatedly to cheat him. Hosea borrows this motif, but characterizes Israel/Jacob as sinful in that Israel's statement, "in all my gain no offense is found in me that would be sin *(ḥēṭʾ),*" in that verse 8 [NRSV: 7] sets the terms by which verse 9 is read, i.e., Israel is a cheat and his protests of innocence in verse 9 [NRSV: 8] are false. Altogether, these

verses build the prophets case that Israel has done wrong in establishing a relationship with Assyria and Egypt, and therefore must change
to avoid punishment from YHWH.

YHWH'S REMINDER TO ISRAEL OF DIVINE FIDELITY:
12:10-12 [NRSV: 12:9-11]

YHWH resumes speaking in Hos 12:10-12 [NRSV: 12:9-11] with a reminder to Israel of YHWH's fidelity to and continued care for Israel.
YHWH's statements are connected syntactically to the prophet's statements in verses 3-9 [NRSV: 2-8] by a conjunctive *waw*, "and." This aids in
establishing YHWH's commitment to the relationship and willingness to
accept the return of Israel (see verse 7 [NRSV: 6]). By demonstrating
YHWH's commitment to Israel, the passage attempts to lay a basis for
calling upon Israel to remain committed to its relationship with YHWH
and with Aram (see below on verses 12, 13-15 [NRSV: 11, 12-14]).

YHWH begins with the self-identification formula in verse 10 [NRSV:
9], "I am YHWH, your G–d, from the land of Egypt," that is addressed
directly to Israel in second person address form. The statement functions not only as a means to identify YHWH to the audience, but to do so
by reminding them of YHWH's actions on behalf of Israel, i.e., the Exodus from Egyptian slavery. YHWH follows immediately with a statement of the intention again to cause Israel to dwell "in tents as in the
appointed days *(kimê môʿēd)."* This statement appears to be a reminder
of YHWH's care for Israel during the period of wilderness wandering
when the people lived in tents as they traveled through the wilderness
from Egypt to the promised land. Once again, the image conveys
YHWH's care for Israel during a period of vulnerability. The reference to
"tents" has been the subject of discussion as some scholars have attempted to associate dwelling in tents with the festival of Sukkoth, in
which the people would dwell in "booths" *(sukkôt)* or temporary shelters in the vineyards while bringing in the grape and olive harvests.[128]
Others object because tents are not the same as "booths," but this
misses an essential point of the image. Sukkoth traditionally commemorates not only the grape and olive harvest, but the period of Israel's
wilderness wandering as well. The "booths" are understood to be representative of the tents or temporary shelters in which Israel lived
while in the wilderness. Furthermore, the reference to "the appointed
days" indicates a festival occasion, as the Hebrew word *môʿēd*, "appointed time, place," normally designates the appointed time or place

---

[128] For discussion, see Davies, *Hosea,* 279–80.

for festival celebration (Deut 31:10; Lev 23:2, 4, etc.; Num 15:3; 29:39; Ezek 36:38; 46:9; and Exod 33:7; Num 12:4; Deut 31:14, etc.).

The premise of YHWH's continuous care for Israel appears in verse 11 [NRSV: 10] as well in which YHWH refers to the prophets sent to Israel. YHWH employs a first person direct address style to state to the people, "and I spoke to the prophets, and I multiplied visions, and by the hand of the prophets I spoke in metaphors (*ʾădămmeh*)." The last statement is particularly problematic, and many translate it as a reference to YHWH's intention to destroy Israel, "and through the prophets I will bring destruction" (NRSV). This translation presupposes that the verb *ʾădămmeh* is derived from the root *dmh II*, "to cease, cause to cease, destroy," which appears frequently in Hosea (Hos 4:5, 6; 10:7, 15), but this root never appears in the *piel* conjugation. When conjugated in *piel*, it always derives from *dmh I*, "to be like, resemble," and conveys an attempt to think, devise, or make comparisons. Insofar as prophetic speech (and particularly that by Hosea) frequently employs metaphors and similes to make points concerning G–d's actions in the world, this statement expresses a fundamental aspect of prophetic speech and thereby conveys G–d's attempts to provide continuous care for the people by making the divine viewpoint known through the prophets.

Verse 12 [NRSV: 11] is especially problematic. Its third person form suggests that it is not a continuation of YHWH's speech in verses 10-11 [NRSV: 9-10], but the unspecified "they" ("they shall surely come to nothing, etc.") requires that "the prophets" in verse 11 [NRSV: 10] must be the referent for these statements. Verse 12 [NRSV: 11] must therefore continue YHWH's speech. The NRSV translates verse 12a [NRSV: 11a], "In Gilead, there is iniquity, they shall surely come to nothing," but this ignores the particle *ʾim*, "if," at the beginning of the statement and the perfect conjugation of the verb *hāyû*, "they were." The statement should read, "If Gilead is iniquity, they were nothing/worthless." Most interpreters consider the statement to refer to some sort of wrongdoing in Gilead associated with idolatry or the institution of kingship in Israel,[129] but these views fail to consider the role of Gilead in the Jacob tradition. Gilead is where Laban overtakes Jacob as he returns with his family and belongings to the land of Israel. After the two men resolved their differences concerning the disappearance of Laban's household gods, they made a treaty between themselves (Gen 31:44) and marked it by erecting a pillar and "a heap of witness" (*galʿēd*), which provides a pun for the name Gilead (Gen 31:45-46). The pillar and the "heap" (*gal*) apparently mark the mutually agreed border between Israel and Aram as they specify that no one from either country shall pass this border to

---

[129] E.g., Wolff, *Hosea*, 215.

do evil (Gen 31:52). This narrative apparently serves as an etiological story for the creation of a treaty or alliance between Israel and Aram. Much as Genesis 28 explains the origins of the Beth El sanctuary, Genesis 30–31 explains the origins of the tribes, etc.

Such an alliance is symbolized by the marriage between Jacob and Rachel (and Leah) as well as by Isaac and Rebekah; indeed, the Pentateuch looks to Aram as the homeland of the patriarchs and matriarchs. It is noteworthy, therefore, that Israel and Aram were allied in 853 B.C.E. when they formed the basis of a coalition that fought the Assyrian monarch Shalmaneser III when he tried to cross the Orontes River at Qarqar.[130] Although Shalmaneser III was stopped at this time, the coalition later broke apart as the Aramean king was overthrown, and Aram and Israel subsequently went to war. By 842 B.C.E., Jehu overthrew the Omride dynasty in Israel, with the support of the prophets Elijah and Elisha, who apparently also supported the Aramean revolt as indicated by YHWH's message to Elijah to anoint Jehu king over Israel and Hazael king over Aram (1 Kgs 19:14-18). The anticipated relationship between Israel and Aram collapsed, however, as Israel suffered invasion by the Aramean king Hazael (2 Kgs 10:32-36). Jehu's conflict with Aram apparently instigated (or resulted from) his alliance with Assyria. An Israelite alliance with Assyria would have provided the basis for the wealth and power of the Jehu dynasty, but it also would have severely weakened Aram. Insofar as Israelite tradition looks to Aram as the homeland of the ancestors associated with YHWH, this constitutes a fundamental betrayal of YHWH's will in the eyes of Hosea. According to Hosea, Aram is Israel's natural ally, as specified by the treaty between Jacob and Laban, not Israel's enemy. If the covenant with Aram at Gilead is iniquity, then the prophets, such as Elijah and Elisha, were false. Hosea clearly opposes such a notion.

YHWH's speech continues with a reference to the prophets' sacrifices of bulls at Gilgal. Gilgal is well known as the site where Joshua encamped at the time of the conquest and celebrated Passover (Joshua 5).[131] It was known for the twelve stones that signified the federation of the tribes of Israel, but its location near Jericho and the Jordan River also marked the eastern border of Israel with the Trans-Jordanian regions inhabited by the tribes of Manasseh, Gad, and Reuben. Indeed, it was these territories that Israel and Aram fought over during times of

---

[130] For discussion of the historical background, see A. K. Grayson, "Assyria: Ashur-Dan II to Ashur-Nirari V (934–745 B.C.)," *CAH* 3/1, 238–81, esp. 259–69. See also M. Elat, "The Campaigns of Shalmaneser III against Aram and Israel," *IEJ* 25 (1975) 25–35.

[131] See Wade Kotter, "Gilgal," *ABD* II:1022-1024.

war. Gilgal is also the site where the prophet Samuel judged Israel (1 Sam 7:16, with Beth El and Mizpah), together with the people anointed Saul as king (1 Sam 11:12-15), and revoked Saul's kingship for encroaching upon his right to perform the sacrifices at Gilgal (1 Sam 13:8-15). The site is also associated with Elijah's ascent into heaven (2 Kgs 2:1-4). Some argue that the Gilgal associated with Samuel is another site north of Beth El, but this is unclear. It is clear, however, that Gilgal is a cultic site associated with prophets such as Samuel, Elijah, and Elisha, who sometimes performed sacrifices there. This is not unusual as ancient prophets or seers were known to perform sacrifices as part of their oracular ritual (see Numbers 22–24; 1 Kings 18).

The final portion of this verse (12b [NRSV: 11b]) notes that the altars of the prophets are like "heaps" *(gallîm)* in the furrows of the field. This is obviously a disparaging reference to the altars of the prophets, which indicates their worthlessness. The reference to "heaps" clearly calls to mind the "heap of witness" that marks the border between Aram and Israel, and revisits the initial statement that if Gilead is iniquitous, the prophets were worthless. Verse 12b [NRSV: 11b] must be understood in relation to the previously mentioned Gilead and Gilgal and the role that these sites play in defining the borders of Israel with Aram and the Trans-Jordan, i.e., if the borders of Israel do not stand, then the words of the prophets that YHWH sends to care for Israel (verse 11 [NRSV: 10]) are worthless.

HOSEA'S EXPLANATION OF YHWH'S REMINDER OF DIVINE FIDELITY
AND REITERATION OF ISRAEL'S CONTINUED REJECTION:
12:13–13:3 [NRSV: 12:12–13:3]

Hosea builds upon YHWH's statements concerning divine care for Israel and the need to preserve Israel's relationship with Aram by pointing to Jacob's (and Israel's) capacity to change in Hos 12:13-15 [NRSV: 12:12-14]. The prophet employs references to both the Jacob and the Exodus traditions in making the point that Israel must observe its relationship with Aram or suffer the consequences. The prophet begins in verse 13 [NRSV: 12] with a reference to Jacob's flight from Aram, when Jacob gathered his wives, concubines, children, and cattle in order to depart from Laban's household and return to the land of Israel (Genesis 31). The second part of the verse, "and Israel served for a woman/wife, and for a woman/wife he watched (sheep)," is particularly controversial in that (largely male) interpreters view this as a reference to Jacob's humiliation, enslavement, just punishment, etc.[132]

---

[132] An exception is Peter Ackroyd, "Hosea and Jacob," *VT* 13 (1963) 245–59.

Such interpretations are motivated, however, by some rather sexist viewpoints concerning the relationships between men and women and by the assumption that Jacob is a deceitful and sinful character throughout the Jacob tradition. Such understandings of this verse overlook the marked emphasis in the tradition concerning Jacob's love for Rachel and the fact that he does not lie or attempt to deceive others after he meets her; rather, figures such as Laban and Esau attempt to deceive or threaten him after this point in the narrative. The reference to Israel's/Jacob's service for a woman points to the manner in which Jacob became an "honest" man, viz., his love for Rachel compelled him to change. The implicit message of this verse is that if the ancestor Jacob could change, so can the Israel or Hosea's day. This point is made especially clear by the use of the name "Israel" rather than "Jacob" in verse 13 [NRSV: 12].

Hosea then turns to the Exodus tradition in verse 14 [NRSV: 13] in which he states that YHWH brought Israel up from Egypt by a prophet and that Israel "was watched" by a prophet. This provides a sort of a complement to the previous reference to Jacob's flight from Aram in that both traditions portray Israel returning to the land of Israel after having experienced oppression or difficulties in a foreign land. Furthermore, the use of the verb *šmr*, "to watch, observe," provides a further link between the two verses that highlights the motif of care and protection for Jacob/Israel. By noting the care of the prophet, i.e., Moses, for Israel in the Exodus, Hosea recalls YHWH's earlier statements concerning the role of the prophets in communicating with Israel and thereby testifying to YHWH's continual care of the people. In the present instance, YHWH's care for the people constitutes the motivation or the premise for their potential return to YHWH. Just as YHWH cared for Israel in the past, so YHWH cares for Israel in the present.

The prophet's statements in verse 15 [NRSV: 14] then emphasize Israel's responsibility for keeping its commitments, especially to Aram. The NRSV translates this verse, "Ephraim has given bitter offense *(hikᶜîs ʾeprayim tamrûrîm)*, so his L–rd (sic., his lord) will bring his crimes down on him and pay him back for his insults." The translation does not adequately convey the meaning of the Hebrew, however, in that it does not indicate the word play represented by *tamrûrîm*. When derived from the root *mrr*, the term means "bitter" (cf. Jer 6:26; 31:15), which underlies the NRSV translation, but when it is derived from the root *tmr* it refers to "signposts" or "piles of stones" (see Jer 31:21). When read in relation to the use of the Jacob tradition, particularly in regard to the heaps of stones that marked the boundary between Israel/Jacob and Aram/Laban, the term calls to mind once again the issue of the covenant/treaty between Israel and Aram that formalized their borders. In this instance, verse 15a [NRSV: 14a] indicates that if Ephraim "provokes" or "violates" its boundary with Aram, it will suffer for its actions. Verse 15b [NRSV: 14b] reads literally, "its blood he shall forsake upon himself, and his lord will return his shame to him," i.e., Israel's blood will be shed as a result of such shameful behavior. Hosea appears to know fully well the consequences of violating an international treaty. Most employed a ceremony in which the parties to the treaty walked between the bloodied pieces of animals that were sacrificed for the occasion in order to indicate that the same fate would befall those who violated the terms of the treaty (cf. Jer 34:17-20; Genesis 15).[133] If Israel violates its treaty with Aram, its blood will be upon its own head.

Hosea then turns to images of death and punishment for Israel in Hos 13:1-3. The absence of a clear syntactical join at the beginning of this text and the lack of explicit reference to the previous verses suggests that this may be the beginning of an originally independent unit that was redactionally placed in its present position. When read in relation to the present context, however, Hos 13:1-3 follows naturally from 12:13-15 [NRSV: 12:12-14] in that it specifies the scenario of death and punishment that will overtake Israel if it fails to heed the prophet's message and maintain its relationship with YHWH and with Aram.

Verse 1 is particularly instructive in that its reference to Ephraim's death for involvement with Baal suggests a reference to either the golden calf tradition of Exodus 32–34 or the Baal Peor apostasy in Numbers 25 that would continue the sequence of references to Israel's history, particularly in relation to the Exodus tradition, in Hos 12:13-15 [NRSV: 12:12-14]. Verse 1a clearly posits the preeminence of the tribe of Ephraim. When Jacob adopted Joseph's sons Manasseh and Ephraim as his own, he gave Ephraim the blessing of the first born and thereby gave Ephraim preeminence over his older brother Manasseh (Gen 48:8-20). The reference to trembling when Ephraim spoke seems clearly to allude to Ephraim's dominant position over the other Israelite tribes in later times, and is illustrated most clearly by Ephraim's threats against other tribes, e.g., Manasseh/Gideon and Gad/Jephthah, when it was not given a leading role in campaigns against Israel's enemies (see Judg 8:1-3; 12:1-6). Verse 1b indicates that Israel "incurred guilt through Baal," i.e., worshiped Baal, and died. The reference in verse 2 to the construction of idols and the kissing of the calves suggests that the golden calf episode of the wilderness tradition stands behind this episode, especially since Moses called upon the Levites to kill those who worshiped the calf (Exodus 32–34). Many have suggested that the verse refers to the Baal Peor episode in which Israelite worshipers of Baal

---

[133] See Michael L. Barré, "Treaties in the ANE," *ABD* VI:653-6, esp. 654.

were killed (Numbers 25), but the primary instigator in this narrative who was slain by the priest Phineas ben Eleazar, Zimri ben Salu, was from the tribe of Simeon. Furthermore, the tradition does not highlight worship of idols but focuses on the Israelites' sexual relations with the Moabite/Midianite women instead.

The introductory particle, "and now," in verse 2 indicates that the prophet is concerned not only with past tradition, but with the present as well. The portrayal of continued sin, the construction of engraved idols from silver, etc., corresponds well to the portrayal of the golden calf at Beth El (and Dan, 1 Kgs 12:25-33) as well as that of the wilderness tradition. The reference to the kissing of the calf by the people also calls to mind the worship of Baal by the Omride dynasty of Israel, whose supporters were said to have kissed Baal (1 Kgs 19:18). The Omrides were overthrown by Jehu, who had their supporters gathered at a Temple to Baal and then burned the Temple (2 Kgs 10:18-27). Although Jehu is initially portrayed as an opponent of Baal, his later alliance with Assyria and that by his successors qualifies him as a supporter of Baal in the eyes of Hosea. The reference to "the sacrifices of Adam," mistranslated as "sacrifice to these" in the NRSV, may well refer to the bloodbath that brought Jehu to power. In any case, the prophet views Israel's idolatry as a continuing problem, and announces punishment in verse 3, which is introduced by the particle "therefore" to indicate the consequences of Israel's actions. He employs ephemeral images to convey Israel's projected passing, viz., morning mist or fog, early morning dew, chaff that blows away on a threshing floor, and smoke drifting away through a lattice. The prophet's reliance on natural images is consistent with his portrayal of YHWH as G–d of the natural world as well as of the human world.

YHWH'S ANNOUNCEMENT OF PUNISHMENT FOR ISRAEL: 13:4-14

YHWH's speech in Hos 13:4-14 takes up the theme of Ephraim's death in 13:1 to project the divine self as the source of death for Israel, insofar as YHWH will bring about the death of children coming to birth in verses 12-14. This contention is particularly important in relation to the previously mentioned worship of Baal in 13:1-3. Baal is the source of life in Canaanite religion, both in the natural and in the human worlds. Much of the mythology concerning Baal represents his overcoming of death, often portrayed as the god Mot, in order to ascend from the netherworld and to bring new life to creation. As Baal is the god of the storm or rains, the time of Sukkoth would be a time especially associated with Baal's ascent from the netherworld as symbolized by the return of the rains and the growth of new life. By claiming to be the source of death and life for Israel, YHWH claims the role conceived for Baal.

YHWH begins in verses 4-5 with a direct address to Israel. The initial self-revelation formula, "and I am YHWH your G–d, from the land of Egypt," identifies YHWH as the sustainer of Israel from the time of its formative experience as a nation in the Exodus from Egypt. Although the NRSV translates this statement with past tense verbs, "Yet I have been the L–rd your G–d," this does not convey the continuing sense of relationship between YHWH and Israel as indicated by the Hebrew which lacks any form of the verb "to be." The formula is similar to the one that introduces the Ten Commandments, "I am YHWH your G–d, who brought you out of the land of Egypt, out of the house of slavery" (Exod 20:2; Deut 5:6-7), and the various formulae that appear in priestly literature, e.g., "I am YHWH your G–d" (Lev 19:10, 34), "I am YHWH" (Lev 19:12, 14), "you/they shall know that I am YHWH" (1 Kgs 20:13; Ezek 25:7), etc. The statement functions as a means to express the identity and revelation of YHWH, and to assert that YHWH is the cause of events or statements associated with the formula. The subsequent statement, "and know no G–d but me, and besides me there is no savior," echoes the second statement of the Decalogue, "you shall have no other gods besides me" (Exod 20:3; Deut 5:7). The reference to YHWH as "savior" indicates that YHWH alone protects the people Israel from threats. The reciprocal nature of the relationship is expressed in verse 5 where YHWH states, "I knew you in the wilderness, in the land of drought." The verse expresses the tradition of YHWH's marriage to the bride Israel in the wilderness (cf. Jer 2:2-3) in that YHWH the husband "knew" Israel the bride. The image of sustenance, particularly in YHWH's claims to the role assigned to Baal, is expressed by the reference to the land of drought as YHWH provides water and food for Israel in the wilderness traditions (e.g., Exod 15:22–17:7; Numbers 11). Such assertions play upon Hosea's portrayal of YHWH as the husband who provides for his wife Israel (cf. Hos 2:3-11 [NRSV: 2:1-9]).

YHWH's speech then employs a third person perspective in reference to Israel in verses 6-8. The audience is not specified, although it is no longer Israel. Again, the Deity employs metaphors from the world of nature to express the intention to punish Israel. The initial statement in verse 6aα is difficult grammatically, but refers to YHWH's feeding Israel or pasturing them like sheep until they were full, "when they were pastured and became full." After they are full, however, "they raised their heart," i.e., they became arrogant and forgot YHWH. YHWH then lays out plans to punish Israel as a result of their forgetting YHWH in verses 7-8. The translation of the initial statement, "so I will become like a lion to them," masks a reference to the deity's name as revealed to Moses in Exodus 3. The Hebrew term *wāʾĕhî*, "and I will be," is a variant of the term *ʾehyeh*, "I am/will be," that appears in YHWH's response to Moses when he requests the divine name, *ʾehyeh ʾăšer ʾehyeh*, "I am who I am" (Exod 3:14). The term appears again in the second part of Exod 3:14 when YHWH tells Moses to say that *ʾehyeh*, "I am," has sent him to Pharaoh. This reference calls to mind YHWH's role in the Exodus in keeping with YHWH's initial statement in Hos 13:4, and thereby recalls YHWH's care for Israel at the time of the Exodus and beyond. But the message is very different here in that the deity intends to convey punishment for Israel instead. YHWH employs the metaphors of a lion and leopard who "lurk" by the side of the road in order to attack and maul those who pass by. This imagery is important for two reasons. First, the Assyrian kings frequently employ lion imagery to describe their own bravery; indeed, the statement "I will lurk" (*ʾāšûr*) constitutes a pun in Hebrew on the name "Assyria" (*ʾaššûr*). Second, the Judean royal house of David frequently employs the image of the lion for itself as the lion is the symbol of the tribe of Judah. YHWH also employs the metaphor of a bear that has lost its cubs, which makes it even more terrifying as an enraged animal that attacks those who might be responsible. The image is known in northern prophetic traditions as Elisha is said to have called out she-bears from the woods to maul boys who were mocking his baldness (2 Kgs 2:23-25). The statement, "and I will tear out the enclosure of their heart," clearly conveys the terror and threat of the situation. YHWH then returns to the imagery of the lion who will eat them there and the wild beast who will split them open. The imagery of a lion waiting by the road to maul those who come by is associated with the Beth El sanctuary, as the Judean man of G–d who condemned Jeroboam for building the Beth El altar was killed by a lion for disobeying G–d's instructions (1 Kgs 13:20-32).

YHWH then returns to a second person address style directed to Israel in verses 9-11. Verse 9 is extremely difficult grammatically, and is frequently emended so that it can be translated, "I will destroy you (*šiḥatîkā*), O Israel; who can help you?" (NRSV).[134] The verse reads literally, "He has destroyed you (*šiḥetkā*), O Israel, for in me is your help." The emendation involves only a minor repointing of the vowels, but the ancient versions apparently provide no indication that this is how the text is to be read. Some take the term *šiḥetkā* as a noun so that the verse reads, "your destruction, O Israel, is because in me is your help." Despite the difficulties, the basic intent is clear in that the verse indicates that Israel is destroyed because it has not recognized YHWH as its "help" or deliverer.

[134] See MacIntosh, *Hosea* 535–6.

The essential thrust of this statement is then applied to the issue of Israel's kingship in verses 10-11. The NRSV translates verse 10a, "where now is your king, that he may save you? Where in all your cities are your rulers of whom you have said . . . ," but this does not represent the Hebrew text accurately. The Hebrew term *ʾĕhî*, "I am," appears once again at the beginning of the verse. The NRSV understands this as a variation of the term *ʾayyēh*, "where?" but this does not account for the presence of the same term in verse 7 above. The verse should read, "I am your king, then, who will deliver you in all your cities, and (I am) your rulers/judges to whom you said, 'give to me a king and officers.'" The verse remains grammatically difficult, but it apparently represents YHWH's attempt to identify the divine self as the true power behind the king and judges of the people. YHWH's dissatisfaction with the king and other leaders of the people is quite clear, in keeping with Hosea's general condemnation of northern Israel's monarchy and leadership throughout the book. Many have noted the correspondence of verse 10b with 1 Sam 8:4-6, in which the people of Israel demand that Samuel appoint a king because his sons are unfit as judges or rulers, "appoint for us, then, a king to govern us like other nations" (1 Sam 8:5b).[135] Again, YHWH's dissatisfaction with the request for a king is evident in this context as well in that YHWH is portrayed as the "king" of the people who is now rejected (1 Sam 8:7). In the present context, YHWH reasserts the divine right to kingship because the kings chosen by the people have failed in their responsibilities. YHWH makes an ironic statement concerning the future kingship of Israel in verse 11, "I will give you a king in my anger, and I will taken (him) in my wrath." The NRSV translates this as a past tense statement in the belief that the verse refers to the Assyrian deposing of King Hoshea in 724 B.C.E. (2 Kgs 17:1-6), but the verbs are clear imperfect and therefore refer to future or incomplete action. Verse 11 is a threat, not a statement of fact, and it suggests that the next king of Israel will be the king of Assyria.

YHWH returns to a third person speech about Israel in verses 12-14. The deity employs the imagery of human childbirth to express the punishment that Israel will suffer as a result of its rejection of YHWH. In doing so, it recaps several important themes. First, is the claim over fertility and life in the natural world that is normally associated with Baal. In keeping with his role as the bringer of life in Canaanite religion, Baal promotes human childbirth. But YHWH makes it clear in this context that it is YHWH, not Baal, who decides such matters of life and death. Second, the theme recaps the birth of Hosea's/YHWH's children that introduces the book of Hosea as a whole. In the present context, Israel's

---

[135] E.g., Yee, "Hosea," 290.

children will die. Third, the theme also recaps the imagery of human childbirth in the Exodus tradition. According to Exodus 1, the Hebrew women bore numerous children despite the attempts of the Pharaoh to restrict Israelite growth and even to kill their first born males. YHWH makes it clear that things will be different this time.

The portrayal of Israel's inability to bring children to birth appears first in verse 12 in which YHWH states that Ephraim's "iniquity" is "bound up" or "hemmed in" (*ṣārûr*) and that "its sin" is "hidden." The terms "iniquity" and "sin" apparently are intended to convey the identity of the unborn children as "children of harlotry" as expressed at the beginning of the book (see Hos 1:2) whom YHWH will not allow to come to birth. Verse 13 expresses the inability of the children to be born. They are characterized as "unwise" sons because they are not able to place themselves properly in the birth channel to allow for a successful birth. Modern readers must remember that children were frequently stillborn in ancient societies, whereas now the practice of Caesarian birth ensures life for many children who would otherwise have died in antiquity. YHWH then makes the statement, "from the hand of Sheol I ransom them; from death I redeem them," which indicates YHWH's power over death, should YHWH choose to employ it. The NRSV attempts to convey this power, and YHWH's choice in the matter, by translating these statements as questions. Verse 4bα is difficult, however, in that it reads literally, "I am (*ʾĕhî*) your plagues, O Death; I am (*ʾĕhî*) your destruction, O Sheol." Again the Hebrew term *ʾĕhî* appears, which the NRSV attempts to render as "where?" But once again, the use of this term asserts that YHWH is the true source behind the power of death. This is clear in the final statement of verse 14, "compassion is hidden from my eyes," i.e., YHWH is not going to save the lives of the unborn children. They will die because YHWH has decided not to act this time.

HOSEA'S ANNOUNCEMENT OF SAMARIA'S DESTRUCTION:
13:15–14:1 [NRSV: 13:15-16]

Hosea builds upon YHWH's message of punishment against Israel in Hos 13:4-14 by announcing the impending fall of Samaria, capital of the northern kingdom of Israel. The prophet draws upon language and imagery from the Exodus tradition, sexual innuendo, the natural world, and common portrayals of the savagery of a conqueror.

The initial statement in verse 15aα^1-5, "Although he may flourish among the rushes," should read literally, "for he shall bear fruit between brothers." The difference in the translation relates to the Hebrew term *ʾaḥîm*, "brothers," which is probably an attempt at a plural rendition of the Hebrew word *ʾāḥû*, "reeds" (cf. Gen 41:18).[136] The reading, "brothers," however, is probably understood by the Masoretes as a reference to the arousal of enmity between brothers in general or between Ephraim and Judah. In any case, such an understanding of the expression would convey the emerging conflict in eighth century Syria-Israel that would eventually see the destruction of the northern kingdom. A reference to sprouting between the reeds, however, would engage the imagery of the natural world in which the winds would first stir reeds prior to demonstrating their full destructing force. An interesting twist in the tradition, this indicates a potential reference to Moses, the deliverer of the Exodus tradition, who was placed in a basket by his mother and floated down the Nile where he was found "among the reeds" *(bassûp)* by the daughter of Pharaoh (Exod 2:3). Such an allusion in the present case would indicate that in contrast to the Exodus tradition, no deliverance could be expected from Yнwн.

The following phrases in verse 15aα[6-11], "the east wind shall come, a blast from Yнwн rising from the wilderness," likewise conveys the role of the natural world in relation to the Exodus tradition. The "east wind" of "a wind from Yнwн" in the Exodus tradition dries up the Reed Sea so that Israelites are able to cross on dry land, and then reverses itself to cover the pursuing Egyptian chariotry with the waters of the sea (Exodus 14–15). Indeed, "the east wind" or "a wind from Yнwн rising from the wilderness" is a reference to the previously mentioned *hamsin* or *sharav,* a dry desert wind much like the southern California Santa Ana winds, that characteristically appear in Israel during the transition from the wet to the dry seasons. They are known for their withering dryness that threatens to kill plant life and for their sometimes destructive force as they can blow at high speeds. Insofar as Sukkoth marks the end of the dry season and the beginning of the rainy season, the *hamsin/sharav* may be normally associated with the festival. In short, Hosea employs the natural changes of the climate at Sukkoth to make his point that Yнwн will bring destruction upon the kingdom. This message appears in the last phrases of verse 15aα[12-15], "and his fountains shall dry up, his spring shall be parched." This conveys the destructive force of the east winds upon water, but it also alludes to human sexuality and fertility as "fountain" and "spring" frequently serve as metaphors for female sexuality (cf. Prov 5:18; Lev 20:18; 12:7 ("fountain," *māqôr;* and Prov 5:16; Cant 4:12, 15; Ps 87:7, "spring," *maʿyān*). Whereas the Hebrew midwives were fertile when Pharaoh tried to suppress childbirth among them, such fertility will not appear in Hosea's Israel.

[136] See MacIntosh, *Hosea*, 552.

Verse 15b applies the preceding images of destruction to the northern Israelite kingdom with a reference to the plundering of its treasuries and its valuables or "every precious thing." Such allusions to wealth obviously recall the trading alliance made by Israel with Assyria and Egypt (cf. Hos 11:5; 12:2 [NRSV: 12:1]). They also reverse the motif of Israel's plundering the Egyptians as they departed Egypt at the time of the Exodus (Exod 12:35-36).

Finally, Hos 14:1 [NRSV: 13:16] describes Samaria's impending destruction. It begins with a reference to Samaria's incurring guilt for rebellion against G–d, which recalls the motif of Israel's rebellions against YHWH in the wilderness during the time of the Exodus. The prophet then describes how Israel shall fall to the sword, how its little ones shall be dashed in pieces, and how its pregnant women shall be ripped open (cf. Hos 10:14). The imagery commonly appears in descriptions of the brutality of an oppressor (2 Kgs 8:12; Isa 13:16, 18; Nah 3:10), but in the context of the book of Hosea, it represents the final destruction of the children that are born to Israel and to Gomer.

Hosea's Appeal for Israel's Return to YHWH and Rejection of Assyria: 14:2-9 [NRSV: 14:1-8]

Hosea 14:2-9 [NRSV: 14:1-8] constitutes the culmination of the prophet's speeches in Hos 9:1–14:1 [NRSV: 9:1-13:16] in particular as well as in the book as a whole. By appealing to Israel to "return" to YHWH and to reject its alliance with Assyria, Hos 14:2-9 [NRSV: 14:1-8] recounts the primary theme of the book, rejection of YHWH in favor of relations with Assyria, and seeks its reversal. There is no explicit allusion to the marriage of Hosea and Gomer; the text is concerned fundamentally with the relationship between YHWH and Israel but various allusions to the metaphors of marriage and sexuality continue to express that relationship.

Although many past scholars have seen this passage as a secondary addition to the book from post-exilic times, more recent scholars are increasingly seeing it as the work of the prophet himself.[137] It thereby constitutes the rhetorical goal of the prophet's speeches, i.e., to convince the Israelite audience to abandon its alliance with Assyria and thereby to return to YHWH. Most of those who hold this view, however, maintain that the passage must have been composed at some time during

[137] See Göran Eidevall, *Grapes in the Desert: Metaphors, Models, and Themes in Hosea 4–14* Coniectanea biblica. Old Testament series (Stockholm: Almqvist & Wiksell, 1996) 208.

the Assyrian invasions of Israel in 733 or 724–722/1 B.C.E. as the fall of Israel has already taken place.[138] This view is based largely on the interpretation of the statement in v. 2 [NRSV: 1], "for you have stumbled in your iniquity." This verse does not describe Israel's destruction as an established fact. The verb "to stumble" is frequently employed by prophets and others as a means to charge Israel with wrongdoing, but it does not necessarily entail destruction or punishment. Rather it presents the premise on which the prophet argues his case, viz., Israel has committed iniquity and must change in order to reestablish its relationship with YHWH. The call for return makes little sense if Israel is already destroyed. There would be no nation left to repent, and the notion of a surviving remnant, commonly expressed in Isaiah, is absent in Hosea. Likewise, the statement in v. 4 [NRSV: 3] that "Assyria shall not save us" would be incomprehensible in the context of Assyrian invasion; the audience would already well know that Assyria has not come to save them. Furthermore, it does not refer to the destruction of Israel or invasion by Assyria at all. It makes a great deal of sense if the prophet argues against making or continuing an alliance with Assyria. His assertion through the mouth of the people that Assyria will not save Israel thereby points to the potential consequences of such a relationship. The setting for such an argument would be at a time when Israel's longstanding relationship with Assyria under Jehu dynasty would come into question, i.e., at the time of Shallum's assassination of Zechariah or Menahem's assassination of Shallum. An alternative setting would be at the time of Pekah's assassination of Pekahiah.

The prophet begins in Hos 14:2-4 [NRSV: 14:1-3] with his own appeal for Israel's return to YHWH. The initial imperative, *šûbâ yiśrā'ēl*, "return, O Israel," employs an emphatic imperative form to signal a new component of his message, the possibility that Israel might avoid the punishment outlined in the book. By appealing for Israel to return "to YHWH your G–d," Hosea frames the issue in explicitly theological terms although verse 4 [NRSV: 3] will make it clear that a political element is involved as well. The motivation for the appeal to return, "for you have stumbled in your iniquity," charges that the people have sinned. The reversal of such "sin" on the part of the people therefore constitutes the prophet's rhetorical goal.

Hosea continues with three further imperatives in verses 3-4 [NRSV: 2-3]. The first two are joined by a conjunctive *wāw*, "take words with you and return unto YHWH." The first statement is somewhat enigmatic because the Hebrew word *dĕbārîm* means both "words" and "things." The following statements proposed by the prophet in verses 3b-4 [NRSV:

---

[138] E.g., Davies, *Hosea*, 300–1; Wolff, *Hosea*, 234.

2b-3] apparently suggest that the people should appeal to YHWH in a liturgical context with a combination of prayers or cultic statements and sacrifices. The repeated call to "return to YHWH" suggests that such actions constitute repentance on the part of the people.

The third imperative, "say to him (YHWH)," conveys the prophet's instructions concerning the liturgical appeal for repentance on the part of the people in verses 3b-4 [NRSV: 2b-3]. There are a number of problems in this section. The first component of the statement, "take away all guilt," is an attempt to render the syntactically jumbled *kol-tiśśā' 'āwōn*, literally, "all you shall lift/forgive iniquity."[139] The term *kol*, "all," generally serves as an adjective, however, and should modify *'āwōn*, "iniquity." In the present context, however, it seems to function as an adverb. The statement, "accept that which is good," is clearly a statement to be directed by the people to YHWH as it is formulated in a masculine singular imperative. It therefore constitutes an appeal by the people to accept their offering. The statement, "and will offer the fruit of our lips," follows the LXX version and its attempt to read *pārîm*, "bulls," as *pĕrî*, "fruit," a metaphorical reference to the people's oral petitions to YHWH. The LXX misses the significance of the role of sacrifice in such petitions, however, as the Levitical laws for the expiation of sin or guilt clearly call for the petitioner to bring an animal sacrifice to the altar (see Lev 3:1-17; 4:1–5:13; 5:14-26). This is reinforced by the use of the verb *šlm*, "to repay, offer," which is frequently used to describe the presentation of a sacrifice to complete a vow (Deut 23:22; 2 Sam 15:7; Pss 50:14; 66:13). Although the syntax remains difficult, the reference to "our lips" expresses the combination of sacrifice and oral prayer or petition. Verse 4 [NRSV: 3] then expresses the heart of the issue, i.e., return to YHWH entails rejection of the Assyrians. By stating publicly that "Assyria will not save us," Hosea calls upon the people to refute publicly their alliance with the Assyrians as a condition for the restoration of their relationship with YHWH. The statement, "we will not ride upon horses," suggests that the Assyrians have called upon Israel to provide armed forces for service in the Assyrian army, a common stipulation of Assyrian treaties with subject or allied nations. The specific occasion is not mentioned, but Aram pressed continuously for allies against Assyria during the eighth century. The Assyrians would have called upon their allies such as Israel to provide troops in an effort to put down Aramean challenges, and this may well have sparked the assassination of the Jehu dynasty monarch Zechariah or the pro-Assyrian Pekahiah. Verse 4b [NRSV: 3b] returns to issues of apostasy against YHWH by referring to the people's penchant for worshiping idols and

---

[139] For discussion, see MacIntosh, *Hosea*, 561.

calling them "our G–d." Some observance of the Assyrian king or gods would be required in the process of treaty making as the gods of both nations were generally called as witnesses to the pact.[140] The final statement, "in you the orphan finds mercy," employs a common ancient near eastern motif to convey the view that YHWH, and not Assyria, is the true source of mercy and justice.[141]

The prophet then presents YHWH's projected response of acceptance to the people's appeal. In this manner, the prophet encourages the people to adopt his proposed course of action. YHWH states the basic premises of the speech in verse 5 [NRSV: 4]. The statement, "I will heal their disloyalty," employs a medical metaphor to indicate YHWH's willingness to repair the relationship with Israel. The statement, "I will love them freely," alludes to the marital metaphors that appear at the beginning of the book in order to convey YHWH's willingness to accept Israel once again. The explanatory statement, "for my anger has turned from them," can hardly be understood in the context of the Assyrian invasions of Israel in 733 and 724–722/1 B.C.E. Rather, it forms part of the effort to convince the people that a return to the relationship with YHWH is still possible.

Many interpreters have noted the affinities between the language of verses 6-8 [NRSV: 5-7] and that of the Song of Songs.[142] It focuses especially on the imagery of natural growth, flowering, and fertility, and thereby conveys a further allusion to themes of sexuality and marriage that introduce the book of Hosea. The use of tree imagery is particularly noteworthy, not only for its allusions to fertility and natural growth, but for its political symbolism as well. Ancient Assyrian iconography frequently employs the "sacred tree" as a symbol of the divine world order, and the Assyrian king is frequently portrayed alongside or in place of the tree in order to symbolize that order as well.[143] The use of such tree imagery here is intended to score a rhetorical point. By employing the Assyrians' own motifs for order and security, Hosea argues that YHWH and not Assyria is the true source of Israel's security. Under YHWH's care, Israel will flourish as a well-watered tree with its roots

---

[140] See M. L. Barré, "Treaties in the ANE," *ABD* VI:653-6.

[141] F. C. Fensham, "Widow, Orphan, and the Poor in Ancient Near Eastern Legal and Wisdom Literature," *JNES* 21 (1962) 129–39.

[142] See Landy, *Hosea,* 169–76; Yee, "Hosea," 296; Eidevall, *Grapes,* 213–8.

[143] A. Tångberg, "'I am like an evergreen fir; from me comes your fruit': Notes on Meaning and Symbolism in Hosea 14,9b (MT)," *SJOT* 3 (1989) 81–93; I. J. Winter, "The Program of the Throne Room of Ashurnasipal II," *Essays on Near Eastern Art and Archeology in Honor of Charles Kyrle Wilkinson,* ed. P. O. Harper and H. Pittman (New York: Metropolitan Museum of Art, 1983) 15–32.

and branches spread out and its fragrance apparent to all. This further underscores the premise of verses 2-4 [NRSV: 1-3], viz., that return to YHWH entails rejection of Assyria.

YHWH begins in verse 6 [NRSV: 5] by employing the simile of "dew" to describe the divine relationship to Israel. This is particularly important in relation to Baal imagery in that the dew or water in general represents Baal's efforts to provide water that will enable the earth to flourish. This is frequently expressed in sexual terms, i.e., the dew and rain represents Baal's semen that impregnates his consort, Astarte/Asherah or the earth. The simile of the "lily" (*šôšannâ*) employs an image that is fundamental to the portrayal of the maiden in Song of Songs (Cant 2:2, 16; 4:5; 6:2, 3; 7:3 [NRSV: 7:2]), so that the statement, "he shall blossom like the lily," alludes to Israel's bright future as YHWH's "bride." The imagery shifts to that of the tree in verses 6b-8aα, [NRSV: 5b-7aα] and emphasizes the imagery of the trees of "Lebanon," which were known in Israel and throughout the ancient Near East for their strength, majesty, and abundance. The prophet begins by comparing the striking of the roots of Israel to the (trees of) Lebanon, and follows by presenting the spreading shoots (*yōnĕqôtāyw*; n.b., *yōnēq* can also refer to a suckling baby) as the tree grows. The comparison of the tree to the "beauty" (*hôd*) of the olive tree employs a term that frequently describes the majesty of the king (Pss 45:4 [NRSV: 45:3]; 21:6 [NRSV: 21:5]; Zech 6:13) or YHWH (Ps 104:1; 1 Chr 29:11; Hab 3:3). The comparison of its fragrance to Lebanon returns to the initial theme of majesty, and the concluding image of people sitting in its shade conveys security, protection, and serenity (cf. Mic 4:4). The imagery then shifts back to more generalized fertility with references to the growing of grain, the blossoming of a garden, and the fragrance (lit., remembrance) like the wine of Lebanon. The combined images of olive, grain, and wine represent the three staples of agricultural production and Temple sacrifice in Israel (cf. Deut 18:4; 14:23).

The prophet's presentation of YHWH's speech concludes with a final appeal to Israel in verse 9 [NRSV: 8]. YHWH addresses Ephraim directly with a rhetorical question that asserts that YHWH has nothing to do with idols. Instead, YHWH asserts that YHWH, and not the idols, answer and look after Israel. The concluding statement once again compares YHWH to a green, leafy cypress tree that provides the fruit that Israel needs.

Concluding Exhortation to the Reader: 14:10 [NRSV: 14:9]

Hosea 14:10 [NRSV: 14:9] is not the work of the prophet, but the work of a later editor or writer who comments upon the significance of the prophet's words. The language derives from the sphere of wisdom, and it is designed to encourage the discerning reader to find YHWH's wisdom and righteousness in the work of Hosea.[144] The writer subtly appeals to the ego of the reader to identify oneself as wise, understanding, etc., in order to push an agenda that sees YHWH's actions in relation to the destruction of the northern kingdom of Israel as righteous. The fall of Israel would naturally raise the issue of theodicy, i.e., was G–d righteous in destroying the northern kingdom? By asserting that "the ways of YHWH" are "right" and that "the upright walk in them," the writer steers the reader to the conclusion that YHWH was justified and that those who sin will reach the opposite conclusion. This is clearly written by someone of great piety, but such a viewpoint may be challenged in light of the modern experience of the Shoah or Holocaust, viz., are the victims of destruction morally responsible for their suffering and deaths? The issue might be posed differently, viz., even in the face of disaster, YHWH is still there.

[144] See G. T. Sheppard, *Wisdom as a Hermeneutical Construct*, BZAW, vol. 151 (Berlin and New York: Walter de Gruyter, 1980) 129–36.

FOR FURTHER READING

COMMENTARIES

Andersen, Francis I., and David Noel Freedman. *Hosea*. Anchor Bible, 24. Garden City: Doubleday, 1980.

Davies, G. I. *Hosea*. The New Century Bible Commentary. Grand Rapids: William Eerdmans, 1992.

Jacob, Edmond. "Osée." in Edmond Jacob, Carl-A. Keller, and Samuel Amsler. *Osée–Joël–Amos–Abdias–Jonas*. Commentaire de l'ancien Testament, XIa. Geneva: Labor et Fides, 1992.

Jeremias, Jörg. *Der Prophet Hosea*. Das Alte Testament Deutsch, 24,1. Göttingen: Vandenhoeck & Ruprecht, 1983.

Landy, Francis. *Hosea*. Readings. Sheffield: Sheffield Academic Press, 1995.

MacIntosh, A. A. *Hosea*. The International Critical Commentary. Edinburgh: T & T Clark, 1997.

Mays, James Luther. *Hosea*. Old Testament Library. Philadelphia: Westminster, 1969.

Rudolph, Wilhelm. *Hosea*. Kommentar zum Alten Testament, XIII/1. Gütersloh: Gerd Mohn, 1966.

Stuart, Douglas. *Hosea–Jonah*. Word Biblical Commentary, 31. Waco: Word, 1987.

Wolff, Hans Walter. *Hosea: A Commentary on the Book of the Prophet Hosea*. Trans. Gary Stansell. Hermeneia. Philadelphia: Fortress, 1974.

Yee, Gale A. "The Book of Hosea: Introduction, Commentary and Reflections." *The New Interpreter's Bible: Volume VII: Introduction to Apocalyptic Literature, Daniel, The Twelve Prophets*, ed. Leander E. Keck et al. *The New Interpreter's Bible*. Vol. 7. Nashville: Abingdon, 1996, 195–297.

STUDIES

Balz-Cochois, Helgard. *Gomer. Der Höhenkult Israels im Selbstverständnis der Volksfrömmigkeit. Untersuchungen zu Hosea 4,-5,7.* Europäische Hochschulschriften, XXIII. Frankfurt am Main: Peter Lang, 1982.

Brenner, Athalya, ed. *A Feminist Companion to the Latter Prophets.* Sheffield: Sheffield Academic Press, 1995.

Buss, Martin J. *The Prophetic Word of Hosea.* Beiheft zur Zeitschrift für die Alttestamentliche Wissenschaft, 111. Berlin: A. Töpelmann, 1969.

Daniels, Dwight R. *Hosea and Salvation History.* Beihefit zur Zeitschrift für die alttestamentliche Wissenschaft, 191. Berlin and New York: Walter de Gruyter, 1990.

Davies, Graham I. *Hosea.* OT Guides. Sheffield: Sheffield Academic Press, 1993.

Diedrich, Friedrich. *Die Anspielungen auf die Jakob-Tradition in Hosea 12,1–13,3. Einliteraturwissenschaftlicher Beitrag zur Exegese früher Prophetentexte.* Forschung zur Bibel, 27. Würzburg: Echter, 1977.

Eidevall, Göran. *Grapes in the Desert. Metaphors, Models, and Themes in Hosea 4–14.* Coniectanea Biblica; Old Testament Series, 43. Stockholm: Almqvist & Wiksell, 1996.

Emmerson, Grace I. *Hosea: An Israelite Prophet in Judean Perspective.* Journal for the Study of the Old Testament Supplement Series, 28. Sheffield: JSOT Press, 1984.

Gelstand, A. "Kingship in the Book of Hosea," *Oudtestamentische Studiën* 19 (1974) 71–85.

Good, Edwin M., "The Composition of Hosea," *Svensk Exegetisk Årsbok* 31 (1966) 21–63.

Kuan, Jeffrey Kah-jin. *Neo-Assyrian Historical Inscriptions and Syria-Palestine.* Jian Dao Dissertation Series, 1. Hong Kong: Alliance Bible Seminary, 1995.

Kuhnigk, Willibald. *Nordwestsemitische Studien zum Hoseabuch.* Biblica et Orientalia, 27. Rome: Biblical Institute, 1974.

Naumann, Thomas. *Hoseas Erben. Strukturen der Nachinterpretation im Buch Hosea.* Beiträge zur Wissenschaft vom Alten und Neuen Testament, 131. Stuttgart: W. Kohlhammer, 1991.

Neef, Heinz-Dieter. *Die Heilstraditionen Israels in der Verkündigung des Propheten Hosea.* Beiheft zur Zeitschrift für die Alttestamentliche Wissenschaft, 169. Berlin and New York: Walter de Gruyter, 1987.

Nissinen, Martti. *Prophetie, Redaktion und Fortschreibung im Hoseabuch. Studien zum Werdegang eines Prophetenbuches im Lichte von Hos 4 und 11.* Alter Orient und Altes Testament, 231. Kevelaer: Butzon & Berker; Neukirchen-Vluyn: Neukirchener, 1991.

Nyberg, H. S. *Studien zum Hoseabuche.* Uppsala: A.-B. Lundequist, 1935.

Rowley, H. H. "The Marriage of Hosea." *Men of G–d: Studies in Old Testament History and Prophecy*. London: Thomas Nelson, 1963, pp. 66–97.

Seifert, Brigitte. *Metaphorisches Reden von G-tt im Hoseabuch*. Forschungen zur Religion und Literatur des Alten und Neuen Testaments, 166. Göttingen: Vandenhoeck & Ruprecht, 1996.

Sherwood, Yvonne. *The Prostitute and the Prophet: Hosea's Marriage in Literary-Theological Perspective*. JSOTSup Series, 212; Gender, Culture, and Theory, 2. Sheffield: Sheffield Academic Press, 1996.

Utzschneider, Helmut. *Hosea. Prophet vor dem Ende*. Freiburg: Universitätsverlag; Göttingen: Vandenhoeck & Ruprecht, 1980.

Wacker, Marie-Theres. *Figurationen des Weiblichen im Hosea-Buch*. Herders Biblische Studien, 8. Freiburg: Herder, 1996.

Yee, Gale A. *Composition and Tradition in the Book of Hosea: A Redaction Critical Investigation*. Society of Biblical Literature Dissertation Series, 102. Atlanta: Scholars Press, 1987.

JOEL

JOEL

Overview

Joel is the second book in the Masoretic version of the Book of the Twelve where it follows Hosea and precedes Amos. In the Septuagint sequence of the Twelve, it occupies the fourth position immediately following Micah and preceding Obadiah. The reasons for the variation in order are not fully understood, and they are complicated by the absence of any specific indication of historical setting in the book of Joel. Joel clearly envisions a threat against Jerusalem and Judah on the "Day of YHWH" that stems from a combination of natural elements, i.e., a plague of locusts that threatens the natural order of creation and the crops that sustain human beings in the land, and enemy nations that are prepared to assault Jerusalem. It calls upon the people of Jerusalem and Judah to repent, although it identifies no wrongdoing on their part, and projects YHWH's answer or intervention, again on the "Day of YHWH," to eliminate the threats from locusts and enemy nations so that the land and nation may be restored and secure forever.

The placement of Joel in the MT and LXX versions of the Book of the Twelve appears to be the result of the overall theological conception that informs each respective version.[1] Many argue that the LXX appears

---

[1] For discussion of the meaning and significance of the order of the Book of the Twelve in both the Masoretic and Septuagint versions of the book, see Ehud Ben Zvi, "Twelve Prophetic Books or 'The Twelve': Some Preliminary Considerations," *Forming Prophetic Literature: Essays on Isaiah and the Twelve in Honor of John D. W. Watts*, ed. J. W. Watts and P. R. House, JSOTSup, vol. 235 (Sheffield: Sheffield Academic Press, 1996) 125–56; Barry Alan Jones, *The Formation of the Book of the Twelve: A Study of Text and Canon*, SBLDS, vol. 149 (Atlanta: Scholars Press, 1995); Marvin A. Sweeney, "Sequence and Interpretation in the Book of the Twelve," paper to be published in a volume of essays on the Book of the Twelve edited by James D. Nogalski and the author. For specific discussion of Joel, see Marvin A. Sweeney, "The Place and Function of Joel in the Book of the Twelve," *Society of Biblical Literature 1999 Seminar Papers* (Atlanta: Scholars Press, 1999) 570–95; James D. Nogalski, "Joel as

to presuppose a roughly chronological order in which the eighth century prophets, Hosea, Amos, and Micah, appear first, followed by Joel, Obadiah, and Jonah, and the rest of the Twelve. But there are problems with this understanding in that a synchronic reading of the Twelve would place Amos before Hosea, insofar as Amos identifies the prophet's activities with the reigns of Jeroboam and Uzziah (Amos 1:1) whereas Hosea locates Hosea's activities in the reigns of Jeroboam, Uzziah, Jotham, Ahaz, and Hezekiah (Hos 1:1). Likewise, Joel and Obadiah may be associated with ninth century figures, such as Jehoshaphat of Judah (Joel 4:2, 12 [NRSV: 3:2, 12]; 2 Chr 20:20-26) and Elijah's associate Obadiah (1 Kgs 18:1-19). Although chronology is generally influential in the overall sequence of the Twelve in the LXX, another principle appears to take precedence which is concerned fundamentally with Israel, the nations, and Jerusalem. Hosea, Amos, and Micah are all concerned with the fate of the northern kingdom of Israel as an example for Judah; Joel, Obadiah, Jonah, Nahum, and Habakkuk are all concerned with the actions of the nations vis-à-vis Jerusalem and Judah; and Zephaniah, Haggai, Zechariah, and Malachi are concerned with the overall restoration of Jerusalem. Within the LXX sequence, Joel outlines a clear threat against Jerusalem by both nature and the nations, and it projects YHWH's actions to remove that threat. Insofar as Joel follows Hosea, Amos, and Micah (citing the latter Amos and Micah), and precedes Obadiah and the other books concerned with the nations and Jerusalem (citing Obadiah, Jonah, Nahum, and Zephaniah), Joel presents the paradigm by which Jerusalem will be threatened by the nations and ultimately restored. Such a role is bolstered by its anonymous character; the threat to Jerusalem in Joel may be read against Assyrian, Babylonian, or even Persian conquest of or hegemony over Jerusalem.

The sequence of the Masoretic version of the Twelve likewise is not based upon chronological considerations. Whereas the LXX makes clear distinctions between Israel, the nations, and Jerusalem in its ordering of the books, the MT is concerned with Jerusalem and Judah throughout. Thus Hosea points to the experience of northern Israel as an example for Judah, and Joel follows immediately with its scenario of punishment and restoration for Jerusalem on the "Day of YHWH." Again, the anonymity of the threat comes into play, but the identity of Jerusalem and Judah as the object of the threat and restoration is very clear. The balance of the MT Book of the Twelve bears this out. Amos looks to the punishment of northern Israel as an opportunity to restore the "fallen booth of David" (Amos 9:11-15); Obadiah condemns Edom for

'Literary Anchor' for the Book of the Twelve," paper to be published in a volume of essays on the Book of the Twelve edited by James D. Nogalski and the author.

its actions against Jerusalem; Jonah projects G–d's mercy for Assyria despite the threat it later poses to Israel and Jerusalem; Micah posits the fall of northern Israel as a model for the fall and restoration of Jerusalem; Nahum points to Assyria's judgment for its arrogant treatment of Jerusalem; Habakkuk calls for the punishment of Babylon for similar reasons; Zephaniah calls for the purification of Jerusalem; Haggai calls for the rebuilding of the Temple; Zechariah presents the process of Jerusalem's restoration; and Malachi calls for the final cleansing of the city. Joel cites Amos, Obadiah, Jonah, Micah, Nahum, and Zephaniah, and thereby establishes its relationship with the books that follow in the MT sequence.[2] Within the MT version of the Book of the Twelve, Joel presents the paradigm for Jerusalem's punishment and restoration as a fundamental question to be addressed within the Twelve as a whole.

Apart from his mention in Joel 1:1, nothing is known of the prophet Joel ben Pethuel. He is not named elsewhere in the Hebrew although the name Joel appears in several other contexts. Joel is the name of one of the sons of Samuel who perverted justice (1 Sam 8:2); an early descendant of Simeon (1 Chr 4:35); an early member of Reuben (1 Chr 5:4); a Gadite chief (1 Chr 5:12); the father of Heman, a Kohathite singer (1 Chr 6:18 [NRSV: 6:33]); the father of Elkanah, another Kohathite singer (1 Chr 6:21 [NRSV: 6:36]); a chief from Issachar (1 Chr 7:3); the brother of Nathan and one of David's soldiers (1 Chr 11:38); the chief of one hundred thirty Levites who bore the ark for David (1 Chr 15:7, 11); the father of Heman, one of David's Levitical singers (1 Chr 15:17); one of the Levites of the Gershom family under David and Solomon (1 Chr 23:8); the son of Jehieli who was in charge of the Temple treasury (1 Chr 26:22); an officer of the half tribe of Manasseh under David (1 Chr 27:20); a Levite in the reign of Hezekiah who helped to resanctify the Temple (2 Chr 29:12); a son of Nebo who put away his foreign wife in the time of Ezra (Ezra 10:43); a Benjaminite leader in Jerusalem under Nehemiah (Neh 11:9). The name of Joel's father, Pethuel, is otherwise unknown.

The absence of historical references in Joel makes it extremely difficult to place the book or the prophet historically.[3] Dates have been suggested which range from the ninth to the fourth centuries B.C.E. The earlier proposals associate the condemnation of Egypt with Pharaoh Shishak's campaign against Israel and Judah following the death of Solomon (1 Kgs 14:25-29) and the condemnation of Edom with the

---

[2] For discussion of the citations of other biblical texts in Joel, see Siegfried Bergler, *Joel als Schriftinterpret*, BEATAJ, vol. 16 (Frankfurt/Main: Peter Lang, 1988); Wolff, *Joel and Amos*, 10–12.

[3] For summaries of the discussion concerning the date of Joel, see Rex Mason, *Zephaniah, Habakkuk, Joel*, OT Guides (Sheffield: JSOT Academic Press, 1994) 113–6; Allen, *The Books of Joel, Obadiah, Jonah and Micah*, 19–25; Crenshaw, *Joel*, 21–9.

Edomite revolt against Jehoram (2 Kgs 8:20-22). Some have argued for a seventh-sixth century date, based upon evidence of Philistine, Greek, and Phoenician trading activity with Jews in the seventh century. Others point to the role played by Greek, Syrian, Philistine, and presumably Phoenician slave traders through the Persian and Hellenistic period (1 Macc 3:41; 2 Macc 8:11). Indeed, the majority of scholars date Joel to the fifth or fourth century B.C.E., based largely upon its literary allusions to texts that date from the late-monarchic period to the early Persian period: Isa 13:6 (Joel 1:15); Ezek 30:2-3 (Joel 1:15); Mic 4:1-4/Isa 2:2-4 (Joel 4:10 [NRSV: 3:10]); Zeph 1:14-15 (Joel 2:1-2); 2 Chr 20:20-26 (Joel 4:2, 12 [NRSV: 3:2, 12]); and the many references to Obadiah in Joel 3–4 [NRSV: 2:28–3:21] (see also the citation of Amos 1:2; 9:13 in Joel 4:16, 18 [NRSV: 3:16, 18]).

This is by no means a secure date. Trade between Seba and Israel/Judah was strong during the monarchic period, but declined in the fifth century. Edom ceased to exist during the fifth–fourth centuries as the Edomites were displaced by Nabataeans. Egypt posed no threat to Judah in the fifth-fourth centuries. It is possible that an earlier version of Joel from the late-seventh century was updated in later times to present a scenario of judgment against all the nations in the Valley of Jehoshaphat/Decision. The concerns with Egypt, Edom, Philistia, and Phoenicia are best placed in the late-seventh century, when Egypt threatened Judah's emerging sovereignty under Josiah in the wake of Assyria's collapse. During this period, Judah was interested in restoring rule over Edom and Philistia, although it was never able to achieve this aim. Phoenicia would have remained in the Egyptian orbit, and the Greeks were known to have begun trade with Phoenicia and the Philistines during the seventh century.

Joel is frequently perceived as a proto-apocalyptic book because of its anonymity and its correlation of natural and human events.[4] Indeed, its portrayal of the portents in heaven and earth at the "Day of YHWH," i.e., the darkened sun and stars, a moon turned to blood, and the pouring out of the divine "spirit" on "all flesh" prior to the judgment of the nations suggests an apocalyptic scenario. The "Day of YHWH" is well known in Israelite/Judean tradition as a day of threat against enemies and as a day of punishment against Israel or Judah (see e.g., Amos 5:18-20; Isaiah 2; 13; Zephaniah). The following commentary demonstrates that this imagery draws upon the experience of the dry east desert wind, the *Ḥamsin* or *Sharav*, that appears in Israel at the time of the transition from the dry summer season to the wet winter season, and vice versa. The effects of this wind are frequently to darken the sun and

---

[4] Otto Plöger, *Theocracy and Eschatology* (Oxford: Basil Blackwell, 1968) 96–105.

stars and to make the moon appear red as the wind blows dust and debris, blocking a view of the sky. The destructive force of the winds is taken as a demonstration of the power of YHWH to punish or to deliver the land and people of Israel. The wind both threatens crops and people, and it delivers Israel from enemy attack so that in Israelite/Judean tradition, it becomes a symbol for YHWH's punishment and restoration of Israel (Isa 27:2-13) as well as YHWH's punishment of the nations that threaten Israel (e.g., Egypt or Assyria, etc.; see Exodus 14–15; Isa 11:11-16). It is not a sign of the eschatological culmination of world history; rather, it is a recurring event in the natural cycles of the land of Israel from antiquity to the present that was understood as a symbol of YHWH's ongoing simultaneous commitment to punish wrongdoing and to protect the righteous.

Overall, the book of Joel equates the threat posed to Israel by nature, employing a locust plague to symbolize that threat (Joel 1:2-20), and by enemy nations (Joel 2:1-14). It likewise combines the world of nature and human nations when it portrays YHWH's judgment against the nations as a time when the sickle will be applied to "harvest" the soldiers of the nations and to make the wine vats overflow for their wickedness (Joel 4:9-17 [NRSV: 3:9-17]). Many scholars argue that the book does not stem from a single author, but that the earlier material in chapters 1–2 was expanded by later authors in chapters 3–4 [NRSV: 2:28–3:21].[5] Nevertheless, the present form of the book constitutes a coherent literary entity despite the potential history of its composition. The literary structure and genre of the present form of the book is based upon YHWH's response to national lamentation at a time of threat.[6] Some view Joel as an antitheocratic prophet whose eschatological viewpoint was intended to critique the Temple establishment,[7] but his use of liturgical forms and his assertion that YHWH will protect Jerusalem from outside threat indicates that he stands squarely within priestly circles,[8] perhaps as a prophetic Temple singer.[9] Following the

[5] See Mason, *Zephaniah, Habakkuk, Joel*, 103–12.

[6] For discussion of the cultic character of the book, see A. S. Kapelrud, *Joel Studies* (Leipzig: Otto Harrassowitz, 1948); G. W. Ahlström, *Joel and the Temple Cult of Jerusalem*, VTSup, vol. 21 (Leiden: Brill, 1971); G. S. Ogden, "Joel 4 and Prophetic Responses to National Laments," *JSOT* 26 (1983) 97–106.

[7] Plöger, *Theocracy*, 96–105; Wolff, *Joel and Amos*, 8–12.

[8] See Stephen L. Cook, *Prophecy and Apocalypticism: The Post-Exilic Social Setting* (Minneapolis: Fortress, 1995) 167–209, who argues that Joel is not the product of marginalized writers opposed to the Temple cult, but was written within pro-Temple priestly circles that stood at the center of post-exilic Judean society.

[9] See R. J. Tournay, *Seeing and Hearing G–d in the Psalms: Prophetic Liturgy from the Second Temple Period in Jerusalem*, JSOTSup, vol. 118 (Sheffield: JSOT Press, 1991).

superscription for the book in Joel 1:1, it comprises two basic parts. Joel 1:2–2:14 contains the prophet's calls to communal lamentation concerning both the plague of locusts (Joel 1:2-20) and the threat of enemy invasion (Joel 2:1-14). Joel 2:15–4:21 [NRSV: 2:15–3:21] contains the prophet's announcement of YHWH's response to the people, i.e., that YHWH will protect them from the threats. Joel 2:15-20 reports YHWH's response to the people. Joel 2:21–4:8 [NRSV: 2:21–3:8] reassures both nature and the people that the fecundity of the land will be restored and the nations that threaten the land will be defeated. Joel 4:9-21 [NRSV: 3:9-21] contains the prophet's call to the nations to assemble for judgment as YHWH carries out the divine promise to restore the land and nation.

The Superscription: 1:1

The superscription for the entire book of Joel appears in Joel 1:1. Superscriptions stand as structurally independent and generically distinct entities within the larger context of prophetic books in that they are designed to introduce and to identify the material that follows.[10] In the prophetic books, they generally identify the genre of the following literature, the identity of the prophet to whom the work is attributed, and the historical setting to which the work is ascribed. Joel 1:1 identifies the following material as "The word of YHWH which was unto Joel ben Pethuel." The "word of YHWH" *(dĕbar yhwh)* is a typical designation for prophetic speech or writing, although it does not employ some of the more technical terminology, such as "vision" *(ḥāzôn;* Isa 1:1; 2:1; Obad 1; Nah 1:1) or "pronouncement" *(maśśāʾ;* Isa 13:1; Nah 1:1; Hab 1:1). Joel 1:1 is the most basic form of a relatively common formulation among the superscriptions of prophetic books that appears elsewhere in Hos 1:1; Mic 1:1; Zeph 1:1; and LXX Jer 1:1. Variant forms appear in Jer 1:2; Ezek 1:3; Jonah 1:1; Zech 1:1; Hag 1:1; and Mal 1:1. The formulation appears to be a derivation from the formula, "and the word of YHWH was unto X," which frequently introduces prophetic oracles in biblical literature.

Apart from the book of Joel, nothing is known about the prophet Joel ben Pethuel. The name Joel is generally taken to mean, "YHWH is G–d," although it could also mean, "YHWH swears," derived from the root *ʾlh,* "to swear." It is the name of one of the sons of the prophet Samuel

---

[10] See Gene M. Tucker, "Prophetic Superscriptions and the Growth of the Canon," *Canon and Authority,* ed. B. O. Long and G. W. Coats (Philadelphia: Fortress, 1977) 56–70.

(1 Sam 8:2; 1 Chr 6:18[32]; 15:17), and it appears throughout Chronicles and Ezra-Nehemiah in the genealogies of Simeon (1 Chr 4:35); Gad (1 Chr 5:12); Reuben (1 Chr 5:4, 8); Isaachar (1 Chr 7:3); Manasseh (1 Chr 27:20); David's heros (1 Chr 11:38); the Levites (1 Chr 6:21[36]; 15:7, 11; 23:8; 26:22; 2 Chr 29:12), and among the contemporaries of Ezra (Ezra 10:43; Neh 11:9). The name Pethuel is otherwise unknown, although the LXX renders it as Bethuel, the father of Rebekah and nephew of Abraham (Gen 24:15). The superscription identifies no historical setting for the prophet, which complicates attempts to place the book historically, nor does it designate him as a prophet.

YHWH's Response of Mercy to Judah's Communal Complaint: 1:2–4:21 [NRSV: 1:2–3:21]

The body of the book of Joel is structurally and generically distinct from the superscription in Joel 1:1, and therefore constitutes the second major structural unit of the book as a whole. Joel 1:2–4:21 [NRSV: 1:2–3:21] is formulated as "YHWH's response to Judah's communal complaint," which employs the "call to communal complaint/lamentation," a liturgical form in which the community is summoned to the Temple or another suitable location to appeal to YHWH for deliverance at times of national crisis or threat (cf. 2 Sam 3:31; 1 Kgs 21:9, 12; Amos 5:16b; Ezra 8:21; Jonah 3:7-8; Isa 23:1-14; Jer 4:8; 6:26; 14:2-22; Psalms 44; 60; 79; 89; 2 Chr 20:3).[11] The call to complaint included summons to repentance as well (see Joel 2:12-14). Although some may distinguish a summons to complaint from a summons to repentance, repentance is inherent in the complaint as the community must present itself as righteous or willing to become so in order to appeal to YHWH. In the case of Joel, the threat is identified both in terms of a natural disaster, a locust plague that threatens the crops and well-being of the people, and a military threat that is identified with the "Day of YHWH," in which YHWH makes war against enemies (cf. Isaiah 2; 13; Amos 5:18-20). The association between the locusts and the enemy assault suggests that both identify the same threat, which takes place both in nature and in the human world (cf. the threat of locusts in Amos 7:1-3, which symbolizes the threat of enemy invasion). Such an equation between the natural and human

---

[11] Cf. H. W. Wolff, *Joel and Amos*, Hermeneia (Philadelphia: Fortress, 1977) 120–4, who identifies the call to communal lament in Joel 1:5-14, and J. L. Crenshaw, *Joel*, AB, vol. 24C (New York: Doubleday, 1995) 82, who labels Joel 1:2-20 a summons to lament and return to YHWH.

realms appears in the Exodus tradition (see esp. Exodus 15), the song of Deborah (Judges 4–5); the work of Deutero-Isaiah (Isaiah 40–55), Ezekiel, and elsewhere. Joel 1:2–4:21 [NRSV: 1:2–3:21] breaks down into three major components: 1) Joel 1:2-20, which calls the people to lament concerning the threat of the locust plague; 2) Joel 2:1-14, which calls upon the people to lament concerning the military threat of the Day of YHWH; and 3) Joel 2:15–4:21 [NRSV: 2:15–3:21], which projects YHWH's answer to the people's plea and announces that YHWH will turn back the threat by showing signs in nature and by defeating the army that threatens Jerusalem and Judah. The first section is introduced by a summons to the elders and inhabitants of the land to assemble in order to petition YHWH, and each of the subsequent sections is introduced by the formula, "Sound the Shofar (ram's horn) in Zion," which calls the people to gather at the Temple for cultic services. The first two sections highlight the threat for which the people appeal to YHWH, and the third section projects YHWH's response to the threat and deliverance of the nation.

The Call to Communal Complaint Concerning the Threat of the Locust Plague: 1:2-20

Joel 1:2-20 calls for the people to assemble at the Temple in Jerusalem in order to appeal to YHWH for deliverance from a locust plague which threatens to destroy the crops of the land and the livelihood of the nation. The passage draws heavily upon the language and themes of the locust plague narrative in the Exodus traditions (Exod 10:1-20) in an effort to present the threat posed to Jerusalem and Judah as a renewed occurrence of the ancient locust plague against Egypt, except that this time Judah and Jerusalem are the victims of YHWH's actions.[12] The structure of the passage is evident in a series of imperative verbs that introduce each major sub-unit of the passage, viz., 1:2-4, 5-7, 8-10, 11-12, and 13-20. The progression of sub-units focuses on the initial premise or threat posed by the locusts (1:2-4); the threat posed to the wine and grape crop (1:5-7); the threat posed to the people of the land and to the grain and drink offerings at the Temple (1:8-10); the threat posed to the grain crops and the trees of the land (1:11-12); and finally calls for a fast because the Day of YHWH is near (1:13-20).

---

[12] See Bergler, *Joel als Schriftinterpret*, 247–94.

THE BASIC PREMISE: THE THREAT POSED BY LOCUSTS: 1:2-4

The passage opens with an example of the "call to instruction" or "summons to hear," "Hear this, O elders, give ear, all inhabitants of the land," a typical form that is designed to call the audience's attention to a discourse that is to follow.[13] The form appears frequently in the wisdom literature to introduce the words of a parent/teacher (e.g., Prov 4:1; 7:24). The form also appears in the context of diplomatic discourse to introduce the words of an envoy (2 Kgs 18:28-29) or it may be employed by a singer to introduce a song (Judg 5:3). It appears especially frequently in the prophetic literature to introduce an oracular speech by a prophet (e.g., Hos 4:1; Amos 3:1; Mic 6:1; Isa 1:10; Ezek 6:3). In the present case, it is directed to the "elders" and "all the inhabitants of the land." No kings or other national leaders are mentioned. Many have speculated that this indicates a setting in the post-exilic period when the monarchy had ceased to function. It appears to be a summons to the people at large, regardless of the status of their leadership. The mention of the elders appeals to the leaders of the people of the local village or town level, although it should be noted that the elders of the people are often assembled to make major decisions, such as the selection of a king (2 Sam 5:1-5), or to represent the people before G–d or political authorities (e.g., Exod 24:9-18; Ezra 5:9; 6:8, 14). The term, "inhabitants of the land," calls to the people of Jerusalem and Judah in general.

The prophet then employs a rhetorical question in verse 2b to heighten the importance of the situation to his audience, "has such a thing happened in your days or in the days of your ancestors?" The answer is obviously "no," but the asking of the question functions as a rhetorical means by which the prophet asserts that such an event has never taken place before. He further heightens the point in verse 3 by calling on the audience to tell their children about this event so that their children will in turn pass the story on to their children and to succeeding generations. In this regard, the prophet employs a motif commonly associated with the Exodus traditions, i.e., to tell your children what YHWH has done (Exod 12:26-27; 13:8, 14; Deut 6:20-23; cf. Deut 4:9; 6:6-7).

Finally, the prophet states the major premise of his speech in verse 4, viz., the locusts are devouring the crops of the land and thereby threaten destruction. Locusts are a regular occurrence in Israel during the spring, generally sweeping through north Africa, the Sinai peninsula, and on into Israel itself where they lay eggs from which even

[13] See Wolff, *Joel and Amos*, 20; idem, *Hosea*, 65–6.

more locusts hatch.[14] The prophet seems to employ terminology that refers to the various stages of a locust's growth: "the cutting locust" (*gāzām*; literally, "biter, chewer") may refer to a young locust prior to full maturity; "the swarming locust" (*ʾarbeh*; literally, "multiplier") designates the locust in full maturity; "the hopping locust" (*yeleq*; probably, "jumping") designates hatched larva that still lacks wings; and "the destroying locust" (*ḥāsîl*; probably, "finishing") designates larva that are just beginning to develop wings. Swarms of locusts are known to fill the skies like a cloud, and such swarms are capable of bringing economic ruin and starvation on an agrarian population that must produce crops in order to survive.

When read in relation to the Book of the Twelve as a whole, the locust imagery seems to anticipate that of Amos 7:1-3, which portrays a locust plague devouring the entire land of Israel. There is no lexical correspondence between the two passages, however, which suggests that the relationship between them is thematic and constituted only by literary placement.

THE THREAT TO THE GRAPE HARVEST AND WINE: 1:5-7

Having stated the basic premise, the prophet then turns to the specific effects of the locust plague, viz., the destruction of the grape crop and the wine that is produced. Grapes (and wine) were part of the staple Israelite crop and diet in antiquity as grapes and wine are included among the three first fruit offerings that are due to YHWH annually at the Temple (see Deut 14:22-23; 18:3-4; cf. Exod 23:19; 34:26). The prophet begins with a series of imperatives that call upon those who drink wine to wake up, weep, and wail. The tone is somewhat mocking as he indicates that they are "drunkards" (verse 5) who perhaps do not realize what is happening to them on account of their preoccupation with wine. The characterization of a prophet's audience as blinded or ignorant drunks likewise appears in Isa 5:8-24; 28:1-29; and Zeph 1:12-13 where it also provides a means to chastise the audience and motivate them to action. The reference to the cutting off of "sweet wine" (*ʿāsîs*) employs the term that is derived from the root *ʿss*, "to press, crush," and is commonly used in reference to the grape juice that is freshly pressed from the grapes. The term thereby evokes images of the gathering and first pressing of grapes at the harvest when the success or failure of the growing season will be apparent to all.

---

[14] For a discussion of locusts in general and their representation in the ancient Near East and Israel, see Y. Palmoni, "Locust," *IDB* III:144-8.

The reason for the call to the "drunks" is apparent in verse 6, which equates the locust plague with a military invasion of the land. Y<small>HWH</small> is apparently the speaker here as the verse refers to the "nation" that has come up against "my land." The metaphor of the locusts therefore establishes a relationship between a threat to the natural growth of the land and the threat posed by a strong and numerous nation. The link is not only metaphorical, however, as ancient armies lived off the land of the nations that they invaded, swarming over the fields and vineyards like locusts and devouring everything in sight (cf. the portrayal of the Assyrian invasion of Israel in Isa 7:18-25). The metaphorical portrayal of the enemy nation continues in verse 6b which compares them to a lion with fangs. Verse 7 explicitly mentions the ruin of the vineyards and fig trees, which may be attributed either to locusts or to an enemy army (n.b., Deut 20:19-20, which prohibits Israelite warriors from destroying the tree of a land that they attack in order to preserve the capacity of the land to provide food for its inhabitants). It also recalls the imagery of Y<small>HWH</small>'s ruined vineyard in Isa 5:1-7. Finally, the imagery of stripped bark and whitened shoots recalls the effects of a locust plague on the vines, and no doubt is an image with which the ancient audience was quite familiar.

THE THREAT TO THE PEOPLE OF THE LAND
AND THE OFFERINGS AT THE TEMPLE: 1:8-10

The prophet next addresses the people metaphorically as a "virgin" dressed in sackcloth who wails at the loss of her husband. The initial imperative *ʾĕlî*, "wail!" is a feminine singular imperative form that establishes the metaphorical presentation of the people as a virgin. A great deal of ink has been spilled, largely by male commentators, over the use of the term *bĕtûlâ*, "virgin," for a woman who mourns the loss of her husband.[15] Some argue that the term actually designates a young woman who is not technically a virgin, and many note the designation of Anat, the Canaanite goddess of passion, the hunt, and war, as *btlt*, "virgin," in Ugaritic poetry even though she clearly is not a virgin. Others note Deut 22:23-24, which prescribes penalties against a man who lies with a "betrothed woman" who is a virgin. Because she is treated as a married woman for whom the bride price is not yet paid and the marriage is not yet consummated (cf. Deut 20:7), the reference to a virgin who mourns her dead husband can be considered as a reference to a betrothed woman. It is noteworthy that Judg 21:15-24 refers to a Benjaminite

[15] For a summary of the discussion, see Crenshaw, *Joel*, 97–8.

practice at the Shiloh sanctuary in which the young men would hide at the time of the grape harvest (viz., the festival of Sukkoth or Booths) in order to wait for the maidens who would dance in the vineyards and take them as their brides. Although the imagery is one of complete spontaneity, some of these unions were undoubtedly planned beforehand by the couples involved, and perhaps even by their families, so that a betrothal would have been possible in anticipation of a marriage at Sukkoth. Such a scenario might well explain the association between wine and a virgin mourning her young husband; whereas Sukkoth was a time of celebration for the harvest of grape and wine and the making of marriage, the locust plague and the invasion by a foreign nation turns it into a time of mourning. As Sukkoth is the time of the onset of the fall rains, it is also possible that some sort of mourning ritual might be associated with the festival in Canaanite religious practice. Baal, the Canaanite god of rain and storm, is mourned by women when he descends into the netherworld during the dry season of the land of Israel. Such mourning by women brings him back to life at the beginning of the rainy season so that the crops will grow for another year. This is expressed in mythology when he is rescued from the netherworld by Anat or another goddess figure (see the Sumerian myth of Inanna's descent to the netherworld to rescue Dumuzi and the Babylonian descent of Ishtar to rescue Tammuz).[16]

Verse 9 turns to the consequences of invasion, whether by locusts or by enemy nations, and mourning for the Temple. In times of economic want and poor crops, both the grain and drink offerings for the Temple will be cut off. Ancient Judean tithing practice calls for a tenth of all the nation's crop of grain, wine, and oil to be offered at the Temple as a form of tax that supports the priesthood and the state at large (Lev 27:30-33; Num 18:8-32, esp. 12; Deut 14:22-29; 18:1-8; 26:1-15).[17] As the priests and Levites do not hold land of their own, the tithes and other offerings at the Temple constitute their primary source of support; when the land and people suffer, so do the Temple and its priests. This is made very clear in verse 10 which notes the devastation of the land, and specifically refers to the devastation of grain, wine, and oil.

THE THREAT TO THE GRAIN CROP: 1:11-12

The prophet addresses the farmers and vintners once again in Joel 1:11-12 with the imperatives, "be dismayed" (literally, "be ashamed")

---

[16] See W. J. Fulco, "Ishtar," *ABD* III:521-2; *ANET* 52–7, 106–9; D. Wolkstein and S. N. Kramer, *Inanna, Queen of Heaven and Earth* (New York: Harper & Row, 1983).

[17] See M. Weinfeld, "Tithe," *Encyclopaedia Judaica* 15:1156-62.

and "wail." The choice of the term "be ashamed" *(hōbîšû)* may be intended as a pun on *hôbîš,* "(the wine) dries up," in verse 10. The basic categories of grain, wheat and barley are listed as the crops (literally, "harvest") of the field that are ruined. Verse 12 returns to the previously mentioned grapevine and fig tree (see verse 7). It then specifies the various fruit trees that are destroyed, "pomegranate," "(date) palm," and "apple." The description of the trees is similar to those mentioned by the spies that Moses sent into the land of Canaan, i.e., grapes, figs, and pomegranates (Num 13:23). The final statement of verse 10 emphasizes that the destruction of grain and fruit coincides with the destruction of "joy" among "the sons of Adam," i.e., human beings suffer at the loss of the crops.

APPEAL FOR FASTING AND MOURNING ON THE DAY OF YHWH: 1:13-20

The prophet sums up his call for a communal complaint concerning the locust plague by appealing to the priests and the people to fast and mourn at the approach of the Day of YHWH. Although the Day of YHWH is generally believed to be a day of celebration for YHWH's beneficence and protection of Israel or Judah from enemies, prophetic tradition in general tends to present it as a day of threat against Israel and Judah in which YHWH comes to attack the people on account of some wrongdoing rather than to protect them from threat (cf. Amos 5:18-20; Isaiah 2; 13; Zeph 1:2–2:3).[18] The passage does not refer to any sin or wrongdoing on the part of the people, however, and the cause of the threat must remain unexplained. Such a contention can be very problematic theologically because it fails to identify a cause, but it does correspond well to the realities of human existence in which catastrophe frequently comes upon people without moral reason.

The prophet begins with a sequence of imperative commands addressed to the priests that call upon them to put on sackcloth and mourn. Sackcloth is a very crude and course cloth that is worn at times of mourning in ancient Israelite and Judean culture (see Gen 37:34; 2 Sam 3:31; 1 Kgs 21:27; Jer 4:8; 6:26; 49:3) in order to symbolize the mourner's removal from normal society and pursuits as well as his/her downcast status as the result of death. It is particularly significant that the priests are called upon to don sackcloth as their normal dress for service on the altar is white linen and other accouterments (Exodus 28), and priests are not normally permitted to mourn for the dead as

---

[18] For discussion of the "Day of YHWH" traditions, see R. H. Hiers, "Day of the L–rd," *ABD* II:82-3; A. J. Everson, "Day of the L–rd," *IDB[S]* 209–10.

death compromises their purity and holy status (Lev 21:10-12; 10:4-7; Numbers 19). The seriousness of the threat is accentuated not only by the behavior of the priests, but by the cause of their mourning, viz., the catastrophe has reached such proportions that the normal Temple ritual, the presentation of grain and drink offerings, is disrupted. Insofar as the Temple and its service symbolize the stability of creation, all creation has come to a halt.

The prophet's second set of imperatives follows immediately in verse 14 and is likewise directed to the priests. He calls upon them to "sanctify a fast," i.e., to declare a fast day or a day of mourning, and to "call a solemn assembly *(ʿǎṣārâ)*." The term *ʿǎṣārâ*, "solemn assembly," is derived from the root *ʿṣr*, "to stop, restrain, retain," and signifies the cessation of all normal activities for the purpose of cultic observance (Lev 23:36; Num 29:35; Deut 16:8; Isa 1:13; Neh 8:18). It frequently refers to standing festivals, such as the last day of Maṣṣot/Passover (Deut 16:8) or Sukkoth (Lev 23:36; Num 29:35), but no specific holiday is named here. The purpose of the fast is to gather the entire people, elders and inhabitants of the land, to lament to G–d in the current crisis.

The lamentation proper appears in verses 15-20 in which the prophet speaks on behalf of the people to outline the sufferings of the people on the Day of YHWH. He begins with the interjection, "alas *(ʾǎhāh)* for the day!" which employs the standard particle employed in situations of mourning or lamentation (Josh 7:7; Jer 4:10; 14:13; Ezek 4:14; 9:8) or shock and surprise (Judg 6:22; 11:35; 2 Kgs 3:10), and thereby constitutes an appropriate introduction to a lament. The basis for the lamentation is identified by the causative *kî* in verse 15b, "because *(kî)* the day of YHWH is near," which employs language typical to the announcement of the approaching Day of YHWH (Zeph 1:7, 14; Isa 13:6; Ezek 30:2-3). The second element of this statement, "and as destruction from the Almighty it comes," employs a pun on the words *šōd*, "destruction," and the divine name *šadday*, "Shaddai, the Almighty" (cf. Gen 17:1; 28:3; 35:11) to make its point that YHWH is the source of the calamity. The prophet underscores the point that catastrophe has arrived with a rhetorical question in verse 16 that asserts that the disaster is right "before our eyes," i.e., food is cut off from the Temple together with joy and celebration. He then specifies the losses in verse 17, viz., seeds die in the clods of earth, and as a result of the inability of plants to grow, the storehouses and granaries are empty for lack of grain. He then turns in verse 18 to the animals on which the people depend, viz., the animals groan, cattle wander about aimlessly for lack of pastureland, and the flocks of sheep are destroyed (literally, "incur guilt, are wasted"). The use of the *niphal* form of the root *ʾšm*, "to incur guilt, be wasted," indicates the moral ambiguity of the situation, those who suffer must be guilty, but the passage does not identify the sin of the people (or the sheep!) that caused this calamity.

The prophet concludes the lament with his own appeal to G–d in verse 19, "Unto you, O Yнwн, I cry!" and follows up with a metaphorical depiction of a wilderness or steppe land ravaged by fire, in which all the pasturage and trees are destroyed. Such a phenomenon occurs periodically in Israel during the dry summer season when dead and shriveled vegetation easily catches fire. The imagery also anticipates Amos's second vision in Amos 7:4-6, in which he sees fire devouring the entire land. The lack of rain and fertility also affects the animals, whom the prophet depicts as "panting after" (*ᶜrg*) Yнwн, because all the streams of water have dried up and fire consumes the pastureland. At this point, the issue is not only a locust plague; all creation has come to a halt.

The Call to Communal Complaint
Concerning the Threat of Invasion: 2:1-14

The second major component of the prophet's oracles is his call to communal complaint concerning the threat of invasion in Joel 2:1-14. This is clearly the human counterpart to the natural threat of locust plague in Joel 1:2-20, and demonstrates the inseparable link between natural and human events in the prophet's perspective concerning the impending "Day of Yнwн." The passage falls into two major structural components, each of which begins with the prophet's quotation of a statement by Yнwн followed by the prophet's own statements. Thus, verses 1-11 comprise a theophanic portrayal of the threat posed to the land by Yнwн's invading army, including statements by both Yнwн (v. 1a) and the prophet (verses 1b-11), and verses 12-14 comprise the call to appeal to Yнwн by both Yнwн (verses 12-13aα) and the prophet (verses 13aβ-14).

THEOPHANIC PORTRAYAL OF THE THREAT POSED
TO THE LAND BY YHWH'S ARMY: 2:1-11

The portrayal of Yнwн's invading army begins with Yнwн's own statement of warning in verse 1a to "Blow the trumpet in Zion; sound the alarm on my holy mountain!" The first person pronoun in the reference to "my holy mountain" demonstrates that Yнwн is the speaker. When read together with the parallel expression "Zion," it demonstrates that the speech is set in the Jerusalem Temple. The blowing of

the "trumpet" or Shofar (*šôpār*, literally, "ram's horn") frequently signals a call to war or approaching danger (Hos 8:1; Judg 3:27; 6:34; 7:8,
16), but it also signals a call to cultic observance at the Temple (Lev 25:9;
Pss 47:6 [NRSV: 47:6]; 81:4 [NRSV: 81:3]; 98:6; 150:3; 2 Chr 15:14). In the
present instance, it presupposes both the threat of the Day of YHWH and
the call to appeal liturgically to YHWH for respite.

The prophet then provides an extended description of the threat
posed to the land by the "Day of YHWH," employing characteristic elements of theophany, which combine the motif of cosmic upheaval and
the imagery of military invasion to portray YHWH's approach.[19] Other
examples of theophanic texts appear in Hab 3:3-12; Nah 1:2-6; Pss 97:2-
5; 114:3-7; and Judg 5:4-5. The description begins with the trembling of
all the inhabitants of the land at the approaching "Day of YHWH,"
which indicates the rhetorical interest in provoking a sense of fear and
awe of the Deity in the audience. The statement that the "Day of YHWH
is coming, it is near . . ." resembles that of other descriptions of the
day in Isa 13:6 and Zeph 1:14.[20] Indeed, the portrayal of the day as one
of "darkness" (*ḥōšek*), "gloom" (*ʾăpēlâ*), "clouds" (*ʿānān*), "thick darkness" (*ʿărāpel*), and "blackness (*šaḥar*) spread over the mountains" recalls the language of storm and dark cloud that is characteristic of Zeph
1:15-16 as well as other theophanic descriptions (e.g., Exod 19:16; Isa
8:20–9:1). The imagery likewise conveys a sense of awe and power, and
it appears to be replicated in the holy of holies of the Jerusalem Temple
by use of incense clouds and the veil that shields out light (cf. 1 Kgs 8:1-
13; Isaiah 6). The statement, "a great and powerful army comes" (literally, "a people, great and strong"; *ʿam rab wĕʿāṣûm*) establishes the
character of the threat as an invading army (cf. Isaiah 13; Habakkuk 3),
and verse 2b indicates that nothing comparable has ever been seen in
the past or will ever be seen in the future. This leads to a portrayal of
fire both preceding and following the army, a common motif in ancient
Near Eastern mythology which often portrays fire, plagues, or other
calamities preceding and following an enemy force or cosmic threat.[21]

---

[19] For a full discussion of theophany, see Jörg Jeremias, *Theophanie. Die Geschichte
einer alttestamentlichen Gattung*, WMANT, vol. 10 (Neukirchen-Vluyn: Neukirchener,
1965); cf. M. A. Sweeney, *Isaiah 1-39*, 541; T. Hiebert, "Theophany in the OT," *ABD*
VI:505-11.

[20] For a discussion of the relation between Joel 2:1-11 and Isaiah 13, see Wolff, *Joel
and Amos*, 47. For a more detailed discussion of Joel's dependence on Isaiah 13 and
Zephaniah in relation to the "Day of YHWH" motif, see Bergler, *Joel als Schriftinterpret*,
131–69.

[21] See for example the portrayal of the advance of the gods who bring about the
flood in the Gilgamesh epic; *ANET* 94; cf. Thomas W. Mann, *Divine Presence and
Guidance in Israelite Traditions* (Baltimore: Johns Hopkins University Press, 1977).

The devastation is emphasized by the portrayal of the land "like the garden of Eden" (see Genesis 2) prior to the army's approach and "like a desolate wilderness" from which nothing escapes after it has passed.

The imagery turns to horses and chariotry, another common motif in theophanic texts (Hab 3:8; Ps 68:17), in verses 4-6. The expression, "they have the appearance of" (literally, "like the appearance of") recalls similar language in Ezekiel 1 (e.g., Ezek 1:26, "like the appearance of sapphire stone"). The images of "horses," "war horses" (cavalry), and "the sound of chariotry" on the mountains leads the reader back into the images of fire that devours stubble (cf. verse 3) and "a powerful army" (literally, "a strong people," cf. verse 2) with which the passage began. The reaction of the victims employs the verb *ḥwl*, "to whirl, writhe (in pain), tremble, wait anxiously," which also appears in Isa 13:8 to describe the victims of the "Day of YHWH" as writhing in pain like a woman in labor. The flushed or reddened *(pāʾrûr)* faces of the victims likewise recall the burning faces of the victims in Isa 13:8.

Following the approach of horses and chariotry, verses 7-10 describe the invading forces as they climb over the walls and through the windows and otherwise ravage the city that is under assault. Verse 7a describes the rush of infantry during the assault, and their attempts to scale the walls of the city. Verse 7b conveys the unrelenting nature of the enemy columns as they move in rank, and do not abandon their formations. The statement, "they do not swerve from their paths," reads literally, "they do not pledge their paths." The use of the verb *ʿbṭ*, "to pledge,"[22] indicates that the enemy soldiers do not pay someone else to take their position in the ranks, i.e., they have no fear and do not seek to escape the devastating effects of a frontal assault on a fortified city which would inevitably cost the lives of many attacking soldiers (cf. 2 Sam 11:14-25). Verse 8 continues the portrayal of the disciplined and unflinching movement of the attacking soldiers as they overwhelm the defenses of the city and march through the weapons, i.e., spears, arrows, and other projectiles, intended to stop them. The statement, "and (they) are not halted," employs the verb *bṣʿ*, "to break off," which also means "to take a bribe, unrighteous gain," and further suggests that the attacking soldiers will spare no one, even if the victims offer to pay for their lives. Verse 9 describes the sacking and looting of the city as the invading troops run upon the walls and climb up on the houses and through the windows like thieves. Verse 10 recalls the cosmic dimensions of the "Day of YHWH" with reference to the quaking earth, trembling heaven, and the darkened sun, moon, and stars. All creation

---

[22] Terms derived from the root *ʿbṭ* are normally used in reference to a pledge made to guarantee a loan, e.g., Deut 15:6; 24:10-13.

responds to the assault as the passage returns to the initial imagery of darkness (cf. verses 1b-2a).

Finally, verses 1-11 close with a portrayal of YHWH's cry to the divine army, summoning it to war, in verse 11aα. The three succeeding *kî*, "because," clauses provide the reasons for YHWH's cry with its anticipation of victory: because YHWH's army (literally, "camp") is numerous; because those who carry out YHWH's command are numberless; because the "Day of YHWH" is great and terrible. The concluding rhetorical question, "who can endure it?" sums up the reason for YHWH's victory, viz., the preceding theophany portrays an overwhelming assault that no one can withstand.

THE CALL TO APPEAL TO YHWH FOR MERCY: 2:12-14

As YHWH's army is poised to strike in the preceding pericope, verses 12-14 offer the audience a chance to "return" to YHWH and thereby avoid the projected consequences of the "Day of YHWH." The passage identifies no crime or sin from which the people might return; it simply presupposes that if YHWH is ready to strike, the people must have done something to deserve such a terrible punishment. Such a theology can be very problematic as the modern experience and theological discussion of the Shoah demonstrates.

The prophet presents YHWH's appeal to the audience to return in verses 12-13aα. The oracular formula, "says YHWH" (*nĕ'ūm yhwh*, literally, "utterance of YHWH"), identifies the prophet as the speaker who quotes a statement by YHWH. The statement begins with the adversative conjunctive phrase, "yet even now" (*wĕgam 'attâ*), which demonstrates that the following statements presuppose the situation portrayed in the preceding pericope but that an alternative is now at hand even as the assault is set to begin. The initial statement of YHWH's last minute appeal to the people, "return to me (*šubû 'ādî*) with all your heart," borrows language from Deuteronomic and Deuteronomistic formulations calling for repentance or a return to YHWH (Deut 30:10; 1 Sam 7:3; 1 Kgs 8:48; 2 Kgs 23:25), but the fundamental call for return appears in prophets such as Hosea (Hos 3:5; 14:2), Amos (Amos 4:6-11, which contains five instances of the formula, "'and you did not return to me,' utterance of YHWH" [*wĕlō' šabtem 'āday nĕ'ūm yhwh*], analogous to that of Joel 1:12), and Jeremiah (Jer 3:10; 24:7). YHWH specifies that the return should be made with "fasting," "weeping," and "mourning," thereby recalling the motifs of Joel 1:13-14. Verse 13a plays upon the reference to "returning with all your heart" by specifying that the people should tear their hearts, not their garments. The tearing of garments is a characteristic sign of mourning (2 Sam 3:31), but Y‌HWH's call to tear the heart attempts to reach the innermost depths of being among those in the audience. Many commentators take this as a warrant to charge ancient Judean mourners with empty ritualism,[23] but this charge is heavily laden with NT theological polemics against Jews and entirely misses the point of an action that is taken to express the grief within. Y‌HWH's words are intended to convey the reality of mourning, not charge those who mourn with hypocrisy.

The prophet resumes with his own appeal to return to Y‌HWH in verses 13aβ-b as indicated by the third person references to Y‌HWH. Again, the appeal identifies no sin on the part of the people, but the basis for the appeal is expressed through the statement, "for he is gracious and merciful, slow to anger and abounding in steadfast love, and relents from punishing." This in fact reflects the reality of a great deal of suffering in the world for which no cause is ever known or identified. Rather than appeal to a notion of divine justice for relief, the prophet cites the well-known formula spoken at the time of Y‌HWH's self-revelation to Moses in Exod 34:6-7,

> Y‌HWH, Y‌HWH, a G–d merciful and gracious, slow to anger, and abounding in steadfast love and faithfulness, keeping steadfast love for the thousandth generation, forgiving iniquity and transgression and sin, yet by no means clearing the guilty, but visiting the iniquity of the parents upon the children and the children's children, to the third and the fourth generation.[24]

Joel 2:13b is one of eight clear citations of this formula (see also Num 14:18; Pss 86:15; 103:8; 145:8; Nah 1:3; Jonah 4:2; and Neh 9:17, 31b). Although this formula was frequently reinterpreted to emphasize Y‌HWH's justice (see Deut 5:9-10; 7:9-10; Nah 1:2-3), the present formulation eliminates the references to punishment in Exod 34:6-7 in order to highlight divine mercy. The five qualities listed include "graciousness" (*ḥannûn*), which refers to the concern shown by a superior to an inferior (Exod 22:26) [NRSV: 22:27]; "merciful" (*raḥûm*), which is based on the Hebrew word for "womb" (*reḥem*) and indicates parental love; *ʾerek ʾappayim*, "slow to anger," or literally, "long of anger"; "abounding in steadfast love" (*rab-ḥesed*), which refers to fidelity or loyalty; and "relents from punishment" (*niḥām ʿal hārāʿâ*), literally, "be sorry over evil" or "forgiving wrong action." Given the lack of cause for the terrible punishment that is described in Joel, this is appropriate as mercy,

[23] Wolff, *Joel and Amos*, 49; Crenshaw, *Joel*, 135.

[24] For discussion of this issue, see Crenshaw, *Joel*, 135–8; Michael Fishbane, *Biblical Interpretation in Ancient Israel* (Oxford: Clarendon, 1985) 335–50.

rather than justice, is the basis on which the people might make an appeal. The formulation in Joel is identical to that in Jonah 4:2, and it is noteworthy that Jonah also focuses on the issue of divine mercy in relation to justice.[25]

The uncertainty or arbitrariness of the punishment is highlighted by the prophet's concluding question in this pericope, "Who knows whether he will not turn and relent . . .?" The question, "who knows?" is rhetorical in that nobody knows what G–d will do (cf. the use of the question in 2 Sam 12:22; Jonah 3:9; Ps 90:11; Qoh 2:19; 3:21; 8:1; Esth 4:14), and it functions in a manner similar to that of the Hebrew particle *ʾulay*, "perhaps" (see Amos 5:15). Basically, the prophet argues to the audience that they have nothing to lose as the certainty of punishment is clear even if its cause is not. Repentance, a grain offering, and a libation to YHWH may well result in YHWH's leaving a blessing in place of an assault.

The Prophet's Announcement of YHWH's Response to Protect People from Threats: 2:15–4:21 [NRSV: 2:15–3:21]

Following upon the presentation of the summons to communal complaint concerning the locust plague and the invasion of the land, the prophet announces YHWH's response to the people in Joel 2:15–4:21 [NRSV 2:15–3:21]. The entire unit constitutes an announcement of deliverance to the people in that it proclaims that YHWH will restore the natural fertility and bounty of the land and defeat the invaders who threaten its security. Most interpreters view the structure of this unit somewhat differently in that Joel 2:15-17 is frequently seen as the conclusion to the previous unit because it calls upon the people to gather at the Temple for a fast, whereas the material beginning in Joel 2:18 focuses specifically on YHWH's response.[26]

Several factors call for a reconsideration of this view. First, the initial calls in Joel 2:15-17 to "Blow the trumpet (Shofar) in Jerusalem," "sanctify a fast," and to "gather the people, . . . assemble the aged/elders," take up not only the initial call of Joel 2:1, "Blow the trumpet (Shofar) in

---

[25] For a study of the interrelationship between Joel and Jonah, see Bergler, *Joel als Schriftinterpret*, 213–45.

[26] For discussion of the structure of Joel, see Crenshaw, *Joel* 29–34; Leslie Allen, *The Books of Joel, Obadiah, Jonah and Micah*, NICOT (Grand Rapids: Eerdmans, 1976) 39–43.

Zion," but elements from Joel 1:2-20 as well, i.e., "Hear this, O elders/ aged, give ear, all inhabitants of the land" (1:2) and "Sanctify a fast, call a solemn assembly. Gather the elders/aged and all the inhabitants of the land" (1:14). Joel 2:15-17 does not simply provide a rhetorical inclusio for Joel 2:1-14, but it recalls elements from Joel 1:2-20 as well. Second, in recalling elements from the previous units of the book, Joel 2:15-17 does not simply sum up the preceding text, but it looks forward as well so that it constitutes an introduction to the following material. It does not call the people together for the purpose of lamentation; that has already been accomplished in Joel 1:2-20 and 2:1-14. Rather, it calls the people together so that they may hear YHWH's answer to their complaint in Joel 2:18–4:21 [NRSV: 2:18–3:21]. Whereas Joel 2:1-14 announced the "Day of YHWH" as a day of coming threat to the people, the question posed to YHWH in Joel 2:15-17 points to YHWH's anticipated action to deliver the people from threat, viz., "Spare your people, O YHWH, and do not make your heritage a mockery, a byword among the nations. Why should it be said among the people, 'Where is their G–d?'" Furthermore, the beginning of the announcement of YHWH's response in Joel 2:18 is linked syntactically to Joel 2:15-17 by a *waw-consecutive* construction, "Then YHWH became jealous for his land and had pity on his people . . ." The material beginning in Joel 2:18 is meant to be read together with 2:15-17, whereas the disjunctive imperatives in Joel 2:15-17 indicate that it is the beginning of a new unit. Finally, Joel 2:1-14 concludes with the request to "return" to YHWH and the speculation that YHWH will show mercy for such a request. Joel 2:15–4:21 [NRSV: 2:15–3:21] comprises precisely such an attempt to appeal to YHWH for mercy together with YHWH's answer.

A succession of syntactically disjunctive introductory imperatives in Joel 2:15-16; 2:21-22; and 4:9-11 [NRSV: 3:9-11] define the three major sub-units of this text. Joel 2:15-20 reports YHWH's response to the people's plea for mercy. Joel 2:21–4:8 [NRSV: 2:21–3:8] reassures the land and animals as well as the people of Zion that YHWH will restore fecundity to all creation and deliver the nations from its foreign oppressors. Joel 4:9-21 [NRSV: 3:9-21] contains the prophet's call to the nations to assemble themselves at the Valley of Jehoshaphat for YHWH's judgment, which in turn will lead to the restoration of fertility in the natural world together with Judah's and Jerusalem's eternal security.

YHWH's Response to the People's Appeal for Mercy: 2:15-20

Joel 2:15-20 presents YHWH's response to the people's appeal for mercy. It contains two major components. Joel 2:15-17 comprises the prophet's summons of the people to a cultic assembly at the Temple so that they might petition YHWH to deliver them from the power of the nations. Joel 2:18-20 contains the report of YHWH's response to the petition indicating the intention to provide the people with crops and to deliver them from an oppressor who comes from the north.

Joel 2:15-17 begins with a series of imperatives in verses 15-16a that call upon the entire people to assemble for a cultic occasion. The first, "blow the trumpet in Zion," calls for the blowing of the ram's horn or Shofar, which is a standard signal to the people to assemble either for cultic assembly or for war. The Shofar is blown as part of the cultic procession around the city of Jericho (Josh 6:4), to announce the Levitical Jubilee year (Lev 25:9), as part of YHWH's theophany on Mt. Sinai (Exod 19:16, 19), at King Asa's renewal of the covenant at the festival of Shavuot (Pentecost) following in victory over Zerah the Ethiopian (2 Chr 15:14), and in various psalms in which YHWH is proclaimed king or festival occasions are observed (Pss 47:6 [NRSV: 47:5]; 81:4 [NRSV: 81:3]; 98:6; 150:3). The command to "sanctify a fast" signals a cultic observance of public confession of sin or as an expression of contrition at a time of threat (Jer 36:6; Isa 58:3; 1 Kgs 21:9, 12; 2 Chr 20:3; Ezra 8:21; Esth 9:31, etc.). The command to "call a solemn assembly" employs the term *ʿăṣārâ*, which is derived from the root *ʿṣr*, "to stop," and indicates that the assembly calls for the cessation of normal activities. The commands to assemble or gather the people, the congregation, elders, the infants, and those still sucking their mothers' breasts indicates that the entire people is to be called out at this time of national emergency. This point is underscored by the statement that the groom is to come out from his chamber, i.e., the place where he would take his bride after the wedding to consummate the marriage (Judg 15:1; 2 Sam 13:10; 2 Kgs 9:2; Cant 1:4), and that the bride should come out from under her "canopy" *(ḥuppâ)*, a characteristic feature of Jewish weddings to this day (cf. Ps 19:6 [NRSV: 19:5]). Deuteronomy 20:7; 24:5 exempt newlywed men from military service, but the nature of the threat dictates that even this command from Mosaic law be overturned.

Verse 17 defines the location of the ceremony between the "vestibule" or "porch" *(ʾûlām)*, i.e., the initial entry hall of the Temple, and the altar (cf. 1 Macc 7:36). This would be the open area immediately in front of the Temple where sacrifices were normally made (cf. 1 Kgs 8:64). In the present case, sacrifices would be part of the ritual to appeal to YHWH for mercy. The priests will conduct the ceremony of lamentation as indicated by their weeping. Their appeal is quoted in full. The call upon YHWH to "spare/have pity" *(ḥûsâ)* upon the people employs a term that is generally used in reference to weeping (Deut 7:16; 13:9 [NRSV: 13:8]; Ezek 5:11; 7:4) and compassion for those who suffer (Jonah

4:10-11; Neh 13:22). The petition refers to the people as Yʜwʜ's "herit-age/inheritance/property" *(naḥălâ)* which should not be put to shame or made into a mockery *(ḥerpâ;* cf. Deut 28:37; Jer 25:9-10). This language recalls the statement in Exod 19:5 that Israel is Yʜwʜ's "treasured possession" *(sĕgullâ).* The motif of mockery appears once again in the statement, "to be a byword among the nations," which reads literally, "for nations to rule/mock *(limšol)* them." The statement is a pun in that the verb *mšl* means both "to rule" and "to represent, be like," and the noun can mean "parable, proverb" (cf. Jer 24:9 in which *ḥerpâ,* "reproach/shame," and *māšāl,* "byword," are used together. The final question posed by the priests, "Why do they say among the nations, 'where is their G–d?'" presupposes that the god of a nation would never allow such disaster to take place. Either G–d is powerless to stop the tragedy or G–d allowed it to take place. If G–d is not powerless, then G–d must have abandoned or betrayed the people. Many would argue that such abandonment is a punishment for sin, but the book of Joel identifies no sin on the part of the people.

Joel 2:18-20 reports Yʜwʜ's response to the people's petition, indicating Yʜwʜ's intention to restore the crops and to defeat the invader. The passage employs *waw-consecutive* verbs at the outset, "and Yʜwʜ became jealous for his land and had compassion on his people," to indicate that Yʜwʜ has already given his answer. This use of past perspective is often identified as the "prophetic perfect," and indicates the speaker's conviction that deliverance is already assured by Yʜwʜ's past statement. The reference to Yʜwʜ's "jealousy" or "zeal" reveals a dilemma in Joel's thought. On the one hand, Yʜwʜ brings punishment upon the people even though no sin is identified; on the other hand, Yʜwʜ's "zeal" for the people is such that Yʜwʜ will protect them from assault. Such a dilemma is inherent in the notion of a single all powerful G–d, i.e., both good and evil must come from G–d and must somehow be rationalized as aspects of a single divine will.

Yʜwʜ's answer is reported in verses 19-20. The initial statement in verse 19a promises the return of the basic crops that were the staples of Israel's diet and offerings at the Temple, grain, wine, and oil (Deut 14:22-23). Such a promise reverses the effects of the locust plague that threatened the land in the first major component of the book (Joel 1:2-20). Yʜwʜ's second statement in verse 19b promises that the people will no longer be given over to the nations for shame, which recalls the people's petition in verse 17 as well as the portrayal of the "Day of Yʜwʜ" in Joel 2:1-14. Verse 20 identifies the enemy of the people as "the northerner," which raises some rather interesting questions concerning the identity of the oppressor in the book of Joel. The "northerner" may be understood in relation to various prophetic statements that identify enemy invasion by a "foe from the north" (Jer 1:13-15; 4:6; 6:1, 22; Ezek 38:6, 15; 39:2), which of course may be identified with either the Assyrian or the Babylonian empires. Although these empires lay geographically to the east of Judah, the difficult passage through the northern Arabian desert required that Assyrian or Babylonian armies approach Judah by traveling along the so-called fertile crescent, i.e, by way of Aram/Syria, so that they would advance against Israel and Judah from the north. Alternatively, various mythical traditions place YHWH's home in the north (e.g., Isa 14:13; Ps 48:3 [NRSV: 48:2]), which draws upon Canaanite traditions that placed El's home on Mount Zaphon (Mount "North"). This statement reflects the ambiguity of the military threat against Judah. On the one hand, Joel 2:1-14 identifies YHWH's army as the cause of the threat on the "Day of YHWH," but this passage presupposes that the threat comes from a foreign invader who will be defeated by YHWH. It should be noted that "Day of YHWH" and other prophetic traditions frequently associate enemy armies as the agents of YHWH's punishment, but once the punishment is complete, the foreign army becomes the target of YHWH's wrath (e.g., Isaiah 2; 5–11; 13–14). A similar shift appears to take place in Joel that is related to the question of YHWH's punishment or abandonment of the people. On the one hand, YHWH brings the calamity; on the other, YHWH delivers the people from it.

The demise of the enemy is described in the balance of verse 20. The enemy will be expelled to "parched and desolate land," in contrast to the people of Judah who will enjoy renewed fecundity in the land of Israel. The depiction of the obviously broken enemy army may draw upon mythological traditions like the Babylonian Enuma Elish in which the enemy is described as a sea dragon (Tiamat) whose body is carved in two by Marduk to create heaven and earth.[27] In the present instance, the "front" or "vanguard" of the army is cast into the "eastern sea," i.e., the Dead Sea, which is known as one of the most parched and inhospitable places in Israel. Its "rear" or "end" is cast to the western sea, i.e., the Mediterranean, which is not particularly parched, but is far away from Judah. The image is that of a split army or body that is cast to the farthest borders of the land of Israel. The "stench" and "foul smell" would be characteristic of a battle field in which the bodies of the dead lie unburied, but foul smells are also easily recognizable at the Dead Sea, and the odor of the Mediterranean would be noticeable to people who normally live in the highlands of Judah. In any case, Joel employs the natural features of the land of Israel (and the seas) to characterize the fate of the enemy, so that both nature and human events re-

---

[27] For a translation of the Enuma Elish, see *ANET* 60–72, 501–3.

main coterminous as at the beginning of the book. The final statement of verse 20, "for he has done great things," is frequently taken as a reference to Yhwh, but the syntax of the statement clearly calls for it to be understood in relation to the enemy.[28] In this case, it should be understood as a reference to the enemy's arrogance (cf. the portrayal of the arrogance of the enemy in Isa 10:5-19 and Hab 2:6-19).

Yhwh's Reassurance to Restore Creation and Deliver the Nation from Oppressors: 2:21–4:8 [NRSV: 2:21–3:8]

Joel 2:21–4:8 [NRSV: 2:21–3:8] constitutes an extended prophetic announcement of salvation. The prophet conveys Yhwh's reassurance to both the land and animals of creation and the people of Zion that creation will be restored and the nation delivered from its oppressors. The unit includes three basic components: 1) a reassurance oracle in Joel 2:21-27 concerning the restoration of creation and the deliverance of the nation; 2) a prophetic announcement in Joel 3:1-5 [NRSV: 2:28-32] concerning Yhwh's signs and wonders among the people and creation; and 3) a prophetic announcement in Joel 4:1-8 [NRSV: 3:1-8] concerning Yhwh's judgment of the nations that threaten Jerusalem and Judah.

Yhwh's oracle of reassurance to creation and the people of Zion in Joel 2:21-27 begins in verses 21-22 with a two-fold address to the land and the animals concerning Yhwh's intentions to restore creation. Each verse begins with a statement of the reassurance formula, "do not fear, O soil" (verse 21), and, "do not fear, you animals of the field" (verse 22), which is typically employed in the cultic context of prophetic oracular inquiry to signal Yhwh's statements or action on behalf of a party in distress (see Isa 37:5-7; cf. Isa 7:4-9; 41:8-13, 14-16; 43:1-7; 44:1-5; Psalms 12; 35; 91; 121). In each case, an explanatory *kî* provides the reason for the reassurance. Verse 21 reassures the land or soil and calls upon it to rejoice. The reason for such optimism appears in the latter part of the verse which states that "Yhwh has done great things." This is apparently a word play upon the last statement of verse 20 which also ascribes great deeds to Yhwh, but verse 21 makes it very clear that Yhwh is the one who does great things. Verse 22 reassures the animals of the field that the land or soil will produce the vegetation and fruit that they need to live on and to eat. Thus the latter part of the verse states that the wilderness pastures will grow once again and the fruit trees, fig trees, and grapevines will again produce their fruit. The latter part of the

---

[28] See Wolff, *Joel and Amos*, 55.

statement is particularly important in relation to the transition to the military threat against the nation in the following pericopes (see esp. 4:1-8 [NRSV: 3:1-8]). The statement, "the fig tree and vine give their full yield," employs the term *ḥayil*, "yield, power, strength," which is used for the "strength" or "yield" of a tree and as a designation for military "strength" or an army.

Verses 23-24 then shift to the people of Zion whom the prophet calls upon to rejoice in a manner analogous to the land in verse 21. No reassurance formula appears at this point, but the expression, "be glad and rejoice (in YHWH your G–d)," is nearly identical to the expression in verse 21. Once again, this demonstrates Joel's perspective that the natural and the human worlds are inextricably intertwined. The reason for the rejoicing is provided in verses 23aβ-24, viz., that YHWH has given rain and that the threshing floors and wine/oil vats are overflowing with produce, viz., grain/corn, wine, and oil. The expression, "early rain for your vindication," is particularly problematic. The Hebrew term *ʾet hammôreh liṣdāqâ* has been particularly problematic. The noun *môreh* can mean "teacher," and the expression may have influenced the Qumran sect. The sect wrote the Dead Sea Scrolls and referred extensively to "the righteous teacher" who led the sect and defined its teachings during its early years.[29] In the present context, the expression clearly refers to rain (cf. Ps 84:7 [NRSV: 84:6]), although the noun *yôreh* is more commonly employed (cf. Deut 11:14; Jer 5:24; Hos 6:3). The term *liṣdāqâ*, "for righteousness," does not refer to moral qualities, but simply indicates that the early rain will fall in its season, i.e., according to its place in the natural order of creation. The statement, "the early and the later rain, as before," indicates that this is the general meaning of the expression.

The passage shifts to a speech by YHWH in verses 25-27, which contains three distinct statements by YHWH, linked by *waw-consecutive* verbs, that are directly addressed to the people and concern YHWH's intention to restore what was lost in the prior locust plague. YHWH's first statement in verse 25 promises to repay the people for the "years that the locusts have eaten." The expression, "and I will repay you," expresses irony in that the verb *šlm* is frequently employed in a cultic context to express the vows or other obligations that are "repaid" or "owed" to YHWH (Deut 23:22 [NRSV: 23:21]; 2 Sam 15:7; Pss 50:14; 56:13 [NRSV: 56:12]; Hos 14:3 [NRSV: 14:2]; Isa 19:21). Otherwise, the term is employed in legal context in reference to restitution or compensation for a loss or a crime (Exod 21:34; 22:1-5, etc.). The reference to "years" apparently refers to the annual harvest that was lost to the locusts. The

[29] Ibid., 63–4.

various types of locusts, apparently named according to the stages of growth in a locust's life cycle, are enumerated as in Joel 1:4. Yhwh states the expected results of the "repayment" to the people in verse 26, viz., they will eat and be satisfied, and they will praise the name of "Yhwh your G–d." The statement refers to Yhwh's wondrous acts on behalf of the people and the fact that the people will never again be put to shame. This statement, however, runs swiftly by the assertion in the first part of the book that Yhwh is the one who brought the plague in the first place and then delivered the people from it. Once again, no specific crime or sin by the people is mentioned. The final result appears in verse 27 when Yhwh states that the people will once again "know" that Yhwh is in the midst of Israel. Yhwh follows with a statement of the self-identification or recognition formula, "and I am Yhwh your G–d and there is no other," which is frequently employed to identify Yhwh as the source of action in both the human and natural worlds (Exod 6:7; 7:5, 17; 8:18 [NRSV: 8:22]; 1 Kgs 20:13, 28).

The Prophet's Announcement Concerning Yhwh's Signs and Wonders: 3:1-5 [NRSV: 2:28-32]

Joel 3:1-5 [NRSV: 2:28-32] builds upon the recognition formula of Joel 2:27 by presenting the prophet's announcement concerning Yhwh's signs and wonders. Yhwh speaks in verses 1-4 [NRSV: 28-31], and the prophet speaks in verse 5 [NRSV: 32]. This pericope employs motifs from the Exodus tradition in which Yhwh sends "signs and wonders" against the Egyptians so that Israel would know that Yhwh is its G–d (see Exod 6:1-9; 7:1-7). It especially builds upon motifs and imagery associated with the eighth and ninth plagues, viz., locusts (Exod 10:1-20) and darkness (Exod 10:21-28), in order to create a theophanic depiction of Yhwh's power over creation and the divine ability to redeem the nation Israel.

Yhwh's speech in verses 1-4 [NRSV: 28-31] begins with the conjunctive phrase, "then afterward *(wĕhāyâ ʾaḥărê-kēn),*" which establishes a direct link to Yhwh's statement of the recognition formula in the previous unit. Thus, the various signs and portents announced in Joel 3:1-5 [NRSV: 2:28-32] come as a direct result of Zion's recognition of Yhwh. Yhwh states the intention to pour out the divine "spirit" upon all flesh. Many see this as reference to the prophesying of all people in the following statements.[30] To a certain extent this is warranted as the "spirit"

---

[30] Douglas Stuart, *Hosea-Jonah,* WBC, vol. 31 (Waco: Word, 1987) 260–1; contra. Wolff, *Joel and Amos,* 67; Crenshaw, *Joel,* 164–5.

of Yʜᴡʜ often prompts prophecy in the Hebrew Bible (cf. 1 Sam 10:6; 19:20-24), but exclusive focus on the "spirit" of G–d in relation to prophecy forces the reader to overlook another dimension of this text. The Hebrew term *rûaḥ*, translated here as "spirit," literally means "wind." Indeed the notion of "spirit" has its roots in much later Christian theological constructs concerning the essence or nature of G–d. When read as "wind," this recalls an important element of the locust plague in Exodus 10, i.e., the strong east wind that brought the locusts upon Egypt (Exod 10:13) and the west wind that carried them away (Exod 10:19). The east wind in particular is to be identified with the *Ḥamsin* (Arabic) or *Sharav* (Hebrew), a strong dry desert wind, much like the Santa Ana winds of southern California, that blows in from the deserts at times of seasonal transition in Israel, either from the dry summer to the wet winter in October or from the wet winter to the dry summer in April.[31] These winds can be very destructive as they reach high speeds, and they frequently blow in a great deal of dust and debris that blocks out or darkens the sun and causes the moon to appear as a deep red or blood-like color.

Indeed, the image of the *Ḥamsin/Sharav* appears to underlie much of the imagery of cosmic transformation in this passage, but it is combined with the imagery of prophecy once again to demonstrate the interrelatedness of the natural and the human worlds in the book of Joel. Verses 1-2 [ɴʀsᴠ: 28-29] are designed to demonstrate that all people will prophecy or see visions when the "spirit/wind" of G–d is poured out (cf. Isa 32:15-20). The list of persons involved, sons and daughters, elders, young men, slaves and maid servants, is intended to be comprehensive. This phenomenon appears to project a return to a much earlier or ideal time prior to the establishment of Israel as a nation ruled by a king in its own land, such as the Exodus and wilderness period when the seventy elders of Israel began to prophesy when the "spirit" of G–d descended upon them (Num 11:25) or the period prior to the time of Samuel and the emergence of the first king, Saul, when 1 Sam 3:1 states that the word of Yʜᴡʜ and visions were rare at that time.

To a certain extent, the passage attempts to portray a return to a state prior to creation, either of the natural world order or of the nation Israel, which of course enables both Yʜᴡʜ and Israel/Judah to start all over again on a new basis. The portents in the heavens and on the earth recalls both the use of heaven and earth as the comprehensive designation for all creation (Gen 1:1; 2:1, 4) and the actions of Yʜᴡʜ in the Exodus narrative that forced Pharaoh to free the Hebrew slaves and that prompted the creation of Israel as a nation and its covenant with Yʜᴡʜ

---

[31] See "Israel, Land of (Geographical Survey)," *Encyclopaedia Judaica* 9:189-90.

(Exod 6:1-9; 7:1-7). The images of "blood, fire, and columns of smoke," appear to be destructive at first sight and suggest the motif of YHWH's battles against the nations that oppress Israel in the following passages. But these images are also the images of the altar at the Jerusalem Temple. Animals are slaughtered for sacrifice, and the treatment of blood is an important part of the sacrificial ritual. Once the animal is slaughtered and prepared for the altar, it is set on fire and consumed entirely, resulting in a thick column of smoke that will stand over the site of the Temple complex. Although the imagery is destructive, it is also constructive in the sense that the Temple sacrificial ritual is intended to maintain or to restore the order of the created world. In a similar manner, the *Ḥamsin* or *Sharav* that darkens the sun and causes the moon to appear red as blood is both destructive and transformative in that it marks the transition from one season to another; one reality is destroyed as another emerges. Altogether, such transformation in both the natural and the human world is labelled as the coming "Day of YHWH" in verse 4 [NRSV: 31].

From the perspective of the book of Joel, such transformation marks the end of the threat posed by the locusts to the natural world or more specifically to the harvest and the means by which human beings might live in the world of creation. It also marks the end of the threat posed by the nations whom YHWH brings to attack Judah. The prophet attempts to introduce an aspect of human causation to this process in verse 5 when he states that "everyone who calls upon the name of YHWH will be saved (*yimmālēṭ*)." Literally, the verb *yimmālēṭ* means "will escape," which suggests the theologically problematic premise that those who are the victims of natural (or human) disaster somehow deserved their fates, whereas those who survived must be righteous. Indeed, the notion of an escaped righteous remnant that survives YHWH's/ Assyria's/Babylon's punishment of Jerusalem is fundamental to the theological perspective of the book of Isaiah and other writings, and stands as the basis for portraying the restoration of Jerusalem in the post-exilic period as an act of YHWH (see Isa 4:2-6; 6:1-13; 10:20-26, etc.). Joel likewise uses this premise to argue that YHWH will save those "in Mount Zion and in Jerusalem" who escape and call upon YHWH. He then turns the concept around to claim that YHWH will likewise call upon them.

In making these assertions concerning the survival of a remnant in Jerusalem, Joel 3:5 draws upon Obad 17–18, which is concerned with YHWH's judgment against Edom.[32] Thus the statement in Joel 3:5b [NRSV: 2:32b], "for in Mount Zion and in Jerusalem there shall be those

---

[32] For discussion, see Bergler, *Joel als Schriftinterpret* 301–3.

who escape *(kî bĕhar ṣîyôn ûbîrûšālayim tihyeh pĕlêʾâ)*, as YHWH has said *(kaʾăšer ʾām yhwh)*, and among the survivors *(ûbaśśĕrîdîm)* shall be those whom YHWH calls," whereas Obad 17–18 reads,

> But on Mount Zion there shall be those that escape *(ûbĕhar ṣîyôn tihyeh pĕlê â)* and it shall be holy; and the house of Jacob shall take possession of those who dispossessed them. The house of Jacob shall be a fire, the house of Joseph a flame, and the house of Esau stubble; they shall burn them and consume them, and there shall be no survivor *(wĕlōʾ yihyeh śārîd)* for YHWH has spoken *(kî yhwh dibbēr)*.

Joel has clearly reworked the material from Obadiah in order to emphasize Jerusalem together with Zion, and to eliminate the references to Jacob and Joseph, the ancestors of the northern kingdom of Israel, as well as Esau, the ancestor of Edom. Insofar as Edom becomes a symbol for the nations opposed to YHWH in prophetic literature (e.g., Isaiah 34; 63:1-6; Mal 1:2-5), it would appear that the author of Joel adapted the anti-Edom material in Obadiah to provide the link between the threat posed by the locust plague and that posed by the enemy nations. The premise of an attack against Edom/the nations in Obadiah is removed in Joel, in order to emphasize the motif of YHWH's defense of Zion/ Jerusalem and the protection of a righteous remnant that dwells therein.

Prophetic Announcement of YHWH's Judgment against the Nations that Threaten Jerusalem and Judah: 4:1-8 [NRSV: 3:1-8]

Joel 4:1-8 builds upon the premise of YHWH's defense of Jerusalem and Judah to construct a scenario in which YHWH will gather the nations that have oppressed Jerusalem and Judah for punishment. The passage begins with the formula, "for then, in those days and at that time *(kî hinnēh bayyāmîm hāhēmmâ ûbāʿēt hahîʾ)*." The formula links the pericope syntactically to Joel 3:1-5 [NRSV: 2:28-32], and emphasizes that the scenario presented in the following material must follow directly upon Joel 2:21-27 as a result or consequence of YHWH's reassurances and Judah's recognition of YHWH. The passage draws heavily upon the book of Obadiah once again, but it also employs the tradition of King Jehoshaphat's defeat of the Moabites, Ammonites, and inhabitants of Mount Seir (Edom) in the Valley of Berakhah ("Blessing") in 2 Chr 20:20-26. The author of this passage seems to be interested once again in using traditions concerning the defeat or punishment of specific nations in order to posit YHWH's punishment of all the nations that have taken captives from Jerusalem and Judah, but the author is also interested in targeting specific nations for actions that are perhaps at issue during the author's own time. The passage contains two basic components: Joel 4:1-3 [NRSV: 3:1-3] presents a general punishment of the nations gathered at the Valley of Jehoshaphat, and Joel 4:4-8 [NRSV: 3:4-8] focuses specifically on YHWH's recompense for Sidon, Tyre, and the Philistines because they sold Judeans as slaves to foreign nations.

As noted above, the introductory formula, "for then, in those days and at that time *(kî hinnēh bayyāmîm hāhēmmâ ûbāʿēt hahîʾ),*" posits a time in the future when the remnant in Jerusalem and Judah recognizes YHWH. At that point, YHWH promises to "restore the fortunes of Judah and Jerusalem." The expression, "I (will) restore the fortunes *(ʾāšîb ʾet šĕbût),*" reads the word *šĕbût* as a derivation from the root *šwb*, "return" (i.e., "restore," cf. Amos 9:14; Job 42:10; Ezek 16:53; Ps 126:4). The expression is frequently read as "I will restore the captivity," which takes *šĕbût* from the root *šbh*, "to make captive" (cf. Jer 29:14; Ezek 29:14; 39:25; Zeph 3:20). The latter meaning appears to be the emphasis of the present context. YHWH's promise to "gather all the nations and bring them down to the Valley of Jehoshaphat" for judgment clearly draws upon 2 Chr 20:20-26, which describes YHWH's defeat of Ammonites, Moabites, and inhabitants of Mount Seir (Edom) who threatened Jerusalem and Judah. No Valley of Jehoshaphat is mentioned here, nor is one otherwise known. The name derives from the role played by King Jehoshaphat in this narrative who told his people to believe in YHWH and YHWH's prophets, and led his army against the enemy as it sang hymns of praise to YHWH. Once the enemy was defeated, the Jerusalemites and Judeans were able to take the booty of the enemy in the Valley of Blessing and to return to Jerusalem in cultic procession. The reference to the Valley of Jehoshaphat is apparently intended to recall a defeat of nations (including Edom) in which the victory is attributed to YHWH; the people's role was to praise YHWH in cultic procession. Apparently, Joel envisions a similar role for the people in their recognition of YHWH.

The grounds for YHWH's judgment against the nations are that they have scattered or exiled YHWH's "inheritance" Israel among the nations and divided the land among themselves. The use of the term Israel is important here because it encompasses all of Israel, not only Judah and Jerusalem, and thereby includes the exile of the northern kingdom of Israel by the Assyrians as well as the later exile of Judah by the Babylonians. Joel 4:3 [NRSV: 3:3] once again draws upon Obadiah in describing the actions of the nations against Israel.[33] The statement reads, "and

---

[33] Ibid., 305–6.

(they) cast lots for my people *(wĕʾel ʿammî yaddû gôrāl)*, and traded boys for prostitutes, and sold girls for wine, and drunk it down *(wayyištû),"* whereas Obad 11b reads, "and foreigners entered his gates and cast lots for Jerusalem *(wĕʿal-yĕrûšālayim yaddû gôrāl)*, you too were like one of them," and Obad 16a, "For as you have drunk on my holy mountain, all the nations around shall drink *(yištû)*." Both passages from Obadiah describe actions attributed by the prophet to Edom at the time of the Babylonian conquest of Jerusalem. Once again, Joel draws upon the images of Edom's crimes against Jerusalem to portray a more generalized picture of the nations' crimes against Israel.

The second part of this pericope in Joel 4:4-8 [NRSV: 3:4-8] focuses specifically on Tyre, Sidon, and the Philistines for their role in selling Jerusalemites and Judeans as slaves to the Greeks and Sabaeans. Many have noted that this situation appears to presuppose the well-known involvement of the seafaring Phoenicians (Tyre and Sidon) and the Philistine seacoast (just south of Phoenicia and northern Israel) in the sale of slaves throughout the Mediterranean world. Wolff points out that Phoenician slave trading with Greece was especially well-known in the fifth and fourth centuries B.C.E., and many view this text as a later reference in Joel to such practice.[34] Slave trading with the Sabaeans of the southern Arabian peninsula is not attested, however, after the fifth century B.C.E., which might suggest an earlier date. Indeed, Assyrian records indicate contact with the Ionians (Greeks) as early as the eighth century B.C.E., and Greek trading colonies were established along the Philistine sea coast as early as the seventh century.[35] Joel's references might suggest a situation that existed in relation to the Babylonian exile, if not before, and that continued through the fourth century B.C.E. and beyond (cf. 1 Macc 3:41; 2 Macc 8:11). It is noteworthy that the oracles against the nations in the book of Amos 1–2 include oracles directed against Philistia (Amos 1:6-8) and Tyre (Amos 1:9-10), which accuse both nations of carrying entire communities into exile so that they might be handed over to Edom. Given Joel's interest in reworking material from Obadiah, which condemns Edom, it is possible that Joel was likewise influenced by the two Amos passages in formulating this particular unit.

[34] Wolff, *Joel and Amos*, 77–8.

[35] For discussion, see Jane Waldbaum, "Early Greek Contacts with the Southern Levant, ca. 1000–600 B.C.: The Eastern Perspective," *BASOR* 293 (1994) 53–66. Note that the seventh century Yavneh Yam Inscription, which is often seen as a site associated with Greek trade, contains an appeal by a debtor for the return of his garment.

Joel 4:4-8 [NRSV: 3:4-8] is linked to 4:1-3 [NRSV: 3:1-3] by the particle *wĕgam,* "and also," which suggests to many interpreters that the passage is a secondary insertion into the text of Joel 4:1-3, 9-21 [NRSV: 3:1-3, 9-21].[36] Considering the focus on all the nations in Joel 4:1-3 [NRSV: 3:1-3], the issues raised in 4:4-8 [NRSV: 3:4-8] appear to be an afterthought that specifies the more general charges of the preceding passage. It is formulated as a speech by YHWH, who begins with a direct question to the Phoenicians and Philistines, "What are you to me, O Tyre and Sidon, and all the regions of the Philistia?" As the following material demonstrates, the force of the question is not so much to devalue these peoples as it is to ask why they take such actions against YHWH's people, i.e., what do they have against YHWH? The following question makes this clear, "Are you paying me back for something?" Many interpreters have speculated that the Phoenician and Philistine actions were undertaken as revenge for Israel's or Judah's domination of these regions during the periods of the Israelite monarchy, i.e., under David and Solomon, Jeroboam II, etc., but this misses the rhetorical point of the question.[37] It doesn't matter what the cause of the action is. YHWH's statement is intended to assert rhetorically that their actions are undertaken as a means to pay back YHWH or Israel, and thereby becomes the basis for YHWH's paying back the Phoenicians and the Philistines. YHWH's statement in verse 4bβγ makes this clear, "If you are paying me back, I will turn your deed back upon your own heads, swiftly and speedily." Once again, Joel draws upon statements from Obadiah.[38] The question, "And also, what are you to me O Tyre and Sidon *(wĕgam mâ-ʾattem lî sōr wĕsîdôn)*?" presupposes Obad 11bβ, "you too were like one of them *(gam-ʾattâ kĕʾahad mēhem),*" which accuses Edom of complicity in Babylon's conquest of Jerusalem. Likewise, Joel 4:4b [NRSV: 3:4bγ], "If you are paying me back, I will turn your deeds back upon your heads swiftly and speedily *(qal mĕhērâ ʾāšîb gĕmulkem bĕrōʾšĕkem),*" draws upon Obad 15b, "As you have done, it shall be done to you; your deeds shall return on your own head *(gĕmulkā yāšûb bĕrōʾšekā),*" which refers to YHWH's punishment against Edom for its role in Jerusalem's fall.

Verses 5-6 then begin to specify the crimes of the Phoenicians and Philistines. Verse 5 refers to YHWH's silver, gold, and rich treasures that these nations have taken into their own temples. One must bear in mind that temples in the ancient world were generally the repositories for national wealth. Verse 6 then refers to the sale of Judeans and Jerusalemites to the Greeks or Ionians, thereby "removing them far from

[36] Wolff, *Joel and Amos,* 74–5.
[37] Crenshaw, *Joel,* 179–80.
[38] Bergler, *Joel als Schriftinterpret,* 306–7.

their own border *(lĕmaʿan harhîqām mēʿal gĕbûlām)*." This last statement
draws upon Obad 9b, "so that everyone from Mt. Seir will be cut
off *(lĕmaʿan yikkāret-ʾîš mēhar ʿēśāw)*, and Obad 7aα, "All your allies
have deceived you, they have driven you to the border *(ʿad-haggĕbûl
šillĕḥûkā)*."[39] Again, both references from Obadiah portray Edom's
punishment for its role in Jerusalem's conquest.

Verses 7-8 contain YHWH's announcements of the intent to restore
the exiled Jerusalemites and Judeans to their homeland and to punish
the nations that sold them in the first place. The statement, "But now I
will rouse them to leave the places to which you have sold them," indicates that YHWH will set the captives in motion so that they might return. The following statement, "and I will turn your deeds back upon
your own heads *(wahăšibōtî gĕmulkem bĕrōʾšĕkem)*," draws once again
from Obad 15b, "As you have done, it shall be done to you; your deeds
shall return on your own head *(gĕmulkā yāšûb bĕrōʾšekā)*."[40] The complete reversal of the roles of the Phoenicians and Philistines with those
of the exiled Judeans and Jerusalemites is expressed in verse 8, which
looks forward to the time when Judeans will sell the sons and daughters of the Philistines and Phoenicians to the far off land of the Sabaeans.
The land of Seba was located in the southwestern Arabian peninsula in
modern Yemen (cf. Gen 10:7; 1 Chr 1:9).[41] Sabeans were known for their
extensive caravan trade connections (see Ps 72:10; cf. Isa 43:3), particularly in gold and precious stones (see Isa 60:6; Jer 6:20; Ezek 27:22-23).
They are believed to have been active from the tenth to the fifth centuries B.C.E., but afterwards they went into a long period of decline. The
statement in Joel 4:8aβ-b [NRSV: 3:8aβ-b], "and they will sell them to the
Sabeans, to a nation far away; for YHWH has spoken *(kî yhwh dibbēr)*,"
appears to derive from Obad 18aβ-b, "they shall burn them and consume them, and there shall be no survivor of the House of Esau, for
YHWH has spoken *(kî yhwh dibbēr)*."[42] Although there is little lexical
equivalence apart from the YHWH speech formula, both passages presuppose the utter destruction of the enemy nations that abused Judah
and Jerusalem. As Seba is probably about as far away as one could expect to go in the world of ancient Judah, it adequately expresses the
sentiment of complete destruction for Judah's and Jerusalem's oppressors. The YHWH speech formula confirms this as a word from YHWH,
and verifies the promise that YHWH makes.

---

[39] Ibid., 308.
[40] Ibid., 306–7.
[41] See W. W. Müller, "Seba," *ABD* V:1064.
[42] Bergler, *Joel als Schriftinterpret*, 308–10.

Prophet's Summons of Nations to Judgment by YHWH: 4:9-21 [NRSV: 3:9-21]

The book of Joel concludes in Joel 4:9-21 [NRSV: 3:9-21] with the prophet's summons to the nations to assemble themselves for judgment, which will result in the restoration of the natural world of creation and the eternal security of Jerusalem and Judah. This projects the resolution of the two major threats that were presented in the first part of the book: the plague of locusts that threatened to destroy the natural world (Joel 1:2-20) and the attack of nations that threatened to destroy Jerusalem and Judah (Joel 2:1-14). The prophet is the speaker throughout this unit, although he presents several statements by YHWH in verses 12, 17, and 21a, to underscore his points. The passage includes two basic components. Verses 9-12 summon the nations to judgment, and verses 13-21 project the results, i.e., defeat for the nations and the restoration of nature and Judah/Jerusalem. Again, this passage cites language from Obadiah and other prophetic writing, such as Micah and Amos, to portray YHWH's actions.

Joel 4:9-12 [NRSV: 3:9-21] summons both the nations and YHWH to the Valley of Jehoshaphat where YHWH will judge the nations. The passage is based upon the typical form of a summons to battle that is characteristically employed to call out soldiers for war (cf. Judg 3:28; 4:6-7; Jer 46:9; 49:14, 28, 31; etc.).[43] It includes a series of five imperatives addressed by the prophet to various parties including the nations, their warriors, and YHWH. It begins with a general summons in verse 9aα, "Proclaim this among the nations," which calls attention to the following summons directed to the individual parties. The summons to the nations and their warriors appears in the four imperative statements of verses 9aβ-11a. The first, "prepare war," reads literally, "sanctify war" (cf. Jer 6:4), and presupposes the setting of holy war in which YHWH fights on behalf of the people and a priest sanctifies the army as an agent of YHWH (see Deut 20:1-20; cf. Isa 13:3 in which YHWH's warriors are called "consecrated ones"). The prophet then calls for the arousal of the warriors in verse 9b. These statements are sometimes associated with Obad 1b, "We have heard a report from YHWH, and a messenger has been sent among the nations: 'Rise up! Let us rise against it for battle!'" (cf. Jer 49:14, which includes a similar statement), but the lexical relationship is not very close.[44] In verse 10a, he reverses the call for the destruction of weapons in Mic 4:3bα and Isa 2:4bα, although his

---

[43] Robert Bach, *Die Aufforderungen zur Flucht und zum Kampf im alttestamentlichen Prophetenspruch*, WMANT, vol. 9 (Neukirchen: Neukirchener, 1962).

[44] Bergler, *Joel als Schriftinterpret*, 313–5.

language varies slightly from these texts, "Beat your plowshares into swords, and your pruning hooks into spears (*rĕmāḥîm*; but *ḥănîtôt* in Mic 4:3bα and Isa 2:4bα)." The reversal of this text enables Joel to have an even greater rhetorical impact upon his audience in that the double appearance of the phrase in Mic 4:1-5 and Isa 2:2-4 probably indicates that the earlier oracle was well-known (cf. Zech 8:20-23, which also presupposes the oracle in Mic 4:1-5 and Isa 2:2-4). This is clearly no time for peace, but a time for war; even the weak declares himself to be a warrior. In contrast to the preceding section, which targeted only Phoenicia and Philistia, the summons in verse 11a clearly is directed to all the nations. The prophet then turns to YHWH in verse 11b, calling upon the Deity, "there, bring down your warriors, O YHWH." This command recalls the portrayal of the attacking army in Joel 2:1-14 as an army sent by YHWH on the "Day of YHWH" (cf. the portrayal of YHWH's army in Isaiah 13). It is sometimes associated with Obad 9a, "Your warriors shall be shattered, O Teman," but the relationship is primarily thematic.[45] Finally, verse 12 explains the reasons for the summons: the nations are to go up to the Valley of Jehoshaphat where YHWH states the intention to subject them to judgment. At this point, the literal meaning of the name Jehoshaphat, "YHWH will judge," appears to underlie the perspective of this passage. The previously cited narrative in 2 Chr 20:20-26, concerning YHWH's defeat of the nations threatening Jerusalem in the time of King Jehoshaphat, likewise informs the perspective of this passage. Because the vocabulary and motifs are similar, the verse may be derived from Obad 21 which portrays YHWH's judgment of Edom, "Those who have been saved shall go up to Mount Zion to rule (literally, "to judge") Mount Esau; and the kingdom shall be YHWH's."[46]

Joel 4:13-21 then projects the course and outcome of YHWH's judgment against the nations. Verses 13-14 employ the imagery of harvest to portray the threat posed to the people by the nations as the enemy warriors are cut down like grain and their blood fills vats much like the new wine and oil. Verse 13 includes a series of three imperatives that call for the "harvesting" or destruction of the enemy warriors. The command, "Put in the sickle for the harvest is ripe," presupposes the imagery of standing grain that is cut down at harvest time to portray the fall of the enemy soldiers. The command, "Go in, tread, for the wine press is full, the vats overflow, for their wickedness is great," presupposes the imagery of grapes being tread at harvest time, which symbolizes the blood shed by the fallen enemy warriors. It is noteworthy that the Hebrew word, "vat(s)," is *gat*, which corresponds to

---

[45] Ibid., 315–6.
[46] Ibid., 318–20.

the name of one of the Philistine cities, Gath. The term may relate to the mention of the Philistines in Joel 4:4-8. Likewise, the Hebrew word for "harvest," *qāṣîr*, relates assonantally to the Hebrew word for Tyre, *ṣōr*, in Joel 4:4-8. Verse 14 portrays the crowds in the "Valley of Decision" as the Day of YHWH draws near. The imagery of crowds presupposes the many people who would fill the land at the time of harvest in order to bring in the new crops. The name, "Valley of Decision," is a very clear word play on the motif of harvest and judgment as *ḥārûṣ*, "decision," is derived from a root that also means, "to cut, sharpen" (cf. the use of the verb in Lev 22:22 and the noun, "trench, moat," in Dan 9:25). At this point, the Valley of Jehoshaphat becomes the Valley of Decision as the judgment is made and the punishment is carried out. The statement, "for the Day of YHWH is near in the Valley of Decision," relates to Obad 15a, "For the Day of YHWH is near against all the nations."[47]

Verses 15-21 then present YHWH's response to the threat. The imagery of cosmic disruption appears once again in verse 15 as the sun, moon, and stars darken. This imagery signals a reversal of creation in that the lights of the heaven will no longer shine (see Gen 1:14-19), but the imagery also presupposes the effects of the dry desert winds called the *Ḥamsin* or *Sharav*, i.e., YHWH's "east wind" which serves as the Deity's weapon against those who threaten creation and Israel (cf. Gen 8:1; Exod 10:13; 14:21; Isa 11:15; 17:13; 27:8). The prophet cites Amos 1:2a in the first part of verse 16, "YHWH roars from Zion, and utters his voice from Jerusalem, and the heaven and the earth shake." By adding the reference to the shaking of heaven and earth, the prophet indicates that all creation is effected by YHWH's response. The prophet continues with a statement concerning YHWH's protection of the people, that apparently draws upon the language of the Psalms, "But YHWH is a refuge (*maḥăseh*) for his people, a stronghold (*ma'ôz*) for the people of Israel" (cf. Ps 46:2a [NRSV: 46:1a], "G–d is our refuge [*maḥăseh*] and strength [*wā'ôz*]"; see also Pss 14:6; 61:4 [NRSV: 61:3]; 62:8-9 [NRSV: 62:7-8]; 71:7; 73:28; 91:2, 9; 94:22; 142:6 [NRSV: 142:5]; 27:1; 28:8; 31:5 [NRSV: 31:4]; 37:39; 52:9 [NRSV: 52:7]; 60:9 [NRSV: 60:7]; 108:9 [NRSV: 108:8]; Nah 1:7; Isa 25:4). This introduces YHWH's statement in verse 17, "So you shall know that I, YHWH your G–d, dwell in Zion, my holy mountain, and Jerusalem shall be holy and strangers shall never again pass through it." As noted above in the discussion of Joel 2:27, the first part of this statement is an example of the self-identification or recognition formula, which identifies YHWH as the cause of action in creation and human events. The statement reiterates YHWH's promise of security to Jerusalem as the city is the holy site of YHWH's Temple, which is not to

---

[47] Ibid., 316.

be profaned by strangers (cf. Isa 1:7). Verse 17 appears to draw upon motifs from Obad 16–17, which refer to the alien invasion of "my holy mountain," and state that Mount Zion "shall be called holy." It likewise relates to Obad 11, "on that day strangers carried off his wealth."[48]

Finally, Joel 4:18-21 [NRSV: 3:18-21] projects a future in which the natural bounty of the land will reappear and Judah and Jerusalem will be secure. It begins with the standard formula employed in prophetic literature to point to a future event, "in that day" (literally, "and it shall come to pass in that day; *wĕhāyâ bayyôm hahû*ʾ; cf. Isa 7:18, 23; 10:20, 27; Jer 4:9; 30:8; Hos 1:5; Amos 8:9; Mic 5:9 [NRSV: 5:10]; Zeph 1:10; Zech 12:3, 9; 13:2, 4; 14:6, 8, 13; etc.). Many consider the formula to refer to an eschatological event, but it merely indicates the future.[49] In the present context, it would signify the coming "Day of YHWH." The portrayal of the mountains and hills dripping new wine and flowing with milk, together with the portrayal of the streams of Judah flowing with water, draws upon the role of the Jerusalem Temple as the source for fertility in creation (see Ezekiel 47; Zech 14:8 [cf. Zech 13:1]; Psalms 46; 65; Isa 33:17-22). It builds upon the mythological traditions concerning the Gihon stream as the source of water for Jerusalem, which in turn projects the city and the Temple as the source of water for all creation (see also Gen 2:10-14; 1 Kgs 1:33, 38, 45; 2 Chr 32:30; 33:14; see also the "Waters of Shiloah" in Isa 8:6; Ps 104:10). The "fountain" from Jerusalem will water the Wadi Shittim. A wadi is a stream bed or arroyo that is normally dry in the summer, but overflows with water during the rainy winter season. No Wadi Shittim is known in biblical tradition, but Shittim is the site where the people of Israel turned to Baal and the Moabite women in Num 25:1-15. Shittim is located east of the Jordan River, which presents geographical difficulties as this would require that the water from Jerusalem flow across the Jordan. But the Jordan flows into the Dead Sea in this region, and it is possible that Joel envisions the transformation of the dry wilderness of the Jordan Valley and Dead Sea as a result of YHWH's actions on the "Day of YHWH." The reference to Shittim would suggest that the water not only secures the fertility and new growth of the world, but it also plays a role in symbolizing the renewal or restoration of the people of Jerusalem and Judah.

Verse 19 contrasts the fate of Egypt and Edom, both of which will become desolate because of the violence that they did against Judah,

---

[48] Ibid., 303–5.

[49] For a thorough study of temporal formulas in the Hebrew Bible, see Simon J. DeVries, *From Old Revelation to New: A Tradition-Historical and Redaction-Critical Study of Temporal Transitions in Prophetic Prediction* (Grand Rapids and Cambridge: Eerdmans, 1995).

with the abundance portrayed for Judah and Jerusalem in verse 18. The statement may draw upon Obad 10, which condemns Edom "for the slaughter and violence done to your brother Jacob."[50] Egypt is the traditional foe of the Exodus which is defeated by YHWH at the Sea (Exodus 14–15; cf. Isa 11:10-16; 12:1-6). The mention of Egypt's and Edom's shedding "innocent blood" is somewhat incongruous as Joel 1–2 presents the locust plague and the invading army as divine actions on the "Day of YHWH." Although the call for repentance in Joel 2:12-14 appears to assume some guilt on the part of the people, these chapters never identify a sin by Jerusalem and Judah that prompted such action. Verse 20 portrays the security of Judah and Jerusalem, "But Judah will be inhabited forever, and Jerusalem for all generations." Such a motif is a standard theme of the Zion traditions in which YHWH promises to defend Zion and the Davidic monarch against the nations (Psalms 2; 46; 47; 48; 89). Verse 20 may also draw on the language of Isa 13:20 concerning the downfall of Babylon on the "Day of YHWH," "It will never be inhabited or lived in for all generations," thereby reversing the fate reserved for YHWH's/Jerusalem's enemies on the "Day of YHWH." Finally, verse 21 presents YHWH's stated promise to avenge the blood of the innocent, "I will avenge their blood, and I will not clear the guilty," which may play upon the themes of the oracle against Edom in Jer 49:12a, "For thus says YHWH, 'If those who do not deserve to drink the cup still have to drink it, shall you be the one to go unpunished? You shall not go unpunished; you must drink it.'" It also appears to serve as a rejoinder to YHWH's stated intention to have mercy in Joel 2:13, in that this statement assures the audience that YHWH will indeed punish the guilty in keeping with the latter part of YHWH's attributes in Exod 34:6-7, "yet by no means clearing the guilty, but visiting the iniquity of the parents upon the children and children's children to the third and the fourth generations." The notice by the prophet that "YHWH dwells in Zion" draws once again on the Zion tradition concerning YHWH's protection of Jerusalem and stands as a guarantee for Jerusalem's and Judah's future security (cf. Joel 4:17; Ezek 48:35).

---

[50] Bergler, *Joel als Schriftinterpret*, 310–2.

FOR FURTHER READING

COMMENTARIES

Achtemeier, Elizabeth. "The Book of Joel: Introduction, Commentary, and Reflections," *The New Interpreter's Bible. Volume VII: Introduction to Apocalyptic Literature, Daniel, The Twelve Prophets.* Ed. by Leander E. Keck et al., 299–336. Nashville: Abingdon, 1996.

Allen, Leslie C. *The Books of Joel, Obadiah, Jonah, and Micah.* New International Commentary on the Old Testament. Grand Rapids: Eerdmans, 1976.

Crenshaw, James L. *Joel.* Anchor Bible, 24C. New York: Doubleday, 1995.

Jacob, Edmond, Carl-A. Keller, Samuel Amsler. *Osée, Joël, Amos, Abdias, Jonas.* Commentaire de l'Ancien Testament, XIa. Geneva: Labor et Fides, 1992.

Ogden, Graham S., and Richard R. Deutsch. *Joel and Malachi: A Promise of Hope, A Call to Obedience.* International Theological Commentary. Grand Rapids: Eerdmans; Edinburgh: Handsel, 1987.

Rudolph, Wilhelm. *Joel–Amos–Obadja–Jona.* Kommentar zum Alten Testament, XIII/2. Gütersloh: Gerd Mohn, 1971.

Stuart, Douglas. *Hosea-Jonah.* Word Biblical Commentary, 31. Waco: Word, 1987.

Wolff, Hans Walter. *Joel and Amos.* Trans. W. Janzen, S. Dean McBride, and C. A. Muenchow. Hermeneia. Philadelphia: Fortress, 1977.

STUDIES

Ahlström, G. W. *Joel and the Temple Cult of Jerusalem.* Vetus Testament Supplements, XXI. Leiden: E. J. Brill, 1971.

Bergler, Siegfried. *Joel als Shriftinterpret.* Beiträge zur Forschung des Alten Testaments und des Antiken Judentums, 16. Frankfurt am Main: Peter Lang, 1988.

Coggins, Richard. "An Alternative Prophetic Tradition?" *Israel's Prophetic Tradition: Essays in Honour of Peter Ackroyd*. Ed. Richard Coggins, Anthony Phillips, and Michael Knibb. Cambridge: Cambridge University Press, 1982, pp. 77–94.

Kapelrud, Arvid S. *Joel Studies*. Uppsala: Lundqvist: Leipzig: Otto Harrassowitz, 1948.

Mason, Rex. *Zephaniah, Habakkuk, Joel*. Old Testament Guides. Sheffield: JSOT Press, 1994.

Ogden, Graham S. "Joel 4 and Prophetic Responses to National Laments," *Journal for the Study of the Old Testament* 26 (1983) 97–106.

Plöger, Otto. *Theocracy and Eschatology*. Trans. S. Rudman. Oxford: Basil Blackwell, 1968.

Prinsloo, Willem S. *The Theology of the Book of Joel*. Beiheft zur Zeitschrift für die alttestamentliche Wissenschaft, 163. Berlin and New York: Walter de Gruyter, 1985.

AMOS

AMOS

Overview

Amos is the third book in the Masoretic version of the Book of the Twelve and the second book in the Septuagint version. It follows naturally from the book of Joel in the Masoretic order in that Joel is especially occupied with the threats posed to Jerusalem by both natural catastrophe, particularly locusts (Joel 1–2), and enemy nations, whereas Amos points to his vision of locusts devouring the land (Amos 7:1-3) as a sign from YHWH of impending punishment at the hands of an enemy nation. Likewise, just as Joel envisions the deliverance of Jerusalem and the restoration of fertility to the land, with particular emphasis on the mountains that drip sweet wine (Joel 4:18 [NRSV: 3:18]), so Amos sees the eventual outcome of Israel's punishment in the restoration of a state ruled by a Davidic monarch and natural fertility and agricultural bounty in which the mountains drip with sweet wine (Amos 9:11-15). Amos also points forward to the book of Obadiah, which is especially concerned with the judgment of Edom, by emphasizing the need to punish Edom at the end (Amos 9:12) and at the beginning (Amos 1:11-12). All three books focus on the theme of the Day of YHWH as a day of punishment (Joel 1:15; Amos 5:18-20; Obad 15). Amos also follows naturally from Hosea in the Septuagint version of the Book of the Twelve. Whereas Hosea outlines the basis for Israel's punishment and restoration in terms of its relationship with YHWH, Amos points specifically to the Beth El sanctuary as a major problem that turns Israel away from YHWH and that must be removed. It also points forward to Micah in that Micah presents the punishment and restoration of northern Israel as the model for the punishment and restoration of Jerusalem and Judah, whereas Amos sees the restoration of the Davidic state in all Israel as the ultimate outcome of Israel's punishment. All three of the

Septuagint's initial books, Hosea, Amos, and Micah, present the works of prophets who lived during the eighth century B.C.E.

The prophet's oracles must be set against the background of the rise of the Israelite state under the rule of Jeroboam ben Joash (786–746 B.C.E.).[1] During the course of his reign, Jeroboam II was able to secure his nation against external threat and to extend its borders from Lebo Hamath in Aram or Syria to the north and the sea of the Arabah (i.e., Gulf of Aqabah) to the south (2 Kgs 14:25). The northern kingdom of Israel was apparently allied with the southern kingdom of Judah under the rule of Uzziah/Azariah ben Amaziah (783–742 B.C.E.), although Judah must be considered as a junior partner in the relationship as it had been forced to acknowledge Israel's suzerainty since the reigns of Jehoash/Joash ben Jehoahaz of Israel (801–786 B.C.E.) and Amaziah ben Joash of Judah (800–783 B.C.E.; see 2 Kgs 14:8-14). Like Jeroboam, Uzziah was able to extend his influence during this period by following upon his father Amaziah's defeat of the Edomites (2 Kgs 14:7) with the rebuilding of Elath and its restoration to Judah (2 Kgs 14:22). Israel's traditional enemies, Aram and Philistia, were quiet during this period as they lacked the power to challenge the combined Israelite and Judean states. Israel's alliance with Assyria during this period, dating from the reigns of Jeroboam's great-grandfather Jehu (842–815 B.C.E.) and father Jehoash, no doubt contributed to Israel' security. Furthermore, Assyria was too preoccupied with its own internal problems to pose much of a threat to anyone during the first half of the eighth century B.C.E.[2]

Although Israel appears to have been secure during Amos' lifetime, the prophet consistently points to the upcoming punishment and exile of Israel at the hands of enemy nations. The reasons for the prophet's condemnation of Israel appear to lie in his Judean identity and the relationship between Israel and Judah during this period. Amos was a sheep herder and tender of sycamore trees who lived in the Judean town of Tekoa, situated south of Jerusalem along the edge of the Judean wilderness overlooking the descent to the Dead Sea. As Judah was subservient to Israel during this period, the Judean state would be ex-

---

[1] For discussion of the general historical period of Amos, see Herbert Donner, "The Separate States of Israel and Judah," *Israelite and Judean History*, ed. J. H. Hayes and J. M. Miller, OTL (Philadelphia: Westminster, 1977) 408–14. For an overview of critical problems in the study of the book of Amos, see A. G. Auld, *Amos*, OT Guides (Sheffield: JSOT Press, 1986).

[2] For discussion of Assyria during this period, see the work of A. K. Grayson in *Cambridge Ancient History 3/1. The History of the Balkans: The Middle East and the Aegean World, Tenth to Eighth Centuries B.C.*, ed. J. Boardman et al. (Cambridge: Cambridge University Press, 1982).

pected to pay a certain amount of tribute to Israel each year to meet the expenses of the administration, defense, and expansion of the larger Israelite empire. Most of this burden would fall upon the population of Judah, from which the Judean monarchy received its own resources for support. In an agrarian economy, this means that the people of Judah would have to pay a share of their agricultural harvest and animal stock to both the Judean and the Israelite monarchies.[3]

The need to pay tribute to northern Israel would account for Amos' presence in Beth El at the time of the festival of Sukkoth. Beth El was the royal sanctuary of the northern kingdom of Israel, situated just north of its border with Judah, and it would be here that Israel would collect tribute, offerings, and other revenues that were due it from Judah and from its own population. Israelite farmers were required to appear at the sanctuary three times during the year, at the festivals of Sukkoth (Tabernacles), Shavuot (Weeks), and Pesach (Passover), in order to pay the annual tithe of their produce that was due to the state (see Exod 23:14-19; 34:21-26; Deut 16:16-17; cf. Lev 27:30-33; Num 18:8-32; Deut 14:22-29; 18:1-8; 26:1-15; 1 Sam 8:10-18).[4] Amos' oracles and visions include reference to his following a heavily laden cart of grain (Amos 2:13) and the harvest of summer fruit (Amos 8:1-3), both of which presuppose the time between Shavuot and Sukkoth during the summer and early fall when the grain and fruit harvests come in.

But Amos' visions also point to economic hardship caused by natural catastrophe. He refers to a locust plague that destroyed the crops shortly after the king's mowings (Amos 7:1-3) and a fire that consumed the land (Amos 7:4-6), apparently leaving little for the people to eat. Nevertheless, he was still compelled to pay the full share of annual tribute at Beth El, and this apparently motivates his condemnation of the northern kingdom of Israel and the Beth El sanctuary. He points to the poverty of the people, who are sold for a pair of sandals, whose garments are taken in pledge, who are subject to fines for failing to pay off their debts, and who are continually cheated in the purchase of grain and other essentials (Amos 2:6-8; 8:4-6). He sees a very wealthy ruling class in Samaria, the capital of the northern kingdom, which lives on the backs of poor farmers such as himself (Amos 4:1; 6:1, 4-7) and does not relent in its demands for wealth even when the people face crop failure and potential starvation. He points to the mourning rituals observed at Beth El during Sukkoth, as worshipers would engage in

---

[3] For general background discussion, see Daniel C. Snell, "Taxes and Taxation," *ABD* VI:338-40; Michael L. Barré, "Treaties in the ANE," *ABD* VI:653-6.

[4] For discussion of the tithe, see Moshe Weinfeld, "Tithe," *Encyclopaedia Judaica* 15:1156-62.

lamentation to bring about the fall rains, and argues that Israel would indeed mourn when YHWH brought about the punishment of the state for its treatment of the poor (Amos 5:1-2; 8:9-14).

Overall, Amos calls for the destruction of the Beth El Temple, as it symbolizes Judah's subjugation to Israel and the Israelite monarchy's mistreatment of the people. The prophet points to the Day of YHWH as a time when punishment will be visited by YHWH against Israel (Amos 5:18-20), and he emphasizes that Israel's leaders will face exile at the hands of an enemy nation (Amos 5:27; 6:7). Many see this is a reference to an impending threat from Assyria, which was known for its practice of exiling leading elements of conquered populations, but Amos nowhere mentions the Assyrian empire as a threat. Instead, he emphasizes the imagery of earthquake (Amos 8:8; 9:5; cf. 9:1-4), the locust plague (Amos 7:1-3), and fire (Amos 7:4-6) as the means to convey YHWH's punishment of the nation. Indeed, the superscription states that Amos spoke two years before the earthquake (Amos 1:1), which would have provided some sense of confirmation for his message. As for the Assyrians, they did not begin to threaten Israel until after the ascension of Tiglath Pileser III to the Assyrian throne in 745 B.C.E., but this was well after the time of Amos. Nevertheless, Israel's alliance with Assyria, which enabled both Assyria and Israel to control Aram, had begun with the subjugation of Jehu to Shalmanezer III, and Amos could speculate that Assyria would someday threaten Israel once again.

Indeed, the present form of the book of Amos is organized to present an argument for Beth El's destruction and an exhortation to seek YHWH in Jerusalem.[5] The argument begins with a relatively broad perspective, but it focuses increasingly upon Beth El itself. Following the superscription to the book in Amos 1:1, the balance of the book appears in Amos 1:2–9:15. It begins with the motto in Amos 1:2, which points to YHWH's roaring from Zion and Jerusalem and the withering of Carmel in northern Israel as the basic theme of the book. The oracles concerning the nations in Amos 1:3–2:16 point to YHWH's condemnation of the nations that comprised Jeroboam II's empire as a basis to draw the audience into the climax of the series which condemns Israel itself for its abuse of its people. Amos 3–4 present a sermon by the prophet in which he points specifically to Israel's abuse of the poor, and Amos 5–6 then present another sermon by the prophet in which he calls upon the people to change their ways, seek YHWH, and thereby avoid the punishment that will otherwise overtake them. Finally, the vision reports in

---

[5] See Marvin A. Sweeney, "Formation and Form in Prophetic Literature," *Old Testament Interpretation: Past Present and Future. Essays in Honor of Gene M. Tucker*, ed. J. L. Mays, D. L. Petersen, and K. H. Richards (Nashville: Abingdon, 1995) 113–26.

Amos 7–9 point to the agricultural reverses faced by Judean farmers and the prophet's interpretation of the various signs associated with these reverses and the requirement to present offerings at Beth El as signs of YHWH's decision to bring about punishment. The vision reports culminate in the call for the destruction of the Beth El temple and the restoration of Davidic rule over all of Israel (including Judah). Many have argued that the book of Amos is the result of a long period of composition;[6] indeed, the third person superscription in Amos 1:1 and the narrative concerning the prophet's confrontation with the priest Amaziah at Beth El demonstrate that someone other than the prophet composed the book in its present form. Nevertheless, the argument for the destruction of Beth El and the restoration of Davidic rule expresses well the perspective of the prophet.[7] Such an argument would have been well received during the reigns of the Judean kings Ahaz (735–715 B.C.E.), Hezekiah (715–687/6 B.C.E.), and later Josiah (640–609 B.C.E.) when Judah sought to restore Israel to the rule of the Davidic dynasty. Amos would also have been read in the post-exilic period as a manifesto for the restoration of Davidic rule in the aftermath of the nation's exile (cf. Haggai).

The Superscription: 1:1

The superscription for the book of Amos appears in Amos 1:1.[8] In contrast to the bulk of the material in the book which is formulated as a series of speeches by the prophet addressed to an ancient audience, Amos 1:1 appears in a third person archival or reporting style that is addressed to a reading audience. It is structurally and generically distinct from the following material in that it is designed to introduce and identify the body of the book as "the words" of the prophet Amos. It is therefore not a part of Amos' work, but the work of a later author or editor who played a role in composing the book in its present form. Throughout the rest of the book, only the statement, "and he said," in Amos 1:2aα[1] and the report of Amos' confrontation with the priest Amaziah at Beth El in Amos 7:10-17 appear to be written in an objective

---

[6] See especially Wolff, *Joel and Amos*, 106–13.

[7] For discussion of the political dimensions of Amos, see especially Max E. Polley, *Amos and the Davidic Empire* (New York and Oxford: Oxford University Press, 1989).

[8] For discussion of superscriptions in prophetic books, see Gene M. Tucker, "Prophetic Superscriptions and the Growth of a Canon," *Canon and Authority*, ed. B. O. Long and G. W. Coats (Philadelphia: Fortress, 1977) 56–70.

narrative style that is addressed to a reading audience. Nevertheless, Amos 1:1; 1:2aα[1]; and 7:10-17 shape and present the book of Amos so that the whole is now addressed to a reader, even though Amos' original speeches may have been addressed orally to an audience of his contemporaries. Together, they indicate that the basic structural and generic divisions of the book are the superscription in Amos 1:1, which identifies the following material as "the words of Amos" and the presentation of Amos' words in Amos 1:2–9:15.

Amos 1:1 provides several pieces of information that aid in identifying the contents of the book as "the words of Amos." The first is the use of the term, "the words of Amos," to identify this material generically. Prophetic literature frequently employs the designation, "the word of YHWH," in the superscriptions and other narrative introductions in the prophetic books to identify the following material as prophetic oracles (see LXX Jer 1:1; Hos 1:1; Joel 1:1; Mic 1:1; cf. Mal 1:1). Only the MT version of the book of Jeremiah employs a similar formulation, "the words of Jeremiah ben Hilkiah . . ." Otherwise, the form appears, frequently as a title, in the context of historical works, e.g., "the words of Solomon" (1 Kgs 11:41); "the words of Nehemiah" (Neh 1:1) and in collections of proverbs or wisdom sayings, e.g., "the words of the wise" (Prov 22:17); "the words of Agur" (Prov 30:1); "the words of Lemuel" (Prov 31:1); "the words of Qohelet" (Qoh 1:1). There have been attempts to associate Amos with wisdom circles,[9] but the term appears to be a very general generic designation for a collection of sayings that can be applied either to prophetic, ruling, or wisdom figures and perhaps to others.

The name of the prophet appears without reference to his father. Although many of the superscriptions to the prophetic books identify the prophets by personal name and the name of the father (i.e., Isaiah, Jeremiah, Ezekiel, Hosea, Joel, Jonah, Zephaniah, Zechariah), others provide only the personal name of the prophet (i.e., Obadiah, Micah, Nahum, Habakkuk, Haggai, Malachi). The name Amos is derived from the verb root, ʿms, "to carry, protect, serve, save," and thereby refers to YHWH's protection, viz., "protected, carried (by YHWH)." Apart from the book of Amos, the name is otherwise unattested in the Hebrew Bible. The name Amaziah is derived from the same root (2 Chr 17:16).

Amos is identified professionally as one "who was among the shepherds of Tekoa." NRSV translates the term, nōqēd, as "shepherd," but this misrepresents the true meaning of the word. The Hebrew term rōʿeh is the usual term for "shepherd," but nōqēd elsewhere designates King

---

[9] E.g., Wolff, *Joel and Amos*, 90–106; idem, *Amos the Prophet: The Man and His Times* (Philadelphia: Fortress, 1973).

Mesha of Moab (2 Kgs 3:4) who paid tribute to the king of Israel with the wool of a hundred thousand lambs and a hundred thousand sheep. The term appears in both Akkadian and Ugaritic in reference to a herdsman or breeder of cattle and sheep. This corresponds well to Amos' description of himself in Amos 7:14 as a "herdsman" or "cattleman" *(bôqēr)*. Given the use of the term *nōqēd* in relation to a Moabite king, it seems best to consider this term to be a reference to a major "herdsman" or "dealer in cattle." This might explain Amos' presence in Beth El. Amos is a resident of the Judean town of Tekoa, which is located about five miles south of Bethlehem and twelve miles south of Jerusalem on the edge of the wilderness area to the east (see 2 Chr 20:20, which refers to the wilderness of Tekoa). He would normally be expected to travel to Jerusalem in order to present his offerings at the Jerusalem Temple. But Judah was allied as a vassal with Israel during the reigns of Kings Uzziah of Judah and Jeroboam ben Joash of Israel, and it seems likely that Amos served as one of those who would present a portion of the Judean agricultural and animal produce as tribute to the suzerain Israel at the royal sanctuary at Beth El. His designation as *nōqēd* would suggest his importance as a leader or at least a principle person in such a delegation over against the more common *rōʿeh.*

The phrase, "which he saw concerning Israel," qualifies the initial reference to "the words of Amos." As noted above, this designation does not identify the nature of the words specifically, but the use of the verb, *ḥzh*, "saw," indicates their prophetic nature. The root *ḥzh* is generally translated in reference to visionary experience, although it is clear that the term also includes the perception of auditory elements as well. It generally refers to prophetic or oracular visions and auditions (Ezek 12:27; 13:16; Num 24:4, 16), the perception of G–d (Exod 24:11; Job 19:26, 27; Pss 11:4; 17:15), and intense observation of the stars (Isa 47:13), the work of G–d (Job 36:25), etc. The phrase takes special care to note that Amos was concerned with Israel, i.e., the northern kingdom of Israel, but it does not mention Judah at all. This is not surprising as Amos appears only at Beth El, the royal sanctuary of the northern kingdom of Israel, and his oracles are directed primarily to the northern kingdom.

The superscription places Amos' words chronologically in the reigns of the Judean king Uzziah (783–742) and the Israelite king Jeroboam ben Joash (786–746). This was a period of great prosperity and security for the combined kingdoms of Israel and Judah. From the time of Jeroboam's father Joash (alternatively Jehoash) and Uzziah's (alternatively Azariah) father Amaziah, Judah had been tied to Israel as a vassal as a result of Jehoash's siege of Jerusalem and the forced submission of Amaziah (2 Kgs 14:8-14). By the time of Jeroboam and Uzziah, the two kingdoms appear to work in tandem. Jeroboam is clearly the senior partner, as indicated by the description of his kingdom, "from the entrance of Hamath as far as the Sea of the Arabah" (2 Kgs 14:25), which ranges from Syria in the north to the Red Sea in the south and includes the territory of Judah. This period precedes the time of the Assyrian onslaughts against the Syro-Israelite region by Tiglath Pileser III (745– 727 B.C.E.), and represents a time when Aram was contained by Israel's alliance with Assyria. The superscription also notes that Amos delivered his words "two years before the earthquake." Earthquakes are not unusual in this region. Therefore, the reference must be to a major earthquake that was remembered for generations (cf. Zech 14:4-5, which refers to this earthquake). Excavations at Hazor have uncovered evidence of a major earthquake that caused extensive damage to the city about 760 B.C.E.[10] Most exegetes therefore place Amos in relation to the period of the mid-eighth century B.C.E.

Presentation of the Words of Amos: Exhortation to Seek YHWH: 1:2–9:15

Many scholars argue that the so-called "motto" for the book in Amos 1:2 must be considered together with the superscription as a structurally independent unit from the following material beginning in Amos 1:3 and as a relatively late addition to the book.[11] This view overlooks the significance of the initial statement, "and he said," at the beginning of verse 2. Although this statement is joined syntactically to Amos 1:1 by the *waw-consecutive* formulation, *wayyōʾmar*, "and he said," it must be considered as the narrator's or editor's introduction to all of Amos' statements in the book, not only to the statement in verse 2. Although Amos 1:3 is syntactically independent of verse 2, it constitutes the next block of Amos' words following the "motto." Amos' words do not end in Amos 1:2; they end in Amos 9:15. The biographical narrative in Amos 7:10-17 does not constitute an element of the editorial superstructure for the book; rather, it is subsumed structurally to the autobiographical presentation of Amos' visions in Amos 7:10-17 where it provides an aside that demonstrates the reaction to Amos' initial visions in Amos 7:1-9, and thereby provides the justification for subsequent visions concerning Israel's or Beth El's projected downfall in Amos 8:1–9:15.

---

[10] Yigael Yadin, "Hazor," *NEAEHL* 2:594-603, 601.

[11] E.g., Wolff, *Joel and Amos*, 116–22; Jeremias, *The Book of Amos*, 11–4.

Amos 1:2 therefore introduces the body of the book of Amos, i.e., the presentation of the words of Amos as indicated in the superscription (Amos 1:1). Following the initial "motto" of the book in Amos 1:2, which introduces the theme of YHWH's theophany from Zion, Amos 1:3–9:15 constitutes the second major component of this material in the form of an exhortation to return to YHWH. The exhortation in turn comprises four major elements:[12] 1) the oracles against the nations and Israel in Amos 1:3–2:16; 2) the sermon directed to the people of Israel that warns of impending punishment in Amos 3:1–4:13; 3) the sermon directed to Israel in Amos 5:1–6:14 that calls upon the people to seek YHWH and live; 4) and the autobiographical vision reports in Amos 7:1–9:15 in which the prophet calls for the destruction of the Beth El altar and the northern Israelite monarchy, and looks toward the restoration of Davidic (and YHWH's) rule over the northern kingdom.

The Presentation of Amos' Motto:
YHWH's Theophany in Zion: 1:2

The editor or narrator of the book presents a statement by the prophet in Amos 1:2 that encapsulates Amos' view of YHWH. Although many interpreters see it as a hymnic fragment drawn from a psalm that might have been a part of the Jerusalem liturgy,[13] it essentially serves as a warning that YHWH is prepared to bring punishment upon YHWH's own land. Insofar as the verse represents a manifestation of YHWH on earth, some have correctly identified it as a theophany or a portrayal of YHWH's manifestation.[14] The portrayal of cosmic disruption, i.e., the drying up or withering of the land, is consistent with other theophanic texts (cf. Nah 1:2-6; Hab 3:3-12; Pss 97:2-5; 114:3-7). The imagery of "the pastures of the shepherds" and "the top of Carmel" is particularly important in relation to "sheepherder" such as Amos. "The pastures of the shepherds" of course speaks to his own interests in tending to sheep and other cattle. The reference to the "Carmel" calls to mind the Carmel mountain range located along the Mediterranean coast of northern Israel just south of Akko (near modern Haifa), although *karmel* in Hebrew refers to any area in which grape vines are planted.

Nevertheless, the northern identification of the Carmel range is important for understanding the perspective of a Judean sheepherder such as Amos. The Carmel represents one of northern Israel's most

---

[12] For discussion, see Sweeney, "Formation and Form."

[13] Wolff, *Joel and Amos*, 122.

[14] Jeremias, *The Book of Amos*, 13–4.

prominent and fertile areas in antiquity, which highlights the importance of a prophet's statement that YHWH will cause the Carmel to dry
up. When considered together with the pastures of the shepherds,
which are found in Amos' own region of Tekoa, the reference to the
Carmel indicates that YHWH's action will affect the entire land of Israel,
including both the northern kingdom of Israel and the southern kingdom of Judah which is allied with Israel at this time. The statement that
YHWH's manifestation appears in Zion or Jerusalem, however, demonstrates his Judean roots as well as his religious and political perspective. Indeed, the portrayal of YHWH's roaring employs the image of the
lion, the symbol of the tribe of Judah (Gen 49:8-12). Zion and Jerusalem,
of course, are the locations of YHWH's Temple and the ruling house of
David. Insofar as Amos calls for the destruction of the Beth El Temple,
i.e., the royal temple of the northern kingdom of Israel (9:1-10), the
death of Jeroboam ben Joash (7:10-17), and the restoration of the "fallen
hut of David," he calls for the reunification of the entire nation Israel
around YHWH's Jerusalem and the Davidic monarchy. Amos is very
much a partisan prophet from the land of Judah who speaks on behalf
of his nation's interests. This perspective permeates the entire book.

The Oracles against the Nations and Israel: 1:3–2:16

Amos 1:3–2:16 constitutes a sequence of oracles against the nations,
including Damascus/Aram (1:3-5), Philistia (1:6-8), Tyre (1:9-10), Edom
(1:11-12), Ammon (1:13-15), Moab (2:1-3), Judah (2:4-5), which culminates in Israel (2:6-16). Each is formulated as a prophetic judgment
speech concerning the nation in question with a relatively standard
pattern of elements.[15] The first is the messenger formula, "Thus says
YHWH," which identifies YHWH as the speaker of the following statement quoted by the prophet. The messenger formula is well-known in
prophetic speech, although it appears to derive from diplomatic discourse in which a king or other figure sends a representative to convey
a message to another party. The messenger begins by identifying the
source of the message, "thus says X," and then proceeds by quoting the
message verbatim (Gen 32:5; Num 22:15-16; 2 Kgs 18:29/Isa 36:14). The
second is the use of a progressive numerical sequence together with the
statement, "I will not cause it to return," in reference to YHWH's decision to punish the nation in question. The progressive numerical statement appears in both biblical and ancient Near Eastern literature, and
generally employs two or more successive numbers to enumerate ex-

---

[15] Cf. Wolff, *Joel and Amos*, 135–9.

amples or qualities of particular phenomenon, e.g., "Three things are too wonderful for me; four I do not understand: the way of an eagle in the sky, the way of a snake on a rock, the way of a ship on the high seas, and they of a man with a girl" (Prov 30:18-19). In this case, the proverb attempts to identify a sequence of marvels in the world, beginning with phenomena of nature and culminating in a timeless example of human interrelations. Other examples appear in Prov 30:15-16; Ps 62:12-13 [NRSV: 62:11-12]; Job 5:19-27; 33:14-15; Sir 50:25-26. The formula, "I will not cause it to return," has provoked extensive discussion because the "it" lacks an antecedent, but it appears to be a reference to YHWH's anger or will to punish, i.e., "I will not revoke the punishment."[16] The third element is a non-formulaic statement of the crime for which the nation is to be punished, which is a basic element of a prophetic judgment speech. The fourth element is a non-formulaic statement of the punishment to be inflicted upon the nation in question, again a basic element of the prophetic judgment speech. The fifth element is a concluding YHWH speech formula, "says YHWH," which again identifies the preceding words as YHWH's and closes the oracle against the nation in question. Of course, not all of the elements are present in each oracle, but they appear consistently enough within this sequence to serve as its characteristic identifying form.

The setting and sequence of these oracles has likewise prompted a great deal of discussion.[17] Various attempts have been made to point to the background of these oracles in relation to Egyptian execration texts, in which a priest pronounces curses upon a series of enemy nations and then breaks a pottery vessel to symbolize its defeat or destruction,[18] or a covenant cursing ceremony in which a prophet pronounces curses upon enemy nations.[19] Both of these proposals are suggestive, although it is difficult to establish precise analogies with the Egyptian ritual and there is no known covenant cursing ceremony against nations in Israelite religious practice. Nevertheless, there are examples in which diviners or prophets pronounce a curse against an enemy nation in time of war. The first appears in the narrative of Balaam's oracles against Israel (Numbers 22–24) in which the Moabite king Balak hires the Mesopotamian diviner Balaam to curse Israel and drive it from his land. Balaam prepares the various sacrifices in preparation for the ritual, but is only able to utter blessings over Israel rather than curses because he is only able to speak

---

[16] See Paul, *Amos,* 46–7, for an overview of discussion.

[17] Wolff, *Joel and Amos*, 135–52.

[18] Aage Bentzen, "The Ritual Background of Amos 1:2–2:16," *OTS* 8 (1950) 85–99.

[19] Henning Graf Reventlow, *Das Amt des Propheten bei Amos*, FRLANT, vol. 80 (Göttingen: Vandenhoeck & Ruprecht, 1962) 56–75.

the word of YHWH. Although this is clearly a satirical narrative that is designed to emphasize YHWH's blessing for Israel as it enters the promised land, it portrays an ancient cursing ceremony against an enemy nation that may well lie behind our present text in Amos. The other example appears in 1 Kings 22, in which Ahab, King of Israel, and Jehoshaphat, King of Judah, assemble their armies for war against Aram. When Ahab inquires of the prophets whether or not he should go up to battle against Ramoth-Gilead, the prophets respond to him that he should go up because YHWH has given it into his hand. This statement is accompanied by a symbolic action in which the prophet Zedekiah ben Henaanah made iron horns for himself to symbolize how Israel would "gore" the Aramaeans. Of course, the prophet Micaiah ben Imlah gave an alternative account of YHWH's will in which he announced that Israel would be defeated and that Ahab would die, but once again, this text serves as a portrayal of the setting of prophetic oracles against nations.

Clearly a war setting stands behind the standard form of the oracles against nations, but no war is evident in the book of Amos. Indeed, Amos portrays the threat as one brought by YHWH against the nations surrounding Israel and Israel itself. There is no hint that Assyria has begun its program of westward expansion, although rumblings in Assyria could well have prompted the prophet's message. Two features of the oracles in Amos are particularly noteworthy with regard to the potential rise of Assyria. First, all of the nations listed in this sequence were allies or even vassals of Israel under Jeroboam ben Joash. As noted earlier, Jeroboam was able to extend his realm from Lebo-Hamath in Syria to the Sea of the Arabah near present-day Eilat (cf. 2 Kgs 14:25). Such a territory encompasses much of Aram, all of Israel, and all of Judah. It would also appear to encompass a great deal of territory east of the Jordan River, including Ammon, Moab, and Edom, as well as the territory of the coastal plain, including much of Phoenicia and Philistia. Jeroboam's reign was a time of power, wealth, and peace, and this security was bought by means of a long-standing alliance between Israel and Assyria that was initiated by Jehu, Jeroboam's great grandfather and the founder of his dynasty. By means of this alliance, Israel and Assyria remained at peace, and they were able to divide Aram and neutralize it as a threat to either nation. Indeed, the identification of the "crimes" of the nations with the Hebrew word *pešʿa*, "transgression," signifies not a moral crime, but an act of political rebellion (1 Kgs 12:19; 2 Kgs 1:1; 3:5, 7; 8:20, 22; Isa 1:2; 2 Chr 10:19; 21:8, 10; Ezek 20:38; Lam 3:42; Hos 8:1).[20] Amos' language suggests that these nations have committed some crime against Israel, their ally or overlord.

[20] Paul, *Amos*, 45.

Second, the sequence of nations suggests a strategy by which Israel could be invaded and conquered by an army approaching from the north. It begins with Damascus/Aram, which is the first major nation situated west of Assyria. One then follows the trade route south from Damascus through the Jezreel Valley of Israel to the coastal plain, and then continues south to Philistia, thereby blocking any attempt by Egypt to intervene. The next move is against Phoenicia, which again blocks Egyptian attempts to intervene by sea. This leaves the trans-Jordanian region open to conquest. Finally, the central hill countries of Judah and Israel, which are the most difficult to take because of the natural protection offered by the terrain, are taken when they can no longer rely on support from their neighbors. Indeed, this strategy was employed by the Aramaeans against Israel when Hazael of Aram besieged Gath, and then turned back to threaten Jerusalem during the reign of Jehoash of Judah (2 Kgs 12:17-18) and later by Sennacherib who besieged Philistia and Lachish in the Shephelah prior to moving against Jerusalem (2 Kings 18–19/Isaiah 36–37). Some have argued that this model does not work because it requires an invading army to pass through the Jezreel Valley of Israel prior to attacking Israel itself, but the example of the Aramaeans demonstrates that it is a very workable strategy.

Indeed, Amos's use of this sequence seems to presuppose the reality of potential invasion of Israel from the north, but this does not become clear until the sequence is complete. Therefore, the rhetorical impact of this sequence must also be considered. Insofar as Amos names nations that are a part of the Israelite orbit and names crimes committed by them against Israel, he appeals to the sense of national pride and moral outrage in his audience by rehearsing actions that these nations have taken against Israel in the past, e.g., the wars between Aram and Israel over the Trans-Jordanian region of Gilead, various actions by Philistia and Tyre against Israel and Judah at the time of the Edomite revolt, Edom's revolt itself, and actions by Ammon and Moab that would have accompanied the wars with either Aram or Edom. Basically, Amos skillfully draws his audience into a mood for condemnation of past atrocities against Israel, but the sequence of nations enables him to encircle Israel and finally to strike at the nation as his rhetorical goal. When he concentrates on surrounding nations, his audience will be very supportive of his efforts, but when he names Judah in Amos 2:4-5 his true goal begins to become clear. Nevertheless, the audience would be committed emotionally at this point as he reaches the culmination of the series, the condemnation of Israel. This oracle comprises the longest oracle of the series, and constitutes the rhetorical goal of the entire speech. In this manner, Amos makes his point in the strongest terms possible by seducing his audience into self-condemnation.

Overall, the oracles against the nations in Amos 1:3–2:16 make their key point, viz., the empire of Jeroboam ben Joash is about to fall. Amos does not identify the threat other than to name Yhwh, but subsequent historical events indicate that the threat comes from Assyria. Perhaps Amos anticipated the rise of Assyria, but the language of the book does not make this clear at all.

The Oracle Concerning Damascus/Aram: 1:3-5

The first oracle in the sequence is directed against Damascus, the capital of ancient Aram (Syria). As noted above, Aram is the first country to the west of Assyria, which would make it the first country to suffer attack in the event of an Assyrian invasion. Indeed, upper Aram was the site of an attempt by Shalmanezer III to expand westward in 853 B.C.E., but he was stopped by an Aramean coalition led by Bar Hadad (a.k.a., Ben Hadad, Hadadezer), which included an Israelite contingent led by Ahab.[21]

Following the formulaic introductory material in verse 3a, verse 3b states that Damascus is to be judged "because they have threshed Gilead with threshing sledges of iron." The metaphorical description of "threshing" a land with "threshing sledges" is well-known as a common depiction of the oppression by one nation of another in Assyrian monumental inscriptions and treaties.[22] Threshing grain is necessary to separate kernels of grain from the chaff, and one of the several ways to do this was by dragging a heavy threshing sledge over the grain in order to crush it and thereby separate the kernels. The image of grain being trampled and crushed in this manner lends itself easily to the depiction of cruel and oppressive conquest by an agriculturalist such as Amos who was accustomed to processing grain in this manner. The identification of Gilead as the victim of such action by Aram stands to reason. Gilead is the Israelite territory east of the Kinneret/Sea of Galilee and the Jordan River that was frequently subject to invasion by Aram. Israel and Aram fought a series of wars during the ninth century B.C.E. for control of this region. During the course of one of these battles, King Ahab of Israel was killed (1 Kings 22) at Ramot Gilead, and his dynasty was eventually overthrown by Jehu as Israel was threatened with the potential loss of the Gilead region (2 Kings 9–10). Israel was not able to reassert control of the region until the reigns of Jehoash/Joash ben Jehoahaz (801–786 B.C.E.) and Jeroboam ben Joash (786–746 B.C.E.),

---

[21] See Pritchard, *ANET*, 278–9.
[22] Paul, *Amos*, 47–8.

when Israel and Assyria were allied, leaving Aram weakened and trapped between the two powers. Indeed, Genesis 31 employs the figures of Jacob and Laban, the eponymous ancestors of Israel and Aram, to describe the determination of the border between the two lands by erecting a "heap of witness" to establish a mutually recognized boundary between them.

Amos' announcement that Aram would suffer for its atrocities in Gilead would no doubt be welcomed by an Israelite audience during the reign of Jeroboam ben Joash, as Israelites would see this as indication that Aram was finally getting all that it deserved for its actions. The imagery of verses 4-5, "I will send fire against the house of Hazael and it shall devour the strongholds of Ben-Hadad; I will break the gate bar of Damascus; I shall cut off the inhabitants from the Valley of Aven, and the one who holds the scepter from Beth Eden, and the people of Aram shall go into exile to Kir," conveys the process of a full frontal assault against a walled city in which flaming torches are shot against the city's defenses, a battering ram is used to break through the barred and fortified gate, the inhabitants and the king are slaughtered, and the survivors deported to another land as captives. This process is well-represented in Assyrian reliefs concerning the siege of the Judean city Lachish by Sennacherib in 701 B.C.E.[23] The references to Hazael and Ben Hadad indicate the names of several Aramean kings during the ninth and eighth centuries. Ben Hadad I was an ally of the Israelite king Baasha (900–877 B.C.E.), but shifted his allegiance to the Judean king Asa (913–873; 1 Kgs 15:18-20). Ben Hadad II was the major opponent of Ahab (869–850), and was assassinated by Hazael in a coup supported by the prophet Elisha (2 Kgs 8:7-15). Hazael's son, Ben Hadad III, was defeated by Jehoash/Joash (801–786 B.C.E.) who reasserted control over the Israelite cities taken by Hazael (2 Kgs 13:22-25).

The reference to the inhabitants of the Valley of Aven, literally, "the Valley of Sin," is understood in LXX as the "Valley of On" (Heliopolis), based upon the same Hebrew consonants (*ʾwn*) as the MT. The LXX designation is generally understood as a reference to Baalbek (i.e., Valley of [*biqʿat*] Baal, not the better known Egyptian Heliopolis) in the center of the "Lebanon Valley," known today as the Beqa Valley, between the Lebanon and ante-Lebanon mountains that define the territory of modern Lebanon. Aram (and later Assyria) sought to control this region in order to allow greater access to the Mediterranean and to coastal trade routes that led to Egypt. "Beth Eden" refers to the Aramean city-state Bit Adini centered around the capital of Tel Barsib, which was situated on the shores of the Euphrates River, some two hundred miles

---

[23] Pritchard, *ANEP,* 372–3.

northeast of Damascus.[24] Its location would make it one of the major Aramean outposts on the Assyrian border, and therefore one of the first Aramean territories to be threatened by Assyria. During the eighth century, it was ruled by an Assyrian governor, and later incorporated as an Assyrian province by Tiglath Pileser III (745–727 B.C.E.). By Amos' time, the "scepter" had already been "cut off" from Beth Eden and given to the Assyrians, which would aid in convincing the Israelite audience that Amos' words concerning the punishment of Damascus were true. The reference to the potential exile of the people of Aram to Kir indicates that the Arameans will be taken back to the land from which they originally came as indicated by the reference in Amos 9:7. The location of Kir is uncertain, but many identify it as a site near Elam, east of Babylonia at the northern portion of the Persian Gulf.[25] This would place the site in the vicinity of ancient Ur, which Gen 11:27-32 identifies as the original home of Abram / Abraham, whose father, Terah, and brother, Nahor, are associated with Aram.

THE ORACLE CONCERNING GAZA / PHILISTIA: 1:6-8

The oracle concerning Gaza and the other Philistine cities is formulated similarly to that concerning Damascus. Gaza is the southernmost of the five Philistine cities (the others are Ekron, Gath, Ashdod, Ashkelon), located along the Mediterranean coast in the present-day Gaza strip, which makes it one of the last major Syro-Israelite outposts along the coastal road to Egypt. Control of Gaza prevents Egypt from interfering in Syria-Israel. Philistia had been taken by David early in the tenth century B.C.E. (2 Sam 5:17-25; 8:1), but it was later able to release itself from Israel's or Judah's control. By the ninth century, Hazael of Aram is reported to have taken Gath as part of his efforts to threaten Jerusalem (2 Kgs 12:17-18). Even prior to this, 2 Kgs 8:22 reports that the Judean city of Libnah revolted against Judah during the reign of Jehoram (849–842 B.C.E.). As Libnah is located in the Judean Shephelah opposite Philistia between Ekron and Gath, it would seem that the Philistines would have had something to do with this revolt, particularly since this was the period immediately after the death of Ahab at Ramot Gilead, when the Arameans had defeated Israel and Judah. Although 2 Kgs 14:23-29 does not indicate that Jeroboam ben Joash conquered Philistia, the expansion of the Israelite kingdom during his reign would suggest to Amos' audience that Israel would control Philis-

---

[24] Paul, *Amos*, 53–4.
[25] For discussion of the site of Kir, see H. O. Thompson, "Kir," *ABD* IV:83-4.

tia. In this regard, Amos' oracle of judgment against the Philistine cities, Gaza, Ashdod, Ashkelon, and Ekron, would suggest to the listening Israelites that Philistia was also getting what it deserved. Scholars have speculated that Gath is absent from the list because it had ceased to exist as a viable city, but this is uncertain.[26]

The cause for Philistia's punishment has provoked a great deal of speculation that the Philistines were involved in some sort of slave trade in the eastern Mediterranean, "because they carried into exile entire communities, to hand them over to Edom."[27] Although such practices were well known in the ancient world and certainly not outside of Philistia's capabilities, the reference to Edom requires consideration. Many speculate that the "slaves" were delivered for work in the copper mines of the region in Edom east of the Arabah, or that the reference to Edom should be emended to "Aram" or some other land.[28] It seems best, however, to consider the reference to the above-mentioned revolt of Libnah against Judah in 2 Kgs 8:20-22, which is mentioned in conjunction with Edom's revolt against Judah. Libnah is a Judean town, and would only revolt under the most extreme circumstances. Such circumstances appear in the aftermath of Aram's defeat of Israel and the death of Ahab at Ramot Gilead. Philistia was clearly open to invasion by Aram in the aftermath of Ahab's death so that it could no longer rely on Israel/Judah for protection or even fear retaliation (cf. 2 Kgs 12:17-18). It would seem that Aram would have exploited this opportunity to prompt Philistia and other territories to revolt against Israel/Judah. The revolt of Edom is important at this point, as Edom had been a key Judean vassal from the time of David (2 Sam 8:13-14); the Edomites had even accompanied Jehoram and Jehoshaphat in their campaign against Mesha of Moab (2 Kgs 3:4-27), and distinguished themselves by blocking the Moabite attempt to escape. But by the reign of the Judean Jehoram, Israel's and Judah's position had suffered markedly, prompting the successful Edomite revolt. The timing of Edom's revolt with that of Libnah suggests that the Philistines were involved; indeed, Philistia and Edom together can threaten the southern borders of Judah in the Shephelah and the Negev desert. This would suggest that Amos' reference to the Philistines handing over an entire "community" (literally, "exile") to Edom might indicate Philistine support or instigation in an Edomite encroachment into Judean territory. Although Jeroboam ben Joash (or the Judean Amaziah; 2 Kgs 14:7) was unable to bring Edom back under Israelite control, he was able to restore the border of Israel

---

[26] Stuart, *Hosea-Jonah,* 312.
[27] Ibid.
[28] Paul, *Amos,* 56–7.

to the Sea of the Arabah, which indicates that he controlled the south-
eastern portions of Judah that would be subject to Edomite threat. Once
again, Amos' Israelite audience would take this as an indication that
Philistia was getting what it deserved for its past actions.

THE ORACLE CONCERNING TYRE/PHOENICIA: 1:9-10

The oracle concerning Tyre appears to be formulated on the model
of the oracle concerning Gaza. In addition to the common formulaic
elements of the oracles against the nations in Amos in general, the first
portion of the statement concerning the basis for Tyre's punishment in
verse 9bα employs vocabulary that also appears in the indictment of
Gaza in Amos 1:7b, viz., "because they delivered entire communities
over to Edom." In addition, verse 7bβ accuses Tyre of having not remembered "the covenant of kinship" as a further basis for punishment.

The similarities between this oracle and that concerning Gaza have
prompted some to argue that Amos 1:9-10 is a secondary addition to
the oracles against the nations to account for the threat that was posed
to Phoenicia by the Babylonian empire and its policy of deporting
major elements from subject populations.[29] This conclusion is unnecessary, however, in that there is sufficient background in the history of
relations between Tyre and Israel to explain the circumstances envisioned in the oracle. The charge that Tyre did not remember "the covenant of kinship" (*bĕrît ʾaḥîm*, literally, "covenant of brothers") is
particularly important in that it points to the treaty relationship that
existed between Hiram of Tyre and both David and Solomon in the
tenth century. Hiram supplied David with material and expertise to
build a palace (2 Sam 5:11), and he supplied Solomon with materials
and expertise to build the Temple (1 Kgs 5:15-32 [NRSV: 5:1-18]). Furthermore, the language employed to describe the relationship between
Hiram and both David and Solomon is the language of ancient Near
Eastern treaties.[30] In 1 Kgs 5:15 [NRSV: 5:1], Hiram is described as one
who always "loved" David. The Hebrew term *ʾōhēb*, "loves," and its
Akkadian cognate *raʾāmu*, "to love," is the standard technical term to
convey faithfulness and loyalty in treaty relationships. Furthermore,
Hiram refers to Solomon as "my brother" in 1 Kgs 9:13, employing a
standard term that is used in ancient parity treaties to signify the relationship between two parties. The use of the same term in Amos 1:9 indicates that the oracle presupposes that Tyre has violated its treaty with

---

[29] Wolff, *Joel and Amos*, 139–41.
[30] For discussion of the treaty language in this oracle, see Paul, *Amos*, 61–3.

Israel. Indeed, Tyre and Sidon were bound to Israel by treaty during the reign of the Omride dynasty (876–842 B.C.E.), as indicated by the marriage of Ahab to Jezebel, the daughter of Ethbaal king of Sidon, and the erection of an altar and temple for the Phoenician Baal in Samaria (1 Kgs 16:31-33; cf. 1 Kgs 18:19). It was only after Jehu's coup against the house of Omri, which saw the assassination of Ahab's son Joram, the Judean king Ahaziah, and Jezebel (2 Kgs 9:14-37), and his execution of the Omride supporters in the Temple of Baal (2 Kgs 10:1-27) that the treaty relationship would have ended. Of course, Phoenicia ceased to support Israel in the aftermath of Jehu's coup, and Jehu was left to face the Arameans alone. Hazael quickly proceeded to occupy the territory of Gilead and Bashan east of the Jordan (2 Kgs 10:32-33), and continued to harass Israel through the reign of Jehu's son Jehoahaz as well (2 Kgs 13:3-7, 22-23) until Jehoahaz's son Jehoash defeated Ben Hadad and re-captured Israel's cities (2 Kgs 13:24-25). Although Jehu overthrew the Omride dynasty and destroyed the Phoenician temple to Baal in Samaria, Phoenicia's failure to come to Israel's aid at the time that Aram occupied Gilead and Bashan would be understood as a violation of its treaty with Israel. Such is the perspective of propagandistic portrayal by a beleaguered monarch to his own people. An entire Israelite population was exiled insofar as it fell under Aramean rule, and the Jehu dynasty would naturally argue that its allies had abandoned them. Some argue that the reference "to Edom" in verse 9b should be changed to "to Aram" in light of Israel's losses to Aram in this period.[31] This is possible as the Hebrew letters *resh* and *dalet* appear to be very similar (n.b., *ʾrm*, Aram; *ʾdm*, Edom). It is also possible that the oracle points to Phoenicia's failure to support Israel and Judah fully in its wars against Aram under Ahab and the subsequent reverses that Israel suffered in the aftermath of Ahab's death. It was after all during this period that Edom and Libnah revolted successfully against Judah (2 Kgs 8:20-22).

THE ORACLE CONCERNING EDOM: 1:11-12

Once again, the oracle concerning Edom in Amos 1:11-12 employs the standard formulaic pattern of Amos' oracles concerning the nations. Several grounds for punishment are listed in verse 11 which indicate Edom's hostile actions against a party identified as "his brother." As the Genesis narratives concerning Jacob and Esau, the eponymous ancestors of Israel and Edom respectively, indicate (Genesis 25–27; 32–33), "his brother" must refer to Israel. Although this would suggest an ethnic

[31] See BHS note.

bond between the two nations, the term apparently indicates a political relationship between them which the Edomites have violated. The statement that Edom "pursued his brother with the sword" calls to mind Isaac's statement that Esau would live by the sword, serve his brother, and eventually free himself from Jacob's control (Gen 27:39-40). This suggests that Genesis 27 looks forward to the situation presupposed by Amos in the present oracle. In this case, it would then refer to some military action by Edom against Israel. As noted in the discussion of the oracles concerning Damascus, Gaza, and Tyre above, Amos presupposes actions taken by these nations against Israel during the ninth century B.C.E., when the Omride dynasty lost control of the Trans-Jordan and was overthrown by Jehu. Biblical sources indicate that Edom had been under Judean control from the time of David (2 Sam 8:13-14), Solomon (1 Kgs 11:15-17), and Jehoshaphat (1 Kgs 22:47; 2 Kgs 3:9-27), but they revolted against Jehoram ben Jehoshaphat of Judah within a few years of the death of Ahab of Israel (2 Kgs 8:20-22). In the early eighth century, Amaziah ben Joash of Judah captured Sela (2 Kgs 14:7), but Judah never regained control of all of Edom.

Biblical sources do not report specific incursions by the Edomites into Judean territory, but this was frequently a problem for Judah throughout its history as indicated by the network of fortresses built to protect Negev trade routes later in the seventh century B.C.E. (cf. 1 Samuel 27; 30, which relate the pattern of Negev raids by various armed groups, such as David's men or the Amalekites).[32] The statement in Amos 1:11b, "and cast off all pity," appears to presuppose atrocities committed during such raids. As indicated by Paul, the Hebrew phrase, *wĕšiḥēt raḥămāyw*, refers to the killing of women (literally, "and he destroyed his wombs," i.e., the "wombs" of "his brother").[33] The latter portion of the verse builds upon this motif by metaphorically portraying Edom as a lion that attacks and guards its prey. The statement, "and he maintained his anger perpetually," employs the verb *ṭrp*, which means "he tore (meat like a lion)" i.e., "his anger tore perpetually." Likewise, the statement, "and kept his wrath forever," should read literally, "and his wrath watched forever," and employs the image of a lion standing watch over its dead prey as it comes back to feed at its leisure. The threat of lions was well known in the Negev and southern Judah throughout antiquity (see David's statements concerning his killing of lions and bears that attacked his father's sheep in the vicinity of Bethlehem; 1 Sam 17:31-37).

[32] See Amihai Mazar, *Archaeology of the Land of the Bible, 10,000–586 B.C.E.* (New York: Doubleday, 1990) 438–44.

[33] Paul, *Amos*, 64–5.

The oracle concludes with the statement that YHWH will send fire against Teman (cf. Jer 49:7, 20; Obad 9) and it will devour the strongholds of Bozrah (Isa 34:6; Jer 49:13, 22), two of the principle cities of the Edomites.

THE ORACLE CONCERNING THE AMMONITES: 1:13-15

The oracle concerning "the sons of Ammon" likewise charges them with atrocities against the people of Israel. The reference to their ripping open "pregnant women in Gilead" once again calls to mind the situation of Israel in the aftermath of the death of Ahab when the Arameans were able to wrest the Trans-Jordan away from Israel. Amos' oracle indicates that Ammonites, whose land was situated east of Gilead around their capital Rabbah (modern Amman), were able to take advantage of the situation to expand their own borders. The oracles portray the coming punishment of Ammon with a combination of images drawn from war and desert winds, i.e., "kindling" fire against the wall of Rabbah, shouting on the day of battle, and "storm on the day of the whirlwind." The kindling of fire calls to mind the ease with which sparks will kindle dry brush at the edge of the Arabian desert. The shouting during battle is of course self-explanatory. The storm and whirlwind imagery employs the image of the *Hamsin/Sharav* or dry east desert wind that sometimes blows with destructive force and blocks the view of the sky. The final statement, "and their king shall go into exile, he and his officials together," appears in a somewhat different form in Jer 49:3, "for Milcom shall go into exile, with his priests and his attendants." The statement in Amos is sometimes emended with the Jeremiah reading (cf. LXX) so that "their king" is read as "Milcom," the god of the Ammonites (1 Kgs 11:5, 33; 2 Kgs 23:13).[34] This is unnecessary, however, as the oracles against the nations in Amos consistently condemn the people and rulers of the countries in question, not their gods. Jeremiah 49:3, which actually reads, "their king," not, "Milcom," may represent an interpretative reading of Amos 1:15.

THE ORACLE CONCERNING MOAB: 2:1-3

The oracle concerning Moab in Amos 2:1-3 charges the Moabites with a crime committed against the Edomites, not against Israel or

---

[34] Cf. Wolff, *Joel and Amos*, 131-2, 161-2, who also rejects the emendation.

Judah. By burning the bones of the King of Edom to lime, the Moabites apparently engaged in a practice that is known among the Assyrians as a means to curse a dead enemy by disinterring the body and desecrating it. Basically, burning the bones to lime means to burn them to dust as the soil of Israel and Jordan is composed largely of eroded limestone. Lime can be used as a cleansing agent or as an element in mortar for building houses,[35] but there is no hint that the Moabites put the lime to use; the action was meant to insult or curse Edom.

There is no known reference to this action. It is noteworthy, however, that following the death of Ahab at the hands of the Arameans at Ramot Gilead, the Moabites appear to be the first nation that revolted against Israel. According to 2 Kgs 3:4-27, Jehoram of Israel, Jehoshaphat of Judah, and the King of Edom embarked upon a campaign to force the King Mesha of Moab to submit to Israel once again, but they failed to accomplish their objective when the Moabite king sacrificed his firstborn son as a burnt offering. The Mesha inscription likewise relates Mesha's successful revolt against Israel and his occupation of Israelite lands in the Trans-Jordan.[36] Although it is somewhat speculative, it is easy to imagine that Moab's successful revolt against Israel became a catalyst to others, such as Edom and Libnah (2 Kgs 8:20-22). It is also possible that Moab took some action against Edom, such as burning the Edomite king's bones, to instigate action against Judah by Edom.

The oracle targets the city of Kerioth, a principle city of Moab (Jer 48:24, 41), which is listed in the Moabite Stone as the site of a sanctuary for the god Chemosh. The oracle calls for the death of Moab (cf. Isa 25:10b-12) amidst the sounds of shouting and Shofar (blast of the ram's horn) during battle. The final judgment against Moab's "ruler" employs the term *šôpēṭ*, "judge," which frequently designates a military or political leader as in the book of Judges.

The Oracle Concerning Judah: 2:4-5

Many scholars argue that the oracle concerning Judah in Amos 2:4-5 must be a secondary addition to the series.[37] Amos is supposed to speak against Israel, not Judah, and an oracle against Judah would undermine the rhetorical impact of his attempt to condemn Israel. The

[35] See W. E. Staples, "Lime," *IDB* III:134.
[36] Pritchard, *ANET,* 320–1.
[37] See Wolff, *Joel and Amos,* 139–41; Jeremias, *The Book of Amos,* 44.

form differs somewhat in that it is shorter than the other examples in the series. Furthermore, the references to rejection of YHWH's Torah and statutes appear to employ Deuteronomic language from the late-monarchic, exilic, or post-exilic period.

It is possible that the oracle has been reworked in keeping with a later interest in the Josianic period to employ the prophecy of Amos as a basis for calling for Israel's return to Davidic rule, but it also makes a great deal of sense for Amos to include an oracle concerning Judah in the original series. It might tip his hand by indicating his intention to target Israel as his ultimate rhetorical goal, but at this point in the series, it is time to provide hints to his audience of his intentions. An oracle against Judah, however, feeds into the same audience perspectives as those against the other nations. Judah is an ally or vassal of Israel in this period, and there had been times when Judah attempted to revolt against Israel (e.g., during the reign of Amaziah; 2 Kgs 14:1-14). As a Judean, Amos could be perceived as engaging in national self-condemnation that would simultaneously have appealed to a northern Israelite audience—he was after all in Beth El to present part of Judah's agricultural tribute to Israel—but it would also have started to raise questions concerning his ultimate intent. The oracle against Judah is only two verses long, and in an oral setting it would not have allowed much time for such speculation. At this point, it would only begin to occur to his Israelite audience that they were his next target, but by the time this realization would have sunk home, his oracle against Israel would have begun.

The oracle accuses Judah of rejecting YHWH's Torah or "instruction," improperly translated in the NRSV as "law." The term conveys instruction in Temple ritual purity or propriety (Hag 2:11-13), political propriety (Hab 1:4), and issues of national history and identity. In the present case, it speaks very generally about disobedience and following the "lies" that led the ancestors astray, but it is not entirely clear what disobedience or lies are presupposed in the oracle. The reference to rejection of YHWH's Torah appears to be somewhat similar to the statement in Isa 5:24, "because they have rejected the Torah of YHWH of Hosts," in which Israel's crime is social abuse in treatment of the poor and failing to rely on YHWH, rather than on military alliance, for protection from outside threat. Insofar as Judah is allied with Israel and Israel is condemned for social abuses much like those of Isa 5:1-24, it seems that Amos may well condemn Judah for its alliance with Israel and its acceptance of Israel's corrupt (from Amos' perspective) practices in treating the poor. By the end of the book, Amos calls for the destruction of the royal Israelite sanctuary at Beth El and the restoration of Davidic rule. From his perspective, Judah has not been true to itself.

THE ORACLE CONCERNING ISRAEL: 2:6-16

The oracle concerning Israel constitutes the climax and rhetorical goal of the entire series of oracles concerning the nations in Amos. It employs the same basic formulation as the other oracles, but the fact that it is directed against Israel rather than a foreign nation catches the audience by surprise as Amos' listeners or readers would presuppose that the entire sequence was directed against Israel's enemies. The culminating focus on Israel at this time is especially pertinent as the reign of Jeroboam ben Joash marked a period of power and security for Israel much like that of the reign of Solomon. But just as Solomon's kingdom fell apart following his reign, so Amos maintains that Jeroboam's kingdom is subject to punishment for crimes of social abuse. In this case the enumeration of three or four "transgressions" on the part of Israel would no longer refer to political rebellion by the nations against Israel, but Israel's wrongdoing in relation to YHWH.

The oracle follows an expanded form of the standard pattern of Amos' oracles against the nations. The messenger formula appears in verse 6aα; the charges against Israel, beginning with YHWH's formulaic statement that Israel's transgressions will not be revoked, appear in verses 6aβ-12; and YHWH's announcement of punishment against Israel appears in verses 13-16.

The charges against Israel in verses 6aβ-12 include a series of statements, linked by *waw-conjunctives*, that specify Israel's actions. Verses 6aβ-8 list examples of Israel's mistreatment of the poor and disadvantaged; verses 9-11 specify YHWH's actions on Israel's behalf, culminating in a rhetorical question that confirms YHWH's beneficent actions on behalf of Israel; and verse 12 returns to Israel's wrongdoing in contrast to YHWH's attempts to act on the people's behalf.

The charges listed in verses 6aβ-8 begin with the formulaic introduction that asserts Israel's wrongdoing, but shifts immediately to specifications concerning the abuse of the righteous and poor. The initial statement, "because they sell the righteous for silver, and the needy for a pair of sandals," has been taken by some interpreters to refer to the bribing of judges to overturn a legal verdict.[38] The basic reason is the use of the term "righteous" (*ṣaddîq*), which is a technical term for one who is judged to be innocent in a legal proceeding, in relation to laws concerning the perversion of justice by judges who accept a bribe (cf. Exod 23:6-8; Deut 16:19; 1 Kgs 8:32). Others have argued that the issue is the sale of the poor in cases of debt slavery, as indicated by the reference to the "needy" in the second part of the statement. According

[38] For discussion, see Paul, *Amos*, 77–9.

to ancient Israelite legal tradition, a person could be sold into slavery to pay off a debt (Exod 21:2-11; Deut 15:1-8). The term of service is specified for a maximum of six years, after which the slave must be released in the seventh year, unless the slave decided to accept permanent service under the master. Essentially, the slave was able to work off the debt. A woman could be assigned as a concubine to a male member of the creditor's family. According to Exod 21:8-11, she could not be sold or released unless the creditor refused to provide for her (cf. Abram's and Sarai's treatment of Hagar in Genesis 16; 21). According to Deut 15:12-18, a woman was released on the same terms as a man. Although interpreters have adopted either of these positions, the passage seems to presuppose both cases as "innocent" and "needy" are presented as a paired reference; the reference to the "righteous" suggests that persons who were legally innocent were being sold into debt slavery, and the reference to the "needy" indicates the reason for the sale. As creditors were able to take the garment of debtor in pledge, it is possible that the reference to sandals indicates that the creditors took even the sandals of the poor as surety against a debt. The law in Exod 22:25-26 envisions such a possibility, but protects the debtor by requiring that the garment be returned at night so that the debtor might have something to sleep in for protection against the cold. Verse 7a confirms this interpretation by pointing to the greed of those who abuse the poor, "they who trample the head of the poor into the dust of the earth, and push the afflicted out of the way." The Hebrew term *haššō'ăpîm*, "translated here as they who trample," can also mean, "they who pant after" (cf. Job 5:5; 7:2; 36:20), to convey the sense of effort made by those who chase their victims down in order to sell them for silver or sandals. The verb is formulated as a participle, so that it appositionally modifies the "they" of verse 6, in order to convey the depiction of the creditors' greed.

The following accusations in verses 7b-8 build upon the initial theme of economic abuse. The statement that "father and son go in to the same girl so that my holy name is profaned," is often taken simply as a sexual crime of incest in keeping with the prohibitions of a father and son engaging in sexual relations with the same woman (Lev 18:8; 20:11, 12). Although incest is still part of the overall scenario envisioned here, there is an issue related to debt slavery as well. The law concerning the treatment of women slaves in Exod 20:7-11 specifies that a man may designate the woman as a concubine for himself, but he may release her it she does not please him. It also states that he may designate the woman for his son, but he must treat her as a daughter-in-law. If he marries another woman, he may diminish her food, clothing, or marital rights. It would appear that verse 7b envisions a situation in which a slave woman's rights have been violated by a man and his son who ignore the sexual boundaries imposed by this law, i.e., whereas the law is designed to prevent incest or abuse and thereby to protect the woman in question, the father and son simply ignore the law as both take her when they please. The reference to profaning the divine Name of YHWH of course presupposes a violation of the natural order of creation as perceived in ancient Israel, viz., incest is not a proper action. The statement in verse 8, they lay themselves down beside every altar on garments taken in pledge, builds upon the sexual imagery of the preceding verse, but it highlights the economic side as well. As noted above, the garments of a debtor could be taken in pledge for a loan, although they had to be returned at night (Exod 22:25-26). The reference to the altar highlights the prior concern with profaning YHWH's Name, after all these actions take place at the Temple where the altar is located. But it is noteworthy that one enters into permanent debt slavery at the site of the Temple or altar, as indicated by Exod 21:6 which requires that the ear of the slave be pierced with an awl when he is brought "to G–d." Verse 8b, "and in the house of their G–d they drink wine bought with fines they imposed," likewise indicates the consumption in the Temple of wine taken as a result of economic abuse. Exodus 21:22 indicates that a fine might be levied against someone who causes a miscarriage or against a man who falsely claims that his bride is not a virgin. It would appear that wine, as a primary agricultural commodity in ancient Israel, could be used to pay fines. Again, the prophet notes consumption of such gain at the Temple to highlight the lack of concern for YHWH's holiness or justice.

Verses 9-11 comprise a series of statements in which YHWH describes acts of divine beneficence on behalf of Israel in a deliberate contrast with Israel's acts that are contrary to YHWH's will. The emphatic "and I" *(wĕʾānōkî)* at the beginning of verse 9 highlights the contrast. YHWH begins with reference to the destruction of the Amorites who preceded Israel in the land, so that the land could be given to Israel. The term "Amorites" refers to the Semitic-speaking semi-nomadic people who migrated into Mesopotamia, Syria, and Canaan from the Arabian desert during the early second millennium B.C.E.[39] The term is derived from the Akkadian *amurru,* "westerners" (from the western Arabian desert or western Syria). The Amorites eventually took control of Mesopotamia —the dynasty of Hammurabi was an Amorite dynasty—and settled extensively in Syria and Canaan. Together with the Canaanites and Hittites, the Amorites are identified as the former occupants of the land of Canaan prior to the emergence of Israel (Ezek 16:3; Gen 15:16; Deut 1:7). Because the Amorites are presented in the Bible as idolaters who committed iniquity (Josh 24:15; Judg 6:10; cf. Lev 18:24-30; 20:23),

---

[39] See G. E. Mendenhall, "Amorites," *ABD* I:199-202.

YHWH destroyed them and gave the land to Israel. The portrayal of the great height of the Amorites corresponds to other biblical traditions that portray the previous inhabitants of the land as giants (Num 13:28; Deut 1:28; 2:10, 21; 9:2; Josh 14:12, 15; 15:14). The portrayal of the Amorites as giant trees, however, may well relate to the imagery of the Asherah beside the altar (cf. Deut 16:21-22). The Asherah was a tree that was intended to represent the presence of Asherah, the Canaanite goddess of the earth and fertility. The Assyrians frequently employed the imagery of a tree to represent the presence of the gods on earth or the king of Assyria. Indeed, Judean prophets employ the imagery of tree to depict the downfall of enemy kings (Isa 10:5-34; Ezekiel 31). Now that Israel behaves in a manner similar to the Amorites, YHWH implies that the same thing can happen to them. The statement that YHWH cut off his fruit above and his roots beneath would be quite familiar to a dresser of sycamore trees like Amos, who constantly had to deal with the threats posed by nature to the fruit trees which helped to provide him with a living.

YHWH follows up chronologically in verse 10 with another statement introduced by the emphatic, "and I" *(wěʾānōkî)* that relates YHWH's bringing the people of Israel out of slavery in Egypt and guidance for forty years in the wilderness. The purpose of YHWH's actions is defined in the last statement of the verse, which returns to the theme of the Amorites, "to possess the land of the Amorite." Verse 11a then continues with YHWH's actions in the land, i.e., to prophets from the people's children and Nazirites from their young men. Numbers 6:1-7 describes a Nazirite as one who makes a special vow to become a Nazirite, literally one who is "separated" or "dedicated" or dedicated to YHWH. A Nazirite drinks no wine or fermented grape juice, does not cut the hair of the head, and does not come into contact with the dead. Insofar as priests do not drink while serving on the altar or come into contact with the dead, the Nazirite conducts the self as a holy figure much like a priest. Samuel, the priest and prophet (1 Samuel 1–3), and Samson (Judges 13–16) were Nazirites. The sequence of YHWH's actions on behalf of Israel culminates in a rhetorical question that is designed to affirm YHWH's beneficence on the part of the people. The oracular formula, "says YHWH," likewise affirms that these statements come from YHWH. YHWH then returns to the accusations against Israel as in verses 6-8, by charging that the people forced the Nazirites to drink wine and commanded the prophets not to prophecy. In both cases, the people themselves, who were the recipients of YHWH's beneficence, deliberately prevented the Nazirites and prophets from doing precisely what they were supposed to do.

Having outlined the charges in verses 6-12, YHWH then turns to an announcement of punishment against the people of Israel in verses 13-16.

The statement begins with the image of a cart loaded down with sheaves of cut grain. Y<small>HWH</small> states the intention to "press" the people much like the heavy grain presses down upon a fully loaded cart. Such an image is to be expected from an agriculturalist like Amos, especially since he appears in Beth El to deliver Judean tribute to Israel. The image is very likely that of a cart loaded with grain that he brought north from Tekoa. The imagery quickly shifts to military themes in an effort to demonstrate that Israel will not be able to defend itself from Y<small>HWH</small>'s judgment, perhaps in the form of an invading army. Verses 14-16 portray the collapse of Israel's own army by playing on the motif of reversal, i.e., the strength of each type of warrior becomes a demonstration of failure. Verse 14 states that flight will perish from the swift foot soldier (or perhaps cavalryman) when attempts to flee; the strong foot soldier will lose his strength; and the "mighty" (i.e., "warrior") will not be able to save his own life. Verse 15 portrays the bowman who will be unable to stand, which is the position in which he shoots his arrows; the runners who will be unable to "save themselves" (literally, "escape"); and the cavalrymen who will be unable to save their own lives (cavalry typically protect the flanks of the foot soldiers). Verse 16 sums up with the statement that "those strong of heart among the warriors will flee naked in that day." This statement not only employs the element of reversal, but the portrayal of fleeing naked warriors reverses the imagery of the rich who would sell the poor for sandals or garments in verses 6-8. The concluding oracular formula, "says Y<small>HWH</small>," once again confirms this as Y<small>HWH</small>'s word.

Prophetic Sermon Concerning the Upcoming Punishment of Israel: 3:1–4:13

Amos 3:1–4:13 constitutes the prophet's discourse or sermon concerning the projected punishment of Israel. It is clearly demarcated by the introductory call to attention addressed to the people of Israel in Amos 3:1-2. A parallel call to attention in Amos 5:1 marks the beginning of a new unit in Amos 5–6 that is designed to convince its audience to return to Y<small>HWH</small> and thereby avoid punishment. The sermon in Amos 3–4 includes a number of disparate elements that together present an argument that punishment will necessarily result from Israel's improper actions.[40] The call to attention in Amos 3:1-2 not only calls upon

---

[40] For discussion of the rhetorical aspects of this text, see especially Yehoshua Gitay, "A Study of Amos's Art of Speech: A Rhetorical Analysis of Amos 3:1-15," *CBQ* 42 (1980) 293–309.

the Israelite audience to listen to the following words of the prophet, but it also establishes Israel's relationship with YHWH as the basis for punishment. Amos 3:3-8 establishes the principle of cause and effect for the passage, i.e., when punishment takes place there must be a cause, and punishment will take place when there is cause. Amos 3:9-11 announces that an enemy will afflict Samaria, and Amos 3:12 follows immediately with an oracle that metaphorically relates Israel's fate to that of a sheep attacked by a lion. The oracle in Amos 3:13-15 identifies the altar at Beth El as the site associated with the sins of Israel and the target of YHWH's punishment. Amos 4:1-3 announces punishment for the women of Israel as well as the men. Finally, Amos 4:4-14 rounds out the unit by employing the genre of priestly Torah or instruction to announce punishment for Beth El and the people of Israel.

THE CALL TO ATTENTION: 3:1-2

Amos 3:1a is a relatively typical example of the call to attention formula that is commonly employed in biblical literature to open a public presentation or address and to direct the audience's attention to the material that follows.[41] It includes a relatively standard set of elements, including the invitation to listen, identification of the addressee(s), and some indication of the nature of the following material. In the present case, the addressees are the people of Israel and the material is identified as the word of YHWH. The call to attention appears in a variety of contexts, such as hymnic praises of YHWH (Judg 5:3), wisdom instruction (Prov 7:24), or diplomatic speech (2 Kgs 18:28-29), and it appears frequently in prophetic literature (Hos 4:1; Mic 6:1; Isa 1:10; Ezek 6:3).

The present example of the call to attention is expanded in verses 1b-2 by several elements that point to Israel's relationship with YHWH as the basis for punishment in the material that follows. Verse 1b specifies the addressees of verse 1a, "concerning you, O people of Israel," with the phrase, "concerning the whole family which I brought up out of the land of Egypt." This specification aids in establishing the relationship between YHWH and Israel. The reference to Israel as "family" (*mišpāḥâ*) employs the same term that appears in YHWH's initial promise of blessing to Abram, "and in you all the families of the earth will be blessed" (Gen 12:3). As indicated by both contexts, the term *mišpāḥâ* is probably best understood as "clan" or "extended family" rather than as "nuclear family." Likewise, the reference to YHWH's bringing Israel

[41] For discussion of the call to attention genre in biblical literature, see Wolff, *Hosea*, 65–6; Sweeney, *Isaiah 1–39*, 544.

out of Egypt recalls the Exodus tradition, which in biblical literature is the formative event of the nation Israel.

The prophet's statement in verse 1 introduces a statement by Yнwн in verse 2, "You only have I known of all the families of the earth; therefore I will punish you for all your iniquities." Again, the quote from Yнwн employs the term *mišpāḥâ* from the initial statement of Yнwн's blessing for Abram in Gen 12:3, which highlights the election of tradition of Israel as Yнwн's chosen people. The statement hardly indicates that Israel will receive special blessings from Yнwн as a result of this relationship. Rather, it indicates that Israel will be singled out for punishment. The prophet once again employs the rhetorical technique of reversal, in that he has taken the motif of Israel's election and reversed it so that it no longer portrays Israel's relationship with Yнwн as a basis for security, but as a basis for threat. The statement is theologically problematic because it singles out Israel for punishment from among other nations. In essence, a higher standard of action is imposed upon Israel, and greater consequences are meted out against Israel as a result of these expectations. In the aftermath of the recent experience of the Shoah or Holocaust, theologians have begun to question assertions that those who suffer punishment must be guilty of sin.

THE PROPHET'S INSTRUCTION SPEECH
CONCERNING CAUSE AND EFFECT: 3:3-8

The prophet continues his sermon in Amos 3:3-8 with an instructional speech that establishes the principle of cause and effect.[42] By this means, he prepares the audience, whether listeners or readers, to accept that if people act contrary to the will of G–d there will be punishment, and if there is punishment then the victims must have committed some sin. The instruction comprises a series of seven paired statements that constitute rhetorical questions, followed by the prophet's concluding statements in verses 7-8 that Yнwн has spoken and that he, Amos, must prophesy. This enables him to build credibility with his audience by establishing the basis on which he speaks as a prophet.

The NRSV provides a rather confusing translation of the first statement in the series, "Do two walk together unless they have made an appointment?" This is an overly literal translation of the verb *hlk* in the statement, *hăyēkĕkû šĕnayim yaḥdāw*, which should read, "do two go together" or "do two belong together." Likewise, the verb *nôʿādû*, "they are appointed," conveys the fact that the two are "appointed" or "be-

[42] See especially Paul, *Amos*, 104–14.

long" together. The entire question thereby reads, "Do two go together unless they belong (together)?" The rhetorical effect of the question is that two things that go together must belong together, thereby stating the principle of cause and effect. The following series then illustrates the general point made in verse 3. Verse 4a points to the fact that a lion roars in the forest when it has its prey, and verse 4b follows up with the similar point that a young lion cries out from its den when it has caught something. Verse 5a states that a bird does not fall from the sky unless it has been trapped, and verse 5b states that a trap does not spring unless it has something to catch. Verse 6a states that people will be afraid when the Shofar (ram's horn) is blown. The Shofar could be used in time of war to warn of approaching danger (cf. Judg 3:27; Josh 6:4-5). Verse 6b then follows with the assertion that YHWH is the cause of any evil that afflicts a city, i.e., when something evil happens to a city, it must be YHWH's punishment. Such an assertion again is theologically problematic, however, in that it essentially assigns blame to the victims of evil, i.e., if you suffer, you deserve it. Finally, verses 7-8 employ the motif of cause and effect to establish Amos' authority to speak. Verse 7 asserts that when YHWH acts, YHWH reveals the divine "secret" to the prophets. The term "secret" *(sôd)* refers to the divine council in which YHWH makes decisions that are not known to humans in general, but may be revealed to prophets (e.g., YHWH's council as described by the prophet Micaiah ben Imlah, 1 Kgs 22:19-23). The prophet then concludes with an analogy in verse 8 that indicates that he must respond when YHWH speaks, "The lion has roared; who will not fear? The L–rd YHWH has spoken; who can but prophesy?" In this manner, Amos establishes his credibility as a prophet.

THE PROPHET'S ANNOUNCEMENT OF A THREAT AGAINST SAMARIA: 3:9-11

In Amos 3:9-11, the prophet turns to the first elements of a prophetic judgment speech against Israel that will constitute the overall flow of the argument for the balance of chapters 3–4. He begins with a version of the instruction to heralds genre, in which emissaries are commissioned to make an announcement or deliver a formal message or proclamation.[43] The prophet calls for a proclamation to "the strongholds of Ashdod" and "the strongholds of the land of Egypt" to assemble their forces for action against Samaria. Samaria, of course, was built in the ninth century B.C.E. as the capital of the northern kingdom of Israel by Omri (876–869 B.C.E., 1 Kgs 16:24). Some translators follow the LXX

[43] Wolff, *Joel and Amos*, 191.

and read "Assyria" in place of "Ashdod," but this is incorrect as later scribes would not likely have mistaken an original reading of Assyria for Ashdod, but they would have mistaken Ashdod for Assyria. The reason for the mention of Ashdod and Egypt in this oracle relates to Assyrian efforts to extend their trading relations into Egypt during this period.[44] Indeed, such an interest later motivated their attempts to invade and conquer Egypt. Ashdod is one of the five major cities of the Philistines. It is situated along the coastal plain nearby to the Mediterranean opposite the Judean city of Libnah, where it commands the trade routes by land and sea to Egypt. According to 2 Chr 26:6, King Uzziah of Judah broke down the walls of Ashdod, Gath, and Jabneh, which would have extended Israelite power into Philistia during the reign of Jeroboam II. As the book of Hosea later indicates, there was an alliance between Israel and Assyria that allowed trade to flow between Assyria and Egypt (Hos 12:2 [NRSV: 12:1]). It seems likely that Amos' call to Ashdod and Egypt envisions the ultimate collapse of friendly trade relations between Israel and Egypt as a consequence of Israel's "sins."

The prophet's instructions in verse 9b that Ashdod and Egypt should be gathered on the hills of Samaria to see the consternation and oppression within apparently refers to the situation within Israel to which the prophet objects. Verse 10 continues the very general portrayal of Israel's lack of righteousness. The reference to storing up "violence" (ḥāmās) and "robbery" (šōd) employs formulaic language that is generally employed in the prophets to describe situations of distress (Hab 1:3; Jer 6:7; 20:8; Ezek 45:9; Isa 60:18). Finally, verse 11 formally announces punishment against Israel. It begins with lākēn, "therefore," which typically introduces the announcement of punishment in a prophetic judgment speech, and continues with the messenger formula, "thus says YHWH" (kōh ʾāmar yhwh), to indicate that the prophet presents a statement by YHWH. The announcement itself is again very general in that it states that YHWH will raise an adversary against Samaria who will "surround" or "go about" the land undermining the nation's strength and plundering its strongholds.

ORACLE CONCERNING THE PUNISHMENT OF ISRAEL: 3:12

Amos 3:12 constitutes a short oracular statement that metaphorically portrays Israel's punishment. It employs the messenger formula, "thus says YHWH," once again to validate the following statement as a

---

[44] See M. Elat, "The Economic Relations of the Neo-Assyrian Empire with Egypt," *JAOS* 98 (1978) 20–34.

word of YHWH. The oracle employs the imagery of a lamb that has been taken from the flock by a lion. The lion tears apart the carcass of the lamb so thoroughly that the shepherd is able only to recover a few severed pieces of the animal, i.e., the legs or thighs, part of an ear. This, of course, presents the fate that Israel can expect as a result of its punishment, i.e., only a few remnants of the people will survive. The reference to the "people of Israel" is specified in verse 12aα[5-6]-b by the statement, "who live in Samaria . . . with the corner of a couch and part of a bed" *(hayyōšbîm běšōmrôn bipʿat mittâ ûbidmešeq ʾāreś)*. The phrase should read literally, "those who sit in Samaria on the corner of a bed and on a damask couch." Some have tried to emend *ûbidmešeq*, "and on damask," to *ûbědammeśeq*, "and in Damascus," in an attempt to provide a parallel with Samaria and perhaps allude to an emerging alliance between Israel and Aram which materialized by 735 B.C.E.[45] There is no real textual evidence for such an emendation, however, and there is no indication that Aram and Israel were allied in the middle of the eighth century. The phrase apparently expresses the resentment of a poor man like Amos against the rulers of Israel in Samaria who can afford such furnishings for their homes. Amos, on the other hand, suffers agricultural reverses (Amos 7:1-6) and yet must bring a portion of his crop to Beth El (Amos 8:1-3) to pay his part of Judah's tribute to Israel as its overlord.

THE PROPHET'S CALL FOR WITNESSES AGAINST ISRAEL: 3:13-15

Amos 3:13-15 constitutes a call by the prophet for witnesses against Israel. Biblical law calls for a minimum of two witnesses to convict someone charged with a crime (Deut 19:15-21), and verses 13-15 appear to presuppose such a need in relation to Israel. The formulaic introduction, "Hear and testify against the house of Jacob," makes this concern clear. The northern kingdom of Israel is frequently referred to as Jacob as the patriarch Jacob is the eponymous ancestor of Israel, who founded the sanctuary at Beth El (Genesis 28), fathered the ancestors of all the tribes of Israel (Genesis 30–31), established relations with both Aram (Laban) and Edom (Esau), and was named Israel after wrestling with a divine figure (Gen 32:22-32) and after receiving YHWH's promise of the covenant at Beth El (Gen 35:1-15). The oracle employs the oracular formula and YHWH's full designation of lord of armies (e g , 1 Sam 17:45), "says the L–rd, YHWH, G–d of Hosts" *(něʾum ădōnāy ʾělōhê hasseḇāʾôt)*. Verse 14 states that YHWH will specifically target the altar at Beth El for

---

[45] For discussion, see Rudolph, *Joel–Amos–Obadja–Jona*, 159–60; Wolff, *Joel and Amos*, 196; Paul, *Amos*, 120–2.

punishment, which is apparent in the final visions of Amos (Amos 8–9) as well. The characteristic imagery of the four-horned altar appears in this oracle (cf. Exod 27:2; 38:2; Ezek 43:15; Zech 2:1-2 [NRSV: 1:18-19]), as the horns that shall fall to the ground when they are cut off by the at- tacking enemy soldiers. Again, the perspective and resentment of a poor man against the rich appears in verse 15 when Amos announces that the winter and summer houses, as well as the houses trimmed in ivory will be destroyed. Winter and summer houses refer to the fact that Israel's climate is variegated, especially with respect to the hill country of Samaria and Jordan valley. During the winter, the hill coun- try of Samaria is cold and rainy, while the Jordan Valley is warm and much more dry. If one sought to escape the chill and wetness of winter, one could always build a house in the Jordan Valley in the vicinity of Jericho or even south by the Dead Sea. Amos' home in Tekoa was not far from the Jordan Valley, and perhaps he saw winter houses that were built by wealthy and powerful Israelites near his home. The houses of ivory are well known from excavations at the Omride palace in Samaria (cf. the reference to Ahab's ivory palace in 1 Kgs 22:39) in which large quantities of ivory were found.[46] Apparently, the ivory carvings were inlaid into furniture and walls as very costly decoration for the palace. Once again, a poor man like Amos would notice such ostentatious displays of wealth, and call for their destruction as punish- ment against those to whom he paid his tribute or taxes. The oracle concludes with another example of the oracular formula, "says YHWH" (*nĕʾum yhwh*).

THE PROPHET'S ANNOUNCEMENT OF PUNISHMENT AGAINST THE WOMEN OF SAMARIA: 4:1-3

The prophet turns to an announcement of punishment against the women of Samaria in Amos 4:1-3. Although this pericope begins with a formal call to attention analogous to those of Amos 3:1 and 5:1, it does not mark the beginning of a new unit within the larger structure of the book of Amos. Rather, it marks a new sub-unit within Amos 3:1–4:13 that takes up the punishment of the women of Samaria within the over- all context of punishment against Israel in general (Amos 3:1, 12, 14; 4:5, 12) and Samaria in particular (Amos 3:9, 12).[47] Much like Isaiah

---

[46] For discussion and bibliography, see Eleanor Ferris Beach, "The Samaria Ivories, Marzeah, and Biblical Text," *BA* 56 (1993) 94–104.

[47] See Klaus Koch and others, *Amos. Untersucht mit den Methoden einer struktu- ralen Formgeschichte*, AOAT, vol. 30 (Kevelaer: Butzon & Becker; Neukirchen-Vluyn: Neukirchener, 1976) II:23.

who announces punishment against the women of Jerusalem (Isa 3:16-24; 3:25–4:1) as well as the men (Isa 3:1-15; 3:25–4:1), Amos recognizes that any scenario of punishment against the nation of Israel will have an impact on both men and women.

The prophet is the speaker throughout this pericope. He employs the formal call to attention to draw the audience's attention to "the word of YHWH" concerning "the cows of Bashan." This metaphor apparently alludes to the imagery of the well fed and plump cattle who graze in the rich pastures of the region of Bashan plain (see Deut 32:14; Ezek 39:18; Ps 22:13 [NRSV: 22:12]), located in the Trans-Jordan on the banks of the River Yarmuk east of the Sea of Galilee (modern Golan Heights). The prophet's use of this image plays upon the relative size of the cattle and the fact that they are continuously engaged in the consumption of food. He applies the image quite clearly to the capital city of Samaria in order to convey Samaria's consumption of resources from throughout the lands of Israel and Judah. This enables him easily to turn to the issue of the oppression of the poor and needy, who must support the needs of the cows of Bashan or the women of Samaria. In this instance, Amos would call to mind his own situation as a Judean shepherd and farmer, who is called upon to provide a portion of his flocks and crops to the northern kingdom of Israel as payment of Judah's tribute to its overlord. This motif is expressed very clearly in the prophet's "quotation" of the women "who say to their husbands, 'bring something to drink.'" This may allude to the motif of idle drunkenness as well (cf. Amos 2:8, 12). In this manner, the prophet establishes the grounds for the punishment that will follow.

After characterizing the women of Samaria in verse 1, the prophet turns to YHWH's plans for punishment in verses 2-3. He does not quote YHWH's words as indicated in verse 1—YHWH's words will appear in verses 4-12—but he speaks about YHWH's oath to bring punishment against the Samarian women. He begins with the oath formula, "The L–rd YHWH has sworn by his holiness," which certifies that YHWH has sworn to act as stated (Ps 89:36 [NRSV: 89:35]; cf. Deut 6:13; Josh 2:12; Isa 62:8; Jer 49:13).[48] By stating that YHWH has sworn "by his holiness," the prophet indicates that YHWH's holy character is at stake, and thereby guarantees YHWH's promise of action. He also employs a typical formula that looks toward the future, "the time is surely coming upon you" (cf. Amos 8:11; 9:13; 1 Sam 2:31; 2 Kgs 20:17; Jer 7:32; 30:3; 31:31, 38), to indicate the cataclysmic change that will affect Israel and the lives of its women. This change is graphically displayed in verses 2b-3, which describe the fate of the women at this time. Verse 2b states that

[48] See Wolff, *Joel and Amos*, 205.

they will be "taken away with hooks, even the last of you with fish-hooks." This statement presupposes the imagery of dead bodies that are carried away for burial or disposal from the field where they have fallen. The latter part of the statement reads literally, "and your back parts in fish pots," in that *sîrôt* means both "hooks, thorns" or "pots."[49] The terminology plays upon the imagery of the cows' plumpness as well as that of fishing by which many people make their living from the Sea of Galilee. The prophet then turns to the imagery of exile or captivity in verse 3 as the women are led out through the breaches in the city's protective wall to captivity. They proceed, each before the other, in keeping with Assyrian portrayals of captives being led out of a captured city in straight lines.[50] The statement, "and you shall be flung out into Harmon," is problematic in that the active *hiphil* verb *wĕhišlaktenâ*, "and you shall cast out," is sometimes read as a passive *hophal wĕhošlaktenâ*, "and you shall be cast out."[51] The reference to Harmon is likely intended as Mt. Hermon, the snow-capped mountain that defines the northern border between Israel and Aram near the region of Bashan. In any case, the verse clearly conveys the imagery of captives being led off to foreign exile from their home country. The focus on Hermon suggests that the conqueror comes from the north, which could allude to Assyria or even to Aram.

THE PROPHET'S INSTRUCTION (TORAH) CONCERNING THE PUNISHMENT OF BETH EL: 4:4-13

Amos 4:4-13 constitutes the prophet's Torah or instruction concerning the punishment of Beth El and indeed Israel. It employs a combination of genres, including priestly Torah or instruction,[52] the prophetic judgment speech,[53] and the liturgical hymn of praise,[54] but it reworks

[49] For a thorough discussion of the meaning of the term, see Paul, *Amos*, 130–2.

[50] See Pritchard, *ANEP* 365, which portrays female captives being led away from Hamath by Shalmanezer III. See also figs. 366, 373, which portray male captives marching in a line carrying their belongings in bags.

[51] See Wolff, *Joel and Amos*, 204.

[52] For discussion of the priestly Torah genre in this passage, see Wolff, *Joel and Amos*, 211–2. See also J. Begrich, "Die priesterliche Torah," *Werden und Wesen des alten Testaments*, ed. P. Volz, BZAW, vol. 66 (Berlin: Töpelmann, 1936) 63–88; C. Westermann, *Basic Forms of Prophetic Speech* (Cambridge: Lutterworth; Louisville: Westminster John Knox, 1991) 203–4; Sweeney, *Isaiah 1–39*, 528.

[53] Westermann, *Basic Forms of Prophetic Speech*, 129–209; Sweeney, *Isaiah 1–39*, 533–4.

[54] See F. Crüsemann, *Studien zur Formgeschichte von Hymnen und Danklied in Israel*, WMANT, vol. 32 (Neukirchen-Vluyn: Neukirchener, 1969); E. Gerstenberger,

them in order to produce a prophetic instruction that ultimately announces Yʜᴡʜ's punishment of Beth El despite the people's continued worship at the site. The passage comprises two basic structural components. The prophet employs the priestly Torah genre in Amos 4:4-5 to instruct the people to continue to sin by bringing their sacrifices, tithes, thank offerings, and vows to Beth El. He then combines the liturgical hymn of praise with its repeated refrains together with the standard prophetic judgment speech to present Yʜᴡʜ's announcement of punishment against Beth El. Amos 4:4-13 thereby displays significant elements of satire, irony, and parody in that it instructs the people to engage in standard forms of worship at the sanctuary and employs standard liturgical forms of praise for Yʜᴡʜ, but asserts that the site will suffer despite the people's efforts. The basic reason, that they did not return to Yʜᴡʜ, is ironic in that it recalls the prophet's initial instruction to worship at Beth El.

The prophet's parody of the priestly Torah in Amos 4:4-5 draws upon a standard priestly form which is designed to convey the priests' instructions to the people concerning proper holy conduct and worship of Yʜᴡʜ. Whereas priestly Torah instructs the people in the proper treatment of animals for sacrifice or consumption (Lev 7:22-25; Deut 14:4-8), priestly and personal purity (Lev 21:1-24; 15:1-33), and moral conduct (Lev 19:1-37), Amos calls upon the people to come to Beth El and Gilgal in order to transgress! Amos is the speaker in this passage, but the concluding oracular formula in verse 5 indicates that he conveys Yʜᴡʜ's statements. The instructions take up a standard priestly regimen of sacrifices and offerings to be presented at the temple. The morning sacrifices *(zebaḥ)* are part of the daily ritual at the Temple (Leviticus 3). The tithes *(maʿăśēr)*, a presentation of one tenth of one's annual income at the Temple, is a fixed requirement by which the people support the Temple establishment and state (Numbers 18; Deut 14:22-29; cf. 1 Sam 8:15, 17). The thank offering *(tôdâ)* is a sub-category of sacrifice that is offered to give thanks to Yʜᴡʜ for some benefit (Lev 7:12-15). It is generally presented in the form of bread or cakes that accompanies the meat sacrifice, and it is to be burned on the third day (Lev 7:17-18). The freewill offering *(nĕdābâ)* likewise accompanies the sacrifice as an extra gift to the Temple (Lev 7:16; Num 15:3; Ezek 46:12). The prophet's instruction to "proclaim" or "publish" (i.e., "announce") the freewill offering indicates the means to publicize such a voluntary gift, much like the modern practice of pledging a gift for a synagogue or church fund drive. Yʜᴡʜ's final statement, "for so you love to do,

Psalms, Part 1, with an Introduction to Cultic Poetry, FOTL, vol. 14 (Grand Rapids: Eerdmans, 1988) 16–9.

O people of Israel," indicates that these are well-established practices on which the prophet draws to condemn the people. Although many see this as a prophetic indictment of ritual action in general,[55] there is nothing inherently wrong with the practices that are outlined here; they are standard means to offer worship, praise, and honor to YHWH. Rather, Amos' polemics against Beth El and the northern kingdom throughout the rest of the book demonstrate that he objects to northern Israel's domination of southern Judah. Insofar as Beth El is the royal sanctuary of the northern kingdom (1 Kings 12–13) and Gilgal is the site associated with Israel's conquest of the land of Canaan (Joshua 5) and the institution of the northern monarchy of Saul (1 Sam 11:14-15), these sites attract special condemnation from a Judean prophet who opposes northern Israel's hegemony over the south.

The second part of the prophet's Torah appears in Amos 4:6-13 in the form of a prophetic judgment speech that draws upon the liturgical hymns of praise and the historical reviews.[56] The prophetic judgment speech is a standard form that lays out the grounds for judgment and follows up with a statement of YHWH's intention to bring punishment as a consequence of the people's actions. The liturgical hymns of praise are designed to laud YHWH for YHWH's role as creator, deliverer, etc., and frequently employ a repeated refrain such as "for his steadfast love endures forever" which appears throughout Psalm 136 (cf. Ezra 3:10-11). Psalm 136 also constitutes an example of the historical review in that it presents an overview of YHWH's acts of deliverance on behalf of Israel as a basis for its praise of YHWH (cf. Psalm 106), although the historical review might also be employed to detail Israel's transgression against YHWH as a means to explain some change in YHWH's actions, such as the rejection of Joseph and the choice of Judah for the site of the Temple and the Davidic house (Psalm 78). In the present case, verses 6-11 detail Israel's rejection of YHWH through the repeated refrain, "'yet you did not return to me,' says YHWH" (verses 6, 8, 9, 10, 11), and verses 12-13 announce YHWH's intention to punish the people as a result. Verses 6-11 likewise employ the historical review to detail YHWH's actions against the people, i.e., withholding food or rain, bringing locusts, pestilence, and invaders, causing natural disaster, etc., as a means to convey YHWH's attempts to demonstrate the need for Israel to return, prior to the identification as the creator in verses 12-13.

This, of course, raises theological questions concerning the prophet's portrayal of YHWH in that YHWH is portrayed throughout the passage as a threat to the people rather than as a sustainer. Amos apparently

---

[55] E.g., Stuart, *Hosea–Jonah*, 337–8.
[56] For discussion of the historical review, see Sweeney, *Isaiah 1–39*, 521.

had experienced reverses due to natural disasters, such as the lack of rain, earthquake, etc., and saw them as YHWH's attempts to warn the people to change.[57] The five oracular statements by YHWH in verses 6, 7-8, 9, 10, and 11 describe a succession of problems that a farmer or sheepherder in ancient Judah or Israel might experience in a very bad year. In verse 6, for example, YHWH states that the people were given "cleanness of teeth" and "lack of bread." The first statement must be understood in relation to the second, viz., cleanness of teeth results from having no food to put in one's mouth. Modern readers must bear in mind that ancient farmers and shepherds are entirely dependent upon their natural environment; if the crops do not grow and the flocks do not increase, there is no food. The oracular statement in verses 7-8 emphasizes this problem; viz., if there is no rain, the cities and fields suffer for lack of water that enable people to drink and crops to grow. Without rain, the land withers. The statement also highlights YHWH's role as creator and master of nature. YHWH decides whether or not to grant rain to the people. In the present passage, YHWH is dissatisfied and expresses that dissatisfaction by withholding rain. In order to provide some incentive to the people, the rain is withheld selectively; some cities get it and others do not. Although the people wandered from one city to another looking for water, they did not return to YHWH, at least in the opinion of the prophet. The oracular statement in verse 9 indicates that YHWH brings "blight" and "mildew" on the people's many gardens and vineyards. "Mildew" (*yērāqôn*) may better be understood as a form of withering as the root *yrq* means "to become yellow, pale," although it frequently means "to become green." A dresser of sycamore trees such as Amos (Amos 7:14) would be intimately familiar with such problems. His reference to the locusts that devour fig and olive trees likewise speaks to his experience, especially since he employs a locust plague as the basis for his vision of YHWH in Amos 7:1-3. The oracular statement in verse 10 refers to a pestilence that affected the people, much like the plagues that YHWH sent against Egypt in Exodus 7–11. Indeed, the reference to "the manner of Egypt" indicates that Amos is well aware of the Exodus plague tradition and has turned it against the people (cf. Amos 2:10; 9:8). He also refers to the death of Israel's young men by the sword and the captivity of horses, an apparent reference to Israel's vulnerability to raiding parties that harass outlying settlements. Amos' home in Tekoa is located close to the edges of the Dead Sea Wilderness of Judah and the Negev desert,

[57] For detailed discussion of this passage and traditio-historical analysis of the disasters portrayed therein, see Hans Barstad, *The Religious Polemics of Amos*, VTSup, vol. 34 (Leiden: E. J. Brill, 1984) 67–75.

which frequently suffered such raids from the Edomites or the ancient bedouin who traveled through these dry and largely unsettled regions. The reference to "the stench of your camp" refers to the Israelite or Judean dead who were left to rot after having been ambushed. Finally, the oracular statement in verse 11 refers to a natural catastrophe on the scale of the one that destroyed Sodom and Gomorrah (Genesis 18–19). The superscription of Amos (1:1) places his activity "two years before the earthquake," but it is likely that other tremors were already starting to affect the land and cause damage. The metaphorical comparison of the people to "a brand snatched from the fire" indicates that the people survived the catastrophe, but that it should stand as a warning of what could come.

Amos 4:12-13 constitute YHWH's announcement of punishment against the people, although verses 6-11 indicate that in the prophet's view, YHWH has been bringing punishment all along. The verse begins with the characteristic "therefore" *(lākēn)* that marks the transition from accusation or cause to punishment or effect in the prophetic judgment speech. The wording of YHWH's statement indicates that YHWH's punishments will continue as they have in the past, albeit perhaps in larger scale. The statement, "prepare to meet your G–d," employs terminology that would normally be employed in the context of cultic worship, e.g., the verb "prepare" *(hikkôn)* appears elsewhere as a term used to describe the preparation of a sacrifice (Zeph 1:7; cf. Ezra 3:3) and the verb "to meet, call" *(qrʾ)* expresses the desire to call upon the name of YHWH (Gen 4:26; 12:8; 2 Kgs 5:11; Jer 10:25; Ps 79:6) or refers to those "invited" or "called" to a sacrifice (Zeph 1:7; 1 Sam 9:13). The expression thereby expresses the irony of the initial call to "come to Beth El" in verse 6; the people will indeed "meet" YHWH, but it will be for punishment, not for worship. Finally, the hymnic fragment in verse 13 further conveys the prophet's parody of liturgical form.[58] It is a typical liturgical description of YHWH's role as creator of the natural world and master of human events. The concluding statement, "YHWH, the G–d of Hosts, is his name," identifies YHWH as creator and master, and employs the title of YHWH that is closely associated with the ark of the covenant and later the Jerusalem Temple (1 Sam 17:45; 2 Sam 5:10; Isa 37:16; Jer 7:3, 21; etc.). Whereas the title Sebaot, "Hosts," suggests YHWH's protective armies, YHWH remains a threat to the people throughout this passage.

---

[58] Many see the hymnic fragments of Amos (cf. Amos 5:8-9; 9:5-6) as portions of a larger liturgical piece that Amos incorporated into his work or that were added by a later redactor. For discussion, see Wolff, *Joel and Amos,* 215–7; Paul, *Amos,* 152–3.

Prophetic Parenesis:
Seek YHWH *and Reject Beth El: 5:1–6:14*

Amos 5:1–6:14 constitutes the prophet's parenetic sermon that calls upon the people of Israel to seek YHWH and reject Beth El, and thereby avoid the punishment that will come upon the nation if it continues in its present course of action. Parenesis is a generic address form that attempts to persuade an audience to adopt a specific viewpoint or to engage in a specific course of action.[59] In order to achieve its ends, parenesis employs both admonition, which warns the audience to avoid an undesirable course of action or point of view, and exhortation, which attempts to encourage the audience to accept a desirable course of action or point of view. In the present instance, Amos 5:1–6:14 calls upon the audience to seek YHWH in two exhortational sections (5:4-6, 14-15), but these sections do not specify what seeking YHWH entails other than to seek goodness, reject evil, and establish justice. Elsewhere in the passage, the prophet points to the perversion of legal justice in the gates (5:7, 10, 12) and abuse of the weak and poor by the strong and rich (5:9, 11). Both of these themes appear throughout the book of Amos as an expression of the prophet's social position as a Judean agriculturalist who must help to pay Judah's tribute to its suzerain Israel. This enables the reader to understand the nature of the prophet's warning not to seek Beth El, Gilgal, or Beer Sheba (5:5), insofar as all of these sites are sanctuaries that were important to the northern kingdom's ability to promote its understanding of YHWH and to collect revenues from the people of the land in the form of offerings at the temples. This suggests that Amos' agenda is the rejection of northern religious and political authority and the return of the nation to YHWH at the Jerusalem Temple.

Although most interpreters maintain that these chapters contain a disparate collection of short, oracular speech units, Amos 5:1–6:14 constitutes a coherent formal and rhetorical unity. The passage is demarcated initially by the call to attention formula in Amos 5:1, "Hear this word that I take up over you in lamentation, O House of Israel," and by the beginning of the vision reports in Amos 7:1–9:15. The internal structure of the passage is based upon the motif of lamentation, introduced in verses 1-3 and continued in verses 16-17, which points to the upcoming downfall of the nation of Israel and its consequences for its cultic and political leadership. Although many see Amos 5:1-17 as a coherent rhetorical unit, based upon its chiastic structure and the return to the

---

[59] Sweeney, *Isaiah 1–39*, 527.

initial motif of mourning and lamentation in verses 16-17,[60] the material in verses 16-17 actually serves as the introduction to the balance of
the unit. Amos 5:1-15 constitutes the fundamental parenesis of the passage in that it combines elements of mourning for the downfall of Israel
(verses 1-3), exhortation to seek YHWH (verses 4-6, 14-15), and condemnation of the abuse of justice and power by the strong against the weak
(verses 7-13). Insofar as Amos 5:16-17 begins with the particle *lākēn,*
"therefore," it builds upon the form of the prophetic judgment speech
to point to the consequences of Israel's downfall and the failures of its
leaders by stating that lamentation will fill the cities and the land.[61] Two
major woe speeches then follow in Amos 5:18-27 and 6:1-14 that illustrate the consequences for both the cultic leadership of northern Israel
and the political leadership of the nation. Amos 5:18-27 points to the reversal of the Day of YHWH, apparently a cultic observance of YHWH's
protection of the nation, into a time of threat when YHWH will act to
threaten the nation, reject its cultic establishment, and carry the people
to exile beyond Damascus. Likewise, Amos 6:1-14 points to the political
leadership of the country that seems secure in power and wealth, in
order to assert that the nation will be decimated and oppressed by a
foreign power throughout the extent of Jeroboam ben Joash's kingdom.

THE PROPHET'S FUNDAMENTAL PARENESIS:
SEEK YHWH AND REJECT BETH EL: 5:1-15

The fundamental parenetic portion of the prophet's sermon appears in Amos 5:1-15, which is designed to convince the audience to
"seek YHWH" and to reject the sanctuaries at Beth El, Gilgal, and Beer
Sheba. The passage demonstrates the prophet's ironic use of the lamentation genre, i.e., he calls upon the audience to mourn the fall of the
"maiden Israel," but it is clear throughout the balance of the passage
that the fall of Israel will take place in the future if the nation does not
change its course of action. The parenesis therefore serves as a warning
to the people to adopt the prophet's recommended course of action: rejection of the northern sanctuaries and leadership and return to YHWH
at Jerusalem, including both the Temple and the house of David. His
condemnation of the abuse of justice and wealth attempts to point to
the corruption of both the religious and the political leadership of
northern Israel and those in Judah who acquiesce to Israelite rule.

[60] J. De Waard, "The Chiastic Structure of Amos V 1–17," *VT* 27 (1977) 170–7.
[61] For discussion of the prophetic judgment speech, see Sweeney, *Isaiah 1–39,*
533–4.

The initial sub-unit of the passage in verses 1-5 employs a lament over the fall of the maiden Israel as a basis to call upon the audience to seek YHWH. The presentation of the lament appears in verses 1-2, and two *kî* ("because") clauses in verses 3 and 4-5 introduce successive statements by YHWH that point to the expected results of such lamentation, i.e., the military defeat of Israel (verse 3) and the recognition by the nation of the need to return to YHWH (verses 4-5).

Verse 1 employs the formal "call to attention" formula to direct the audience's attention to the lamentation proper that appears in verse 2.[62] The term *qînâ*, "lamentation," is a technical term that designates a formal poetic dirge or lamentation song, such as David's lament at the deaths of Saul and Jonathan (2 Sam 1:17-27) or Ezekiel's laments concerning the princes of Israel (Ezek 19:1-14) or Pharaoh (Ezek 32:1-16). The formal dirge is characterized by a special poetic or "Qinah" meter that employs an initial three beats followed by two additional beats, which appears in Amos 5:2, e.g., verse 2a, *nāpĕlâ* ("fallen"), *lōʾ-tôsîp* ("not again"), *qûm* ("to rise"); *bĕtûlat* ("[is] the maiden"), *yiśrāʾēl* ("Israel").[63] The dirge metaphorically portrays the nation Israel as a young maiden who has fallen, and has no one to raise her up. The image appears to draw on various cultic images of women who mourn for the dead, e.g., the women who weep for the Babylonian vegetation god Tammuz so that he might rise from the underworld to inaugurate the rainy season (Ezek 8:14-15) or the daughter of Jephthah who mourned for her own death when she was to be sacrificed to satisfy a vow by her father (Judg 11:34-40). The motif is also expressed by the death of Rachel in the vicinity of Beth El (Gen 35:16-21), the weeping of Rachel for her dead children (Jer 31:15), the tradition that associates weeping with Beth El or Bochim, "weeping" (Judg 2:1-5), and the burial of Rachel's nurse Deborah at Allon Bakuth ("oak of weeping") near Beth El (Gen 35:8), all of which indicate some sort of ancient mourning ritual associated with women at or in the vicinity of Beth El. It is impossible to reconstruct this ritual with the evidence at hand, but it appears that the prophet draws upon this tradition in the formulation of this sermon. Based upon his viewing of women mourning at Beth El, he constructs an image of Israel as woman, lying on the ground in lamentation, as a metaphor for the nation Israel.

Verse 3, introduced by *kî*, "because," and a version of the messenger formula, then conveys the significance of this image for the nation in the prophet's quotation of a statement by YHWH, i.e., Israel will be decimated by its enemies. The statement employs military terminology in that Israelite military groupings are organized by tens, hundreds, thousands,

[62] For discussion of the call to attention, see ibid., 544.
[63] Ibid., 518–9.

etc. (cf. Exod 18:21, 25; Num 31:14). Verses 4-5, likewise introduced by *kî*, "because," and a version of the messenger formula, then conveys the prophet's aims for Israel's response, i.e., that they will seek YHWH and thereby avoid the catastrophe outlined in verse 3. The first person formulation of the statement in verses 4b-5 makes it very clear that the prophet quotes a statement by YHWH. YHWH presents going to Beth El, Gilgal, and Beer Sheba as very clear alternatives to the command to "seek me." Each of these sanctuaries was under northern Israelite control during the eighth century B.C.E., and would have been sites for the collection of offerings that would support the northern Israelite cultic establishment and state.[64] This would suggest that Amos' intention was to call for a return to the Jerusalem Temple and Davidic rule (cf. Amos 9:11-15). Although many argue that verses 4-5 should be grouped with verse 6 because of the concern with seeking YHWH, verses 4-5 are tied syntactically to verses 1-3 by the introductory *kî* whereas verse 6 is syntactically independent. Furthermore, the concern with seeking YHWH in verses 4-5 is formulated as a statement by YHWH, whereas verse 6 is clearly formulated as a statement by the prophet.

The prophet's sermon then continues with two sub-units in verses 6-13 and 14-15, each of which begins with the exhortation to "seek YHWH" or to "seek good." Together, these statements convey the prophet's primary purpose in addressing his audience.

Verses 6-13 begin with the basic statement of the prophet's premise in verse 6, formulated as the dual command to "seek YHWH and live," followed by a statement that threatens destruction for "the house of Joseph" and Beth El. The imagery of fire breaking out against the "house of Joseph" is a very real threat at the time of Sukkoth, the transition from the dry to the rainy season. At this point, the land remains dry and susceptible to fire as the rainy season approaches. Indeed, the prophet's vision of fire consuming the land (Amos 7:4-6) may recall just such an outbreak of fire prior to the rains. The designation of Israel as the "house of Joseph" is particularly pertinent as Joseph is the father of Ephraim and Benjamin, the two tribes that populate the central hill country of Israel and in whose territory the sanctuary at Beth El is located.

Verses 7-13 then follow upon the statement of the prophet's premise by identifying and characterizing those with whom the prophet's ser-

---

[64] Note also the inscriptions and drawings found at Kuntillet Ajrud or Horvat Teiman, apparently the site of an ancient way station along the trade routes through the Sinai to Egypt. The inscriptions, written on pottery, include the statement, "I bless you by YHWH of Samaria and his asherah," which indicates northern Israelite presence along these routes during the eighth century B.C.E. (Philip J. King, *Amos, Hosea, Micah: An Archaeological Commentary* [Philadelphia: Westminster, 1988] 104–6; Ze^ʾev Meshel, "Kuntillet ʿAjrud," *ABD* IV:103-9).

mon is concerned, viz., the leadership of the nation that enjoys the wealth brought by working people such as Amos. Overall, this section is designed to remind the leadership of who is actually in charge, i.e., YHWH, and that their actions run contrary to the principles of justice established by YHWH. These concerns are raised in two successive sub-units in verses 7-9 and 10-13. Verses 7-9 are introduced by a syntactically independent, participially formulated statement that characterizes the leadership of the nation. Verses 10-13 continue the characterization of the leadership with a prophetic judgment speech that builds upon the motifs introduced in verses 7-9 of the abuse of justice and power.

Verses 7-9 refer to the leadership of the nation as "you that turn justice into wormwood, and bring righteousness to the ground." The NRSV begins the statement with "Ah," as though the Hebrew particle *hôy*, "woe!" introduced the section, but this misrepresents the statement. The imagery is relatively self-explanatory. Wormwood is a bitter tasting shrub that lies close the ground; consequently, justice and righteousness fall to the ground. The hymnic characterization of YHWH in verse 8 is somewhat problematic as scholars often consider it as a hymnic fragment that has been placed in context to conclude a major section of Amos. But verse 8 does not conclude a major section; it simply follows the first statement of characterization, and identifies YHWH as the true power in the universe to those addressed in verse 7. By pointing to YHWH as the maker of the Pleiades and Orion, the one who turns darkness to light and light to darkness, and as the one who controls the waters of the earth, verse 8 identifies YHWH as the essential power of the universe and thus as the true source of justice and righteousness that the leaders of the nation now overturn. In this respect, verse 8 works together with verse 6 to convince the audience that a turn to YHWH is essential.[65] Finally, verse 9 must be considered as a continuation of verse 8. The initial participle *hammablîg*, "he who causes to flash up, spread," is masculine singular, and must therefore follow directly upon the masculine singular participles of verse 8 that characterize YHWH. Furthermore, the motif of bringing destruction upon the strong and upon the fortress conveys YHWH's power to bring the security of the state and its leaders to an end. Verse 9 thereby builds upon the portrayal of YHWH as creator in verse 8 by pointing to YHWH's ability to destroy and punish as well.

Verses 10-13 then turn to a third person portrayal of the leadership of the nation. Verse 10 returns to the basic themes of verse 7 by pointing

---

[65] Verse 8 is frequently identified as a hymnic fragment (Wolff, *Joel and Amos*, 240–1), although the reference to Pleiades and Orion raises questions as to its Israelite character. It is possible that Amos used portions of hymns sung at Beth El in constructing his oracles, but reworked them to serve his own purposes.

to their opposition to "one who reproves in the gate" and their abhor-rence of "one who speaks the truth." Legal cases or complaints were heard by judges in the gates of ancient Israelite cities (Deut 21:19; 25:7; Ruth 4:11). The Hebrew term *môkîaḥ*, "one who reproves," is based on the root *ykḥ* which is frequently employed in legal contexts to refer to one who brings charges or raises questions in court (Gen 31:37, 42; 1 Chr 12:17; Isa 2:4; 11:3, 4; Ps 94:10; Job 9:33; 16:21). Likewise, "one who speaks the truth" would refer to a witness in a legal setting. The passage fol-lows up on this statement with a brief prophetic judgment speech in verse 11 which points to abuse of the poor as the grounds for punish-ment in verse 11a, and then announces the punishment in verse 11b, in-troduced by *lākēn*, "therefore," by stating that the leaders will not enjoy the houses they have built and the vineyards that they have planted. A statement by Yhwh, as indicated by its first person formulation, ap-pears in verse 12. The initial *kî*, "because," indicates that it functions as a means to reinforce the prophetic judgment speech in verse 11 by as-serting that Yhwh knows the sins of the leadership, specifically, the af-fliction of the righteous *(ṣaddîq)*, the taking of bribes (cf. Exod 23:8), and the perversion of justice for the poor (cf. Exod 23:6). The term *ṣaddîq*, "righteous," is a legal term that designates innocence as a result of a lawsuit (cf. Exod 23:7-8). Verse 13 states the consequences of the sins of the leaders by stating that the prudent one will remain silent in such a time, i.e., it's too dangerous to challenge such actions. When Amos made such an attempt, he was reported to the king and expelled from Beth El (Amos 7:10-17).

Finally, the prophet's exhortation resumes in Amos 5:14-15 with a two-fold parenetic appeal to seek what is good and reject what is evil. The first statement is formulated as an imperative, "seek good and not evil that you may live." It employs the verb *diršû*, "seek," based on the root *drš*, which appears frequently in reference to oracular inquiry and worship (Gen 25:22; 1 Sam 28:7; Isa 8:19; Deut 18:11; Zeph 1:6; 1 Chr 16:11; Pss 9:11 [NRSV: 9:10]; 22:27 [NRSV: 22:26]; 34:5, 11 [NRSV: 34:4, 10]; 119:2, 10). It also refers once again to the need to seek Yhwh and live (Amos 5:6), indicating the life and death situation that the prophet an-ticipates for the nation. He reinforces this point by stating that perhaps Yhwh will be with you. Apparently, the prophet refers to the presup-position of the leadership of Israel, i.e., that Yhwh is with them as they have said. At various points in biblical literature, Yhwh states "I will be with you" as a means to emphasize the relationship between Yhwh and Israel and the promise of divine protection (cf. Gen 26:3; Deut 20:4; Isa 7:14; 8:10; Ps 46:8, 12 [NRSV: 46:7, 11]). Amos does not see such a promise as an unconditional guarantee, but as part of a reciprocal rela-tionship in which Israel has obligations to Yhwh as well. The imperative in verse 15 represents the counterpoint to that in verse 14, "hate evil and love good, and establish justice in the gate." The statement clearly has in mind the correction of legal abuses that were taken up in verses 7-9 and 10-13. Again, the conditional element in Amos' thought appears in the second half of the verse when he suggests that just action on the part of the leadership may result in YHWH's favor toward "the remnant of Joseph." Joseph is the ancestor of the tribes of Ephraim and Benjamin. Although the term "remnant" *(šĕʾērît)* can refer to those left after some disaster, the noun *šĕʾēr* can also mean "flesh" or "blood relation" (Lev 18:12; 20:19; Num 27:11; Prov 11:17), which indicates that the term can also refer to the descendants of Joseph.

The Prophet's Statements Concerning the Consequences of Failure to Seek YHWH: Lamentation in the Land: 5:16–6:14

As noted above, Amos 5:16–6:14 constitutes the second major unit of the prophet's parenesis in Amos 5:1–6:14. Verses 16-17 play an especially important role in that they point to the consequences of the failure to heed the prophet's warnings in verses 1-15, and thereby introduce the two woe speeches in Amos 5:18-27 and 6:1-14 that describe the consequences in detail. They begin with the particle *lākēn,* "therefore," which demonstrates that they introduce a section that takes up the previously mentioned consequences. Furthermore, the expanded messenger formula indicates that these consequences are authorized by YHWH. YHWH's statement then follows with a description of the lamentation or mourning that will engulf the land if the nation does not change. Indeed, the projected image in verse 2 of Israel as a maiden fallen in mourning would be realized among all the people of the land. YHWH refers to mourning in the squares and streets of the cities, and notes that the mourning will extend to the farmers in the field and to the vineyards. The exclamation, "Alas! alas!" *(hô-hô)* is analogous to the statement of mourning in 1 Kgs 13:30, "Alas, my brother" *(hôy ʾāḥî).* The concluding speech formula, "says YHWH," again emphasizes that YHWH authorizes such punishment.

THE PROPHET'S WOE SPEECH AGAINST THE CULTIC LEADERSHIP OF THE NATION: 5:18-27

The first of the two woe speeches then follows in Amos 5:18-27, which focuses especially on the condemnation of the cultic leadership of the nation.[66] The passage begins with a woe speech by the prophet in verses 18-20 in which he warns those who wait for the "Day of YHWH" that it will be a day of darkness or punishment and not light or deliverance.[67] The prophet's presentation of a speech by YHWH then follows in verses 21-27 in which YHWH states opposition to cultic action without justice and concludes with a threat to exile the people beyond Damascus.

The prophet's woe speech in verses 18-20 has prompted a great deal of discussion because of its focus on the "Day of YHWH." Although this motif appears throughout prophetic tradition (cf. Isaiah 2; 13; Ezekiel 30; Joel 2; Zeph 1:14-18; 2:1-3), scholars have been unable to point to a specific observance or setting by which to understand the day. Suggestions include a tradition of popular eschatology, an annual New Year festival that celebrates YHWH's kingship and defeat of enemies, holy war traditions, theophanic traditions, covenant and treaty curse traditions, and various historical settings that involved military action.[68] Most agree that Amos 5:18-20 is the earliest reference to the "Day of YHWH," and consequently, many see it as an expression of Amos' sense of irony and reversal. It is clear that the prophet presents the "Day of YHWH" as a day for which people in Israel wait in expectation of benefits from YHWH. The prophet identifies his addressee as "you who desire the day of YHWH," which indicates its positive significance, but he begins his address with a "woe" (*hôy*) statement that always conveys warning, danger, and the threat of punishment (see esp. Zech 2:10 [NRSV: 2:6]; cf. Isa 1:4; 3:11; 5:8-24; 10:5; 28-33; Nah 3:1; Hab 2:6-20; Zeph 3:1), and follows up with a rhetorical question that challenges the premises of those who wait for the day, "Why do you want the day of YHWH? It is darkness, not light." Clearly, the prophet presupposes that the audience expects light or something positive from YHWH on the "Day of YHWH," but he announces that darkness or something negative will ensue. The threat of danger is made especially clear in verse 19 when the prophet makes an analogy between the day and the experience of a man who flees from a lion, only to be caught by a bear, and then enters a house, leans against the wall thinking he is safe, and is bit by a snake. The concluding rhetorical question in verse 20 emphasizes that the day is one of darkness and not light, again representing the threatening aspects of the day. The emphasis on the imagery of "light" (*ʾôr*) and "darkness" (*ḥōšek*) as well as "gloom" (*ʾāpēl*) and "brightness" (*nōgah*) points especially to the theophanic traditions of ancient Israel and

---

[66] For discussion of the woe speech form, see Sweeney, *Isaiah 1–39*, 543.

[67] For discussion of the "Day of YHWH," see Paul, *Amos*, 182–4; Richard Hiers, "Day of the L–rd," *ABD* II:82-3; K. J. Cathcart, "Day of YHWH," *ABD* II:84-5.

[68] Paul, *Amos*, 182–3.

the imagery of inner sanctum or "Holy of Holies" in an Israelite temple where the presence of YHWH is represented.[69] The imagery and vocabulary of light and darkness is especially prominent in the theophanic traditions in relation to the imagery of storm and the emergence of light or the sun that follows upon the dark storm clouds (see Exod 19:16-24; Deut 33:2-3, 26-29; Hab 3:3-15; Ps 68:7-8, 31-34). Such imagery is generally linked not only with the manifestation or revelation of YHWH, but with YHWH's defeat of enemies and the granting of rain and fertility to the land. It also represents the imagery of the Temple, in which the central hall is filled with incense and the Holy of Holies, which houses the ark of YHWH in the Jerusalem Temple, is generally portrayed as a place of darkness and gloom (Lev 16:1-14; 1 Kgs 8:1-13). These images, of course, relate to the Jerusalem Temple. Although we have no clear images of the Beth El Temple, the common three room structure of temples in ancient Canaan and Israel suggests that Beth El would have had a Holy of Holies which housed the golden calf as a representation of the mount of YHWH (1 Kgs 12:26-33), much as the ark served as the throne of YHWH (1 Sam 4:4; 2 Sam 6:2; 2 Kgs 19:15; Pss 80:1; 99:1; cf. Isa 66:1). The image of the young Samuel sleeping before the ark in the Temple at Shiloh suggests a similar function for the northern sanctuaries. Whereas Amos' audience would look to the "Day of YHWH" as a time when "light" would emerge from "darkness" or YHWH would emerge from the "darkness" to deliver the nation, Amos focuses especially upon the imagery of darkness to point to a time of punishment for the nation of Israel and not deliverance. Once again, Amos shows himself to be a master of irony and reversal in his articulation of his prophetic message.

Taking a cue from the cultic or Temple setting of the "Day of YHWH" in verses 18-20, verses 21-27 then present YHWH's critique of cultic action that is not accompanied by justice. The interpreter must bear in mind that the ancient Israelite temple was not only a place for ritual celebration, sacrifice, and worship, but that the Temple was also perceived to be the source for instruction concerning YHWH's expectations of justice in Israelite and Judean society. Thus, the revelation of the Torah at Sinai represents the revelation of Torah in the Jerusalem Temple (Exodus 19; cf. Isa 2:2-4/Mic 4:1-5); the prophet and priest Samuel also serves as a judge in Israel (1 Sam 7:15–8:3); a slave who desires to remain a permanent slave is brought to the sanctuary for such a declaration (Exod 21:1-6); Moses the Levite appoints the judges of Israel (Exodus 18); and Levitical priests serve as judges at the sanctuary in the final court of appeal (Deut 17:8-13). YHWH's indictment of cultic practice

---

[69] Theodore Hiebert, "Theophany in the OT," *ABD* VI:505-11.

in verses 21-27 presupposes the close interrelationship between sanctuary and justice.

The first person address forms in verses 21-27 indicate that YHWH is the speaker in this passage, although the concluding speech formula in verse 27b demonstrates that the prophet conveys YHWH's speech. The speech represents another example of Amos' use of irony and reversal in that it appears to be dependent upon the prophetic oracle of salvation. Such oracles are generally presented in a cultic setting, following an appeal to YHWH for help in a time of danger (e.g., Isa 37:14-35/2 Kgs 19:14-34; cf. Exodus 3). Rather than delivering a message of YHWH's salvation or deliverance in the face of danger, YHWH's speech in verses 21-27a conveys a message of rejection and threat that presupposes the cultic setting in which the plea to YHWH would have been made. It states YHWH's abhorrence and rejection of all the basic elements of the Israelite cult. The term "your festivals" (*ḥaggêkem*) employs the technical term for the three major festivals of the Israelite cultic and agricultural year, viz., Pesach (Passover, the beginning of the grain harvest), Shavuot (Weeks or Pentecost, the conclusion of the grain harvest), and Sukkoth (Booths or Tabernacles, the conclusion of grape and olive harvest and the beginning of the rainy season; see Exod 23:14-19; 34:22-26; Deut 16:13-17). The term "your solemn assemblies" (*ʿaṣṣĕrōtêkem*) employs the technical term for the seventh day of Pesach (Deut 16:8) and the eighth day of Sukkoth (Lev 23:36; Num 29:35), both of which are special holidays that mark the conclusion of each festival. The terms "whole burnt offerings" (*ʿōlôt*) and "your grain offerings" (*minḥōtêkem*) in verse 22 take up the technical references for the daily meat and grain offerings at the Temple (Leviticus 1; 2). Likewise, the "offerings of well-being of your fatted animals" (*šelem mĕrîʾêkem*) is a variation of the term employed for the "offerings of well-being" (*šĕlāmîm*) that was presented for special occasions and eaten by both priests and lay people (Leviticus 3; 7:15, 28-34; cf. 1 Sam 10:8; 11:15; 2 Sam 6:17-18).

YHWH's command to remove song and melody appears in verse 23. Music, including the playing of instruments and the singing of psalms, was a regular part of Temple worship (2 Sam 6:12-19; 1 Kgs 1:34, 39-40; 1 Chronicles 15–16; Psalms 149; 150). Indeed, the book of Psalms is thought by many to represent the hymnbook of the Jerusalem Temple. Having stated rejection of cultic observance and commanded the cessation of cultic music, YHWH states expectations for justice and righteousness. The statement employs the imagery of water, which is an important feature of Temple worship at the time of Sukkoth as the festival marks the beginning of the rainy season and represents YHWH's commitment to provide life and fertility for the land. The Jerusalem liturgy and psalms frequently make reference to the gushing forth of springs and rivers (Pss 104:10-17; 107:35-38), and northern shrines would have a similar concern with water and fertility (1 Kings 18; cf. Judg 5:19-21). In this case, Amos draws upon a long tradition in which fertility for the land and justice for the people are considered together with the cultic worship of G–d (Psalms 40; 50; 68; 72; 147) as both are necessary for the sustenance of human life.

YHWH continues with a reference in verse 25 to the sacrifices and grain offerings presented by the people during the forty years of their wilderness wanderings. The present statement might be read as a contrast to the worship of the pagan gods Sakkuth and Kaiwan in verse 26. One must recall, however, that the Pentateuch presents this period as one of rebellion against YHWH, including the building of the golden calf (Exodus 32–34); the rejection of YHWH's promises of the land (Numbers 10–14); the rebellion of Korah (Numbers 16); and the apostasy at Baal Peor (Numbers 25). It would appear then that YHWH cites the sacrifices of the wilderness period as an indication that sacrifice alone does not constitute a proper relationship to YHWH, especially when the people reject YHWH and turn to other gods. Sakkuth (literally, "Sikkuth" in Amos 5:26) is a Mesopotamian astral deity, identified with Ninurta, who served as one of the chief deities of the Mesopotamian pantheon.[70] Ninurta's high position explains the reference to Sakkuth in this verse as "your king." Ninurta is associated with Saturn and especially with water and its management in the form of floods, storms, dams, irrigation channels, etc. 2 Kings 17:30 indicates that Sakkuth was brought to Israel by Babylonians who were settled in the land by the Assyrians following the destruction of the northern kingdom of Israel. Kaiwan (literally, "Kiyyun" in Amos 5:26) is an Akkadian appellation of the star god Saturn, which is frequently associated with justice as symbolized by the steadiness of Saturn's orbit. The reference to the people's carrying these gods apparently reflects the ancient practice of carrying images of gods in procession through the streets as part of a cultic observance (cf. Isaiah 46). In this case, it would contrast with the Israelites' carrying the ark through the wilderness. Finally, YHWH states in verse 27a that, as a result of such apostasy, YHWH will exile the people beyond Damascus. Most interpreters take this as a cryptic reference to Assyria, although Amos never mentions Assyria in the book. The reader must bear in mind that Israel was allied with Assyria during the reign of Jeroboam ben Joash. Amos' reference of such exile could well be an implicit critique of Israel's foreign relations, although such a concern is much more characteristic of his younger contemporary Hosea.

[70] Samuel A. Meier, "Sakkuth and Kaiwan," *ABD* V:904; William J. Fulco, "Ninurta," *ABD* IV:1119.

THE PROPHET'S WOE SPEECH CONCERNING THE
POLITICAL LEADERSHIP OF THE NATION: 6:1-14

The prophet's woe speech concerning the political leadership of the northern kingdom of Israel follows in Amos 6:1-14. By focusing on the political leadership of the nation, it complements the woe speech in Amos 5:18-27 by pointing to the power that stands behind the temple at Beth El and the power that is entrusted with the military and economic security of the people. Although interpreters are prone to point to the prophet's statements in this material as signs of the self-indulgence of the Israelite monarchy and its supporters, one must remember that the portrayal of Israel's leadership here represents the viewpoint of a Judean farmer and shepherd who is compelled to offer his produce at Beth El. Excavations at Samaria indicate that the ruling class of northern Israel was relatively wealthy; the Samarian ivories that were once inlaid in furniture, implements, etc., testify to the wealth of their owners.[71] Nevertheless, such wealth is not unusual for an ancient monarch and his immediate circle; it does not constitute a moral comment on the character of the monarchy. Amos' portrayal is bound to be polemical and unflattering. It reflects the resentment of a man who sees others as idle and secure, while he has to work hard for a living and pay a very high tribute that supports such a lifestyle and other aspects of the nation's activities. Nevertheless, the interpreter cannot draw conclusions as to the moral corruption of the Israelite state. Rather, one must recognize that this is how the prophet chooses to portray its leaders.

The form of Amos 6:1-14 is once again the woe oracle, which is designed to announce a warning to those who are addressed, in this case, the ruling classes of northern Israel and southern Judah. The overall pattern of the oracle, however, appears to be that of the prophetic judgment speech insofar as verses 1-6 outline the wrongdoings of the ruling classes that constitute the basis for punishment, and verses 7-14, introduced in typical judgment speech form by the particle *lākēn*, "therefore," outlines the consequences that will befall the leaders of Israel and Judah as a result of their actions. In this case, the prophet points to exile (verse 7) and the rise of a nation that will oppress the people of Israel (verse 14).

Verses 1-6 outline the basis for YHWH's decision to bring an oppressive foreign nation. The initial woe statement of these verses is clearly addressed to the leadership of both the northern kingdom of Israel and the southern kingdom of Judah as indicated by the phrases, "those who are at ease in Zion," and "those who feel secure on Mount Samaria."

---

[71] King, *Amos, Hosea, Micah: An Archaeological Commentary,* 139–49.

There has been a great deal of discussion concerning the prophet's address to the leadership of Judah in that the bulk of his statements are addressed exclusively to the northern kingdom of Israel. Many speculate that the passage is the work of a much later author or that a later editor has included the reference to the leaders of Judah in light of much later threats to the southern kingdom, such as the Babylonian exile.[72] Nevertheless, one must keep in mind the political situation of Amos' day. Judah and Israel were allied during the mid-eighth century as Judah had been a vassal state of Israel since the reigns of Amaziah of Judah (800–783 B.C.E.) and Jehoash of Israel (801–786 B.C.E.) as indicated by Amaziah's forced submission to Jehoash in 2 Kgs 14:11-14. Although Amos was Judean, his call for the reestablishment of Davidic rule over all Israel (Amos 9:11-15) indicates that he could not have agreed with the continued submission of Judah to Israel during the reigns of Uzziah of Judah and Jeroboam ben Joash of Israel. His condemnation of the leadership of southern Judah would reflect his dissatisfaction with their acceptance of subordinate status. It further reflects the prophet's fears of foreign attack. The kingdoms of Jeroboam and Uzziah may be secure for the moment, but Amos points to a potential threat that both need to consider.

The prophet points to the position of political power that Israel and Judah enjoyed during the mid-eighth century. 2 Kings 14:25 states that Jeroboam restored the border of Israel from Lebo Hamath to the sea of the Arabah, i.e., from Hamath in upper Aram/Syria to the depression south of the Dead Sea that falls into the Gulf of Aqaba, and Amos 6:14 demonstrates that the prophet has precisely these borders in mind. Obviously, Israel and Judah controlled an empire much like that of David and Solomon. As verse 1b indicates, the leadership of the choicest nations has come to Israel to pay respects and presumably tribute. Nevertheless, the prophet employs a rhetorical question in verse 2 to point to the fact that Israel controls a relatively small territory, and in fact, Israel and Judah are minor states themselves. He asks that the Israelite and Judean leadership look to Calneh, Hamath, and Gath, and consider whether these kingdoms are better than those controlled by Israel and if their borders are greater than those of Israel. The rhetorical answer, of course, is that they are not and that the leadership of Israel and Judah must recognize that they are under as great a threat as the one faced by these nations.

The exact significance of this statement continues to puzzle scholars, however, as Calneh, Hamath, and Gath are presumably under the control of Israel during the mid-eighth century B.C.E. Calneh, referred to as Calno in Isa 10:9, is the north Syrian city of Kullani (Akkadian) or

---

[72] Wolff, *Joel and Amos*, 269–70.

ʿAmq (Aramaic), the capital of a minor state known as Pattin/Hattin/
Unqi in the lower valley of the Orontes River.[73] Hamath Rabbah (cf. Isa
10:9), modern Hama in Syria, was an important Syrian city state situated between Hattin/Pattin and the city state of Damascus.[74] Gath, was
one of the five Philistine cities that controlled the coastal plain west of
Judah.[75] Indeed, Gath was a key strategic location in that it controlled
entrance to the coastal plain opposite the Judean city of Lachish, which
sometimes served as a second capital for the Judean kings (cf. 2 Kgs
14:17-20). Nevertheless, these cities were not taken by the Assyrians
until the latter part of the eighth century when Tiglath Pileser III (745–
727 B.C.E.) initiated the western campaigns that resulted in the expansion of the Assyrian empire. Indeed, Calneh (Calno) and Hamath were
not conquered until 738 and the Philistine cities were threatened or
taken at several occasions, beginning in the Syro-Ephraimitic War (735–
732 B.C.E.) and continuing through Sennacherib's invasion (701 B.C.E.).

It would seem that Amos points to a line of conquest that begins in
the north with Calneh, continues through Hamath, and concludes in
Gath. Indeed, such a strategy had been employed in the mid-ninth century by the Assyrian king Shalmanezer III, who invaded upper Syria,
defeated Hattin/Pattin, and was stopped in the vicinity of Hamath,
and by the Aramaean king Hazael who had controlled Israel and Judah
by taking Gath (2 Kgs 12:17-18). None of these cities had been conquered in Amos' day, but past experience provided a guide for the
present. Calno, Hamath, and Gath had been taken before by invading
armies coming from the north, either from Assyria or from Aram. Jeroboam's empire extended as far north as Hamath. If the Assyrians were
to invade upper Syria, which was immediately adjacent to the Assyrian
homeland, and continue along the same routes that Aram had used to
invade Israel in the past, would Israel be able to stop them? Amos' rhetorical questions assert that it would not.

Amos then returns to his addressees in verses 4-6, the wealthy class
that indulges itself in food, drink, and song, while the threat of foreign
invasion looms on the horizon. This theme is stated in verse 3 in reference to those who "put far away the evil day," which of course results
in the arrival of violence. The prophet refers to those who "lie on beds
of ivory" and "lounge on their couches," which again calls to mind the
Samarian ivory carvings that were once inlaid in what must have been
very costly furniture.[76] Such couches were generally employed as din-

---

[73] Paul, *Amos*, 201–2; Samuel A. Meier, "Calneh," *ABD* I:823-4.
[74] Paul, *Amos*, 202–3; Marie-Louise Buhl, "Hamath," *ABD* III:33-6.
[75] Joe D. Seger, "Gath," *ABD* II:908-9.
[76] King, *Amos, Hosea, Micah*, 139–49.

ing furniture in the ancient world as well as for general lounging. The prophet refers also to the sumptuous meals, including the lambs chosen from the flock and the calves that were left to fatten in stalls rather than roam the hillsides to feed. Verse 5 presents the prophet's mocking portrayal of the plucking at harps, as the revelers apparently consider themselves in comparison to David. The prophet portrays the leaders drinking wine and anointing themselves with oil. The use of the term *mizrāq*, "bowl," is not merely the common bowl or cup *(kôs)*, but is the term used for sacred vessels that are employed for ritual sacrifice elsewhere in the Bible (Exod 27:3; 38:3; Num 4:14; 7:13; 1 Kgs 7:50; Neh 7:70, etc.). The use of the term here may indicate an attempt to charge the leadership with sacrilege of some sort; others suggest that the prophet depicts a cultic observance such as the *Marzeah*.[77] But the absence of cultic themes elsewhere in the passage indicates that the term merely refers to the use of expensive dishware, analogous to the use of expensive furnishings, such as ivory couches. The reference to anointing with oil is a common means for cleansing the skin in antiquity, particularly among those who had the income to afford such extras. The oil would function much like soap, and it could be perfumed with herbs and spices as well.

Finally, the prophet concludes this section with the statement that the leadership of Israel and Judah is not grieved over "the ruin of Joseph." Joseph, of course, is the ancestor of the central tribes of Ephraim and Benjamin in whose territory the sanctuary at Beth El is situated. No actual ruin of Joseph needs to be identified. The prophet merely anticipates the consequences for a nation whose leaders pay more attention to feasting than they do to their borders. Ironically, the leadership is initially referred to as "at ease" and "secure" in verse 1, but they do not look after the security of the state.

Verses 7-14 then outline the consequences for Israel of the leadership's lack of attention to the security of the nation. The prophet begins with a reference to the exile of the nation, in which the leaders will be at the head of the exiles. It was common Assyrian practice to deport the leading elements of a conquered population as a means to destabilize local leadership and to assert Assyrian control. As those who were responsible for the welfare of the state, and who neglected that welfare for revelry, Amos would note that Israel's leaders will bear the brunt of Assyrian measures.

The prophet elaborates upon this statement of Israel's punishment in the following verses, beginning with a quote of YHWH's oath to allow

---

[77] King, *Amos, Hosea, Micah*, 137–61; Hans M. Barstad, *The Religious Polemics of Amos*, VTSup, vol. 34 (Leiden: E. J. Brill, 1984) 127–42.

the nation to be attacked in verses 8. The combination of the oath formula and the oracular formula validates the statement as that of YHWH. YHWH's statement concerning divine abhorrence and hatred for the "pride of Jacob" and Jacob's "strongholds" calls into question Israelite belief in the security of its hold over its empire. The expression "pride of Jacob" *(gĕʾôn yaʿăqōb)* apparently refers to the aura of might, power, and wealth that would characterize the nation, and the reference to the strongholds would refer to the palaces and fortifications that were built to ensure and to protect that might, power, and wealth. Nevertheless, YHWH intends to "deliver up the city and all that is in it." The *hiphil* form of the verb *sgr*, here translated as "to deliver up," means literally "to close up" in reference to the besieging of a city.

Verses 9-10 then graphically describe the aftermath of attack when a house is searched for survivors and then burned to protect the living from the rotting corpses of the dead. There are some elements of parody present in these verses and in the following material in that they suggest that the house may be identified with the Beth El temple.[78] Verse 9 states the initial premise of the scenario, viz., that ten people are left in a house, presumably following the exile and punishment announced in verses 7-8, and that they die. Interpreters have pointed out that it would be unusual to have ten people left in a house, and suggest that the number may indicate a minimum number of people required to carry out a worship service, based upon the requirement of a minyan, or ten men who are required for worship in Judaism. The requirement for a minyan is a much later practice within Judaism, and it is not certain that such a requirement existed in the eighth century B.C.E. Indeed, the number ten may refer to the previous decimation of the nations (cf. Amos 5:3). The portrayal does play upon concepts of sanctity associated with temple and priesthood. Verse 10 describes the actions of an "uncle" or "kinsman" (Hebrew, *dôd*, literally, "uncle," but it may also refer generally to a relative) who comes to remove the dead from the house; apparently he burns the structure to purify the site from the effects of corpses who have been left to rot for some period of time and then removes the bones for proper interment. He calls out to see if anyone is alive in the house, and learns that no one is alive. The narrative does not make it clear to whom he calls or who answers him if everyone in the house is dead! His final statement, "Hush! We must not mention the name of YHWH," presupposes the need to protect the sanctity of the Name of YHWH by not bringing it into contact with the dead. This is expressed in several texts, particularly in relation to the priesthood. Numbers 19:11-22 specify that anyone who comes into contact with the

---

[78] Jeremias, *The Book of Amos*, 116–7.

dead will be unclean for seven days, and must cleanse oneself on the third and seventh days. It further specifies that such a defiled person may have no contact with the tabernacle/temple. If such a person should defile the tabernacle/temple, then that person is cut off from the community entirely. Likewise, a priest may not come into contact with the dead unless it is a blood relative, and the high priest may not even come into contact with the body of a father or mother (Lev 21:1-15), because such contact would profane the name of G–d (Lev 21:6) and the sanctuary of G–d (Lev 21:12). Similar regulations apply to Nazirites, who consecrate themselves to YHWH for specified periods of time (Num 6:6-8). The expression *has*, "Hush!" indicates the concern with YHWH's holiness as well, in that it is employed in prophetic tradition to signal the presence of YHWH in the Temple or the beginning of sacrifice (Hab 2:20; Zeph 1:7; Zech 2:17; cf. Amos 8:3, which likewise calls for silence in the presence of dead bodies). The expression, "to mention the name of YHWH," *lĕhazkîr bĕšēm yhwh*, generally refers to calling upon or invoking the name of YHWH or another god (Isa 26:13; 48:1; Exod 23:13).

Verses 11-12 then follow with an explanatory reiteration of the grounds for such punishment in the form of a reversed prophetic judgment oracle. Verse 11 begins with causative *kî*, "because," which indicates the intention to explain the situation portrayed in verses 9-10. Verse 11 then relates YHWH's command to shatter houses large and small. Whereas verse 11 conveys the punishment, verse 12 conveys the basis for punishment in the form of a rhetorical question and its explanation. The question reads, "Do horses run on rock? Or does one plough with oxen?" The present wording of the question is problematic. Whereas the first part of the question makes perfect sense, viz., of course horses do not run on rock, the second part of the question makes no sense at all because there is nothing unusual about ploughing with oxen. Consequently, interpreters have sought to emend the verse by repointing the active verb "plough" *(yaḥărōš)* as a passive *niphal* form *(yēḥārēš)*, and by redividing the consonants of "with oxen" *(babbĕqārîm)* to produce the expression, "with the ox the sea" *(babbāqār yām)*.[79] The result is a rhetorical question that makes perfect sense, "Or (does one) plough the sea with the ox?" Of course not! Nevertheless, there is no textual evidence for such rewording of the text. One might suggest that one does not plough with horses and oxen together (cf. Deut 22:10), but the grammar and syntax of the question would be very awkward. In any case, the question is intended to be understood as a rhetorical question that asserts that such an action is unthinkable. It thereby introduces the

[79] Wolff, *Joel and Amos*, 284; Paul, *Amos*, 218–9.

following statement in verse 12b, "but you have turned justice into poison (Hebrew, *rō'š*, "poppy") and the fruit of righteousness into wormwood," such overturning of justice and righteousness is equally unthinkable and yet that is precisely what happened. According to the prophet, this is the cause of punishment.

The prophet concludes this sermon with reference to YHWH's decision to bring an enemy nation against Israel to oppress the nation and presumably take it into exile (cf. verse 7). He begins with a portrayal of the people's rejoicing over the conquest or defeat of two Ammonites or Aramaean cities, Lo-debar and Karnaim. There has been a great deal of discussion concerning the identity of these cities based upon the presumption that they represent Jeroboam ben Joash's efforts to restore the borders of Israel from Lebo Hamath to the Sea of the Arabah (2 Kgs 14:25).[80] Lo-debar is associated with an Ammonite city mentioned in 2 Sam 17:27; 9:4, 5; Josh 13:26, which is likely identified with Tell el-Hammeh in the northern regions of Gilead north of the Jabbok River. Karnaim is an Aramaean city located in the region of the Bashan, east of the Sea of Galilee, and identified with Sheik es-Saʿad on a tributary of the Yarmuk River. The prophet notes the self-confidence of people who rejoice and claim to have taken the cities by their own strength, but both names convey puns that parody the celebration. Lo-debar of course means literally, "no thing" or "nothing," indicating that the people have conquered nothing. Karnaim means "two horns," and the statement that the people "taken for ourselves Karnaim" parodies the seizing of the horns of the Temple altar for protection against enemies (cf. 1 Kgs 2:28). Although the people have "taken the horns," they will not be protected from the enemy that YHWH sends against them. This is clear in verse 14 when YHWH states the intention to raise a nation against Israel. At no point does Amos identify the nation, but the earlier portrayals of the pattern of conquest in Amos 1–2 and the references to exile in Amos 5:27 and 6:7 make it clear that the nation is Assyria. The use of the term "oppress" *(lḥṣ)* recalls the oppression of the Egyptians against the Israelite slaves in Egypt (Exod 3:9; cf. Deut 26:7), and states that it will include all of the nation from Lebo Hamath to the Wadi/Stream Arabah. Of course, this recalls the entire extent of Jeroboam's kingdom from Lebo Hamath to the Sea of the Arabah (2 Kgs 14:25). Some have argued that the Wadi Arabah and the Sea of the Arabah are not the same, but this is a minor quibble over terminology as the intent to portray the entire kingdom of Jeroboam ben Joash is clear. The use of the oracular formula, "utterance of YHWH, G–d of Hosts," authorizes this as a statement by YHWH.

---

[80] Paul, *Amos*, 219–20.

The Visions of Amos:
Call for the Downfall of the Northern Dynasty and Temple
and the Rise of the Davidic Monarchy over Israel: 7:1–9:15

The concluding unit of the book of Amos appears in chapters 7–9, which present the visions of the prophet. These chapters have been the subject of a great deal of discussion as scholars have attempted to identify the nature of the prophet's visionary experience and the literary structure and compositional history of the unit.[81] Fundamental to this discussion is the question as to whether Amos was commissioned as a prophet in these visions or if the visions represent successive revelations to him throughout his prophetic career. For the most part, scholars have concluded that the visions do not represent Amos' call. He is not commissioned to go and speak to Israel, there is little mention of the reasons for YHWH's efforts to punish the nation in the visions themselves, and the prophet appears already to presuppose a role as an intermediary between YHWH and the people. Furthermore, the literary forms of the visions suggest a multi-staged process of composition. The first four visions in Amos 7:1-3, 4-6, 7-9; 8:1-3 are grouped in two pairs according to similarities in their respective literary forms, and the fifth vision in Amos 9:1-6 is formulated differently from the previous four. The visions appear to have been supplemented with a narrative report in Amos 7:10-17 concerning Amos' confrontation with the priest Amaziah at Beth El and, in Amos, with oracular material concerning YHWH's intention to bring judgment against the nation, and YHWH's intention to restore Davidic rule in Amos 9:7-15. Various reconstructions of the process and setting of literary composition have been put forward, most of which argue that unit reaches its final form in the post-exilic period. Many see the final oracle concerning the restoration of Davidic rule as an example of post-exilic messianic hopes, but recent recognition of the religious and political differences between the northern kingdom of Israel and the southern kingdom of Judah in the monarchic period have led some to maintain that the final form of the unit derives from some time in the pre-exilic period.[82]

Although Amos 7–9 may well be a composite literary unit, an attempt to analyze its synchronic literary features is essential for both the synchronic and diachronic interpretation of the text. For the most part, redaction-critical models for the formation of Amos 7–9 have played an inordinate role in the interpretation of this textual block as scholars

---

[81] For summaries of the discussion, see Auld, *Amos*, 16–24; Paul, *Amos*, 222–5.

[82] E.g., Paul, *Amos*, 288–95; Sweeney, "Formation and Form in Prophetic Literature," 124–5.

have focused on the visions themselves as the primary structural mark-
ers of the unit. Such a procedure reflects the presupposition that the visions, or at least the first four, represent the earliest stage or stages in
the compositional history of this text whereas the narrative in Amos
7:10-17, and the oracular material in Amos 8:4-14 and 9:7-15, represent
later expansions of the original visions. Certainly, the narrative must
have been written by someone other than the prophet as its objective
reporting style differs markedly from the first person autobiographical
style of the visions, but the literary form of the oracular material may
also derive from the prophet. Furthermore, the oracular material in
particular adds a rhetorical dimension to the text in that it points to the
fact that the purpose of Amos 7–9 is not simply to report the visionary
experiences of the prophet, but to employ them as part of a larger strategy to convince its audience to adopt the viewpoint of the prophet that
the northern Israelite dynasty and the Temple at Beth El must fall and
that the nation of Israel must be restored under Davidic rule as an expression of the will of YHWH. Insofar as the oracular materials in Amos
8:4-14 and 9:7-15 build upon the vision reports in Amos 7:1–8:3 and 9:1-
6 respectively to achieve this end, Amos 8:4-14 and 9:7-15 must be
viewed as texts that are central to the primary goals of the passage.

These considerations point to a very different view of the literary
structure of Amos 7–9 in that each block of visions is followed immediately by an oracular section that draws out the meaning of the prophet's
visions and explains their significance in relation to YHWH's intentions
concerning the nations Israel and Judah. Although it supplements the
vision concerning the wall in Amos 7:7-9, the narrative concerning the
prophet's confrontation with Amaziah in Amos 7:10-17 aids in focusing
the reader's attention on the northern monarchy and priesthood, and
thereby aids in building the case that Jeroboam and Beth El must fall and
that Israel must be united around the Davidic house (and presumably
the Jerusalem Temple). Thus, the literary structure of Amos 7–9 includes
two basic components. The first is the presentation of the first four visions in Amos 7:1–8:14, including the presentation of the visions themselves in Amos 7:1–8:3 followed by the oracular discourse in Amos 8:4-14.
The second is the presentation of the fifth vision in Amos 9:1-6 followed by the oracular discourse in Amos 9:7-15. There is a natural progression to the visions that points to the life experience of the prophet
and many like him as the basis for such a message. Amos 7:1-3 and 7:4-6
point to the difficulties faced by Judean and Israelite farmers and shepherds in paying the revenues required by the state, i.e., a plague of locusts
and fires that have destroyed much of the crops and pasturage have left
the people in severe economic straits. Amos 7:7-9 (plus 7:10-17) and 8:1-3
employ the symbols of a newly plastered wall and the harvest of summer

fruit to point to the reasons for YHWH's decision to bring the northern monarchy and the Beth El Temple to an end. These reasons are clearly articulated in the prophet's oracular discourse in Amos 8:4-14. Finally, Amos 9:1-6 employs the images of fire, blood, and death that are characteristic of an altar in operation to call for the final destruction of the temple at Beth El and the monarch who supports and authorizes it. This vision informs the prophet's oracle concerning the punishment of Israel and the rise of the house of David in Amos 9:7-15.

Altogether, the presentation of the prophet's visions in Amos 7–9 also points to the rhetorical goal of the book as a whole.[83] The indictment of the nations in Amos 1:3–2:16 is designed to draw the audience's attention to the sins of northern Israel. Amos 3–4 lay these sins out in detail as a basis for YHWH's decision to punish the state. Amos 5–6 point to the possibility of repentance if the people will seek YHWH. Finally, Amos 7–9 define what seeking YHWH means, i.e., the removal of the northern Israelite dynasty and cultic establishment and the restoration of the house of David over all Israel. Such goals are consistent with the initial motto of the book in Amos 1:2 which presents YHWH as a lion roaring from Jerusalem/Zion against the north. The book presents a Judean political and religious critique of the north and a statement concerning the future course of the nation, i.e., it must return to Judean rule and religious observance.

THE FIRST FOUR VISIONS:
THE BASIS FOR YHWH'S DECISION TO BRING DOWN
JEROBOAM AND BETH EL: 7:1–8:14

As noted above, Amos 7:1–8:14 presents the first four of Amos' vision reports in Amos 7:1–8:3 followed by the prophet's oracular discourse in Amos 8:4-14 that builds upon the visions to point to YHWH's decision to bring punishment against Israel. The visions are grouped in pairs that are formulated similarly and that convey similar content.[84]

The first pair of visions appear in Amos 7:1-3 and 7:4-6. Both vision reports are formulated in a first person autobiographical style that presents Amos himself as the narrator who recounts his own visionary experiences. Both passages employ the same introductory formula, "Thus my L–rd YHWH showed me, and behold . . ." followed by a

[83] Sweeney, "Formation and Form in Prophetic Literature," 117–25.

[84] For discussion of the formal features of vision reports, see Sweeney, *Isaiah 1–39*, 542; B. O. Long, "Reports of Visions among the Prophets," *JBL* 95 (1976) 353–65; F. Horst, "Die Visionsschilderungen der alttestamentlichen Propheten," *EvT* 20 (1960) 193–205.

participially based description of YHWH's actions that provide the bases for the visions. In both cases, the prophet raises the question, "How can Jacob stand? He is so small!" This results in YHWH's decision to turn back the punishment, expressed formulaically, "YHWH relented concerning this; 'It/This also shall not be,' said YHWH." Similar uses of the verb *hir'anî*, "he (YHWH) showed me," in relation to prophetic visionary experience appear in 2 Kgs 8:13; Jer 24:1; Zech 2:3 [NRSV: 1:18]; 3:1 (cf. Exod 27:8; Isa 30:30).

In the first vision in Amos 7:1-3, YHWH shows Amos a horde of locusts that will threaten the crops of the land. YHWH employs the verb *yôṣēr*, "forming, creating," to describe the divine action. The term can be used for both human action, such as creating a pot (Isa 29:16; Jer 18:4; Isa 44:9; Hab 2:18) or devising a course of action (Ps 94:20), or for divine action, such as the creation of human beings (Gen 2:7, 8), animals (Gen 2:19), Leviathan (Ps 104:26); dry land (Ps 95:5), the mountains (Amos 4:13), etc. Locust plagues are well known throughout the ancient near eastern and contemporary worlds as a threat to agriculture and thus to human subsistence. In the present case, the locusts are particularly threatening in that they are formed "at the beginning of the time of the latter growth," i.e., at a time when crops that were planted later than the earlier planting of wheat or grain would begin to sprout. Such later planting would include various vegetables that would supplement the basic grain diet. This is an especially vulnerable time in that the grain crops had already begun to grow and mature, making it possible for the locusts to destroy two very important sources of food for an agriculturally based population. The threat is especially acute in that it arises immediately after the time of "the king's mowings," i.e., after the time that the king has already taken the share that will be devoted to the support of the state (cf. 1 Sam 8:11-18, esp. 14-15; 1 Kgs 4:7–5:8). Whereas the king would have his share, very little would be left for the people. In an agrarian culture, this could well mean starvation. When Amos implores YHWH to forgive the people and call back the punishment, YHWH relents. This may well reflect a setting prior to that presupposed by the oracles against the nations in which YHWH repeatedly states, "I will not revoke the punishment/cause it to return" (e.g., Amos 2:6). The oracle appears at the beginning of the sequence of Amos' visions, and suggests that a locust plague may well have prompted the agriculturalist to speak out against the northern monarchy. After all, he still had to provide his share of crops to the king despite the difficulties he faced with the locusts.

The second vision in Amos 7:4-6 depicts YHWH "calling for judgment by fire." There have been various attempts to emend the text from *lārib*, "for judgment," to *lāhābet*, "for a flame of (fire)," or *lirbîb*, "for a shower of (fire)," based upon claims of semantic or syntactic irregularities in the verse, but there is no support for such emendations in the versions.[85] The phenomenon of fire would be a very common threat to farmers in the dry season of Israel when the land is parched for lack of water and any vegetation is so dry and wilted that it can quickly erupt into a flame that can consume acres of land. Southern California, which has a climate similar to that of Israel, experiences such fires every summer. The oracle employs a combination of mythological imagery and earthly reality to describe the scope and impact of such a natural disaster. On the one hand, the fire consumes "the great deep" *(tĕhôm rabbâ)*, a term that recalls the primordial waters prior to creation (Gen 1:2; Ps 104:6), but it also consumes "the land" *(haḥēleq)*, literally, "the portion, tract, share (of land)," that would be the holding of an individual Israelite/Judean farmer or family. The threat of fire to crops is again made quite clear with the use of this term; apparently, Amos experienced fire on his land during the dry season when some crops are still undergoing harvest. The results of such fire would be devastating for an agrarian economy. Once again, Amos asks YHWH to desist because Jacob is so small, and once again YHWH relents.

The second pair of visions appear in Amos 7:7-9(10-17) and 8:1-3. Both are formulated similarly with the same basic introductory formula as the previous pair, "Thus he/my L–rd YHWH showed me and behold . . ." followed by a description of an activity or an object, in these cases, YHWH standing beside a wall and a basket of summer fruit respectively. In both cases, YHWH asks the prophet, "What do you see, Amos?" and Amos replies with the appropriate answer (cf. Jer 1:11-12, 13-14). YHWH then applies the answer to a statement that conveys a sense of punishment against Israel and follows up with the phrase, "I will never again pass them by," i.e., "I will not forgive them again." The vision then concludes with an oracular statement that conveys the punishment, either in relation to destruction of Israel's high places and sacrifices and the death of Jeroboam (Amos 7:9) or the portrayal of wailing and dead bodies in the temple (Amos 8:3). The first vision introduces the narrative concerning Amos' confrontation with Amaziah (Amos 7:10-17) and the second vision precedes the oracular material in Amos 8:4-14.

The vision report in Amos 7:7-9 has been particularly problematic because interpreters have been uncertain as to the meaning of the term *ʾănāk*, frequently translated as "plumbline."[86] The vision depicts YHWH

---

[85] See Wolff, *Joel and Amos*, 292–3; Rudolph, *Joel–Amos–Obadja–Jona*, 232–3.

[86] See Paul, *Amos*, 233–6, Auld, *Amos*, 19–20, for overviews of the discussion. See also H.G.M. Williamson, "The Prophet and the Plumb-Line. A Redaction-Critical Study of Amos vii," *OTS* 26 (1990) 101–21.

standing by "a wall of *ănāk*," translated in NRSV as "a wall built with a plumbline," with "*ănāk* in his hand." The term is a *hapax legomenon* in this particular passage in the Hebrew Bible, which has been traditionally taken to mean "lead." Lead is frequently used as a weight for a plumbline, an architect's or builder's tool used to ensure the straightness of a wall so that it will not collapse under its own weight as it is built higher and higher. In the present case, the plumbline is taken as an indicator of Israel's moral straightness, i.e., YHWH measures Israel, finds it lacking, and then uses the image to introduce an oracle that speaks to the destruction of Israel's high places and monarchy. The term *ănāk* has been recently studied in relation to its Akkadian cognate *annaku*, "tin," and it has been proven conclusively that *ănāk* can not possibly mean, "lead," but can only mean, "tin."[87] This presents problems for the traditional interpretation of the verse as tin does not provide a suitable weight for use in a plumbline. Various attempts to reinterpret the term in relation to YHWH's standing by a tin wall, with perhaps a tin instrument in the divine hand, are entirely unsatisfactory. Tin provides no useful function when used to cover a wall, nor can it be used to make any kind of useful weapon or instrument for working on a wall. Objections to the meaning "lead" include the fact that biblical Hebrew has a standard term for "lead," i.e., *ʿōperet*, but it also has a standard term for "tin," i.e., *bĕdîl* (Num 31:22). Zechariah 4:10, where *hāʾeben habbĕdîl*, "the tin stone," is used to describe a plummet, demonstrates that tin could be employed for a plumbline, but the problem of the "wall of tin" remains.

A frequently overlooked meaning for the term, however, is "plaster."[88] The verb root *ʾnk* appears in Rabbinic Hebrew with the meaning, "to rub, polish, finish, to glaze vessels, to line (with onyx)."[89] The noun form *ănāk/ʾênāk*, "onyx, glaze," is also attested in Rabbinic Hebrew. Walls in ancient Israel were frequently made from a combination of stone, either dressed or undressed, and sun dried brick. Various forms of plaster could be used to seal crevices in stone and brick walls, and it would be particularly important to do so at the end of the summer and the beginning of the rainy season when the summer fruit harvest was brought in (cf. Amos 8:1-3). In this case, the vision would refer to a plastered wall, and YHWH would be standing with plaster in the divine hand to represent the repair work that would take place at this time of year. As in the visions of the locusts, the fire, and later the basket of summer fruit, such a sight would be well known to a man like Amos.

[87] B. Landsberger, "Tin and Lead—The Adventures of Two Vocables," *JNES* 24 (1965) 285–96.

[88] See Andersen and Freedman, *Amos*, 756–9.

[89] See Marcus Jastrow, *A Dictionary of the Targumim, the Talmud Babli and Yerushalmi, and the Midrashic Literature* (Brooklyn: P. Shalom, 1967) 85.

Nevertheless, the meaning of such a symbol remains to be defined. Amos sees YHWH by a plastered wall with plaster in the divine hand. When Amos replies to YHWH's question that he has seen "plaster," YHWH employs the term to state, "See I am setting *ʾănāk* ("plaster?") in the midst of my people Israel." Such an image would hardly explain the destruction of the sanctuaries and the northern monarchy. But the vision in Amos 8:1-3 might provide a clue in that Amos sees "summer fruit" *(qāyiṣ),* which provides the basis for a pun on the word "end" *(qēṣ),* which in turn describes what YHWH is bringing upon the people Israel. The parallel with Amos 8:1-3 suggests that *ʾănāk* in Amos 7:7-9 might provide the basis for a pun. Two are possible. In the first case, the consonants for *ʾănāk* are also the consonants for *ʾānōkî,* "I," which would suggest that YHWH intends to set the divine self in the midst of Israel to carry out the punishment. The awkwardness of such a pun, however, renders the attempt unlikely. A more likely approach to consider the assonance of the term *ʾănāk* with *ʾănāḥâ,* "lament, sighing, mourning," i.e., YHWH intends to place "mourning" or "lamenting" in the midst of Israel.[90] This would explain the following statement concerning the destruction of Israel's high places, sanctuaries, and king. It would also speak to the theme of mourning that is associated with the sanctuary at Beth El in biblical tradition. Such mourning would be particularly prominent at the end of the summer season as lamentation would symbolize the mourning for the dead world as a means to bring about the rainy season and new life.

The final oracular statement of the vision in verse 9 states that the high places of Isaac, the sanctuaries of Israel, and Jeroboam would all be destroyed or put to the sword. The reference to Isaac is somewhat enigmatic as the patriarch is normally associated with Beer Sheba rather than the north (Gen 26:32-33; 28:10). It should be recalled that Isaac is the father of both Jacob (Israel) and Esau (Edom), and that Judah controlled Edom during the ninth century as a vassal of Israel (2 Kgs 3:4-27; 8:20-22). Even after Edom's revolt, Israel continued to control Judah and it very likely controlled trade through Beer Sheba as well. In such a circumstances, Isaac would well symbolize the unity of both northern Israel and southern Judah as one family or nation.

The narrative in Amos 7:10-17 concerning Amos' confrontation with Amaziah, the priest at the Beth El sanctuary, is tied structurally to the report of Amos' third vision in Amos 7:7-9.[91] This is clear from both the syntax of the passage, which begins with a conjunctive *waw-consecutive*

[90] See Stuart, *Hosea-Jonah,* 373.

[91] See Peter Ackroyd, "A Judgment Narrative Between Kings and Chronicles? An Approach to Amos 7:9-17," *Canon and Authority,* ed. G. W. Coats and B. O. Long (Philadelphia: Fortress, 1977) 71–87.

narrative formulation that joins the passage to verses 7-9, and the contents of the passage in which Amaziah responds to the oracle concerning the death of Jeroboam and the destruction of Israel's sanctuaries in verse 9. Although it is not joined structurally to the first two vision reports, the narrative relates to both of them in that the locust plague and the fire would have special significance for a herdsman and dresser of sycamore trees (verse 14). The third person descriptive formulation of the narrative, in contrast to the autobiographical form of the vision reports, demonstrates that Amos is not the author of the passage. It was clearly composed by someone else with an interest in presenting the career of the prophet—we will never know by whom—but it nevertheless relates to the vision reports in that it aids in establishing the social and historical context in which Amos presented his message. Based upon the visions outlined in these chapters, the narrative asserts that Amos challenged the political and religious establishment of the northern kingdom of Israel, and that like the prophet Jeremiah in Jerusalem (Jer 36:5), he was banned from prophesying in the Beth El temple for his efforts.

The narrative also functions as a means to validate Amos' prophetic message. This is particularly pertinent in ancient Israel because biblical tradition recognizes the possibility that prophets may not always speak a true message from G–d.[92] Deuteronomy 18:15-22 establishes criteria by which one might recognize a true prophet, viz., when the prophet's words come true then the prophet must speak a true word from YHWH. Likewise, the narrative concerning the prophets Micaiah ben Imlah and Zedekiah ben Chenaanah in 1 Kings 22 demonstrates that YHWH is capable of giving a false message to prophets in order to serve divine purposes. In retrospect, it may be relatively easy to determine the validity of a prophetic message by applying the criteria of Deut 18:15-22, but this provides little assistance to the contemporaries of a prophet who must make a decision as to whether or not the prophet's statements are valid. This issue is addressed in a number of narratives that are formulated similarly to Amos 7:10-17 in which the validity of a prophet's message is established in relation to a confrontation with an opponent of the prophet.[93] Examples include the confrontation between Micaiah ben Imlah and Zedekiah ben Chanaanah in 1 Kings 22;

---

[92] For discussion of the issues involved in the problem of prophetic conflict or true and false prophecy in the Hebrew Bible, see James L. Crenshaw, *Prophetic Conflict*, BZAW, vol. 124 (Berlin: Walter de Gruyter, 1971); James A. Sanders, "Hermeneutics in True and False Prophecy," *Canon and Authority*, ed. G. W. Coats and B. O. Long (Philadelphia: Fortress, 1977) 21–41.

[93] Sweeney, *Isaiah 1–39*, 518.

the confrontation between YHWH, represented by the prophet Isaiah ben Amoz, and the Assyrian king in Isaiah 36–37/2 Kings 18–19; and the confrontation between Jeremiah ben Hilkiah and Hananiah ben Azzur in Jeremiah 28. In all cases, the narrative presents the contrasting viewpoints of the primary protagonists and confirms the message of the prophet by narrating the death of the prophet's opponent or a third figure who fails to heed the message of the prophet, i.e., King Ahab of Israel dies in battle when he ignores Micaiah's warning that Israel will be defeated, the Assyrian Sennacherib is assassinated by his sons when he fails to acknowledge YHWH's sovereignty as articulated by Isaiah, and Hananiah dies when he continues to assert against Jeremiah that Babylon will be overthrown in two years. In a similar manner, the death of Amaziah in Amos 7:10-17 validates Amos' message that King Jeroboam of Israel will die and that the nation will ultimately go into exile. This, of course, prepares the reader for the following material in chapters 8 and 9 in which the prophet points to the downfall of northern Israel and the Beth El temple and the rise of the house of David.

The narrative begins with a notice in verse 10 that Amaziah, the priest at Beth El, reports to King Jeroboam that Amos has conspired against him. Amaziah is not identified as the high priest, but the examples of other priests in other Israelite sanctuaries, e.g., Eli at Shiloh (1 Samuel 1–4); the Levite in the house of Micah (Judges 17); Jonathan ben Gershom ben Moses at Dan (Judg 18:27-31); Abiathar or Ahimelek ben Abiathar and later Zadok ben Ahitub at Jerusalem (2 Sam 8:17; 1 Kgs 2:26-28, 35), indicate that he may well have functioned as such. The charge of conspiracy is particularly pertinent in that the ruling dynasty of Jehu, of which Jeroboam was the fourth king, came to power when Jehu assassinated Jehoram of Israel, the last ruler of the Omride line, and Ahaziah of Judah, whose mother was the Omride princess Athaliah (2 Kings 9–10). Furthermore, Jeroboam's son Zechariah was ultimately assassinated in a conspiracy by Shallum ben Jabesh (2 Kgs 15:8-12), who was in turn assassinated in a conspiracy by Menahem ben Gadi (2 Kgs 15:13-16). Menahem's son Pekahiah was assassinated by Pekah ben Remaliah (2 Kgs 15:23-26), and Pekah was assassinated by Hoshea when the Syro-Ephraimitic War turned sour (2 Kgs 15:29-31). Amaziah's statement that "the land is not able to bear all of his words" suggests that conditions in Israel were ripe for the overthrow of the king, as subsequent events confirm. The evidence for Amaziah's charges is presented in verse 11, in which the priest reports Amos' words to the king, "Jeroboam shall die by the sword, and Israel must go into exile away from this land." The statement reads literally, "Jeroboam shall die by the sword, and Israel will surely go into exile from upon its land." Interpreters have noted the discrepancy between Amos' statement in verse 9 and Amaziah's report of Amos' statement in verse 11, but there is very little importance to the difference. Amaziah's report accurately represents Amos' statement that Jeroboam would die by the sword (cf. verse 9), and other statements concerning the exile of Israel (Amos 5:27; 6:7). Others note that Amos' prediction did not come true, i.e., Jeroboam died a natural death, but his son Zechariah was assassinated. This disturbs some interpreters who wish to protect Amos' identity as a true prophet, but even Amos states in verse 14 that he is not a prophet! Readers must keep in mind that prophets speak about what is possible; they do not always state what actually will be. The fact that Amos' statement did not come true literally should not detract from his prophetic status, even if he states that he is no prophet (which happens to be another incorrect statement!).

The narrative does not report Jeroboam's response to Amaziah's charges. It only hints at the king's response when it presents Amaziah's command to Amos in verses 12-13 that he should leave Beth El and prophesy instead in Judah. Many presuppose that the narrative suggests that Jeroboam (or Amaziah) did not consider Amos to be a very serious threat because he did not have the prophet killed. There are exceptions, e.g., Ahab (1 Kings 21), but ancient Israelite kings were not barbarians who simply murdered people willfully.[94] The fact that Amos was banned from Beth El, much like Jeremiah was later banned from speaking in the Jerusalem Temple (Jer 36:5; cf. Jeremiah 7; 26), indicates that Jeroboam took the threat seriously enough. Several aspects of Amaziah's command deserve notice. First, he refers to the prophet as "seer" (ḥōzeh), a title that some take as a derogatory term to indicate Amaziah's lack of respect for Amos.[95] The term carries no such overtones, however, as it is a standard professional designation for a prophet or oracle giver in both ancient Israel/Judah and in the pagan world. Other prophets in the Bible are called "seer," such as Gad (2 Sam 24:11; 1 Chr 21:9; 2 Chr 29:25); Heman (1 Chr 25:5); Jedo (2 Chr 9:29); Iddo (2 Chr 12:15); and Jehu ben Hanani (2 Chr 19:2). The term is often used in parallel with "prophet" (nābîʾ; 2 Sam 24:11; 2 Kgs 17:13; Isa 29:10; cf. Isa 30:10, which places it in parallel with rôʾeh, also translated as "seer"). It appears also in eighth century inscriptions in reference to pagan "seers," such as those invoked by King Zakir of Hamath[96] and in refer-

---

[94] Even Ahab was convinced to murder Naboth by his pagan wife, Jezebel, which helps to demonstrate the dangers of marrying a pagan wife as understood in the Deuteronomistic History (cf. Deut 7:1-7).

[95] For discussion of the term ḥōzeh, see Paul, Amos, 240–1.

[96] H. Donner and W. Röllig, Kanaanäische und Aramäische Inschriften (Wiesbaden: Otto Harrassowitz, 1962–64) I:202:12.

ence to Balaam in the Deir ʿAlla inscription.[97] The meaning of the root *ḥzh* means "to perceive," by both seeing and hearing.[98] The term may well designate an oracle diviner, which would be a type of prophet in the ancient world. Amaziah's demand that Amos "flee away to the land of Judah" suggests that indeed there is some element of threat. The verb *brḥ*, "flee," certainly indicates that Amos should not tarry. Furthermore, the command presupposes Amos' Judean identity, and hints that his Judean status may have something to do with his threats against king, sanctuary, and state. These concerns appear once again in the closing words of Amaziah's command when he emphasizes that Beth El is "the king's sanctuary" and "the temple of the kingdom." Although Beth El appears to have been founded as an Israelite sanctuary well before the period of the dual monarchies (cf. Genesis 28; 35), Jeroboam ben Nebat established it together with Dan as an official state sanctuary at the outset of his rule over the northern kingdom of Israel (1 Kings 12–13). When Amaziah orders Amos to return to Judah, he in essence tells him to go to his home country. Furthermore, the qualification that he should prophecy there in order to "earn your bread there," literally, "eat bread there," suggests that he considers Amos to be a professional prophet who earns his living by delivering oracles. This is not unusual in that the role of prophet was a professional status in the ancient world. Basically, Amos is banned from speaking at Beth El and told to go home. He need not be killed; the ban from speaking at Beth El effectively silences him. Readers must keep in mind that ancient temples provided ready-made audiences for prophets at festival time. With his audience taken away, the prophet's attempts to convey a message are undermined. Once again, the example of Jeremiah is instructive. When he is banned from speaking at the Temple, he has his message written down so that it can be read by someone else at the Temple (Jeremiah 36). Speaking on street corners is apparently not an adequate substitute.

The presentation of Amos' response to Amaziah in verses 14-17 is designed to impress upon the reader and Amaziah that Amos' prophetic message is genuine despite his lack of professional prophetic

[97] J. Hoftijzer and G. van der Kooij, *Aramaic Texts from Deir ʿAlla*, Documenta et Monumenta Antiqua, vol. XIX (Leiden: Brill, 1976).

[98] Cf. the use of the root in Isa 1:1, "The vision of Isaiah ben Amoz which he saw concerning Judah and Jerusalem . . ."; cf. Isa 2:1; 13:1; Obad 1; Nah 1:1; Hab 1:1. These examples indicate that *ḥzh* refers to both visual and auditory experience as the verb is used to qualify "vision" (Isa 1:1), "word" (Isa 2:1), and "pronouncement" (Isa 13:1; Nah 1:1; Hab 1:1). In all cases, the term introduces prophetic oracles. Cf. Jepsen, "חזה," *TDOT* IV:283.

status. The first part of the response emphasizes his statement, "I am not a prophet, and I am not a son of a prophet." The term "son of a prophet" is well recognized as an indication of professional status rather than biological descent as indicated by the use of the term to designate prophetic guilds (1 Kgs 20:35; 2 Kgs 2:3, 5, 7, 15; 4:1, 38; 5:22; 6:1; 9:1). Many have attempted to suggest that Amos means that he *had not been* a prophet, but that he *was* one now, but this ignores the fact that Hebrew verbless clauses do not indicate time. It further undermines the force of the statement. Amos emphasizes that his profession is that of "a herdsman" and "dresser of sycamore trees," i.e., he is a farmer, not a prophet. But he continues by stating that YHWH took him from following the flock and commanded him to prophesy to the people of Israel. Such a claim is reminiscent of the one made by YHWH through Nathan on behalf of David, "I took you from the pasture, from following the sheep to be prince over my people Israel" (2 Sam 7:8). It suggests an attempt to appear as a simple person who, with no thought of personal advancement or motivation, responded to a spontaneous call by YHWH to serve in a special and authoritative capacity. It thereby strengthens the claim to authority on the part of the prophet (or the king), i.e., he didn't want the job, but he was compelled by G–d to do it anyway.

Having made the claim for divine authority in verses 14-15, Amos then turns to an oracle concerning Amaziah in verses 16-17. The oracle is formulated as a prophetic judgment speech that is identified as "the word of YHWH." It begins with an opening instruction to Amaziah in verse 16a to hear YHWH's word, and the oracle follows in verses 16b-17. The grounds for punishment are stated in verse 16b when Amos reiterates Amaziah's command that Amos not prophesy. Having stated his case that he speaks the word of YHWH, he throws Amaziah's words back in his face. They are not an exact quotation of Amaziah's words, but they express the basic thrust of the priest's command. As noted above in relation to Amaziah's quotation of Amos' words in verses 9 and 10, precision in quotation is hardly necessary. Once again, Amos identifies Israel as the "house of Isaac," which might indicate the united kingdoms of Israel and Judah (cf. Amos 7:9). He then presents an announcement of punishment in verse 17, which is identified by the characteristic particle *lākēn*, "therefore," and the messenger formula, "thus says YHWH," which again identifies the statement as a word of YHWH. The announcement emphasizes several key points that emphasize both the personal consequences for Amaziah and the national consequences for Israel. First, he states that Amaziah's wife "shall become a prostitute in the city." This is a very misleading translation in that it suggests some moral fault on her part. The reality of a woman's experience in a time of war and conquest by a foreign enemy is that she will likely be raped by enemy soldiers (or even by men of her own people) or forced into sexual relationships in order to save her life. Second, he states that Amaziah's sons and daughters will fall by the sword. Children are too young to be of any use to a conqueror and are considered simply as extra mouths to feed. There is no compassion when enemy troops run rampant through a conquered city. Hence, children of the enemy are killed. Third, Amos states that Amaziah's property will be divided up and parceled out by line, i.e., it will be measured and given as spoil to the conquering soldiers. This statement is remarkable in that Amaziah is a priest and presumably a Levite. Levites were not to own property in ancient Israel, but derived their income from the offerings brought by the people to the Temple or from special Levitical cities (see Numbers 18; Deut 18:1-8; Joshua 21; 2 Chronicles 31). 1 Kings 12:31 charges that Jeroboam ben Nebat appointed non-Levites as priests at Beth El and Dan, but this may be a Judean polemic against the northern kingdom and priesthood. Fourth, Amos states that Amaziah will die in "an unclean land." This means that he will die in a foreign country, and presupposes that he will be exiled as a result of Israel's defeat. Priests were expected to be "holy" and to serve in the sanctuary as a "holy" place. By maintaining the holiness of the sanctuary, the land also was considered to be holy. A foreign land would, of course, lack the presence of an Israelite sanctuary and be considered unclean. Finally, Amos states what had been his main thesis, that Israel would be exiled from its land. Once again, he appears to presuppose the threat posed by the Assyrian empire, which was known for its practice of deporting the leading elements of a conquered population in order to deprive the nation of its leadership and thereby to prevent the possibility of revolt.

The fourth vision report in Amos 8:1-3 employs the same formal features as the third vision report in Amos 7:7-9. Once again, the vision is based upon the prophet's experience as an agriculturalist and his development of a pun based upon the vision to express the message that he wishes to convey. It begins in verse 1 with the statement that YHWH shows him "a basket of summer fruit," in Hebrew, *kĕlûb qāyiṣ*. "Summer fruit" (*qāyiṣ*, literally, "summer") refers to the fruit that is harvested at the transition to the rainy season around the time of Sukkoth in the seventh month and perhaps the eighth month of the year.[99] When asked by YHWH what he sees, Amos responds that he sees a basket of summer

---

[99] The Gezer calendar associates "summer fruit" (*qṣ*) with the last month of the year. As the new year begins in the seventh month (or perhaps the eighth month; cf. 1 Kgs 12:32), the harvest of summer fruit would coincide with Sukkoth. For a translation of the Gezer calendar, see Pritchard, *ANET* 320.

fruit. YHWH then answers, "The end has come upon my people Israel," in which the word "end," *qēṣ* in Hebrew, expresses a pun on the word *qāyiṣ*, "summer fruit." Apart from paranomasia, the two terms have nothing to do with each other as *qāyiṣ* is derived from the root *qyṣ*, "to be hot, to awaken," and *qēṣ* is derived from *qṣṣ*, "to cut off." Paul notes that the northern Israelite dialect may well have rendered the pronunciation of *qāyiṣ* somewhat similar to *qēṣ*.[100] In any case, the association of the two terms makes the meaning of the vision clear; the prophet sees the "summer fruit" that is brought to the Temple at Beth El at Sukkoth and understands it as a sign from YHWH that the "end" of the northern kingdom of Israel is coming. As in Amos 7:7-9, YHWH concludes with the statement, "I will never again pass them by," i.e., "I will not again relent (concerning the punishment)." The vision report concludes in verse 3 with an oracular statement concerning the mourning over all the dead bodies that will litter the area as a result of the punishment. The NRSV renders the statement, "The songs of the Temple will become wailings in that day . . .," which attempts to render the Hebrew accurately. Interpreters have noted, however, that the noun *šîrôt*, "songs," does not provide a suitable subject for the verb *wĕhêlîlû*, "and they shall wail," in that the verb normally requires a subject that carries out the wailing. Many have therefore emended *šîrôt* to *šārôt*, "singing women," based upon 2 Sam 19:36 [NRSV: 19:35], which refers to both singing men and singing women, and 2 Chr 35:25, which refers to the singing men and women who sang laments for the dead king Josiah.[101] There is no textual evidence for such an emendation, however, and the NRSV translation must stand despite its awkwardness. The oracular formula identifies YHWH as the speaker of this statement, which continues with the portrayal of the many corpses cast out in every place. The concluding command, "Be silent!" recalls the command for silence that appears at a time of YHWH's manifestation in the Temple (Hab 2:20; Zech 2:17 [NRSV: 2:13]; cf. Neh 8:11), at a time of sacrifice on the "Day of YHWH" (Zeph 1:7), and in the presence of the dead (Amos 6:10). Although the command generally presupposes a cultic setting of theophany in the Temple, its use here is ironic because it signals the impending destruction of the Beth El temple and the deaths of its worshipers as YHWH imposes punishment upon the northern kingdom.

The cultic setting is presupposed throughout the oracle in Amos 8:4-14 in which the prophet announces YHWH's punishment against the people of Israel. Many interpreters consider these verses to be a collection of originally separate literary or speech units, i.e., verses 4-7, 8, 9-

[100] Paul, *Amos*, 254; cf. Andersen and Freedman, *Amos*, 796.
[101] Rudolph, *Joel, Amos, Obadja, Jona*, 238.

10, 11-12, 13-14,[102] or variations of these groupings, but the consistent theme of impending punishment, the cultic motifs that permeate the entire section, and the references in verses 9, 11, and 13 to a future time in which the punishment will be realized indicate that these verses are to be read together as a single unit concerned with the impending punishment of Israel. Verses 4-6 establish the basis for the punishment, and verses 7-14 outline the measures that will be taken against the people.

Verses 4-6 begin with the call to attention formula that is directed against those who will suffer YHWH's punishment. They are identified initially as "you that trample on the needy and bring to ruin the poor of the land." The use of the verb šʾp, "to trample," to characterize those who abuse the poor recalls the prophet's earlier statement in Amos 2:7 in which he addresses "those who trample upon the dust of the earth, on the head of the needy." The care of the poor and needy is a fundamental responsibility of kingship throughout the ancient Near East (cf. Exod 23:10-11; Deut 15:7-11).[103] The verb sʾp also means, "to pant after," which emphasizes the greed or passion with which the leadership of the nation oppresses its people.

The prophet places a quotation in the mouths of those whom he would accuse in verses 5-6 to illustrate their willingness to neglect the cultic requirements of YHWH at the Beth El sanctuary in order to pursue their oppression of the poor. The first statement is actually a pair of questions, "When will the new moon be over so that we may sell grain; and the Sabbath, so that we may offer wheat for sale?" They presuppose the observance of the new moon and the Sabbath as holy days on which no work is to be performed. The new moon, of course, is the first day of the month for which a special sacrificial offering at the Temple is required (Num 28:11-15; cf. Num 10:10; 29:6; Ps 81:4 [NRSV: 81:3]). There is no explicit prohibition of work in the various cultic calendars, but this passage clearly presupposes that normal work and commercial activity are not permitted. The observance of the new moon is noted by other eighth century prophets, i.e., Hosea (Hos 2:13) and Isaiah (Isa 1:13, 14), and it appears in narratives relating to other pre-exilic contexts, such as 1 Sam 20:1-34; 2 Kgs 4:23, as well as exilic or post-exilic settings, such as Ezek 45:17; Isa 66:23; Neh 10:34 [NRSV: 10:33] (cf. 1 Chr 23:31). The Shabbat is the seventh day of the week which commemorates the creation of the world (Gen 2:1-3; Exod 20:11) or the Exodus from Egypt (Deut 5:15). Work is explicitly prohibited on the Shabbat (Exod 20:8-11; 23:12; 34:21; 35:2-3; Lev 23:3; Deut 5:12-15; cf. Jer 17:21-27;

---

[102] See Wolff, *Joel and Amos*, 324.

[103] Cf. F. C. Fensham, "Widow, Orphan, and Poor in Ancient Near Eastern Legal and Wisdom Literature," *JNES* 21 (1962) 129–39.

Neh 13:15-22), and a special offering is required to be sacrificed at the Temple (Num 28:9-10). Like the new moon, the Shabbat is noted by other eighth century prophets, including Hosea (Hos 2:13) and Isaiah (Isa 1:13-14), and it is mentioned in relation to the ninth century prophet Elisha (2 Kgs 4:23). The prophet's placement of these words in the mouths of those whom he would condemn clearly portrays them as having little regard for cultic observance despite their appearances in the Temple, which in ancient Israel and the Near East in general, is generally regarded as the site where the justice of YHWH or other gods is taught and carried out (cf. Isa 2:2-4; Mic 4:1-5; cf. Exodus 19, which presents Mt. Sinai as YHWH's abode or Temple).

The quotation continues with a statement that the addressee intends to "make the ephah small and the shekel great" and to use "false balances." The ephah was an ancient dry measure used especially for grain, equivalent to 20.878 quarts. The shekel was a standard measure of weight used for silver or gold, equivalent to 176.29 grains.[104] The intent is clear, i.e., to reduce the measure of grain sold to the customer and to increase the price. The use of false balances and the general misrepresentation of goods is strictly prohibited in Israelite law (Lev 19:35-37; Deut 25:13-16). The monarchy and priesthood are generally considered to be the authorities responsible for the enforcement of such standards (cf. Deut 17:8-13, 18-20; cf. 2 Sam 12:1-25; 1 Kgs 3:16-28). Finally, the prophet concludes the quotation with statements of the intention to buy (literally, "sell") "the poor for sliver and the needy for a pair of sandals" and to sell "the sweepings of the wheat." Basically, these statements further portray attempts to abuse the poor economically. If a person in ancient Israel could not pay a debt, he or she would have to enter into debt slavery to work off the debt. Such arrangements were limited to a maximum of six years for a man (Exod 21:1-6; Deut 15:12-18), but a woman might serve all of her life if she was designated for marriage by the owner (Exod 21:7-11; contra Deut 15:12-18, which specifies the same six year term as for a man). At the end of the designated time, the debtor was to be released from service unless he or she declared a desire to remain a slave forever. By pointing to the sale of persons for silver, Amos points to accepted practice, but the reference to a pair of sandals suggests that people were being impressed into debt slavery for relatively small obligations. Nevertheless, it should be noted that sandals and other forms of clothing might be considered a

---

[104] For these equivalencies, see H. G. May and B. M. Metzger, eds., *The Oxford Annotated Bible with the Apocrypha* (New York: Oxford University Press, 1965) 1530–1, but cf. M. A. Powell, "Weights and Measures," *ABD* VI:897-908, who points to the uncertainties in establishing precise equivalences for ancient Israelite measures.

significant amount as Exod 22:25-27 indicates that a mantle could be taken as a pledge for a debt (although it must be returned at night; see also Deut 24:10-13).[105] The "sweepings of wheat" refers to the chaff that falls when grain is processed. Such chaff is generally useless as food, but it can fill out a bag when placed in the bottom out of view.

Verses 7-14 then take up YHWH's plans to punish the nations for these offenses. The prophet begins with a statement of YHWH's oath never to forget the deeds of the "pride of Jacob." The term "pride of Jacob" is of uncertain meaning, but it likely refers to the overall might and reputation of the northern kingdom of Israel, particularly of its leadership. This statement sets the tone for the following material in verses 8-14 that specifies YHWH's intentions to bring punishment upon the nation for the wrongdoings outlined in verses 4-6.

The prophet's announcement of punishment in verses 8-14 once again demonstrates his tendency to draw conclusions concerning YHWH's intention to bring punishment upon the people from his observations of the natural world. He begins in verse 8 with a rhetorical question that notes the trembling or shaking of the land, the mourning of its inhabitants, and its rising and sinking like the Nile River of Egypt. It seems very clear that he employs the imagery of an earthquake to portray YHWH's judgment. The superscription of the book (Amos 1:1) states that Amos spoke "two years before the earthquake," but the imagery of the land rising and pitching like the Nile is unmistakable. We cannot know if this description is based upon the prophet's experience of a real earthquake at the time that he spoke or if he simply employs the imagery of past experience, either his own or of others, but he clearly sees natural phenomena as indicators of YHWH's actions in relation to the human world. The initial phrase of the question, "on account of this," clearly ties catastrophe to the actions of the people conveyed in verses 4-6 and points to the earthquake as YHWH's punishment of the people for wrongdoing.

The prophet continues with a portrayal of natural events that convey YHWH's punishment in verses 9-10. These verses are tied syntactically to verse 8 by the *waw-consecutive* formulation of the introductory statement, "and it shall come to pass on that day." The NRSV does not adequately convey the Hebrew *wĕhāyâ*, "and it shall come to pass," which together with the formulaic *bayyôm hahhûʾ*, "on that day," conveys the future orientation of the events that will take place. The appearance of the oracular formula, "utterance of my L–rd YHWH," indicates that

---

[105] Cf. the Mesad Heshavyahu or Yavneh Yam inscription in which a man sues his creditor to return a mantle taken by a certain Hoshaiah ben Shobai (Pritchard, *ANET* 568).

the prophet quotes an oracle by YHWH. The initial statement in verse 9b plays upon the theophanic and Exodus traditions of ancient Israel in that it portrays a solar eclipse as an act of YHWH to punish the land. This, of course, reprises one of the plagues visited upon the Egyptians at the time of the Exodus (Exod 10:21-29), and may reflect the prior reference to the rise and fall of the Nile as an image for earthquake. The portrayal of the darkening of the sun is also characteristic of theophanic traditions that emphasize dark clouds, thunder, and lightening as expressions of YHWH's manifestation (Exodus 19; Ezekiel 1; Habakkuk 3). YHWH then turns to the people in verse 10 and states that their festivals will be turned to mourning and their songs to lamentation. Once again, this appears to build upon the tradition of mourning associated with worship at Beth El as noted previously in references to the grave of Rachel's nurse Deborah *Allon-bacuth*, "the oak of weeping" (Gen 35:8); the association with the death of Rachel (Gen 35:16-21); the naming of the region as Bochim, "weeping" (Judg 2:1-5); and the motif of Rachel weeping for her children (Jer 30:15). It is possible that Beth El employed rites of mourning at the time of Sukkoth to mark the transition of the dry to the rainy season analogous to those of Mesopotamian or Canaanite religion that mourned for the dead fertility god Tammuz/Dumuzi or Baal/Aqhat whose ascent from the netherworld with the aid of Ishtar/Inanna (the Queen of Heaven) or Anat/Paqhat marked the beginning of rain and fertility in the land (cf. Jeremiah 44; Ezekiel 8).[106] Of course, we cannot be sure as to the nature of such rites at Beth El, but it does appear that YHWH/the prophet makes ironic use of such a tradition of mourning. The donning of sackcloth and shaving the head were typical signs of mourning (Gen 37:34; 1 Kgs 20:31; 21:27; 2 Kgs 6:30 for sackcloth; Lev 21:5; Isa 3:24; 15:2; Mic 1:16 for baldness). Mourning for an only child indicates an especially grievous and bitter situation that would last well beyond the conclusion of the mourning period, especially in a society that placed such importance on the birth of children to carry on the father's name and inheritance (cf. Genesis 15; 21; 22).

Two further paragraphs in verses 11-12 and 13-14 specify the calamity that will overtake the people on the day of punishment. Verses 11-12 begin with the formulaic statement, "behold, the days are coming," which announces future events (cf. Amos 4:2; 9:13).[107] It is fol-

---

[106] See the Mesopotamian "Descent of Ishtar to the Netherworld" (*ANET* 106–9); the Sumerian "Inanna's Descent to the Nether World" (*ANET* 52–7); the Ugaritic "Poems about Baal and Anath" (*ANET* 129–42); and the Ugaritic "The Tale of Aqhat" (*ANET* 149–55).

[107] For a thorough study of passages in which this formula appears, see Simon De Vries, *From Old Revelation to New: A Tradition-Historical and Redaction-Critical Study of*

lowed by another occurrence of the oracular formula, which identifies the following statements as oracles from YHWH. The motif here is hunger, which follows naturally from the concern with the instability of the natural world expressed in the previous verses. It also builds upon the motif of mourning, especially insofar as the mourning expresses ritual portrayals of the inauguration of the rainy season. Effectively, YHWH's statement represents an ironic reference to such rites in that they will be ineffective. YHWH states that the people will not suffer hunger and thirst as a result of the failure of the rains and fertility to come to the land, but that they will suffer "hunger" and "thirst" for the words of YHWH, i.e., they will recognize that they have not listened to YHWH and that this is the cause of their present difficulties. The portrayal of the people's wandering from sea to sea and from north to east is intended to convey their wandering to every conceivable place to search out the word of YHWH. Sea to sea would refer to the Mediterranean in the west and either the Sea of Galilee or the Dead Sea in the east. From north to east might also allude to the Sea of Galilee and the Dead Sea. One must keep in mind that travel to the south leads only to the Negev desert. The punitive intent of the statement is clear enough, but it is highlighted by YHWH's statement that the people will search for the word of YHWH, but they will not find it.

The final paragraph in verses 13-14 builds upon the motifs of hunger and thirst as well as upon the earlier motifs of mourning and ritual celebration. The paragraph begins with the formulaic *bayyôm hahû᾽*, "on that day," which signifies the future.[108] It portrays the young women and young men fainting from thirst, which plays once again into the motif of rain and fertility at the time of Sukkoth. It is possible that the rites of Beth El called for the young men and women to go out into the fields and vineyards at this time, not only to gather the harvest but also to give expression to mourning and renewed life at the transition of the season. The narrative concerning the Benjaminite men who find their wives from the maidens of Shiloh who go out into the vineyards to dance at the time of the festival to YHWH (i.e., Sukkoth) suggests that fertility might also be portrayed by the marriage of young men and women who go out into the fields at this time. Obviously, YHWH's statement here has another outcome in mind as their thirst indicates a lack of water. The causes are outlined in verse 14. They are sworn to a god characterized as "the guilt of Samaria," and make vows by "the life of your G–d, O Dan" and "the way of Beer Sheba." Many have argued

---

Temporal Transitions in Prophetic Predictions (Grand Rapids: Eerdmans, 1995) esp. 74–85.

[108] See De Vries, *From Old Revelation to New*, esp. 38–63.

that *ʾašmat šōmrôn*, "the guilt of Samaria," should be read as *ʾăšîmat šōmrôn*, "Ashimah of Samaria," which is a reference to the Aramaean deity Ashima' (*ʾăšîmāʾ*) brought by the men of Hamat to Israel in the aftermath of the fall of the northern kingdom (2 Kgs 17:30).[109] The name would have been reread as *ʾašmat šōmrôn* in order to polemicize against the deity. There is no textual evidence that Ashima' is the intended reference, however, and the names of the other deities in verse 14, "life of your G–d, O Dan," and "the way of Beer Sheba," do not seem to hide proper names. In each case, the location or association of the deity is determinative in the prophet's or YHWH's estimation. Samaria is the capital of the northern kingdom, Dan is the sanctuary at the northern border of Israel, and Beer Sheba is the sanctuary at the southern border of Judah. It appears that the references are intended to encompass the entire land of Israel, including its Judean ally / vassal, and to delegitimate the worship of G–d under the auspices of the northern Israelite state. Jerusalem is not mentioned, which suggests that the prophet intended to argue that YHWH could only be understood and worshiped properly in relation to the Jerusalem Temple. Until the people of the northern kingdom returned to YHWH at Jerusalem, all would be lost as they would fall, not to rise again (cf. Amos 5:2).

THE FIFTH VISION:
CALL FOR THE DOWNFALL OF THE BETH EL TEMPLE
AND THE RISE OF THE HOUSE OF DAVID: 9:1-15

The presentation of Amos' fifth vision and its associated oracular material concerning the call for the destruction of the Beth El Temple and the reestablishment of the fallen House of David in Amos 9:1-15 constitutes the climax of the vision reports in Amos 7–9 and indeed of the book as a whole. Many have noted that the distinctive form of the vision report, which begins with the statement, "I saw my L–rd standing beside the altar, and he said, . . ." marks the fifth vision for special consideration.[110] Furthermore, in contrast to the previous reports, YHWH does not speak directly to the prophet, but makes a general announcement concerning the downfall of Beth El. Although some interpreters mistakenly take the formal differences as grounds for viewing this material as the work of later writers,[111] the distinctive form of the

[109] For a thorough study of the issues posed by the references to the gods in this verse, see Barstad, *The Religious Polemics of Amos*, 143–201.

[110] E.g., Jeremias, *Amos*, 154–5.

[111] E.g., Karl Budde, "Zum Text und Auslegung des Buches Amos," *JBL* 43 (1944) 46–131; 44 (1925) 63–122, 100; cf. the discussion in Rudolph, *Joel, Amos, Obadja, Jona*, 243.

fifth vision demonstrates its culminating role in relation to the previous four vision reports. This vision expresses the core of the prophet's message of judgment against the northern kingdom and his view that the nation's future lies only in a return to Judean political and religious institutions.

The presentation of the fifth vision comprises two basic components. Amos 9:1-6 presents the vision concerning the projected downfall of the Beth El Temple per se together with a hymnic segment that acknowledges YHWH's power over creation and the world at large. Amos 9:7-15 presents oracular material that elaborates upon verses 1-6 by identifying YHWH as the One who will bring punishment upon Israel and who will see to the ultimate security and natural fertility of the nation under Davidic rule.

The presentation of the fifth vision in Amos 9:1-6 begins with the vision report proper in verses 1-4. Employing a first person autobiographical form similar to that in the prior vision reports, the prophet reports seeing YHWH standing beside an altar, understood from the general context of Amos 7-9 to be the altar at the Beth El Temple, as the Deity makes an announcement that calls for the destruction of the Temple and its worshipers. The contents of the vision must be understood in relation to the visual imagery of an ancient Israelite altar in operation. Animals are being slaughtered and cut apart, blood flows as it is drained from the carcasses prior to the sacrifice, and a heavy column of smoke and fire rises from the altar as the sacrifices are burned. Altogether, the imagery is one of death and destruction, and this imagery informs the portrayal of the Temple's destruction in the prophet's vision.

YHWH's announcement begins with commands to "strike the capitals until the thresholds shake" and to "shatter them upon the heads of all of them." The imperative form of these commands presents some problems. The addressee of the masculine singular form of *hak*, "strike," is uncertain, although it could be simply an unspecified command. The masculine singular imperative form *ûběṣaʿam*, "and shatter them," means literally, "and cut them off." The NRSV misinterprets the latter statement as a command to "shatter/cut off" the heads of all of the people, but the expression means to cut off the capitals from the tops ("heads") of the columns. The overall scenario presupposes a structure in which a roof is supported by columns. Atop the columns are capitals that bear the main weight of the roof, and the columns in turn are supported by "thresholds" or bases that distribute the weight for better support. The imagery here focuses on the weak points of the structure at both the tops and the bottoms of the columns, i.e., when the capitals are struck and cut off, the roof collapses, and when the thresholds shake, the columns collapse. The underlying imagery appears to be that of an earthquake that is able to bring about such destruction and that ought to be considered as an act of YHWH.

Following the command to destroy the Temple structure, YHWH then concentrates on the slaughter of the worshipers who attempt to flee and escape the destruction. A combination of military and mythological language is employed. They will be slain by the sword no matter how far they attempt to flee. The reference to their attempts to escape to Sheol, i.e., the ancient Israelite realm of the dead, or to heaven expresses metaphorically that there is to be no escape from YHWH. The references to attempts to hide at the top of the Carmel mountain range, located along the northern Israelite Mediterranean coast south of modern Haifa, or the floor of the sea, likewise expresses the futility of such attempts to flee as YHWH will search them out or command the sea serpent, i.e., the mythological Leviathan tamed by YHWH (cf. Isa 27:1; Pss 74:14; 104:26; Job 40:25–41:3 [NRSV: 41:1-9]), to bite them. The Deity returns to the specter of enemy assault and victory in verse 4 by stating that the people will be killed even if they are taken as captives by their enemies, and sums up with the statement, "I will fix my eyes on them for harm and not for good." There will be no hope for those whom YHWH chooses to punish.

The hymnic passage in verses 5-6 is joined to the vision report in verses 1-4 by a *waw-conjunctive*, which indicates that the two segments must be read together. The hymn conveys YHWH's power to bring about destruction in the cosmos, and it thereby validates YHWH's ability to bring about the punishment of the Beth El Temple and the people as portrayed in verses 1-4. It begins with a statement of YHWH's name, "and my L–rd, YHWH of Hosts," which employs the military term *sĕbāʾôt*, "hosts, armies," to convey YHWH's destructive power. In typical form, it then presents a series of three statements based upon participles that convey YHWH's destructive and creative attributes more specifically. In the first statement, YHWH "touches" the earth and it "melts" or "dissolves," its inhabitants "mourn," and the earth rises and falls like the Nile (cf. Amos 8:8, where similar imagery is employed to convey YHWH's power). In the second statement, YHWH builds "his stairs" in the heavens and founds "his vault" upon the earth. The Hebrew term *maʿălôtāyw*, "his steps," is frequently emended to *ʿălîyātô*, "his upper chambers," or simply understood as such,[112] but this overlooks the role that "steps" play in an ancient Temple structure. Ramps or steps were a common feature in Mesopotamian ziggurats upon which temples were placed. Jacob's vision of YHWH at Beth El in Gene-

---

[112] Rudolph, *Joel, Amos, Obadja, Jona*, 242; Wolff, *Joel and Amos*, 336–7.

sis 28 presupposes a "ladder" or "ramp" *(sullām)* extending from earth to heaven at the site of what was to become the Beth El Temple. Exodus 20:26 forbids the priests to use "steps" when ascending upon the altar in order to protect their modesty. Likewise, the platform of the Second Temple was built with ramps that are placed behind the now sealed Huldah gate of Temple platform ruins in Jerusalem to allow access to the Temple. The foundation "vault" *(ʾăguddâ),* derived from the root *ʾgd,* "to bind together," refers to some foundation structure at the base of the ramp, perhaps analogous to the Herodian enclosure of the ruined Second Temple platform. Although nothing is known of the structure of the Beth El Temple, the hymn in Amos 9:5-6 likely describes structural features that were probably a part of the Beth El Temple. Finally, the third statement describes YHWH's power to call to the waters, pour them out upon the earth, and thereby bring about the power of the flood to destroy the earth. The hymn ends with a recapitulation of YHWH's name, viz., "YHWH is his name."

Amos 9:7-15 presents oracular material that elaborates upon the meaning of the vision presented in Amos 9:1-6. Overall, it presents a scenario of judgment against Israel which is consistent with the judgmental perspective of the vision, but it also points to the restoration of the nation under Davidic rule. This constitutes the overall goal of Amos' diatribes against Israel; YHWH does not simply announce the destruction of YHWH's own people, but points to a future in which Israel is constituted along the lines that YHWH (and Amos) desire.

The passage begins with a set of rhetorical questions that are directed by YHWH to Israel. The oracular formula indicates that the prophet conveys YHWH's questions to the people. The questions are designed to demonstrate that Israel is no different from other nations, in that YHWH will move the people of Israel wherever YHWH wishes to move them. This challenges Israel's sense of chosenness and security in that it raises questions concerning the divine promises to the ancestors that the people would live in the land of Israel as a people specially bound to YHWH. The first question, "Are you not like the Ethiopians to me, O people of Israel?" challenges the notion of chosenness or a special relationship with YHWH in that Ethiopians lived in a land that was at the edge of Israel's known world, and Israelites were aware that Ethiopians appeared to be very different from the Israelites due to their black skin (cf. Jer 13:23). By comparing Israel to Ethiopia, YHWH asserts that Israel is just as distant and strange to YHWH as Ethiopia is to Israel. The second rhetorical question, "Did I not bring Israel up from the land of Egypt, and the Philistines from Caphtor and the Arameans from Kir?" likewise calls into question Israel's sense of a special relationship with YHWH. The Exodus tradition is the foundational tradition of Israel's identity as a distinctive nation, but the question asserts that YHWH has acted in a similar capacity for other peoples as well. The Philistines were brought from Caphtor, usually identified as Crete (cf. Jer 47:4; Ezek 25:16; Zeph 2:5),[113] and the Arameans were brought from Kir, usually identified as a region near Elam (cf. Amos 1:5; 2 Kgs 16:9; Isa 22:6).[114] The point is especially strong in that the other nations listed, Philistia and Aram, were among Israel's closest neighbors, with whom they were frequently at odds. Nevertheless, it underscores the point made by the hymn in Amos 9:5-6, if YHWH is the creator of the universe, YHWH controls the fates of other nations as well.

In verses 8-15, the prophet then presents YHWH's scenario of judgment and restoration for Israel. The basic premise is stated in verse 8, which first conveys YHWH's intention to punish and then qualifies that statement by asserting that YHWH will not destroy the nation entirely. The first part is unequivocal, "The eyes of my L–rd YHWH are upon the sinful kingdom, 'and I will destroy it from the face of the earth.'" Israel is identified as sinful, and YHWH states the intention to destroy Israel, but the particle *ʾepes kî*, "except that," introduces YHWH's qualification, "except that I will not utterly destroy the house of Jacob." The oracular formula emphasizes that this is YHWH's statement. Although many see this as the work of a later hand from the post-exilic period,[115] the following portrayal of YHWH's intention to punish only the wicked and to rebuild following the punishment provides some sense of a justifiable rationale for the prophet's oracles. YHWH does not abandon the promises to the ancestors of Israel, nor does YHWH give up by leaving Israel only to destruction. Rather, YHWH's actions are presented constructively as a means to address a problem and to correct it by punishing the guilty and rebuilding with what is left.

Verses 9-10 are syntactically joined to verse 8 by an explanatory *kî*, and they elaborate upon the process of punishment and destruction portrayed in the first part of verse 8. YHWH's speech employs the metaphor of the sieve to portray the process by which Israel will be shaken among all the nations, i.e., YHWH will bring the nations to shake or punish Israel and the punishment will be so thorough that no one will escape just as a pebble does not drop from the sieve. The metaphor is drawn from Amos' agricultural experience, i.e., grain had to be sifted as part of the process by which it was removed from the chaff and other foreign matter, and prepared for sale or consumption (cf. Amos 8:6b). Verse 10 specifies that "all the sinners of my people" shall be killed by

---

[113] Richard S. Hess, "Caphtor," *ABD* I:869-870.
[114] Henry O. Thompson, "Kir," *ABD* IV:83-84.
[115] Jeremias, *Amos*, 162, 164–65.

the sword. This of course attempts to address the moral problem of the suffering of an entire nation by asserting that only the guilty will in fact die. The converse, that those who die must be guilty, presents even greater moral problems, however, as those who have attempted to rationalize the Shoah or the Holocaust will recognize. The sinners are identified as those who maintain that no evil can overtake the nation, i.e., those who believe that YHWH will protect the nation. Although such persons are condemned, one may ask if this is just; YHWH had guaranteed fidelity to Abraham, Isaac, and Jacob. Why should they not expect YHWH to keep the divine promise?

Amos 9:11-15 then shift to the theme of the restoration of the House of David and the people of Israel. The passage is introduced by the *bayyôm hahû*, "in that day," which relates to the time of punishment outlined in verses 9-10. Verses 11-12 focus specifically on the restoration of the Davidic house, which is portrayed metaphorically as "the fallen booth (*sukkâ*) of David." The image of the "booth" is particularly pertinent to the setting of Amos' oracles and vision in relation to the festival of Sukkoth, as this is the period when Israelite farmers go out into the vineyards and dwell in temporary structures known as Sukkoth or booths so that they might bring in the grape harvest (Lev 23:39-43; Neh 8:13-18). Each year, the Sukkah must be repaired or rebuilt, i.e., its sides must be patched and its foundation and supporting structures repaired so that it will be able to serve as a temporary residence for another season of the grape harvest. The statement, "and you shall build it as in the days of old," aids in conveying the double entendre of the metaphor in that it facilitates a transition from a concern with building a Sukkah to rebuilding the old Davidic empire by reestablishing Davidic rule over Edom and other nations that are called by YHWH's name (cf. 2 Sam 8:1-14, esp. 13-14). The Edomites had revolted from Davidic rule during the reigns of Solomon (1 Kgs 11:14-22) and Jehoram (2 Kgs 8:20-22). Although he did not succeed in restoring Davidic rule over all of Edom, Azariah (i.e., Uzziah; cf. 2 Kgs 15:1-7) was able to reestablish Judean rule over Elath (2 Kgs 14:21-22). As Azariah/Uzziah was king over Judah during Amos' career, it would appear that this success may well have suggested to the prophet that the time was ripe for the restoration of Davidic rule over all of the people of Israel. Certainly the characterization of Edom as "the remnant of Edom" would suggest such a scenario in which Amos expected Uzziah to follow up by conquering the rest of Edom as well as other nations that once had stood within the Davidic orbit. The oracular formula indicates that this is a statement by YHWH.

Verses 13-15 then shift to the restoration of the people of Israel. They are introduced by the formula, "behold the days are coming," which again signals the future orientation of the scenario portrayed herein, and another instance of the oracular formula again identifies this as a word of YHWH. In keeping with the setting of Sukkoth, the language continues to draw upon the metaphorical portrayals of agriculture and especially viticulture to express the restoration of the nation. Verse 13 states that one who plows shall overtake the one who reaps and the one who treads grapes shall overtake the one who sows the seed. Both images indicate that there will be so much agricultural bounty in the land that the work of plowing and reaping and treading and planting will consume every available moment; there will be no break in the agricultural work cycle for lack of anything to do. The results bear this out as the mountains and hills are portrayed as gushing forth new wine (cf. Joel 3:18 [NRSV: Joel 4:18]). Verse 14 shifts to general themes of Israel's restoration. YHWH's statement, "I will restore the fortunes of my people Israel," is frequently understood as, "I will restore the captivity of my people Israel," and used to justify those who see the passage as a post-exilic addition that points to messianic restoration. The Hebrew expression *lĕhēšîb šĕbût* is well-known in pre-exilic contexts,[116] but it could easily be read as an oracle for the restoration of Israel in the post-exilic period as well. Both of its components are derived from the root *šûb*, "to return," and connote "restoring the returning" in the sense of restoring general welfare. In this case, it expresses the building of ruined cities and the planting of crops. The reference to the planting of vineyards and drinking their wine and the making of gardens and eating their fruit of course recalls the common expression that each person shall sit under vine and fig tree without fear (cf. 2 Kgs 18:31; Isa 36:16; Mic 4:4; Zech 3:10). The metaphor of planting relates well to the setting of Sukkoth, and it is applied once again to YHWH's promises of security to Israel in verse 15, i.e., YHWH promises to plant Israel upon their own land and never again to pluck them up (cf. Jer 1:10; 18:7; 31:28). The passage presupposes YHWH's prior punishment of the people which will be redressed at the time that Davidic rule is restored. The concluding speech formula identifies the passage as a word of YHWH.

---

[116] See the discussion in Paul, *Amos* 294.

FOR FURTHER READING

COMMENTARIES

Amsler, Samuel. "Amos," *Osée, Joël, Amos, Abdias, Jonas.* By Edmond Jacob, Carl-A. Keller, and Samuel Amsler, 157–247. Commentaire de l'ancien Testament XIa. Geneva: Labor et Fides, 1992.

Andersen, Francis I., and David Noel Freedman. *Amos.* Anchor Bible 24A. New York: Doubleday, 1989.

Bič, Miloš. *Das Buch Amos.* Berlin: Evangelische Verlagsanstalt, 1969.

Gowan, Donald E. "The Book of Amos: Introduction, Commentary, and Reflections," *The New Interpreter's Bible. Volume VII: Introduction to Apocalyptic Literature, Daniel, The Twelve Prophets,* ed. Leander E. Keck et al; 337–431. Nashville: Abingdon, 1996.

Hayes, John H. *Amos, the Eighth Century Prophet: His Times and Preaching.* Nashville: Abingdon, 1988.

Jeremias, Jörg. *The Book of Amos: A Commentary.* Trans. D. W. Stott. Old Testament Library. Louisville: Westminster John Knox, 1998.

Koch, Klaus, et al. *Amos. Untersucht mit den Methoden einer strukturalen Formgeschichte.* Alter Orient und Altes Testament 30/1-3. Neukirchen-Vluyn: Neukirchener, 1976.

Mays, James Luther. *Amos: A Commentary.* Old Testament Library. Philadelphia: Westminster, 1969.

Paul, Shalom. *Amos.* Hermeneia. Minneapolis. Fortress, 1991.

Wilhelm Rudolph. *Joel–Amos–Obadja–Jona.* Kommentar zum Alten Testament XIII/2. Gütersloh: Gerd Mohn, 1971.

Soggin, J. Alberto. *The Prophet Amos: A Translation and Commentary.* Trans. John Bowden. London: SCM, 1987.

Stuart, Douglas. *Hosea-Jonah.* Word Biblical Commentary 31. Waco: Word, 1987.

Wolff, Hans Walter. *Joel and Amos.* Trans. W. Janzen, S. Dean McBride, Jr., and C. A. Muenchow. Hermeneia. Philadelphia: Fortress, 1977.

STUDIES

Auld, A. G. *Amos*. Old Testament Guides. Sheffield: JSOT Press, 1986.

Barstad, Hans M. *The Religious Polemics of Amos*. Vetus Testamentum Supplements 34. Leiden: E. J. Brill, 1984.

King, Philip J. *Amos, Hosea, Micah—An Archaeological Commentary*. Philadelphia: Westminster, 1988.

Markert, Ludwig. *Struktur und Bezeichnung des Scheltworts. Eine gattungskritische Studien anhand des Amosbuches*. Beiheft zur Zeitschrift für die alttestamentliche Wissenschaft 123. Berlin and New York: Walter de Gruyter, 1977.

Plein, Ina Willi-. *Vorformen der Schriftexegese innerhalb des Alten Testaments*. Beiheft zur Zeitschrift für die alttestamentliche Wissenschaft 123. Berlin and New York: Walter de Gruyter, 1971.

Polley, Max E. *Amos and the Davidic Empire*. New York and Oxford: Oxford University Press, 1989.

Rottzoll, Dirk U. *Studien zur Redaktion und Komposition des Amosbuches*. Beiheft zur Zeitschrift für die alttestamentliche Wissenschaft 123. Berlin and New York: Walter de Gruyter, 1996.

Sweeney, Marvin A., "Formation and Form in Prophetic Literature," *Old Testament Interpretation: Past, Present, and Future. Essays in Honor of Gene M. Tucker*. Ed. James Luther Mays, David L. Petersen, and Kent Harold Richards, 113–26. Nashville: Abingdon, 1995.

Wolff, Hans Walter. *Amos the Prophet: The Man and His Background*. Trans. F. R. McCurley. Philadelphia: Fortress, 1973.

OBADIAH

OBADIAH

Overview

Obadiah is the fourth book in the Masoretic version of the book of the Twelve and the fifth book in the Septuagint version. It follows the book of Amos in the MT where it builds upon the imagery of the restoration of the Davidic kingdom and its possession of the remnant of Edom (Amos 9:11-12) by presenting an oracle that calls for the exiled remnant of Israel to dispossess Edom on account of its treachery against Jerusalem. Like Joel and Amos, it is fundamentally concerned with the "Day of YHWH," but Edom is now the object of YHWH's wrath rather than the nations at large (Joel 1:15) or Israel (Amos 5:18-20). Obadiah precedes the book of Jonah, which tempers the vengeful spirit of Obadiah by pointing to the fact that YHWH can show mercy even to Assyria, one of Israel's most fearsome enemies, when it repents of its actions. Within the MT, Obadiah thereby points to a central concern with Jerusalem's fate, including its judgment by the nations and its restoration once the judgment is complete. In the LXX, Obadiah follows the books of Hosea, Amos, and Micah, which are concerned with the punishment of the northern kingdom of Israel as a model for the eventual fate of Jerusalem and Judah. Obadiah follows Joel, which outlines both natural and human threats to Jerusalem in very general terms prior to announcing YHWH's judgment of the nations that threaten Jerusalem.[1] In addition, Joel alludes to Obadiah at numerous points. Obadiah then relates Jerusalem's punishment specifically at the hands of Edom, and points to the time when the exiles of Israel and Jerusalem will be able to respond in kind to Edom for its crimes. Again, Obadiah precedes Jonah, which notes that even a bitter enemy such as Assyria can repent when given the opportunity to do so.

[1] See Bergler, *Joel als Schriftinterpret*, 295–333.

The book of Obadiah provides little overt evidence that would help in establishing its historical setting.[2] It provides no information concerning the prophet Obadiah other than his name. Rabbinic tradition attempted to identify Obadiah with the northern Israelite palace official from the time of King Ahab (869–850 B.C.E.) who assisted the prophet Elijah and hid one hundred prophets of YHWH (bSanhedrin 39b). Although Obadiah 20 refers to Israelite exiles from the Phoenician city of Zarephath, which establishes an analogy with Elijah who was sheltered by a widow from Zarephath (1 Kgs 17:8-24), the identification can not be established. There is no evidence that the northern Obadiah was a prophet, and the book of Obadiah, with its focus on Jerusalem, appears to be the work of a Judean. Furthermore, the name Obadiah is very common in the Hebrew Bible. It means simply "one who serves YHWH," and it is applied to some twelve individuals throughout Israel's and Judah's history (1 Kgs 18:4; 1 Chr 3:21; 7:3; 8:38; 9:44; 9:16; 12:9; 27:19; 2 Chr 17:7; 34:12; Ezra 8:9=1 Esdr 8:35; and Neh 12:25). Although several are priests or Levites, none of them may be identified as a prophet. Nevertheless, it is noteworthy that Edom broke its long-standing alliance with Judah from the days of David (2 Sam 8:13-14; 2 Kgs 3:4-27) during the ninth century reign of Jehoram ben Jehoshaphat (849–842; 2 Kgs 8:20-22) which left Jerusalem exposed to attack by the Arameans during the reign of Jehoash ben Ahaziah (837–800 B.C.E.; 2 Kgs 12:17-18). Furthermore, the Judean king Amaziah ben Jehoash (800–783 B.C.E.) was able to mount a counterattack against the Edomites which saw the fall of their capital in Sela (2 Kgs 14:7; cf. Obad 3), and Azariah (a.k.a. Uzziah) ben Amaziah was able to restore the port city of Elath at the northern edge of the Gulf of Aqabah to Israelite/Judean control (2 Kgs 14:22). Nevertheless, Judah was never able to reestablish full control over Edom.

The present form of the book is designed to present a condemnation of Edom as a result of its treachery against Jerusalem and to point to the return of the exiles of Israel and Jerusalem as the agents who will carry out Edom's punishment and restore YHWH's kingdom.[3] Following the superscription in Obad 1a, which simply identifies the book as

---

[2] For an overview of discussion concerning the interpretation of the book of Obadiah, see R. Mason, *Micah, Nahum, Obadiah*, 85–108.

[3] For earlier attempts to establish the structure or literary form of Obadiah, see esp. T. H. Robinson, "The Structure of the Book of Obadiah," *JTS* 17 (1916) 402–8; W. Rudolph, "Obadja," *ZAW* 49 (1931) 222–31; and more recently, Josef Wehrle, *Prophetie und Textanalyse. Die Komposition Obadja 1–21 interpretiert auf der Basis textlinguistischer und semiotischer Konzeptionen*, ATSAT, vol. 28 (St. Ottilien: EOS, 1987).

"the vision of Obadiah," Obad 1b-21 presents the oracle concerning Edom. This oracle is a standard example of the oracles against the nations, which is formulated as a messenger speech in which the prophet conveys Yнwн's words concerning Edom. The messenger formula in Obad 1bα$^{1\text{-}5}$ introduces the prophet's presentation of Yнwн's words in Obad 1bα$^{6\text{-}12}$-21 in which the prophet includes his own comments together with those of Yнwн. Within the prophet's presentation, Obad 1bα$^{6\text{-}12}$-7 constitutes the call to punish Edom, and Obad 8–21 constitutes the prophetic announcement of punishment against Edom. The later text includes a general summation of announcement of Edom's punishment in verse 8, the grounds for punishment in verses 8-14, and the announcement of punishment proper, introduced by causative *kî*, in verses 15-21.

Most scholars identify Obadiah as an exilic or post-exilic book because of its focus on the punishment of Edom for its betrayal of Israel and Jerusalem at the time of the Babylonian invasions. Edom apparently took part in the pillaging of Jerusalem at the time of the Babylonian conquest of the city (cf. Psalm 137, esp. verse 7; Isa 34:5-17; 63:1-6; Jer 49:7-22; Ezek 25:12-14; 35:2-15; Mal 1:2-5; Lam 4:21-22), and 2 Kgs 25:4-5 and Jer 39:4-5 indicate that the Babylonians captured King Zedekiah ben Josiah (597–587 B.C.E.) as he fled Jerusalem towards the Arabah (i.e., the border with Edom), which might suggest that the Edomites played some role in preventing his escape or that they failed to come to his aid (cf. Obad 14, but see also Jer 40:11 which mentions Judean refugees in Edom). Jeremiah 27:3 indicates that the Edomites had a treaty with Judah at this time, which would explain the sense of a betrayal as well as the treaty references and language of Obad 12–14, 16. Obadiah 7 refers to Edom's betrayal by its own allies, which might suggest that the Babylonians turned on Edom at some point following the destruction of Jerusalem. Indeed, the Babylonian king Nabonidus (556– 539 B.C.E.) mounted a major campaign against Edom which may have destroyed the Edomite city of Bozrah and hastened the process by which the Edomite kingdom disintegrated during the sixth and fifth centuries B.C.E. By the fourth/third centuries B.C.E., Edom had disappeared and a new Nabatean kingdom had taken its place.

A key element in determining the historical setting of the book is the oracle against Edom in Jer 49:7-22, which includes elements, especially in verses 7, 9, and 14-16, that are parallel to Obad 1–7.[4] The text is arranged somewhat differently in the two versions and there are a number of textual variants between their parallel statements. Various

---

[4] See esp. the discussions of Ben Zvi, *Obadiah*, 99–109; Wolff, *Obadiah and Jonah*, 37–42.

arguments have been put forward that Obad 1–7 is based upon Jer 49:7-22,[5] that Jer 49:7-22 is based upon Obad 1–7,[6] or that both presuppose a common earlier text.[7] Most scholars opt for the last proposal due to the difficulties in establishing a ninth century setting for Obadiah, the clear references to Edom's treachery against Jerusalem at the time of the Babylonian defeat of Judah, and the difficulties in establishing the interdependence of the Jeremiah and Obadiah texts.

Several features of Obadiah and Jer 49:7-22 indicate that Obadiah is indeed dependent upon Jer 49:7-22, and that the present text of Obadiah is a later reworking of a much earlier oracle. The present form of Obadiah clearly presupposes an exilic or post-exilic setting as indicated by the references to the exiles of both Israel and Jerusalem in Obad 19–21. Furthermore, Obad 19–21 appears to be an elaboration of earlier material in Obad 16–18. Obadiah 16–18 closes with the YHWH speech formula, "for YHWH has spoken," which indicates the end of an oracular unit. Obadiah 19–21 likewise reinterprets the problematic references to the "house of Jacob" and the "house of Joseph" in Obad 18, both of which refer to the northern kingdom of Israel, as the exiles of Israel and Jerusalem. These verses also indicate that the Negev and the Shephelah, both of which are Judean territories, will dispossess the land of Ephraim and Samaria, both of which are northern territories. Although Obad 16–18 presupposes an Edomite betrayal of an alliance with Jerusalem or Judah, the Edomites broke alliances with Judah in both the ninth and the early sixth centuries. It is noteworthy that verses 16-18 make no reference to Jerusalem's destruction, only to its suffering, and they state that the "house of Jacob" and the "house of Joseph," both of which are northern entities, will take action against Edom. The northern kingdom of course did not exist during the sixth century, but Judah was an ally and vassal of northern Israel from the reigns of Ahab of Israel (869–850 B.C.E.) and Jehoshaphat of Judah (873–849 B.C.E.) through the time of the Syro-Ephraimitic War (735–732 B.C.E.). Indeed, Ahab and Jehoshaphat went to war against Aram together (1 Kings 22), Jehoshaphat made peace with Israel (2 Kgs 22:44), Jehoshaphat and Jehoram made war together with Edom against Moab (2 Kings 3), Jehoshaphat's son Jehoram married Ahab's daughter Athaliah (2 Kgs 8:18), and Joash

---

[5] Bert Dicou, *Edom, Israel's Brother and Antagonist: The Role of Edom in Biblical Prophecy and Story*, JSOTSup, vol. 169 (Sheffield: JSOT Press, 1994) 58–73; Raabe, *Obadiah*, 22–31.

[6] Brian Peckham, *History and Prophecy: The Development of Late Judean Literary Traditions*, Anchor Bible Reference Library (New York: Doubleday, 1993) 678–90.

[7] Ben Zvi, *Obadiah*, 108–9; Wolff, *Obadiah and Jonah*, 38–40.

[NRSV: Jehoash] of Israel forced Amaziah of Judah to submit when the latter attempted to revolt against Israel (2 Kgs 14:8-14). Edom's revolt against Judah (2 Kgs 8:20-22) and Amaziah's defeat of the Edomites (2 Kgs 14:7, 22) took place while Judah was an ally and vassal of northern Israel.

Although Jer 49:7-22 and Obad 1–7 share a great deal of language, they clearly presuppose different situations. Jer 49:7-22 condemns Edom, and emphasizes the fear that Edom inspires (Jer 49:16). But in pointing to YHWH's future punishment of Edom, it provides no specific grounds for punishment nor does it envision concrete action other than vague threats of YHWH's warfare against the Edomites. Obadiah, on the other hand, points to Edom's violation of a treaty with Judah (Obad 12–15), Edom's betrayal by its own allies (Obad 7), and calls for punishment against Edom not only by YHWH (Obad 1–7, 8), but by northern Israel acting on behalf of Judah (Obad 16–18) or by a combined Israel and Judah (Obad 19–21). Jeremiah 49:7-22 appears to reflect the frustration of a prophet whose people is defeated and can do nothing about the Edomites other than call upon YHWH, but Obadiah envisions a course of action in which either a restored Israel or a restored Israel and Judah can take action for themselves together with YHWH.

It is also noteworthy that Obad 1–7 appears to reflect a somewhat more organized text that emphasizes Edom's arrogance and impending downfall, and that reworks or summarizes elements from Jer 49:7-22. Whereas the messenger formula in Jer 49:7-22 appears in the middle of the prophet's discourse in verse 12, it appears at the beginning of the Obadiah discourse even though it creates some literary tension. Likewise, the summons to battle appears only in verse 14 of the Jeremiah text, but it appears immediately following the messenger formula at the head of Obadiah's oracle in verse 1, thereby setting the theme of the entire book of Obadiah as action that will be taken against Edom. Furthermore, it employs the pronoun "we" rather than the "I" of Jeremiah, and thereby suggests that the prophet speaks on behalf of the people and calls upon them to take part in the upcoming action against Edom. Whereas Jer 49:15 refers to Edom's "humiliation (despised) among humankind," thereby reflecting the setting of Jer 49:7-22 in the midst of Jeremiah's oracles against the nations at large, Obad 2 states only that Edom is "very humiliated/despised," enabling the oracle to focus only on Edom. Whereas Jer 49:16 refers to the fear that Edom strikes in others as well as its arrogance, Obad 3 eliminates any sense of Edom's power to focus exclusively on its unfounded arrogance by which it deceives itself into believing that it is powerful, and adds Edom's statement, "who will bring me down from there?" to highlight its conceit. Whereas Jer 49:16 employs the particle *kî* to present Edom's

sense of grandeur as a fact (i.e., "*for* you make high your nest . . ."),
Obad 4 employs the particle *ʾim* and reworks the statement to make it
conditional and to emphasize Edom's attempts at self-aggrandizement
(i.e, "*if* you soar aloft like the eagle and *if* between the stars your nest is
set . . ."). Whereas Jer 49:9 begins with references to Edom's being
robbed, Obad 5–6 presents the robbing of Edom as a consequence of
YHWH's summons to war and adds language to accentuate Edom's vulnerability to such plundering by enemies. Finally, Obad 7 emphasizes
the fact that Edom's allies have turned against it, and it employs the
initial statements of Jer 49:7 to assert that there is no wisdom in Edom.
In addition, Obad 7 draws upon Jer 38:22, "your trusted friends have
seduced you (*hissîṭûkā;* cf. Obad 7, *hiššîṭûkā*, "deceived you") and have
overcome you." In short, Obad 1–7 draws upon Jer 49:7-22, but it reworks the material from Jeremiah to point decisively to YHWH's action
against Edom, Edom's self-deceptive arrogance as the cause of its
downfall, its vulnerability, and ultimately its foolishness. In addition,
the summons to war directed to the prophet's audience speaks to the
situation presented in Obad 19–21 in which the prophet calls upon the
exiles of Israel and Jerusalem to take action against Edom.

It would appear that Obad 1–7 and 19–21 share a common interest
in envisioning action on the part of the people of Israel and Judah
against Edom. Furthermore, both texts appear to presuppose a late-
exilic or post-exilic setting in that Obad 1–7 is based upon Jeremiah and
Obad 19–21 presupposes the exile of both Israel and Judah. This is all
the more striking in that Obad 8–18 comprises a self-contained prophetic judgment speech against Edom. As noted in the following commentary, Obad 8 presents a general overview of the entire oracle, i.e.,
that YHWH will punish Edom because of its slaughter, Obad 9–14 presents the specific grounds for which Edom is to be punished, and Obad
15–18 presents a detailed portrayal of the process by which the punishment will be carried out. The grounds include Edom's standing aside
while foreigners do violence against Jacob, dividing the spoil of Jerusalem, and even taking part in the plunder and cutting off fugitives.
The punishment is carried out by a restored Jacob and Joseph that act
on behalf of Jerusalem. Although many maintain that this presupposes
the Babylonian pillaging of Jerusalem, it also expresses the Aramean
assaults against Israel in the aftermath of Ahab's death (2 Kgs 6:8–7:20)
and the Aramean siege of Jerusalem in which King Jehoash was forced
to empty the treasures of Jerusalem in order to buy off the Arameans
(2 Kgs 12:17-18). Edom had already revolted against Judah by this time,
and may well have entered the Aramean orbit (cf. Amos 1:3-5, 11-12,
which presuppose both Aramean and Edomite action [among others]
against Israel).

Uncertainties remain, i.e., Edomite participation in the Aramean actions against Israel is not documented, but it is clear that Edom did not come to Israel's or Judah's aid at this time. A ninth century setting does explain why northern Israel should be the agent to act against Edom on behalf of Jerusalem and Judah, however, as Judah was Israel's vassal. The oracle against Edom in Obad 8–18 may well have been delivered at the time that Ahaziah of Judah was preparing for his assaults against the Edomites. The later material in Obad 1–7 and 19–21 would have been added in the aftermath of the Babylonian assaults against Edom during the reign of Nabonidus (556–539 B.C.E.). In such a scenario, the later author of Obadiah reworked Jeremiah's early oracle against Edom in Jer 49:7-22 to emphasize a call to arms on the part of the Israelite and Jerusalemite exiles, Edom's betrayal by its Babylonian allies, and Edom's arrogance and foolishness in trusting Babylon. The earlier material in Obad 8–18 would have been reread to express Edom's betrayal of its alliance with Israel/Judah, its action against Jerusalem at the time of the Babylonian conquest of the city, and the expectation that Israel, i.e., "Jacob" and "Joseph" would take action against Edom for its betrayal. Finally, Obad 19–21 was added to reinterpret Obad 16–18 so that it would point to exiled Israelites and Jerusalemites as those who would return to the land, take control of Edom, and reestablish YHWH's kingdom. Such a conception of Israel's restoration fits well with the circumstances of the late-sixth century, when Cyrus of Persia initiated the return of exiled Judeans to the land of Israel so that they might rebuild Jerusalem and the Temple (cf. Isaiah 40–55; Ezra 1–6) and the returning exiles would have anticipated the restoration of a Davidic kingdom in the aftermath of the restoration of the Temple (Haggai; cf. Zechariah 1–8).

Superscription: 1a

The superscription for the book of Obadiah appears in Obad 1a as simply ḥăzôn ʿōbadyâ, "the vision of Obadiah." The term ḥāzôn, "vision," appears in the superscriptions for the books of Isaiah (Isa 1:1), "the vision of Isaiah ben Amoz which he saw concerning Judah and Jerusalem in the days of Uzziah, Jotham, Ahaz, and Hezekiah, kings of Judah," and Nahum (Nah 1:1), "An oracle concerning Nineveh. The book of the vision of Nahum the Elkoshite." Although the term is generally translated as "vision," it refers to both visual and auditory perception as indicated by its placement in the superscriptions of prophetic books that present prophetic oracles together with visual experience. The basic Hebrew root ḥzh, and the Aramaic root ḥzy, from which the

Hebrew term is derived, likewise mean "to see/perceive."[8] Hence, the term might best be understood as a reference to the "perception of Obadiah" or "the revelation of (i.e., made to) Obadiah."

Because the superscription provides no details pertaining to the prophet other than his name, relatively little can be said about Obadiah.[9] The name means "one who serves/worships YHWH," and it appears to be a relatively common name in the Hebrew Bible. Although the name is attested for some twelve individuals throughout all periods of biblical history, it appears most frequently in the books of Chronicles and Ezra-Nehemiah (see 1 Kgs 18:4; 1 Chr 3:21; 7:3; 8:38; 9:34; 9:16; 12:9; 27:19; 2 Chr 17:7; 34:12; Ezra 8:9/1 Esdr 8:35; Neh 12:25). Rabbinic tradition attempts to identify Obadiah with the northern Israelite palace official during the reign of Ahab who assisted the prophet Elijah (1 Kgs 18:1-16; bSanhedrin 39b). Although this Obadiah is described as sheltering one hundred prophets of YHWH during Jezebel's persecution of those loyal to YHWH, there is no indication that he is himself a prophet. Attempts to date Obadiah to the ninth century must therefore remain tenuous for lack of information. Because Psalm 137 clearly identifies Edom's participation in the Babylonian destruction of Jerusalem in 587 B.C.E., attempts to date the book to the period of the Babylonian exile have generally been much more successful.

As a superscription, Obad 1a introduces and identifies the material that follows in Obad 1b–21. It must therefore be considered generically and structurally distinct from the balance of the book.[10]

The Oracle Concerning Edom: 1b–21

Obadiah 1b–21 constitutes the prophet's presentation of an oracle by YHWH concerning Edom. At its most basic generic level, Obad 1b–21 must be considered as an example of the oracles concerning the nations that appear so frequently in prophetic literature (e.g., Numbers 22–24; Isaiah 13–23; 34; MT Jeremiah 46–51; LXX Jeremiah 26–31; Ezekiel 28–32; Amos 1:3–2:16; Nahum; Zeph 2:4-15).[11] The genre is well known throughout the ancient Near East as well. It is apparently derived from situations

---

[8] Cf. A. Jepsen, "חזה," *TDOT* 4:280-90, esp. 281, 284.

[9] For surveys of the proposals for the dating of Obadiah, see Wehrle, *Prophetie und Textanalyse*, 9–12; Raabe, *Obadiah*, 47–56.

[10] Gene M. Tucker, "Prophetic Superscriptions and the Growth of the Canon," *Canon and Authority*, ed. G. W. Coats and B. O. Long (Philadelphia: Fortress, 1977) 56–70.

[11] See Sweeney, *Isaiah 1–39*, 528–9.

of oracular inquiry during a war in which a monarch consults Yhwh through the prophets concerning a course of action against an enemy nation (e.g., Numbers 22–24; 1 Kings 22; cf. 2 Sam 2:1). It also appears in liturgical poetry that is concerned with announcing Yhwh's sovereignty over other nations and the world at large (Psalms 2; 46; 48; 76). Oracles concerning foreign nations may appear in a variety of specific forms.

The form of Obadiah is somewhat complicated.[12] The messenger formula in Obad 1bα$^{1-5}$, "thus says my L–rd Yhwh concerning Edom," demonstrates that Obad 1b–21 is formulated as a messenger speech, although the following statement in Obad 1bα$^{6-12}$-β, "we have heard a report from Yhwh, and a messenger has been sent among the nations . . ." can hardly be considered as a speech by Yhwh. It is instead a speech by the prophet that demonstrates the prophet's role in conveying Yhwh's words. Although a great deal of the material in Obad 1b–21 is presented as first person speech by Yhwh, the prophet's words appear throughout the oracle as a means to introduce, explain, and elaborate upon the meaning of the words of the Deity. A combination of formal and thematic criteria indicate that this speech comprises two basic components. Obadiah 1bα$^{6-12}$–7 constitutes the prophet's vision of Yhwh's intention to punish Edom, formulated as a call to attack Edom that is sent by messenger to unnamed parties. Obadiah 8–21 then constitutes an example of a prophetic announcement of judgment against Edom that follows up on Obad 1bα$^{6-12}$–7 by pointing to the causes for Edom's punishment in its treachery against Jacob/Israel and Jerusalem in particular (Obad 8–14) and by specifying the punishment that will come upon Edom as a consequence of its actions (Obad 15–21).

The Messenger Formula: 1bα$^{1-6}$

Obadiah 1bα$^{1-6}$, "thus says my L–rd Yhwh concerning Edom," is based upon the standard messenger formula, "thus says X," that is expanded by an indication of the subject of the message, i.e., Edom.[13] The term *le°ĕdôm*, "concerning Edom," appears as the superscription for the oracle concerning Edom in Jer 49:7-22, which shares much common terminology with Obad 1–7. Normally, the messenger formula precedes direct speech by the party named by the formula. Verse 1bα$^{6-12}$-β, however, is not a speech by Yhwh as indicated by the third person reference to

---

[12] For a discussion and survey of the problems relevant to the formal interpretation of the book, cf. R. Mason, *Micah, Nahum, Obadiah*, 97–104.

[13] See Sweeney, *Isaiah 1–39*, 546; Westermann, *Basic Forms of Prophetic Speech*, 98–115.

YHWH, i.e., "we have heard a report from YHWH . . ." The identity of those referred to by "we" is never made clear, although the context indicates that the prophet must be the speaker of this particular statement. Perhaps he quotes a statement made by others or he speaks on behalf of the audience to which he presents this oracle. Many scholars have attempted to resolve the tension in this verse by moving the messenger formula to another location or by emending the text in various ways,[14] but there is absolutely no textual support for any displacement or emendation. Rather, the formula must be considered as an indication by the prophet that YHWH has revealed the following material to him, although he apparently feels free to embellish YHWH's statements with his own comments. The occurrences of the oracular formula in verses 4 and 8 together with the various third person references to YHWH in verses 15, 18, and 19-21 indicate that the prophet is the speaker who conveys YHWH's words throughout the book.

The Prophet's Presentation of YHWH's Oracle Concerning Edom: 1bα[6-12]–21

As noted above, Obad 1bα[6-12]–21 constitutes Obadiah's presentation of YHWH's oracle concerning Edom. In verses 1bα[6-12]–7, the prophet presents a call to battle that is supported by YHWH's statements of the intention to punish Edom.[15] Verses 8-21 then constitute a prophetic announcement of punishment against Edom that outlines the actions for which Edom is to be punished (verses 8-14) and the turns to the consequences that Edom will suffer as a result of its actions (verses 15-21).

The Prophet's Presentation of the Call to Punish Edom: 1bα[6-12]–7

The prophet begins his presentation of the vision from YHWH with the call to punish Edom in Obad 1bα[6-12]–7. The unit is held together thematically by the concern with punishment to be visited by YHWH upon Edom, whereas beginning in verses 8-10, the concern shifts to identifying the reasons why Edom should be punished. The rhetorical question in verse 8 likewise signals a shift in perspective in that it raises the question as to whether YHWH is really going to carry out the punish-

---

[14] E.g., Wolff, *Obadiah and Jonah,* 33, 45; Watts, *Obadiah,* 38, 44.

[15] Sweeney, *Isaiah 1–39,* 539; Bach, *Die Aufforderung zur Flucht und zum Kampf im alttestamentlichen Prophetenspruch,* 51–91, esp. 52–3, 61.

ment outlined in verses 1bα⁶⁻¹²–7 as a basis for turning to the reasons why Edom deserves such treatment. Obadiah is the speaker throughout this pericope although he quotes YHWH's words throughout verses 2-7.

The unit begins with the prophet's quotation of a general alarm that has been raised concerning the report of a word from YHWH. Although the statement employs the pronoun "we," it provides no clue as to the identity of the speakers. As noted above, he either quotes a statement made by others who have heard a report of a summons to battle against Edom or he speaks as one of the audience to which he addresses his oracles. The corresponding statement in Jer 49:14 employs "I," an obvious reference to Jeremiah, but there is no indication that Obadiah is joined by others in hearing this statement. The statement also makes reference to the sending of a "messenger," although the usage of the Hebrew term *sîr* elsewhere suggests as a reference to ambassadors or envoys sent from one nation to another (cf. Isa 18:2; 57:9; cf. Prov 13:17; 25:13). The statement, "Rise up! Let us rise against it for battle," is a typical example of the summons to war formula, which appears in situations where soldiers are called upon to prepare for battle against an enemy (cf. Judg 3:28; 4:6-7; Jer 46:9; Joel 4:9 [NRSV: 3:9]; Mic 4:13). The "it" against which the soldiers rise is Edom as indicated in the messenger formula. Joel 4:9a, 11a [NRSV: 3:9a, 11a] appears to allude to the summons to war in Obad 1bα and Jer 49:14.[16]

Following the prophet's statements concerning the summons to war, verses 2-7 then shift to his presentation of a speech by YHWH who announces the current threat that the Deity proposes to visit upon Edom. Verses 2-3 provide general statements that YHWH intends to make Edom the "least among the nations" and "utterly despised." This clearly presupposes an element of reversal in that YHWH points to Edom's "proud heart" or arrogance that has deceived them into thinking that they are immune from such threats. The reference to Edom's arrogance is based upon the image of Edom's dwelling set high "in the clefts of the rock *(selaʿ),*" an obvious reference to the Edomite fortress city of Sela that was conquered by Amaziah and renamed Joktheel (2 Kgs 14:7). Based upon the LXX reading of *petrōn* ("rock") for *selaʿ*, Sela has been frequently identified throughout the centuries with the Nabatean rock city of Petra or the site of Umm el-Bayyarah, which is situated on a rocky peak above Petra.[17] The actual site of Sela appears to be es-Sela, about 2 ½ miles northwest of Bozrah, just east of the Dead Sea, which was settled during the ninth–seventh centuries B.C.E. The

---

[16] See Bergler, *Joel als Schriftinterpret*, 313–5.

[17] See A. F. Rainey, "Sela (of Edom)," *IDB[S]* 800; Wann M. Fanwar, "Sela," *ABD* V:1073-4.

self confidence of the Edomites is expressed in YHWH's quotation of
their rhetorical question, "who will bring me down to the ground?"

Of course, the rhetorical answer to this question is YHWH. This is
expressed in a series of three questions that are posed to the Edomites
by YHWH in verses 4-6 and that are designed to demonstrate YHWH's
power and Edom's vulnerability. The first (verse 4) employs the imagery of an eagle, known to dwell in the high cliffs of Edom, to express
Edom's inability to get away from YHWH, even if they "soar aloft like
the eagle" or set their "nest . . . among the stars." YHWH asserts flatly,
"from there I will bring you down." The oracular formula at the end of
verse 4a confirms that the prophet is the speaker who presents YHWH's
speech. The second question (verse 5a) poses the possibility that
thieves or plunderers could come to Edom by night and take whatever
they like. The question and its answer presuppose that the heights of
Sela will not prevent thieves from climbing up stealthily by night to rob
the Edomites, i.e., Edom is in fact vulnerable. The third question (verses
5b-6) employs the imagery of the grape harvest to show that Edom
would be picked clean, i.e., just as those who harvest a vineyard leave
only a few berries that the poor may then glean from the vineyard (see
Exod 23:10-11; Lev 19:9-10; 23:22; Deut 24:19-20, 21-22). Again, Edom is
vulnerable and will be left destitute.

Up to this point, the source of Edom's self-deception and vulnerability has not been made clear, but verse 7 states it forthrightly. Edom
will be driven to its borders in flight by its own allies (literally, "men of
your covenant") on whom it depended for protection. The verse goes
on to state that Edom's "confederates" (literally, "men of your peace")
have deceived and prevailed over them, eating their bread and setting
traps for them. The reference to "those who ate your bread" is difficult
in that the Hebrew text states only "your bread," but the context makes it
clear that Edom's allies have deceived her and are now "eating Edom's
lunch." The motif of deception of course recalls the initial statement in
verse 3 that Edom's "proud heart" or "arrogance" has deceived her.
Verse 7 concludes with YHWH's statement, "there is not understanding
of it," which is perhaps better rendered, "there is no understanding in
it (i.e., Edom)," i.e., the Edomites have been fools.

Prophetic Announcement of Judgment Against Edom: 8-21

Obadiah 8–21 is based in the prophetic announcement of judgment
genre, although it takes great liberties with the standard form of the
genre. Normally, the genre first presents some accounting of the actions
that serve as the grounds for judgment and then follows up with an an-

nouncement of judgment per se.[18] Both of these fundamental elements are present in Obad 8–21, but the passage actually begins with YHWH's statements of the intention to punish Edom (verses 8-9) together with statements that identify the causes of this punishment (verses 10-14). The full announcement of judgment against Edom actually appears in verses 15-21, which are introduced by causative *kî* in verses 15 and 16 and thereby tied syntactically to verses 10-14. This complicates an assessment of the structure of this passage considerably. Indeed, closer examination of verses 8-21 indicates that there are two major structural components: Obad 8-9, which provides an introduction to and basic summation of the issues posed by the prophetic announcement of punishment, and Obad 10–21, which constitutes the formal prophetic announcement of punishment. This assessment of the structure of Obad 8–21 is based upon the syntax of the passage and the MT reading of *miqqāṭel*, "from/because of the slaughter," at the end of verse 9.

Obadiah 8–9 is formulated as the prophet's presentation of YHWH's rhetorical question that asserts that the Deity will indeed punish Edom "in that day." The oracular formula in verse 8 demonstrates that the prophet quotes YHWH, and the introductory interrogative particle demonstrates that YHWH's statements are formulated as a question, i.e., "'Shall I not indeed on that day,' utterance of YHWH, 'destroy the wise out of Edom . . .?'" The references to YHWH's destruction of the "wise from Edom" and "understanding from Esau" plays upon the concluding statement of verse 7 that there is no understanding in Edom to begin with as demonstrated by its gullibility in allowing its own allies to undermine its security. The reference to Esau, Edom's eponymous ancestor, is particularly appropriate. The Genesis narratives concerning Esau show him to be gullible in that he foolishly sells his birthright to Jacob for a bowl of lentil soup (Gen 25:29-34) and allows Jacob to trick Isaac into giving him the blessing of the first born that was rightly due to Esau (Genesis 27). Likewise, the references in verse 9 that Teman's "warriors shall be shattered" and that "everyone from Mount Esau will be cut off," recall the motifs of defeat in battle that are signaled in Obad 1bα[6-12]–7. Teman is probably a regional designation for Edom that is based upon the name of Esau's grandson, Teman ben Eliphaz ben Esau (Gen 36:9-11, 15, 42; 1 Chr 1:36, 53). The appearance of the term *miqqāṭel*, "from/because of the slaughter," at the end of verse 9, however, presents problems.[19] It is grammatically parallel to the term *mēḥămas*,

---

[18] See Sweeney, *Isaiah 1–39*, 533–4; Westermann, *Basic Forms of Prophetic Speech*, 129–209.

[19] For discussion of these problems, see Ben Zvi, *Obadiah*, 124–8; Wolff, *Obadiah and Jonah*, 35.

"from/because of violence," at the beginning of verse 10, and it is therefore frequently grouped together with *mēḥāmas* in the textual versions and translations, including the NRSV, so that it forms a part of the introduction to the delineation of Edom's misdeeds in verses 10-14. It is possible that the *hapax legomenon miqqāṭel* is the original introduction to verse 10 and that *mēḥāmas* was added as a gloss to explain the term. Nevertheless, *miqqāṭel* must be read as the conclusion to verse 9 in the present form of the MT because it lacks any syntactical connection to verse 10. Rather, it presents the explanation why YHWH has decided to shatter Teman's warriors and cut off everyone from Mount Esau, i.e., "because of the slaughter." The nature of the slaughter is unspecified, but verses 10-14 make this clear by elaborating upon *miqqāṭel*.

Obadiah 10–21 then constitutes the formal prophetic announcement of punishment against Edom that explains the preceding statements in verses 8-9. The entire passage is held together syntactically by a series of conjunctions, but the causative *kî*'s in both verses 15 and 16 mark the major shift from crime to punishment within the passage. Verses 10-14 specify the actions committed by Edom against his brother Jacob, i.e., Israel, that are the cause of the punishment that it will suffer. Verse 10 is a fundamental statement of Edom's guilt and punishment, "for/because of . . . the violence done to your brother Jacob, shame shall cover you, and you shall be cut off forever." Once again, this verse plays upon the Genesis tradition of Jacob and Edom as Israel's and Edom's eponymous ancestors,[20] but it reverses the motif in that it is no longer Jacob that wrongs Esau as in the Genesis narrative, but Esau that wrongs Jacob. In the Genesis narrative, Esau threatened to kill Jacob for taking his father's blessing, which prompted Jacob's flight to Aram (Genesis 27), but upon Jacob's return, he was able to persuade his brother not to harm him (Genesis 33). But in Obadiah, Esau has indeed carried out violence against Jacob, which violates the agreement established between them (cf. Gen 33:1-17). Verse 11 specifies the crimes committed by Edom/Esau against Israel/Jacob. Edom stood aside while foreigners plundered Israel, entered Israel's gates, and cast lots for Jerusalem. The casting of lots for Jerusalem refers to the arbitrary division of captives and spoil plundered by enemy soldiers (cf. Joel 4:3 [NRSV: 3:3]; Nah 3:10). Clearly, Edom did not support Israel or Jerusalem at a time when Israel/Jerusalem was attacked, defeated, and plundered by a foreign enemy. Because of these actions, Edom is con-

---

[20] For a discussion of the role of Jacob, Esau, and Laban as the eponymous ancestors of Israel, Edom, and Aram in the Jacob narratives, see my study, "Puns, Politics, and Perushim in the Jacob Cycle: A Case Study in Teaching the English Hebrew Bible," *Shofar* 9 (1991) 103–18.

sidered as one of the enemy. Such a statement presupposes some obligation on the part of Edom to come to Israel's aid.

Verses 12-14 then present a series of eight prohibitions that provide greater detail concerning Edom's actions against Israel. The prohibitions seem to be modeled loosely on the style of the prohibitions contained within the Ten Commandments (cf. Exodus 20; Deuteronomy 5) so that they rhetorically express what Edom must not do. The style likewise reflects the prohibitions that are found in a treaty between nations in the ancient Near East.[21] This stylistic aspect underscores Edom's obligations to Israel as an ally and thereby emphasizes that Edom grossly violated whatever treaty might have bound the two nations together. Verse 12aα prohibits Edom from "gloating over" (literally, "look on") his "brother" in his misfortune, i.e., Edom is obligated to come to Israel's aid when attacked. Verse 12aβ prohibits Edom from rejoicing over Judah's ruin. Verse 12b forbids Edom from "boasting" (literally, "make great your mouth") at a time of distress. Verse 13aα prohibits Edom from entering the gates of my (YHWH's) people at the time of "their calamity" (ʾêdām). The Hebrew term ʾêdām, "their calamity," constitutes a pun on the name of Edom (ʾĕdôm). Verse 13aβ prohibits Edom from "gloating" over Israel's (literally, "his"; NRSV reads "Judah's") disaster. Verse 13b prohibits Edom from taking spoil from Israel. Verse 14a prohibits Edom from standing at the crossroads to cut down Israel's fugitives. This plays upon the stipulation of most treaties that call upon an ally to capture and return any enemy fugitives to the king with whom it is allied.[22] In this case, Edom treats its ally as an enemy. Verse 14b likewise prohibits Edom from handing over the survivors to the enemy that has defeated Israel. Clearly, these stipulations point to the fact that Edom has not proved to be a reliable ally for Israel, but instead has turned against its brother in treachery.

Obadiah 15–21 then shifts to the prophet's presentation of YHWH's announcement of punishment against Edom. The introductory kî's that appear in both verses 15 and 16 establish the role of verses 15-21 in spelling out the consequences of the actions delineated in verses 10-14. Verse 15 introduces the theme by relating it to the approaching "Day of YHWH" against all the nations. The "Day of YHWH" tradition in the prophets of ancient Judah and Israel apparently presupposes a time when YHWH will act against the enemies of Israel (cf. Isaiah 13; Ezek 30:1-19), although it is frequently turned against Israel itself (Isaiah 2;

---

[21] See Michael L. Barré, "Treaties in the ANE," *ABD* VI:653-6, esp. 655; Simo Parpola, "Neo-Assyrian Treaties from the Royal Archives of Nineveh," *JCS* 39 (1987) 161–89, esp. 175–7.

[22] E.g., "The Treaty between KTK and Arpad," *ANET* 659–61, 660.

Joel 2; Amos 5:18-20; Zephaniah 1).[23] The phraseology of this particular
statement, "for the Day of YHWH is near *(qārôb)* against all the nations,"
is a stereotypical example of the language employed for the "Day of
YHWH" tradition in prophetic literature, such as that of Isa 13:6; Joel 1:15;
4:14 [NRSV: 3:14]; Zeph 1:7, "for the Day of YHWH is near"; Ezek 30:3,
"for a day is near, the Day of YHWH is near"; and Zeph 1:14, "for the great
Day of YHWH is near" (cf. Deut 32:35, "because the day of their [i.e.,
Israel's enemies] calamity is at hand"). As in Isaiah 34, Obadiah turns the
Day of YHWH against Edom. The statement, "as you have done, it shall
be done to you," restates the basic principle of ancient Israel's and
Judah's system of justice, i.e., "any [who maims another] shall suffer
the same injury in return" (literally, "just as he has done, so shall it be
done to him"). The principle is expressed in the famous series that calls
for "a life for a life, an eye for an eye, a tooth for a tooth, etc." (Lev
24:16-22; Exod 21:23-25; Deut 19:21). The same principle appears in Joel
4:4, 7 [NRSV: 3:4, 7] employing language similar to that of Obad 15b.[24] Just
as Edom stood by and actively participated while Israel and Jerusalem
were ravaged and decimated, so Edom will be attacked in the future.

Verses 16-21 then elaborate upon this principle by pointing to the
survival of a remnant of Israel that will then turn on Edom and carry
out the punishment. Verses 16-18 present this elaboration in relation to
the remnant of Israel that will be saved in Jerusalem, and verses 19-21
point to the exiles of both Israel and Jerusalem as the parties who will
carry out the judgment.

Verses 16-18 begin with a reference to Edom's drinking on YHWH's
holy mountain, i.e., Mount Zion or the site of the Jerusalem Temple.
Most interpreters take this to be a reference to Edom's punishment for
its role in the defeat of Judah or to its desecration of the site of the
Temple at the time of the Babylonian conquest of Jerusalem in 587
B.C.E.[25] There is no indication, however, that the Temple has been destroyed or that Mount Zion has been occupied by Edomites. Rather,
drinking (from a cup), together with feasting and other signs of mutual
bonding, is part of the ritual that seals a treaty or covenant between
two nations in the ancient world.[26] Such actions appear in the context of

---

[23] See Richard H. Hiers, "Day of the L–rd," *ABD* II:82-3; K. J. Cathcart, "Day of
YHWH," *ABD* II:84-5.

[24] Bergler, *Joel als Schriftinterpret,* 306–7.

[25] See Ben Zvi, *Obadiah,* 179–84; Raabe, *Obadiah,* 202–4; Wolff, *Obadiah and Jonah,*
64–5; Stuart, *Hosea-Jonah* 420; Watts, *Obadiah,* 57–8.

[26] See "The Vassal Treaties of Esarhaddon," *ANET* 534–41, esp. 536, which lists
"drinking from the cup" as part of a series of actions that signify the ratification of
treaty.

Israel's covenant with YHWH as Moses, Aaron, Nadab, Abihu, and the seventy elders join YHWH on Mount Sinai for a banquet of eating and drinking (Exod 24:9-11), and the nations will join YHWH on Mount Zion for a banquet of eating and drinking that will mark YHWH's relationship with all the peoples (Isa 25:6-10). Obadiah apparently refers to Edom's treaty with Israel/Jerusalem, which would have been sealed with such feasting and drinking on Mount Zion. Such a relationship is presupposed either by Edom's alliance with Israel during the tenth and ninth centuries B.C.E. (cf. 2 Sam 8:13-14; 1 Kgs 11:14-22; 2 Kgs 3:9-27) or Edom's alliance with Judah in the early sixth century B.C.E. (Jer 27:3). The prophet then expands the reference to all the nations, thereby including all nations who were similarly allied with Israel/Judah during its time of affliction, and maintains that those nations who drink continually and gulp down their drink (i.e., who eagerly concluded treaties with Israel but failed to provide support when Israel was attacked) will ultimately be no more. In this manner, Edom's projected judgment becomes a symbol in later times for all those nations who betrayed or persecuted Israel in similar fashion (cf. Isaiah 34; 63:1-6). Verse 17 posits that "those who escape" (*pĕlêṭâ*, literally, "an escape") will constitute a "holy" remnant of Israel on Zion that will enable the house of Jacob to regain "their possessions" (*môrāšêhem*). Many interpreters, including the translators of the NRSV, read *môrāšêhem* as *môrîšêhem*, "those who dispossessed them," with LXX, the Qumran Murabba'at Scroll, and other versions to emphasize Israel's vengeance against Edom and the nations.[27] Such a reading is in keeping with the following statements in verse 18, but the MT reading of verse 17 makes good sense as it stands. Joel 3:5 [NRSV: 2:32] (cf. Joel 2:3) appears to allude to the statements in Obad 17–18 concerning the escapees in Jerusalem.[28] Verse 18 then employs the metaphor of fire catching flame in tinder to portray the house of Jacob as a fire, the house of Joseph as flame, and the house of Esau as stubble. Once the "stubble" catches fire, it will be consumed until there is no survivor left of the house of Esau, thereby reversing the status of the escaped remnant of Israel on Zion and their enemies in Edom who left them in this condition. Such a portrayal goes well beyond the principle of verse 15b, "as you have done, so shall it be done to you." The distinction between the house of Jacob and the house of Joseph is noteworthy in that it points to a conception of Israel that is centered in Jacob and especially the Joseph tribes, i.e., Ephraim and Manasseh, which suggests that the author has in mind the northern kingdom of Israel, i.e., an Israel that is based upon the central hill country of northern Israel

---

[27] Wolff, *Obadiah and Jonah,* 60; Rudolph, *Joel, Amos, Obadja, Jona,* 311.
[28] Bergler, *Joel als Schriftinterpret,* 301–3.

and its dependencies in Judah and the other tribes.[29] Finally, the formula, "for YHWH has spoken," both closes off the oracle and identifies YHWH as its source.

Verses 19-21 then portray a scenario in which the natural forces of the Negev, the Shephelah, and the land of the central Israelite hill country will overtake the Edomites, the Philistines, and the Gilead region, and thereby enable the remnant of Israel and Jerusalem to reestablish themselves in these regions. The concluding YHWH speech formula in verse 18 indicates that the prophet is the speaker here. The scenario articulated in these verses implies divine action in that the land itself becomes an agent that will overcome Israel's enemies. Verse 19aα states that the Negev will dispossess the Mountain of Esau and that the Shephelah will dispossess the Philistines. The Negev is the desert region of southern Judah that was frequently the target of Edomite raids and encroachment. Effectively, the Negev itself will swallow up the Edomites. Likewise, the Shephelah, the rolling low hill country of southwestern Judah, will dispossess the Philistines who have encroached upon Judean territory. Verse 19aβ-b then states that the Negev and Shephelah will likewise possess the "field of Ephraim" and the "field of Samaria and Benjamin," which implies Judean control over the territory of the former northern kingdom as the Negev and Shephelah were part of Judean territory. The verse likewise asserts that Benjamin will dispossess Gilead, i.e., the territory east of the Jordan River that was assigned to the half tribe of Manasseh, Reuben, and Gad in Numbers 32; Deut 3:8-22; and Josh 13:8-32. Benjamin is far removed from the Gilead and would have to travel through Samaria and Ephraim to reach it, but the statement recalls the Benjaminite King Saul's special relationship with Jabesh Gilead in the territory of the Gilead (cf. 1 Samuel 11; 31). Insofar as 1–2 Chronicles continually identifies Judah *and* Benjamin as the tribes who survived the Assyrian deportations of northern Israel and who constitute the remnant of Israel in the post-Assyrian period, this statement reflects the perspective of the late- or post-exilic period that Judah and Benjamin together would see to the restoration of all Israel to the land.

Indeed, verse 20 points to "the exile(s) of this fortress of the people of Israel who are Canaanites as far as Zarephath" and "the exile(s) of Jerusalem who are in Sepharad" to regain possession of the cities of the Negev. This verse is brimming with textual and interpretative problems.[30] The reference to "this fortress/rampart *(haḥēl hazzeh)* of the people of Israel . . ." is frequently read as "the exiles of the Israelites

---

[29] Cf. Ben Zvi, *Obadiah*, 190–5.
[30] For a thorough discussion of these problems, see Ben Zvi, *Obadiah*, 211–23.

who are in Halah *(ḥālâ)*." Halah is a city in Assyria to which northern Israelites were exiled following the Assyrian conquest of the kingdom in 722 B.C.E. (see 2 Kgs 17:6; 18:11), but this proposal creates tremendous grammatical problems in that it does not account satisfactorily for *hazzeh*, "this." Ben Zvi notes that *hēl* refers to "territory" or "bounds" in 1 Kgs 21:23 rather than to "fortress" or "rampart."[31] It seems best then to read verse 20 as a statement that "the exile of this territory of the people of Israel who are Canaanites as far as Zarephath," those people of the northern Israel kingdom who lived in the Phoenician/ Canaanite territories as far as Zarephath would join the exiles of Judah who are in Sepharad in regaining possession of the Negev. Zarephath, i.e., Sarepta, was a Phoenician port city located south of Sidon and north of Tyre.[32] The prophet Elijah was sheltered by a widow from Zarephath (1 Kgs 17:8-24), which enabled him to return to northern Israel and play a part in the overthrow of the Omride dynasty. As many exiles of northern Israel apparently found shelter in this region as well, the author of Obadiah apparently sees them as a source for the renewal of Israel in the period following Edom's betrayal. Sepharad is now a term employed in modern Hebrew and in Rabbinic literature for Spain, but in biblical Hebrew it may refer to Sardis, the capital of the ancient Lydian empire in east central Turkey, which was apparently the home of some Judean exiles. It may also be identified with a Median city east of Assyria.[33] During the late-eighth and seventh centuries, a string of fortresses was built in the Negev to protect trade routes, perhaps from Edomite harassment, and in the aftermath of Judah's demise in the sixth century, the Edomites moved in and took control of this territory.[34] In any case, the references to exiles in Zarephath and Sepharad and to the cities of the Negev express the author's hope that exiles will return from great distances to reclaim the cities of the Negev and thereby to reestablish Israel in place of the territory taken by the Edomites. The author is clearly Judean and sees Judah's restoration as the beginning of the restoration of all Israel. Verse 21 expresses such sentiments in that it calls for "deliverers/saviors" *(mōšiʕîm)*, the term employed in the book of Judges for the judges who delivered Israel from foreign oppression, to go up to Mount Zion in order "to judge/ rule" *(lišpōṭ)* Mount Esau. Joel 4:12 [NRSV: 3:12] expresses similar sentiments in relation

---

[31] Ibid., 220–1.

[32] See Ray L. Roth, "Zarephath," *ABD* VI:1041.

[33] John D. Wineland, "Sepharad," *ABD* V:1089-90.

[34] For discussion, see Mazar, *Archaeology of the Land of the Bible*, 441–3; J. R. Bartlett, *Edom and the Edomites*, JSOTSup, vol. 77 (Sheffield: JSOT Press, 1989); idem, "Edom," *ABD* II:287-95.

to the nations in general.[35] As a result, the kingdom shall be Yhwh's, which of course allows for the restoration of the Israelite/Judean kingdom.

[35] Bergler, *Joel als Schriftinterpret*, 318–20.

FOR FURTHER READING

COMMENTARIES

Allen, Leslie C. *The Books of Joel, Obadiah, Jonah, and Micah*. The New International Commentary on the Old Testament. Grand Rapids: Eerdmans, 1976.

Cogan, Mordechai, with Uriel Simon. *Ovadya, Yona*. Miqra' leYisrael. Jerusalem: Magnes, 1992.

Coggins, Richard J., with S. Paul Re'emi. *Israel among the Nations: Nahum, Obadiah, Esther*. International Theological Commentary. Grand Rapids: Eerdmans, 1985.

Keller, Carl-A., with Edmond Jacob and Samuel Amsler. *Osée, Joël, Amos, Abdias, Jonas*. Commentaire de l'ancien Testament XIa. Geneva: Labor et Fides, 1992.

Pagán, Samuel, "The Book of Obadiah: Introduction, Commentary, and Reflections," *The New Interpreter's Bible. Volume VII: Introduction to Apocalyptic Literature, Daniel, The Twelve Prophets*. Ed. Leander E. Keck et al., 434–59. Nashville: Abingdon, 1996.

Raabe, Paul R. *Obadiah*. Anchor Bible 24D. New York: Doubleday, 1996.

Rudolph, Wilhelm. *Joel–Amos–Obadja–Jona*. Kommentar zum Alten Testament XIII/ 2. Gütersloh: Gerd Mohn, 1971.

Stuart, Douglas. *Hosea-Jonah*. Word Biblical Commentary 31. Waco: Word, 1987.

Watts, John D. W. *Obadiah: A Critical and Exegetical Commentary*. Grand Rapids: Eerdmans, 1969.

Wolff, Hans Walter. *Obadiah and Jonah*. Trans. Margaret Kohl. Continental Commentaries. Minneapolis: Augsburg, 1986.

STUDIES

Ben Zvi, Ehud. *A Historical-Critical Study of the Book of Obadiah*. Beiheft zur Zeitschrift für die Alttestamentliche Wissenschaft 242. New York: Walter de Gruyter, 1996.

Dicou, Bert. *Edom, Israel's Brother and Anatogonist: The Role of Edom in Biblical Prophecy and Story*. JSOTSup 169. Sheffield: JSOT Press, 1994.

Mason, R.. *Micah, Nahum, Obadiah*. OT Guides. Sheffield: JSOT Press, 1991.

Robinson, T. H. "The Structure of the Book of Obadiah," *JTS* 17 (1916) 402–8.

Rudolph, W. "Obadja," *ZAW* 49 (1931) 222–31.

Snyman, S. D. "Cohesion in the Book of Obadiah," *ZAW* 101 (1989) 59–71.

Wehrle, Josef. *Prophetie und Textanalyse. Die Komposition Obadja 1–21 interpretiert auf der Basis textlinguistischer und semiotischer Konzeptionen*. Arbeiten zu Text und Sprache im Alten Testament 28. St. Ottilien: EOS, 1987.

Weimer, Peter. "Obadja. Eine redaktionskritische Analyse," *BN* 27 (1985) 35–99.

JONAH

JONAH

Overview

The book of Jonah is the fifth book in the Masoretic version of the Book of the Twelve and the sixth book of the Septuagint version. It follows Obadiah in the Masoretic text and functions as a means to temper Obadiah's diatribes against Edom with a demonstration of YHWH's capacity for mercy toward the city of Nineveh. It precedes the book of Micah in the MT, which is concerned with the judgment of the northern kingdom of Israel as a model for that against the southern kingdom of Judah as well as with the ultimate restoration of Israel and Judah around the Jerusalem Temple and the royal house of David. Insofar as Jonah points to YHWH's mercy for Nineveh, it prepares for Micah's scenario of destruction and restoration for Israel and Judah. After all, Nineveh in later times was the capital of the Assyrian empire which initiated this process by conquering the northern kingdom of Israel and deporting many of its key inhabitants. Jonah also follows Obadiah in the LXX where it once again tempers the message of YHWH's judgment against Edom, understood as a symbol of the nations, with a message of mercy for Nineveh, likewise understood as a symbol for the nations. In addition, it takes up the question posed in Joel 2:12-14 as to whether YHWH will respond to repentance by relenting from an earlier decision to punish.[1] It precedes the book of Nahum, however, which celebrates YHWH's destruction of Nineveh for its crimes against Israel, YHWH, and the world at large, and thereby points to the necessary interrelationship of YHWH's justice together with YHWH's mercy. YHWH can show mercy to Nineveh when it repents, but YHWH will punish Nineveh when it sins.

[1] Cf. R. B. Salters, *Jonah and Lamentations*, 26.

The portrayal of the prophet in the book of Jonah draws upon the reference to the prophet Jonah ben Amittai in 2 Kgs 14:25. According to the Kings account, Jonah had foreseen the greatness of the restored kingdom of Israel under the rule of Jeroboam ben Joash (786–746 B.C.E.), who established Israelite rule from Lebo-Hamath in Aram/Syria to the Sea of the Arabah/Gulf of Aqaba during the first half of the eighth century B.C.E. This notice provides little information about the prophet, stating only that he was from Gath-Hepher, which has been identified with the site of Tel Gath Hefer approximately four kilometers east of Sepphoris in the Galilee.[2] The Kings narrative leaves open the question whether Jonah ben Amittai lived at the time of King Jeroboam II or prior to his reign.

There is little evidence to maintain that the book of Jonah presents a historical account of events in the life of the prophet, no matter when he may have lived. The narrative is permeated with elements of irony and parody,[3] e.g., a prophet of YHWH flees from YHWH in an attempt to avoid carrying out his prophetic commission; the pagan characters of the narrative, including both the sailors of the ship and the king and people of Nineveh, acknowledge YHWH and repent concerning their real or imagined wrongdoings; a great fish swallows Jonah for three days until he prays to YHWH and acknowledges YHWH's power; and YHWH saves the city of Nineveh, later the capital of the Assyrian empire which ultimately destroys the northern kingdom of Israel. Other elements also point to its fictionalized or exaggerated character: the sea stops raging when Jonah is thrown overboard; it takes three days to walk through the city of Nineveh; and even the animals of Nineveh are included in the rituals of mourning and repentance of the city. Other features must also be considered. The name Jonah, *yônâ* in Hebrew, means "dove," which symbolizes the capriciousness and lack of direction that characterize both YHWH and Jonah in this narrative (cf. Hos 7:11-12). The name of Jonah's father, Amittai, *ʾămittay* in Hebrew, means "my truth" or "true." Nineveh was the capital of the ancient Assyrian empire and the major symbol of its power, but it did not become the capital until the reign of Sennacherib (705–681 B.C.E.), long after the Assyrian empire destroyed Jonah's homeland, the northern kingdom of Israel. Overall, the book of Jonah is not designed to present a historical account of the experiences of the prophet Jonah ben Amittai; it is designed to make a point concerning the character of YHWH.

[2] Raphael Greenberg, "Gath-Hepher," *ABD* II:909-10.
[3] See now David Marcus, *From Balaam to Jonah: Anti-prophetic Satire in the Hebrew Bible*, BJS, vol. 301 (Atlanta: Scholars Press, 1995).

There has been tremendous debate concerning the intended meaning or message of the book of Jonah.[4] Many interpreters have construed the issues posed by Jonah as the conflict between universalism and particularism within the Jewish community, i.e., does G–d's grace and salvation apply to the Gentiles in general or only to the Jews?[5] A certain element of anti-Jewish polemic enters into this discussion as Jonah is frequently portrayed as selfish and petulant in questioning why YHWH should show mercy to Nineveh and asserting that YHWH's mercy should be granted only to Israel. The question of YHWH's mercy to Gentiles is of course a part of the concern of the book of Jonah, but it is mistaken to focus exclusively on the role of the nations in relation to YHWH. Rather, the question is YHWH's trustworthiness and fidelity to YHWH's own promises. Jonah is known in Kings as a prophet who foresees the rise of Jeroboam's kingdom and Israel's greatness, but as a prophet of YHWH he would also presumably be aware that Israel would one day fall to the Assyrian empire—certainly the reading audience of the book is aware of this fact. As the narrative indicates, he is placed in a position in which he is expected to proclaim judgment against Nineveh, but he knows that YHWH will ultimately show mercy to Nineveh when they repent. Although many see Jonah's anger as a selfish concern for his own reputation as a prophet, the narrative does not raise the issue of Jonah's reputation nor does it question the principle of YHWH's mercy to Gentiles in general. Instead, it points to YHWH as a G–d who will first say one thing and then reverse course to do another—in this case, YHWH condemns Nineveh and then forgives it.[6] The issue is all the more pertinent in that Assyria will ultimately destroy the northern kingdom of Israel during the latter part of the eighth century B.C.E., which thereby calls into question YHWH's promises (and mercy) to Israel. Furthermore, the book of Nahum makes it very clear that in its oppression of Israel and Judah, Nineveh commits crimes of bloodshed. By forgiving Nineveh in the time of Jonah, i.e., during the eighth century reign of Jeroboam II or before, YHWH prepares for Israel's destruction by freeing a city with a known reputation for sin. Why does YHWH do this?

To a certain extent, the answer is that YHWH is sovereign over all creation and nations, and a figure such as Jonah has little basis on which to challenge YHWH's actions.[7] Nevertheless, YHWH has good reason to act as YHWH does. When confronted with genuine repentance,

---

[4] For an overview of discussion on Jonah, see Salters, *Jonah and Lamentations,* 13–62.

[5] Ibid., 51–62.

[6] See Terence Fretheim, "Jonah and Theodicy," *ZAW* 90 (1978) 227–37.

[7] Ibid.

which YHWH constantly calls for in the prophetic tradition, how could YHWH deny mercy? Although the reader is aware that Assyria will ultimately destroy Israel, in the temporal perspective of the narrative such an event remains in the future and it cannot be certain whether or not such destruction will take place. YHWH and Jonah may be aware that it will, but the narrative presupposes the principle of the human choice to do right or wrong (cf. Genesis 3). Just as Nineveh chose to repent, so it might choose not to destroy Israel. Fundamentally, the choice is up to Nineveh, not YHWH or Jonah, and YHWH must grant Nineveh the right to chart its own course, even if that means potential risk to Israel. Fundamentally, the book of Jonah grapples with a fundamental reality of human existence, i.e., evil happens despite YHWH's promises of righteousness and mercy. In this case, Assyria destroyed Israel and YHWH must hold some responsibility for allowing Nineveh/Assyria to be in a position to carry out such an act. By pointing to the principle of YHWH's mercy as the basis for YHWH's decision, the narrative holds out some hope that YHWH's mercy might also be shown to Israel.

Indeed, such questions are particularly pertinent in relation to the Babylonian destruction of Jerusalem and the Temple and the deportation of major elements of the Judean population in the sixth century B.C.E. Although Jonah is a northern prophet, the references to the Temple in the Psalm of Jonah and the concern with the city of Nineveh, which only became the capital of Assyria after the destruction of northern Israel, point to a setting and reading (or hearing) audience for the book in southern Judah. During the sixth and fifth centuries B.C.E., in the aftermath of the Babylonian exile and the continued subjugation of Judah to foreign rule, many would question YHWH's trustworthiness and fidelity to the relationship with Israel and Judah. The fact that the Persians ruled Judah from Babylon, the capital of the former Babylonian empire that had carried out the destruction of Jerusalem and exile of its people, would be especially important in relation to the portrayal of Nineveh as a great and sinful city that is not destroyed. Although prophets had called for Babylon's destruction (e.g., Isaiah 13–14; 21; Jeremiah 50–51), Babylon was not destroyed, but survived through 486 B.C.E. as the Persian administrative center for the western portions of the Persian empire. In such a situation, Judeans would demand an explanation as to why YHWH had not seen fit to carry out the threats of punishment made against Babylon by Isaiah and Jeremiah.

Jonah is designed to address that question. Furthermore, in drawing upon other biblical traditions,[8] such as the creation narratives in Genesis, the Exodus narratives concerning YHWH's confrontation with

[8] A. Feuillet, "Les sources du livre de Jonas," *RB* 54 (1947) 161–86.

Pharaoh and Moses' confrontation with YHWH, the Elijah narratives concerning his distress and revelation from YHWH, etc., the book of Jonah engages in a dialogue with earlier biblical traditions concerning the character of YHWH and YHWH's relationship with Israel. By pointing to YHWH's merciful character, Jonah acknowledges YHWH's sovereignty over the entire world of creation and the nations, and holds out the possibility that YHWH's mercy will be shown to Israel once again. During the early post-exilic period in the fifth century B.C.E., such a message would help to support efforts to rebuild Jewish life in Jerusalem and Judah.[9] The enduring character of such a message is evident in the role that the book or figure of Jonah continue to play in Judaism, Christianity, and Islam.

There has been a great deal of discussion concerning the literary integrity of the book, particularly in relation to the Psalm of Jonah in chapter 2.[10] Although the psalm draws upon earlier language and images from the book of Psalms and may indeed be earlier, it is well integrated into the present literary context. It functions within the present form of the book of Jonah, which is designed to raise the issue of YHWH's (and Jonah's) trustworthiness in its two major and parallel components. Jonah 1–2 presents Jonah's attempt to flee from YHWH's prophetic commission to speak against Nineveh and Jonah's ultimate recognition of YHWH's power when he is swallowed by the fish, thereby denying him even death as an opportunity to escape YHWH. Jonah 3–4 then presents Jonah's attempt to carry out his commission only to see it frustrated by YHWH's decision to grant mercy to Nineveh when it repents. The ensuing encounter between YHWH and Jonah establishes YHWH's prerogative to grant mercy to Nineveh and thereby to reverse the earlier divine message. The question that then remains for the reader is whether or not YHWH will show mercy to Israel.

Concerning Jonah's Attempt to Flee from YHWH: 1:1–2:11

The first major component of the book of Jonah is Jonah 1–2, in which Jonah attempts to escape from YHWH's commission to speak against Nineveh only to find himself in the belly of a great fish. In this manner,

---

[9] Although some scholars point to the relatively late dating of the language of Jonah, especially its affinities to Aramaic elements, more recent studies dispute this criterion. See esp. George Landes, "Linguistic Criteria and the Date of the Book of Jonah," *Eretz Israel* 16 (1982) 147–70.

[10] See Salters, *Jonah and Lamentations*, 28–40.

Jonah learns that YHWH is all powerful and that it is impossible to escape or hide from the Deity. The function of Jonah 1–2 is largely preparatory in that it is designed to set the scene and to prepare the reader for Jonah 3–4, in which the primary encounter between YHWH and Jonah takes place. Nevertheless, it parallels Jonah 3–4 in several respects. Both Jonah 1–2 and 3–4 begin with a notice that the word of YHWH comes to Jonah and that the prophet is commissioned to speak out against Nineveh. As a result of these attempts to commission Jonah to speak, something entirely unexpected happens: in Jonah 1–2, Jonah attempts to flee from YHWH rather than to carry out his instructions; in Jonah 3–4, Nineveh, a city with one of the worst reputations for evil in the entire Hebrew Bible, actually repents and seeks YHWH's forgiveness. In both narratives, the unexpected events set the scene for an encounter between Jonah and YHWH: in Jonah 1–2, a great fish swallows Jonah and he implores YHWH for mercy; in Jonah 3–4, Jonah sulks concerning YHWH's decision to show mercy to Nineveh and YHWH must show him that such action also expresses YHWH's character as an all powerful and merciful G–d.

The literary structure of Jonah 1–2 comprises three basic sub-units, each of which begins with action by YHWH that provides the basis for action on the part of the other major protagonists in the narrative. Jonah 1:1-3 presents YHWH's initial commission of Jonah to speak to the city of Nineveh and Jonah's attempt to flee from YHWH by sea. Jonah 1:4-16 presents YHWH's creation of a storm at sea which threatens the ship on which Jonah travels, and the encounter between Jonah and the ship's sailors who do everything possible in an attempt to save both themselves and Jonah but are eventually compelled to throw Jonah overboard. Finally, Jon 2:1-11 relates both how Jonah is swallowed by a great fish and his prayer to YHWH that acknowledges YHWH's power and appeals to YHWH for deliverance from danger.

YHWH's Initial Commission to Jonah and Jonah's Attempt to Flee: 1:1-3

Jonah 1:1-3 conveys YHWH's initial commission to Jonah and Jonah's attempt to flee from YHWH by sailing as far away as he could get by ship. The book lacks a formal superscription, but YHWH's commission is expressed through a typical example of the prophetic word formula,[11] "now the word of YHWH came to Jonah ben Amittai saying . . ." (liter-

---

[11] See Sweeney, *Isaiah 1–39*, 546–7.

ally, "and the word of YHWH was to Jonah ben Amittai saying . . ."). The formula combines the phrase *dĕbar yhwh*, "the word of YHWH," with the verb *hyh*, "to be, happen," and the preposition *ʾel*. It normally functions as a means to relate the reception of a prophetic word by a prophet in a narrative context (e.g., 1 Sam 15:10; 1 Kgs 6:11) or to introduce a quotation of prophetic oracle that immediately follows (e.g., Jer 7:1; 11:1). It sometimes appears as part of a first person statement by a prophet (e.g., Jer 1:4, 11; Ezek 6:1). It also appears frequently as the superscription for a prophetic book (Hos 1:1; Joel 1:1; Mic 1:1; Zeph 1:1). It does not function as a superscription in Jon 1:1, however, because it serves as a means to initiate narrative action within the literary context of the Jonah narrative.

The choice of Jonah ben Amittai as the major protagonist of the narrative speaks to its character as both a prophetic narrative and an example of satire or parody. Jonah ben Amittai is well known as a prophet in the time of King Jeroboam ben Joash of the northern kingdom of Israel. According to 2 Kgs 14:25, Jonah was the prophet who predicted Jeroboam's great success in restoring the borders of Israel from Lebo-Hamath in the north (i.e., Aram or Syria), until the Sea of the Arabah in the south (i.e., the Gulf of Aqabah). The large extent of Jeroboam's kingdom, including both northern Israel and southern Judah, ruled by his ally or vassal Uzziah, rivaled that of the combined kingdom of David and Solomon. 2 Kings 14:25 also indicates that Jonah is from Gath-Hepher, a small walled town in the Galilee (Tel Gath Hefer) some four kilometers east of Sepphoris that was occupied until the period of the Assyrian invasions and again in the Persian period.[12] The name Jonah means "dove" *(yônâ)*, and the term is used elsewhere as a metaphor for Israel's senselessness and fickleness in flitting back and forth between Assyria and Egypt (Hos 7:11-12) and for its ultimate return to YHWH (Hos 11:11). His father's name, Amittai *(ʾămittay)* means, "(my) truth" or "true." It is noteworthy that the term *yônâ* can also mean "oppressiveness," as indicated by its use in relation to Jerusalem in Zeph 3:1. The double entendre seems to be entirely appropriate here. Jonah lacks direction, i.e., he is a prophet and yet he flees from YHWH when YHWH instructs him to speak a prophetic word to Nineveh. When he finally does speak the required word in Jonah 3, Nineveh repents and is saved, which enables it ultimately to destroy the northern kingdom of Israel. In this respect, the term applies also to the character of YHWH, who spares Nineveh after declaring its judgment and then allows it at a later time to oppress and destroy the northern kingdom of Israel. This sense of capriciousness would be particularly evident to the

---

[12] See Raphael Greenberg, "Gath-Hepher," *ABD* II:909-10.

figure of the prophet Jonah, who anticipates the glory and power of the
northern kingdom of Israel under Jeroboam ben Joash and then plays a
role in the deliverance of Nineveh, the later capital of the Assyrian empire which ultimately destroyed the kingdom of Israel.

YHWH's commission to Jonah in verse 2 is entirely in keeping with
the expectations of judgment against a city that has one of the most
sordid reputations of any in the Bible (see Nahum). Nineveh was the
administrative capital of the neo-Assyrian empire from the time of
Sennacherib (704–681 B.C.E.) until its destruction by the Babylonians
and Medes in 612 B.C.E.[13] Ironically, it was not the capital at the time of
Israel's destruction in 722/721 B.C.E., but it came to symbolize Assyria
during the apex of its power in the seventh century. The city was located on the east bank of the Tigris River not far from the base of the
Kurdish mountains at the site of the modern city of Mosul in Iraq.
Under Sennacherib, the city was extensively rebuilt with a magnificent
royal palace and a processional way from the palace to the Tigris. The
circumference of the ancient city walls was approximately 7.75 miles,
which corresponds well to its description as a "great city" in Jon 1:2.
The cuneiform presentation of the name Nineveh, *NINA* in Sumerian,
resembles the sign *ÈŠ*, "temple, house," within which appears the sign
HA, "fish."[14] It would appear that the cuneiform form of the name, or
folk traditions associated with it, played some role in suggesting the
motifs of the present Jonah narrative.

Finally, verse 3 indicates that Jonah undertakes action that is entirely unexpected from a prophet of YHWH. Rather than speak against
Nineveh as instructed, Jonah flees from YHWH toward Tarshish, and
books passage on a ship at the port of Yaffo (Joppa). Scholars have debated the location of Tarshish.[15] Many identify it with Tartessos in
Spain or Tarsus in Asia Minor as well as just about every other major
port in the ancient Mediterranean. Some have also noted the potential
correspondence of the name to the Greek term *tarsos*, "oar."[16] The fact of
the matter is that no one is entirely sure where Tarshish was located or
if its location is even meaningful in relation to the common expression
"ship of Tarshish" in the Hebrew Bible (Isa 2:16; 23:1, 14; 60:9; Ezek
27:25; 1 Kgs 22:49/2 Chr 20:36, 37; 1 Kgs 10:22/2 Chr 9:21). The term
probably simply refers to a sea-going ship, so that in the Jonah narrative, the prophet's attempt to flee to Tarshish simply indicates that he is
trying to get as far away from YHWH as one can possibly get. Yaffo

---

[13] A. Kirk Grayson, "Nineveh," *ABD* IV:1118-9.

[14] Sasson, *Jonah*, 71.

[15] David W. Baker, "Tarshish," *ABD* VI:331-3.

[16] Sasson, *Jonah*, 79.

(Joppa), located at the southern boundaries of modern Tel Aviv, was a major port city from the second millennium B.C.E. through the Roman period and beyond.[17] It was assigned initially to the tribe of Dan (Josh 19:46), and it was the port through which cedars of Lebanon were imported for the construction of both the first and second Temples (2 Chr 2:16; Ezra 3:7). The verb *yrd*, "to go down," appears twice in verse three, in reference to Jonah's "going down" to Yaffo and to his "going down" into the ship (not represented in the NRSV) to escape from the presence of YHWH. The use of this verb is noteworthy not only for its continued repetition in the narrative (see also verse 5) and its assonantal relationship to the verb for Jonah's deep sleep (*rdm*, verses 5, 6), but for its contrast with the verb *ʿlh*, "to go up," which is normally employed for travel to Jerusalem and the Temple so that one may encounter the presence of YHWH (e.g., Isa 2:3/Mic 4:2; Jer 31:6; Ezra 1:3; 7:7). Again, Jonah is trying to get as far away from YHWH as he can.

Jonah's Encounter with the Sailors during the Storm: 1:4-16

Jonah 1:4-16 then narrates YHWH's casting a storm upon the sea to threaten the ship in which Jonah is traveling, and Jonah's interaction with the sailors as they desperately try to save themselves. There are strong elements of parody and satire in this section as well. In contrast to the usual divine role of the creator who overcomes chaos, the sea, and sea monsters to bring about order in the world (cf. Genesis 1; Exodus 15; Isa 11:15-16; 27:1; 43:14-21; Job 38–41; Psalms 74; 104), YHWH actually creates chaos on the sea in order to catch the fleeing Jonah who is completely beyond YHWH's control. There is a certain note of desperation in YHWH's actions as the Deity "hurled *(hēṭîl)* a great wind" upon the sea in an effort to stop Jonah. In effect, YHWH disrupts the created order itself in order to catch a prophet who does not fulfill his proper function. The verb *hēṭîl*, "to hurl," or *ṭûl*, "to cast," is normally used in reference to the throwing of a javelin (1 Sam 18:11; 20:33) or the slinging of a stone (cf. Jer 22:26). It is generally used in a punitive sense when applied to YHWH, e.g., YHWH's reference to Jehoiachin's being hurled into exile (Jer 22:28) or the threats to hurl Judah into exile (Jer 16:13) and Pharaoh to the ground (Ezek 32:4). YHWH here is depicted as a god who has lost control, much like Zeus in Greek mythology who hurls thunderbolts at those who anger him. Likewise, the reference to the ship that "threatened to break up" indicates a sense of parody. The verb

---

[17] Jacob Kaplan and Haya Ritter Kaplan, "Joppa," *ABD* III:946-9.

ḥšb, "to consider," here translated as "threatened," is applied to an inanimate object for the only time in the Hebrew Bible. Normally, one would expect YHWH or Jonah to "consider" their actions, but neither YHWH nor Jonah fill such self-conscious roles in the narrative. It is left to the ship to think about what is to be done next.

Verses 5-16 then turn to the interaction between the crew of the ship and Jonah as the sailors attempt to save themselves and the ship. Throughout this encounter, the sailors show remarkable self-restraint, concern for the safety and welfare of Jonah, and even reverence for YHWH, whereas Jonah seems to be little concerned with the fate of those around him, his own responsibility as a prophet of YHWH, or even his own well-being. Again, this is ironic because the prophet is the one in biblical traditions who is normally concerned with such matters, but in Jonah, it is the sailors who undertake such concerns, even if it is motivated by fear for their own safety. Verse 5 begins by noting the fear of the sailors and their actions to try to save themselves, including their crying out to their own (pagan) gods and their jettisoning the ship's cargo into the sea in order to lighten the ship and thereby save it. The verb ṭûl is employed once again to describe the sailors' throwing the cargo overboard, which establishes a parallel between their action and YHWH's earlier "hurling" of the wind upon the sea, i.e., both act out of desperation to save either their own lives or the power to control creation. In contrast to the sailors, Jonah "had gone down" (yārad) into the "innermost reaches of the ship" (yarkĕtê hasĕpînâ), translated as "hold" by the NRSV, where he fell fast asleep. The verb yārad, "had gone down," once again emphasizes Jonah's movement away from YHWH as indicated in verse 3, which contrasts markedly with the normal role of the prophet. The verb employed to describe his sleep, the niphal or passive form of rdm, generally describes a trance-like state or deep sleep, such as that employed for Daniel when he had his visions of the end time interpreted to him by angelic figures (Dan 8:8, 18; 10:9). The noun derived from the verbal root, tardēmâ, "deep sleep," describes Adam's deep sleep when YHWH created Eve from his rib or side (Gen 2:21), Abram's trance when he had the vision of Israel's future enslavement in Egypt (Gen 15:12), or the sleep that produces visions of the night (Job 4:13; 33:15). Although the term can describe deep sleep in general (1 Sam 26:12; Prov 19:15; Isa 29:10), it frequently comes from YHWH and suggests the type of trance state that would produce a prophetic vision. Jonah the prophet, however, has no such visions; he merely goes to sleep to escape his prophetic task. In this regard, he is dead to the world and to YHWH's commission. The irony of Jonah's status and actions is emphasized in verse 6 when the crew draws near to him, much as people in ancient Israel would approach a prophet for some request

(1 Sam 10:5-14; 1 Kgs 14:1-18; 22:5-6; 2 Kgs 4:18-37; 19:1-9; 23:11-20), to ask him to call upon G–d and save their lives. The nature of their questions points both to his prophetic status and to his refusal to act as a prophet. They ask him, "What are you doing sound asleep *(nirdām)*?" which highlights the trance-like prophetic sleep into which Jonah has fallen, and they demand that he arise and call upon his G–d just as a prophet is expected to do (cf. Elijah in 1 Kings 18, who calls upon YHWH in a time of crisis). The motivation is that perhaps Jonah can persuade YHWH to reconsider the situation so that they will not die, i.e., they appeal to Jonah to intercede with YHWH on their behalf, just as prophets normally are expected to do in a time of crisis. Notably, Jonah does not respond to their request. His silence is resounding at this point; he is a prophet, but he does not speak. His lack of response is all the more ironic when compared to the questions that Elijah poses to the prophets of Baal at Mount Carmel when Baal does not respond to their pleas, e.g., "perhaps he is asleep and must be awakened" (1 Kgs 18:27).

Having received no response from Jonah, the sailors begin to take matters into their own hands in verse 7. They propose to cast lots in order to identify the cause of their distress. The casting of lots, i.e., the throwing of some inanimate object in order to learn the divine will, is well known in ancient Israelite and near eastern cultures. It is employed to select Saul as king in 1 Sam 10:16-26, to apportion land among the tribes of Israel (Num 26:55), to identify Achan as the man responsible for stealing the spoil from Jericho (Josh 7:14), and to identify Jonathan as the one who violated Saul's oath not to eat until the Philistines were defeated (1 Sam 14:42). The sailors are unable to learn the divine will from the prophet Jonah, so they are forced to employ other means. Of course, the casting of lots identifies Jonah as the cause of the problem. The sailors then address Jonah once again in verse 8 in an attempt to understand why their lives are threatened. Their questions are expressed more as demands than as pleas for help in verse 6, i.e., "Tell us why this calamity has come upon us." Their questions turn to Jonah's identity as they attempt to understand who this stranger is among them and why he presents such a threat. The questions concerning his occupation, the land from which he comes, and the identity of his people are all designed to establish his identity, but they are of course rhetorical questions when considered from the perspective of the reader. He is a prophet, and he is Israelite. Curiously, he identifies himself not as an Israelite, but as a Hebrew in verse 9. The term is known elsewhere in the Hebrew Bible, but it is generally employed to describe the status of Israelites prior to the time that they had their own land and had established themselves as a nation, i.e, Abram is described as a Hebrew in Gen 14:13 prior to YHWH's granting him land by covenant (Genesis 15) and his purchase of land in Canaan (Genesis 23). Joseph and his brothers are called Hebrews while in Egypt (Gen 39:14; 43:32), and the Israelite slaves are likewise called Hebrews in Egypt (Exod 1:16, 19; 3:18, etc.). The Israelites are referred to as Hebrews until they free themselves from Philistine control (1 Sam 4:6, 9; 13:19; 14:21; 29:3, etc.), and an Israelite who is forced into debt slavery is also referred to as Hebrew (Deut 15:12; Jer 34:9). The term is frequently seen as a cognate to Akkadian *habiru/apiru*, which refers to landless persons who stand outside of settled civilization and law, but the identity is disputed.[18] Nevertheless, the usage of the term in Hebrew indicates someone who resides outside of their own land, and this status well expresses Jonah's situation as he flees from his own land and his own G–d. He expresses this situation when he states that he "worship(s) (literally, "fears") YHWH, the G–d of heaven, who made the sea and the dry land." Once again, his response is ironic in that his fear of YHWH prompts him to flee, and yet YHWH's identity as G–d of heaven, who made the sea and the dry land, demonstrates that Jonah will be unable to escape from YHWH no matter where he goes. Even so, YHWH the creator is unable to control Jonah.

Upon hearing Jonah's answer to their questions, the sailors again are afraid and ask Jonah in verse 10 what he has done. The question is of course rhetorical because no answer is provided; indeed, the reader already knows what Jonah has done and the narrative does not need to repeat this information. The narrative provides only what is necessary, i.e., that the sailors know that Jonah is fleeing from YHWH because he told them so. They then discuss the matter among themselves, in order to determine what shall be done to quiet the sea around them. All the while, the narrative builds the sense of threat by reminding the reader that the sea was becoming more and more tempestuous. The sailors will have to act soon or die.

At first glance, Jonah's proposal in verse 12 that the sailors throw him into the sea appears to be a noble gesture of self-sacrifice by one who recognizes his own role in bringing calamity upon others. But on closer examination, it demonstrates Jonah's continued refusal to take responsibility not only for his prophetic role, but indeed, even for his own life. YHWH's creation of the storm is not intended to kill anyone, although it certainly threatens to do so. Rather, it is intended as a means to prompt Jonah to carry out his prophetic assignment. Seeing the disruption of creation around him, he shows contempt for his own life,

---

[18] See Niels Peter Lemche, "Habiru, Hapiru," *ABD* III:6-10 and "Hebrew," *ABD* III:95, for overviews of the discussion.

i.e., he would rather die than carry out YHWH's commission to speak a word of judgment against Nineveh. Jonah knows very well why the sea is raging—it is because of him as he says—and yet he still refuses to undertake the action that is necessary to still it. Just as both he and YHWH have lost control of the situation, he proposes that the sailors again demonstrate their own loss of control by "hurling" him into the sea, just as YHWH "hurled" the great wind upon the sea and the sailors earlier "hurled" cargo overboard. This would, however, entail their committing murder. Again, YHWH doesn't want Jonah's life, YHWH wants Jonah to speak.

The sailors seem to sense this as demonstrated by their actions in verse 13. Rather than comply with Jonah's request, they redouble their efforts to save themselves by attempting to row the ship back to shore. They do not even answer Jonah's proposal; it's simply not worthy of comment from their perspective. Ironically, their actions constitute an attempt to save Jonah as well as themselves. Normally, it is the prophet's role to attempt to save the people from some divinely-inspired disaster or punishment, but here, it is the pagan sailors who attempt to save a prophet of YHWH who refuses to speak. Nevertheless, they are unable to overcome the power of the raging sea. The greatest irony then appears in verse 14 as the pagan sailors begin to call upon YHWH for deliverance. They employ a standard form of invocation in a time of distress, "Please *(ʾānnâ)*, O YHWH, we pray *(nāʾ)*, do not let us perish on account of this man's life . . ." (cf. Exod 32:31; 2 Kgs 20:3/Isa 38:3; Pss 116:4, 16; 118:25; Neh 1:5, 11; Dan 9:4). The reason for their earlier refusal to throw Jonah overboard becomes clear when they ask YHWH not to hold them guilty of shedding innocent blood. Again, the role of prophet and people is reversed as the (pagan) people refuse to commit a crime after the prophet has asked them to do so. They acknowledge YHWH's power and sovereignty once again by reiterating that YHWH does as YHWH pleases.

Having cleared themselves of responsibility before YHWH, the sailors then take the action that they had struggled so desperately to avoid, i.e., they "threw" *(wayĕṭiluhû)* Jonah overboard. At once, the sea ceased from its raging (i.e., anger), which of course alludes to YHWH's anger at Jonah. In another display of irony, verse 16 notes that the pagan sailors feared YHWH greatly, apparently much more so than YHWH's own prophet, and that they engaged in standard forms of worship including the making of sacrifices and the vows to YHWH. Vows are a commonly employed means symbolically to repay YHWH for divine help in a time of crisis, such as Jacob's vow for YHWH's protection while journeying (Gen 28:20; 31:13) or Hannah's vow for the birth of her son Samuel (1 Sam 1:11).

Jonah's Prayer to Yhwh from the Belly of the Fish: 2:1-11

Jonah 2:1-11 presents Jonah's prayer to Yhwh from the belly of a great fish that has swallowed him. The NRSV follows the LXX and Vulgate in renumbering Jon 2:1 as Jon 1:17 and grouping it together with the narrative material in the first chapter. The reason for such a change would be that Jon 2:1 is written in a narrative form which resembles that of Jon 1:1-16 whereas Jon 2:2-11, renumbered in NRSV, LXX, and Vulgate as Jon 2:1-10, contains the poetically styled prayer of Jonah. This change creates problems, however, in that it suggests that Yhwh's appointing of a fish to swallow Jonah is a response to the sailors' prayers, sacrifices, and vows, rather than simply Yhwh's next act to pressure Jonah into complying with the divine will. Furthermore, although Jonah's prayer appears in poetic form, the literary framework of the prayer in Jon 2:2-3aα¹ [NRSV: 2:1-2aα¹] and 2:11 [NRSV: 2:1-10] is written in narrative form. As noted above, Jon 2:1-11 [NRSV: Jon 1:17–2:10] follows the basic structural pattern of Jon 1:1-3 and 1:4-16 in that Yhwh initiates the action to which the major protagonists of the narrative respond. In this case, Yhwh appoints a fish to swallow Jonah in verse 1 [NRSV: 1:17], Jonah responds with prayer in verses 2-10 [NRSV: 2-9], and Yhwh speaks to the fish who vomits up onto dry land Jonah in verse 11 [NRSV: 10].

The narrative begins with Yhwh's appointing the fish to swallow Jonah. Although the sailors had already recognized Yhwh's power and provided proper worship and acknowledgment, Jonah had not done so, and more importantly, had still not complied with the divine command to speak against Nineveh. Although Jonah apparently felt that he would be able to escape Yhwh's commission by his own death, Yhwh makes it clear to him that there will be no escape. Rather than kill him or let him die, Yhwh imprisons Jonah in the belly of the fish to demonstrate further that there is nowhere in the world, even death, where Jonah can flee (cf. Amos 9:2-3, who states that Yhwh will find the wicked even if they descend into Sheol or to the bottom of the sea). The verb "provided" is best translated as "appointed" or "assigned" (*mnh*), and further indicates Yhwh's authority over all creation. Although the fish is widely understood to be a whale, the Hebrew text uses only the word *dāg*, "fish." The popular concept of "whale" is apparently derived from the LXX, which employs the term *tou kētous* (nominative, *to kētos*), "the sea monster," which has come to be understood as whale. The notice that Jonah was in the "belly" (literally, "intestines") of the fish for three days and three nights has prompted some discussion. It has been taken as a typical reference to a long period of time (cf. 1 Sam 30:11-15), simply as an expression of the Hebrew fondness for the number three, or a mythological reference to the time it takes to descend to the netherworld.[19] The span of time corresponds roughly to the "three days" it takes to walk across the city of Nineveh (Jon 3:3), which would support the notion that it expresses a long period of time. It should be noted that a three-day journey expresses the length of time it takes to travel to YHWH's presence for worship in the Exodus tradition (cf. Exod 3:18; 5:3, 8, 23; 15:22). Insofar as Jonah expresses a desire to return to the presence of YHWH in the Temple, the reference to three days and nights in the belly of the fish also conveys the sense of separation from YHWH.

Verses 2-10 [NRSV: 2-9] then present Jonah's prayer to YHWH. Verses 2-3aα[1] [NRSV: 1-2aα[1]], "then Jonah prayed to YHWH his G–d from the belly of the fish, saying . . ." constitute the introductory narrative framework for the prayer proper in verses 3aα[2-4]-10 [NRSV: 2aα[2-4]-9]. Interpreters have noted that the Hebrew term for "the fish" changes from the masculine form *haddāg* in verse 1 to the feminine form *haddāgâ* in verse 2 [NRSV: 1].[20] Although this shift remains problematic, Jonah's presence in the belly of the fish suggests the imagery of pregnancy for the fish and new birth or new creation for Jonah. There has been extensive debate concerning whether or not the prayer was written by the same author as the rest of the narrative. Several reasons for viewing the prayer as an independent composition are cited.[21] The situation of the psalm differs from that of the narrative in that Jonah is now in the Temple and not in the belly of the fish. The language of the psalm differs in that it does refer to the fish or to Jonah's flight from YHWH, but employs the liturgical language of the Temple. The pious and humble Jonah of the prayer does not correspond to the stubborn Jonah of the narrative who resists YHWH continuously both before and after the prayer.

Although the prayer may well have been composed for some other occasion or literary setting, these tensions are important to consider in relation to the present literary context. The setting and liturgical language of the Temple evident in the prayer demonstrate an important element of narrative perspective, i.e., the narrative is written from a Judean perspective about a northern prophet and his relation to YHWH. The fact that northern Israel was destroyed and never reestablished, whereas Judah was reestablished following the Babylonian exile, is an important interpretative element in this story. By portraying Jonah's

---

[19] See Trible, "Jonah," 504–5; Sasson, *Jonah*, 152–4; George M. Landes, "The Three Days and Three Nights Motif in Jonah 2:1," *JBL* 86 (1967) 446–50; James S. Ackerman, "Satire and Symbolism in the Song of Jonah," *Traditions in Transformation: Turning Points in Biblical Faith*, ed. Baruch Halpern and Jon D. Levenson (Winona Lake: Eisenbrauns, 1981) 213–46.

[20] Trible, "Jonah," 505; Sasson, *Jonah*, 155–6.

[21] See esp. Wolff, *Obadiah and Jonah*, 128–31.

struggle with YHWH in relation to YHWH's decision to spare Nineveh, which ultimately symbolizes the future destruction of northern Israel, the narrative raises questions for the reader as to why YHWH allows evil to happen at all. YHWH had the capacity to destroy Nineveh, and chose not to, leaving Assyria to destroy northern Israel in the future. Jonah, after all, was a northern prophet who foresaw the restoration of the northern kingdom under Jeroboam II. By pointedly emphasizing Jonah's presence in the Temple, the present form of the narrative speaks to the situation of the Judean reader, who questions why YHWH allows evil to take place, e.g., the destruction of Jerusalem and the Temple, and who is left only with the answer that YHWH will deliver the victim of such evil when the victim turns to YHWH. The prayer itself does not provide a reason why evil happens—the narrative is intended to address that issue—but the prayer expresses the only recourse available to one who is overwhelmed with suffering, i.e., turn to YHWH as the only power capable of deliverance. Judah had seen the destruction of Israel. When faced with similar destruction at the hands of the Babylonians, it was left only with the option of turning to YHWH in the hope that YHWH would respond.

Nevertheless, the dissonance between the character of Jonah in the narrative and the character of Jonah in the prayer must also be considered. Jonah is completely humble and pious in the prayer, but entirely resistive and recalcitrant in the narrative. The Jonah of the prayer knows that he is in trouble, and does what he must to get out. He acknowledges YHWH's power, his separation from YHWH, and his deliverance from calamity as though it had already taken place, but he never acknowledges his own guilt or takes responsibility for his own troubles. Jonah is trapped—he is after all in the belly of the fish—but the dissonance between the prayer and the narrative indicates only that Jonah recognizes his situation and does what he must to escape. Perhaps he is truly repentant, after all he obeys YHWH's command after he is released from the belly of the fish, but he is still angry and with good reason. Indeed, like Job, Jonah has a case against YHWH as indicated subsequently in the narrative; why should he condemn Nineveh when he knows that YHWH will forgive Nineveh and that Assyria will ultimately destroy his own nation? Likewise, Nineveh itself will be destroyed by the Babylonians and Medes in 614 B.C.E. Why not condemn it now? The same questions might be posed by a Judean reader, i.e., why did YHWH allow the Babylonian empire to survive and ultimately to destroy both Nineveh and the Jerusalem Temple from which Jonah prays. As the all-powerful master of creation, YHWH could have prevented this, but chose not to.

The prayer itself continues to express the irony and parody of the narrative. It is formulated as a psalm of thanksgiving, in which the singer thanks YHWH for deliverance from some calamity. But Jonah is not delivered; he is still in the belly of the fish and presumably faces death if he does not get out. Perhaps he understands after all that YHWH does not intend to kill him, but intends only to demonstrate to him that he cannot escape YHWH's power and will—Jonah *will* condemn Nineveh whether he likes it or not. Jonah was ready to die as indicated by his willingness to be thrown overboard, and his presence in the belly of the fish demonstrates that he cannot escape YHWH even by death. YHWH will not let him die, and he can remain in the belly of the fish for as long as he likes. It won't do him any good, however, as YHWH is still waiting for him to fulfill his prophetic commission. By expressing his deliverance as though it had already taken place, Jonah explicitly acknowledges YHWH's power and implicitly accepts YHWH's will that he speak against Nineveh. He does not have to agree with such action, but he will carry it out because he really has little choice.

Jonah's prayer is based in the thanksgiving psalm genre,[22] but it presents the various elements that typically appear within the genre according to its own three part scheme. Overall, it emphasizes the person of the prophet, and relates his perspectives concerning both his distress and YHWH's actions in response to his situation. Each segment of the psalm therefore begins with an emphatic first person reference to the prophet, in which the prophet relates his own statements and situation and then continues with reference to YHWH's actions on his behalf. The segments include a notice of the prophet's call to YHWH for assistance, together with a summation of YHWH's response and an account of YHWH's role in bringing about this calamity (verses $3a\alpha^{2\text{-}4}$-4 [NRSV: $2a\alpha^{2\text{-}4}$-3]), an account of the prophet's distress and YHWH's actions on his behalf (verses 5-9 [NRSV: 4-8]), and a statement of the prophet's thanks, sacrifices, and vows to YHWH in response to YHWH's deliverance.[23]

The notice of the prophet's call to YHWH and the summation of YHWH's response and actions in verses $3a\alpha^{2\text{-}4}$-4 [NRSV: $2a\alpha^{2\text{-}4}$-3] serves as a general introduction to the psalm. It is actually formulated as a report of both the prophet's and YHWH's actions, and thereby looks back to the situation of distress and deliverance. One might presuppose that the prophet has already been delivered, but the reader knows from the narrative context that this is not the case. Given the literary setting of the psalm, it must be understood as a portrayal of the prophet's confidence

---

[22] For discussion of the thanksgiving psalm genre, see Erhard S. Gerstenberger, *Psalms Part 1, with an Introduction to Cultic Poetry*, FOTL, vol. XIV (Grand Rapids: Eerdmans, 1988) 14–6; Frank Crüsemann, *Studien zur Formgeschichte von Hymnus und Danklied in Israel*, WMANT, vol. 32 (Neukirchener: Neukirchener Verlag, 1969) 210–84.

[23] Cf. Sasson, *Jonah*, 166.

that YHWH either will act or is already acting to save him, but it must also be considered as another example of irony and parody in that the prophet also points to YHWH as the cause of his distress. The first half of this text in verse 3aα$^{2-4}$-b [NRSV: 2aα$^{2-4}$-b] is presented in a parallel, repetitive first person singular style, and emphasizes the prophet's appeal to YHWH and YHWH's response. Verse 3aα$^{2-4}$ [NRSV: 2aα$^{2-4}$] relates the prophet's calling to YHWH (*qārā᾽tî*, "I called") from his distress, and reports that YHWH answered (cf. Ps 120:1, which employs the same phrase but with a slightly different word order). Verse 3b [NRSV: 2b] differs in that it is formulated as a direct address to YHWH, but it likewise relates that the prophet cried out for help (*šiwwatî*, "I cried out for help") from the belly of Sheol, and that YHWH (i.e., "you") heard him. The reference to the prophet's crying out from "the belly of Sheol" might suggest his current location in the belly of the fish, although the terminology differs completely. Nevertheless, it appears in the current literary context to be a metaphorical representation of his situation. Sheol after all is the realm of the dead, and Jonah will die if he does not emerge from the fish. The second half of this segment in verse 4 [NRSV: 3], which is joined to the first half by the *waw-consecutive* construction of the verb *wataŝlîkēnî*, "and you cast me," then describes YHWH's actions in concrete terms. It therefore presents YHWH's action against Jonah as a consequence of his call to YHWH for assistance. Rather than describe YHWH's actions of deliverance, it focuses on YHWH as the cause of the prophet's distress by relating how YHWH cast him into the heart of the sea so that "flood" (literally, "river") surrounds him and the waves and billows pass over him. The syntactical characteristics of the text thereby reverse the normal temporal sequence of the contents so that the cause of Jonah's affliction, i.e., YHWH, is mentioned only after the notice of his call to YHWH for help. YHWH thereby emerges as both Jonah's deliverer and tormentor. Given its syntactical relationship to verse 3aα$^{2-4}$-b [NRSV: 2aα$^{2-4}$-b], this statement must be considered as a very self-serving critique of YHWH's actions by the prophet; he relates how YHWH placed him in a situation of threat but says nothing about his own actions that led to this turn of events.

The second major segment of the prayer in verses 5-9 [NRSV: 4-8] begins with an emphatic first person reference to the prophet's own actions, "Then I said (*wa᾽ănî ᾽āmartî*) . . ." Once again, the prophet points to his own piety and longing for YHWH in his situation of distress. Having already accused YHWH of being the source of his affliction, he now turns to YHWH as the only power capable of delivering him from it. Nevertheless, he never alludes to his own role in bringing this situation about. The segment contains four syntactically independent basic subunits in verses 5, 6-7, 8, and 9 [NRSV: 4, 5-6, 7 and 8] that take the reader through the basic sequence of events concerning the prophet's pleas, suffering, and deliverance.

The first sub-unit in verse 6 [NRSV: 5] relates the prophet's distress at his separation from YHWH. He notes that he is "driven away" from YHWH's sight, and expresses his longing once again to gaze upon YHWH's holy Temple. In the perspective of the Judean reader, the verse refers of course to YHWH's Temple in Jerusalem, but this only serves as a means to highlight Jonah's own disingenuous nature. He is a prophet from the northern kingdom of Israel, which revolted from Davidic rule long before the purported time of Jonah. Furthermore, the reader knows that Jonah is attempting to flee from YHWH. If he really wanted to appear before YHWH in the Temple, he would not have booked passage on a ship headed for Tarshish!

The second sub-unit in verses 6-7 [NRSV: 5-6] then relates Jonah's impending death and YHWH's action to save his life. The imagery is that of one who is drowning, and is entirely appropriate for the present context in that Jonah was tossed into the sea by the sailors. The NRSV translation, "the waters closed over me," does not fully convey the sense of mortal danger expressed in Hebrew, "the waters closed over me unto (the) throat/breath (*ʿad nepeš*)." The "deep" that surrounds him employs the Hebrew term *tĕhôm* that expresses the state of the earth prior to YHWH's acts of creation (Gen 1:2), so that Jonah's impending death is presented as a reversal of creation. The portrayal of Jonah with weeds bound to his head has prompted some surprise among interpreters who wonder how such a thing could happen in the belly of the fish,[24] but the image pertains to one who is washed up on shore after drowning in the sea. One must bear in mind that the fish is Jonah's vehicle of deliverance. If he remains inside, he might die, but the fish prevented him from dying three days earlier when he was thrown into the sea. Verse 7 [NRSV: 6] employs the imagery of descent to Sheol or the netherworld, i.e., he is going down to the world of the dead who are barred from reentering the world of the living. The *waw-consecutive* verb *wataʿal*, "and you brought up," in verse 7b [NRSV: 6b] points to YHWH's rescue of Jonah as he sinks into the sea and death, "yet you brought my life up from the Pit, O YHWH, my G–d." The "Pit" (*šaḥat*) refers to the grave or destruction. Jonah here acknowledges YHWH as his G–d, and thereby acknowledges YHWH's power to control his fate.

The third segment in verse 8 [NRSV: 7] recapitulates Jonah's experience of near death and YHWH's deliverance, but it emphasizes his own piety. As his life fades away, he states that he remembered YHWH. Following his earlier statement that YHWH cast him into the sea in the first

---

[24] Cf. Wolff, *Obadiah and Jonah*, 136.

place (verse 4) [NRSV: 3], one might wonder how he could forget! Nevertheless, the statement emphasizes Jonah's acknowledgement of YHWH. The *waw-consecutive* verb *wattābô*, "and it came," links Jonah's statement in verse 8b [NRSV: 7b] that his prayer came to YHWH to verse 8a [NRSV: 7a]. Again, it emphasizes Jonah's piety and action, as his payer comes to YHWH's holy Temple.

The fourth segment in verse 9 [NRSV: 8] refers to idol worshipers who forsake "their true loyalty." Although the NRSV understands this as a reference to their betrayal of YHWH, there is no reason to believe that they were ever bound to YHWH in the first place. Rather, the statement refers to idol worshipers who forsake their loyalty to their idols when they see the power of YHWH. In the present literary context, verse 9 [NRSV: 8] relates the actions of the sailors who acknowledged YHWH and made sacrifices and vows to the Deity when they saw what YHWH did to Jonah. Verse 9 [NRSV: 8] therefore constitutes the concluding statement of a sequence of action that began in verse 5 [NRSV: 4], i.e., Jonah recognizes that he is lost; the waves close over him, YHWH rescues him, he prays to YHWH, and the pagans acknowledge YHWH as well.

The final major section of the prayer appears in verse 10 [NRSV: 9], which begins with the emphatic *waʾănî*, "but I," as in verse 5 [NRSV: 4]. Again, it emphasizes Jonah and his piety as he relates his thanks to YHWH, his sacrifices, and his payment of vows in return for YHWH's deliverance. Ironically, Jonah now follows the example of the pagan sailors who feared YHWH, made sacrifices, and made vows to YHWH in Jon 1:16. Jonah, the prophet of YHWH, must learn from the example of pagans.

The narrative concerning Jonah's prayer ends in Jon 2:11 [NRSV: 2:10] with the simple statement that YHWH spoke to the fish, and it vomited Jonah up onto dry land. The reference to "dry land" (*yabāšâ*) picks up the creation motif underlying the narrative as the dry land emerges from the deep at creation (Gen 1:9). Having been delivered from the sea and death, Jonah experiences his own new creation.

Encounter between YHWH and Jonah Concerning YHWH's Mercy for Nineveh: 3:1–4:11

The second major component of the book is Jonah 3–4, in which YHWH and Jonah have their primary encounter concerning YHWH's decision to forgive the people of Nineveh. Whereas Jonah 1–2 prepared the reader (and Jonah) to recognize YHWH's power over all creation, this portion of the book points to YHWH's capacity for mercy in exercising that power as well as to the role of human repentance in prompting

Yhwh's mercy. Jonah 3–4 presents a deliberate parallel with Jonah 1–2 in order to demonstrate the interrelationship within the narrative between the concerns for Yhwh's power and mercy as well as the human capacity for repentance and self-correction. As in Jonah 1–2, Yhwh calls upon Jonah to speak a message of judgment against Nineveh for its wrongdoing. In contrast to Jonah 1–2, Jonah carries out the divine commission, but he is not prepared for the result, i.e., Nineveh's repentance. Upon seeing Nineveh's repentance, Yhwh demonstrates divine power in a manner very different from Jonah 1–2 in that Yhwh chooses not to carry out the previously announced punishment of the city.

This prompts an interaction between the prophet and Yhwh in which Jonah protests Yhwh's decision to show mercy and thereby to contradict the prophetic word delivered by Jonah. During the ensuing interaction between Yhwh and Jonah, Jonah demands that Yhwh take his life (cf. Jonah 1–2 in which Jonah offers his life to save the sailors) but Yhwh arranges a demonstration of the principle of divine mercy. Yhwh creates a plant to shade Jonah from the daytime sun and heat, and then destroys it once Jonah comes to enjoy the comfort that it offers. By pointing to Jonah's compassion for a plant that is of so little consequence to the world, Yhwh makes the point that compassion can also be shown to the people of Nineveh and even to their animals (cf. Jonah 1–2 in which Yhwh had the capacity to kill Jonah for his defiance, but chose not to do so). In sum, the encounter demonstrates an important principle of (divine) power and mercy: power may be exercised by its use or by refraining from its use, i.e., the capacity for (divine) mercy is what makes (divine) power truly efficacious.

The literary structure of Jonah 3–4 is fairly straightforward. Jonah 3:1-10 relates Yhwh's renewed commission to Jonah and its outcome, i.e., the repentance of the people and king of Nineveh and Yhwh's decision not to punish them. Jonah 4:1-11 then relates the encounter between Jonah and Yhwh over Yhwh's decision to show mercy to Nineveh. The narrative ends with Yhwh's rhetorical question to Jonah, and more importantly to the reader, in which Yhwh asserts the right to show mercy, even to those who have committed (or will commit) evil or to those who do not have the capacity to decide. This assertion encapsulates the essential point of the entire book.

Yhwh's Renewed Commission to Jonah and Its Outcome: 3:1-10

The second portion of the book begins with a statement that is nearly identical to the first statement of the book, viz., "(and) the word of Yhwh came to Jonah a second time saying . . ." The only difference between Jon 3:1 and 1:1 is the substitution of the word *šēnît*, "a second time," for *ben-ʾămittay*, "son of Amittai." Otherwise, the same prophetic word formula is employed, thereby helping to convey the parallel or repetitive nature of the situation, i.e., Jonah gets a second chance to carry out Yhwh's commission. The content of the commission likewise proceeds along the lines of the initial commission in Jon 1:2, viz., "Get up, go to Nineveh, that great city, and proclaim to it the message that I tell you." The commission in Jon 3:2 is identical to that of Jon 1:2 up to the occurrence of the verb *ûqĕrā*, "and proclaim." Afterwards, the pronoun *ʾēleyhā*, "to it," varies slightly from the *ʿāleyhā*, "against it," of Jon 1:2, and the balance of the statement merely refers in summary fashion to the earlier commission, i.e., "the message that I tell you." The formulation of this phrase, however, is noteworthy in that the participial formation of the verbal statement indicates a present action on the part of Yhwh, not a past action, i.e., *ʾānōkî dōbēr ʾēleykā*, literally, "I am speaking (to) you." Some have noted that Jonah's rendition of the message to Nineveh varies from that of Jon 1:2 by the specification that Nineveh will be punished in forty days,[25] but the formulation of Jon 3:2 more likely indicates the perspective of Yhwh's renewed commission to the prophet, i.e., Yhwh commissions him once again in the present.

Jonah 3:3-4 portray Jonah's response to Yhwh's renewed commission. Whereas he fled the first time, he immediately arises and carries out Yhwh's instruction this time. The statement emphasizes the size of the city of Nineveh as "an exceedingly large city" (literally, "a great city to G–d") that required three days for a person to walk across it. This piece of information is noteworthy for two basic reasons. First, ancient Nineveh actually was an enormous city.[26] At the height of its size and influence as capital of the Assyrian empire during the seventh century B.C.E., Nineveh occupied an area of some 1850 acres, its walls measured approximately 7.75 miles or 12.5 km in circumference, and its width was approximately 3 miles. This, of course, does not require a three-day journey to cross, unless one stops frequently to browse or chat. Some interpreters who take this statement literally have attempted to maintain that it refers to greater Nineveh, including all of its suburbs or outlying fields, etc.[27] Ancient Babylon, at 2500 acres, was actually larger. The point of the figures was not to present the actual size of the city, but to convey its enormous size and to justify Jonah's stopping in

---

[25] Trible, "Jonah," 511–2. She also notes that the message in Jon 3:4 lacks a prophetic messenger formula.

[26] See A. Kirk Grayson, "Nineveh," *ABD* IV:1118-9; Sasson, *Jonah*, 230–1.

[27] See Sasson, *Jonah*, 230; Allen, *The Books of Joel, Obadiah, Jonah and Micah*, 222–3.

the midst of the city, after only one day's journey, so that he could witness Nineveh's repentance first hand. Second, the reference to a three-day journey to cross the city corresponds to the three days that Jonah spent in the belly of the fish, and thereby aids in establishing some sense of parallel between Jonah 3–4 and 1–2. Whereas the three days in the belly of the fish symbolized Jonah's distance from YHWH, and indeed his nearness to YHWH even at such a distance, the three days required to traverse Nineveh likewise conveys Jonah's return to YHWH, and indeed his distance from YHWH even as he returns. In this respect, the description of Nineveh as "a great city to/for G–d" aids in conveying Jonah's relationship to YHWH while in the midst of his journey through the city.

The reference to the forty days remaining until Nineveh is overthrown merely indicates that Nineveh has plenty of time to change its ways. The use of forty in relation to units of time is a somewhat formulaic reference for a long time in the Hebrew Bible, e.g., the forty days that the flood remained on the earth (Gen 7:12, 17); the forty years of wandering in the wilderness (Num 14:33); forty years of peace in the land during the time of the Judges (Judg 3:11; cf. 4:30); the forty years of David's reign (1 Kgs 1:11; 1 Chr 29:27); etc. The use of the verb *nepāket*, "overturned," in reference to the projected punishment of Nineveh employs the same root that is commonly applied to the destruction of Sodom and Gomorrah (Gen 19:21, 25, 29; Deut 29:22; Jer 20:16; 49:18; Amos 4:11; Lam 4:6). The use of the verb thereby aids in characterizing Nineveh as an exceedingly wicked city, as well as an exceedingly great one, and thereby makes its repentance all the more remarkable and worthy of recognition by G–d.

Jonah 3:5-9 then describes Nineveh's repentance, first by the men of Nineveh (verse 5) and then by the king who calls upon all humans and animals in the city to do likewise (verses 6-9). The wording of the statement in verse 5 that conveys the repentance of the men of Nineveh is especially noteworthy. The NRSV reads, "and the people of Nineveh believed G–d," but the statement reads more literally, "and the men of Nineveh believed in G–d *(wayyaʾămînû ʾanšê nînĕwēh bʾlhym)*." Although some have noted that the reference to G–d rather than to YHWH indicates that the pagan people of the city merely acknowledged some form of divine power consistent with their own religious perspectives,[28] the statement as presently worded indicates belief in G–d akin to that demonstrated by the sailors on the ship in Jonah 1. Furthermore, upon hearing Jonah's proclamation, they immediately declare a fast and put on sackcloth, both of which are common signs of mourning,

---

[28] E.g., Trible, "Jonah," 513.

sorrow, and repentance in the ancient world (cf. 1 Kgs 21:9, 12; Jer 36:6; Ezra 8:21; Esth 4:3; 9:31; etc., for fasting; Gen 37:34; 1 Kgs 20:31; 2 Kgs 19:1, 2/Isa 37:1, 2; etc., for sackcloth). All around him, the Israelite prophet Jonah sees pagans acknowledging G–d, but he, a prophet of YHWH who presumably has more immediate contact with and understanding of G–d, has difficulties in coming to terms with YHWH's demands and actions. Such a portrayal serves the purposes of the book as it places the Israelite, or more properly the Judean, reader who is striving to understand YHWH and divine action in the place of Jonah.

Verses 6-9 then describe what takes place when word of Jonah's message reaches the king of Nineveh. His reaction is all the more remarkable in that elsewhere, the king of Assyria is portrayed as an arrogant, boasting monarch, who not only defies YHWH and threatens Jerusalem, but argues that his power is greater than YHWH's because he has been able to defeat the god of Israel/Judah just as he defeated the gods of other nations (Isa 10:5-34, 36-37/2 Kings 18–19; cf. Isa 14:3-27; Nahum 2–3). The portrayal of the king's repentance emphasizes his sovereignty and his control over the animals of creation as well as human beings, and thereby presents him as a potentially self-styled rival to YHWH who, like the sailors and men of Nineveh before him, recognizes YHWH's power. He rises from his throne, removes his robe, puts on sackcloth, and sits in the dust or ashes (cf. Job 2:8; Dan 9:3; Esth 4:1, 3). The throne is a clear symbol of sovereignty, and the term for "robe," Hebrew *ʾadderet*, is derived from a root that means "glory" or "greatness" and thereby alludes to the king's power (cf. Josh 7:21, 24, which alludes to a fine Babylonian mantle [Shinar is the location of Babylon]). The term for "robe" or "mantle" also describes the garment worn by Elijah (1 Kgs 19:13, 19; 2 Kgs 2:8, 13, 14), which might suggest that the king of Nineveh here has greater "prophetic" insight than does Jonah. His decree that all people and animals in the city follow his example by fasting and donning sackcloth demonstrates his own power over the inhabitants of the city, but he willingly acknowledges that YHWH's is greater. The Hebrew term for "decree," *ṭaʿam*, literally means, "taste" (i.e., in reference to the "whim" or "mood" or "will" of the king), and thereby forms a pun with the verb *ṭʿm*, "to taste," which is employed in his decree that humans and animals will not "taste" anything or drink water. To a certain extent, the king's decree is absurd in that he orders the animals not to eat or drink, but the device is employed to accentuate his power over those in the city and thereby provides a basis for comparison with YHWH that emphasizes his willing submission to YHWH's authority. Verse 8 emphasizes the repentance of the people of Nineveh who cry out to YHWH and turn from the violence that they were accustomed to practice. The concluding question of this section in verse 9, "who knows? G–d may relent and change his (sic) mind; he may turn from his fierce anger, so that we do not perish," expresses the people's hope that YHWH will indeed exercise the divine capacity for mercy. The people's question/statement takes up the well-known characterization of YHWH in Exod 34:6-7, "YHWH, YHWH, a G–d merciful and gracious, slow to anger, and abounding in steadfast love and faithfulness, keeping steadfast love for the thousandth generation, forgiving iniquity and transgression and sin, yet by no means clearing the guilty, but visiting the iniquity of the parents upon the children and the children's children, to the third and fourth generation." Although the statement in Exod 34:6-7 emphasizes both YHWH's compassion and capacity for punishment or justice, the people's statement in Jon 3:9 emphasizes only YHWH's compassion and capacity to forgive.[29] This is entirely in keeping with the purpose of the narrative at this point, which is to emphasize YHWH's mercy, but as the preceding material in Jonah demonstrates, YHWH's mercy must be understood in relation to YHWH's capacity for punishment. Together, both punishment and mercy define the two components of justice. The people of Nineveh hold out the hope that by turning from evil, justice may be served through compassion rather than through punishment.

Finally, Jon 3:10 relates YHWH's observation of the Ninevites' repentance and YHWH's decision not to carry out the punishment. The wording of the verse deliberately plays upon the formulaic statements concerning YHWH at creation, viz., "When G–d saw what they did (literally, "their deeds," *ʾet maʿăśêhem*) . . ." (cf. for example, Gen 1:31, "and G–d saw everything that he had made [*ʿāśâ*], and indeed, it was very good") so that YHWH's action in forgiving the Ninevites might be compared to YHWH's observation of the goodness of creation. This continues the hyperbole of the king's decree that even the animals must fast and wear sackcloth in order to express the repentance of the people of Nineveh. By employing such hyperbole, the narrative conveys the complete and sincere repentance and sorrow of the people of Nineveh. What else can YHWH do but forgive them?

YHWH's Assertion of the Right to Mercy in Encounter with Jonah: 4:1-11

Jonah 4:1-11 presents the encounter between YHWH and Jonah that results from YHWH's decision to forgive the people of Nineveh and thereby reverse the earlier message of judgment against them delivered

---

[29] Cf. Fishbane, *Biblical Interpretation*, 345–7.

by Jonah. Verse 1 introduces the key motif of this encounter: Jonah's anger at Yhwh for having reversed the divine message. The NRSV does not adequately convey Jonah's emotions at this turn of events with the translation, "but this was very displeasing to Jonah." The statement, *wayyērāʿ ʾel yônâ rāʿâ gĕdôlâ wayyaḥar lô*, should be rendered, "but this was extremely bad to Jonah, and he burned (with anger)." There is a great deal of speculation that Jonah's anger is prompted by his own selfishness and embarrassment at having his prophetic message reversed, but as the following discussion will show, he is angry at Yhwh for not following through on an announcement of punishment. The issue is not Jonah's selfishness or embarrassment, but Yhwh's reliability. The reader must bear in mind that Nineveh or Assyria would one day destroy Jonah's homeland and carry its people off into exile.

Verses 2-3 present Jonah's prayer to Yhwh. Again, this presents a parallel to Jonah 1–2 in that Jonah once again prays to Yhwh when he finds himself in a situation of distress. Earlier, Jonah was in the belly of a fish. Now, he is in a quandary because he announced a prophetic message that Yhwh would destroy Nineveh. As in Jonah 1, he expresses his willingness to die. Like Elijah before him who sits under a broom tree and prays to die at a time of crisis (1 Kgs 19:4), Jonah experiences a similar loss of confidence.[30] But also like Elijah, who experienced a revelation of Yhwh on Mt. Horeb, Jonah will also receive a revelation. Jonah's revelation will be of a very different character than that of Elijah, but this contributes to the irony of the book and its preoccupation with the question of theodicy in that Jonah's revelation is that Yhwh is capable of showing mercy to a nation that will ultimately destroy Jonah's own homeland. Although some have questioned Jonah's character because he declines to kill himself,[31] the reader must keep in mind that suicide is absolutely anathema in Judaism because it shows scorn not only for the sanctity of life but for G–d who gives life as well. Jonah does not defy G–d out of arrogance; he is unwilling to challenge the life that Yhwh grants him, but asks that Yhwh take it back. His fundamental problem is Yhwh's self-contradiction, and if Yhwh chooses to contradict the divine self by failing to follow through on an earlier divine word, then Jonah must consider the possibility that Yhwh will fail to follow through in granting him life as well. And so he asks that Yhwh take it back. In presenting his prayer to Yhwh, Jonah highlights Yhwh's contradiction of the prophetic message delivered to Nineveh by Jonah. By stating, "is this not what I said while I was still in my own country?" Jonah provides a reason for his earlier flight from Yhwh.

---

[30] Cf. A. Feuillet, "Les sources du livre de Jonas," *RB* 54 (1947) 161–86, esp. 168–9.
[31] Trible, "Jonah," 518.

Jonah's statement presupposes an earlier conversation between Jonah and Yʜᴡʜ at the time of Jonah's initial commission to speak a message of judgment against Nineveh, but the text of Jonah does not provide the reader with that conversation. Perhaps the words were never spoken or perhaps the narrator chose not to present this conversation until this point for specific reasons. It seems unlikely that Jonah would expect to get away with lying to Yʜᴡʜ; whether the words were spoken or not, the reader must take this as an accurate indication of Jonah's motivation to flee. By declining to provide this information at the outset, the narrator initially builds up Jonah's character as one who is rebellious, but the objection is valid. Jonah raises the question of Yʜᴡʜ's integrity, and claims this as his reason for fleeing, i.e., he knew that Yʜᴡʜ would not carry out the divine word. He cites as the reason for this conclusion the well known statement concerning Yʜᴡʜ's merciful character from Exod 34:6–7, "for I knew that you are a gracious G–d and merciful, slow to anger, and abounding in steadfast love, and ready to relent from punishing." As noted in the discussion of the question posed by the king of Nineveh in Jon 3:9, the references to Yʜᴡʜ's capacity to punish in Exod 34:6-7 are entirely missing in Jonah so that the issue focuses on Yʜᴡʜ's capacity to forgive when wrongdoers repent and change their ways.[32] Furthermore, Jonah's statement revises the statement in Exod 34:6-7: it refers to Yʜᴡʜ's "graciousness" (*ḥannûn*) prior to Yʜᴡʜ's "mercy" (*raḥûm*); it refers to Yʜᴡʜ's "steadfast love" (*ḥesed*), but eliminates reference to Yʜᴡʜ's "truth" (*ʾemet*); and it adds a reference to Yʜᴡʜ's forgiveness from wrongdoing. Altogether, these changes present a much softer side of Yʜᴡʜ than does Exod 34:6-7, i.e., it emphasizes "grace" (literally, "favor"), "steadfast love," and forgiveness, includes "mercy," and eliminates "truth" and "punishment." Jonah thereby points to Yʜᴡʜ as a god who will forgive, but who is not willing to carry out punishment when it is due. In this manner, he questions Yʜᴡʜ's character and capacity for justice, and thereby concludes that it is better to die than to live. If a prophet cannot depend upon Yʜᴡʜ to make a just decision, then there is little reason for him to live. Again, Jonah as a prophet is expected to know that Assyria will destroy his homeland Israel.

Verse 4 presents Yʜᴡʜ's simple response to Jonah's request for death, "is it right for you to be angry?" The ɴʀsv does not convey the true sense of the question, however, as *hahêṭîb* actually means, "is it better?" or "is it good?" Yʜᴡʜ does not question whether or not it is right for Jonah to be angry; as the narrative indicates, he has ample reason. Instead, it questions whether or not his anger will do him any good.

---

[32] See Fishbane, *Biblical Interpretation*, 345–7.

Jonah does not answer YHWH's question, which indicates that it is meant to be a rhetorical question; anger will not do him any good. Perhaps his refusal to answer also demonstrates the depths of his anger and sense of betrayal by YHWH. Instead in verse 5, he simply leaves the city of Nineveh, makes himself a small hut or sukkah to sit under for protection from the sun, and waits to see what will happen in Nineveh. Jonah is through with talking, either to Nineveh or to YHWH. This is all the more remarkable and ironic for a prophet, for whom speech with both people and YHWH is a primary function. He does remain to see, however, which suggests that he has some expectation that perhaps YHWH will keep the divine word after all. As YHWH has forgiven Nineveh, there is no need for further action unless YHWH changes the divine mind once again.

YHWH's response to Jonah's silence and action is silence and action in return. Rather than attempt to speak further to Jonah, which is clearly useless at this point, YHWH appoints a "castor bean plant" to grow up over Jonah and to provide shade for his head and to protect him "from his discomfort." The NRSV translation, to protect him "from his discomfort," does not adequately convey the pun expressed by the Hebrew term *mērā'ātô*, "from his evil." Clearly, what Jonah is doing is not necessarily the right thing to do, at least from YHWH's or the narrator's perspective! There has been an endless amount of ink spilled over the meaning of the term *qîqāyôn*, here rendered as "bush" or "castor bean plant" *(ricinus communis)*. Robinson thinks that it could be an Assyrian loan word best rendered as "gourd" (cf. LXX) or even a nonsense word coined specifically for this story, but ultimately, he is unable to decide.[33] In fact, the identity of the plant is not that important; rather, its function in the narrative is the crucial fact on which to concentrate. YHWH acts to provide Jonah with shade. After all, Jonah had already built a sukkah to provide shade for himself, so there was clearly a need. As verse 6b indicates, Jonah was extremely pleased with the plant. It is not entirely clear why he should be so pleased, but the statement concerning his pleasure contrasts markedly with the earlier statement concerning his anger in verse 1. Jonah charges YHWH with inconstancy in divine statements and actions, but Jonah is clearly subject to some mood swings himself.

YHWH's next actions in verses 7-8a are to appoint a "worm" to destroy the "castor bean plant" and a "sultry east wind" to beat down on Jonah's head now that his shade is gone. Both of these actions clearly demonstrate YHWH's mastery over creation. YHWH creates the plant as

---

[33] For a full survey of the options, see Bernard P. Robinson, "Jonah's Qiqayon Plant," *ZAW* 97 (1985) 390–403.

well as the creature who eats from it and ultimately leads it to its destruction. This is nothing more than an expression of the natural order of the world. Likewise, the "sultry east wind" is well known as the Ḥamsin or *Sharav* of the land of Israel, a dry desert wind like the Santa Ana winds of southern California that dissipate moisture in the air and the will to act by humans and animals.[34] The east wind is capable of blocking out the sun with the dust that it raises, and it can frequently become destructive as it blows harder. It is featured in the Exodus narrative where it divides the Red Sea (Exod 14:21), and elsewhere where it serves as an expression of YHWH's power (Exod 10:13; Isa 11:15; 27:8; Ps 48:8 [NRSV: 48:7]). Again, it is a feature of the natural order of the world in Israel, as it appears every fall and spring at the transitions between the rainy and dry seasons. As a result of YHWH's actions, Jonah becomes "faint" *(wayyitʿallāp),* which recalls the earlier statement in his prayer, "as my life was ebbing away *(bĕhitʿallēp),* and suggests that Jonah could actually die from exposure to the sun. In verse 8b he asks to die and reiterates that his death is better than his life. Again, such a request represents complete rejection of life and of YHWH, although Jonah is still unwilling to take his own life. To a certain extent, he acknowledges YHWH's power once again as he did after being swallowed by the fish. YHWH is master of creation, and YHWH is master of Jonah. Jonah is in the same position that he was in at the end of chapter 2.

In verse 9a, YHWH asks Jonah once again whether his anger is better for him (cf. verse 4). YHWH qualifies the question, however, by specifying Jonah's anger in relation to the loss of the castor bean plant. Obviously, YHWH created and destroyed the plant to make a point, and to elicit from Jonah a response to the earlier question concerning his anger. Jonah's response is both adamant and concise. He is angry enough to die over the loss of the plant. For Jonah, YHWH's actions concerning the plant mirror those of YHWH's actions concerning Nineveh, i.e., YHWH begins one course of action, only to step back and reverse it completely. The destruction of the castor bean plant merely demonstrates YHWH's capriciousness. To Jonah, the prophet of YHWH who is to speak the divine word, YHWH is simply unreliable.[35]

Finally, YHWH explains the divine actions undertaken in relation to both Nineveh and the castor bean plant in verses 10-11. YHWH begins by pointing out Jonah's "concern" for the bush, for which he did nothing, even though it lasted only from one night to the next. The verb *ḥûs,* here translated as "comfort," actually means "pity," which better conveys YHWH's emotions in relation to the Ninevites. YHWH points to

---

[34] See "Israel, Land of," *Encyclopaedia Judaica* 9:189-90.
[35] Cf. Fretheim, "Jonah and Theodicy," 227–37.

Jonah's "pity" for the castor bean plant as a means to illustrate YHWH's own "pity" for the people and animals of Nineveh. Even though he did no work to create it or raise it, Jonah took delight in the castor bean plant and regretted its destruction. All the more so for YHWH, who actually did the work to create some 120,000 people in the city of Nineveh. YHWH's role as creator and master of the world comes once more into play, as the Ninevites were understood to be a people that only a parent could love in biblical tradition. The destruction of Israel by Assyria would hardly endear the Ninevites to Israel in biblical tradition. The Jonah narrative highlights this sense of disdain by pointing to the complete stupidity or helplessness of the Ninevites, they do not know their right from their left. Furthermore, the inclusion of animals not only speaks to YHWH's role as creator, but it also provides a not so subtle comparison for the Ninevites. Nevertheless, YHWH is their creator and loves them. As a result, YHWH is more than willing to show compassion to them, especially when they finally do something right by hearing Jonah's prophetic message and repenting from their evil. Nineveh may be an evil city, but even the most wicked people in the world are capable of repentance according to the book of Jonah, and they should have the chance to repent and be spared from punishment. In YHWH's eyes, to do otherwise would be a waste. Furthermore, YHWH's statement provides a perspective on prophecy in the Hebrew Bible. Prophets do not only announce judgment in the Hebrew Bible—although they are frequently understood this way—but they announce comfort and the possibility of repentance from evil as well. This helps to define the purpose of a prophetic announcement of judgment in the Hebrew Bible. It does not announce irrevocable judgment; that would be a pointless waste of human beings who are created by G–d and have the capacity to discern right from wrong (cf. Genesis 3). Rather, human beings must employ that capacity to discern right from wrong, even in the aftermath of wrongdoing. By pointing to the potential consequences of wrongdoing, prophets point to potential punishment, but they also call upon their audience to change its ways and thereby to avert punishment. The book of Jonah is designed to teach this fundamental facit of prophecy to its readers.

FOR FURTHER READING

COMMENTARIES

Allen, Leslie C. *The Books of Joel, Obadiah, Jonah, and Micah*. The New International Commentary on the Old Testament. Grand Rapids: Eerdmans, 1976.

Cogan, Mordechai, with Uriel Simon. *Ovadya, Yona*. Miqra' leYisrael. Jerusalem: Magnes, 1992.

Fretheim, Terence. *The Message of Jonah: A Theological Commentary*. Minneapolis: Augsburg, 1977.

Keller, Carl-A., with Edmond Jacob and Samuel Amsler. *Osée, Joël, Amos, Abdias, Jonas*. Commentaire de l'ancien Testament XIa. Geneva: Labor et Fides, 1992.

Limburg, James. *Jonah: A Commentary*. Old Testament Library. Louisville: Westminster John Knox, 1993.

Rudolph, Wilhelm. *Joel–Amos–Obadja–Jona*. Kommentar zum Alten Testament XIII/2. Gütersloh: Gerd Mohn, 1971.

Sasson, Jack M. *Jonah*. Anchor Bible 24B. New York: Doubleday, 1990.

Stuart, Douglas. *Hosea-Jonah*. Word Biblical Commentary 31. Waco: Word, 1987.

Trible, Phyllis. "The Book of Jonah: Introduction, Commentary, and Reflections," *The New Interpreter's Bible. Volume VII: Introduction to Apocalyptic Literature, Daniel, The Twelve Prophets*. Ed. Leander E. Keck et al; 461–529. Nashville: Abingdon, 1996.

Wolff, Hans Walter. *Obadiah and Jonah*. Trans. Margaret Kohl. Continental Commentaries. Minneapolis: Augsburg, 1986.

STUDIES

Feuillet, A. "Les sources du livre de Jonas," *RB* 54 (1947) 161–86.

Fretheim, Terence. "Jonah and Theodicy," *ZAW* 90 (1978) 227–37.

Gunn, David M., and Danna Nolan Fewell. *Narrative in the Hebrew Bible.* The Oxford Bible Series. Oxford: Oxford University Press, 1993.

Lacocque, André, and Pierre-Emmanuel Lacocque. *Jonah: A Psycho-Religious Approach.* Studies on Personalities of the Old Testament. Columbia: University of South Carolina Press, 1990.

Lux, Rüdiger. *Jona. Prophet zwischen "Verweigerung" und "Gehorsam."* FRLANT 162. Göttingen: Vandenhoeck & Ruprecht, 1994.

Magonet, Jonathan. *Form and Meaning: Studies in Literary Technique in the Book of Jonah.* BBET 2. Bern: Herbert Lang; Frankfurt/Main: Peter Lang, 1976.

Marcus, David. *From Balaam to Jonah: Anti-prophetic Satire in the Hebrew Bible.* Brown Judaic Studies 301. Atlanta: Scholars Press, 1995.

Payne, David. "Jonah from the Perspective of Its Audience," *JSOT* 13 (1979) 3–12.

Person, Raymond F., Jr. *In Conversation with Jonah: Conversation Analysis, Literary Criticism, and the Book of Jonah.* JSOTSup 220. Sheffield: Sheffield Academic Press, 1996.

Salters, R. B. *Jonah and Lamentations.* OT Guides. Sheffield: JSOT Press, 1994, pp. 13–62.

Schmidt, Ludwig. *"De Deo." Studien zur Literaturkritik und Theologie des Buches Jona, des Gesprächs zwischen Abraham und JHWH in Gen 18,22ff. und von Hi 1.* BZAW 143. Berlin and New York: Walter de Gruyter, 1976.

Steffen, Uwe. *Die Jona-Geschichte. Ihre Auslegung und Darstellung im Judentum, Christentum und Islam.* Neukirchen-Vluyn: Neukirchener, 1994.

Wolff, Hans Walter. *Studien zum Jonabuch.* Biblische Studien 47. Neukirchen-Vluyn: Neukirchener, 1965.